Music in American Life

*A list of books in the series
appears at the end of this book.*

Shoshone
Ghost Dance
Religion

Shoshone Ghost Dance Religion

Poetry Songs and Great Basin Context

Judith Vander

University of Illinois Press
Urbana and Chicago

Publication of this book was supported by grants from the Sonneck Society for American Music and the National Endowment for the Humanities, an independent federal agency.

This book is printed on acid-free paper.

Library of Congress Cataloging-in-Publication Data

Vander, Judith.
    Shoshone ghost dance religion : poetry songs and Great Basin
context / Judith Vander.
        p.   cm. — (Music in American life)
    Includes bibliographical references and index.
    ISBN 0-252-02214-9 (cloth : acid-free paper)
    1. Shoshoni Indians—Music—History and criticism. 2. Shoshoni
Indians—Music. 3. Ghost dance. 4. Shoshoni Indians—Religion.
I. Title. II. Series.
ML3557.V34   1997
782.42162'974—dc20   95-41755
                                                                         CIP
                                                                         MN

In memory of
Emily Hill and Dorothy Tappay

We always sing those Ghost Dance songs. Our place looks real good. That's what that means. It makes seeds grow. That's the kind of song it is, it ain't just a song. It's a religious song that you sing to God.

—Emily Hill (1978)

Behind all religions lies nature. It lurks equally behind the buried cults of Neanderthal man, Cro-Magnon hunting, and in the questions of Job and in the answering voice from the whirlwind.

—Loren Eiseley, *The Lost Notebooks of Loren Eiseley*

Contents

Illustrations follow page 284

Preface

The purpose of this book is threefold. First, and foremost, it presents the music and text of 130 Ghost Dance songs of the Wind River Shoshone. As amplified in the introduction, the Shoshone term for these songs is *Naraya*. These songs, along with seventeen Naraya published in a previous monograph, *Ghost Dance Songs and Religion of a Wind River Shoshone Woman* (1986), complete the corpus of Naraya music of Emily Hill and her half sister, Dorothy Tappay, which I taped over a six-year period on the Wind River Reservation in Wyoming. This presentation includes all comments by the singers concerning the meaning and imagery of the song texts.

The focus of this book differs from the earlier monograph mainly because of the wealth of material presented here and the special opportunity it offers as a consequence. The succession of song texts, each a short poetic statement of Shoshone Ghost Dance belief, creates a text of larger proportions akin to one long and complicated song cycle. Themes and images appear and reappear in variant forms and combinations. Through the process of accretion, a rich panorama of Shoshone concerns and religious belief comes into view. Themes, images, concerns, and beliefs guide my presentation of Naraya songs in this publication.

Beverly Crum, a native Shoshone speaker and linguist, has used the term "poetry songs" in reference to social dances and their texts: "Poetry songs are composed in an elevated and figurative form of language. They are often detailed descriptions of what the authors observed in their environment, with several levels of meanings" (Crum 1980:5). I am happy to extend the use of this term to Naraya song texts, which share these qualities.

The second purpose of this book is to place the songs and religion within the cognitive, conceptual worlds of Wind River Shoshone culture, the 1890 Ghost Dance religion, and, most important, the broader frame of Great Basin culture.

Third, expanding the analytical framework and conclusions of my 1986 monograph, the book presents a detailed study of the music and texts.

I met Emily Hill and Dorothy Tappay during my first summer of fieldwork on the Wind River reservation in 1977. I was learning about Shoshone music and culture in preparation for writing a master's thesis on Shoshone ceremonial music (Vander 1978). At that time Emily, sixty-six years old, was caring for Dorothy, who, although only fifty-seven years old, had been an invalid for many years due to an accident. Emily and Dorothy sang three Naraya songs during my first interview with them. I was immediately intrigued by the music and texts of these songs; they differed markedly from other songs Shoshones sing. Over the next two summers Emily and/or Dorothy sang an additional fourteen Naraya songs for me. By 1980 neither woman could sing. So, instead, Emily played some of the tapes that she had made, over the years, of Dorothy and herself singing Naraya songs. In the summers of 1981 and 1982 Emily allowed me to make copies of all her tapes. Together we went over the texts for translation and meaning. After Dorothy's death in 1982, I lived with Emily during the summer as we continued our work. Because her hearing was failing, however, her participation became increasingly difficult. It was to be the last time we worked together. With the exception of 1985, I visited Emily every summer after that until her death in 1988, but, sadly, it was hard to communicate much more than our joy in seeing one another during these visits.

Although it is true that there are still a few elderly Shoshones who remember and can sing Naraya songs, their dwindling repertoire is no longer rooted in Ghost Dance belief. To my knowledge, Emily and Dorothy were the last of their people to believe in the Shoshone Ghost Dance religion. This publication fulfills my deep obligation to the two women and to the preservation of the material that they placed in my safekeeping.

For a variety of reasons, some of which will be discussed later, it was not possible to translate every word of every song. Emily was able to provide full, or almost full, literal translations for 105 songs (including the 17 from *Ghost Dance Songs*) and partial translations for an additional 25. Phonetic transcriptions of 17 songs for which Emily had neither translation nor comments appear in appendix B.

For further refinement of the Shoshone texts I sought the assistance of Gladys Hill, Emily's daughter-in-law, who helped me with both translation and orthography. In some instances Gladys also provided Shoshone words as spoken in everyday language, when they varied from those forms used in the song texts. For comparison, these versions are presented side-by-side with their sung counterparts in the glossary (appendix C) at the end of this book. The differences between sung and spoken words are an important subject that I examine, among other topics, in chapter 8.

I am not a linguist. There remain many ambiguities and questions concerning the orthography, syntax, and grammar that Emily, Gladys, and I could not resolve. Therefore, I view these transcriptions of the texts in their sung version as a first presentation. It is my hope that other scholars and people who are fluent in Shoshone will follow me, using their skill to bring out the texts' subtleties of meaning and artistry of poetic form. In order to facilitate this, all the tapes of these songs are deposited at the Library of Congress, the Archives of Traditional Music at Indiana University, and the University of Wyoming. One can also hear four Naraya songs sung by Emily and Dorothy on the cassette tape that accompanies my book *Songprints: The Musical Experience of Five Shoshone Women* (1988). (See songs 1, 2, 3, and 12 in appendix A of the present volume.)

The seventeen songs in my *Ghost Dance Songs* (1986) were numbered chronologically, according to the order in which Emily and Dorothy sang them for me. Because the songs in the present book are a continuation of the total collection of Naraya songs sung by both women, I number the first song here as song 18. There is, however, no chronological order to the songs in this book. The tapes that Emily made and that I copied were made approximately over a ten-year period. I do not know their chronology. The ordering of the texts in this publication derives from my classification of their topics and imagery.

So that all the Naraya texts that I have recorded from Dorothy and Emily are contained in a single volume, I have included the literal translations for songs 1–17 in appendix A.

Emily and Dorothy's Naraya repertoire constitutes the majority of published songs for this genre. There are, in addition, fewer than two dozen Naraya songs, provided by other singers, that have been recorded and/or published by me or by other researchers. I have recorded ten songs from four other Shoshones; eight of these songs are identical to ones that Emily and Dorothy sang, and the ninth is a variant. (I will note in chapters 2–7 whenever I have multiple recordings of a song.) The tenth song is exceptional. I have published it previously and analyzed how its text and music differ from those of all other Naraya songs (Vander 1988:63, 64). I have been able to translate and transcribe the texts and music for two of four Naraya songs recorded by other researchers: a 1909 recording of Dick Washakie by Edward Curtis (Archives of Traditional Music at Indiana University, accession no. 57-014-F) and a 1951 recording of Cyrus Shongutsie by Willard Rhodes (Library of Congress record: AAFS L38). These two songs are identical to ones that Emily and Dorothy sang and I will likewise note in chapters 2–7 which songs they duplicate. In chapter 10, I present four Naraya texts that Demitri Shimkin collected in 1937 and subsequently published. While these four songs do not appear in Emily and Dorothy's repertoire, their form and imagery are completely congruent with it.

Acknowledgments

As with my first monograph, I hope this work pays honor to Emily Hill and Dorothy Tappay, whose friendship has meant so much to me. I am particularly grateful to two native Shoshone speakers, Gladys Hill and Rupert Weeks, both now deceased, who worked with me in the translation of these texts. I also thank all my friends of the Wind River Shoshone community who took me in over many summers, patiently answered my questions, and made me feel at home. I acknowledge a special debt of gratitude to James Mooney, whose monumental Ghost Dance study served as inspiration for my own work. I offer this book as a centennial tribute to him and to the publication, in 1896, of *The Ghost-Dance Religion and the Sioux Outbreak of 1890*.

Within the contemporary community of scholars, I dedicate this book to the memory of the anthropologist Demitri Shimkin. He was a beloved mentor to me from the start and an inspiration, both in his scholarship and his deep humane concern for all people. He freely offered his support and expertise—all invaluable to me during long years of solitary work. I thank Charlotte Frisbie, also an anthropologist, for her encouragement and friendship over the years. I benefited from her experience, knowledge, and keen sense of humor. I gratefully acknowledge the prodigious effort of both Charlotte Frisbie and Michael Hittman, who read through the manuscript and offered many insightful suggestions for improving it.

I am also grateful to other scholars for permission to reprint both published and unpublished material from their work: Figure 1 and Southern Paiute song texts, reprinted from *Anthropology of the Numa: John Wesley Powell's Manuscripts on the Numic Peoples of Western North America*, edited by Don D. Fowler and Catherine S. Fowler (Washington, D.C.: Smithsonian Institution Press, 1971), pp. 6 and 122–28, respectively, by permission of the publisher, © 1971. Southern Paiute song texts and songs reprinted from *The Collected Works of Edward Sapir*, volume 4, edited by Regna Darnell and Judith Irvine (Berlin: Mouton de Gruyter), pp. 623–24, 627, 632–35, 638–39, 642–43, 652–57, 659, 683, 691, 697, and 707, by permission of the publisher, © 1994. Unpublished song texts and other data from 1937 fieldnotes by Demitri Shimkin, courtesy of Tauby Shimkin. Figure 2 reprinted from Wick Miller, "Uto-Aztecan Languages," in *Handbook of North American Indians*, edited by William C. Sturtevant, vol. 10: *Southwest*, edited by Alfonso Ortiz (Washington, D.C.: Smithsonian Institution Press, 1983), p. 114, by permission of the publisher, © 1983. Figure 4 reprinted from Demitri Shimkin, "Eastern Shoshone," in *Handbook of North American Indians*, vol. 11: *Great Basin*, edited by Warren L. D'Azevedo (Washington, D.C.: Smithsonian Institution Press, 1986), p. 310, by permission of the publisher, © 1986. Northern Shoshone song texts and Ghost Dance songs reprinted from Sven Liljeblad, "Oral Tradition: Content and Style of Verbal Arts," and Thomas Vennum, Jr., "Music," in *Handbook of North American Indians*, vol. 11 (Washington, D.C.: Smithsonian Institution Press, 1986), pp. 648 and 703–4, respectively, by permission of the publisher, © 1986. Figure 5 reprinted from James A. Goss, "A Basin-Plateau Shoshonean Ecological Model," in *Desert Research Institute Publications in the Social Sciences* 8 (Reno: University of Nevada, 1972), p. 128, by permission of the author, © 1972. Round Dance song texts reprinted from a 1988 paper, "Southern Paiute Round Dance Songs," by Robert J. Franklin and Pamela A. Bunte, by permission of the authors. Retranslation of Lakota Ghost Dance song texts reprinted from William K. Powers, *Voices from the Spirit World* (Kendall Park, N.J.: Lakota Books, 1990), pp. 20, 23, 27, 32, 42, 45, 48, and 56, by permission of the author, © 1990. Naraya songs 1–17, which I first published in *Ghost Dance Songs and Religion of a Wind River Shoshone Woman*. Monograph Series in Ethnomusicology, no. 4 (Los Angeles: University of California, 1986), appear in appendix A of the present book in slightly modified form, with permission of the publisher.

I am indebted to Judith McCulloh, executive editor at the University of Illinois Press, for her longstanding interest and help in publishing my work, and to Carol Bolton Betts, who edited the manuscript with meticulous care.

I cannot adequately thank my husband, Arthur, for making my work possible. Beyond moral and financial support, I thank him for his intellectual involvement with my work—bringing to bear his own scientific expertise. The book and I have richly profited from his many editorial and computer skills.

I gratefully acknowledge and thank the National Endowment for the Humanities for its support of my research on the reservation. I also thank the Endowment, as well as the American Council of Learned Societies, for fellowship support during the writing of the book. May this work be a fitting tribute to all. I, alone, take full responsibility for any errors of fact or interpretation contained herein.

I offer this book to the reader in the spirit of J. Henri Fabre, who, at the end of his tenth and final volume of *Souvenirs Entomologiques,* wrote, "If we had to wait until we knew every detail of the question studied, no one would venture to write the little that he knows. From time to time, a few truths are revealed, tiny pieces of the vast mosaic of things. Better to divulge the discovery, however humble it be. Others will come who, also gathering a few fragments, will assemble the whole into a picture ever growing larger but ever notched by the unknown" (Fabre 1991:66).

Key to Orthography

The following are used in my transcriptions of Naraya song texts and Shoshone spoken words. The orthography used in the quoted works of other scholars follows their use, which usually employs International Phonetic symbols.

a	as in f*a*ther
a:	long *a*, etc.
e	as in p*a*y
ë (ə)	as in *a*bove
i	as in el*i*te
ï (ɨ)	as in s*i*t
o	as in n*o*
ȯ (ɔ)	as in l*a*w
u	as in l*u*te
ü (ѡ)	as in p*u*t
ai	as in Th*ai*land
oi	as in n*oi*se
x	Scottish *ch* in loch
I, etc.	final whispered sounds
~	nasalization
ʔ	glottal stop
ʰ	aspiration

Accent generally falls on the first syllable and every other syllable after that.

Note on Textual Transcription and Translation

Because of the sung poetic nature of the Naraya song texts, I have felt it imperative to be faithful to the sounds of the words in performance. My transcription, therefore, is phonetic rather than phonemic. I have made no attempt to standardize my transcription for any given word or morpheme. For example, the Shoshone word for fog is pronounced differently in different songs and my transcriptions reflect it: *vagïna*, in song 36 and *bagana*, in song 40. Similarly, *-tsi*, a diminutive suffix in song 18, appears alternately as *-zi* in song 71.

I am aware that my orthography differs from that used by Wick Miller and other linguists who are Shoshone specialists, especially in my choice of consonants. This is, of course, because I lack linguistic training and must depend solely on how I hear the words. I often use b, d, and g where Miller uses p, t, and k. However, I do note with interest that Miller has made the following comment on this issue: "Sometimes the p, t, and k sound like English b, d, and g" (W. Miller 1972:6). So it often seems to me, and thus my transcription.

The reader will notice that there may be several different forms of a Shoshone word for which the English translation is identical. This is true for spoken language, where there are long and short forms of the same word. The Shoshone language also creates new compound words by joining together two or more word stems. All of these features appear in Naraya song texts. In addition, in some instances, the song forms may be different from what a Shoshone speaker might expect to see. This is especially true of words that in their sung form add vocable infixes or suffixes to them, lengthening rather than shortening the word in unusual ways. I will analyze these differences between sung and spoken language in chapter 8. The Shoshone-English portion of the glossary (appendix C) presents every form of a word as it appears in the song texts: for each alphabetical entry, the sung form or forms are given first; a longer spoken form, if I know one, follows, in brackets; and then the English translation is given. The English-Shoshone portion of the glossary refers the reader only to the first Shoshone word, if there are more than one, in the preceding Shoshone-English portion.

A word about hyphens is also appropriate here. I use hyphens in my transcriptions in order to bring out the different aspects of word construction: the stems of compound words; vocable infixes and suffixes; stem reduplications; and nasalization. The reader will note that in some instances, the placement of hyphens in a word of textual transcription does not agree with its placement in the lyrics accompanying the music. For example, in song 20, *sogap-ade* appears as *so-go-pa-de* in the lyrics. I have tried to relate the texts as closely as possible to the spoken words from which they derive. However, when the text appears as lyrics, musical elements may dictate slight differences in the syllabic division of a word and thus the difference between the text and the lyrics.

Other signs and abbreviations that appear in the translation of the texts are as follows:

n-	nasal insert
in-	nasal insert
um-	nasal insert
s.r.	stem reduplication
e.d.	ending duplication
s. or suff.	suffix
a.s.	affectionate suffix
d.a.s.	diminutive affectionate suffix
v. or voc.	vocable
v.s.	vocable suffix
?v.s.	could be a vocable suffix or meaningful suffix or another word in compound construction
-[ ]-	vocable infix
e.v.	ending vocable
abb. e.v.	abbreviated ending vocable
grass/green	grass and/or green
?	unknown Shoshone letter or word
?*dua* or ?child	questionable Shoshone or English word
(GH)	suggestion by Gladys Hill
(RW)	suggestion by Rupert Weeks

Key to Musical Transcriptions

6th verse · Indicates which repeat of the song has been transcribed

 · B♭ throughout the song with no implication of scale or key

 · Written accidentals for notes are maintained throughout the remainder of the entire section and do not carry across the barline into the next section

 · Original starting note

 · Pitch lowered or raised by no more than a quarter tone

 · Note released by portamento fading down to an indefinite pitch

 · Note released by portamento fading up to an indefinite pitch

 · Portamento between notes

 · Slurs indicate that a word, syllable, or vocable sustains through the music until the next word, syllable, or vocable appears

$\dfrac{3}{8}$ ♪ = one beat, underlying rhythmic organization of threes (or multiples thereof) but not invariable, and with no implied barline/accent pattern

$\dfrac{2}{4}$ ♩ = one beat, underlying rhythmic organization of twos (or multiples thereof) but not invariable, and with no implied barline/accent pattern

, Brief rest for breath without direct rhythmic significance

Pulsations on a tone without breaking the tone

Another representation of pulsation

> Accent

(>) Lesser accent

Softer dynamic level for smaller notehead

‖○‖ Tonic note

Rhythmic representation of the relative total durations of all pitches used in a song

Marks the end of a musical section

Marks a subdivision within the musical section

Three dots indicate an omitted portion of music in the middle of an excerpt

a, b Sections of song

a^1, a^2 Standardized variant forms of a musical section

Shoshone
Ghost Dance
Religion

Introduction

The Wind River Shoshone Ghost Dance, or *Naraya*, has been viewed traditionally as one particular rendering of the widespread 1890 Ghost Dance religion started by the Northern Paiute prophet Wovoka. In fact, the Naraya is richly complex, the creation of cultural and individual overlays, dovetailings, congruencies, sympathetic vibrations, and overtones. The organizational form of the book will imitate its subject and use all of these components to isolate and identify the elements and essence of the Naraya.

Wind River Shoshone History

Wind River Shoshones have two distinctly different cultural heritages—Great Basin and Plains. Their origins can be traced at least to the thirteenth century in the southwestern portion of the Great Basin, near Death Valley (E. Johnson 1975:16–18; Warren and Crabtree 1986:191). Wind River people are but one small group of the Shoshones, who are members of the Uto-Aztecan linguistic family. (See figure 1, a map showing the distribution of Shoshone speakers, and figure 2, a map showing the distribution of Uto-Aztecan languages.) For all, survival was precarious in the dry, harsh environment of the Basin. Shoshones gathered food for their daily diet, supplementing this with hunting and fishing when possible. The search for food was a primary concern, reflected in the names that Shoshones used to distinguish one another, for example, Mountain Sheep Eaters, Salmon Eaters, and Pine Nut Eaters (Hoebel 1938:410–12). These names, which derived from different geographic areas and their regional resources, were not permanent. People who moved on from one area to another assumed, in the process, the relevant food-name from their new territorial home (Harris 1940:43; E. Johnson 1975:7; Liljeblad 1957:56; Park 1938:622, 623; Powell 1971:38, 287n.141; Steward 1939:262; Steward 1970:141, 142; Steward and Wheeler-Vogelin 1974:

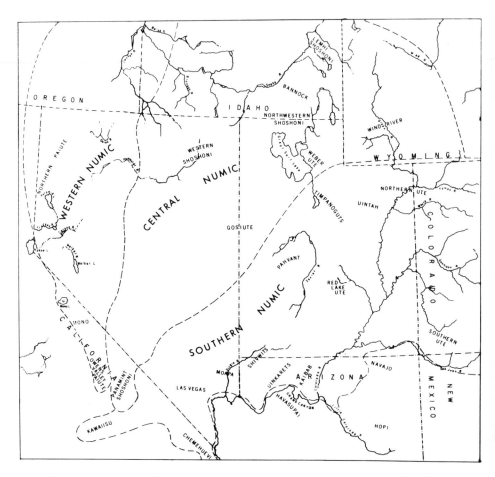

Figure 1. Location of Numic tribes and linguistic groups. From Powell 1971:6.

54, 55). Water was also a prime concern. As we will see, these ancient and basic needs remained central to the Naraya.

Over time, Shoshones separated into four major divisions, with cultural differentiation overlaid upon their common heritage. Ancestors of the Wind River Shoshones moved eastward across the Rocky Mountains and onto the Plains by the early 1500s. They were one of the first groups on the northern Plains to acquire horses in the early 1700s (Shimkin 1986a:309; Shimkin 1986b:517), and being the easternmost group, they were sometimes referred to as Eastern Shoshones.

They, in turn, split in two, and the group that moved down to the Southern Plains became known as Comanches (Shimkin 1940:19). Shoshones who moved up into Idaho were called Northern Shoshones while those who continued to live close to their ancestral origins in Nevada and California were Western Shoshones.

Mounted, the Wind River Shoshones (henceforth, unless otherwise

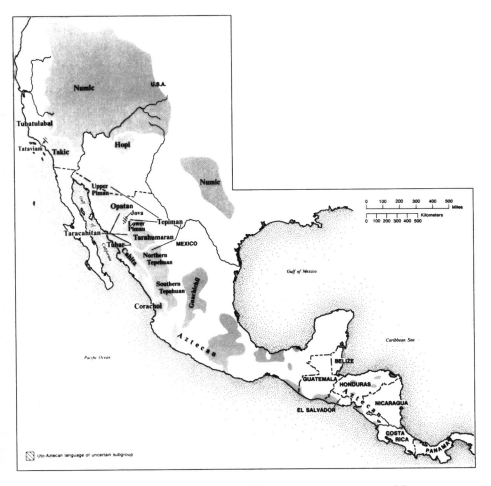

Figure 2. Approximate distribution of Uto-Aztecan languages and language groups at the time of the first European contact. Not mapped are groups for which no linguistic data survive. From W. Miller 1983:114.

noted, I will simply refer to them as the Shoshone) were full participants in Plains life as nomadic hunters in search of buffalo and as
warriors contending for hunting grounds and horses. From 1780 to
1825 they were pushed west of the Rockies by the Blackfeet, who by
that time had acquired not only horses but guns. Sickness, another
scourge during this same period and a challenge to Shoshone survival,
also profoundly influenced the development and orientation of Shoshone religions, including the Naraya.

However, Euro-Americans posed the principal threat to Shoshone
survival in the nineteenth century. Washakie, a strong leader during
this period, skillfully managed Shoshone accommodation to the
United States government. In 1868 he and other Shoshone leaders
signed a treaty establishing the Wind River Reservation on a fragment
of traditional Shoshone territory. "The period from 1885 to 1905 was
a cruel time for the Shoshones, . . . The buffalo were gone, the government placed the Northern Arapaho—traditional enemy of the
Shoshone—on the reservation, government rations were lowered,
agricultural attempts which had at first flourished subsequently failed,
and a measles epidemic brought death to many Shoshone children . . ." (Vander 1986:5).

Recoiling from these traumas, Shoshones were receptive to influences from many new sources. From Euro-America came Mormon
proselytizing and the successful establishment of an Episcopalian
mission. From intertribal contacts with the Crow, Gros Ventre, and
Cree came new dances such as the Women's Dance and Wolf Dance
(Shimkin 1942:456–67). Contact with the Comanche and Arapaho led
to the introduction of the Peyote religion, an all-night ceremony for
health, general welfare, and religious insight (Stewart 1987:193–94).

> The old Sun Dance was renewed, combining old beliefs, Christian sym-
> bolism, and addressing the grave problems of health and tribal disuni-
> ty which marked the times. Beliefs forged in the heat of that painful
> time of cultural flux and physical hardship soon crystallized and cooled.
> They form the mold for Shoshone beliefs in the twentieth century. . . .
> Livelihood today comes from a variety of farming, ranching, leasing,
> and employment on and off the reservation, all supplemented by the
> per capita allotment of tribal income derived from oil and gas royal-
> ties. (Vander 1986:5)[1]

Despite the Wind River Shoshones' long history and participation
on the Plains, scholars continue to classify them as Great Basin people. Language, myth, and other cultural practices support this viewpoint. However, I was slow to recognize this because my focus had

always been on music. Songs that Shoshones sing today—in conjunction with the Sun Dance, War Dance, Round Dance, and ceremonies—are all clearly in the Plains musical style and, with few exceptions, relate to Plains life and culture. I knew that Naraya songs were different; their musical style was Great Basin. But it was only after I had studied all the song texts in this book that I fully understood the extent to which Great Basin culture continued to inform Wind River Shoshone culture. Naraya religion and poetic expression are Great Basin to the core.

The Ghost Dance Movements

The 1890 Ghost Dance movement began with the Northern Paiute, a Great Basin people, and spread rapidly to other groups within the Basin and across the Plains. To understand this movement and its relationship to the Naraya, one must go back to its precursor, the 1870 Ghost Dance movement.

The 1870 Ghost Dance Movement

In the best of times, Northern Paiute life in the Great Basin was difficult. Neither 1870 nor 1890 was the best of times. This is important for understanding the genesis of both Ghost Dance movements and their dissemination. Euro-American expansionism set in motion a long destructive chain of events—the advent of explorers, horses, trappers, missionaries, slavers, overland migrations, railroads, mining, cattle ranches, disease, forts, federal troops, wars, treaties, and reservations—that ravaged the land and the cultures it had once supported (Malouf and Findlay 1986:499–516).

In his study of the 1870 Ghost Dance, Hittman writes, "Ethnographic data on the Northern Paiute can be interpreted that the *food quest* and the *shamanistic-curing complex* were two of their cultural foci, . . . Deprivation was experienced on the Walker River Reservation because early reservation life disrupted these two cultural foci, thereby providing the seed bed from which arose the 1870 Ghost Dance" (Hittman 1973:256–57).

Thus, around 1869, Wodziwob, a Northern Paiute prophet of the 1870 Ghost Dance, dreamed that a train was coming from the east, and he began to preach at large traditional gatherings, such as at the time of the pine nut harvest or the communal rabbit hunt, or at gatherings he called (Du Bois 1939:5, 6). On all of these occasions, Northern Paiutes danced what was called the Round Dance (described in detail in chapter 1). Thus, Wodziwob's prophecies became an add-on to the Round Dance. Before or after the dance, he went into a trance, traveled to the spirit land, and communicated with the dead (Du Bois 1939:5–7). In this way he learned that the Northern Paiute dead were coming back to life in three or four years (Du Bois 1939:3). Although he later denied that he had prophesied the return of the dead, his disciples did; there is even evidence suggesting a tradition of such prophets among the Northern Paiute before Wodziwob's time (Du Bois 1939:3, 4). People were to do the Round Dance, use paint, and bathe—all old and traditional activities (Du Bois 1939:6, 7). The source for new songs that were to accompany the 1870 Round Dance likewise followed traditional patterns, in this case, the way to acquire spiritual knowledge. Wodziwob learned the songs while transported to the spirit world in a trance (Du Bois 1939:6, 7).

Although Wodziwob was later to become a well-known shaman, he was not one at the time of the 1870 Ghost Dance. In any case, the prediction of the return of the dead in mass numbers, with specific reference to the Paiute recently deceased from epidemics, went well beyond the claims or power of the shaman, who ordinarily resurrected an unconscious patient by going into a trance and recovering the lost soul. Du Bois reported one informant's recollection of Wodziwob's words as follows: "Our fathers are coming, our mothers are coming, they are coming pretty soon. You had better dance. Never stop for a long time. Swim. Paint in white and black and red paint. Every morning wash and paint. Everybody be happy" (Du Bois 1939:4).

Wodziwob further lept to the prophecy of the restoration of Northern Paiute land, its grasses, seeds, and pine nuts, a return to the time before it was ravaged by cattle and settlers. In doing so, he clearly went beyond the traditional prayers for rain, seeds, and health spoken at the conclusion of Round Dance performances. We learn Wodziwob's vision for the natural world from the report of Frank Campbell, a non-Indian employee on the reservation at the time and a witness to one of Wodziwob's trances and its revelation. Campbell said: "Upon reanimation he gave a long account of his visit in the spirit to the Supreme Ruler, who was then on the way with all the spirits of the departed dead to again reside upon this earth and change it into a paradise. Life was to be eternal, and no distinction was to exist between races" (Mooney [1896] 1991:703).

In 1872, an Indian agent named Bateman wrote a report concerning the 1870 Ghost Dance by the Walker River Reservation Paiute. Bateman, like Campbell, underscored the restoration of the natural world as a key element in Wodziwob's prophecy. Bateman reported what seemed ludicrous to him, "the farce that God was coming in the mountains beyond with a large supply for all their wants, of what Indians most desire, game, and withal transform the sterility of Nevada to the fertility and beauty of Eden. (All would admit a glorious transformation, but over which in prospect they would dance.)" (*Annual Reports of the Commissioner of Indian Affairs to the Secretary of the Interior*, quoted in Hittman 1973:260).

Hittman suggests that Wodziwob's 1870 Ghost Dance had two principal meanings for the Walker River Reservation Paiutes. First, it was a "curing rite writ large," an attempt to resurrect those recently deceased from typhoid and measles epidemics in 1867 and 1868 (Hittman 1973:262). Second, it was a restorative rite for the ecosystem, a returning to nature in its aboriginal state (Hittman 1973:262, 263).

The 1870 Ghost Dance drew on ancient Northern Paiute–Great Basin traditions and religious complexes, shamanism and the Round Dance, both sources of power that could affect health and fertility in the natural world. Wodziwob layered on top of them prophecies and expanded potencies in response to the accumulated woes of the late 1860s (Hittman 1973:258–64). Pushing to the limit and beyond, Wodziwob used traditional sources of power and ceremony in order to accomplish the extraordinary.

Regarding the form and religious meaning of the Round Dance, Hittman writes, "The essential and overwhelming similarities between the 1870 Ghost Dance and the traditional Round Dance enable us to imagine the relative ease with which Wodziwob could have grafted the religious movement he founded upon Paiute culture" (Hittman 1973:264). (As we will see, this comment is equally appropriate to the 1890 Ghost Dance.)

Hittman also explains how belief in the resurrection of the dead—an unexpected element of the 1870 Ghost Dance religion, given the strong ritual avoidance of the dead by Northern Paiutes—may derive from Wodziwob's personal history. He cites evidence that Wodziwob originated from Fish Lake Valley. Unlike the Walker River Paiutes, who never even mentioned the name of the deceased after death, Paiutes from Fish Lake Valley and Owens Valley performed an annual mourning ceremony (the "cry dance") anywhere from one to four years after the death of a person. In the late 1860s the population of the Walker River Reservation increased and became diverse as people from other Paiute groups immigrated there. Wodziwob was part of this influx as were others with a background in the mourning ceremony (Hittman 1973:264–66). Hittman writes, "Thus it is suggested that

either Wodziwob attempted to introduce the annual mourning ceremony at the Walker River Reservation, or that the 1870 Ghost Dance
functioned as such for 'Mono Pi-Utes' living there" (Hittman 1973:
267).

Cultural dislocation and deprivation afflicted many tribes, creating fertile ground for the 1870 Ghost Dance. It was soon disseminated
west to many tribes in California (Du Bois 1939:map facing p. 1, 129;
Gayton 1930:81–82; Kroeber 1904:32; Kroeber 1925:868), throughout
the Basin, including to the Western Shoshone, and north to the
Northern Shoshone (Jorgensen 1986:661). By 1870, the Wind River
Shoshones were performing this Ghost Dance, and they continued
to do so through the early 1880s (Jorgensen 1972:75, 77; Jorgensen
1986:661). Indeed, Colonel Brackett's 1879 report on Shoshone "Religion, Superstitions, and Manners" may very well be an allusion to
annual performances of the 1870 Ghost Dance by the Wind River
Shoshones. As with Bateman's report, Brackett's comments reflect the
Euro-American condescension toward Native Americans that was
common to his time, culture, and position: "Almost every summer
they get thoroughly frightened by some prophet's predicting the
speedy end of the world. Old and young mount their ponies and
crossing the mountains, assemble near Bear River, where they go
through a series of dances, incantations, and rites until they are almost beside themselves in excitement. This excitement disappears as
quickly as it makes its appearance, and then all hands pack up again
and bundle themselves off home as contented as can be" (Brackett
1880:332).

At home on the Walker River Reservation, the 1870 Ghost Dance
movement was short-lived. Significantly, the last performance of the
dance, in 1871, also marked the date of its unfulfilled prophecy (Hittman 1973:268). There is evidence that even Wodziwob became disil-
lusioned. A reported subsequent visit he made to the land of the dead
was said to have revealed only silent shadows, with no promise of
returning life (Hittman 1973:269).

Others rejected both prophet and movement after they learned
that on some occasions Wodziwob resorted to trickery in order to
convince his followers, for example, secretly exploding dynamite
while he deceitfully claimed communication from the dead (Du Bois
1939:5).

A final reason for the downfall of this religious movement among
the Northern Paiutes is equally pragmatic and ecologically oriented.
In place of depending on dance and ceremony to bring back the
plants, animals, and subsistence patterns of the past, Paiutes began

to develop new skills as farmers. Despite problems of flooding on their land, they persisted in their efforts and by 1874 had achieved relative success in agriculture (Hittman 1973:268).

Although Wovoka's father, Numu-tibo'o,[2] has been mentioned as an assistant to Wodziwob (Du Bois 1939:3), his exact role in the 1870 Ghost Dance is not known definitively (Hittman 1990:29). In any case, Wovoka was thirteen or fourteen years old in 1870 and could have learned of the religion, if not directly then second-hand, independent of his father's influence (Hittman 1990:96). In any event, the 1870 Ghost Dance contributed a religious prophetic base for the 1890 Ghost Dance.

The 1890 Ghost Dance Movement

In 1889,[3] as the earth itself lay in darkness during a solar eclipse, Wovoka (known also as Jack Wilson) lay unconscious with a severe fever and dreamed: "When the sun died, I went up to heaven and saw God and all the people who had died a long time ago. God told me to come back and tell my people they must be good and love one another, and not fight, or steal, or lie. He gave me this dance to give to my people—Wovoka" (Mooney [1896] 1991:764).

Based on interviews with Wovoka in 1892, Mooney summarized Ghost Dance doctrine:

> The great underlying principle of the Ghost Dance doctrine is that the time will come when the whole Indian race, living and dead, will be reunited upon a regenerated earth, to live a life of aboriginal happiness, forever free from death, disease, and misery. On this foundation each tribe has built a structure from its own mythology, and each apostle and believer has filled in the details according to his own mental capacity or ideas of happiness, with such additions as come to him from the trance. Some changes, also, have undoubtedly resulted from the transmission of the doctrine through the imperfect medium of the sign language. The differences of interpretation are precisely such as we find in Christianity, with its hundreds of sects and innumerable shades of individual opinion. The white race . . . has no part in this scheme of aboriginal regeneration, and will be left behind with other things of earth that have served their temporary purpose, or else will cease entirely to exist . . . . Believers were exhorted to make themselves worthy of the predicted happiness by discarding all things warlike and practicing honesty, peace, and good will, not only among themselves, but also towards the whites, so long as they were together.
>
> . . . The mythology of the doctrine is only briefly indicated, but the principal articles are given. The dead are all arisen and the spirit hosts are advancing and have already arrived at the boundaries of this earth,

led forward by the regenerator in shape of a cloud-like indistinctness. The spirit captain of the dead is always represented under this shadowy semblance. The great change will be ushered in by a trembling of the earth, at which the faithful are exhorted to feel no alarm. (Mooney [1896] 1991:777, 782)

An 1890 interview by Arthur Chapman with Captain Josephus, a Northern Paiute policeman on the Walker River Reservation, leaves open to question Mooney's contention that whites were not to be included in the Ghost Dance prophecy. They were, at least, clearly present in two seminal trance-visions by Wovoka as described by Josephus: "God came and took him to heaven and showed him everything there; . . . both Indians and whites who were all young; . . . God came and took him to heaven again, and he saw all the Indians and white people who had died heretofore, that they were all young, and having a good time, dancing, etc." (Hittman 1990:198).

Without question, Wovoka urged peaceful relations between Indians and whites in this world (Hittman 1990:99–102). Any hostility toward whites expressed in Ghost Dance performance developed after the religion spread east onto the Plains. To my knowledge, there is no explicit statement by Wovoka that excluded whites from the new world to come. Tassitsie, a Wind River Shoshone man who traveled to Nevada in 1890 to learn the Ghost Dance, told Shimkin: "Wilson [Wovoka] made no claim that the white people would blow away" (Shimkin 1942:457).[4]

Hittman analyzes the controversy concerning the place of whites in Ghost Dance prophecy: "Although Mooney took care to distinguish between the pacific nature of Wovoka's doctrine and its radical reinterpretation on the Plains, sweeping conclusions in chapter 10 of this grand work [specifically, the exclusion of whites in the Ghost Dance prophecy] could have altered our own consciousness" (Hittman 1992:158). Mooney's "sweeping conclusions" place a Plains filter on Ghost Dance doctrine and through it subsequent generations of Americans have viewed the Ghost Dance.

Hittman supplies another explanation in this matter: "America's fascination with the Plains and its corresponding disdain for Great Basin 'Digger' Indians" (Hittman 1992:159). Euro-American prejudice toward Plains and Great Basin cultures, which regarded one with fascination and the other with disdain, was born of nineteenth-century experience. D'Azevedo summarizes this dichotomy:

To the White immigrants of the 1850s and 1860s who had a grudging respect for the mounted warriors of the eastern and northern plains,

the small scattered groups of Western Shoshone, Northern and Southern Paiute, and Washoe beyond the Wasatch Mountains were perceived
as the most wretched of the earth, a people depicted as roaming the
land on foot to scratch out a meager survival on roots, seeds, and small
animals.... These attitudes reflected a familiar pattern of American
conquest of the continent in which those who put up the most formi-
dable resistance to domination [for example, Plains tribes such as the
Lakota] became romanticized in historical lore ... while the generally
peaceable and helpless were despised and ignored. All but a few of the
remnant groups in the Great Basin and California in this period (referred to derogatively as Diggers) fared badly in this process. (D'Azevedo
1986a:2)

Details of Ghost Dance performance were written down in 1891
by an Arapaho man (Casper Edson) listening to Wovoka address a
Cheyenne and Arapaho delegation. As freely rendered by Mooney,
Wovoka instructs: "When you get home you must make a dance to
continue five days. Dance four successive nights, and the last night
keep up the dance until the morning of the fifth day, ... I want you
to dance every six weeks. Make a feast at the dance and have food
that everybody may eat. Then bathe in the water. That is all" (Mooney
[1896] 1991:781).

Wovoka expressed such moral teachings as, "Do no harm to any
one.... Do not tell lies" (Mooney [1896] 1991:782). Tucked into the
beliefs and practices of the religion was also a promise concerning
weather: "There will be a good deal of snow this year and some rain.
In the fall there will be such a rain as I have never given you before"
(Mooney [1896] 1991:781). (Seemingly irrelevant, the power to predict and influence weather has, in fact, great significance to the Ghost
Dance religion as conceived by Wovoka, and its meaning will unfold
in a later discussion.)

From what is known of Wovoka and the history of the 1890 Ghost
Dance religious movement, one can discern some of the disparate elements, in addition to the 1870 Ghost Dance movement, that were
fused to create it. First and most important, Wovoka was securely en-
culturated in his own Northern Paiute heritage, and the major relevant aspects of this heritage—shamanism and the Great Basin Round
Dance—will be described in detail in chapter 1. However, much of
Wovoka's boyhood was spent with an adoptive white family, the Wil-
sons. They were religious Presbyterians who read aloud from the Bible in the evenings (E. Johnson 1975:45). The appearance of God as
the source of knowledge and power in Wovoka's Ghost Dance vision,
and the emphasis on love, peace, and nonviolence as part of Ghost

Dance morality, suggest Christian influence. In fact, this is one example of many in which two systems, in this case Christian and
Northern Paiute, share congruences and dovetail with one another.
In the Paiute origin story a first Father and Mother have four children who quarrel and fight so much that the Father is forced to separate the family permanently. Tears of the saddened Father over the
breakup of his family were the origins of springs in various parts of
Paiute territory (E. Johnson 1975:15; Lowie 1924b:200–209). Love,
peace, and nonviolence are as much an implied lesson of this story
as they are explicit in Christ's sermons; each reinforces the other.
Similarly, Ghost Dance predictions of earthquakes and upheaval,
presaging the return of the dead and the advent of the new world,
carry overtones of Christian apocalyptic images for the end of the
world and Judgment Day.

Views concerning the relationship between Wovoka and Christ
differed dramatically, not only between Wovoka and his followers but
among various tribal groups of Ghost Dancers. After interviewing
Wovoka, Mooney stated, "He makes no claim to be Christ, the Son
of God, as has often been asserted in print. He does claim to be a
prophet who has received a divine revelation" (Mooney [1896]
1991:773). Hittman believes that the Northern Paiute people of Smith
and Mason Valleys in Nevada did not perceive Wovoka as Christ
because the Paiutes lacked exposure to Christian teaching (Hittman
1990:191). Other tribal groups, however, did identify Wovoka with
Christ. For example, Northern Cheyennes who talked about the Ghost
Dance to Grinnell in 1890 referred to the religion simply as the
"Dance to Christ" (Grinnell 1891:62, 65). Wovoka became "Father"
in Plains Ghost Dance songs and in the many letters addressed to him
by his followers (Dangberg 1957:288–95; Mooney [1896] 1991:959).
Here, too, Northern Paiute, Great Basin, and other Indian traditions
and terms of reverence elide with Christian terminology. *Nümi´naǎ´*,
"Our Father," was the Paiute ancestor in the origin story mentioned
above (E. Johnson 1975:15; Mooney [1896] 1991:1051).

Christ as healer and performer of miracles resonates sympathetically with Wovoka as shaman and such miracles as he performed.
Testimony from a Lakota[5] delegation member attested to Wovoka's
miraculous power to resurrect buffalo killed by the delegation as they
journeyed home (Mooney [1896] 1991:797). (See note 5 for an explanation of my use of the name "Lakota" versus "Sioux" in this book.)
A Northern Cheyenne account of an ever-replenishing bowl of buffalo meat at a Ghost Dance performance (Grinnell 1891:66) comes
closer still to Gospel stories of Christ feeding crowds with a single loaf
of bread and an ever-full bowl of wine.

Mormon settlement in the West and active missionary work with many Indian tribes uniquely reinforced Ghost Dance doctrine. American Indians were embraced as descendants of the "ten lost tribes" of Israel from the "righteous branch of Joseph" and were included within Mormon prophecy (Mooney [1896] 1991:792). Wovoka's prophecy of the return of the dead meshed with Mormon prophecy that some of the "lost" Israelites were frozen in the north and would melt and come back to life one day (Mooney [1896] 1991:703). The imminent fulfillment of this prophecy motivated further proselytizing by the Mormons among various tribes (Mooney [1896] 1991:703, 704). In turn, and unwittingly, the promised rewards for Mormon baptism and church attendance—that "old men would all become young, the young men would never be sick" and that "in the future life they will meet their friends gone before"—meshed with Ghost Dance prophecy (Mooney [1896] 1991:704; Shimkin 1939:17). In an even more explicit connection between the two religions and their prophecies, Joseph Smith Jr., prophet and founder of Mormonism, predicted that in 1890 a Messiah would come to the American Indians (Mooney [1896] 1991:792, 793).

Beyond doctrinal congruence between Mormonism and the Ghost Dance religion was behavioral congruence. Garold Barney writes that "to appreciate fully the Mormon movement, the Saints should be understood as a 'singing-dancing people'" (Barney 1986:38). Mormons danced side-by-side with Indians during Ghost Dance performance, each with overlapping yet separate visions of the event and its meaning (Mooney [1896] 1991:818).

Garold Barney also points out that unlike other prophetic movements that may have influenced the 1870 and 1890 Ghost Dance movements, Mormonism alone was "geographically tied" to it (Barney 1986:70). As West notes, "With the exception of California, Mormons occupied areas that were still largely inhabited by the Utes, Paiutes, and Shoshone; this fact alone necessitated a policy of goodwill towards the Indians and caused Brigham to reaffirm to the people, 'They are the seed of Abraham, and God is ever their God'" (West, quoted in Barney 1986:56). Bailey writes that Northern Paiutes of eastern Nevada who were inculcated with Mormon doctrine became fast adherents of the 1890 Ghost Dance (Bailey 1957:99, 121–22).

Genoa, Nevada, a site of Mormon settlement in 1852, was just sixty miles northwest of Smith and Mason valleys, home area to Wovoka (Hittman 1990:84). However, there is no documentation to indicate that Wovoka or any other Northern Paiutes living in Smith and Mason valleys or on the Walker River Reservation converted to Mormonism at that time[6] (Hittman 1990:85).

Besides Euro-American influence, other Indian cultures and prophets may also have contributed to the 1890 Ghost Dance. For example, one possible source of influence was the interior Plateau area in the northwest. According to Spier, beliefs among the indigenous Indian cultures concerning world destruction, renewal, and the return of the dead en masse could be traced back at least to the early eighteenth century (Spier 1935:5, 24). The beliefs expressed in the Prophet Dance complex of those northwest Plateau cultures became overlaid with Christian elements by the 1830s and in that form influenced the Ghost Dance religion[7] (Spier 1935:19, 20). The core of this complex consisted of belief in the destruction and renewal of the world and the return of the dead, which would be hastened by the performance of a dance that imitated the dance of the dead (Spier 1935:5).

The beliefs of Smohalla, an Indian prophet from the Columbia region of Washington, exemplified the later Christianized version of the Prophet Dance complex (Spier 1935:46). His religion appeared around 1860, approximately ten years prior to the first Ghost Dance movement. Smohalla, like Wodziwob and Wovoka, went into a trance and visited the spirit world, where he learned that all the dead were coming back to life (Mooney [1896] 1991:718, 721). Smohalla challenged the Euro-American relationship to the earth, asking: "You ask me to plow the ground! Shall I take a knife and tear my mother's bosom?" (Mooney [1896] 1991:731). Hittman points out the dissonance between this strong antifarming stance and the vigorous engagement of Walker River area Paiutes as farmers and ranchers in the late nineteenth century (Hittman 1990:79). He seriously questions the impact, if any, of Smohalla on Wovoka.

Mooney, in his study of the Ghost Dance religion, provides biographical and doctrinal details of Smohalla and other important Indian prophets who preceded Wovoka. His discussion of John Slocum and the Shaker religion of Puget Sound is pertinent, especially in light of the fact that Paiutes and perhaps Wovoka himself had contact with the religion while picking crops in Washington and Oregon (Bailey 1970:41; Hittman 1990:80). The Shaker religion was also a syncretism of Indian (Squaxin) and Christian (Catholic and Presbyterian) religious beliefs (Bailey 1957:51–56; Mooney [1896] 1991:755). Like Wovoka, Slocum became ill and "died." In this state he went to the gates of Heaven and learned about God and the upright moral life one must lead in order to enter Heaven. Slocum came back to life after this experience and began preaching these religious, moral instructions, which became the basis for the Shakers' religion (Mooney [1896] 1991:746, 747).

From his first-hand observation of Ghost Dance performances, Mooney saw connections between the hypnotic state of Ghost Dancers and the hypnotic trance experience of Slocum and his followers, which was manifested by nervous twitching (Mooney [1896] 1991:762). This connection went beyond physical likeness to similarity of function—preventing and curing disease (Mooney [1896] 1991:762). In the Ghost Dance, hypnotic trance also helped one achieve communication with the dead. Mooney cites evidence that Wovoka might have learned the art of hypnotism directly from two Shakers with the skill to heal (Mooney [1896] 1991:763). However, as Hittman comments, one need not look afar for the source of Wovoka's trances. "Until any evidence which is solid and verifiable can be put forward, this case for direct borrowing of Wovoka's trances from Shakerism must lie in abeyance, especially in light of the fact that trances were part and parcel of traditional Numu [Northern Paiute] culture" (Hittman 1990:80). Blowing, another practice of Shakers in order to "blow away badness," and brushing sin away with the hands would likewise have seemed familiar to Wovoka, although in Great Basin shamanistic practices it would have been to blow and brush away illness rather than sin (Mooney [1896] 1991:748, 761; Park 1938:56).

There can be no doubt that by 1890 all Native American cultures had endured great deprivation as a result of contact with Euro-Americans. The severe repercussions of disease, death, war, and cultural dislocation were devastating. It is easy to understand the appeal of Wovoka's prophecy. What Indians in 1890 would not fervently wish for the return of their dead, for immortality, and for a new paradise of nature? Beyond this immediate appeal, the completion of a transcontinental railroad in 1869, which included the right of free passage for all Indians, was crucial for the rapid spread of the religion as well as its further development on the Plains (Dangberg 1968:23, 26). Indians literally overrode their reservation borders, which had been designed to contain them. Rumor of the new religion prompted delegations from many Plains tribes, such as the Cheyenne, Northern and Southern Arapaho, Lakota, and Kiowa, to visit Wovoka and learn about the religion firsthand. Plains tribes enthusiastically embraced the Ghost Dance religion, and in so doing they changed it.[8]

Mooney reported:

Different dates have been assigned at various times for the fulfillment of the prophecy. Whatever the year, it has generally been held, for very natural reasons, that the regeneration of the earth and the renewal of all life would occur in the early spring. . . . The messiah himself has set several dates from time to time, as one prediction after another failed to materialize, and in his message to the Cheyenne and Arapaho, in August, 1891, he leaves the whole matter an open question. The date universally recognized among all the tribes immediately prior to the Sioux outbreak was the spring of 1891. (Mooney [1896] 1991:777–78)

Eventually the date was pushed to the "unknown future" (Mooney [1896] 1991:778).

The tragic massacre of the Lakota who were performing a Ghost Dance at Wounded Knee in 1890 was widely publicized at the time, and contributed to the disillusionment with and abandonment of the religion. Even Wovoka played a part in this. In 1891 a council of five tribes met in Oklahoma and heard the devastating report of Apiatan, a Kiowa man who had recently made the pilgrimage to meet the Ghost Dance prophet. Wovoka told Apiatan that "he had preached to Sitting Bull and others and had given them a new dance, but that some of them, especially the Sioux, had twisted things and made trouble, and now Apiatan had better go home and tell his people to quit the whole business" (Mooney [1896] 1991:913).

Many tribes, perhaps most, abandoned the Ghost Dance, but not all. The religion continued in various forms well into the twentieth century. Lesser's 1933 study of Pawnee Ghost Dance performance in connection with the Hand Game (Lesser [1933] 1978) supported Mooney's contention that each tribe developed its own form of Ghost Dance belief in accordance with its mythology and the evolution of new interpretations as a consequence of individual dream experience. Kehoe documented Ghost Dance belief and performances by "Dakota Sioux" of Canada until 1950 (Kehoe 1968:301). In this realization, elements of traditional Dakota religion, such as the pipe, sweetgrass, and eagle feathers, were integrated with the Ghost Dance (Kehoe 1968:301). Shimkin and I have each documented Wind River Shoshone Naraya belief and performances in this century (Shimkin 1953:458; Shimkin 1986a:325–27; Vander 1986; Vander 1988:11–27, 60–64, 133–35, 210–11). As will be described next, Dorothy Tappay's and Emily Hill's belief endured until their deaths in the 1980s.

The Naraya

Emily Hill's Description of the Naraya

Because of Dorothy Tappay's ill health, most of my interviews concerning all aspects of the Naraya religion were with Emily Hill. My relationship with Emily developed further as she became a principal

participant in a separate study of the musical experience of five Shoshone women (Vander 1988).

Born in 1911, Emily Hill lived her entire life on the Wind River
Reservation in Wyoming. After attending the government boarding
school on the reservation through high school, she married and had
three children. Ultimately she and her husband were divorced. Emily
lived to see a large and growing brood of grandchildren and great-
grandchildren, although she outlived her own children.

Dorothy—Emily's widowed half sister—was Emily's lifelong partner. The two women shared a hard-working independent life together,
raising hay, gardening vegetables, and tending animals. After a serious accident in the mid-1950s, Dorothy became confined to her bed.
By that time Emily had already become a medicine woman, taught
at first by an elderly Indian woman and later through her own dreams
of particular plants and their medicinal uses. Emily cared for Dorothy
until the latter's death in 1982. Their separation was not long; Emily
died in 1988.[9]

Emily and Dorothy began attending Naraya performances in the
1920s, when they were children. The religious beliefs and convictions
born of this experience lasted a lifetime, although the religion ceased
to be practiced by others on the reservation in the late 1930s.

As introduction to the first Ghost Dance song that Emily and
Dorothy ever sang for me, in 1977, Emily commented: "The white
man asked him, asked that [Indian] person, 'What's that song?' He
said, 'Ghost Dance song.' But it ain't Ghost Dance, it's a religious
song. In those days Indians [just] started talking English. They don't
really know [it]. They just say Ghost Dance song. That's why that
person told the white man."

The following year, Dorothy added her explanation. "I think they
call it Ghost Dance this way. You know that Ghost Dance song sings
about our Father in Heaven and sings about the angels and sings
about the spirit. That's why they call it Ghost Dance."

Despite their irritation with this incorrect convention, Emily and
Dorothy did, in fact, say "Ghost Dance," when speaking in English.
However, *Naraya,* which literally refers to the particular shuffling step
of the Ghost Dance, is the native term that Shoshones use for the
religion and its music. Henceforth, I will use "Naraya" when referring to the Shoshone Ghost Dance, and "Ghost Dance" when referring to the religion as practiced by other tribes.

Remarks by Emily Hill about the Naraya appear throughout this
book. Some are long; they move in fits and starts; there is repetition
within a narrative and between narratives spoken at different times.

But without question they have power, and there is meaning in the subtly different nuances of focus and expression. Inexact repetition, a major characteristic of Naraya musical style (Vander 1986:17–22, 42), is part of Emily's pattern of speech and, consequently, intrinsic to the book's presentation.

Over and over again Emily taught me three functions of the Naraya: to assure abundance of water, plants, and animals; to prevent illness and destructive storms; and to cure illness. Emily and Dorothy repeatedly emphasized that of these three functions of the Naraya, renewal of the natural world—water, plants, and animals—was primary.

Well, we said, let's sing those prayer songs. Those songs that our old-timers longway, far away was ever born. Long before our fathers and our great grandmother and fathers before they're ever born. That song was here, put here on this world for the Indians. So they used to always have a Ghost Dance—songs. They say they have big large dance. And they dance about four, five days. Our grandparents and our mother's grandparents—their grandparents—way back the songs been put on this world. For the Shoshones, Shoshones from Nevada and people from Idaho. That song belongs to us. Bannocks[10] and us. Those [Shoshone] people from Nevada. And I told Gladys [Hill], we [Emily and Dorothy] put those songs here because nobody's singing it. This, our land here, Shoshones, Wyoming. That song belongs to Shoshones, Wyoming. That's put here a long time. We got some of those songs and we'll sing it! They say when you sing those songs it makes berries grow! And makes grass grow. Make water run. That's what they say. It makes water, won't get dried up. Grass grow and berries grow, plenty of berries for in the fall. Everything: fish, anything. Sing for them. Let them, our elk and deer and all them. That's what it's for. It ain't any kind of song. It's for that. So our land won't get dry! Our berries won't dry up and die off. That's what it means. (Emily 1982)

Them songs is for, it's for the grass to grow again and grow good and trees grow good, green. Flowers grow good and berries, our berries. Some people say when our trees and grass and no berries—old people says, "Well, we'll dance. We'll make our earth come, grow up and make more water, more water." *Datevuntëg* means wake 'em up, wake 'em up. That song is for that. Them Nevada Indians, Nevada Shoshones, Johnny Dick [a Naraya leader from Nevada who settled on the Wind River Reservation] says, "My [Western Shoshone] people says, well, let's have our berries, have berries on our earth. Let the water run, let the grass grow again. Let's dance and make our earth and everything, roots what we eat on our ground—let 'em come alive again." That's what Johnny Dick said. (Emily 1982)

And when you dance, when Indians dance in springtime it makes their grass grow, your river—so you have enough water all year. Berries, things like that. (Dorothy 1978)

You know it's songs about trees and Mother Nature and the mountains and the hills and the birds, anything. River and berries and all that. That's the song they sing of that. (Dorothy 1978)

EMILY: When you sing that song, when you dance, Mother Nature's going to give all the berries. They're going to grow good. And water too.
DOROTHY: Helps everything to grow.
EMILY: We always sing those Ghost Dance songs. Our place looks real good. That's what that means. It makes seeds grow. (Emily and Dorothy 1979)

Emily also described the second function of the Naraya—the prevention of disease: "You hear white people down different states some place, way down there east or someplace—they got measles, they got flu, they got some kind of a disease. One of the old Indians, he sleep and then dream about it. That kind of a flu or measles or some kind of a sickness that's some kind of hard cough. It's coming, coming to us. Just like air, it's coming, coming this way. Let's dance! We just make it go back."

Actions at the end of a dance reinforced this preventive function, extending it to destructive storms as well as disease.

JUDY: "Did people wear blankets when they danced, or a shawl?"
EMILY: "Yes."
JUDY: "Did they shake out the blankets at the end of the dance?"
EMILY: "Uh huh. Shake blankets".
JUDY: "And that shakes away . . ."
EMILY: [patted her body and then blew across the open palm of her hand] "That means take the sickness away."
JUDY: "So it was to help against disease, measles, and things like that."
EMILY: "Yeah, that same thing too. And you can—storms, too."
JUDY: "To help that storm shouldn't be too bad or hurt people?"
EMILY: "Not too bad, yeah. These songs protect people from heavy storms, winter storms. All these songs."
JUDY: "Did they stamp their feet [at the end of the dance]?"
EMILY: "Stomped the rain away, sick."

In addition to renewal and preventive roles, the Naraya songs and dance also served a third, curative function. Emily remarked: "When you don't feel good, when you feel sick or something, you dance with them. You feel good then."

On another occasion Emily's focus moved from Naraya dance to songs.

EMILY: "When you don't feel good, you get out, you feel better when you sing it."

JUDY: "They make you feel good when you sing them?"

EMILY: "Yeah."

However, this curative function received much less attention in Emily's discussions with me than the first two functions.

Encompassing these three functions, Emily told me several times that Naraya songs are religious prayer songs. Witherspoon's statements about the potency of ritual language in Navajo culture are relevant to Shoshone and Great Basin use of language: "*In the Navajo view of the world, language is not a mirror of reality: reality is a mirror of language.* The language of Navajo ritual is performative, not descriptive. Ritual language does not describe how things are; it determines how they will be" (Witherspoon 1977:34). Language creates its own articulated reality. This applies to all the texts of all the Naraya songs. Unlike Judeo-Christian prayer, Naraya prayer is not framed in the form of a petition. It does not ask for berries and water. It simply images them in song.

Picking up this theme that Naraya songs are religious prayer songs, Emily once suggested an alternative name for the Naraya. "You could call it *nasündainïkëp*[11] ['prayer dance']," she said. This catches the essence and moves the boundary of prayer even beyond language and music. Prayer is song-text-dance, a powerful and inseparable union capable of imposing its vision, its will, on the natural world. Song, text, and dance separate only in my conversation with Emily, but not in Naraya performance, Naraya prayer.

Emily also described, more briefly, the form the dance took. Certain men sponsored Naraya performances when they received a dream instructing them to do so. Dreams were also the sources of new songs. Naraya dances would then take place on four consecutive nights, ending in the daytime of the fifth day and followed by a feast. When men and women danced together, they held hands and alternated around the circle, moving clockwise with a shuffling side step. After the song ended, the women moved back a step or two and waited for the next song to begin before moving up again and joining hands with the men. The sponsor and other song leaders would lead off the singing, joined by other dancers who knew the song and wished to sing. There was no drum or any other instrumental accompaniment.[12] A final quitting song signaled the end of the dance (Vander 1986:8–9).

As stated at the beginning of this chapter, the Naraya is traditionally viewed simply as the Wind River Shoshone rendering of the 1890 Ghost Dance movement. Remarkably, however, Emily's perceived functions of the Naraya do not include the unique and central functions of the Ghost Dance, namely the return of the dead and the coming of a new world. Indeed, for Emily the Naraya was a very ancient and purely Shoshone religion, and she denied any non-Shoshone influences on the Naraya, including any by Wovoka. For reasons to be described later in this chapter, I believe that Emily's view is in large part correct. Nevertheless, there are several lines of evidence that support a significant influence of the 1890 Ghost Dance religion on the Naraya.

First, there is documentation for direct Wind River contacts with Wovoka. In 1910, one year prior to Emily's birth, Wovoka attended a Naraya performance, given in his honor, on the Wind River Reservation (Shimkin 1942:457). Hultkrantz reports that another visit by Wovoka occurred in 1916 and/or 1917 (quoted in Hittman 1990:128). Shimkin learned from Moses Tassitsie that he had been one of several Shoshones who traveled to Mason Valley, Nevada, to visit Wovoka and learn more about the religion soon after its inception (Mooney [1896] 1991:807, 808; Shimkin 1942:457).[13] Second, and most tellingly, a small number of Emily's Naraya song texts (presented in chapter 2) do express specific aspects of Wovoka's Ghost Dance doctrine and belief. Third, there is the limited testimony concerning the form and function of the Naraya provided by Wind River Shoshones other than Emily, to which I now turn.

Descriptions of the Naraya by Other Wind River Shoshones

The earliest mention of the Naraya in scholarly literature was by Mooney, who transcribed the name as *Tänä´räyün* or *Tämänä´rayära* and translated it as "'everybody dragging,' in allusion to the manner in which the dancers move around the circle holding hands, as children do in their ring games" (Mooney [1896] 1991:791). Lowie transcribed the name as *Naroya* in his 1915 study of Wind River Shoshone dances. He wrote:

> The *na´roya* might be danced at any season of the year. The Shoshone believe it always keeps storming when the dance is performed; thus last winter (1911) it was snowing all the time because of several performances. Any man might give the dance if some member of his family was smitten with a cold or some more serious disease; to drive this away the performers would shake their blankets at the close of the ceremony. Ha´wi recalled several instances where sick people attended the dance and also shook their blankets when the headman bade the participants do so. Both men and women took part; the men first formed a circle, then each woman would step between two men, all interlock-

ing fingers. Sometimes there were so many dancers that a larger concentric circle, or part of one had to be formed. Within the (smaller) circle, though not in the center but rather near the circumference, there
was a pine tree; this remained standing and was used for subsequent
ceremonies. The dance might be performed either in the daytime or at
night; in the latter case a big fire was built in the center of the circle,
or sometimes on the outside. In the early days the ceremony lasted five
consecutive nights, only final performance took place in the daytime.
Nowadays the Shoshone only dance for one or two days. The dancers
move clockwise. There is no musical instrument; the performers move
in accompaniment to their own singing. At the close of the ceremony
all go to take a bath. (Lowie 1915:817)

Shimkin did fieldwork on the Wind River Reservation in 1937 and
received information on Naraya performance in the years prior to
World War II. I quote now primarily from unpublished data that he
sent me in 1977. (A small selection of material from Toorey Roberts
given below has been previously published; see Shimkin 1986a:327.)

Polly Shoyo, born ca. 1845: The special *dukurka* (Mountain Sheep
Eaters of the Wind River Rockies and Yellowstone, DBS) dance was the
Narayar or Round Dance. It is now called the Ghost Dance. . . . "I know
the *Narayar* (Round Dance) from way back. But lately, I had heard that
if they keep on dancing that way, the dead would come back and the
white people would vanish—blow away. In the old days, nobody faint-
ed at the dance, but then a man or woman would drop, as though in a
faint. At that time he or she would have a dream, talk to some person,
get medicine (i.e., *poh,* or supernatural powers, DBS). When the Bannocks
came, they told them it was the dead that made them faint. It was not
the Shoshoni pattern. Fainting in the dance started only with the Bannocks (ca. 1890, DBS). I didn't believe this myself. That's the reason I
didn't believe it; they never did it before (in a Round [Naraya] Dance)."

Moses Tassitsie, born 1852: *Narayar*—originated in Nevada, in Jack
Wilson's country after the treaty at Fort Bridger (1863) when the Shoshone moved to Wind River. He knew of a Nevada Indian who came
here to visit and give this dance: *ke nawaga* Doesn't Give Grub; also
started the dance in Idaho. They were told the dance causes the dead
to come closer; they would come to life sometime. The dancers would
stop, shake their blankets, pound their chests to eliminate illness. (This
is also described in Shoshone myth.)

Tassitsie saw Jack Wilson when he was an old man in Nevada. He
never said white people would blow away. After the *Narayar* had been
introduced, it became a religious dance; it has been known to cause
people to be cured. It is danced here only rarely, maybe once in four
months. At the [1937] Sun Dance some Bannocks and a few Shoshone
danced it for an hour.

Pandora Pogue, born 1863: *Narayar*—a big religious dance; They are

God's songs. Every song is supposed to kill disease and help bring the
dead back.

Toorey Roberts, born 1881: *Narayar*—he just picked it up as a boy.
Zebulon Taylor (b. 1899), Mort Pogue (b. 1874), and he are the only
ones to have the songs, without which the dance can't be held. The
purpose is to chase illness through shaking it off (*nawawai*). Usually,
it's at the Post [Fort Washakie] with all the people who want to dance
for their good; especially, his own family, Zebulon's and Steve Tappay's
(born 1879). [Steve Tappay was Dorothy's father and Emily's step-father.]
Others sit around. The dance is held at full moon, and during the three
winter months. Mostly, they dance four nights but with bad luck, only
three nights. . . .

Prior to the dance a fire is lit. People don't dress in a special way;
just have a blanket. No formal way of starting; the leader (and others
with songs) knows one to four songs each. They change around. One
leads, others follow; no instruments. When the dancers get tired and
sleepy, they shake blankets, sing one long song and then circle the fire
twice instead of once as otherwise for each song. [Note in Shimkin's
figure 1 the counterclockwise direction of the concluding two circles.
If my information is correct, this differs from the clockwise motion of
all the dances that preceded it.[14]]

The cedar (*wāpit*) in the center was used in the old days. Toorey did
not know of the *apï nïkar* ["Father Dance"].

Toorey has been leading the dance about five years, i.e., since 1932.
William Washington (born 1854, deceased by 1937) used to lead, but
switched to Peyote and quite the *Narayar*. Zebulon and Mort started
with Toorey. Carl Wise (b. 1880) and Tinzant Coando (b. 1888) sometimes come in now.

While none of the Shoshones that I interviewed in addition to
Emily could sing anywhere near the number of Naraya songs that
Emily and Dorothy could, some did remember a few songs. They also
described to me their remembrance of Naraya performance and its
purpose. The reader can glimpse their differing emphases of many of
the same elements that Emily and Dorothy described and the differing relationships that Shoshones had to the religion.

Richard Engavo was in his eighties when I interviewed him in 1979
and 1980. Born in the late nineteenth century, he would have been
approximately twelve or more years older than Emily. I did not record
his relevant comments, but he alluded to two functions of the Naraya: preventing illness and bringing back the dead. Richard observed
that winter performance of the Naraya actually brought on colds and
illness rather than prevented them and for this reason he rejected the
Naraya. I refer the reader to chapter 5, where I quote in full his one
Naraya story, which he found amusing.

Ethel Tillman, born circa 1903, was eight years older than Emily. She remembered going to Naraya performances in a horsedrawn wagon with her parents when she was about six. This would have been around 1909, twelve years earlier than Emily's introduction to the religion in 1921, when she was ten.

ETHEL: "Johnny Dick used to be one to sponsor the dance. And then there was another old fellow, I can't think of his name. . . . Well, they'd tell the people that they were going to have a dance. . . . Sometimes some of these old people would dream if they had this dance or dream about that they're going to give this dance. And dream about it and maybe there's some kind of disease that's coming to the tribe or something that's bad that's coming to the people. That's the only part that I know of. The older men used to announce it to the people. Be watching out, there's something that's coming up. They know. The old people did. . . . And they'd hold this dance to prevent it from coming around. They knew about it before anybody knew about it. . . . That some of these people would dream about it. . . . [Ethel said that people did not shake out their blankets at the end of the dance.] Then after the song's over with they all shake their feet and, you know, pound their hands, and you know, get the sickness or something away. [Ethel patted her body with her hands and then opened her hands with palms up and blew across them, i.e., blowing all sickness away.] . . . That's all they did. And then they'd dance to that. It's kind of like a prayer dance, anyway. And that's how they danced that a long time ago."

JUDY: "Was there also an idea that dead people were going to come back?"

ETHEL: "They used to say that. They still used to say that they're going to come, come back, come alive again some day. That's all they used to say, that they were coming back."

JUDY: "Also, was there a notion that it would help things in nature? That berries would come—was there a notion of that?"

ETHEL: "Yes, everything. Come along, so we'd have plenty to eat and plenty of this and that to eat. . . Round Dance, that's what we used to call it. That was the Round Dance, that was Naraya. It used to be a Round Dance [*Naraya,* being the Shoshone word]. . . . But I don't know how it ever got to be Ghost Dance [in English]."

JUDY: "Did people here make up [Naraya] songs?"

ETHEL: "No they had song for it."

JUDY: "Did the song come from—"

ETHEL: "Nevada. The old people used to sing them quite a lot."

JUDY: "When they sang those songs from Nevada, could you understand all the words, or is their language a little bit different?"

ETHEL: "No, they have the same language that we have, Shoshone language. We could understand it. It's [i.e., Naraya song texts] mostly the songs like up in the mountain or something like that, or tree or something like that—that that song was mostly like."

JUDY: "Something from nature."

ETHEL: "Something from nature. That was the songs that came out that way. Like the ground [etc.]."

JUDY: "What do you think was the meaning of those words?"

ETHEL: "Well, that's the meaning of the people what's living to be blessed or something, I don't know. But it was a meaning to them as a dance on this Round [Naraya] Dance." . . . It's kind of religious dance. . . .

"Anybody from the young kids on up, they used to all get in there and dance. . . . It was fun, you know. They danced and they laughed and had fun. . . .

"I wished I had got a tape, but see, there was no tape, nothing like that then. You can get a lot of those songs from down Nevada. 'Cause they're the ones that sing this and dance this mostly down there."

Ethel's description of the overall Naraya schedule differed in two ways from Emily's: according to her the dance lasted only two consecutive nights (performed about every two weeks) and there was no feast at the conclusion of the final dance. As to the age of the Naraya, Ethel commented simply, "I don't know 'cause I was too young. Anyway, I kind of grew up with it."

VN was born around 1917 and is approximately six years younger than Emily. He is a male singer who sings with drum groups that perform for the Sun Dance and powwow. I recorded him singing a song identical to Emily's Naraya song 1. (See appendix A.) Although only an occasional participant, he shared some of his Naraya observations with me.

VN: "I don't know too much about Ghost Dances because I never was too much involved in it. . . . I only took part just to be doing it. The others they go into it more seriously. . . .

"Well, it's been here all this time. Mostly people from down this other way, Nevada, they generally come up here. They're great for that Ghost Dancing. They didn't actually introduce it but they kept it moving here. . . . I don't know if it started here or not. Most of them used to dance it. Those people that settled here from that part of the country [Nevada]. They always were great for Ghost Dances. They know most of those songs."

JUDY: "Did you have any notion what the meaning was at that time?"

VN: "I'm pretty vague on that. There were some spiritual attach-

ments to it. Like the singing of the words, you know. . . . Not like a
regular church singing or anything like that. But it had some significance like that. After a certain kind of song they're all singing, then
they all start beating, like do this [patting themselves with their
hands]."

JUDY: "That's kind of what they do at Sun Dance?"

VN: "Yes, they do. This person, whether he's leading or not, or just
somebody that's singing it, when he gives the word, that means to
do that to your person. He gives a short—I wonder whether it's a
prayer or not. It's something like a prayer anyway. But more like a
blessing than a prayer. . . . They used to pat certain area of their bodies, whatever, to be blessed. From there they go on—dance as long
as they want. . . . They'll just keep dancing and dancing. When they
run out of a song they start on another one. When they stop they
do that, pat each other [themselves]. They start another song and go
on again. They dance for hours and hours."

JUDY: "Did they hold hands [in the dance]?"

VN: "Some of them do but most of them don't They just stand side
by side. That's the way they dance, with shuffling steps, sideways."

JUDY: "Is it almost like a [contemporary powwow] Round Dance
[step]?"

VN: "Similar to it."

JUDY: "How was it different?"

VN: "Well, because you do your own singing [i.e., the dancers provide their own musical accompaniment]. You don't [do] the steps like
you do in Round Dancing. You just have side-motion stepping in the
Ghost Dance. Clicking your heels, in other words."

Another Shoshone person, Angelina Wagon, demonstrated this
difference to me. Both dances are in a circle formation with all dancers facing the center. The side-stepping motion and its rhythm are
also the same. The pattern is: first, step to the side on the left foot
on count one and hold it there for count two. Second, bring the right
foot next to the left foot on count three. In the powwow Round
Dance, an up-down motion is added to this pattern. As the right foot
moves next to the left on count three, the dancer slightly flexes the
knees. When the left foot moves out to the left for the next step on
counts one and two, the dancer straightens the knees and comes back
to the full upright position. According to Angelina and VN, the Naraya dance step did not include the flexing and straightening of the
knees. They both also recalled that men clicked their boot heels together on count three, when the right foot came into position next
to the left.

VN said, "Naraya means the steps. It actually means the dance it-self. It refers to the step and the dance itself."

Angelina Wagon, born in 1921, is ten years younger than Emily and was a childhood friend of Dorothy. I recorded her singing seven Naraya songs (five of which are identical to Emily's Naraya 1, 85, 117, 118, and 135B, and one of which is textually a close variant of Emily's Naraya 86 and 87).

JUDY: "Did you attend some of those Naraya?"

ANGELINA: "Yes, I attend some of them." . . .

JUDY: "Were they like the Sun Dance in that they were religious?"

ANGELINA: "They were religious, you know. They tell some people to put it up, just like Sun Dance. It's for healing, or they put it up for somebody, to heal them. They would dance for four nights. It's got a meaning to that. It might be in a building or out in the open, maybe out in the brush someplace, in a circle, just dancing. There was a fire on the outside or in the center. They would hold hands, and they could get partners, too, or maybe just ladies dance. It de-pends on what they think. Well, they just go dance, oh, probably in the evening, not too long—probably until about 12:00 or 1:00 A.M. Some of them had a feast at the end. Some will furnish food like having a feast with them, you know, it's been said to him or her. It's got meanings to that. . . .

"They got to find those [Naraya] songs. They got to have a real meaning for it, too. ["Finding" songs is her terminology for learning a song and its meaning in a dream. Angelina distinguishes these songs and this process from that of ordinary composed songs.] They just come from people to people. I don't know where that song started from [Naraya song 117, which she had just sung for me]. My old people, they sing those. I learned those songs from them a long time ago."

Angelina's remembrances of Naraya performances document the transition from a religious to a social dance as well as the eventual disappearance of even the social form of Naraya.

ANGELINA: "When I used to go to them dances, you put your blan-ket over you. Maybe you got your boyfriend in there with you. That's that kind of dance that one is. Some might be religious in it, too. Or some just go up there—either way, whatever they think, you know. . . . It was someplace in the '40s that kind of quietened [*sic*] down. Some of the people around here, I don't think they give that dance. I don't know why. Maybe the people that all gave that dance passed on and all that. But these young people, they never did get that dance. Maybe they don't know the songs or something. Not like them old people that used to give them dances. I think some of that still goes on in Idaho, because they give that dance. Last year [1980] my uncle gave that dance back there. They still have that dance, but us people here, we don't do it."

HS is a participant in all important community events. He dances and sings for the powwow, sings for the Sun Dance, and often is in charge of many of the activities outside the Sun Dance lodge that are crucial for support of the ceremony. I can only guess his age, which I judge to be similar to Angelina's, give or take a few years.

HS: "That's a Shoshone dance, too, Ghost Dance. In the night they would go out there by the river and make fire and have a blanket. That's where they catch girls, you know. These menfolk, you know. You have to put her underneath his blanket. They're going to dance all night. After they're through with the song they have to shake their leg, you know, just kind of pound on the ground. That's what they used to do."

JUDY: "Was there a meaning to that?"

HS: "They try to wake the dead ones underneath the ground. It's what they want to come. That's what it means. A lot of them like that. What I got in my head, not too many of them [Naraya songs]. But I hear a lot of it. But I never keep it in my head, you know. I was too young to keep it in my head. . . . them real Ghost Dance songs, it means you're singing on that mountain or ground or something like thundering or something like that. See, like when it's like this, rainy, you know, rainy looking. [HS then sang a song identical to Emily's Naraya song 26.] See that's the way it goes. Like it's raining, you know."

JUDY: "Did they used to shake their blankets at the end of the song?"

HS: "No, just their legs."

Despite a host of differences in all of these accounts of Naraya performance and its meanings, I believe one can see that, in fundamental ways, they are consistent with Emily and Dorothy's account of the religion. All agree that the religion addressed concerns for health. All agree that there were other "meanings," even if they either didn't know them or didn't choose to articulate them. We see rainy weather conditions mentioned in some accounts and growing plant foods in others. The one striking difference is that some, but not all, mentioned a belief in the return of the dead, whereas Emily and Dorothy never included this point in their teachings to me.

However, as will be described below, several Naraya songs the two women sang did, in fact, refer to the return of the dead and a coming new world, and Emily translated these texts for me. Why were these points of doctrine always omitted in their discussions?

It seems to me now that it was because Emily and Dorothy believed in the Naraya in a daily ongoing sense that other Shoshones did not. Emily pointed to the greenness of her own lawn as validation for the continuing efficacy of the Naraya and the Naraya songs that she and Dorothy sang. Both women sang Naraya songs in winter to avoid catching colds. Emily even attributed my speedy recovery from a rafting accident to the many tapes of Naraya songs that I had in my house. If there had been dates in the past for the resurrection of dead Shoshones, these dates had surely come and gone. I surmise that this particular belief had been discredited in the eyes of Emily and Dorothy. The two women abandoned the one tenet but not the remainder of the religion. The Naraya remained living faith for them throughout their lives.

Other Shoshones, however, abandoned the religion. Shoshone performances of the Naraya continued until the late 1930s. As they petered out they became abbreviated add-ons after the conclusion of the Sun Dance. In the process they lost their religious meaning and function and became essentially social in nature (Shimkin 1953: 451).[15] Eventually, they were dropped completely.

Ethel Tillman recalled the last Naraya performance she attended and the reason she learned for its ultimate abandonment.

ETHEL: "The last dance I remember, Johnny Dick gave a dance down by the river and we went down there. We were on the car then. ... There wasn't too many people in it at that time then dancing. That's the last dance that I know of. That was around 1934 or '35. It's in the thirties anyway, in that time. That's the last that Johnny Dick gave that dance. After that nobody didn't go to anything like that then after that. He called for them to come dance but seemed like they faded away from that. And then that done away with that."

JUDY: "Why do you think that faded out?"

ETHEL: "Well, because I was told. I asked about that, asked John Dick when he was still living—he came over and visited with me. He said the Indians, that young ones now growing don't know the songs too well. ... That was why, he said. He said they didn't know the songs."

Emily blamed young people's disrespectful and foolish behavior at Naraya performances, as well as the growing interest in another rival religion, the Peyote Religion, alternately referred to as the Native American Church.[16]

Theses

The abundance of Naraya song texts in this book and Emily's comments on them provide rich new data that, I believe, document the Great Basin imprint on the Naraya and the Ghost Dance religion in its original Paiute conception. When I published my monograph based on seventeen Wind River Shoshone Naraya songs and texts in 1986, I tried to place Naraya texts within the context of published Ghost Dance songs, principally Mooney's collection ([1896] 1991). To my puzzlement the fit was poor. Shoshone texts were different and I could only conjecture why this was so (Vander 1986:57–61). I did, however, note the close correspondence between Shoshone and Northern Paiute song texts. Significantly, Northern Paiutes are a Great Basin culture, not Plains, which comprise the bulk in Mooney's publication. It was not until I analyzed the much larger number of Naraya songs described in the present book and reexamined the large collection of song texts published by Mooney that I began to see more clearly the differences between the two collections. Simultaneously, I read extensively about Great Basin culture, cradle of Shoshone culture as well as Northern Paiute origins of the Ghost Dance religion. These two factors together provided the key to my new understanding, which both supports Emily's statements concerning the ancient origins of the Naraya in ways that I never dreamed and informs anew the 1890 Ghost Dance religious movement itself. Two interrelated theses summarize this understanding.

First, the Naraya was largely a Wind River Shoshone religious tradition whose origins predated the 1890 Ghost Dance movement. Specifically, I believe that the Naraya can be traced back to ancient religious practices of the Great Basin Round Dance. Wovoka's prophetic doctrines then added an additional layer of meaning and purpose to Naraya performance.

Second, there was not a single homogeneous Ghost Dance religion, but rather two distinct branches: Great Basin—the root branch, to which the Naraya belong—and Plains. Because the Plains tribes did not share in the Great Basin Round Dance tradition, they took Wovoka's prophetic doctrines and elaborated them according to their own Plains traditions and worldview.

I do not mean to imply by the second thesis that the renderings of the 1890 Ghost Dance by the various Great Basin peoples were identical. The Round Dance tradition itself and its religious practices were not identical from tribe to tribe, and the degree to which Great Basin peoples adhered to Wovoka's doctrine probably varied as well. Similarly, the lumping together of all the Plains tribes into one category is an oversimplification. Mooney alludes to this point when he writes that each tribe took the basic Ghost Dance foundation and "built a structure from its own mythology" (Mooney [1896] 1991: 777). Powers's long study with the Lakota reinforces this point. He writes that "although the Ghost dance is frequently referred to as a movement, there was very little connection between the Ghost dance of the Lakota and that of other tribes" (Powers 1990:12).

The bifurcation of the two branches—Great Basin and Plains—is clearly seen in a comparison of all extant texts of Plains Ghost Dance songs and Great Basin Ghost Dance songs, of which the Naraya are by far the largest collection. A quantitative formal comparison is given in chapter 10, and I will present here only the most striking differences. First, people, often from the first-person perspective (Liljeblad 1986:647), appear in almost every Ghost Dance song of Plains tribes published by Colby (1895), Mooney ([1896] 1991), Curtis ([1923] 1968), and Densmore ([1929] 1972). In contrast, people rarely appear in Naraya and Southern Paiute songs (Sapir 1994) and are totally absent in nine published Northern Paiute songs (Mooney [1896] 1991:1052–55).

It is not just the presence or absence of people, however, that separates Great Basin and Plains Ghost Dance song texts. This is but one identifiable aspect among many, being one expression of a different underlying nexus and orientation. If we understand place and time from the 1890 Ghost Dance perspective, there is a spirit world where all the dead have gone. It is a collective communal past. There is also a present world where one performs the Ghost Dance and its accompanying songs. In this present world, peaceful behavior and Ghost Dance belief and performance were to be the bridge and catalyst to resurrecting the dead, carrying them along with living Ghost Dance believers to yet a third world—the new world of the future, a world free from death and sickness and presaged by thunder and earthquakes. Plains Ghost Dance songs place people predominantly within these three worlds of place and time, especially the spirit world. Even such pastimes of the present world as games and gambling all take place in the spirit world with dead friends and relatives (Mooney [1896] 1991:962, 964, 990, 994, 995, 1000, 1002, 1005–8, and 1036). Song topics derived from everyday life, such as buffalo meat, bow and arrows, and tipis, were allusions to the old nomadic Plains life, which by 1890 was finished. Plains Ghost Dance songs, both in the doctrinal worlds of the religion and in their vision of the everyday world, look to the past. Finally, and most important, the world of nature plays a relatively small part in Plains Ghost Dance songs; it is a minor character.

If we now turn to Ghost Dance songs of the Northern Paiute, the Southern Paiute, and the Wind River Shoshone, a different pattern and focus come into view. People and cultural references to everyday life are virtually absent. The majority of topics and images here center on the natural world: water in many forms, mountains, grass/greenery, trees, and rocks. This is the underlying nexus and orientation that sharply distinguish the Great Basin branch of the Ghost Dance from the Plains branch. We see this most clearly in Naraya songs.

Perhaps one particular Naraya text best catches both the essence of Naraya song texts and the distinctions made so far. Naraya song 82 is the sole text that mentions buffalo, this despite the fact that Wind River Shoshones were full participants in Plains life, which centered, to a large degree, on the buffalo and its nomadic movement.

> Our buffalo ground ground ground *ena,*
> ?Greasewood water-?black leaves [in damp salty ground],
> ?Greasewood water-?black leaves [in damp salty ground] *ena*
> *yaiyowainda.*

EMILY: "White salty ground—those stickers that looks like—they're tall but they're different from sagebrush [?greasewood]. That's what they eat, those buffaloes."

Naraya song 82 conjures up an ecological scene in compressed poetic form. It suggests a particular type of salty alkaline soil, a particular sticker plant, greasewood, that grows in it, and its relationship as a food source for the buffalo. This, then, is "buffalo" ground. But note that Plains life is not evoked here. The buffalo is not imagined being hunted as it is in "Sioux" Ghost Dance songs 16 and 17 from Mooney ([1896] 1991:1070, 1071). Nor is the buffalo imagined in the spirit world as it is in "Sioux" Ghost Dance song 4 from Mooney ([1896] 1991:1064) and Kiowa Ghost Dance song 11 from Mooney ([1896] 1991:1086).

Naraya texts sing of nature for nature, carefully observed habitats of land, plant, and animal life. They do not hark back to the old days on the Plains but are a continuation of modes of thought and behavior from the more distant Basin origins of the Wind River Shoshone. They are of the same stuff as Wovoka's Ghost Dance vision, which also took shape and meaning within the cognitive world of the Great Basin. All lead back to conceptions of nature, the relationship of people to the natural world, and, most relevantly for this study, the religious expressions in shamanism and the Round Dance. Indeed, the close familial relationship of the Naraya and Wovoka's religion to religious forms and meanings of the Great Basin, especially the Round Dance, defines, in large part, the differences between the two branches of the 1890 Ghost Dance movement.

The evolution of a distinct Plains version of the Ghost Dance provides an example of congruence and dovetailing between different belief systems, a contact that led to creative development. Plains tribes, like Great Basin tribes, had their own cultural traditions for visions. On the Plains, men went on vision quests in order to acquire power for success as hunters, warriors, and healers. One sought vision and power alone in nature, abstaining from food and drink, and asking for pity and help from a spirit helper (Lowie [1954] 1963:170–75; Powers 1977:91–93; Wallace and Hoebel [1952] 1986:155–59). In their own performance of the religion, Plains Ghost Dancers also went into a trance and received songs with texts in their own language. The form of the dance and the musical style of these songs remained that of the Basin Round Dance—distinctly different from Plains musical style—but the content of the texts became a Plains interpretation of the Ghost Dance, its own vision of the spirit land of the dead, this world of the living, and the newly restored Plains world to come.

Child of the past, the Naraya song inhabits a different place and time from that of the Plains Ghost Dance song. The place is the natural world, the time, the present, which looks to the near future: tomorrow's berries. Nature fills Naraya song texts, the ecosystem that surrounds and supports Wind River Shoshone life. Nature, with no reference to the I of the eye that beholds, is both subject and object. To sing of the fertile, verdant world is to act on it, to help bring it into being. In a discussion of a Kwakiutl Song of Salmon, Hymes remarked that the song symbolized the North Pacific Coast's "sense of concreteness and of participant maintenance in relation to nature and gods" (Hymes 1965:331). This concreteness and this relationship aptly characterize the Naraya and its songs.

I am not the first scholar to make a connection between the Great Basin Round Dance and the Naraya. Mooney reported what Wind River Shoshones told him about the origins of the Naraya: "However novel may have been the doctrine, the Shoshoni claim that the Ghost dance itself as performed by them was a revival of an old dance which they had had fully fifty years before" (Mooney [1896] 1991:809). As noted earlier, in 1915 Lowie described what he termed the *Naroya,* which he had been told was an old dance (Lowie 1915:817). Spier (1935:24) and

Park (1941:192), citing Mooney and Lowie respectively, affirmed the connection of the Naraya to the Round Dance. Finally, Shimkin concluded that the Ghost Dance of 1890 among the Wind River Shoshone was a minor variant of well-established Shoshone ceremonies. He observed, "The concept of the return of the dead was the sole special feature" (Shimkin 1953:433n.41).

However, because of a paucity of data, the connection drawn by all these scholars between the Naraya and earlier traditions such as the Round Dance was never fully developed. Privileged with an extensive repertoire of songs and accompanying interviews about the religious intent of Naraya performance, I am able to develop this connection in ways that were previously not possible.

In conclusion we may ask: What precisely did the 1890 Ghost Dance mean to the Wind River Shoshone? As stated above, in my view the Naraya was an old religious tradition based on the Great Basin Round Dance, with a body of song texts and a religious significance similar to those that Emily Hill and Dorothy Tappay sang and described to me. The religious practice may possibly have been relatively quiescent for a period of time, but in any case it took on new life as the basis of the Shoshone variant of the 1890 Ghost Dance movement. Wovoka's Ghost Dance doctrine overlaid it, enfolding within the Naraya its predictions for the return of the dead and the destruction of this world at the advent of a pristine new world. But for the Shoshones this new world differed from the present world only by being an idealized version of it. Whether the Shoshones were singing for berries and water and good health in one or the other seems almost immaterial. In either case they sang for life itself rather than for a way of life that had vanished on the Plains. The Ghost Dance movement came and went but the Naraya endured. Traces of Ghost Dance doctrine and images remained in Naraya songs but were significantly absent in Emily's and Dorothy's religious beliefs.

I cannot emphasize too strongly that speculations about the Naraya as performed in 1890 are largely an extrapolation from the repertoire and interpretations of two women who came to the religion thirty years later. Additional supporting data relevant to this question are the small number of other extant Naraya songs and, more indirectly, the equally small number of extant Ghost Dance songs of other Great Basin peoples. As described in chapter 10, all these songs are either identical or analogous to those in Emily's and Dorothy's repertoire with regard to their imagery.

In summary, Naraya songs have two aspects, and in this they occupy a special place within published Native American song texts.

They contain Ghost Dance references and allusions, and in one sense they are the largest collection since Mooney's collection of Ghost Dance songs published in 1896. In another sense, they are a twentieth-century connection to the ancient religious Round Dance traditions of the Great Basin, for which there are very few published examples at all.

Organizational Overview

At this point the reader should know the overall organization of the rest of the book. Chapter 1 focuses on key aspects of the Great Basin context, emphasizing power in Nature, shamanism, and the Round Dance. This background material provides the basis for my understanding of the Naraya and my thesis regarding the Ghost Dance.

Chapters 2–7 present the 113 Naraya song texts for which I provide translations. The distribution of songs among these chapters flows from the following analysis: I first analyzed all songs (including the previously published 17 songs in appendix A), placing their topics and imagery in a table (see table 1). I then tallied and ranked these topics and images for all songs; these findings are summarized in table 2.

The 320 topic-imagery elements divide into two unequal groupings, each with a distinctly different focus and frequency within the repertoire. The smaller portion clusters around what is usually considered Ghost Dance belief and Ghost Dance worlds: resurrection of the dead from their spirit world and the advent of a pristine world to come presaged by thunder and earthquakes. The larger portion centers on the natural world, this world, in all its multitudinous forms, textured and colored through a prism of the Great Basin worldview.

Unlike a scientific measurement of physical properties, a count of topics and imagery is bound to contain a certain amount of overlap and even arbitrariness of its categories. For example, I divide water, the most common element in Naraya songs, into two types: ground water (for example, rivers and pools) and weather-related water (fog, rain, and snow). The category for animals, which does not include birds as they are numerous enough to warrant their own category, has a subdivision for offspring, as does the bird category. Trees and/or wood are a large separate category from green vegetation, the latter with subdivisions for food plants and flowers. In a few instances an element is double-counted; for example, pine nut in Naraya song 121, is counted with both trees and in the food plant subcategory of green vegetation.

Table 1. Topic Images of Naraya Song Texts Using Songs 1–10 (Appendix A).

Song	1	2	3	4	5	6	7	8	9	10
water	X		X			X	X			
ground (rivers, etc.)						X	X			
weather (fog, etc.)	X		X							
mountains	X						X	X		X
animals (excluding birds)					X			X		
young animals								X		
greenery, grass, vegetation						X				X
trees or wood					X		X			
earth										
birds						X				
immature birds										
rocks										
sun or day		X		X						
sky										
food plants										
people		X						X		
Our Father							X	X		
new world										
night										
Morning Star										
Milky Way										
wind										
dead relatives		X						X		
earthquake										
mountain road for spirit										X
medicinal power										
soul			X							
flowers										
spirit world										
resurrection		X								
thunder										
whirlwind								X		
thunder										
silver										
Naraya performance										
white paint (<u>evi</u>)										
sickness										
sacred power										
feather										

Table 2. Frequencies of Naraya Topics and Imagery

Ghost Dance Belief and Worlds		This World: Nature	
Our Father	5	water	52
new world	4	ground 27	
dead relatives	4	weather 25	
medicinal power	3	mountains	45
soul	2	animals (excluding birds)	34
resurrection	2	young 7	
spirit world	2	greenery or vegetation	32
mountain road for spirit	2	food plants 10	
thunder	2	flowers 2	
sacred power	2	trees or wood	29
earthquake	1	birds	17
whirlwind	1	immature 3	
Naraya performance	1	earth	17
song	1	rocks	15
sickness	1	sun or day	14
morning star	1	sky	7
		Milky Way	6
		people	6
		wind	5
		night	3
		silver	2
		feather	2
Total	34		286

Morning star is part of the natural world, but in table 2 it appears on the Ghost Dance side of the ledger because of its strong Ghost Dance association. The same is true for earthquake, thunder, and whirlwind. Despite the fuzzy edges of the categories and their placement, I believe that the table reveals something of the range and predilection of poetic choices as well as the underlying focuses of concern addressed by the Naraya.

In order to determine the chapter in which to place a particular song text, I selected what seemed to me to be the text's central image or topic—admittedly difficult and arbitrary because most texts include more than one topic or image. Indeed, I wish to emphasize that the essence of Naraya song texts is this multiplicity of topics within a single song—the coherent ecological clustering of place, water, plant and animal life—always specific and compressed. One hundred thirteen texts: one hundred thirteen microscopic worlds.

Chapter 2 presents the relatively small number of Naraya texts that express the prophecy and teachings of Wovoka. All other texts, in chapters 3–7, deal with nature. Chapter 3 presents a sampling of texts with the most frequent image in Naraya songs, water. Chapter 4 presents texts about fog, mountains, and rocks. Chapter 5 presents texts with animals; chapter 6, texts with plants and greenery. Last and least in table 2, texts with a sky focus—texts that mention the sun, stars, and night—are presented in chapter 7.

With the exception of chapter 2, all these chapters that present song texts begin with the Shoshone texts and literal interlinear English translations. Following each song text are all the comments that Emily or Dorothy made about it, as well as very brief comments by me when essential for clarification of the text.

I leave the texts as literal translations—ambiguities of meanings are unresolved and the Shoshone word order, which may differ from that of English, is presented as it is. Despite the roughness of the literal translation, which is quasi-English, or Shoshone-English, I believe that something of the authentic poetic essence still shines through, perhaps more brightly, more truly so.

The texts and accompanying comments are at the heart of the book and the Naraya. Poets or readers who want this unalloyed essence may choose to read just these parts of chapters 2 through 7.

In each chapter, following all the song texts and the women's explanation of them, is a section called "Commentary." Naraya texts are small in scale, usually just two different lines with four or five words per line. Their spareness is part of their poetic nature. Emily's textual commentaries explain the meaning, as she understood it, for the outsider; however, they are just a beginning. Each word of text—water, mountain, grass, blackbird—is a self-contained world of associations and connotations for the generations of people who have performed the Naraya. Although Emily and Dorothy's Naraya repertoire is primarily a Wind River Shoshone document, it is not exclusively so. Some of the songs they sang came from Idaho Shoshones and even Nevada Shoshones. However, even more to the point is the Great Basin origin of the Wind River Shoshone people themselves. It lies at the base of their cultural heritage. I have, therefore, culled the scholarly literature and drawn on my own fieldwork experience in order to supply something of the rich Wind River Shoshone and Great Basin contexts that frame each word. I have spread my net widely, considering aspects of daily life, power, and myth. This is not to imply that Emily or any other individual knew or knows all of the material presented in my commentaries. Rather, the entire culture to which individual participants belong is collectively imbued with this knowledge.

In my commentaries it is as if I were trying to add overtones to a fundamental pitch, the subtle vibrating series of tones that in large part color and determine perception of pitch. My goal is a prose overtone series for the reader, one that brings the pitch of the text in tune with Wind River Shoshone and Great Basin experience and perception of it.

Chapter 2 is exceptional in its order of presentation of song texts and commentaries. Because these texts fit into an integrated religious drama, I intersperse my contextual commentaries between individual song texts, following Emily's and Dorothy's comments, rather than reserving them for the end of the chapter. I lead the reader through the scenes of the drama, supplying what seem to me to be the appropriate Ghost Dance, Wind River Shoshone, and Great Basin backdrops.

The last three chapters of the book are analytical. Chapter 8, "Textual Analysis," examines such things as differences between sung and spoken language, rhythm, rhyme, vocables, and personification. Chapter 9, "Musical Analysis," examines the musical characteristics of the songs—their melody, rhythm, tonality, phrase delineation and relationships, text setting, and repetition. Chapter 10, "Song Text Comparisons: Naraya with Great Basin and Plains Ghost Dance," provides a sampling of texts for comparison and contrast with those of the Naraya. The similarity between Naraya and other Great Basin texts and the dissimilarity between Naraya and Plains Ghost Dance texts help validate my basic theses: the schism of the Ghost Dance religion—Great Basin and Plains—and the shared background and character of Wovoka's Ghost Dance with the Naraya.

1 | *Great Basin Context: Power in Nature, Shamanism, and the Round Dance*

JUDY: "Your parents went to the Ghost Dance?"

EMILY: "Uh huh."

JUDY: "Did they talk about when it came to this reservation, or was it a long, long time ago?"

EMILY: "That Ghost Dance, it belongs here. It's no place [i.e., it's from no other place]. It's been going on all them years. I don't know how many hundred years they had it. People long time ago, they dance it. When they died the rest dance. It's been going on that way. I don't know how many hundred years. It ain't just started a few years ago. It's been how many—well, it's been put here on this world for the Indians. Long time ago, maybe I don't know how many hundred years ago."

There is justice in Emily's sense of time in this regard. Despite a long history on the Plains and active participation in Plains culture, Shoshone culture in Wyoming retains much religious and cognitive heritage from its Great Basin ancestry. This heritage is the key to understanding the Naraya, the Northern Paiute conception of the Ghost Dance religion, and the familial relationship of these two to one another.

I will, therefore, summarize some of the evidence that supports the well-recognized similarity between Shoshone and Paiute culture in the Great Basin, as well as the important continuities in contemporary Wind River Shoshone culture. Then, I will turn to the principal occasions for large gatherings in the Basin—shamanistic performances and Round Dances. I explore their religious significance: the relationship of people to the natural world and the concept of power that underlies it. These form the ancient cultural matrix of the Naraya.

The Great Basin region lies in Nevada, Utah, western Colorado, and parts of Oregon, Idaho, and Wyoming. The Sierra Nevada and Rocky Mountains bound it on the west and east, respectively. In the center of the Great Basin, Western Shoshones ranged between the Northern Paiutes to the west and Southern Paiutes to the southeast (D'Azevedo 1986a:ix; E. Johnson 1975:14). All these groups were neighbors in a dry environment, moving about in small groups, wresting a hard livelihood from the land, its plants and animals, wherever possible (Steward and Wheeler-Voegelin 1974:42, 44). Each spoke a language from the Numic branch of the Uto-Aztecan language family, and the languages were closely related. There was much intermingling among the groups, with no sharp boundaries to separate them. Wick Miller writes, "There are today much coming and going between the [Western] Shoshone and Northern Paiute populations, and the boundary reflects only a difference in language, not culture" (W. Miller 1986:29).

Other scholars corroborate close cultural identity between Shoshones and Paiutes: their intermingling in the past as well as in more recent times (Harris 1940:44; Lowie 1924a:193; Powell 1971:100; Steward 1938:161, 172; Steward 1970:132; Steward and Wheeler-Voegelin 1974:76) and the intermarriages that resulted from it (E. Johnson 1975:5; Steward 1938:124, 132; Steward and Wheeler-Voegelin 1974:8, 9, 13, 14, 111). The groups participated in each other's communal hunts and festivals; for example, Western Shoshones attended the Walker River Paiute fish run. They learned songs from one another (thus, a Shoshone doctor's song appears in the repertoire of an Owens Valley Paiute man [Steward 1933:278]), and also language, Northern Paiute, Ute, and Southern Paiute being the most common second languages for Western Shoshones (W. Miller 1986:29).

In the outside world of other Indian tribes and non-Indians, Shoshones and Paiutes were commonly called by one undifferentiated name, Snakes (Mooney [1896] 1991:1056; Stewart 1970:203). In their own Shoshone and Paiute languages and dialects they also used a common term, calling themselves simply "the people," *Numa*[1] (Powell 1971:5). This term referred to each person's social network with shared language and customs (Murphy 1986:305). As noted in the introduction, group names at the smaller, more local level reflected the constant shifting of peoples throughout the Basin in search of food.

The pattern of fluidity within and between Shoshone and Paiute populations was wide ranging. Shoshones from Nevada and northern Utah intermarried with Shoshones of Wyoming and Idaho (Murphy 1986:324, 325). Bannocks, a Northern Paiute people, lived in long association with Shoshones in Idaho. Other Northern Paiutes joined the Bannocks in a continual process. Murphy's comments have specific relevance for the Wind River Shoshone: "It may be further argued that this continuity and exchange of population served in some degree to preserve a more amorphous Basin-type society among the buffalo hunters" (Murphy 1960:332).

Hultkrantz views Wind River Shoshones as "synthesizers and transformers of cultural material derived from both eastern and western sources; their culture is a blend of the two" (Hultkrantz, in Murphy 1960:294). This is the result of Wind River Shoshones' geographic location at the interface of Plains and Great Basin cultures and their complex historical associations in both directions, east and west. The Wind River Shoshones' Great Basin heritage is central to this book's thesis. Two examples can support this connection.

Wind River Shoshone mythology is, in essence, profoundly similar to other Numic Great Basin mythology. Anthropomorphic animal characters such as Coyote, Wolf, and Cottontail are its major personalities. Perhaps the only significant change in these myths by the Shoshones in Wyoming was to locate the stories in the Wind River–Teton intermontane zone (Shimkin 1947c:332). But Shoshone mythology lacks buffalo tales in its subject matter, which is telling evidence for the absence of major Plains influence (Lowie 1909:235, 236).

Another example of Great Basin continuity in Wind River Shoshone life is a cluster of beliefs and practices surrounding menstruation and childbirth. There is perfect congruence. Belief in the power and potential danger of menstrual blood, the separation of menstruating women from their families, the performance of hard work at that time in order to inculcate the value of work, dietary restrictions, and the use of a scratching stick are all well documented in Great Basin literature (Hopkins [1883] 1969:48; Kelly 1932:159, 160, 162, 163; Lowie 1923:145–48; Lowie 1924a:274; Lowie 1924b:211–15; Shimkin 1947a:305; Steward 1943a:280, 324, 343; Steward 1943b: 274). My work with five Shoshone women carries this documentation forward into the 1980s (Vander 1988:13, 14, 199, 200). The correspondence obtains even in such details as the placement of an infant's umbilical cord on an ant's nest in order to foster industriousness in the child (Kelly 1932:158; Steward 1943a:340, 342; Vander 1988: 195).

It is my thesis that the Naraya is one of the most important manifestations of Great Basin continuity in Wind River Shoshone culture. Its form and content draw on elements of Great Basin shamanistic performance and Round Dance (or Circle Dance)[2] celebrations. These occasions, which derived special significance in the Basin, in part, from being two of the relatively infrequent opportunities for larger social gatherings, were simultaneously the principal venues for religious expression. Nature, power, and people are the warp, woof, and shuttle that create the religious fabric of shamanism and the Round Dance. The Northern Paiute Ghost Dance religions and Naraya were woven on the same loom, using strands of these older fabrics and adding some new ones.

Power in Nature

In the Great Basin worldview, every object in nature, be it animate or inanimate, has power: animals, mountains, rocks, caves, springs, lakes, and lightning (Harris 1940:55; Hultkrantz 1981a:39; Hultkrantz 1986: 631; Hultkrantz 1987:47, 51, 60; E. Johnson 1975:45; Liljeblad 1986: 644; Lowie 1909a:223, 224; Park 1938:14, 76; Shimkin 1986a: 325; Steward 1933:312). Great Basin Numic myth richly illustrates this. Thus, a serviceberry branch on a house has power to protect it from thunder (Steward 1943a:353); thunder has power to cure Oriole (Powell 1971:92); mole has power to cause thunder (Steward 1943a:353).

Humans are part of the natural environment. They passively receive power from a guardian spirit (Hultkrantz 1987:52; Park 1938:22; Smith 1939:199; Steward 1934:424) or actively seek a vision by going to a special place in nature associated with power (Harris 1940:57; Kelly 1932:190; Lowie 1924a:294; Park 1938:22, 118; Steward 1943a: 345).[3] Power from the natural world, often identified as a spirit, manifests itself in a dream or vision. Dream and vision are inseparable from human thought, as well as from human speech. Thought sits at the center of power. In myth it makes no difference if a character thinks or speaks a wish. Both equally effect a new reality: the wish comes true. Jay Miller writes of power, "Close to the life force, it was the most cosmic of mediators, pervading the universe and symbolizing thought in its full expanse" (J. Miller 1983:78). The Wind River Shoshone word for "pray" underscores the mind as its key element. *Nanrisundaih* (Tidzump 1970:41) has at its center *su*, an abbreviated form of *sua-*, which is the verbal stem for "to think" (Shimkin manuscript, n.d.).

Power from the natural world communicates and transfers power to people with or as song (Hultkrantz 1956:201; Hultkrantz 1987:54; Liljeblad 1957:32; Mooney [1896] 1991:923; Park 1938:22, 23, 47; Powell 1971:245; Smith 1939:199; Steward 1941:259, 353; Steward

1943:282, 345; Stewart 1941:413; Vander 1986:7; Vander 1988:13; Whiting 1950:28, 30). Other communicated elements include words and instructions, and sometimes dance, as was the case in Wovoka's Ghost Dance vision (Mooney [1896] 1991:772). Miller's characterization of the nature of power suggests the particular appropriateness of song and dance in relationship to it. Power is "the life force—energy. It is not static or concrete, but rather kinetic, always moving and flowing throughout the cosmos, . . . The primary attribute of power is this processual dynamic, . . . [Thus, the] . . . importance of singing and dancing for controlling power by becoming attuned to it since all are rhythmical" (J. Miller 1983:73).

Power from nature given in dream inheres in the waking human performance of song, dance, and words. The correct realization of these three empowered and empowering elements influences the natural world. They affect health, plant and animal food sources, and the weather. Power moves in a circular path from nature to people, from people to nature. This concept, relationship, and set of interrelated concerns permeate Great Basin culture.[4] This is true in Great Basin myth, the Round Dance, the Northern Paiute Ghost Dance, the Naraya, and shamanism.

Critical to the notion of power is its potential for danger. Every instruction given in a dream must be carried out with extreme care and accuracy to avoid disastrous consequences (Park 1938:33, Whiting 1950:47–48). Respect for power and its source in nature is imperative, too; to ridicule thunder is to invite death (Park 1938:19). The person who receives power can choose to use it for good or bad purposes. This is the dark underside of power. Sorcery is a prime example of power used with harmful intention (Kelly 1932:195; Park 1938:43; Whiting 1950:27). Water babies, the *nïnïmbi* or "little people," and whirlwind ghosts, who all had power to kill, embody this dangerous and fearful potential of power.

Shamanistic Belief and Practice Relevant to the Naraya

Joe Green, a Northern Paiute man, clearly articulates the relationship between people, power, and nature in his comments on shamanism. And in a suggestive way, he roots its origins in the mythic world of the past. He said, "Indians were put here on this earth with trees, plants, animals, and water, and the shaman gets his power from them. . . . A long time ago, all the animals were Indians (they could talk). I think that is why the animals help the people to be shamans" (Park 1938:16).

Health

The Great Basin shaman uses power from nature, first and foremost, as a healer. Patients who seek the shaman's services suffer illnesses from three sources—sorcery, intrusion of foreign objects in the body, and soul loss, a particularly important concept for Ghost Dance doctrine (Park 1938:136; Steward 1940:493).

According to Great Basin and Wind River Shoshone belief, each person has a soul, a breathy entity called *mugua* in Shoshone (Hultkrantz 1951:22; Kelly 1932:198; Park 1938:40). The soul's departure from the body causes sickness and loss of consciousness, and this is equated with and defines death (Hultkrantz 1951:21; Hultkrantz 1987:59; Kelly 1932:195; Lowie 1909a:301; W. Miller 1972:37; Mooney [1896] 1991:922; Steward 1943b:275). Shamans seek to restore life by going into a trance or dream and searching for the lost soul in the land of the dead (Kelly 1932:195; Lowie 1924a:294; Park 1938:15, 27, 37, 41, 53). As Lowie described it, "the shaman would lie beside him [the patient] and also 'die' for several hours" (Lowie 1924a:294).[5] If successful, the shaman brings the soul back to the patient, who regains consciousness; the patient is resurrected, as is, indeed, the shaman.

In Northern Paiute terms, the trances of Wovoka and Wodziwob were death, albeit temporary, and the return to consciousness was resurrection.[6] In a letter written to the Commissioner of Indian Affairs, Frank Campbell described being present when Wodziwob was in a trance. Campbell watched as "Indians gathered around him and joined in song that was to guide the spirit back to the body" (Mooney [1896] 1991:703).

Note that it is song that guides the separated "lost" soul back to the body. The importance and power of dreamed song is central to all Great Basin religious experience and expression, including shamanism. Underscoring the importance of song for Shoshone shamans of Nevada, Steward writes, "Vision gave not only spirit helpers, but songs (which were the most potent element in the power)" (Steward 1941:259).

Park reinforces the importance and close connections of dream, power, and song. "The central idea in the acquisition of supernatural power is dream experience. . . . [Nick Downington, a Northern Paiute shaman] . . . learns his songs when the spirit comes and sings to him" (Park 1938:22). Park continues, "There seems . . . to be an emphasis on auditory experience in dreams" (Park 1938:23). Another Northern Paiute shaman, Dick Mahwee, reported a dreamed promise of song. Mahwee said, "You will get your songs when you doctor" (Park 1938:28).

Whether learned previously in a dream or on the spot during a performance, singing is one of the principal activities in curing (Kelly 1932:192; Steward 1940:495). For the application of the shaman's songs and power, it was important to have a large company present. Curing was a public ceremony and all those attending were expected to help the shaman by singing. The shaman's assistant, a so-called "talker," facilitated this process, repeating the song words so that everyone could follow along and join in the singing (Kelly 1932:193; Lowie 1924a:292; Park 1938:50; Steward 1941:413; Steward 1943a: 345; Whiting 1950:40). Park understood this group singing to be a "powerful aid in establishing contact through the shaman with the supernatural forces" (Park 1938:47). Elsewhere he notes, "The words of a shaman's song often refer to the source of power" (Park 1938:58).

Whiting also described the importance of song and its use by Paiute shamans of Harney Valley. The shamans' songs appealed to the power for a diagnosis of the patient's illness (Whiting 1950:40). Song was also key for the shaman's recovery of the soul-breath (Whiting 1950:46). Whiting reported that "song alone without sucking, or by both singing and sucking" was also the remedy for illness from sorcery (Whiting 1950:40). Song had the power to keep ghosts away in the future.

Like song, dance is another potent element in shamanistic performance. Among the Harney Valley Paiutes, "The appeal to the power is always accompanied by vigorous dancing. . . . A few doctors have assistants who dance with them" (Whiting 1950:40). There is evidence that dance, too, might come in a dream (Steward 1933:311, 312; Whiting 1950:28). This was the case with Wovoka in his dreamed meeting with God: "He [God] gave me this dance to give to my people" (Mooney [1896] 1991:764).

We see the importance of dance to shamanism in a Western Shoshone myth in which Coyote dances and says, "Now I am a doctor" (Steward 1943b:274). Dance validates and is integral to Coyote's new status as a shaman. The shaman heals through song and dance (Park 1938:51, 122; Steward 1943a:293). In Gosiute myth, U-na's empowered song and dance resurrect a dead widow and her son (Powell 1971:260). There is even an anecdote about Wovoka, who, after accidentally shooting himself, "sings, and he dances for his self. Gets well, too, by God" (Hittman 1990:288).

Shoshone comments provide insights on the meaning and function of dance within the context of religion, with implications for its use by the shaman as well. Shoshones who traveled to Nevada in 1889 in order to learn more about the Ghost Dance religion returned home to

Wyoming and reported the importance of frequent Ghost Dances, "because the dance moves the dead" (Mooney [1896] 1991:807, 808). Resonating with these notions are the Naraya recollections of an elderly Shoshone man who talked with me in 1978. As quoted in the introduction, HS described how people shook their legs and pounded their feet on the ground at the conclusion of a song. "They try to wake the dead ones underneath the ground. It's what they want to come" (Vander 1986:8). In a similar vein, recall the exhortations of Johnny Dick, a Naraya leader who was quoted by Emily: "Let's dance and make our earth and everything, roots what we eat on our ground—let 'em come alive again." Metaphors of awakening and resurrection were intended for the natural world as well as for people.

These beliefs and metaphors inform another Shoshone religion. Lynn St. Clair, writing for his own Wind River people, explained the meaning of dance in the Sun Dance. "The motion of the dancers is also a prayer, it is a prayer for life and action for a dead body does not move" (St. Clair and St. Clair 1977, quoted in Vander 1988:298). Like brings like; movement brings movement. Life and wakefulness are danced out of death-sleep.

Shamans learn not only song and dance in dreams, but also knowledge of future events, such as an impending epidemic (Kelly 1932:189).[7] As already discussed by Emily, this was also the case for Naraya leaders. Shamans use their power to cure illness as well as to prevent it, at both the personal and community levels. Preventive medicine is an important aspect of shamanistic performance. Here, too, song and dance are the antidotes that drive away epidemics and bad dreams (Park 1938:128; Powell 1971:162). As a Paiute man from Bishop expressed it, the "Indian doctor dances all night to fight the evil spirit, goes after it" (Hulse 1935, notebook 154.2–5, n.p.). Park reports a special dance by a female dancer at a shamanistic performance that served two functions, one of which was to drive away an epidemic (Park 1938:128). Likewise, in myth, Coyote calls a dance in order to drive illness away (Lowie 1909b:274–75).[8]

Blowing sickness away from the body and shaking and brushing it off from clothing are other strategies to drive away disease. They are part of the shaman's repertoire to prevent illness and the audience's repertoire as participants in shamanistic performance (Park 1938:56; Powell 1971:161, 162; Steward 1941:321, 413; Steward 1943:345). The concepts of immunity from illness in the Ghost Dance and prevention of illness in Naraya performance flow from shamanistic tradition, as do the strategies of song, dance, and blanket shaking (Mooney [1896] 1991:803; Shimkin 1939:18, 84).

Words, like the songs in which they are embedded, are also central to the shaman's performance and power. Words in song, speech, and thought create a reality through articulation. Their importance is underscored by the shaman's assistant, whose main task is to repeat every word of the shaman, sung or spoken (Kelly 1932:193; Park 1938:50; Steward 1943a:388; Whiting 1950:40). Words, song, and dance are the three talismans of the shaman's power. Their correct performance affects the physical world. They are critical for addressing concerns of health.

Food: Antelope Charming

Antelope charming is a public five-day performance of song and dance prior to a communal antelope hunt. The shaman is leader throughout its duration (Hopkins [1883] 1969:56; Park 1938:45, 62, 63). However, unlike curing, all participate in the dance for antelope charming.

The potency of words and thoughts come into play even during the preparation of the corral into which the antelope are to be driven. Sarah Winnemucca Hopkins, a Northern Paiute woman, recalled that while making mounds of sagebrush and stone, the people were to "keep thinking about the antelope all the time" (Hopkins [1883] 1969:56). As with dance, like brings like: thought of the antelope brings real antelope. Song words are also instrumental; one text mentions the food of the antelope (Steward 1941:219). Word-food attracts as if it were real food.

Moving closer to the goal of antelope charming, the shaman sings, "'The antelope are coming; I scent them coming through the canyon'" (Kelly 1932:85). The shaman's song directs the movement of the antelope (Kelly 1932:83). Hank Hunter, a Paiute man, described the use of song prior to hunting: "There is also a certain song which is sung during hunting time. This song is believed to be sung to attract the game's attention and for them to come forth to be slain" (Hulse 1935, notebook 153, n.p.).

Other activities believed to attract the animals included use of a gourd rattle made with antelope hooves, an example of musical onomatopoeia (Hultkrantz 1961:201). Surprise Valley Paiute sang, danced, and made noise like an antelope in order to direct the movement of the antelope (Kelly 1932:83). They went further and dramatically enacted the hunt. The shaman wore the head and horns of an antelope while others, in their dance, imitated killing the antelope (Kelly 1932:85).

As with curing, souls are an issue in antelope charming. The shaman's soul departs in order to capture the antelope's soul. "He captured antelope's souls (*süəp:*, breath) so that they were already 'dead' when they entered the corral and could not be frightened" (Steward 1941:220).

Steward's description of antelope charming by Nevada Shoshone captures all these interacting elements of song, dance, words, dramatic play, trance, and souls:

> The shaman rubbed a notched stick tied to the back of a tanned antelope hide, which was stuffed with grass (*watsip*) to resemble an antelope, and sang for about two hours. His song was of a kind of brush (*sisovi*) that antelope eat and about young antelope and their food. People near the shaman also sang. Meanwhile, a line of boys, the tallest near the shaman, the shortest near the opening, danced in imitation of antelope. They finally pretended to be very tired, indicating that the shaman had captured the antelopes' souls. After the dancing, the shaman, if powerful, fell down and bled through his nose (apparently like other shamans, the most powerful of whom go into a trance), proving that he had taken the antelopes' souls. (Steward 1941:219)

Antelope charming is yet another link of continuity between Wind River Shoshone and Great Basin culture. Shimkin learned the following from Moses Tassitsie, a Shoshone man born in 1852:

> [In his grandfather's time there was a] man who had a little drum (some ten inches in diameter) painted red, with a drum stick. He would prepare a place on the ground, sitting toward the east. He would get a little antelope fetus hide with hoofs on it. It would be taken out and put in a sitting position, also looking toward the east. First he beat his drum very fast, then slowly. He sang his song all night, quitting just before dawn. He put away his things. He picked up the hide and pointed it to the west, shaking it. Then in a half-circle to the south and east. Then he's done. Next morning there's a whole head of antelope coming to the campground. His people go out and kill these. (Shimkin 1937)

It is interesting to see the adaptation of antelope charming to Shoshone life on the Plains. Antelope charming became buffalo charming. Polly Shoyo (born circa 1845) described the latter, noting that

> when the people were starving, a medicine man (*pohogant*, i.e., holder of supernatural power, DBS) would be helped by four women and three men to bring game. The seven sat and sang; he danced all night long. They would smoke a pipe all around at first (it was not offered to the directions); then they sang four smoking songs, while the shaman danced. There were no rattles, no drum. He danced back and forth.

Once in a while, he would stop and say: "Now, I want you to bring a lot of buffaloes." Then they smoked, sang four songs, and smoked again. The next morning the shaman would tell the people that he had found the buffaloes. They were at a given place. The people went there, found them, killed them, and were saved. (Shimkin 1937)

Thus, layered on top of Great Basin notions of power that channel through song, dance, and words are Plains elements: the importance of the number four (here, four songs), which, while not true for this ceremony, often refers to the cardinal directions, and the ritual use of the pipe.[9]

Weather

Weather is the third domain of the shaman.[10] There is close connection and overlap among all three areas of shamanistic power: health, food, and weather. Broadly viewed, health is achieved not only by the lack of illness but by the presence of an adequate food supply. Plants and animals that sustain human life are, themselves, sustained by their environment, including the weather conditions that shape and support them. It is as difficult to separate these domains as it is to disentangle the domains of power in song, word-thought, and dance. Although George Briley's account of his father-in-law, Buck Skin Joe, is not about a shaman, it nevertheless illustrates the inseparability of hunting, environment, and weather in Paiute thought, and the direct relationship between people and nature that is effected through song and words. The following is Buck Skin Joe's spiritual song before he went out to hunt:

> On your side slopes.
> Trees quivering they stand.

. . . He asks the wind to please not blow when he is at the [place] where he is to get the deer. He doesn't want the wind to carry the scent of human towards the deer so he pleaded to the wind, and the wind obeys, the wind dies down and every thing get still not a leaf stirs to scare his deer away. He never fails to get his deer when he goes to get it. The following is his song.

> O! ye, [? Only] down ward blow—[p]lease!
> Blow no more
> O! ye, [? Only] down ward blow—[p]lease!
> Blow no more. (Hulse 1935, notebook 154)

For the shaman, the ability to control and predict weather is proof of a "rapport with spirits" (Park 1938:15, 16, 98). Often it was exercised solely as a demonstration of this power and not for communal benefit (Park 1938:60). Wovoka worked within this tradition when he produced melted ice from a July sky (Hittman 1990:213–14).[11] Other accounts of Wovoka's correct weather predictions and fulfilled promise of rain were further proofs of his power (Dangberg 1968:27; Hittman 1990:198–99).[12]

As with every aspect of shamanism, weather power comes in dreams (Kelly 1939:159; Steward 1941:322; Steward 1943a:285). The dreamed source of Wovoka's power was two clouds. Joe Green, a Northern Paiute shaman, adds these details: "One was a straight high cloud. This was for snow. The other cloud was dark and close to the ground. It was for rain" (Park 1938:19). Northern Paiutes today still comment on the extraordinary storm that occurred the day Wovoka died, which reflected both the strength and source of his power (Catherine Fowler, personal communication to author, 1992). This accords with Northern Paiute belief that when a shaman dies, "clouds gather in the sky, rain falls, or other changes in the weather takes place" (Park 1938:69).

Shamanistic control of weather was not used exclusively as proof of power. Many examples in the literature document its use for communal benefit as well (Park 1938:60). In this vein Wovoka promised his Cheyenne and Arapaho visitors, "When you get home I shall give you a good cloud [rain?] which will make you feel good" (Mooney [1896] 1991:781). One way of controlling weather was to speak directly to it, just as Buck Skin Joe did. Shamans might speak to the wind and rain while doctoring (Liljeblad 1986:644), but perhaps the more common use of weather control was in a preventive way, for example, "talking to rain or to a storm and diverting it" (Steward 1943a:28).[13] With an emphasis on the prophylactic, the shaman aims to prevent bad weather, a function parallel to the prevention of epidemics. Naraya performance also served both of these functions.

Shamans went further than just diverting weather. Speaking and singing, they altered it in a variety of ways. Wovoka's power in five songs is a case in point. He had "five songs for making it rain, the first of which brings on a mist or cloud, the second a snowfall, the third a shower, and the fourth a hard rain or storm, while when he sings the fifth song the weather again becomes clear" (Mooney [1896] 1991:772–73).

Several patterns emerge as one studies the many different accounts of shamanistic manipulation of weather for communal benefit. It is intimately connected to the life cycles of plants and animals; more specifically, it seeks to hasten the winter season into spring. Snow melt and warm winds, which accomplish this, are common themes and images in song and prayer (Kelly 1932:201; Steward 1941:322; Steward 1943:346; Stewart 1941:414). The first example of these patterns is from the White Knife Shoshone: "The *Badsai* medicine men had power to control the weather and especially to curtail the winter seasons which, if they lingered, prevented the camp group from starting on its nomadic search for food. . . . An individual with this power went out in a blizzard in early morning, his nude body painted red, and prayed toward the east. That evening the Chinook (South Wind) came and melted the snow" (Harris 1940:59–60).[14]

A second example is from the Paviotso, or Northern Paiute:

> This weather-control is chiefly concerned with causing changes in the elements in order to bring about a badly-needed run of fish in the rivers. It is said that fish may be induced to go up the river in the spring by causing the ice to melt or by bringing about a wind that will force them to the mouth of the river. When ice covers the rivers late in the spring, delaying the run of fish from the lakes, a shaman known to have control over the elements is asked to cause warm weather and rain to melt the ice. Only a few shamans, however, have this power. (Park 1938:60)

Joe Green adds, "The shaman sang and the ice was made to melt" (Park 1938:60).

This pattern carries over into Shoshone myth-telling. At the conclusion of the story there "is a statement obscurely hinting at melting snow, which results from properly told tales" (Shimkin 1947a:330). Myth-telling in the winter was to help bring spring and fertility (Hultkrantz 1976:147). The image of melting snow appears in eight Naraya songs.

Rain was another important focus of weather control (Kelly 1939:159; Steward 1941:322; Steward 1943a:346). Water in every form is the central image in Naraya songs and was a major reason for Naraya performance. The following account (which seems to flow from Dorothy to Emily) relates dance to water and food, much as the Badsai's prayer related to snow melt and food, and the Paviotso shaman's song related to ice melt and fish.

DOROTHY: "And when you dance, when Indians dance in springtime it makes their grass grow, your river—so you have enough water all year. Berries, things like that."

EMILY: "Berries, things like that, to eat. Things to eat, grow."

Some shamans claimed personal invulnerability, another area that proved their possession of power (Park 1934:113; Park 1938:59). In precontact times it was invulnerability to arrows, in postcontact times, invulnerability to bullets (Lowie 1924a:292, 293, 295; Powell 1971:245; Steward 1933:310; Steward 1943a:286; Whiting 1950:28). The shaman had power to "charm" arrow points. Thus, the concept of charming can work in diametrically opposed ways, either attracting (antelope) or repelling (arrows and bullets). It prevents death just as other shamanistic performance and power prevent epidemics and storms. As with all other power, its source is from nature. Northern Gosiute Shoshone sought invulnerability in war from bear power (Steward 1943a: 346). Wind River Shoshone men sought invulnerability from turtle power (Shimkin 1939:88). In an interesting example of the transfer of power from person to person, Yellow Hand, a famous Sun Dance chief, gave the power of invulnerability to Chief Washakie, an important Shoshone leader of the nineteenth century (Shimkin 1939:91).

Wovoka's claim for being inviolate drew on this Great Basin tradition. Wovoka's father was a powerful shaman in his time and, like Wovoka, was said to be bulletproof (Hittman 1990:33). This added weight to Wovoka's claim, because Northern Paiutes believed in the general possibility of the inheritance of shamanistic power and, in the case of Wovoka, many expected this to happen (Hittman 1990: 182).

Wovoka attempted to validate his claim to invulnerability by being shot in public. Dangberg reports that he relied on trickery and fooled his audience (Dangberg 1968:14–15; Hittman 1990:82–84). Edward Dyer, Wovoka's non-Indian friend and secretary, noted the impact of this event via the grapevine. "Naturally news of such a phenomenon as a bullet proof Indian with its possible application by other and more disgruntled Indians soon spread by word of mouth beyond the immediate tribal area and in the course of time reached the Plains Indians and those in Oklahoma Territory" (Hittman 1990:215). Indian delegations from a variety of tribes traveled to Nevada to check Wovoka's invulnerability. They attended Ghost Dance performances and in the process "a sort of religious fervor was generated" (Hittman 1990:215).

Indians were enthusiastic but non-Indians were apprehensive. The army massacre of Lakota Ghost Dancers in 1890 brought the religion, hostility between whites and Indians, and the issue of invulnerability into the headlines of non-Indians' newspapers. Given this swirl of events and the emotional response to them, Wovoka sloughed off his formerly touted proof of invulnerability in an interview with Chapman, an army scout:

CHAPMAN: "What about the time you asked your own brother to shoot at your calico shirt while you stood on a blanket ten feet away just to show off that you were bulletproof and the ball struck your breast and dropped to blanket?"

WOVOKA: "That was a joke." (Hittman 1990:11)

However, the 1890 tragedy at Wounded Knee, in which slaughtered dancers wore "bulletproof" Ghost Dance shirts, was no joke. To Mooney's inquiry, Wovoka "disclaimed all responsibility for the ghost shirt which formed so important a part of the dance costume among the Sioux; . . . and earnestly repudiated any idea of hostility toward the whites, asserting that his religion was one of universal peace" (Mooney [1896] 1991:772).[15] Lakota use of "bulletproof" Ghost Dance shirts was not based on Great Basin traditions—the personal demonstration of shamanistic power. The Lakota built on their own Plains-Teton tradition of warfare. Warriors drew designs learned in dreams onto shields as protection against enemy darts (Lowie 1924b:195). The Lakota "had made the ghost shirt an auxiliary of war" (Mooney [1896] 1991:791). Wovoka disavowed responsibility for bulletproof shirts and any doctrinal implications of an enemy—Indian or white (Mooney [1896] 1991:772). Hostility was antithetical to his doctrine of peace and love, beyond the pale of his context, Great Basin/Northern Paiute shamanism: proof of power through invulnerability (Park 1934:113).

The Round Dance

As stated in the introduction, the form of the 1890 Ghost Dance, as performed by all tribes, very likely derived from the Round Dance of the Great Basin. In addition, I believe that the imagery in the songs and the religious intent of Naraya performance also derived from the Round Dance. It is this that distinguishes the Naraya from the Ghost Dance of other Plains tribes.

The data of many scholars indicate the importance of the Round Dance in Great Basin culture. Performance of the Round Dance was one of the few occasions for large gatherings, and it has an historical depth that can be traced back to pre-European America. We see something of the form and fun of the Kaibab Southern Paiute Round Dance in the account of Frederick Dellenbaugh, an artist who accompanied John Powell on his anthropological expedition down the Green and Colorado Rivers in 1871–72.

We went to the camp one moonlight night, June 6th, to see a sort of New Year's dance. They had stripped a cedar tree of all branches but a small tuft at the top, and around this the whole band formed a large circle, dancing and singing. The dancing was the usual hippity-hop or "lope" sideways, each holding hands with his or her neighbors. In the center stood a man, seeming to be the custodian of the songs and a poet himself. He would first recite the piece, and then all would sing it, circling round at the same time. We accepted their cordial invitation to join in the ceremony, and had a lot of fun out of our efforts, which greatly amused them too, our mistakes raising shouts of laughter. The poet seemed to originate some of the songs, but they had others that were handed down. (Dellenbaugh 1908:178)

It is possible to derive from Dellenbaugh and others the following generalized outline of the Round Dance. It was part of a five-day occasion. Men and women held hands in a circle, dancing clockwise with a side-shuffling step.[16] Some groups erected a center pole with greenery on it in the center of the dance area (Older 1923:37; Steward 1941:352). One account says that "the dancers slightly flex the right knee while stepping to the left" (Liljeblad 1986:646). After the weight transfers to the left foot, the right foot is dragged in place next to the left, thus completing the basic pattern. No drum or other musical instrument accompanied the dance. Rather, dancers accompanied themselves by singing songs that were initiated or taught by a song leader (Powell 1971:248, 270; Steward 1941:353). The musical style of the songs—repeated phrases, narrow melodic range, tonic phrase finals—is characteristic of Great Basin music in general (Herzog 1935a:403, 404; Nettl 1954:15; Vennum 1986:687).[17] Song leaders composed their own songs (Kelly 1932:178; Park 1941:185) and/or received songs with power and religious meaning in dreams (Liljeblad 1986:649; Steward 1941:263, 353). The songs have primarily linguistic texts, and nature in all its multitudinous forms is the principal topic (Crum 1980:5, 17; Liljeblad 1957:39; Liljeblad 1986:647; Powell 1971:121–28; Sapir 1994:627, 632–35, 639, 653, 657, 659).[18]

In the Round Dance there is a male leader (variously referred to in scholarly literature as chief, boss, head man, master of ceremony, or priest). This is noteworthy in the Great Basin, where small family groups moved about to exploit natural resources. It was an egalitarian society with limited opportunities for large groups and leadership on this scale. However, the important seasonal dances provided such an opportunity. The native term for this leader, or chief, on those occasions is "*te'gwani* . . . his main function being 'to talk'"[19] (Steward 1938:169). While the people are singing and dancing, this leader walks around the outside of the circle and speaks. (Examples of these speeches appear later in this discussion.)

As already mentioned in the introduction, there was a male leader for the Naraya whose dream would indicate the time for Naraya performance. He received Naraya songs and was a song leader for the dance. Shimkin reported that Naraya leaders who received Naraya songs in dream were shamans. He identified Frank Perry, from whom he collected Naraya songs, as a powerful shaman (Shimkin 1947c: 350).

With the possible exception of the leader's role, all of the characteristics of the Round Dance described in the above paragraphs are indistinguishable from those of the Naraya. In chapter 9 I will discuss the striking similarity between the small number of published Round Dance song texts and those of the Naraya.

Even the various native names for the Round Dance and the Naraya follow a similar pattern. "The most common term for the Round Dance is formed on the Numic verb 'to dance': Northern Paiute *nigába*, Shoshone *nikappih*, and Southern Paiute *nikkappi*. . . . In Shoshone, there is also the descriptive term *nataya·ti*, literally 'lifting feet together.' . . . Northern Shoshone also has *nuakkinna*, based on a verb *nua-* 'to move' cognate with what Miller (1972) gives as *numa* 'to do the circle dance'" (Liljeblad 1986:646–47).

Mooney learned the Northern Paiute and Wind River Shoshone names for the Ghost Dance, both of which are consistent with this pattern. He reported that they were, respectively, *Nänigükwa*, "dance in a circle" (*nüka*, "dance"), and "*Tänä´räyün* or *Tämanä´rayära*, which may be rendered 'everybody dragging,' in allusion to the manner in which the dancers move around the circle holding hands" (Mooney [1896] 1991:791). I will return later in this chapter to the issue of names and the relationship between the Round Dance and the Naraya.

If, as I believe, the Naraya was a continuation of the Round Dance tradition, this raises the question of whether the Round Dance itself was a religious ritual. The rest of this section analyzes this question.

In contrast to the descriptions of the Round Dance, which are relatively consistent, scholarly interpretation of the dance's function and meaning diverges sharply. The Round Dance brings together—in different proportions for any given dance—social pleasure and religious expression and intent. For Julian Steward, a prominent researcher of Great Basin culture, the presence of one, in some sense, negates or denigrates the other. In the following three quotations, each from a different publication by Steward, note the use and connotation of such words as "incidental," "extra," "minor," and "incipient," words that reflect Steward's Euro-American cultural viewpoint in interpreting data that seemed to lack sharp boundaries between sacred and secular:

> Ritual was everywhere exceedingly limited and practically none attached to economic activities. There were no group ceremonials, except as the round dance was thought incidentally to bring rain, crop fertility, or general well-being. (Steward 1938:45)

> The sole dance of most localities in pre-Caucasian times was the Circle or Round dance, called merely *nukaiyu* or *nukəp,* dance. Though varying slightly in details, in seasons held, and in extra purposes such as rainmaking or producing crop fertility, it was substantially uniform throughout the area and may be considered a distinctively Shoshonean dance. (Steward 1941:265)

> While the ubiquitous circle dance, held whenever enough people were assembled, was essentially recreational, there is slight evidence that in certain localities it was ascribed a minor supernatural significance. Among the Shoshoni and Paiute of northern Nevada and Oregon, this dance was supposed to have a beneficent effect on nature in general. The Pyramid Lake *"Kuyui"* fish festival mentioned previously evidently had minor supernatural significance. But in these and other possible instances of incipient group ceremonialism, the religious features seem to have been incidental to the recreational. (Steward 1974:51)

I will return later in this chapter to Steward's data. They are a major source of information on the Round Dance and, ironically, support the contrary view: that the Round Dance included significant religious meaning and function as well as social pleasure and play.

Liljeblad recognized that there were two viewpoints concerning the religious nature of the Round Dance, and his own writings express both these views. In his most recent writing on Great Basin Round Dance and Ghost Dance songs, in the 1986 *Handbook of North American Indians,* Liljeblad agrees with Steward's interpretation. He finds the absence of piety, abstractions, and religious ideas in the song texts compelling argument for their nonceremonial nature and meaning. He adds that the popularity of the Round Dance "points to its entertainment rather than a sacral function" (Liljeblad 1986:647).

Like Steward, Liljeblad documents religious aspects of the Round Dance yet downplays them in his interpretation: "The Bannock and Northern Shoshone lit their dance fires in the evenings of early summer and therefore called the dance respectively *tamánika* and *tawanikka* 'spring-dance.' It is said to promote health in man and fertility in nature, to make grass, seeds, and pine nuts grow, to melt snow and produce rain. The English name Grass Dance is an allusion to this function. Ritual was incidental and varied and may be looked upon as a matter of afterthought" (Liljeblad 1986:649).

However, in an earlier publication, Liljeblad wrote:

> The so-called "Pinenut Dance" of the Nevada Paiutes, performed in late fall after the pinenut harvest, is clearly a thanksgiving ceremony with dances and prayers to the divine giver. . . . Likewise, "the Spring Dance" or Grass Dance, sometimes called "the Ghost Dance," can still be seen on the tribal dance grounds by the light from fires in the quiet nights of early summer. This dance is the time-honored native ritual dance of the Shoshonean peoples and was originally performed in order to promote health in man and fertility in nature. (Liljeblad 1969:54)

In a broader discussion of American Indian religion, but still part of this same article, "The Religious Attitude of the Shoshonean Indians," Liljeblad writes, "In the view of the Indians, there was a partnership between man and nature. Nature supplied man with what he needed. In return, man performed the rituals in order to promote the growth of nature" (Liljeblad 1969:52). This relationship, already touched upon in my discussion of nature and power, is, I believe, at the heart of the Round Dance tradition and runs through Wovoka's Ghost Dance religion and the Naraya.

Harris's description of a White Knife Shoshone Round Dance fleshes out the scene and its religious aspects:

> From one [hundred] to three hundred people came together for . . . seasonal dances, games and prayers. . . . This six-day gathering had as its primary function, fertility prayers and rites. The camps were arranged in a semi-circle with the open end toward the east. In the center of the circle, a green willow pole, which symbolized the verdure of the earth, was erected, and about this pole the dances were performed.
>
> Just before sunrise, the leader would stand in the center of the camp half-circle, face the east and pray to the sun. He would ask for rain; that the earth bring forth berries, seeds, plants; that the hills be covered with green and growing things; that the streams be stocked with fish; that the valleys and ranges abound with deer, antelope and mountain sheep. In the evening, between performances of the round dance, he would admonish the people to be industrious, the men to provide abundant game and fish, the women to gather seeds and roots. At the conclusion of the dance each individual clapped his hands over his body, from the ankles, over the legs, at the sides, on the breast, over the head, symbolically brushing and shaking off the evil, filth, and disease. (Harris 1940:53)

According to Harris, this prayer is directed to *Apo* [literally, "Father"], "the fountain-head of supernatural power" (Harris 1940:56).

Two Northern Paiute prayers from the Round Dance performed at the Pine Nut Festival (called, Fandango, in more recent times) are examples of its form and character: "'*Numinaa*, we pray to you to help us; help our people; bring us enough of everything to eat; and help us to thrive in happiness. Make us happy and keep our country for us, and save us. Give us lots of rations. We are glad for lots of rations.' The prayer is considered to be more effective if, in advance, someone has brought a dozen or more pine cones. In this case, the chief adds to the prayer, 'Our Father, we pray that the yield of the pine nuts will be great, and that all of them be free of rot and decay'" (Heizer 1970:240).[20]

In 1968, Ivan Northrop, a visitor from McDermott, was asked to give the opening prayer at a Pine Nut festival he attended in Schurz, Nevada. A woman with a helper scattered pine nuts on the ground as he spoke:

> Ladies and gentleman. Our forefathers in early days give us this opportunity to pray for everything that we have for our oldtimers. We pray like when we are going out hunting deer. We pray for 'em. When we are going out hunting for any kind of an animal, we go and pray. And now tonight these folks here tell me to stop up here and pray for them. . . . This old man said that here it's been several years now that the pinenuts haven't come back so we gotta pray or do something for it so that we can get some pinenuts. I guess lot of you pinenut-people knows about pinenuts same as I do back home knowing about buckberries. 'Course we never have no buckberries there for the last 3–4 years, now. Seems just like everything is just frozen up, tighter up. So tonight I'm going to ask God, our Father, who up in heaven, to give us our food back again. Along the line some way there might been a mistake, said the old fellow. This old fellow said it never been used to doing that before. He said that along the line we made a mistake so let's do it again and let's try our best. You all know that pinenuts and all the old timers' food is all fading away. (Margaret M. Wheat Collection, 1968, tape 83)

Park provides strong documentation and affirms the religious nature of the Round Dance. It is clear that the "mistake" alluded to in Northrop's Pine Nut prayer was already recognized and articulated by Northern Paiutes in 1941:

> In addition to its social and recreational functions, the Round Dance is also an occasion for the performance of simple but important religious rites. The repeated statements of nearly all informants that praying or "talking" is one of the chief reasons for giving the dances indicates something of the importance attached by the Paviotso [Northern

Paiute] to this part of the ceremony. These religious practices are simple to an unusual degree, but the dance has clearly the double function of bringing people together for a thoroughgoing good time and for an appeal to vaguely conceived supernatural powers that are thought to control human health and supplies of wild seeds and game. The Paviotso frequently expressed the view that the prayers and "talking for things" are as much a part of the occasion as the dancing. The religious character of these dances is further evidenced by the statement quoted above: "People had to pray for things all the time."

These simple religious observances often have been neglected at the dances given in recent years. The consequences that have followed the failure to observe old practises have been pointed out by several Paviotso. "Nowadays no one asks for pine nuts at the dances. The pine nuts grow but the weather is too hot so they burn on one side. People should talk about pine nuts at the dances as they did in the old days."

Religious expression at the dances is confined to "talking" or praying while the dancers were singing and circling the pole in the Round Dance. A dance leader or head man (sometimes called the dance chief or "boss") selected for the occasion walks around outside the circle of dancers, asking for rain, wild seeds, pine nuts, fish, game, and good health for all. All agree that he is asking aid and blessings from some supernatural force or power. "The chief of the dance talks while the people dance. It is just like praying. He talks about the weather. He asks for rain so the people will have plenty of roots and seeds. He wishes for pine nuts and other foods for the coming year. He talks to some kind of spirit." . . . One informant described additional ritual acts: as the head man walked around the dance circle he scattered seeds or pine nuts on the ground and over the dancers. (Park 1941:186)

In a footnote to this passage, Park adds, "There seems to be no distinction made between the rites and prayers in the spring and those of the dances held [in fall] to celebrate the pine nut harvests" (Park 1941:186).

Prayers spoken while the dance was in progress might also touch on issues of moral values as well—preaching. For example, we learn that, "During the dance Tutuwa talked from time to time, telling the boys not to steal or make trouble and urging people to bring out food for feasts" (Steward 1938:107). As noted earlier, a leader might urge the people to be industrious in their hunting and gathering. It is easy to imagine the accretions to the dance talker's role over time—progressing from praying to preaching to prophesying. Wovoka drew on all three modes. Enfolded within Ghost Dance vision were these words of admonishment to his followers: "God told me to come back and tell my people they must be good and love one another and not fight, or steal, or lie" (Mooney [1896] 1991:764).

Another religious task of the Round Dance leader (a task sometimes performed by helpers in attendance) was to scatter offerings of pine nuts, seeds, or other wild foods during or at the conclusion of the dance. This appears in several Round Dance accounts already quoted. The detail of nuts and seeds scattered on the dancers, as recounted by Park, connects the health of people to an abundance of food. A detailed account by Stewart brings this connection into sharper focus: "The ceremony took place the last morning of the big five-day spring round dance. Just before dawn a half circle was formed at the west side of the dance place by basketry cups filled with Indian food. Each cup contained but one type of food, such as seeds, small pieces of fish or meat, piñon nuts, and so forth. Just as the sun came up the head man took each cup separately, danced around the circle of Indians, sprinkled the food in all directions, and prayed for a good season for all things" (Stewart 1941:427).

Many scholars reinforce Park's religious interpretation in their documentation of multiple forms and meanings of specific Round Dance occasions. Lowie reports the *nū´akin* or *ta-nu´in* among the Lemhi Shoshone. Celebrated in early spring, its "object was to ensure a plentiful supply of food, especially of salmon and berries" (Lowie 1909a:217). Powell reports Northern Paiute festivals in the summer when seeds are ripe and in the fall when pine nuts are ripe, noting, "Every festival has a singing master under the direction of the Priest" (Powell 1971:248). White Knife Shoshones have "festivals for rain, snow, hunting festivals. Generally governed by priests" (Powell 1971:270).

Hittman underscores the religious purpose of the Round Dance and its imprint on the 1870 Ghost Dance. "The 1870 Ghost Dance functioned as a curing rite, and since it was grafted upon the Round Dance, a traditional ceremony whose function was the increase of food supplies, the 1870 Ghost Dance also functioned as an increase rite" (Hittman 1973:248).

Stewart's tally of different aspects of Northern Paiute culture reveals both the religious character and the social nature of the Round Dance. Working with people from fourteen contiguous groups, which he referred to as "bands," he published the following data. Twelve out of fourteen bands believe the purpose of the Round Dance is to make seeds grow; eight believe it makes piñon nuts grow; twelve believe it produces rain. Six give offerings of game at the spring dance, eight offer seeds. All fourteen bands see the dance as an occasion for courting (see Stewart 1941:415, 416).

Hultkrantz argued against Steward's denial of religious meaning in the Round Dance. Referring to Steward's 1938 publication, "Basin-Plateau Aboriginal Sociopolitical Groups," Hultkrantz writes, "In contrast to Steward, I would say that the religio-ecological adaptation in the Basin area was striking and important for the whole culture pattern. In particular, I challenge his view that ritual had practically no connection with economic pursuits. Steward misunderstood the motives of the round dance and thereby misjudged the whole religious configuration in the Great Basin" (Hultkrantz 1976:147, 148). Like Hittman and Park, Hultkrantz sees the increase of food supply as a principal aim of the Round Dance, its "clear religious purpose" (Hultkrantz 1986:634).

In returning to Steward's work itself, the reader should note that it provides important information on religious aspects of the Round Dance.

In his publication on the Northern and Gosiute Shoshone, Steward reports Round Dances that "were usually held spring and fall and were to promote health and make nature fertile. But a special dance might be held in time of sickness or trouble" (Steward 1943a:287). (This dance will be described later in this chapter.)

In his publication on Nevada Shoshone, Steward reports on the various seasons and purposes of the Circle (Round) Dance:

> [Shoshoni of Battle Mountain performed the Circle dance] . . . in the spring when grass was about 4 inches high and called *tawa* (spring) *nuka* (dance), it helped seeds to grow; when held in summer and called *taza* (summer) *nuka*, it helped seeds to ripen. S-Egan: [Shoshoni of Egan Canyon] The fall dance, held prior to pine-nut gathering, made deer plentiful. . . . TP said S-SnRv [Shoshoni of Snake River] people at Owyhee danced as follows: early spring, called *takavi* (snow) *tapazüŋgun* (*tap:*, to trample; *pazüŋgun*, to make dry), to make the snow disappear; in May, called *puip:* (green) *ta* (foot?) *suuŋgun* (to accomplish by means of), to make plants green; when seeds (or, farther south, pine nuts) were ripe, it and the Back-and-forth dance [Bear Dance] were performed ten nights to produce a good harvest. Eureka, according to H, danced the Circle dance six nights; it brought enough rain to lay the dust but not enough to aid plant growth. He once saw a dance at Belmont, probably a circle dance, in which women jumped, throwing grass seeds (*wai*), *Mentzelia* (*kuhwa*), and pine nuts, which they carried in baskets. (Steward 1941:265)

Later in the publication, Steward gives numbered examples of further Circle Dance practices among the Nevada Shoshone:

> 2621. S-Btl M: [Shoshoni of Battle Mountain] dance leader stands in front of his house and "talks" for rain and growth of plants.

2623. S.-Egan, S-SmCr: [Shoshoni of Smith Creek Valley] recent droughts are attributed for recently abandoning round dance.

2628. E-Egan: for summer dance, young pine-nut tree with green cones pulled up by roots and put in center of dance corral; this helps insure good pine nut harvest.

2629. S-SnRv: young juniper or spruce tree. S-RsRi: [Shoshoni on the upper portion of the Reese River and in Ione Valley] according to FSm, also used young juniper tree.

2634. S-BtlM, S-SnRv: singer, called *huvia* (song) *gunt* (possessor or performer), has dreamed special songs.

(Steward 1941:352, 353)

Following the last example, Steward reminds his readers: "Recall that it is in dream that one taps into power, the transfer coming in and as song. This is true for the shaman and the song leader in the Round Dance" (Steward 1941:353). Finally, in this same publication, he writes, "S-BtlM: might dance extra day to insure good fortune of group which had arrived toward end of dance" (Steward 1941:353).[21]

It is no accident that season, food, and Round Dance religious ceremony coincide. This convergence results from an intricate interdependent relationship between two calendars, one determined by nature, the other by people and culture. The fall harvest of pine nuts and the spring run of kuiyui fish follow the natural calendar, and these events provided a food supply adequate to support a large gathering of people. In a land of meager food resources, this abundance of food and people is noteworthy in itself. In fact, there is a suggestive relationship between the traditional length of the Round Dance celebration, usually five days, and food supply.[22] As part of his description of a White Knife Shoshoni Round Dance, or *Gwini* Ceremony, Harris writes, "It was recognized that the food supply would allow for no longer than these five and a half days (camp broke on noon of the sixth day)" (Harris 1940:53; also see Steward 1938:45, 46).

The number five has special significance for the Paiute. Lowie describes it as their "mystic" number, and it has manifestations in other areas of the culture (Lowie 1924a:295; Lowie 1924b:193; Hopkins [1883] 1969:13, 16, 56). Nevertheless, pragmatism joined with mysticism in determining the length of the Round Dance celebration. Food made possible the occasion, which, in turn, gave rise to song, dance, and prayer for the food that was harvested.

Sarah Winnemucca Hopkins remembers that "we had a thanksgiving dance. The day we were to start we partook of the first gathering of food for that summer. So that morning everybody prayed, and sang songs, and danced, and ate before starting" (Hopkins [1883] 1969:40). Powell's notes on the Northern Paiute also refer to this occasion: "The first fruits of the forest, the meadows, the chase, etc. are sacrificed, thanking the *Na-tu´-ni-tu-a-vi*" (Powell 1971:246).

Wind River Shoshones also used to perform a thanksgiving dance in late September or early October. Sarah Olden describes the circle of men, women, and children who moved slowly around a hemlock or cedar tree pole and sang:

> *Na-va-*   *an-day-ab!*
> [*ba* (water)   *doiyav* (mountains)]
> *Na-va-*   *an-day-ab!*
> [water   mountains]
> Send rain on the mountains!
> Send rain on the mountains!

> repeated a thousand times, in which they thanked the Great Father for his bounty and for its continuance. They then asked him to look upon the mountains, the rivers, and the trees, and besought him to send rain upon them and into the rivers. They also entreated him to bid the earth to cease swallowing their fathers, mothers, and children [a poignant reference to sickness and the population decline of the time]. (Olden 1923:37–38)

In this last statement and laced through some of the discussions of the Round Dance already cited is mention of practices and prayers that address concerns for health. In another example of this, Harris states, "The round dance is still performed in much the same fashion as it had been in the past and there is the same ceremonial hand-clapping over the body to rid it of disease" (Harris 1940:109).

At certain times, health or well-being became in and of itself the central focus for Round Dance performance. Thus, we learn that the Lemhi River people held Round Dances "during any period of sickness or other trouble" (Steward 1938:193). Liljeblad reinforces this in "The Religious Attitude of the Shoshonean Indians," noting that "when a person or the group as a whole went through a crisis, there was a dance to be held" (Liljeblad 1969:52).

The use of the Round Dance as a prophylactic even appears in one version of a Comanche myth, "The Hoodwinked Dancers."[23] Coyote tricks his prey, a village of prairie dogs, into dancing on the false pretext of approaching illness. "Coyote said, 'Well, we are going to dance, a bad disease is coming'" (Lowie 1909a:274).

Emily Hill's statements regarding the Naraya show the carryover of this particular aspect of the Round Dance to the Naraya. Likewise, writing of the Wind River Shoshone "*Naroya* [*sic*]," Lowie notes, "Any man might give the dance if some member of his family was smitten with a cold or some more serious disease; to drive this away the performers would shake their blankets at the close of the ceremony" (Lowie 1915:817).

Round Dance literature provides examples of the widening scope of problems that Round Dance performance attempted to redress. Sarah Winnemucca Hopkins recalls the warnings of medicine men who foresaw the limits of traditional prophylactics to avert impending troubles with whites: "Dance, sing, play, it will do no good; we cannot drive it away" (Hopkins [1883] 1969:19). Though this statement is in the context of a failed effort, it still reveals the serious purpose and inseparability of dance, song, and even "play."

However, within the confines of the natural world, people continued to perform the Round Dance to avert storms and other natural disasters. Park tells us that "the dance, held in the spring, is believed . . . to prevent the frost from killing the blossoms" (Park 1941:187). The more common type of weather control involved prayer for rain at the Round Dance. Park notes, "While the dancers are moving in a circle a headman, not necessarily one with supernatural power, walks around praying for rain in order to insure abundant wild products" (Park 1938:60n.18). So important did this aspect seem to Park, that in a subsequent publication he referred to "the Round Dance with its rain-fertility rites as characteristically Paviotso-[Paiute] Shoshoni performance" (Park 1941:193).[24]

I have so far stressed the religious nature of the Round Dance in order to counterbalance what seems to me some scholars' bias against acknowledging it. In rectifying one wrong, however, I do not mean to commit another through neglect. Without question, the Round Dance was also an important social event. As one Paiute person expressed it, "The dance is for a good time" (Park 1941:185). Gambling, games, feasting, and courtship were vibrant parts of the scene, adding other layers of texture to the event. Unmarried girls sought eligible husbands in the dance (Park 1941:185). Sarah Winnemucca Hopkins, herself a Northern Paiute, writes that young women were, in fact, not even allowed to talk to young men who were not cousins, except at festive dances (Hopkins [1883] 1969:45). Beyond courtship, the Round Dance helped produce social cohesion as it "wove a loose net of linkages" (Harris 1940:55). Independent of the varying proportion of religious intent in the Round Dance, and even as this purpose waned in certain documented instances,[25] the social functions of the occasion remained valid and important. Entertainment, humor, courtship, fellowship, group solidarity, cooperation, harmony—these are central to and enhanced by the Round Dance experience.

Nū´akin and the Father Dance

Two specific forms of the Round Dance or Circle Dance, the *Nū´akin* and the Father Dance, have close connections to the Naraya. Indeed, Lowie and Shimkin reported that Wind River Shoshones identified one or both of these dances with the Naraya. I examine them now in order to bring out the similarities and differences among all three and to mention, if not completely clarify, their multiple names and consequent confusion in the scholarly literature.

As noted earlier in this chapter, Lowie reported the *Nū´akin* among the Lemhi Shoshones, danced in early spring to ensure plentiful food, especially salmon and berries:

> Of the dances formerly in vogue at Lemhi, the *nū´akin* . . . seems to have been the most important. Some informants identified it with the *na´dzangai,* or *na´dzangEn;* but others denied any connection between the two, and insisted that the latter was a squaw-dance recently derived from the Nez Perce, though some similarity in the step was admitted. The women wore elk-tooth dresses or their modern equivalents, put red paint on their face, and dyed their hair yellow. . . . The men used *bi´cap* on their face, white clay on their forehead and hair. . . . No drum was used during the performance. The dancers themselves sang, gliding with clockwise movements. . . . As soon as the singing ceased, the women stepped out of the circle, resuming places when a new song was begun. So far as could be learned, there was no difference between the several (according to some two, according to others five) days' performance, which was concluded with a feast. Mr. Faukner, a young half-breed from Ft. Hall, remembers a dance, called grass-dance, which seems to correspond to the *nū´akin,* though he has forgotten the native designation. An immense circle was formed by men and women, neighbors interlocking fingers. The dance continued for several days and nights; the object of the dance was to make the grass grow. [Lowie gave a *nū´akin* song text here; I quote it in chapter 10.] . . . A very vague, general resemblance might be noticed between the style of this song and that of some recorded ghost-dance songs. Together with the informant's statement that some Shoshone called the *nū´akin dzō´a-nò´gakin,* ghost-dance, the slow movement, the characteristic position of the women, and the clasping of hands, it might be taken as evidence of a recent development of the dance. But Mooney's statement, that the Shoshone ghost-dance was merely a revival of an older dance practised fifty years ago, is supported by the testimony of Lemhi informants, reinforced both by the mention of the *nū´akin* in mythology and the explanation of its object. There can thus be little doubt as to its antiquity. (Lowie 1909a:217–18)

Note that in this account Lowie gives four alternate names for the *nū´akin: na´dzangai, na´dzangEn,* grass-dance, and *dzō´a-nŏ´gakin* (ghost-dance).

Steward also received information from the Lemhi Shoshone on their dances:

> Dance 1 in the lists, the grass dance, lacked a drum and was called *nazaŋgünt* (leading) or *nu'a* (side stepping) or *apünukun (ap:,* father). In the afternoon, men went from house to house and encircled the village four times, arriving finally at the dance ground in the center of the camp circle. As the sun sank, each man "brushed evil from himself," while singing, "*Kwinaŋ* (eagle feather) *gwasi* (tail) *hupi* (stick) *nzia* (?)," which was addressed to nature or to the maker of green things. The men went home to eat, then returned to the dance ground in the evening when the dance was performed. The above prayer song was always sung twice in the evening. There were several groups of four singers, each with a leader, who took turns singing. Each time the dancers had made a complete circle, the song stopped and women stepped back behind the men. Sometimes clowns, dressed like old men, their faces painted with mud so that it cracked, and carrying canes, danced for a while. They would pretend to become tired and sit on the side lines. They were called *na* (dress) *zoavitc* ("giant" or ghost person) *naix.* Dancing ceased about midnight. On the fourth night, the chief would announce that they would finish in the morning and that each camp should bring food to a certain place to be cooked for a general feast about noon after which the camp would break up. These dances were usually held spring and fall and were to promote health and make nature fertile. But a special dance might be held in time of sickness or trouble.
>
> This dance was sometimes called *tsoa* (ghost) *nukaiyᵘ* and was performed for protection against ghosts. This is not to be confused with Jack Wilson's ghost dance, which was never introduced to S-Lemhi. (Steward 1943a:287)

Three of Steward's names for the dance (grass, *nazaŋgünt,* and *nu'a*) are almost identical to those reported by Lowie. Elsewhere Steward reports that *nadzangai* (holding hands) was a dance of the Snake River Shoshone, and this would seem to translate one of the alternate names given by Lowie. (I also learned from Gladys Hill that *nazanG,* which means holding hands, was another name used by Wind River Shoshones for the Naraya.) Steward, like Lowie, also reported that the *nu'a* dance was sometimes called ghost dance, which bore no reference to the 1890 religious movement. New to Steward's list of names for the dance was *apünukun,* father dance.

In its form and substance the Naraya was extraordinarily similar to Lowie's and Steward's foregoing descriptions of the *nū´akin.* The dance—even the detail of women stepping back out of the circle between songs—is identical to Emily Hill's description to me of the Naraya. The use of paint in the Naraya, however, was not as extensive as suggested in the above accounts. As far as I know, its only use was by women who might paint the part in their hair red. Certainly the participation of clowns as described by Steward is significantly different from what took place in the Naraya, which, to the best of my knowledge, had none. But most important, the intent of the *nū'akin* dance—to ensure abundance in nature and health for humans—was identical to that of the Naraya.

Steward included *apünukun*, "father dance," as an alternate name in his description of the *nu'a* given above.[26] He was not the first scholar to do so. In 1915 Lowie described the Wind River Shoshone *Naroya* (a word that I believe to be an alternate transcription of Naraya) and I have already quoted his description in the introduction to this book. He also reported the various names given to the dance and its origins:

> This is regarded as an old dance; the meaning of the name is obscure. According to one informant, it is identical with the *ā'pö nöqà* and the *nū'akin;* another Shoshone identified it with the *dzō'a nöqà* and the *nadaí nöqà* of Idaho. The first-mentioned authority gave the following origin account:—
>
> After the Father (*ā'pö*) had created the world, there was a man with his wife and two children. Coyote came along and said, "I am your father and made all these hills and trees. Now I will give you this *ā'pönöqā*." So he taught them the *nā'röya* dance. Coyote was merely fooling the people. (Lowie 1915:817)

Accordingly, in Lowie's publication, *Naroya* was added to the list of different names that purportedly refer to the same dance. Thus *Naroya* [shuffling] = *ā'pö nöqā* (father dance) = *nū'akin* [side-stepping] = *dzō'a nöqà* (ghost dance, but with no reference to the 1890 religion) (Lowie 1915:817). It is important that Park recognized that the *Naroya* as described by Lowie was, in fact, an old form of the Great Basin Round Dance (Park 1941:192). This is in keeping with Mooney's report, quoted in the introduction to this book, that the Naraya was a revival of an earlier Wind River Shoshone dance.

In fact, documentation on the Father Dance as performed by the Wind River Shoshones suggests several significant differences between it and the Naraya. Shimkin writes:

> An ancient form, reported by hearsay by two informants (Polly Shoyo, b. 1845, d. 1938) and Moses Tassitsie (born 1852, d. about 1940), was associated with small pox epidemics in the late eighteenth (about

1781) and early nineteenth centuries (about 1837). According to Polly Shoyo, the Father Dance warded off smallpox. A sponsor's dream initiated the dance, usually in the spring. They started in the morning when the sponsor and his two assistants gave each dancer two bundles of big-leafed sage to hold in each hand. The dancers formed a circle, men and women alternating. In the center, facing east, was the sponsor who prayed 10 prayers and sang 10 prayer songs, so that the children would have no illness. These invocations were addressed to the Sun, Moon, Trees, Queerly Shaped Rocks, Mountains, Berries, Sage, Sky, Waters, and finally Earth. The people stood quietly as he prayed, then hopped up and down with their sage bundles as he sang. In the evening, they quit. (Shimkin 1986a:326)

The intent of this dance—to ward off disease—and its prayers that enfold every part of the natural world have counterparts in the purpose of the Naraya and the contents of its song texts. But the form of the Father Dance is strikingly different from the Naraya. The Father Dance was a ceremony that lasted one day rather than four nights and a concluding fifth morning. The "sponsor," not the dancers, sang the songs. The ten songs and the ten prayers were prescribed sets, unlike the open-ended Naraya repertoire that grew with the number of songs dreamed by its dancers, such as Virginia Grant Bonatsie's song, Naraya song 112.[27] Each dancer held in both hands bunches of sage rather than interlocking their fingers with those of neighboring dancers. Even the dance steps were markedly different. Although men and women alternated in a circle, as in the Naraya, the circle never moved in the Father Dance. Each dancer danced in place. As Polly Shoyo described it, they hopped up and down. Moses Tassitsie elaborated on this point to Shimkin, adding that the dancers bent their knees and then slowly straightened them (Shimkin 1937).[28]

As I have written elsewhere:

> One can follow the fading distinction between the Father Dance and the *Naraya* in the remembrances of the Shoshone people that Shimkin spoke to in 1937. Polly Shoyo, born ca. 1845, . . . distinguished the Father Dance from the *Naraya*. Moses Tassitsie, born 1852, . . . said it was the same as the *Naraya* or Round Dance, and that the *Naraya* originated in Nevada. Charlie Washakie, son of Chief Washakie and born in 1873, said that the Father Dance was the same as the *Naraya* which Shoshones got from the Bannocks. Toorey Roberts, born in 1881, one of the leaders of the *Naraya* in the mid 1930's, knew nothing of the Father Dance. (Vander 1986:13)

Unquestionably, scholars have received confusing and at times contradictory information and their published accounts reflect it. In some instances, as cited above, "Ghost Dance" and "Father Dance" were synonymous but did not refer to the 1890 Ghost Dance religion. For other groups these terms were interchangeable and did refer to the 1890 religion (Steward 1943a:288). It is interesting that Mooney reported the native Comanche name for the 1890 Ghost Dance religion as *A´p-anĕka´ra,* "Father's dance" (Mooney [1896] 1991:791). This term was unique in his study and is important in light of the fact that Comanches were originally Wind River Shoshones who split off from their kin in the early eighteenth century and moved down onto the Southern Plains.

2 | *Naraya Songs Related to the 1890 Ghost Dance Movement*

This chapter presents Naraya songs that express the prophecy and teachings of Wovoka. They are a small percentage of the known Naraya repertoire.

Naraya Song 18

Da - mën nü - wï - tsi da - mën nü - wï - tsi, Da - mën nü - wï - tsi da - mën nü - wï - tsi. Da - mën nü - wï - tsi za - ni sua - no - ve ge- ma - no, Da - mën nü - wï - tsi za - ni sua - no - ve ge- ma - no.

8 repeats

Pitches

Dorothy Tappay
Emily Hill

Damën	*nüwï-tsi*	*damën*	*nüwï-tsi,*
Our	people-(d.a.s.)	our	people-(d.a.s),

Damën	*nüwï-tsi*	*damën*	*nüwï-tsi.*
Our	people-(d.a.s.)	our	people-(d.a.s).

Damën	*nüwï-tsi*	*zani-suano-ve*	*gemano,*
Our	people-(d.a.s.)	good-feeling-(?v.s.)	coming,

Damën	*nüwï-tsi*	*zani-suano-ve*	*gemano.*
Our	people-(d.a.s.)	good-feeling-(?v.s.)	coming.

EMILY: "Our people's coming, they're feeling good. Our people coming. They're glad they're coming." (*Za* and *sua*, literally, "good feeling" or "good thought," can be translated as "glad.")

Thornton has studied the Ghost Dance movement from a demographic standpoint, interpreting the object of the religion—the return of the dead—in terms of a desire for demographic revitalization and survival. He concludes that population decline prior to 1890 and small absolute tribal size are the two key statistics that correlate strongly with Ghost Dance participation (Thornton 1986:28–37). Wind River Shoshone statistics fit these criteria. An estimated population of 1,300 in 1870 declined to 916 in 1890 (Thornton 1986:73) and reached its lowest number, 799, in 1902 (Shimkin 1942:455). The decline in population was accompanied by the continuation of Naraya performance from the nineteenth into the twentieth century.

The unspoken implication of the text of Naraya song 18 is the return of the dead from the spirit world to life on earth. An enigma surrounds the theme of death and resurrection in this song and in the Northern Paiute Ghost Dance movements of 1870 and 1890. The notion of the return of the dead en masse seems inconsistent with the fundamental Shoshone-Paiute-Great Basin understanding of death, the dead, and ghosts.

In this view, death is not an unambiguous, irretrievable event. Death occurs when the soul leaves the body and there is a loss of consciousness. Out of the body, the soul looks like fog, or clouds. As it first journeys up into the sky it is visible only to shamans (Lowie 1924a:297). During this critical period when the soul is in its moist embodiment, the shaman, in a trance, seeks to send his own soul after the patient's soul—to bring it back to the body, consciousness, and life. Resurrection, on an *individual* basis, is the shaman's work. Individual resurrection is also one of the most common wishes and occurrences in Basin mythology, and it is often effected through the use of water or damp ground (Smith 1939:10, 167). In myth and everyday life, moisture and soul correlate positively with the potential for resurrection.

According to myth, however, halfway up in the sky on the soul's journey to Wolf's house, it is met by a "spirit descending on horseback, who then escorts [it] to [its] proper place. The *mu´gua* [soul] then becomes a *dzo´ap,* ghost" (Lowie 1909a:226). The former soul, now a ghost, takes on a new, dry form: it becomes a whirlwind. A point of no return has now been reached. Death is final.

Ghosts of the dead were greatly feared, as were the dead. Ghosts posed a threat to the living as they had the power to steal the soul from the body. "The appearance of a ghost to one who is not a shaman is certain to cause immediate and serious illness, unless precautions are taken to counteract their contaminating influence. For example, when a whirlwind in which ghosts travel is seen, dirt is thrown in its direction and it is driven away with these words: 'Stay away from me. You are no good. I can see you. I know what you are. You go the other way'" (Park 1938:40).[1] Wodziwob's prophecy in the 1870 Ghost Dance, as articulated by one Paiute informant, takes cognizance of Paiute fear of the dead and ghosts. According to that account Wodziwob "predicted that the dead would return in three or four years and that everyone would be badly frightened when the event occurred" (Du Bois 1939:3).

New to both Paiute Ghost Dance movements is the concept of resurrection en masse,[2] and the resurrection of those who had, presumably, passed the point of no return and had become ghosts. How were Shoshones and Paiutes to reverse the wet-dry process and transform dry whirlwinds back into moist, foggy souls? Wovoka clearly made this leap. We read about it in the letters of Cheyenne and Arapaho delegates who listened and wrote down his words as he spoke. "Jueses [Jesus] was on ground, he just like cloud. Every body is alive again" (Mooney [1896] 1991:780). Mooney commented on the constancy of this cloud image for the leader of the returning dead. "The dead are all arisen and the spirit hosts are advancing and have already arrived at the boundaries of this earth, led forward by the regenerator in shape of cloud-like indistinctness. The spirit captain of the dead is always represented under this shadowy semblance" (Mooney [1896] 1991:782). Wovoka's vision transformed dry ghosts back into moist souls, a form in which they were retrievable to consciousness and life.

Beneath attitudes toward the dead and the ghosts of the dead lies the issue of death itself. By returning the dead and thus overriding death, Wodziwob and Wovoka moved counter to Great Basin experience and the wisdom embedded in its mythology. Wolf and Coyote argued the question whether death should be permanent. "Wolf said that when a person died he could be brought back to life by shooting an arrow under him. But Coyote did not agree: he thought it was a bad idea to bring people back to life, for then there would be too many people here and there would not be room for them all. 'No,' he said, 'let Man die; let his flesh rot and his spirit glide away with the wind so that only a heap of dry bones will be left'" (Hultkrantz 1954b:129). Coyote's argument prevailed. It was pragmatic and took account of the most basic ecological relationship between population and land. Death makes room for life.

According to Bailey, Wovoka responded to Coyote's argument during an audience with Sioux and Cheyenne visitors:

> "It has been shown to me that all our dead are to be resurrected. That their spirits will come back from the Other World, join their bodies here on earth, and all will be made whole and alive again."
>
> "Is not the earth too small for this?" asked the interpreter acting for the Sioux and Cheyenne. And his words were in perfectly understandable Paiute.
>
> "My Father tells me that he will do away with heaven. To accomplish this, he will make the earth larger. Much larger. Large enough to contain all of us—and all our people who have died before us." (Bailey 1970:129)[3]

Scholars have suggested a variety of other sources, both Native American and Euro-American, that could account for a doctrine of resurrection en masse emanating from a culture that feared the dead. As described in the introduction, the Christianized version of the Prophet Dance complex and the individual Christian and/or Mormon experiences of Smohalla, Slocum, Wodziwob, and Wovoka affected, in varying degrees, each of their prophetic movements. The resurrection of Christ and the cataclysmic prophecies of resurrection on Judgment Day vibrate sympathetically with native forms of the Prophet Dance complex. Dangberg suggests that both Wodziwob's and Wovoka's visions of happy and benevolent spirits coming back to live on earth were the result of Christian-Mormon influence (Dangberg 1968:10). Happy benevolent spirits supplanted the dangerous whirlwind ghost.

Hittman's explanations for the dissonant resurrection doctrine in the 1870 Ghost Dance movement are pertinent for the 1890 movement and the Naraya, and they bring us full circle to Thornton's demographic study. Hittman points out the significant deprivation of the Paiute caused by Euro-American expansionism. Wodziwob's

1870 Ghost Dance was a curing rite in the most profound sense, in response to epidemics that devastated the Paiute at that time (Hittman 1973:262).

Shoshone people saw death and resurrection in the natural world that surrounded them. "It is said that the moon dies but comes to life again" (Lowie 1924a:309). Wovoka spoke in a similar vein: "When the sun died, I went up to heaven and saw God and all the people who had died a long time ago" (Mooney [1896] 1991:764). The coinciding of Wovoka's trance-coma and an eclipse of the sun must have been a powerful demonstration of death and resurrection, one that linked the sun to Wovoka and to Paiute interpretation of death in its retrievable form.

Naraya song 18 is a transformation text: the dead return to life. Naraya song 19 is also about change, but in this case that change is the aging of the earth.

Naraya Song 19

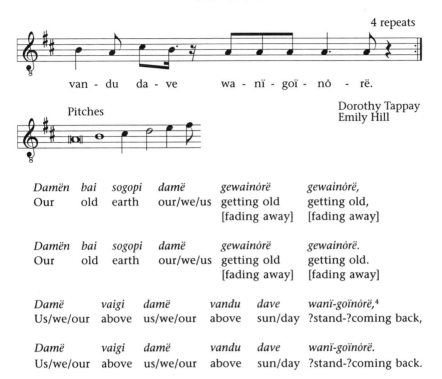

4 repeats

van - du   da - ve   wa - nï - goï - nȯ - rë.

Pitches

Dorothy Tappay
Emily Hill

Damën	*bai*	*sogopi*	*damë*	*gewainȯrë*	*gewainȯrë,*
Our	old	earth	our/we/us	getting old	getting old,
				[fading away]	[fading away]

Damën	*bai*	*sogopi*	*damë*	*gewainȯrë*	*gewainȯrë.*
Our	old	earth	our/we/us	getting old	getting old.
				[fading away]	[fading away]

Damë	*vaigi*	*damë*	*vandu*	*dave*	*wanï-goïnȯrë,*[4]
Us/we/our	above	us/we/our	above	sun/day	?stand-?coming back,

Damë	*vaigi*	*damë*	*vandu*	*dave*	*wanï-goïnȯrë.*
Us/we/our	above	us/we/our	above	sun/day	?stand-?coming back.

EMILY: "Our old earth, just like when the trees, when they get old. *Gewai*, it's 'get old.' You know, you see the trees, they get old, just like people."

Porcupine, a Cheyenne man who visited Wovoka in 1889, reported Wovoka's teachings. "My father told me the earth was getting old and worn out and the people getting bad, and that I was to renew everything as it used to be and make it better" (Mooney [1896] 1991:785). Mooney comments that many tribes held similar beliefs in an aging earth that needed to be renewed, including the "Washo, Pit River, Bannock, and other tribes adjoining the Paiute on the north and west" (Mooney [1896] 1991:785).

The second line of this text remains unexplicated. Is it our relatives above who are waiting for the day to come back? Or is it the sun that is above us, a new day, and a renewed world of nature that is coming back? In 1880 Brackett reported Wind River Shoshone belief in "*Tamapah*, a Sun-Father, who is the Father of the Day and Father of us all, and lives in the sun" (Brackett 1880:330).

This is but one of the multiple meanings for "Our Father," who is the subject of Naraya song 20. In this text we see the beginning of his journey; Our Father moves on and leaves behind the old world of Naraya song 19.

Naraya Song 20

♩ = ca. 84   (5th verse)

Da - më A - pë dïm - be   so - go - pa - de,

Da - më A - pë dï - nam - be   so - go - pa - de.

Sï - na - ve doi - ya yi - yï - gwi - dë,   Sï - na - ve doi - ya

yi - yï - gwi- dë.   Bü - nï - so mi - ëp   pü - do,

Bü - nï - so mi - ëp   pü - do.   Bu - hi   doi - ya - vi yi - yï-

                                                    6 repeats   last repeat

gwi- dë,   Bu - hi   doi- ya - vi yi - yï - gwi- dë.   -gwi- dë.

Emily Hill
Dorothy Tappay

Pitches

Damë Apë   dïmbe   sogop-ade,
Our   Father old   earth/world-(?v.s.),

Damë Apë   dï-   nambe   sogop-ade.
Our   Father ?old ?foot [steps] earth/world-(v.s.)? .

Sïnave   doiya   yiyïgwidë,
Quaking aspens mountains many sitting together,

Sïnave   doiya   yiyïgwidë.
Quaking aspens mountains many sitting together.

Bünïs-o   miëp   püdo,
He himself went   (?voc.),

Bünïs-o   miëp   püdo.
He himself went   (?voc.).

Buhi   doiyavi   yiyïgwidë,
Green mountains many sitting together,

Buhi   doiyavi   yiyïgwidë.
Green mountains many sitting together .

EMILY: "Our Father left the old world and going on through the mountains. There's a green pass where he went. He went through the mountains where it's green."

Emily sang the song again, and added, "It's still there, it says, this pass. That *buhi* ['green'] mountains [Emily had a particular plant in mind, *hunap*] that's I think that tall [about three feet]. That's nothing but that over the mountains and the other road on the other side. They got green pass where he went—his body." Emily's thought returned to the green plant. "Some are low. They're up this way, way up this way. Indians make—it's good for sores."

Another Naraya song (number 10, appendix A) charts the same journey away from this earth. It is the path for the dead soul. Emily said, "When a person dies they go in a dust whirlwind. They go up in the mountains. There's a road for that, there's a green pass through there, where they go" (Vander 1986:53). As will be described in chapter 6, green grass and vegetation of every type are key images that run throughout Naraya song texts. They are part of a cluster of closely associated elements in Great Basin culture: trees, greenery, water, and power (Vander 1995:179–81).

Who is Our Father in Naraya song 20? He is God the Creator, but complexly so as a result of Great Basin heritage, Plains heritage, Christian proselytizing, and Wovoka's religious experience.

Shoshones view "Our Father" as an ancient and indigenous term and concept. Moses Tassitsie explained this to Shimkin: "In those (former) days we only knew the name 'Our Father' to whom we prayed, but since then we have learned His Name from the white people—God" (Shimkin 1939:26). Another Shoshone statement adds conceptual form to the image. "We think about him as the whole sky, he covers the whole world. He is a human being above the sky. His power extends over the whole earth" (Hultkrantz 1956:205). Further, we learn that Our Father's realm is in the western sky in the direction of the setting sun. It was the final destination of the dead soul (Hultkrantz 1981b:40).

This brings us back to the connection between the sun and Our Father, the "Sun-Father" mentioned earlier in a quotation from Brackett. It is a controversial connection. Hultkrantz supports it in an article on Shoshone Sheep Eaters (Hultkrantz 1981a:39) and in a discussion on contemporary Wind River Shoshone religious belief (Hultkrantz 1987:43). However, two Wind River Shoshones sought to dispel this notion, which they felt was a distorted representation. Tom Compton, a Sun Dance chief, explained, "In the Sun Dance there is no worship of the sun. It is through the sun" (Shimkin 1953:463). Dick Washakie, son of Chief Washakie, analyzed the issue further: "The reason the Indian seems to worship the sun to some people is because the Indian believes that the sun is a gift from God, our Father above, to enlighten the world and as the sun appears over the horizon they offer up a prayer in acceptance of our Father's gift" (Hebard 1930:293). One sees this association in the Christianized vision of Toorey Roberts, an important Naraya leader in the 1930s. He saw "Jesus standing in the East with the sun surrounding his head, and underneath him there was a pleasant spot with high green grass and green sagebrush" (Hultkrantz 1969:35).

Our Father is a central figure in Wind River Shoshone religious thought of the past and present. Hultkrantz observes the Wind River Shoshone attempt to reconcile and integrate two diverse configurations of religious belief.[5] Connecting with Plains heritage, one includes Our Father, Mother Earth, and Buffalo (Hultkrantz 1956:211, 212). A second Great Basin configuration presents a confusing array of primal kin relations embodied as animal characters in myth. This series includes father, elder brother, younger brother, Wolf, and Coyote. Even Jesus and Reverend John Roberts, the Episcopalian missionary on the Wind River reservation, are drawn into this fold.

In myth, Wolf, the wise elder brother, and Coyote, the mischievous younger brother, are the creators of people and culture, their heroes and antiheroes. Scholarly accounts document contradictory Shoshone versions of who is who and who created what.[6] Some Wind River Shoshones believed that Our Father created Wolf and Coyote as his brothers. Others believed, variously, that Wolf is Our Father; Wolf is *pia apö,* "great father," and Coyote, *tɛi apö,* "little father" (Hultkrantz 1981b:560). Wolf is God's younger brother who didn't create the world but gave it rulings. Coyote is God's younger brother; Coyote is Creator and father of the Shoshones; Coyote is false creator; Coyote is malicious helper. Within this kin framework, Reverend Roberts was Elder Brother (Olden 1923:90), and Jesus was Our Father's son and also our elder brother (Hultkrantz 1969:35).

Conceptualized in a variety of guises, Our Father was the object of prayer.[7] Shimkin characterizes three key Wind River Shoshone ceremonies—the Father Dance, the Naraya, and the Sun Dance—as "supplications addressed to beneficent beings, particularly Our Father" (Shimkin 1986a:325). In his Sun Dance monograph, Shimkin derives the name of the Father Dance from this practice. Shimkin writes that "Our Father was addressed in prayer by the shaman, whence the name" (Shimkin 1953:433n41). Our Father, or sometimes simply "Father," was also spoken to in prayer by the "talker" at the Great Basin Round Dance. Harris described the White Knife Shoshone concept of *apö* as the apex of an animistic universe, the one who "had the power to bring rain, make plants grow, stock the earth with game and the streams with fish, and to preserve the well-being of the people" (Harris 1940:55, 56). Steward reports "*Ija* (wolf), our father, would tell the dance leader to call a dance (probably Circle dance) in the early spring so that food plants would grow. During the dance, the leader prayed to wolf" (Steward 1941:267). Elsewhere, Steward documents offerings of pine nut mush made from the first nuts gathered that were set aside for "*Ap:*" during the Circle dance (Steward 1943a:288). He also mentions that prayers were directed to the "father" and suggests an intriguing possibility that "father" and nature were interchangeable identities used by Northern and Nevada Shoshones, respectively. He writes that "the 'father' is supposed to give benefit in answer to prayers during Circle dances among Idaho and Utah Shoshoni . . . ; and nature is supposed to be benefited by prayers or 'talking' in many Nevada Circle dances. There is, therefore, the question of whether in the north, 'father' has supplanted 'nature' farther south" (Steward 1941:267).

"Our Father," the ancestral father in Northern Paiute myth, was part of Wovoka's heritage. I have very briefly sketched the outline of this story in the introduction: a first Mother and Father, children, familial strife, and separation. We pick up the story at this point. The ancestral parents then traveled to the mountains, and from there the Father went up into the sky, like Our Father in Naraya song 20, followed by the Mother (Mooney [1896] 1991:1051). The Pine Nut prayer quoted in chapter 1 is addressed to *Nümi´naă´*, "Our Father" of the Northern Paiute.

Bailey asserts that *Numi´na* (his rendering of the same word) was the source from whom Wovoka received the five songs with power to effect different weather conditions and that Paiutes called Wovoka "Our Father" (Bailey 1970:105–6).[8]

Wovoka's prolonged state of coma-trance, in which he seemed dead, and his awakening to consciousness and life paralleled Christ's death and resurrection. His proclaimed talk with God heightened his identification with Jesus. To Ghost Dance believers, Wovoka, Our Father, became Christ, Our Father (Mooney [1896] 1991:784, 1088; Steward 1941:267). Letters to Wovoka were addressed to "Dear father" and "Dear Father in Christ, Jack Wilson" (Dangberg 1957:289, 295). Plains Ghost Dance song texts include many references to "father," "my father," and "Our Father."[9]

There is one final parallel regarding the realm of Our Father that exists in Christian and Great Basin cultural contexts. Both the Christian concept of Our Heavenly Father and the Great Basin vision of Our Father's home locate them in the sky. Toorey Roberts's vision of Christ silhouetted against the sun, which streams out like a halo around his head—a not uncommon representation of Christ—also resonated with the association between father-creator and the sun that appears in Paiute myth (Smith 1939:21). The eclipse of the sun in 1889, its "death," in Wovoka's words, coincided with his own "death." Sun, Christ, and Wovoka—Our Father—all underwent death and resurrection.

In Naraya song 20, Our Father leaves the old earth. In Naraya song 21, a good earth, a new earth, moves in next to and then slowly over the old earth.

Naraya Song 21

♩ = ca. 84

(5th verse)

Da - më tsa   so-go - ven - dë   boi - hoi - ge - no,

Pitches

Dorothy Tappay

Damë	*tsa*	*sogo-vendë*	*boihoigeno,*[10]
Our	good	earth-?next to it (GH)	running slowly,

Damë	*tsa*	*sogo-vendë*	*boihoigeno.*
Our	good	earth-?next to it (GH)	running slowly.

Damë	*ügë*	*sogo-vai-ye*	*nuhiyogeno,*
Our	new	earth-over-(?v.s.)	coming or moving in,

Damë	*ügë*	*sogo-vai-ye*	*nuhiyogenë.*
Our	new	earth-over-(?v.s.)	coming or moving in.

EMILY: "Good news coming towards our earth, moving. A person's kind of running over, running, glad and running. Happy that new song's sang over the earth."

Emily's commentary on the text moves well beyond a literal translation and my capacity to relate every part of it to my transcription. My commentary can focus only on the song words themselves. If a happy runner is, at present, undetected in the text or there by implication, he or she is one of the rare appearances of people in Naraya songs. There are just six other such examples in Emily's repertoire.

I suggest that the subject of this text is the predicted new earth of Ghost Dance prophecy, expressed variously as good earth and new earth in lines one and two. This good or new earth is in the process of replacing the aging old earth of Naraya songs 19 and 20. Old and new are separate entities. Similar language and vision for a new world appear in a song text of the Father Dance of the Snake River Shoshone of Idaho, a dance that supposedly antedated the influence of Wovoka and the 1890 Ghost Dance. The song text says, "The good land is moving toward us; the land where we will never die" (Steward 1941:267).

Ghost Dance texts published by Mooney and Colby also speak of a new earth, for example, in the following Arapaho song, which Mooney titles "1. Opening Song—Eyehe´! Na´nisa´na."

> O, my children! O, my children!
> Here is another of your pipes—*He' eye'!*
> Here is another of your pipes—*He' eye'!*
> Look! thus I shouted—*He' eye'!*
> Look! thus I shouted—*He' eye'!*
> When I moved the earth—*He' eye'!*
> When I moved the earth—*He' eye'!*
> (Mooney [1896] 1991:958)

Mooney comments, "The second reference is to the new earth which is supposed to be already moving rapidly forward to slide over and take the place of this old and worn-out creation" (Mooney [1896] 1991:959). However, a critical difference between this Arapaho Ghost Dance song and Naraya song 21 is the presence and identity of the speaker in the Arapaho song. Here, and in many other Ghost Dance songs, Wovoka, the father or messiah, addresses his "children" (Mooney [1896] 1991:959). Elsewhere, the father gives the new or good earth as a gift to his children (Mooney [1896] 1991:984), predicts its coming (Colby 1895:148), and appears simultaneously with its arrival (Mooney [1896] 1991:1028). But Wovoka, the father, does not appear in any Naraya songs (or any of Mooney's Northern Paiute songs [Mooney (1896) 1991:1052–55]), in contrast to his very frequent appearance in Plains Ghost Dance songs (see chapter 10).

In Naraya song 20, Our Father leaves the aging earth. In Naraya song 22, we see that his destination is the new earth of Naraya song 21.

Naraya Song 22

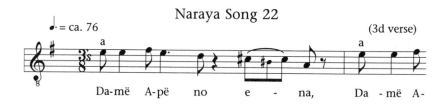

Da-më   A-pë   no   e   -   na,   Da - më   A-

Dorothy Tappay
Emily Hill

Damë	*Apë*	*no*	*ena,*			
Our	Father	?	(e.v.),			

Damë	*Apë*	*no*	*ena.*			
Our	Father	?	(e.v.).			

Damën	*biya*	*nambürü*	*nare-yïzïnórë,*			
Our	mother's	footprints [tracks]	rising, flying up,			

Damë	*ügë*	*sogovi*	*gunwar*	*vaigi*	*yani*	*wainanórë,*
Our	new	earth/world	on the edge/rim	above	?	standing-moving,

Damë	*ügë*	*sogovi*	*gunwar*	*vaigi*	*yani*	*wainano.*
Our	new	earth/world	on the edge/rim	above	?	standing-moving.

EMILY: "That's Our Father, our mother's going behind him, in back of him. *Nare yïzïnör*, that's flying on the new top of the new world, *darïna*, edge of the new world." Gladys Hill elaborated on the last verbal image of the text, *wainano*, from *wïnïnör*. She likened it to a person standing on the back of a moving truck; standing and moving, but not in the sense of walking. In this way our mother and her footsteps fly up behind those of Our Father to the edge of the new world.

On the surface, Naraya song 22 would appear to be a companion text to Naraya song 9 (Vander 1986:56), which I reproduce here:

> Our Father's footprints,
> Our mother's footprints fly up.
> My mother making herself rise, fly up,
> My mother making herself rise, fly up.

EMILY: "Our Father, our mothers, that's when they're gone, when they pass on. . . . She's following Our Father, our mother. That means, you know, a person's gone. She's following where Our Father's going. . . . Rising up like that—I think that's the spirit. Something like that" (Vander 1986:56).

I believe that Emily's comments apply equally to Naraya song 22. The participants of both songs are the same, the journey up in the sky is the same; but what of the destination? Where is Our Father leading our mother? The journey in songs 9 and 22 leads to two different but related realms: the land of the dead and the new world prophesied by Wovoka.

Emily commented about Naraya song 9 soon after her sister Dorothy's death in 1982. "It's a happy song for those kind, where she [Dorothy] is now. The spirits that just leave the world [are] glad to leave this world" (Vander 1986:57). Dorothy's spirit, like that of our mother in the song text, flew up to the land of Our Father and the dead, Our Father's home. This is the destination implied in Naraya song 9.

Many different sources suggest how Wind River Shoshones visualize the land of the dead, its regional placement and geographic features. A consistent pattern emerges. Brackett wrote in his 1879 annual report, "The Wind River Mountains are supposed by the [Wind River Shoshone] Indians to be the home of the spirits, and they believe a person can see the spirit land they will occupy after death, from the top of them. They are fond of describing the beauties of this land, and the enjoyments and pleasures they will find therein: fresh and pure streams; wide prairies covered with grass and flowers, and abounding in deer" (Brackett 1880:330).

Other visions, both in the Sun Dance and in dreams, that were reported to Shimkin reiterate the mountain's location and add a western direction (Shimkin 1939:48, 108). We see some more detailed impressions of this in Tom Compton's Sun Dance vision, in which he first saw a spirit. Compton described it as "Some kind of a hu- man—it floated about a foot and a half above the earth—. . . It floated like a fog" (Shimkin 1953:460). Tom tried to drive it out of the Sun Dance lodge and in so doing, headed toward, perhaps into, the land of the dead. "I found myself on a high mountain. . . . It was a ridge running to the west. The lower half was green with grass, sprinkled with flowers. . . . Even with me was a little stream with tall weeds growing by it" (Shimkin 1953:460).

The particular mountain location is idiosyncratic to the Wind River people, but otherwise Compton's vision is indistinguishable from many other Great Basin descriptions of the land of the dead. It de- scribes an idealized version of the familiar everyday world, a place "where the land is green and fertile and berries and food are always ripe" (Steward 1943a:283).

Cultural differences in diet and livelihood have counterparts in concepts of the land of the dead. For example, in this land there are pine nuts for the Owens Valley Paiutes and buffaloes for the Wind River people (Hultkrantz 1986:637). Brackett elaborates on the Wind River Shoshone version. There are "beautiful squaws to wait upon them; horses, always ready and never tired, to take part in the chase; new lodges supplied with every comfort, and provisions and meat so plentiful that they will never again suffer the pangs of hunger" (Brack- ett 1880:330).

Returning to the tale of Coyote, we learn that after winning the argument for death itself, he further decreed that "the dead go to another world" (Lowie 1909a:239). The act of "following" Our Father after death, expressed in Naraya songs 22 and 9, likewise has prece- dence in Great Basin mythology. We return, too, to the first Paiute man, the Father, and his words just before leaving this earth and his squabbling children: "'When you people die you have to follow me'" (Kelly 1938:372).[11] The tale continues in another telling of it. "He [Father] opened the clouds and told his wife to look through. 'Per- haps you will find some country.' She looked and saw a beautiful valley, green all over. He said, 'I think you had better go through, we'll go to the beautiful country. Perhaps some day the boys will die and come to us. Don't grieve too much.' They went through there. 'Whenever any one dies he'll come to us'" (Lowie 1924c:208). In Mooney's account of this story, we return to the image in Naraya songs 22 and 9. He recounts that "the parents went on to the mountains farther east and there *Nümi´naǎ* went up into the sky and his wife followed him" (Mooney [1896] 1991:1051). After death, people follow the footsteps of Our Father-Creator/Wolf.

Landscape is not the only familiar feature of the land of the dead. Its inhabitants, dead relatives, and their social pastimes and pleasures of this earth continue in the next. Just as the landscape is idealized, so is the socialscape. In three Wind River Shoshone accounts the Naraya, itself, is part of this happy scene. The first is from Rupert Weeks, a Shoshone storyteller. In this tale, grandfather, just before his death, gives solace to the story's two young male characters. "'Do not cry over me; it is getting dark. I can see my relatives and friends; they all have happy faces. I see my father leading the ghost dance, singing. I am coming, Father, I am coming to join—'" (Weeks [1961] 1981:70). George Guina told Shimkin, "After death, an Indian goes to heaven. God makes him take a bath in a willow basket. The spirit now turns into a person and then goes to a camp, where he ghost-dances. While he dances, he feels good, and God says, 'When they have a dance, they will be glad when they dance'" (Shimkin 1947c:331).[12] Years after Guina's statement to Shimkin, Emily told me, "Well, the way they say, the Indians, the spirits when they go to God's home, they still dance it [the Naraya]."

Wind River Shoshones were not unique in embracing this vision of dance and communal pleasure. White Knife Shoshones visualized "a pleasant place with much green grass and shade, dancing, gambling and abundant food" (Harris 1940:66). Steward reports the end of the soul's journey and its arrival at the camp of the land of the dead. "They [souls] passed through a buffalo herd and came to camp where they were bathed, fed, and directed to a big round dance where they saw their relatives" (Steward 1943a:287). Powell reports that, for Southern Numic people, the land of the dead was equally idyllic. "In that land there is no want, no pain, no sorrow. The people are ever engaged in dancing and feasting" (Powell 1971:69). In a subsequent tale of a chief who tries to retrieve his beloved wife from the land of the dead, he discovers the circle dance of its inhabitants to be so enormous as to take many days to complete one revolution (Powell 1971:69). The specific mention of the Shoshone Ghost Dance (the

Naraya) and Round Dance in the land of the dead is another link that reinforces my underlying premise of the close identity between the two.

Destination separates Naraya songs 9 and 22. In Naraya song 9, our mother follows Our Father to the land of the dead, a happy land for those who dwell there and forever leave behind life and loved ones on this earth. For this reason, one Shoshone man commented that it was a "sad song made up for the ones who were gone" (Vander 1986:57). A new world is the destination in Naraya song 22. Conceptually fashioned from the idealized land and socialscape of the dead, the new world promised a reunion of the living with the resurrected dead on a new-old earth.

Figure 3 summarizes the relationship among the three worlds of my previous discussion—the real world, the land of the dead, and the new world—and adds the overlay of Christian terminology, which

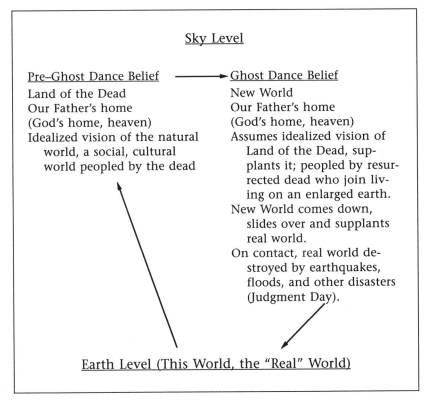

Figure 3. Relationships between three worlds in Ghost Dance doctrine.

will be discussed in connection with Naraya song 23. One should begin reading this figure at the bottom, with the earth level. The new world usurped both the land of the dead and the real world, metaphysically and physically, by engulfing them.

Naraya songs 9 and 22, so similar in imagery, diverge dramatically in destination, in doctrine, and consequently, I conjecture, in their chronology. Naraya song 9 would seem a later song. In it, the New World of Naraya songs 21, 22, and 23 (the latter follows) has faded away, leaving only the Land of the Dead, from which it had been created in the first place. No one returned from that land, certainly not in 1977, when I asked Emily, "But is there an idea that if people dance this dance that dead people will come back to life?" Emily replied, "Some day, some Judgment Day. You'll see your folks that day. Some day . . ." I will return to Emily's use of Christian terminology—Judgment Day.

Naraya Song 23

Emily Hill
Dorothy Tappay

Damën	*tsa*	*sogove*	*naishünde*	*dïvaroi*[13]		*en,*
Our	good	land/earth [heaven]	prayer	edge barely showing		(e.v.),

Damën	*tsa*	*sogove*	*naishünde*	*dïvaroi*		*ena.*
Our	good	land/earth [heaven]	prayer	edge barely showing		(e.v.).

Damën	*ügë*	*sogovi-në*	*nare-nagüx*	*ena,*
Our	new	earth-(?v.s.)	showing up	(e.v.),

Damën	*ügë*	*sogovi-në*	*nare-nagüx*	*en.*
Our	new	earth-(?v.s.)	showing up	(e.v.).

EMILY: "Our land, when you pray on earth, a new earth's coming up, *nani-naguk*. That's *damën*—all of us, our land—prayer, you pray on earth. When you pray your new earth's showing up. *Nai:naguk*, it means it's showing up, another earth. That's a prayer song. When they sing that, they—people that's looking on—all the old people, they get up and dance."

On another occasion Emily connected *tsa* with *naishünde* in the first line of text, describing it as "good, our good land—prayers— prayer land. When you pray, you know what pray means? Well, that's what it means. Just like you're going to church." One year later, the explication continued. Our good land, prayer land, was heaven and God's home. Emily said, "That means our heaven, that's the way they—just showing at the edge, *naishünde gewa:rïn*. The edge is showing. [I asked what word was 'heaven.'] *Damën tsa sogov*, that means that. Up in heaven, that's our *sogopi*. It's coming. I think that means God's home." Emily sang the second line of text and commented, "That's just barely showing, that song is coming, our people." Note Emily's identification of the new world with song and with the coming back of "our people," i.e., dead relatives. I asked if the new earth in the second line was the good earth of the first. It was. When I asked if the new world were God's earth, Emily replied, "Yes, that's where our people all going there, to God's home."

Like the land of the dead, the new world of the Ghost Dance is located up in the sky. In Naraya song 22, the mother rises up to it under her own power. Mooney describes Cheyenne, Arapaho, and Kiowa belief that Ghost Dancers would be carried upward to the new earth "by the aid of the sacred dance feathers which they wear in their hair and which will act as wings to bear them up" (Mooney [1896] 1991:786).

Mooney's mention of wings and the inclusion of "heaven" in Emily's explication of Naraya song 23, as well as her earlier reference to Judgment Day, lead us to Christian imagery and concepts. Heaven, a paradisiacal land of the virtuous dead holding promise of a Judgment Day resurrection, has strong parallels with the new Ghost Dance world in which this is accomplished, and this, in turn, draws on the paradisiacal "heaven" vision for the land and life of the dead, Our Father's home, an idealized version of the real world.

Christian influence among Shoshones and Northern Paiutes goes back to at least the early nineteenth century (Spier 1935:48). In 1883 Sarah Winnemucca Hopkins wrote, "We call heaven the Spirit land" (Hopkins [1883] 1969:15). A Paiute doctor "sings heavenly songs, and says he is singing with the angels" (Hopkins [1883] 1969:16). Angels watch over a sick person and take his or her soul to the Spirit land (Hopkins [1883] 1969:31).[14] Wovoka told Mooney that his Ghost Dance vision with God took place in heaven (Mooney [1896] 1991: 764).

Christian influence on Wind River Shoshone culture also came from the Comanches, who broke off from their Wind River kin in the early eighteenth century and moved down onto the Southern Plains. There they had contact with Spanish Catholicism from New Mexico. Yellow Hand, the Comanche man who brought the Sun Dance to the Shoshones in the early nineteenth century, also bore with him the fruit of this Spanish contact.

George Guina's reference to heaven as the destination of the soul and Emily Hill's mention of heaven in regard to Naraya song 23 are Christian references. However, some caution is necessary, for it is not always clear whether such Christian terms as "angels," "heaven," and "Judgment Day" are anything more than surface translations to help non-Indian interviewers understand native concepts. The point of this is often merely to ensure due appreciation for the religious nature of something, in some sense to legitimize it in another's eyes. For example, Naraya song 6 (appendix A) describes an eagle flying in the sky. Emily gave me an almost literal translation for the line. Her sister, Dorothy Tappay, explained it to me as angels flying in heaven. The depth of meaning and commitment to Christian terms used by Dorothy is a moot point. Nevertheless, there still remains some significance and interest in the translation, a reflection of contact and interaction.[15]

In the case of eagles and angels, we can also see the translation process from the other side, and with different intent. Reverend John Roberts, a lifelong minister on the Shoshone reservation, translated

Christian belief and imagery into native Shoshone belief and imagery in order to proselytize. Olden reports a sermon given to Shoshone girls who attended Roberts's mission school. In it, the Devil and Christ stood at the top of a tall temple in Jerusalem. "The Devil said to Him: 'Cast Thyself down! You won't hurt Yourself! God will hold You up; He under You will protect You!' It is the same when little eagles fly; the large eagle hovers underneath, so they can fall on her and not hurt themselves. 'God's angels will be watching, so that you will not fall.' The teasing, the teasing of this Evil One!" (Olden 1923: 93, 94).

Reverend Roberts translated prayers, the Episcopal service, and a catechism into Shoshone. His translation of Our Father, *"Dam Apua,"* is close to my orthography in Naraya song 22 and to other published renderings of this word (Roberts 1990:1). However, the Shoshone Naraya expressions of good earth, prayer earth, and new earth, which Emily glossed one time as heaven, are "heaven" in a special Naraya–Ghost Dance sense. Reverend Roberts translated "heaven" as *Damuvant* (Roberts 1990:2), literally, "above us." However, Episcopal-Christian heaven, *Damuvant,* does not appear in any Naraya song.[16]

Naraya song 24 serves as coda to a discussion of prayer and especially the Christian influence that preceded it. It is the only song in Emily's repertoire that makes reference to Christ.

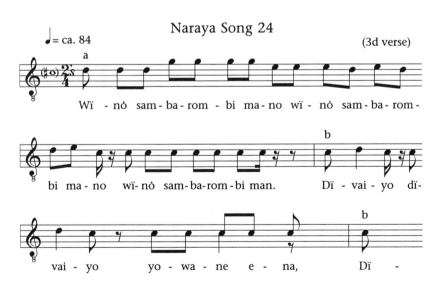

Naraya Song 24

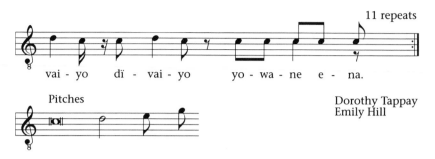

11 repeats

vai - yo   dï - vai - yo   yo - wa - ne   e - na.

Pitches

Dorothy Tappay
Emily Hill

*Wïnȯ sam-baro-mbi mano wïnȯ sam-baro-mbi mano wïnȯ sam-baro-
mbi man.*
Stand ?-water-(v.s.)   ?   stand ?-water-(v.s.)   ?   stand ?-water-
(v.s.)   ?.

[walking on water]   [walking on water]

Dïvaiyo dïvaiyo yowane ena,
?   ?   ?   (e.v.),

Dïvaiyo dïvaiyo yowane ena.
?   ?   ?   (e.v.).

EMILY: "A man from Idaho danced down here for the Ghost Dance. He sang that for them. I don't know if I was alive or not. I think that's from Nevada, that song. That means, you know they have stories about Jesus, after they crucified him, he walked through the ocean. He walked on the water, *ba:noge mano.* That's their word [Nevada, Western Shoshone]. It's something about Christ, they're singing about Christ walked on the water. That's something just the same as they say about the Shoshones here—*ba:rogïnd miyagïnd,* that means coming on the water, walking on the water. I don't know what that last part [the second line of text] means. I think it's in Nevada words. I guess they know what it means. I know that *baru,* coming on water, walking on the water. Jesus walked on the water just like he's walking on the ground."

There are many possible Ghost Dance connections to the story of Christ: Christ as miraculous healer, Christ as provider of food to multitudes, Christ resurrected after death. Nevada Shoshones chose Christ walking on water. Water was an ancient concern in life and a prevalent image in Great Basin literature and Naraya songs.

I turn now to song 25, which, like songs 26–28, centers on the final cataclysmic event in Ghost Dance doctrinal drama: "the predicted spiritual new earth is about to start to come over and cover up this old world. . . . at the moment of contact this world would tremble as in an earthquake" (Mooney [1896] 1991:973). Wovoka psychological-ly prepared his followers for it, telling them, "When the earth shakes do not be afraid. It will not hurt you" (Mooney [1896] 1991:781).

Naraya Song 25

♩ = ca. 88

(4th verse)

Da-më A-pë nï- nam be so - go-ben- de ya-no-me ya - no- me, Da - më A- pë nï-

nam be so - go-ben- de ya- no- me ya- no- me.

En - wad n- doi en - wad n- doi-ya yi - yï- gwi- dë ya-no-me ya-no- me, En - wad n- doi en - wad n- doi-ya

7 repeats

yi - yï - gwi - dë ya - no - me ya - no - me.

Pitches

Emily Hill
Dorothy Tappay

Damën	*Apë*	*nïnam*	*be*	*sogo-bende*	*yanome*	*yanome,*
Our	Father's	?	?old	earth/ground	wavy	wavy,

Damën	*Apë*	*nïnam*	*be*	*sogo-bende*	*yanome*	*yanome.*
Our	Father's	?	?old	earth/ground	wavy	wavy.

Enwad	*n-doi*	*enwad*	*n-doiya*	*yiyïgwidë*	*yanome*	*yanome,*
Rain	mountains	rain	mountains	many sitting	wavy	wavy,

Enwad	*n-doi*	*enwad*	*n-doiya*	*yiyïgwidë*	*yanome*	*yanome.*
Rain	mountains	rain	mountains	many sitting	wavy	wavy.

EMILY: "Our Father's, our old ground. *Yanome* is a wave like that."

Applied to a person, the word *yanome* means "getting dizzy." Gladys Hill defined it as something "wavelike, swirling, wavy." Regarding the second line of the song, Emily simply said, "It's raining."

Naraya song 25 presents an apocalyptic vision of a rainstorm on Our Father's old earth and its many mountains—a waving upheaval.

Measured in human terms, an earthquake, like an eclipse of the sun, is an extraordinary natural event. Interpreted in human terms, it is fraught with meaning. As Mooney noted, "In the New World, as in the Old, the advent of the deliverer was to be heralded by signs and wonders" (Mooney [1896] 1991:660). Native American connections between earthquake and renewed life—death and resurrection—that surrounded the Naraya and Ghost Dance are historically deep and geographically broad. Earliest Aztec sources, which come from sixteenth-century Mezoamerica, are Nahuatl, part of the large Uto-Aztecan language family, of which Shoshone and Paiute are a part. The myth of Quetzalcoatl, god-hero-culture-bringer, is "a myth of regeneration, of death and revival, illustrating the perennial power of nature to make things new. . . . It may foreshadow, or hark back to, the cataclysmic destruction of the universe and its subsequent recreation" (Bierhorst 1974:4).

Spier's study of the Prophet Dance complex (see the introduction to the present book) draws us north to the interior Plateau area and contiguous with the Great Basin. We have moved from the sixteenth to the late eighteenth century and on into the nineteenth. Again, impending destruction and world renewal are central themes. Earthquakes, like falling stars, portend earth's end (Spier 1935:5, 9, 60). Kotai'aqan, the chief supporter of Smohalla's Christianized version of the Prophet Dance complex, interpreted this imminent destruction as a moral judgment: "Notwithstanding all the benefits they enjoyed, there was quarreling among the people, and the earth-mother was angry. The mountains that overhung the river at the Cascades were thrown down, and dammed the stream and destroyed the forests and whole tribes, and buried them under rocks" (Mooney [1896] 1991:721–22).

If Mezoamerica and the Plateau area delimit the south-north axis of this discussion, northern California marks its westernmost extremity. The time is the early 1870s in California, when the first Ghost Dance movement took hold and briefly enthralled its adherents.[17] Scholarly documentation suggests that influences moved back and forth between northern California religion/shamanism and the Ghost Dance. In connection with earthquake prophecy in the Ghost Dance, Du Bois notes that it was a favorite topic of shamanism in northern California. "Apparently this element was amalgamated and maximized in the [1870] Ghost Dance doctrine of north-central California. The various 'worlds' in the mythology of the area provides a native pattern which could easily be dovetailed with Christian ideas concerning the end of the world and the resurrection" (Du Bois 1939:6n.15).

While Ghost Dance belief on the Klamath Reservation lasted just one year, much of its doctrine was incorporated in a new syncretism with older religious practices, known subsequently as the Earthlodge Cult. This religion also prophesied earthquakes, which had the selective capacity to destroy whites and Indians who did not believe in the religion (Nash 1955:421).[18]

In the 1890 Ghost Dance we learn that the Pawnee believed that "the feet of the dancers pounding the earth was symptomatic of the rumblings of the earth which presaged the change" (Lesser [1933] 1978:105). In this understanding, a synchrony of human and physical forces worked within and without the earth.

Finally, in his study of North American shamanism, Park states that earthquakes mark the shaman's death (Park 1938:69). One sees the translation or perhaps straight correspondence of this belief in Reverend John Roberts's Episcopal sermon to his Wind River Shoshone flock. Roberts said, "Then Jesus Christ died. God cannot die. He was God, because there was darkness, night, over the earth in the middle of the day; and the earth shook, and the rocks broke. When an ordinary man dies, nothing like that happens" (Olden 1923:92). The shaman's death and Christ's death bring earthquakes. Christ's death and Wovoka's trance-death brought darkness to the earth. These are truly signs and wonders.

Naraya Song 26

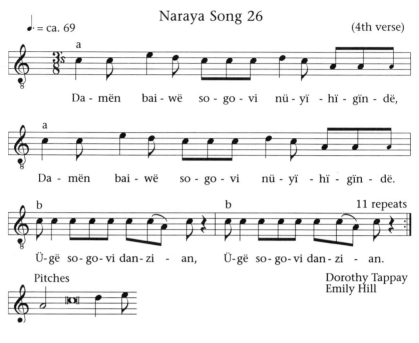

Damën baiwë sogovi nüyïhïgïndë,
Our rain earth shakes with rumbling sound,

Damën baiwë sogovi nüyïhïgïndë.
Our rain earth shakes with rumbling sound.

Ügë sogovi danzian,
New earth crackling [like thunder],

Ügë sogovi danzian.
New earth crackling [like thunder].

EMILY: "Rain, it's, you know, thunderstorm, *baiyu.* It shakes the earth, *nu:yuyïgiwünchits,* noise and shaking, [for example] anything, maybe dynamite. They do them [dynamite explosion], it makes the earth shake. That's what it's like. Rain, thunderstorm makes the earth shake."

Within Great Basin and Plains cultures, thunder and lightning are sources of power. Sky is their element and they are related to the birds who fly there, as will be described in chapter 5. The power of thunder, as in all things, is dangerous. Its destructive potential calls for protective measures. Northern Paiutes drive away thunder by throwing a knife outside the house (Steward 1941:445). A shiny knife draws lightning; like attracts like. When I lived with Emily I discovered another manifestation of this same underlying belief. Emily methodically covered every mirror in her house with towels during a storm. Another protective stratagem against thunderstorms is to place a serviceberry branch on a house (Steward 1943a:353). The power of one cancels the other.

The power of thunder can also serve beneficial aims. Shamans with power to influence weather had dreams of thunder and rain (Kelly 1939:159; Steward 1941:262). Toorey Roberts, a Wind River Shoshone man, could predict weather because he was blessed by spirits with power, lightning spirits being the most important (Hultkrantz 1987:81). Clouds and thunder are potential sources of the shaman's power to heal. Thunder aid is specifically efficacious for diagnosing illness (Park 1938:76, 86). In myth, Thunder (*Ni-mi-ap*) is the doctor who cures Oriole (Powell 1971:92). However, anyone who seeks help from thunder must do so with care and respect. Tom Mitchell, a shaman, warned bluntly, "Anyone who makes fun of thunder will be killed" (Park 1938:19).

Finally, for Northern and Wind River Shoshones, the conjunction of thunder, season, and human response is interpreted as an augur for the future. One account told that "when a child rejoices at the first thunder in the spring, it is an omen that it will live to an old age and enjoy distinction" (Hebard 1930:302; Lowie 1909a:232).[19]

Naraya Song 27

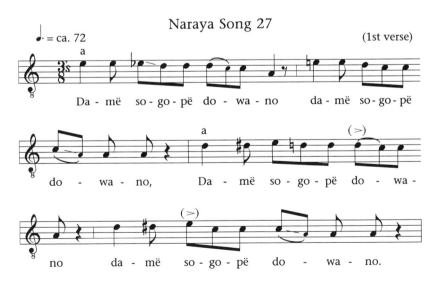

Pitches

Emily Hill
Dorothy Tappay

Damë	*sogopë*	*dowano*	*damë*	*sogopë*	*dowano,*
Our	ground/earth	washing down	our	ground/earth	washing down,
		[pours down] (GH)			[pours down]

Damë	*sogopë*	*dowano*	*damë*	*sogopë*	*dowano.*
Our	ground/earth	washing down	our	ground/earth	washing down.
		[pours down] (GH)			[pours down]

Damën	*doiyavi*	*nuyihïgïn*	*damën*	*doiyavi*	*nuyihïgïn,*
Our	mountains	rumbling-shaking	our	mountains	rumbling-shaking,
		[after thunder]			[after thunder]

Damën	*doiyavi*	*nuyihïgïn*	*damën*	*doiyavi*	*nuyihïgïn.*
Our	mountains	rumbling-shaking	our	mountains	rumbling-shaking.
		[after thunder]			[after thunder]

EMILY: "*Damë sogopë doawegïn,* coming down, sliding down—our ground. From up there. Moving."

JUDY: "Is it like an avalanche?"

EMILY: "Something like that but just when it's raining. *Ndoiyavi niyihïgïn*—that's thundering up the mountains. That's why that ground is wet coming down, sliding down. *Damën doiyavi niyihïgïn,* that's our mountains, it's thundering up there. That's shaking the earth."

Emily's focus in 1981 was on the groundslide. The following year, it shifted to the thunderstorm, the agent that shakes and shifts the earth's surface:

EMILY: "Storm on the mountains. You know water, you know the ground when it's wet—got water running—it means *dogweïngïnt,* washing it down, the rain. That *niyihïgïn* means thunderstorm. You know how it makes noise. That's a thunderstorm up in the mountains. Raining, and it's washing the ground down."

The Southern Paiute Kaibabs had their own song that focused on the coming earthslide. Tony Tillohash sang it in 1910 for Edward Sapir, and it has recently been published as song "No. 195." It consists of the phrase "Coming sliding, coming sliding" (Sapir 1994:656). In his linguistic note on this song, Sapir added that "coming sliding" was a term used for such things as glass, stones, snow, and ice (Sapir 1994:656).

A dynamic and destructive process is at work in Naraya songs 25–27. The old earth is beset by thunderstorms, earthquakes, and slides. Naraya song 28 presents a silent spirit earth.

Naraya Song 28

De - ve - se vai - yo   mu - gu - a so - go - vai - ye,

De - ve - se vai - yo   mu - gu - a so - go - vai.

7 repeats
(>)

Pitches

Dorothy Tappay
Emily Hill

Devese	*vai-yo*	*oi-*	*so-vai-yedu,*
?	on-(?s.v.)	all over	earth-on-(?v.s.),

Devese	*vai-yo*	*oi-*	*sogo-vai-yedu.*
?	on-(?s.v.)	all over	earth-on-(?v.s.).

Devese	*vai-yo*	*mugua*	*sogo-vai-ye,*
?	on-(?v.s.)	spirit/soul	earth-on-(?v.s.),

Devese	*vai-yo*	*mugua*	*sogo-vai.*
?	on-(?v.s.)	spirit/soul	earth-on.

EMILY: "It's about the spirit. This earth is nothing but spirit now, it says."

Emily's explanation stops here. Her comments suggest that death has occurred to the old earth, just as it does to the human body, through the separation and departure of the soul. Earth's soul floats over the corpse of its body. However, this interpretation remains tentative as the text and Emily's spare comments leave room for ambiguity and other interpretations. For example, might not the spirits all over the earth be those of the dead relatives? Have they reversed death's journey of Naraya song 3 (see song 3, appendix A), where the soul appears as fog and is flying up? Is it their souls that have now descended and hover over the earth, awaiting corporeal resurrection?

I have included Naraya songs 29 and 30 in this chapter, which is devoted to texts that express belief in Ghost Dance doctrine and prophecy. However, I recognize that their placement here, especially that of Naraya song 30, is marginal, at best. Naraya songs with Ghost

Dance doctrine include people—the return of dead relatives—and it is for this significant characteristic, one that sets them apart from other Naraya texts, that I have included Naraya songs 29 and 30 in the chapter. They, too, have reference to people: Naraya performance itself in song 29 and human illness in song 30. Lacking any better contextual frame, they are a people-postscript to the chapter proper.

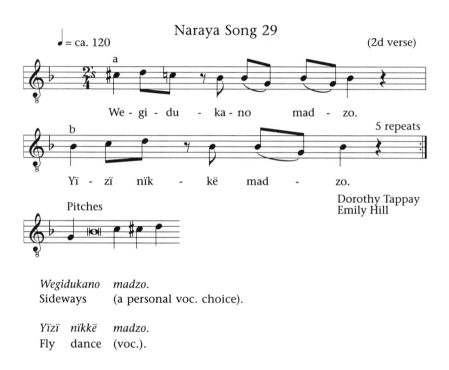

Naraya Song 29

♩ = ca. 120

(2d verse)

a

We - gi - du - ka - no   mad - zo.

b   5 repeats

Yï - zï   nïk - kë   mad - zo.

Pitches

Dorothy Tappay
Emily Hill

Wegidukano   madzo.
Sideways   (a personal voc. choice).

Yïzï   nïkkë   madzo.
Fly   dance   (voc.).

EMILY: "There's an old fellow a long time ago, the folks said, when he sings songs he's got all those *'madzo'* at the end. When he sings like that he has that word at the end of all the songs he sings. That's what the old folks say about him. . . . *Wegipür madz,* that means we're going sideways."

We have already seen flight expressed in Naraya songs. It appears in song 22, in which Our Father and the dead mother fly to the top of the new world. Mooney has documented the importance of crow, eagle, and magpie feathers, which Ghost Dancers wore in their hair and on their clothing while performing the Ghost Dance, enabling them to fly to the new world (Mooney [1896] 1991:970, 999). (See

Mooney's photograph of a Cheyenne Ghost Dance, which I reproduce in one of the photo sections of this book, in which one can see feathers in the dancers' hair.) According to Ghost Dance doctrine, the dance itself was to be an important factor in bringing about Ghost Dance prophecy. In song 29 we see an interesting mix of these beliefs in the combined imagery of Naraya flight-dance.

"Sideways" in this text refers to the direction of the dance step, the side-shuffling motion of dancers as they progress around the circle. It is a text about Naraya performance, describing both its movement and its power: a fly-dance, a flying dance.

In this song notice the use of a vocable ending, which was identified with the old man who was the song's source. His songs were unique in this regard, retaining his individual mark.

Naraya Song 30

Emily Hill
Dorothy Tappay

Yogavit-a	*yogavi,*		
Mucus-(v.s.)	mucus,		

Basiwamb-itta	*yogavi.*		
?Sand-(?v.s.)	mucus.		

Yogai	*yogai*	*yogai*	*yoga.*
Mucus	mucus	mucus	mucus.

Basiwamb-itta	*yogavi,*		
?Sand-(?v.s.)	mucus,		

Basiwamb-itta	*yogavi.*		
?Sand-(?v.s.)	mucus.		

EMILY: "They had a big Ghost Dance a long time ago. A lot of people there. And two guys from Idaho sang that. *Yogep*[h] means something like, you cough that *yogep*[h] in your throat."

JUDY: "Like mucus in your throat?"

EMILY: "Uh huh. . . . It's something about sand—mixed with sand. It's from Idaho, I don't know what it means."

Gladys Hill added that *yogabui* in Shoshone means "gooey stuff in your eyes." She suggested that the mention of sand and mucus in this text might refer to discharge from the eyes.

Whether the intent of this song was to prevent the illness it mentions and/or to cure it, I cannot say. In either case it accords with Emily's explanations of Naraya goals and seems totally unrelated to Ghost Dance prophecy. There is no promise of health in another world to come. Song 30 addresses sickness in this world, here and now. As stated earlier, it is an anomaly in this chapter. Indeed, it is an anomaly within the Naraya repertoire presented in this book.

3 | *Water*

Naraya texts overflow with water, ever present and in every form. It appears as ground or surface water (puddles, streams, and rivers) and sky or weather water (fog, rain, and snow). The linkage of water with every aspect of the natural world—trees and green vegetation, animals, rocks, and mountains—is one of the defining characteristics of Naraya song texts. Because water is ubiquitous in Naraya song texts, it will be subsumed within chapters that focus on other parts of the natural world. I present here only a small sample of water texts to illustrate these linkages.

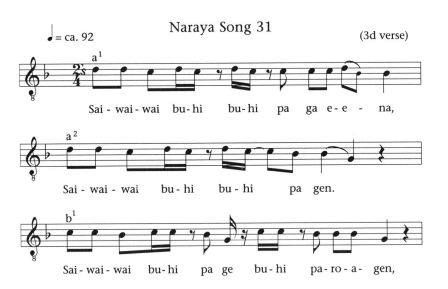

Naraya Song 31   (3d verse)

♩ = ca. 92

Sai - wai - wai bu - hi   bu - hi   pa   ga   e - e - na,

Sai - wai - wai   bu - hi   bu - hi   pa   gen.

Sai - wai - wai   bu - hi   pa ge   bu - hi   pa - ro - a - gen,

Dorothy Tappay
Emily Hill

Saiwai-wai	*buhi*	*buhi*	*pa*	*ga*	*e-ena,*
Melting snow-(e.d.)	green	green	water	?	(e.v.),

Saiwai-wai	*buhi*	*buhi*	*pa*	*gen.*
Melting snow-(e.d.)	green	green	water	(e.v.).

Saiwai-wai	*buhi*	*pa*	*ge*	*buhi*	*paroagen,*
Melting snow-(e.d.)	green	water	?	green	rain shower (GH),

Saiwai-wai	*buhi*	*pa*	*ge*	*buhi*	*paroagen.*
Melting snow(e.d.)	green	water	?	green	rain shower (GH).

Emily and I never discussed this text. Its combined imagery—melting snow, greenery, water, and showers—is common to many Naraya songs.

Naraya Song 32

nó - rë,   Da bi - ya   no - vi   da bi - ya

no - vi   yï - zï - gïh   ha - vi - gï - nó - rë.

6 repeats

Pitches

Dorothy Tappay
Emily Hill

Da	biya	ogwe	yï-tsi		ogwe	nórë,
Our	big	river	?-(? d.a.s.)		river	moving,

Da	biya	ogwe	yï-tsi		ogwe	nórë.
Our	big	river	?-(? d.a.s.)		river	moving.

Da	biya	novi	da	biya	novi	yïzïgïh	havigïnórë,
Our	big	hill	our	big	hill	rising	lying-moving,

Da	biya	novi	da	biya	novi	yïzïgïh	havigïnórë.
Our	big	hill	our	big	hill	rising	lying-moving.

EMILY: "That's about water—river, *ogwe*. It's the river going down under, like this hill, see. Big hills like this, water going under there just like this. Water, big river running underneath, close by the hill. That song's about something like this."

♩ = ca. 96

Naraya Song 33

(3d verse)

Ye va va - ru - kë ye va va - ru - kë- pen- ji,   Ye va va -

ru- kë   ye va va - ru - kë- pen- ji.   Ye va va - ru - kë   ye va

va - ru- kë- pen - ji,   Ye va   va - ru- kë   ye va   va - ru- kë- pen- ji.

Pitches

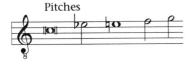

Dorothy Tappay
Emily Hill

Ye	*va*	*varukë*	*ye*	*va*	*varukë-penji,*
?	water	?water rising	?	water	?water rising-(v.s.),

Ye	*va*	*varukë*	*ye*	*va*	*varukë-penji.*
?	water	?water rising	?	water	?water rising-(v.s.).

Ye	*va*	*varukë*	*ye*	*va*	*varukë-penji,*
?	water	?water rising	?	water	?water rising-(v. s.),

Ye	*va*	*varukë*	*ye*	*va*	*varukë-penji.*
?	water	?water rising	?	water	?water rising-(v. s.).

EMILY: "It's about water. You know when water gets kind of pool-
like—it goes around."
JUDY: "Oh, a whirlpool?"
EMILY: "Uh huh, something like that. And some deep places."

I tentatively suggest a connection between *paa-rua-h*—which in the
closely related Comanche language means "to come up," "to rise,"
as water in a creek—and *varuk* in this song text (Canonge 1958:143).

Naraya Song 34

Da - ve ba - ü - wah doi - ya - ve   da - ve ba - ü - wah

doi - ya - ve   e - na,   Da - ve   ba - ü - wah doi - ya - ve

da - ve   ba - ü - wah   doi - ya - ve   e - na.

Won - go sü - gi ba - bai - e - ya we - gïn do - gan - do

16 repeats

da - ve   ba - ü - wah   doi - ya - ve   e - na.

Pitches

Emily Hill
Dorothy Tappay

Dave	*baüwah*	*doiyave*	*dave*	*baüwah*	*doiyave*	*ena,*
Sun/day	rain	mountains	sun/day	rain	mountains	(e.v.),
[sun showers]			[sun showers]			

Dave	*baüwah*	*doiyave*	*dave*	*baüwah*	*doiyave*	*ena.*
Sun/day	rain	mountains	sun/day	rain	mountains	(e.v.).
[sun showers]			[sun showers]			

Wongo	*sügi*	*babaieya*	*wegïn*	*dogando*	*dave*	*baüwah*	*doiyave ena.*
Pine	needles	pools	?side	?low	sun	showers	moun- (e.v.).
				place			tains
				[deep]			

EMILY: "Our mountains, you know, it kind of sprinkles up the mountains like towards the light. That's afternoon showers. It's raining, [but] not too much. And there's—on the mountains—there's them water pools. Just like lakes, but only smaller. You know how it is, puddles under them mountains. And those pine tree leaves all over on the water. Pine needles in the water. That's what it means. Clouds go over, clouds behind that—shadow, shadow on them puddle things. It gives that shade where the water puddles are."

Naraya Song 35

♩. = ca. 69   (5th verse)

Bo- ha gwi-an-zi   bai- gi yï- zï-nȯ- rë,   Bo- ha gwi-an-zi

bai- gi yï - zï - nȯ - rë.   Bu- hi   ba - ga - dï - dë

yï- zï- nȯ- rë,   Bu- hi   ba- ga- dï- dë   yï- zï- nȯ- rë.

Pitches

Dorothy Tappay
Emily Hill

Boha	*gwian-zi*	*baigi*	*yïzïnȯrë,*
Sacred power	eagle-(a.s.)	high	flying,

Boha	*gwian-zi*	*baigi*	*yïzïnȯrë.*
Sacred power	eagle-(a.s.)	high	flying.

Buhi	*bagadïdë*	*yïzïnȯrë,*
Green/grass	small lake, pond	flying,

Buhi	*bagadïdë*	*yïzïnȯrë.*
Green/grass	small lake, pond	flying.

EMILY: "*Boha gwian* means eagle. You know, Indians doctor with that, eagle feathers, you know. *Bohagan* means doctor, Indian doctor. That's why they call it *boha gwia,* that's the eagle, flying over the green grass that's got water—lakes, that's got green all around. It's little lakes. That's what that *boha gwia* is flying over."

Water is part of the landscape in songs 31–35. In these four vignettes we see snow melt and rain showers with greenery, big rivers and hills, showers on the mountains with pine needles floating in pools, and the sacred eagle that flies over small lakes surrounded by grass.

The following is a list of the twenty Naraya songs in which ground water combines with other parts of the natural world.[1]

No.

6	eagle, green water
7	aspen, mountains, and water
11	snow melt on mountains
12	ducks in water
13	snow on mountains
14	snow melt on mountains
47	wet mountains
55	rock in water and mountain
56	rocks and grass under water
76	pine trees by water
79	cattails in swampy ground
88	blackbirds bathing
91	wet rocks
95	"water people" (beaver, fish, ducks, etc.)
96	fish and grass in water
97	goslings in water weeds
99	otter hissing in water
100	otter on rocks under water
119	strawberries in damp earth
129	water splashing at night

Texts that mention weather-related water—for example, song 34—comprise another large category, appearing in nineteen songs. Within this category, fog is an image of such particular importance that I will discuss it separately, in concert with mountains and rocks, in chapter 4.

Commentary

Water is so important to Naraya texts, and so closely related to almost every facet of Shoshone and Great Basin life, that an exposition on the topic serves here as a preface to all the nature texts that follow.

Steward opened his classic study of the Basin-Plateau with an explication of the region's physical setting. "The important features of the natural environment were topography, climate, distribution and nature of plant and animal species and, as the area is very arid, occurrence of water" (Steward 1938:2). His thesis built on this environmental given. "Basin-Plateau activities were related in certain ways to the flora and fauna, topography, climate, and distribution of sources of water. . . . Salient features of the natural landscape are so interrelated with one another and with the cultural landscape that great altitude, heavy rainfall, relative abundance of edible foods, sources of water, and consequently population coincide" (Steward 1938:10).

Names for places and groups of people reflect the importance of water in Basin-Plateau life. Steward points out that "each village was named after some salient feature of its locality. As proximity to water was essential to village location, it was most often named after a spring or creek" (Steward 1938:247). Runoff from mountains, another source of water, also inspired place names; thus, *Saga´namatsibui* was the Surprise Valley Paiute name for the place where the river comes from the mountain into the open country (Kelly 1932:77). In Idaho even a water-derived simile served as a name. *Séhewok´i*, which means "willows standing in rows like running water," referred to a region where the Boise, Payette, and Weiser Rivers emptied into the Snake (Liljeblad 1957:62). On the Wind River reservation today, Shoshones identify major residential locations by the rivers and creeks that cut the land, such as Trout Creek, Sage Creek, and North and South Fork of the Little Wind River.

This same pattern continued when it came to naming different groups of people. Often they were identified by their location and proximity to water. Thus, *pa*, meaning "water" in Paiute and Shoshone, appears in *ankappa·nukkicicimi*, the "red-stream people," a subgroup of the Southern Paiutes (Kelly and Fowler 1986:394). The term "Paiute" itself, widely used in the Basin and beyond, derives from *pa* (water) Ute (Mooney [1896] 1991:1056; Steward 1933:235; Steward 1974:20). *Pa* may also be the root of *panákwate*, the name that Bannock people (a Northern Paiute group in Idaho) use for themselves. Liljeblad writes, "The word may have either meant one (or both) of two things: either 'on the water side' or 'on the west side'" (Liljeblad 1957:22). In a similar vein, "Panamint Shoshone east of Owens Valley call the Owens Valley Paiute *pan·aŋʷi·ti* 'westerners' or '(those) in the direction of the water'" (Liljeblad and Fowler 1986:433).

Water also gave names to seasons. States and forms of water were defining characteristics for the Wind River Shoshone, who linked them to other events in nature as markers of the yearly calendar. Lowie recorded this information, stating:

> The following seasons are recognized:—
> Late in fall—"Little Month" *(tü´ve mö´ə),* when the ice begins to appear
> on the edges of the creeks.

Big Moon *(píə mö´ə)*, creeks are all frozen over, except the middle which
  might be open
Cold Month *(ö´djö mö´ə)*, creeks all frozen.
[March] *Pósitc*, thawing of ice and big snowflakes come down.
ícarừə mö´ə, wolves are having their young and ice has gone from creeks.
mö´dzarừə, mountain sheep have their young and grass is beginning to
  come up.
bádzamak kímiə, water going down.
tồgwetāts, midsummer.

(Lowie 1924a:311)[2]

Water-weather also marked the cultural calendar. For example,
Powell reported that Shoshones of eastern Nevada celebrated a Snow
Festival *(Ta-ka-su-win-ta-ni-kak)* and a Rain Festival *(Pa-i-mun-ta-ni-kak)*
(Powell 1971:270). The Nez Percés and the Northern and Wind River Shoshones danced the Warm Dance *(Yuwai nükai)* in order to bring
warm weather, which would melt the snow (Steward 1943a:287). In
addition, there are connections between rain and the Round Dance,
as discussed in chapter 1.

Water and Power

The belief in water as a source of power is widely held, both within
and beyond the Great Basin.[3] The water could be contained in springs
and lakes (Steward 1940:492; Steward 1941:422; Steward 1943a:347)
or, as in the case of the Owens Valley Paiutes, could be found in snow
and haze (Steward 1933:303). Jay Miller, in his study of Great Basin
religion, identified water as the "keystone of Basin religion because
power, with its affinity for life, was strongly attracted to water" (J.
Miller 1983:78).

Wind River Shoshones seek power at Dinwoody Canyon, the walls
of which bear ancient petroglyphs, and at nearby Dinwoody Lake.
Bull Lake was another such source of power. Hultkrantz reports that
it was the most dreaded sacred spot, a reminder of the double-edged
nature of power (Hultkrantz 1954a:56).

Springs as a source of the shaman's power are richly documented
in Wind River Shoshone and Great Basin literature (Hultkrantz
1954a:56; Kelly 1932:190; Steward 1933:311–12; Steward 1943a:282).
In his study of shamanism, Park noted that "the words of a shaman's
song often refer to the source of power" (Park 1938:58). The text of
the First Shaman's Song, which is a Northern Paiute example, corroborates the importance of water as a source of power for the shaman:
"Noise water-blue-rock on water-blue-rock on stand noise" (Natches
1923:259).

The shaman directly addresses water in its various forms, indeed, all parts of the natural world. This practice relates not only to the shamanistic control of weather but also to shamanistic healing, the focus here. Tom Mitchell, a Northern Paiute shaman, told Park, "The Indian doctors know the wind, clouds, and rain. A shaman talks to them. They are just like people, and they come" (Park 1938:19).[4]

Shamans used water directly on the patient, blowing it from the mouth or sprinkling it with a sagebrush or eagle feathers (Steward 1943a:346, 389; Stewart 1941:414; Whiting 1950:42). They might also sprinkle it around the room during a shamanistic ceremony. Whiting explained this usage by Harney Valley Paiutes, among whom "water is recognized as a purifying agent and is spoken of as being like the human breath" (Whiting 1950:40). Bathing could cure sorcery-induced illness (Whiting 1950:53). Rain, itself, was efficacious. Northern Paiutes used rainwater to cure snake bites (Stewart 1941:443). Wovoka instructed followers to decorate their bodies with red paint and then to wash it off by standing in the rain (Dangberg 1957:286). Snow, placed in the hand during a vision, was another healing agent (Steward 1934:428). Even clouds promoted well-being. Wovoka promised to send a "good cloud" to a visiting delegation after they had returned home, commenting that it would "give you chance to make you feel good" (Mooney [1896] 1991:780).

Northern Paiutes took cold baths to protect themselves against evil (Steward 1934:431). Water was part of the Grouse Creek Shoshone antidote for bad dreams. The person "arises before sunrise, goes east, puts damp earth on his body, and 'talks to the sun against the dream.' As the sun rises, he brushes the earth off toward the sun" (Steward 1943a:389).

The sweat lodge, another institution concerned with health, uses water and steam. Lowie described the Wind River Shoshone sweat lodge in 1924: "Into a round pit were placed hot rocks, and one man would pray over the sick ones who had come in, saying, 'I wish that I and my companions may feel well and have good luck.' He poured water on rocks till steam rose" (Lowie 1924a:308–9). A final use of water occurs at the end of the ceremony when all participants leave the lodge and go for a swim.

Bathing in a river has many purposes, salutary and purifying for body and soul. Wind River Shoshone Sun Dancers bathe in the river before and after the Sun Dance. A Shoshone father bathes in the river after the birth of his child, regardless of the time of year, to ensure that the child will live a long life and be able to endure cold. It is also felt that such bathing prolongs the youthful appearance of the father.[5]

Water, power, and health are also central elements in the Peyote Ceremony of the Native American Church, a religion practiced by many North American Indians, including Shoshone and Great Basin peoples. During the course of the all-night meeting, water is spilled on the ground as an offering, drunk by participants, and rubbed over the body. It is also sprinkled on the ceremonial paraphernalia (Stewart 1944:100).[6] A Shoshone woman explained to me the conclusion of the ceremony at dawn, when a woman brings in the "water of life, and she's the one that puts everybody's prayers together and talks to the Creator for them" (Vander 1988:110). A Kiowa artist described his experience during the Water Song, which is sung at this time, just prior to the end of the meeting: "When the Water Song is sung by a father or priest in the morning, the priest's face disappears and in its place is the Water Bird, singing, perched upon a staff with the peyote gourd or rattle" (Rhodes n.d.:30).

Water, power, and health are central to the Shoshone Sun Dance. Sun Dancers bathe in a river before and after they dance. But they also abstain from food and water in their quest for health and, for some, the power to heal. Conceptually and physically, water is paramount, expressed in the Shoshone name for the ceremony, *taguwënër*, Standing in Thirst (Shimkin 1953:418). Sun Dancers forgo drinking real water in order to be blessed with visionary water—sign and symbol of power. Richard Engavo, an elderly Shoshone man, told me that on one occasion when he took part in the Sun Dance, an old man dancing next to him had a vision of water. (Richard said he felt two drops of water from his neighbor's vision.) Voget documents another Sun Dance example of this vision-water-power connection. He writes that John Truhujo, a Shoshone Sun Dance chief who taught the Wind River version of the Sun Dance to the Crow, fasted and in a vision "saw a 'person' (spirit-being) come out of a lake. This person 'taught him to use this song in all the leading ceremonies as well as the Sun Dance.' . . . For most Crows, the 'water song' dreamed by Truhujo was the favorite when doctoring and when dancing for power" (Voget 1984:211, 259).

One sees the close identification between water and power in other comments about the Sun Dance by Richard Engavo. He recalled that "the Shoshones used to have their Sun Dance in June, when the sweet sage leaves were damp and green. [Now it is generally held near the end of July.] Everything was green and everything was damp. But now, along in July, everything's burned up. Everything has no leaves on it; it's all dried up. Just has no power, nothing in it" (Vander 1988:100–101). An even more explicit reference to water as power appears in a prayer described by a non-Indian anthropologist who danced in the 1966 Shoshone Sun Dance. He reports that the prayer sought blessings from several sources, one of which was "living water" (T. Johnson 1968:6).

At the end of the Sun Dance ceremony, dancers drink special water for the occasion and at this time some water is poured on the ground as an offering to Mother Earth (Hultkrantz 1987:74).[7] The notion of water offerings and blessings are part of generalized beliefs that extend beyond the Sun Dance. While doing fieldwork in 1980, I recorded in my log, "Alberta says to drink water first thing in the morning—get a blessing. She might also drop some water on Mother Earth. She says the old people used to pat water on their heads in the morning" (Vander 1988:100).

There is a countercurrent to the broad stream of water, power, and health. It is the dangerous aspect of water-power, the Water Ghost Being who causes disease (Shimkin 1939:43). Northern Paiutes placated an alternate manifestation, which was equally feared, the water babies who live in streams and springs. People spoke directly to these creatures, saying, "This water in lake is for both of us. Don't hurt me; we're both the same" (Stewart 1941:444). However, power from the water baby was not all negative. People who slept by water might have a dream in which they receive bulletproof power from the water baby. Thus, one dangerous source of power protects against another (Smith 1939:111; Steward 1941:258). It is interesting to note a Northern Cheyenne account in which Wovoka called on the destructive power of water, causing a seven-day rainstorm, which drowned soldiers coming to arrest him (Grinnell 1891:67).

Water in Myth

One sees the importance and power of water reflected in myth. Just as water is instrumental in healing in everyday live, so it is in a Gosiute myth. Water is the cure that drives an evil spirit out of Wolf's wife (Powell 1971:262). Myths of a primeval flood are common throughout the western Basin, including among the Paiute and Western Shoshone (Mooney [1896] 1991:1050; Smith 1939:15). Beaver and Muskrat dive deep below the floodwaters in order to retrieve the mud from which God rolled the earth (Liljeblad 1969:50).

A striking feature of Great Basin myth is the presence of stories that explain the origins of ground water and weather-water from the sky. As already discussed, Paiutes trace the origins of springs to the tears of the first Paiute Father and Mother over the irrevocable breakup of their family due to quarreling (Lowie 1924a:204–5, 207).[8] Moving beyond myth to the text of a Southern Paiute song, "The Home of a River," one learns: "'The edge of the sky / Is the home of the river.' The sky is supposed to rest on the edge of the earth. Chuar-ru-um-pik [one of Powell's informants], in explanation of this song[,] says that the river comes from the sky and returns by way of the horizon" (Powell 1971:122). Note the special relationship of the river to the sky in this text. Linkage between various parts of nature is the rule in the origin myths for water. It is found in a Northern Paiute myth for the origins of snow, hail, and rain. Rattlesnake was able to make these by scratching an overhanging rock, which he lifted to differing heights (Powell 1971:219–20).

The importance of water and its special link to vegetation clearly appear in the following myth, which gives the origin of water itself.

> Once there was no water on earth, and being unable to find any they cried, hoping to bring sufficient water in that way, but it did not. "How will we make water?" they said. This they deliberated about for six days. "We will put no more marks on our arms," they said. Once more they hunted but without success. Then they opened the ground but no water came out. Then they went to a tree and opened it and out came the water. The father tells them that hereafter to look in the green spots on the ground and they will find water and to this day wherever there is a particularly green spot, there is always water to be found. (Powell 1971:219)

Water, in myth, defines people and their state in a variety of ways. In the Shoshone creation story, a woman and her mother give birth to all the Indians. After birth, the women wash all the babies except for one batch. Coyote, the father, washes this batch and tells them, "'You are my children. I am going to stay with you.' If he had washed all the babies, there would have been nothing but Shoshone in the world" (Lowie 1909a:238). Water and the washer mark the birth of Indians and Shoshones. In an analogous fashion, water and the washer also mark death, state and status. Shoshones believe that after death the soul rises to Wolf's house. Wolf washes and revives the soul and it enters into the life of the spirit land (Lowie 1909a:226; Lowie 1924b:101).

It is easy to see the appealing congruence of these beliefs with Mormon baptism of Shoshones, which occurred in 1879. The Indian agent reported:

> During the early part of the summer, quite a number of Shoshones left the reservation for Salt Lake. Not understanding the reason for this mysterious departure, as most of them slipped away in the night time,

I inquired of [Chief] Washakie the cause; his explanation was they were Mormons; they have gone to Salt Lake to get washed, and they can see their departed friends and relatives next summer. I judge from this the Mormons have instructed them to be baptized in the Mormon Church and in the future life they will meet their friends gone before. (*Annual Reports of the Commissioner of Indian Affairs* 1879:168 and 1880:177, in Shimkin 1939:17)

Water is the key ingredient in the portrayal of death and resurrection in myth, a common occurrence in the Great Basin. In Smith's Basin study she noted subtle regional differences in the manner of effecting resurrection. "Revival by putting into water or into damp ground is the most popular method in the Basin. This is frequently combined with the revival-from-part-of-the-body device. Damp ground is used more in tales of the eastern Basin, water in those of the western Basin" (Smith 1939:167). The Wind River Shoshone version of "The Bungling Host," a tale in which Beaver serves up his children to Coyote and then revives them by throwing their bones in water, is one example of resurrection by water (Lowie 1909c:266).[9]

Cause and effect in myth carried over into everyday life. Bailey describes how Paiutes poured water on Wovoka in an attempt to revive him from a trance (Bailey 1957:79). One can view this as a non-Indian remedy for reviving a live person who has lost consciousness, and perhaps that is Bailey's meaning. Or one can see the same sequence from a Paiute standpoint: a person who is unconscious, and therefore "dead," can be resurrected by water, as in myth from the western Great Basin. Is this not like the Wind River Shoshone myth in which Beaver resurrects his dead children by throwing their bones in water (Lowie 1909c:266), or the one in which Coyote resurrects Wolf by soaking his hair in water (Lowie 1924b:213)? Stewart reports that Northern Paiutes carefully throw deer bones into water (Stewart 1941:427). Might this, too, be another example of seeking more live deer in everyday life, in the way that Beaver and Coyote effect resurrection in myth?

4 | *Fog, Mountains, and Rocks*

Fog, mountains, and rocks are closely associated in nature. Naraya imagery in this chapter reflects this relationship.

Naraya Song 36

Dorothy Tappay
Emily Hill

Vagïna	*doiyavi*	*barukande*	*he,*
Fog	mountains	?under water	(v.),

Vagïna	*doiyavi*	*barukande*	*hena.*
Fog	mountains	?under water	(v.).

Vagïna	*vagïna*	*vagïna*	*winogaiye,*[1]
Fog	fog	fog	blown (apart) by the wind,

Vagïna	*vagïna*	*vagïna*	*winogaiye.*
Fog	fog	fog	blown (apart) by the wind.

EMILY: "It's about fog, moving along . . . *Vagïna winoganos sede,* you know, 'they go fast'; 'they go in parts,' like—you know, flowers, blooming, white blooming flowers. Sometimes you see them when it [the wind?] leaves some [petals or seeds] on the back [stem], when it's going along [the wind is blowing and scattering the petals or seeds]. That's what it means." [I believe that Emily is likening the wind-scattering process to the movement of fog in the song text.]

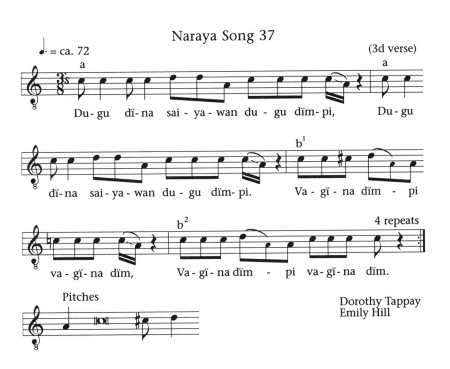

Naraya Song 37

Dorothy Tappay
Emily Hill

Dugu	*dïna*	*saiyawan*	*dugu*	*dïmpi,*
Sky	down	?mesh/sieve(GH), ?wet	sky	rocks,

Dugu	*dïna*	*saiyawan*	*dugu*	*dïmpi.*
Sky	down	?mesh/sieve(GH), ?wet	sky	rocks.

Vagïna	*dïmpi*	*vagïna*	*dïm,*
Fog	rocks	fog	rocks,

Vagïna	*dïmpi*	*vagïna*	*dïm.*
Fog	rocks	fog	rocks.

EMILY: "I like that song. Slow."

JUDY: "You said that *dugu* is 'up in the air'?"

EMILY: "Uh huh. Fog over rocks. Over rocks sitting. Fog, *vago.*"

Although Emily never mentioned the presence of the Milky Way in this text, I call the reader's attention to songs 126 and 127, which appear in chapter 7. In song 126 the Milky Way is presented as rocks in a row in the sky, very similar to the sky rocks in line one of song 37. In her commentary on song 127, Emily said that *dugu saiyag* (or *saiyaganan*) was the term for Milky Way, and this, too, seems similar to *dugu saiywan*, used in this text. "Fog rocks," in the second line of song 37, would be congruent with this interpretation.

Naraya Song 38

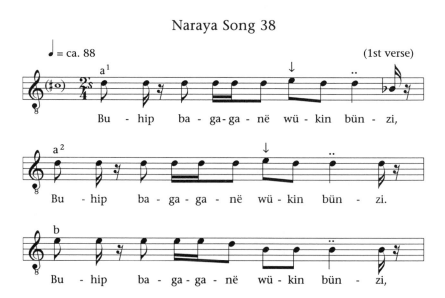

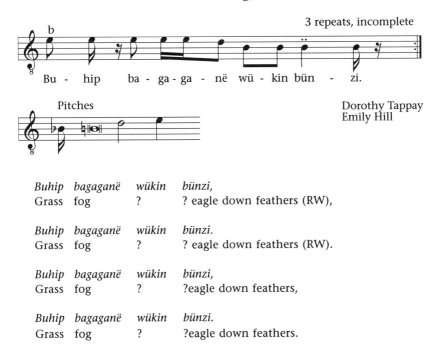

3 repeats, incomplete

b

Bu - hip ba - ga - ga - në wü - kin bün - zi.

Pitches

Dorothy Tappay
Emily Hill

Buhip	*bagaganë*	*wükin*	*bünzi,*
Grass	fog	?	? eagle down feathers (RW),

Buhip	*bagaganë*	*wükin*	*bünzi.*
Grass	fog	?	? eagle down feathers (RW).

Buhip	*bagaganë*	*wükin*	*bünzi,*
Grass	fog	?	?eagle down feathers,

Buhip	*bagaganë*	*wükin*	*bünzi.*
Grass	fog	?	?eagle down feathers.

EMILY: "It's a fog going over it. You seen the green grass with fog going over it. You know when it's green, in the fall? Fog comes and goes over it where the ground's green, sometimes it does."

Naraya Song 39

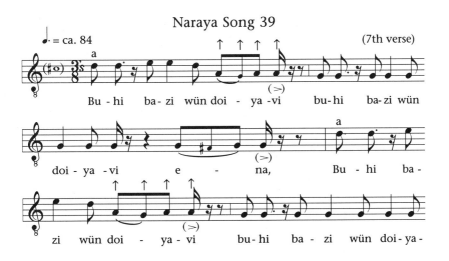

♩· = ca. 84

(7th verse)

a

Bu - hi ba- zi wün doi - ya -vi   bu - hi   ba- zi wün

doi - ya -vi   e - na,   Bu - hi   ba-

zi wün doi - ya - vi   bu-hi ba - zi   wün doi - ya -

Dorothy Tappay
Emily Hill

Buhi	*bazi*	*wün*	*doiyavi*	*buhi*	*bazi*	*wün*	*doiyavi*	*ena,*
Green	fog	?	mountains	green	fog	?	mountains	(e.v.),

Buhi	*bazi*	*wün*	*doiyavi*	*buhi*	*bazi*	*wün*	*doiyavi*	*ena.*
Green	fog	?	mountains	green	fog	?	mountains	(e.v.).

Buhi	*bazi*	*wün*	*doiyavi*	*buhi*	*bazi*	*wün*	*doiyavi*	*buhi*
Green	fog	?	mountains	green	fog	?	mountains	green

bazi *wün* *doiyavi* *ena,*
fog ? mountains (e.v.),

Buhi	*bazi*	*wün*	*doiyavi*	*buhi*	*bazi*	*wün*	*doiyavi*	*buhi*
Green	fog	?	mountains	green	fog	?	mountains	green

bazi *wün* *doiyavi* *ena.*
fog ? mountains (e.v.).

EMILY: "Green mountains got fog. *Buhi doiya baganavi,* green mountains with fog. Fog over green mountain."

Naraya Song 40

(4th verse)

Emily Hill
Dorothy Tappay

Bagana-via bagana-via bagana-via,
Fog-(?v.s.) fog-(?v.s.) fog-(?v.s.),

Bagana-via bagana-via bagana-via.
Fog-(?v.s.) fog-(?v.s.) fog-(?v.s.).

Dugum bagana-vi dugumba wanëkinóra,[2]
Sky fog-(?v.s.) sky blown by the wind,

Dugum bagana-vi dugumba wanëkinóra.
Sky fog-(?v.s.) sky blown by the wind.

EMILY: "*Dugu* means above, *dugu baganavi*, the fog's above. *Dugüm-*

bānr, that's 'above, sky,' that fog was up high. That was the rain—
ba:. It turns into water, you know that."

Henan	*doiyave-dë*	*van³-vagïnan*	*doi*	*seya,*
?	mountains-(?v.s.)	(s.r.)-fog	mountains	?,

Henan	*doiyave-dë*	*van-vagïnan*	*doi*	*seya.*
?	mountains-(?v.s.)	(s.r.)-fog	mountains	?.

Van-vagïnan	*doi*	*van-vagïnan*	*doi*	*seya,*
(s.r.)-Fog	mountains	(s.r.)-fog	mountains	?,

Van-vagïnan	*doi*	*van-vagïnan*	*doi*	*seya.*
(s.r.)-Fog	mountains	(s.r.)-fog	mountains	?.

Emily had no commentary for this song or for Naraya song 42, which she noted was from Idaho.

Naraya Song 42

♩. = ca. 66   (4th verse)

Da hon yon-zi a-vï-tsi-wën,   Da hon

yon-zi a-vï-tsi-wën.   Va-gï-në va-gï-në

va-o-ton-de,   Va-gï-në va-gï-në va-o-ton-de.

Dorothy Tappay
Emily Hill

Pitches

Da   hon   yonzi   avïtsiwën,
?   ?   ?   ?,

Da   hon   yonzi   avïtsiwën.
?   ?   ?   ?.

Vagïnë   vagïnë   vaotonde,
Fog   fog   ?,

Vagïnë   vagïnë   vaotonde.
Fog   fog   ?.

Naraya songs 1 and 3 (Vander 1986:38, 52; see also appendix A) are also about fog. Song 3, also given in chapter 2, likens the soul to fog. Song 1, like several song texts in this section, places fog over mountains, a common occurrence on the Wind River Mountains of the Shoshone reservation and elsewhere in nature.

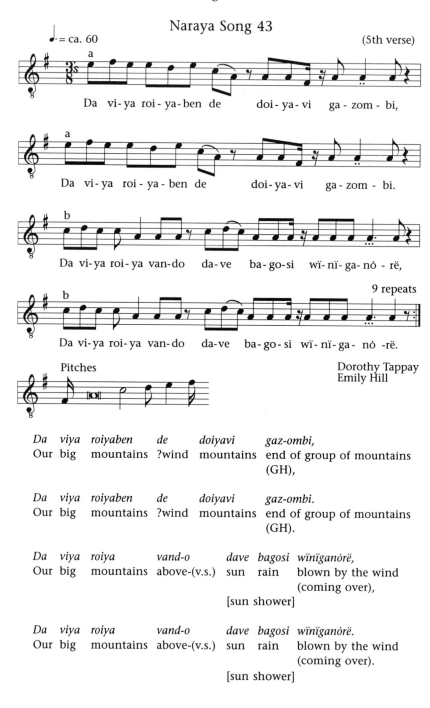

Naraya Song 43

(5th verse)

Dorothy Tappay
Emily Hill

Da   viya   roiyaben   de   doiyavi   gaz-ombi,
Our big   mountains   ?wind   mountains   end of group of mountains
(GH),

Da   viya   roiyaben   de   doiyavi   gaz-ombi.
Our big   mountains   ?wind   mountains   end of group of mountains
(GH).

Da   viya   roiya   vand-o   dave bagosi wïnïganórë,
Our big   mountains above-(v.s.)   sun   rain   blown by the wind
(coming over),
[sun shower]

Da   viya   roiya   vand-o   dave bagosi wïnïganórë.
Our big   mountains above-(v.s.)   sun   rain   blown by the wind
(coming over).
[sun shower]

EMILY: "Windy mountains, our mountains, the windy mountains. It's raining up there on the mountains. *Bagosia* means raining, *bagosiwad* means raining."

JUDY: "You were saying that's about the sun is out and you can see the rain coming down. Wind is blowing in the mountains."

EMILY: "Yeah, *neïd doiyavi* means windy mountains."

Naraya Song 44

In	n-doiya		garïdë	mandu	in	n-(?)	siyu	paiye	yai	oka
?	mountains	sit	onto	?	?		feather	?	?	?

weyawaindë,
(e.v.),

In   n-doiya   garïdë mandu in   n-(?) siyu   paiye yai oka
?   mountains   sit   onto   ?   ?   feather ?   ?   ?
      weyawaindë.
      (e.v.).

In   n-garïdë ?dëdë   mandu garïd oka weyawaindë,
?   sit   ?   onto   sit   ?   (e.v.),

In   n-garïd we ya en   mandu garïd oka weyawain.
?   sit   (? vocs.) onto   sit   ?   (e.v.).

EMILY: "There's something that's blowing around, something up on the mountains. Something like feathers."

This is another Naraya song from Idaho.

Naraya Song 45

♩ = ca. 88   (2d verse)

Da bi-ya doi-ya-vi   bi-ya wan   doi-ya-vi

bi-ya wan doi-ya-vi yai-yo-wain-dë,   Da bi-ya doi-ya-

vi   bi-ya wan   doi-ya-vi   bi-ya wan doi-ya-vi

yai-yo-wain-dë.   Bu-hi wan doi-ya-vi

bu-hi wan doi-ya-vi yai-yo-wain-dë,   Bu-hi wan doi-ya-

2 repeats incomplete

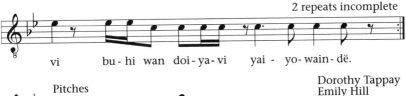

vi   bu - hi   wan doi - ya - vi   yai - yo - wain - dë.

Pitches

Dorothy Tappay
Emily Hill

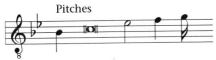

Da biya doiyavi   biya wa   n-doiyavi   biya wa   n-doiyavi
Our big mountains big   two mountains big   two mountains
yaiyowaindë,
(e.v.),

Da biya doiyavi   biya wa   n-doiyavi   biya wa   n-doiyavi
Our big mountains big   two mountains big   two mountains
yaiyowaindë.
(e.v.).

Buhi   wa   n-doiyavi   buhi   wa   n-doiyavi   yaiyowaindë,
Green two mountains green two mountains (e.v.),

Buhi   wa   n-doiyavi   buhi   wa   n-doiyavi   yaiyowaindë.
Green two mountains green two mountains (e.v.).

EMILY: "That's from Idaho. Same kind of song [Naraya], different words [either Northern Shoshone or Bannock]."[4]

JUDY: "Green mountains? Green grass?"

EMILY: "Yeah, same thing. Two mountains sitting together, all green."

Naraya Song 46

♩ = ca. 88   (5th verse)

Do - sa wai   doi - ya - pen - ji,   Do - sa wai

doi - ya - pen - ji.   Bu - hi   doi - ya   e   man - do,

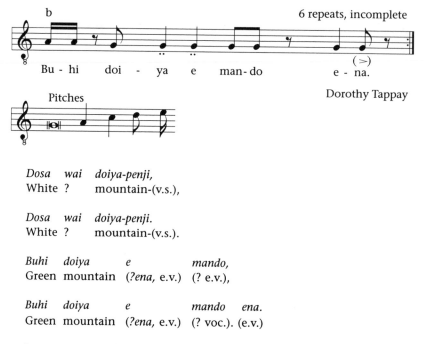

Bu - hi   doi - ya   e   man- do   e - na.

Pitches

Dorothy Tappay

Dosa   wai   doiya-penji,
White   ?   mountain-(v.s.),

Dosa   wai   doiya-penji.
White   ?   mountain-(v.s.).

Buhi   doiya   e   mando,
Green   mountain (?ena, e.v.) (? e.v.),

Buhi   doiya   e   mando   ena.
Green   mountain (?ena, e.v.) (? voc.). (e.v.)

I never reviewed this song with Emily, but its words and forms were very familiar to me by the time I transcribed it. Mountain, its subject, wears two contrasting colors that suggest the progression of the seasons—from winter snowy white, in line one, to spring-summer grassy green, in line two.

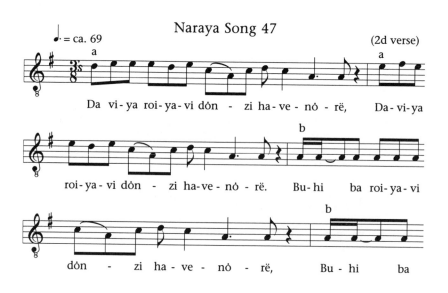

Naraya Song 47

Da vi-ya roi-ya- vi dȯn - zi ha-ve-nȯ - rë,   Da- vi-ya

roi-ya- vi dȯn - zi ha-ve-nȯ - rë.   Bu- hi   ba roi-ya- vi

dȯn - zi ha-ve-nȯ - rë,   Bu - hi   ba

3 repeats, incomplete

roi - ya - vi dòn - zi ha - ve - nò - rë.

Dorothy Tappay
Emily Hill

Pitches

Da	*viya*	*roiyavi*	*dònzi*	*havenòrë,*
Our big		mountains	shining, blooming	lying while moving,

Da	*viya*	*roiyavi*	*dònzi*	*havenòrë.*
Our big		mountains	shining, blooming	lying while moving.

Buhi	*ba*	*roiyavi*	*dònzi*	*havenòrë,*
Green water		mountains	shining, blooming	lying while moving,

Buhi	*ba*	*roiyavi*	*dònzi*	*havenòrë.*
Green water		mountains	shining, blooming	lying while moving.

EMILY: "Big mountains, big mountains sitting there. [Emily sings the second line.] Green mountains, green mountains."
JUDY: "Is that wet grass that's shining [in the second line]?"
EMILY: "Yes."

Naraya Song 48

♩. = ca. 63

(9th verse)

Wa - zan doi-ya-vi wa - zan doi-ya-vi, Wa - zan doi-ya-vi

wa - zan doi-ya-vi. Wa- zan doi-ya - vi, Wa- zan doi-ya - vi.

10 repeats

Dorothy Tappay
Emily Hill

Pitches

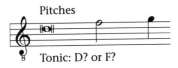

Tonic: D? or F?

Wazan		doiyavi	wazan	doiyavi,
?Game animals [or antelope]		mountains	?game [or antelope]	mountains,

Wazan		doiyavi	wazan	doiyavi.
?Game animals [or antelope]		mountains	?game [or antelope]	mountains.

Wazan	doiyavi,
?Game animals [or antelope]	mountains,

Wazan	doiyavi.
?Game animals [or antelope]	mountains.

Emily identified this as an Idaho song and commented, "They [Shoshone-Bannocks from Idaho] sing about mountains; so do Nevadas [Western Shoshones]."

Naraya Song 49

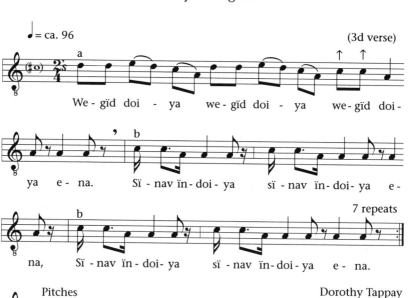

Dorothy Tappay

Wegïd   doiya   wegïd   doiya   wegïd doiya   ena.
Sideways/slanting mountain side   mountain side   mountain (e.v.)

Sïnav   ïn-doiya   sïnav   ïn-doiya   ena,
Quaking aspen   mountain   quaking aspen   mountain   (e.v.),

Sïnav   ïn-doiya   sïnav   ïn-doiya   ena.
Quaking aspen   mountain   quaking aspen   mountain   (e.v.).

EMILY: "*Wegïd doiyav* means sides, kind of side-like. It's got that kind of [aspen] trees on there [the side of the mountain]."

Naraya Song 50

♩. = ca. 63   (3d verse)

He yo na   he yo he yo na he yo he yo   na ne yo,

He yo na ne yo he yo   na ne yo he yo   na ne yo.

Do - sa doi-ya de-ga nu-ga wi ye bo ro   ha-ve-gïn,

7 repeats

Do-sa doi-ya de-ga nu-ga wi ye bo-ro - ha-ve-gïn.

Pitches   Dorothy Tappay
                                 Emily Hill

He yo na he yo he yo na he yo he yo na ne yo,
(vocables),

He yo na ne yo he yo na ne yo he yo na ne yo.
(vocables).

Dosa	*doiya*	*dega*	*nuga*	*wi*[s]	*ye bo ro*	*havegïn,*
White (snow)	mountains	?	foot of mountains	silver	(?voc.)	lying,

Dosa	*doiya*	*dega*	*nuga*	*wi*	*ye bo ro*	*havegïn.*
White (snow)	mountains	?	foot of mountains	silver	(?voc.)	lying.

EMILY: "You make something like a noise. [A reference to the first line of vocables?] *Nugag* means foot of the mountains, where those silvers [deposits are] under the mountains."

Emily noted the close similarity of this song text to that of Naraya song 54, which will appear in the section devoted to rocks, below.

EMILY: "Like the other song, little different words in it."

Naraya Song 51

Ba rün doi-ya ba rün doi, Ba rün doi-ya ba rün doi. Ban-zuk-an doi-ya wa-mi-a-nòr, Ban-zuk-an doi-ya wa-mi-a-nòr.

Pitches

Emily Hill
Dorothy Tappay

Ba	*rün*	*doiya*	*ba*	*rün*	*doi,*
Water	?	mountains	water	?	mountains,

Ba	*rün*	*doiya*	*ba*	*rün*	*doi.*
Water	?	mountains	water	?	mountains.

Banzukan	*doiya*	*wamia-nòr,*
Otter	mountains	?-?while moving,

Banzukan	*doiya*	*wamia-nòr.*
Otter	mountains	?-?while moving.

EMILY: *"Ba run ndoiya,* it's a water mountains. *Banzuk ndoiya*—Otter Mountains. Otter's a *banzuk,* big ones. I seen that kind to Bull Lake, laying on a tree that's big branches. Laying on there and I happened to see it. When it seen us he jumped in the lake. He went a long ways and then stuck his head out, looking back. You know they have their hides for their dancing braids, brown ones."[6]

Naraya Song 52

(6th verse)

♩. = ca. 80

Da - më so - go - pë dï - pë - gai - yu dï - pë - gai, Da - më

so - go - pë dï - pë - gai - yu dï - pë - gai. Dïm - pi dï - pë - gai - yu

dïm - pi dï - pë - gai - yu dï - pë - gai, Dïm - pi

dï - pë - gai - yu dïm - pi dï - pë - gai yu dï - pë - gai.

9 repeats

Emily Hill
Dorothy Tappay

Pitches

Damë	*sogopë*	*dïpëgaiyu*	*dïpëgai,*
Our	earth/ground	flat	flat,

Damë *sogopë* *dïpëgaiyu* *dïpëgai.*
Our earth/ground flat flat.

Dïmpi *dïpëgaiyu* *dïmpi* *dïpëgaiyu* *dïpëgai,*
Rocks flat rocks flat flat,

Dïmpi *dïpëgaiyu* *dïmpi* *dïpëgaiyu* *dïpëgai.*
Rocks flat rocks flat flat.

EMILY: "Ground, earth—it's got rocks covered, flat rocks in ground, rocks under, you know."

Naraya Song 53

Dorothy Tappay
Emily Hill

Tonic: A? or G?

Wainaiyo *wainaiyo,*
Coming down coming down,

Wainaiyo   *wainaiyo.*
Coming down   coming down.

Wazi   *doiya*   *dïmp-vanzingo-óra,*[7]
?Game animals [or antelope] mountains rock-slide-(?),

Wazi   *doiya*   *dïmp-vanzingo-óra.*
?Game animals [or antelope] mountains rock-slide-(?).

Wainaiyo,
Coming down,

Wainaiyo   *wainda.*
Coming down   (ending vocable added for last repeat).

EMILY: "[That's about] walking down the mountains [and] rocks under the ground. *Dïmp-vanzingo*—that's rocks that's under the ground. It shows in some places. The rock is like a sidewalk [i.e., smooth]."

♩. = ca. 69   **Naraya Song 54**   (3d verse)

Dïm- pi tan ga - ra   na - ru - ë dïm- pi ta tsi - yu - wa- no,

Dïm- pi tan ga - ra   na - ru - ë dïm- pi ta tsi - yu - wa- no.

Dïm- pi na - ru - yu - ë dïm - pi na - ru - yu - a gin,

3 repeats, incomplete

Dïm- pi na - ru - yu - ë dïm - pi na - ru - yu - a- gin.

Pitches   Dorothy Tappay
                                      Emily Hill

Dïmpi tan   gara   naruë dïmpi ta   tsiyuwano,[8]
Rocks (?voc.) sitting ?   rocks (?voc.) peeling, slicing,

Dïmpi tan   gara   naruë dïmpi ta   tsiyuwano.
Rocks (?voc.) sitting ?   rocks (?voc.) peeling, slicing.

Dïmpi naruyuë dïmpi naruyuagin (GH),
Rocks   ?   rocks   ?,

Dïmpi naruyuë dïmpi naruyuagin (GH).
Rocks   ?   rocks   ?.

EMILY: "Where rocks sitting and from there just peeling off. *Tsiyu-wano,* it means peeling, you know, in slices, like."

Naraya Song 55

Dorothy Tappay
Emily Hill

Ba-ru	dïmpi	siwai	doiyavi	ba-ru	dïmpi	siwai	doiyavi,
Water-black	rock	?	mountain	water-black	rock	?	mountain,

Ba-ru	dïmpi	siwai	doiyavi	ba-ru	dïmpi	siwai	doiyavi.
Water-black	rock	?	mountain	water-black	rock	?	mountain.

Ba-ru	dïmpi	siwai	doiya	wïto (GH)	doiya	gendë,
Water-black	rock	?	mountain	?shelter/sheltered	mountain (v.),

Ba-ru	dïmpi	siwai	doiya	wïto (GH)	doiya	gendë.
Water-black	rock	?	mountain	?shelter/sheltered	mountain (v.).

Emily often attributed the origin of songs for which she had little or no commentary to Idaho or Nevada. Such is the case for Naraya song 55. She added, "It's something like a black rock or something."

Naraya Song 56

♩ = ca. 104   (2d verse)

So- go- rïm-bim - pi   si   bu- hi pa- ro   wai gon - di,

So - go- rïm- bïm- pi   si   bu - hi pa - ro   wai gon - di.

Pa - ro wai gon - di   pa - ro   wai gon-di   pa- ro wai gon- di,

6 repeats

Pa - ro   wai gon - di   pa - ro wai gon- di.

Emily Hill
Dorothy Tappay

Pitches

Sogo-rïm(bïm)pi   *si*   *buhi* *pa-ro*   *wai*   *gondi,*
Earth-rock   ?leaf (GH) grass   water-deep   down   ?,
                                        under-water (GH)

Sogo-rïm(bïm)pi   *si*   *buhi* *pa-ro*   *wai*   *gondi.*
Earth-rock   ?leaf (GH) grass   under-water   down   ?.

Pa-ro   *wai*   *gondi* *pa-ro*   *wai*   *gondi* *pa-ro*
Under-water   down   ?   under-water   down   ?   under-water
  wai   *gondi,*
  down   ?,

Pa-ro   *wai*   *gondi* *pa-ro*   *wai*   *gondi* *pa-ro*
Under-water   down   ?   under-water   down   ?   under-water
  wai   *gondi.*
  down   ?.

EMILY: "*Sogo-rïmp,* they're in the water. That's what they sing about. They're in the water, the bottom of the water. *Sogo-rïmp* means the sea, under the water at the bottom down there. *Sogo-rïmp* means [a particular kind of rock that looks] all—just like paper—smashed like that. The sea, the sea, it's under that. [Emily sings, '*buhi paro waigondi.*'] With them water there, grass along that."[9]
JUDY: "Green grass?"
EMILY: "Along that water."
JUDY: "Is *waigondi* 'down' or 'under'?"
EMILY: "Yeah. *Paro waigondi,* that's way down, bottom of the water."
JUDY: "Where did you get these [rocks]?"
[Emily had pulled out a few rocks from a can filled with them.]
EMILY: "Way up there at the headgate. I got 'em in the water. You could see different kinds of fishes around there."
JUDY: "Do you do anything with those rocks? Do you just collect them?"
EMILY: "Well, if you want to take some of those rocks, you can take them when you're going home. Show it to your people. Feel it. It's just like cement."
JUDY: "Yeah, real heavy." [To my untrained eye, it looked like sedimentary rock.]
EMILY: "I think there's something in this rocks: copper, gold, silver, something like that. That's why they're heavy. But those ordinary rocks about this size, they ain't heavy. See the hand, fingers." [Emily pointed out patterns in the rocks.]
JUDY: "Just about looks like that, fingerprints."

EMILY: "They call these *dogarïmp*. Just all smashed like, you know, paper smashed. Like that. That's a song about these kind. [Emily then pointed to some rounded rocks.] It protects the house from wind blowing. Evaline, she come over here, she got scared of the wind. It's really—just feels like the wind's going to lift up her house or something. She came over here and I gave her those kind, like that, and told her [to] put it in that sack and hang it up in her house. These are that kind. That's the kind of song that is."

Wi-ïnboro	wi-ïnboro	wi-ïnboro	havegïn,
Silver-?[10]	silver-?	silver-?	lying,

Wi-ïnboro	wi-ïnboro	wi-ïnboro	havegïn.
Silver-?	silver-?	silver-?	lying.

Doiya	*ruka*	*maruk-andu*	*wi-ïnboro*	*havegïn,*
Mountains	under (?deep)	still under it-(v.s.)	silver-?	lying,

Doiya	*ruka*	*maruk-andu*	*wi-ïnboro*	*havegïn.*
Mountains	under (?deep)	still under it-(v.s.)	silver-?	lying.

EMILY: "There's something about the mountains. Beneath the mountains, under the mountains, way under the mountains there's silver. *Wih, wih,* that means *buiwih, buiwih,* silver, gold."[11]

Naraya Song 58

Dorothy Tappay
Emily Hill

Saiwai		*dïmpi*	*tiwoizi*	*saiwai*		*dïmpi*	*tiwoi,*
Snow melting,	wet,	rock	?	snow melting		rock	?,

Saiwai		*dïmpi*	*tiwoizi*	*saiwai*		*dïmpi*	*tiwoi.*
Snow melting,	wet,	rock	?	snow melting		rock	?.

Saiwai		*dïmpi*	*tiwoizi*	*saiwai*		*dïmpi*	*tiwoi,*
Snow melting, wet,		rock	?	snow melting		rock	?,

Saiwai		*dïmpi*	*tiwoizi*	*saiwai*		*dïmpi*	*tiwoi.*
Snow melting, wet,		rock	?	snow melting		rock	?.

EMILY: "I don't think it's ours."
Emily attributes this song to the Fort Hall Shoshones in Idaho.

Naraya Song 59

♩ = ca. 104

(6th verse)

Emily Hill
Dorothy Tappay

Waiyo		*waiyo*	*waiyo*	*wain,*
Going or climbing down		going down	going down	going down,

Waiyo		*waiyo*	*waiyo*	*wain.*
Going or climbing down		going down	going down	going down.

Dosa	*dïmpi*	*garïmbi*	*waiyo*	*wain,*
White	rock	sit	going down	going down,

Dosa	*dïmpi*	*garïmbi*	*waiyo*	*wain.*
White	rock	sit	going down	going down.

EMILY: "Where you're going down, there's a white rock there, just on down, keep going down, down."[12]

Commentary

Fog: Moisture, the Soul, and Feathers

Fog takes two meanings in Naraya songs. A physical phenomenon, it is one manifestation of water, a prime concern and rationale for Naraya performance. As a metaphysical entity, fog's airy moisture—a substance seemingly polymorphous, without substance—assumes other meanings and associations. Underhill writes that "gray fog of winter and blue haze of summer . . . were sources of power for Northern Paiutes" (Underhill 1941:46). As mentioned earlier, Park makes a similar statement, noting that clouds are a potential source of the shaman's power, and he documents this to be the case for Wovoka (Park 1938:19, 76).

The connection of fog and clouds to power is implicit in fog's other connection, to the soul. Breath, which looks like fog in cold air, is identified with the human soul or spirit, the *mugua* that appears in scholarly literature about Paiutes and Shoshones, including Wind River Shoshones (Harris 1940:65, 66; Hultkrantz 1951:22, 26; Lowie 1924a:294, 296, 297; Lowie 1924b:101; Powell 1971:270). Some scholars refer to it as the "life principle" and note its power to survive after the death of the body. This is clearly the case in Powell's Northern Paiute report, in which the soul at death goes out through the nose (Powell 1971:242).

There is consensus on the concept of a soul in its identification with breath, its departure from the body after death, and its subsequent journey to the land of the dead or spirit land.[13] Hultkrantz learned that Wind River Shoshones conceive of a pair of souls: a body or corporeal soul, *mugua*, and a separable soul, *navujieip*, that represents the person in dream (Hultkrantz 1951:41).[14] The first gives motion, the second, intelligent actions. Because the transfer of power occurs in dream, the *navujieip* is both dream and power soul (Hultkrantz 1961:206). It is the *navujieip* that receives sacred songs, songs with power. Lynn St. Clair, who during his life was a well-known chief of the Wind River Shoshone Sun Dance, told Hultkrantz, "in the ghost-dance people learn ghost-songs through their dream, *navujieip*" (Hultkrantz 1951:32). A nineteenth-century Southern Paiute song text is suggestive of the soul as singer and source of song:

P-3[15] (The Spirit)

The spirit	Mo-go´-av
Is swaying and singing	Yan-tu´-na-gi-kai.
	(Powell 1971:125)[16]

The *navujieip*, or separable soul, is associated with or represents the mind. Hultkrantz explains that sometimes *navujieip* and *suap* (breath-soul) may be synonymous (Hultkrantz 1951:40).[17] In a more recent publication, he amplifies the relationship of the souls to life and death, noting that one is "a free soul able to leave the body in dream, the other a soul bound to the body and giving it life. When the free soul leaves for good, the body soul also goes, and that means death" (Hultkrantz 1986:636).[18]

Scholars document Northern Shoshone and Gosiute belief in one soul, the *mugua*, located in the head (Lowie 1909a:226; Lowie 1924b: 101; Steward 1943a:287, 348). Olden adds more precise information about Wind River Shoshone placement for the soul in the head: it was lodged between the eyes (Olden 1923:43). Her discussion of the soul refers solely to the *mugua* and includes no mention of the *navujieip*.

Wind River Shoshone and Great Basin cultures cast the soul in two related images. First and foremost is the image of the soul as fog.[19] We have already encountered it in a Wind River Shoshone Sun Dance vision in which a spirit "floated like a fog" (Shimkin 1939:154). Naraya song 3 (appendix A) sums up this embodiment: soul-fog, soul floats, soul rises up. Northern Shoshone belief is identical. "While rising, they [*mugua*] look like clouds" (Lowie 1909a:226). Recall Wovoka's reference to the cloudlike appearance of Jesus and the dead cited earlier (chapter 2), a journey of souls, but in reverse—back to life. It is interesting to note that the same cloud image appears in Aztec song texts that date from the sixteenth century. As in the 1890 Ghost Dance movement, these texts express desire for resurrection of the dead. Cloud comrades refer to dead comrades. *Mixcoacalli*, house of cloud comrades, is the place where the ghosts come (Bierhorst 1985:24).[20]

I see a flow of associations and images that lead from soul to fog. Soul is breath, breath is fog, therefore, soul is fog. The resemblance between fog/clouds and feathers, on the other hand, is not as immediately apparent.[21] The first time I encountered this observed likeness was in the commentary by Rupert Weeks on Naraya song 38. He thought that the last word in the text might be "eagle down." He suggested that the whole line meant that fog going over green grass looks like eagle down. Wind River Shoshone myth contains the same feather-fog image: "Monster Owl's down-feather, which, donned on one's head, looks like 'a mist floating'" (Shimkin 1947c:334). Great Basin song texts also reveal the perception of fog/clouds and feathers as metaphors for one another. In the following Southern Paiute song texts it is not fog per se, but foglike misty spray from swift water that is equated with feathers.

P-12 (Untitled)

As feathers are drifted	Pi-ya-ni wa-ne-Kwink
So is the foam in the Colorado	Pa-ga´i-ani
Where the creeks run in	Hu-Kwint pan-wi-ton
	(Powell 1971:123)[22]

P-13 (The Storm Creek)

Along the land	Tu-wīp´ pu-a´
A-down the gulch	Na-ru´-yar-u´-kwai
The mountain stream	Wu-nu´-kwin kai´-va
The feathery mountain stream	Piv wa-nu´-kwin kai´va
	(Powell 1971:125)

The connection between clouds/rain and feathers is explicit in the next two song texts.

P-14 (Sunset Clouds)

The red sunset clouds	Un-ka´ pa-ris
Are rolled about	Whu-ka-ri-nu-mi-va
(Like) feathers	Pear´ Ur´ ru-mi
on the Mountains	Kaivw´ ai-mai
	(Powell 1971:124)

P-15 (Untitled)

The rain (or snow) on the mountain	Wa´-ru-im Kai´-vwa
Is like feathers around the head	Wi-geav A-gwim-Kwi-no
	(Powell 1971:128)

Given this perceived likeness between fog/cloud/spray and feathers in the natural world, it is interesting to note corresponding visualizations of the soul after it leaves the body. I have already discussed the soul in the form of foglike entities. The soul is also represented as a feather: a thread or feather plume by Wind River Shoshones (Hultkrantz 1951:24), a fine white or downy feather by Western and Northern Shoshones (Steward 1941:261; Steward 1943a:389).

Wind River Shoshone shamans use feathers as a means of predicting the course of a patient's illness. A feather that does not float and keeps falling means a bad prognosis (Shimkin 1939:80). Feather as soul comes out even more explicitly in the following tragic story told to me by an elderly Shoshone woman. When she was a young woman her toddler suffered a bad fall one day while staying with a babysitter. In the middle of the night the child began to cry inconsolably. Distraught, she took him to a medicine man, who saw a feather all tattered and torn, a representation of the child's soul. From this he realized that chances for survival were slim and that he was impotent to save the child. He informed her of this. She had no further recourse but to return home with her dying child. In a similar vein, but drawn from a Shoshone story rather than real life, the death of Cottontail is marked by the falling of a feather to the ground (W. Miller 1972:47).

Aztecs were part of the same Uto-Aztecan linguistic family as Shoshones and Paiutes and it is fascinating to see in them the same perception that links water spray to feather, and further, the use of these images in connection to soul and death. Bierhorst translated Aztec song texts, which he calls Ghost Songs because they seek the resurrection of dead comrades and warriors. He explains that phrases in the songs, such as "water's midst" or "in the plume water," which correlate closely to Southern Paiute metaphor of feathers for foam from the Colorado River, are actually elliptical references to the Spirit Land (Bierhorst 1985:39). Bierhorst's textual translation of his song 69 describes a victim, a slain warrior, who is "drifting as a feather into Spirit Land" (Bierhorst 1985:349).

Fog, spray, and feather share a weightlessness, a drifting, floating movement, and light color, and they are embodiments of the soul. Another connection to the soul is the location of fog over the mountains in Naraya songs 36, 39, 41 and feather over the mountains in Naraya song 44. As discussed in chapter 2, mountains are the location of the land of the dead. For Wind River Shoshones, this land lies in the Wind River Mountains, "and above all their snow-covered tops were counted as abodes of the spirits and of the dead" (Hultkrantz 1954a:47). Olden described the trip to the western side of the mountain by a Shoshone medicine man in his quest to get a boy's soul back (Olden 1923:28). Brackett reported the soul's ascent of the mountains on its final journey to the land of the dead. "When an old man is dying he finds himself near the top of a high hill on the Wind River Mountains, and, as the breath leaves his body, he reaches the top of it, and there, in front of him, the whole magnificent landscape of eternity is spread out" (Brackett 1880:330).

Mountains: Power and Dreamed Vision

I begin this discussion with mountains in their most basic physical relationships to water and weather. The many Naraya texts that speak of fog, rain, and snow on the mountains are true to meteorological reality. Mountains do gather and catch moisture in the air, which precipitates on them in several forms. The Wind River Shoshone song text (in chapter 1) "Send rain on the mountains!," sung during a thanksgiving dance, clearly recognizes this fact. Mountains are a source of water, which courses down their slopes in water runoff. I suggest that they partake of power in this association with water—the essence of the soul and life, and the prime source of metaphysical power. By their sheer size mountains are extraordinary features of landscape, and they provide habitat for abundant plant and animal life. These, too, are givens, and I believe they all contribute to Great Basin belief in mountains as both source and place of metaphysical power.[23]

Scholarly literature richly documents pursuit of power, especially shamanistic power, on mountains or in mountain caves (Park 1938:108, 110; Steward 1940:492–93; Stewart 1941:443). Spirits of animals and other parts of the natural world that are sources of power live there (Hultkrantz 1987:60; Park 1938:14). Communication with these spirits occurs in dreamed vision, song being one of the most important aspects in the transfer of power in this communication. Park summarizes this experience for Surprise Valley Paiutes, Lemhi, Wind River Shoshone, Seed Eaters, Salmon Eaters, White Knives, some Southern Paiutes, and Utes, in his comments on the Paviotso: "In all of these tribes, the quest is similar to that practised by the Paviotso, a lonely vigil in the mountains unaccompanied by fasting, self-torture, or unusual and prolonged exertion"[24] (Park 1938:118).

The pursuit of power in mountains survives in Comanche thought, even after almost three centuries on the Southern Plains and separation from their kin, the Wind River Shoshones. Gelo analyzes a dichotomy of power according to geographic altitude. High places, such as mountains and knolls, are places of benevolent spirits and good power. In contrast, low places are dangerous places of deficit power and death (Gelo 1990:1, 2, 7).

Mountains are not only the home of spirits, or guardian spirits with power. They, themselves, are sources of power (Liljeblad 1986:644; Park 1938:5; Steward 1933:311–12). For Western Shoshones, Black Mountain has power (Steward 1943b:282); for Owens Valley Paiutes, Birch Mountain and Mount Dana have power (Steward 1933:308). A Paiute man described his experience: "I saw Birch mountain in a dream. It said to me: 'You will always be well and strong'" (Steward 1934:426). For Wovoka and Northern Paiutes, Mount Grant was a mountain with power (Mooney [1896] 1991:765, 1050–51).

Rocks

It is difficult to isolate different parts of the natural world; rocks and mountains create one another through their rise and fall. They share an affinity to power. Wind River Shoshones seek power in Dinwoody Canyon, the rock face of which is incised with ancient petroglyphs (Hultkrantz 1956:200–201; Lowie 1924a:296). This place is a *poha kahni*, "house of power" (Shimkin 1986a:325). Like mountains, rocks are not only a place to receive power, which comes from a variety of sources, but are themselves a source of power. Obsidian is a case in point, tucked into the following observation about Owens Valley Paiute culture. "Individuals' powers embrace most things in nature. Eagle, fox, bat, snow, obsidian, the blue haze sometimes over the valley, and Birch mountain and Mt. Dana in the Sierra Nevada have been powers" (Steward 1933:308).

Rocks are a source of power and are beneficial for health; consequently, they are important to the shaman. Their mention in the text of a shaman's song cited in chapter 3, "Water-blue rock," indicates rock as one source of power to its singer.[25] Northern Paiute shamans provide another example. To effect a cure, they used a "charmstone" that talked to them (Heizer 1970:240). Rocks empower shamans and have the capacity to achieve desired ends by direct application. Thus, a Wind River Shoshone medicine man used a small black stone for two purposes, healing and ensuring that a bullet or arrow would hit its mark (Olden 1923:25).

A Wind River Shoshone woman with whom I worked described how, as a child, she received therapy that utilized rocks. Her mother gathered small pebbles from on top of an ant hill, then warmed and placed them on top of her legs. The woman commented on this therapy by noting the strength of ants to carry loads greater then their own body weight. Unstated, but implied, is the connection of power between ants and rocks, or from ants to rocks, and its transfer to a girl who, in her youth, was weak and sickly. Similarly, Northern Paiutes put rocks around a patient while in the sweat house, or lodge (Steward 1941:379–80).

People also relate directly to rocks in other ways for curative and protective purposes. Hebard reported a Wind River Shoshone example:

> The Shoshones had a tradition relative to an illness. They would pick up a stone as they traveled along moccasin footed, finally depositing it along the trail where other stones had been deposited by other indians [*sic*]; that is, deposited it along the road at different intervals, creating what they called "medicine piles"—believing that by leaving a rock behind them as they journeyed on the trail, their ills, sicknesses and bad feelings towards other indians [*sic*] would be forgotten. One today sees many of these monuments erected to forgotten ills. (Hebard 1930:298)

A history of Walker River Paiutes (Wovoka's people), written for and by themselves, described their traditions surrounding a special "medicine rock." "The People when entering the reservation, leave offerings at the rock and pray for good health" (E. Johnson 1975:94).

The protective power of certain rocks against wind comes out in Emily's discussion of the "earth rocks" or "underwater rocks" mentioned in song 56. Other Wind River Shoshones with whom I have worked have discussed the special powers of *bazidïmpi* (literally, *ba*, "water," *dïmpi*, "rocks"). Gladys Hill described them as agatelike rocks that protect one against thunder. Helene Bonatsie Oldman reported that they are round stones found in water that you put in the corners of the room to prevent wind.[26] Isaac Coando said that if you put them in a sack and hang it in a tree the rocks can stop lightning.

Steward conveys a different yet similar example of the protective power of rocks. Northern Paiutes sprinkle *Tö*, speculorite (*yadupi*), around the house or body for protection against whirlwinds (Stewart 1941:445). Recall that in Great Basin thought, whirlwinds are associated with ghosts, or the souls of the recently dead who travel in the center of a whirlwind to the land of the dead. This use of rocks is reminiscent of Emily's comments for Naraya song 56; however, Emily made no specific reference to whirlwinds. Another Northern Paiute example of the power of rocks over wind appears in myth. Cottontail, using a rock, could both repel and attract winds (Kelly 1938:425).

There is one final insight about rocks and people's relationship to them. Lowie writes that in Shoshone tales, rocks, like animals, were originally people and spoke. The barrier between the living and nonliving worlds vanishes. All speak (Lowie 1924a:228–29). Powell expands on this for the Northern Paiute. "Rocks, trees, sagebrush, etc., were all people once" (Powell 1971:241). They were an Ancient People, called the *Numwad*. Although this mythic time of kinship between all parts of the natural world is past, some vestige of the relationship endures. In their Father Dance of former times, Wind River Shoshones offered ten prayers and ten prayer songs to various parts of the natural world—Sun, Moon, etc. "Queerly Shaped Rocks"[27] was one of the ten to receive prayer and prayer song (Shimkin 1986a:326).

Two recent Wind River Shoshone anecdotes bring out the continued belief in the human or animistic potential of rocks. One person recounted how Jack Guina found a rock and put his thumb in a hole that fit it perfectly. However, when Jack wanted to take his thumb out of the hole, he couldn't. The rock would not "let go" of him for a few days. Finally, the rock "released" his thumb.

Helene Oldman discussed how she likes to bring pretty rocks into her house, but she does not keep them there permanently. She has a sense that they should be free outside. Eventually, she takes the rocks back out or, according to her perception, they "leave."

Great Basin cultures anthropomorphized nature by conferring the power of speech and other human qualities to it. In another example it is the reverse: people identified with natural objects, including rocks. In the late nineteenth century, Sarah Winnemucca Hopkins described the Northern Paiute Festival of Flowers, held each spring. Girls assumed new names derived from different flowers and other plants. "Some girls are named for rocks and are called rock-girls, and they find some pretty rocks which they carry; each one such a rock as she is named for" (Hopkins [1883] 1969:47). The flower and rock girls made a song about their namesakes and strengthened their identification with them. Part of Sarah's song text went, "I, Sarah Winnemucca, am a shell-flower, such as I wear on my dress. My name is Thocmetony. I am so beautiful!" (Hopkins [1883] 1969:47). One wonders about the girl who chose a rock as her namesake. What might her song have said?

5 | *Animals: Ground People, Sky People, and Water People*

Wind River Shoshone and Great Basin taxonomy of the animal kingdom provides the basic three-part organization of this chapter. Using mythic underpinnings, I have determined the first two divisions, "Ground People" and "Sky People." "Water People" is a category recognized by the Shoshone. This taxonomy, which I will discuss later, codes animals according to their environment and behavior—habitats and habits. That animals are "people" is significant; I will come back to this strong human identity several times.

Ground People

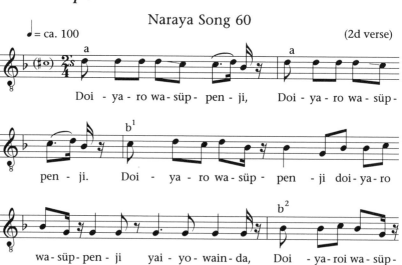

Naraya Song 60

2 repeats, incomplete

pen - ji   doi- ya - ro wa - süp - pen - ji   yai - yo- wain- da.

Dorothy Tappay

Pitches

Doiyaro	wasüp-penji,
Mountains	game animals-(v.s.),

Doiyaro	wasüp-penji.
Mountains	game animals-(v.s.).

Doiyaro	wasüp-penji	doiyaro	wasüp-penji	yaiyowainda,
Mountains	game animals	mountains	game animals	(e.v.),
	-(v.s.)		-(v.s.)	

Doiyaro	wasüp-penji	doiyaro	wasüp-penji	yaiyowainda.
Mountains	game animals	mountains	game animals	(e.v.).
	-(v.s.)		-(v.s.)	

EMILY: "That means, *wasüp*, that means the deer, the elk, and all those things. *Wasüp*, that means all together." Game animals comprise one of the biggest categories in Naraya songs, second only to water in its many forms.

♩ = ca. 70   Naraya Song 61   (6th verse)

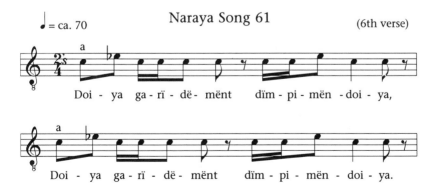

Doi - ya ga - rï - dë - mënt   dïm - pi - mën - doi - ya,

Doi - ya ga - rï - dë - mënt   dïm - pi - mën - doi - ya.

Do - sa gwe - shi ga - rï - dë dïm - pi - mën - doi - ya,

9 repeats

Do - sa gwe - shi ga - rï - dë dïm - pi - mën - doi - ya.

variation:

Dorothy Tappay
Emily Hill

Pitches

Doiya   garïdëmënt   dïmpi-mëndoi-ya,
Mountains sitting there rocks-climbing-(v.s.),

Doiya   garïdëmënt   dïmpi-mëndoi-ya.
Mountains sitting there rocks-climbing-(v.s.).

Dosa gweshi garïdë   dïmpi-mëndoi-ya,
White tail   sit   rocks-climbing-(v.s.),

Dosa gweshi garïdë   dïmpi-mëndoi-ya.
White tail   sit   rocks-climbing-(v.s.).

EMILY: "Going out and climbing the rocks. That's what it means. There's some deer, they go around. They say *dïkant, dïkant,* that means eating around, you know. *Dïmpimandoiyigïn,* it's climbing that rock. *Doiya garïd man,* that's the mountains sitting. *Dïmpimandoiyigïnt,* getting on a rock; *dïmpi garïd man,* that rock sitting there. *Dosa gweshi,* that's white-tailed deer."

JUDY: "And they're climbing on those rocks sitting on the mountain?"

EMILY: "Yeah, you got it right, now."

Naraya Song 62

$\bullet$ = ca. 84

(4th verse)

Dorothy Tappay
Emily Hill

Wadzi-wo	*wadzi-wo*	*wo ya*	*wai*	*ena,*
Antelope bull-(?v.s.)	antelope bull-(?v.s.)	(vocs.)	climbing down	(e.v.),

Wadzi-wo	*wadzi-wo*	*wo ya*	*wai*	*ena.*
Antelope bull-(?v.s.)	antelope bull-(?v.s.)	(vocs.)	climbing down	(e.v.).

Dïva	*n-doiya*	*dïva*	*n-doiya*	*doiya*	*ena,*
Pine nut	mountain	pine nut	mountain	mountain	(e v.),

Dïva	*n-doiya*	*dïva*	*n-doiya*	*doiya*	*ena.*
Pine nut	mountain	pine nut	mountain	mountain	(e v.).

EMILY: "Antelope bulls, sitting on the top of that mountain where there's those—you know those people, they . . . down someplace in Nevada. They pick those nuts off the pine trees, pine nuts, over on Pine

Nuts Mountain. That bull's coming down from there. Sitting there, on the hill and then coming down. Pine nuts, Pine Nuts mountain."

JUDY: "Do people here eat pine nuts?"

EMILY: "Yes, they used to sell them on the reservation, bringing them in sacks. Now they sell them in the stores."

Naraya Song 63

(5th verse)

Dorothy Tappay
Emily Hill

Dïmpi-do	*dïmpi-do*	*waiyo*	*wai*	*gena,*
Rocks-(v.s.)	rocks	coming down	coming down	(e.v.),

Dïmpi-do	*dïmpi-do*	*waiyo*	*wai*	*gena.*
Rocks-(v.s.)	rocks	coming down	coming down	(e.v.).

Wadzi	*to-do*	*wadzi*	*to-do*	*wai*	*gena,*
Antelope bull	(?voc.)	antelope bull	(?voc.)	coming down	(e.v.),

Wadzi	*to-do*	*wadzi*	*to-do*	*wai*	*gena.*
Antelope bull	(?voc.)	antelope bull	(?voc.)	coming down	(e.v.).

I have no commentary from Emily for this song except her belief that it came from either Idaho or Nevada.

Naraya Song 64

$\quad = $ ca. 96 (2d verse)

Da - man doi-yav - no wa - süp-pen - ji   yai yai e - na,

Da - man doi-yav - no wa - süp-pen - ji   yai yai e - na.

Sai - ba-rȯ - tsi wï- në- re sai - ba-rȯ- tsi wï-në-re yai yai e - na,

Sai - ba-rȯ - tsi wï- në- re

sai - barȯ- tsi wï- në- re yai yai e - na. yai-yo- wain-dë.

8 repeats (last repeat)

Pitches

Emily Hill
Dorothy Tappay

Daman	doiyav-no	wasüp-penji	yai yai ena,
Our	mountains-(v.s.)	game animals-(v.s.)	(vocs.) (e.v.),
Daman	doiyav-no	wasüp-penji	yai yai ena.
Our	mountains-(v.s.)	game animals-(v.s.)	(vocs.) (e.v.).

Sai   ba-ró-tsi   *wïnëre*
Melting   water-?black-(d.a.s.)   standing-moving[1]
[Snow melting]/[water-black]   [ref. to tracks]
    sai   ba-ró-tsi   *wïnëre   yai yai   ena,*
    melting   water-?black (d.a.s.)   tracks   (vocs.)   (e.v.),

Sai   ba-ró-tsi   *wïnëre*
Melting   water-?black-(d.a.s.)   standing-moving
[Snow melting]/[water-black]   [ref. to tracks]
    sai   ba-ró-tsi   *wïnëre   yai yai   ena.*
    melting   water-?black (d.a.s.)   tracks   (vocs.)   (e.v.).

EMILY: "It's about the mountains. Mountains and deer and elk and all those animals up there. *Wasüpin, wasüpin,* it means a whole lot of elk, deer, and antelope, and moose."

JUDY: "What else does the song say?"

EMILY: "Our mountains, and our game, you know, they get under these kinds—shades, away from the cold. That's what it means."

JUDY: "Under the trees?"

EMILY: "You know, horses, cattle, when it's cold, they stand behind those trees where it's a windbreak. A windbreak, that's what for elk."

(Our conversation about the second part of the text continued on another occasion.)

EMILY: "Game, mountains, and game *barótsi wïnërëk*—wet, their tracks wet. You know how ground is wet and their tracks. *Sai* means, you know, melting, where the roads are wet where the tracks are. Wet tracks where the side are, the snow melted. *Sai barótsi;* that means, *saigënt* means, you know, snow melting."

JUDY: "What about the *-penji* in the first line?"

EMILY: "Just to make it pretty. Just put 'pretty' on there."

Naraya Song 65

♩ = ca. 88   (4th verse)

Wa - zi dïm - pi   ti - wai - zi   wa - zi dïm - pi   ti - wai - zi,

Wa - zi dïm - pi   ti - wai - zi   wa - zi dïm - pi   ti - wai - zi.

Wa - zi boi   ti - wai - zi   wa - zi boi   ti - wai - zi,

6 repeats

Wa - zi boi   ti - wai - zi   wa - zi boi   ti - wai.

Dorothy Tappay
Emily Hill

Pitches

Wazi	dïmpi	tiwaizi	wazi	dïmpi	tiwaizi,
Game animals	rocks	?	game animals	rocks	?,

Wazi	dïmpi	tiwaizi	wazi	dïmpi	tiwaizi.
Game animals	rocks	?	game animals	rocks	?.

Wazi	boi	tiwaizi	wazi	boi	tiwaizi,
Game animals	road	?	game animals	road	?,

Wazi	boi	tiwaizi	wazi	boi	tiwai.
Game animals	road	?	game animals	road	?.

EMILY: "That's deer and elk and moose, together, they're going along. They're looking for water. They're going along. They roam around where those big rocks are. Where they hide where those big rocks are when they see something."

The translation of this text is problematic. *Wazi*, the first word in both lines of text, may derive from *wazigad,* which means "hide," or, in this case, "hiding" or "hidden"; it could also derive from *wasüpi,* "game animals." Gladys Hill pointed out that in addition, *wazi dïmpi* is a special kind of rock used as protection against such things as wind or thunder. (See chapter 4.)

Naraya Song 66

♩ = ca. 88   (5th verse)

Wa - sü - pit n - du - an - zi   wa - sü - pit n - du - an - zi,

Wa - sü - pit   n - du - an - zi   wa - sü- pit   n - du - an - zi.

Bu - hi   doi - ya - vi- di   bu - hi   doi - ya - vi- di   e - na,

6 repeats, incomplete

Bu - hi   doi - ya - vi- di   bu - hi   doi - ya - vi- di   e - na.

Pitches

Dorothy Tappay
Emily Hill

Wasüpi-t	*n-dua-n-zi*		*wasüpi-t*	*n-dua-zi,*
Game animals	child [offspring]-(d.a.s.)		game animals	child (d.a.s.),

Wasüpi-t	*n-dua-n-zi*		*wasüpi-t*	*n-dua-zi.*
Game animals	child [offspring]-(d.a.s.)		game animals	child (d.a.s.).

Buhi	*doiyavi-di*	*buhi*	*doiyavi-di*	*ena,*
Green	mountains-(v.s.)	green	mountains (v.s.)	(e.v.),

Buhi	*doiyavi-di*	*buhi*	*doiyavi-di*	*ena.*
Green	mountains-(v.s.)	green	mountains (v.s.)	(e.v.).

EMILY: "I was telling you, little elks and little deer. *Wasüpi*, game. They're on the mountains, green mountains, some young ones. They're on the mountains where the green mountains are."

Naraya Song 67

♩ = ca. 104   (6th verse)

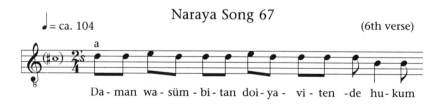

Da - man wa - süm - bi - tan doi - ya - vi - ten -de hu - kum

boi - ya ga - zu mi - ya- gin, Da - man wa - süm - bi - tan doi - ya -

♩.= ca. 66

vi - ten - de hu - kum boi - ya ga- zu mi - ya gin. Bu - hi wü -

wü ha -ve - en - dë, Bu - hi wü- wü ha -ve - en - dë.

Pitches

Dorothy Tappay
Emily Hill

Daman	*wasümbita*	*n-doiyavi-tende*	*hukum*	*boiya*	*gazu*	*miyagin,*
Our	game animals	mountains-(v.s.)	dust	road	edge	walking,

Daman	*wasümbita*	*n-doiyavi-tende*	*hukum*	*boiya*	*gazu*	*miyagin.*
Our	game animals	mountains-(v.s.)	dust	road	edge	walking.

Buhi	*wüwü*	*?nüwü*	*have-endë,*
Green/grass	small amount	?person	lying or showing-(v.s.),

Buhi	*wüwü*	*?nüwü*	*have-endë.*
Green/grass	small amount	?person	lying or showing-(v.s.).

EMILY: "Mountains, where the game are, where the deep, deep roads [are]. A person walking on there, [on the] edge of that, where a little bit of that green grass showing. They're [the game animals] scattered around. Anyway, when they go through there—just like horses and cows—there's a pass through there, through the pass."

Nüwë, "person," and *wüwü,* "a small amount," are similar sounds in Shoshone and are a source of confusion in this text. I believe that Emily's reference to a "person" is her way of explaining something walking on the edge of a "deep" or rutted road. If the word "person" is in this text, its placement between "green grass" and the final verb, "lying," seems odd. I suggest that game animals are the subject of the text, and it is they who walk on the grassy edge of a dusty, rutted, mountain road.

Naraya Song 68

Dorothy Tappay
Emily Hill

Tonic: E? or B?

Yïva	doiyav	wasümbi	ena,
Fall, autumn	mountains	game animals	(e.v.),

Yïva	doiyav	wasümbi	ena.
Fall, autumn	mountains	game animals	(e.v.).

?Hinën ba-ru ?nuki ba-ru ?hinën ge ba-ru
?What water-?black ?running water-?black ?what ? water-?black
yiyïgwïnd yïva ru yiyïgwïnd ena,
many sitting together fall ?black many sitting together (e.v.),

Yïva ru   yiyïgwïnd   ena.
Fall ?black many sitting together (e.v.).

EMILY: "That's about them animals up in the mountains in the fall. *Yïva* means the fall. *Yïvain* means the fall and *domo* is winter. *Da^hwãni* is spring and summer, *daz.*"

Gladys Hill commented that in the fall the herds are fat and their coats are dark. As the text expresses it—water-black, fall-black.

Naraya Song 69

Ye - va wand- zi - a   ye - va wand- zi - a   ye - va wand- zi-

a   e - na.   Ye - va no van du   ye-va no van du

e - na,   Ye - va no van du   ye-va no van du   e - na.

Dorothy Tappay
Emily Hill

Pitches

Yeva   wandzia   yeva   wandzia   yeva   wandzia   ena.
?Autumn   antelope ?autumn antelope ?autumn   antelope (e.v.).
          bulls   bulls   bulls

Yeva   no² van³ du   yeva   no van   du   ena,
?Autumn   hill above young ?autumn hill above young (e.v.),

Yeva   no van   du   yeva   no van   du   ena.
?Autumn   hill above young ?autumn hill above young (e.v.).

EMILY: "It's about those antelope bull. They rest on the side of the hills, with their little ones, all of them—side of the hills. Almost like the other one [song 70]."

Düna-na   vui ya dombina vui ya dombi ena.
Downhill-(?v.s.) ?   ?   ?   ?   ?   ?   (e.v.).

Wandzi   duru   wandzi   durua   wai   ena,
Antelope bulls   young   antelope bulls young   ?down (e.v.),
                 males   males

Wandzi   duru   wandzi   durua   wai   ena.
Antelope bulls   young   antelope bulls young   ?down (e.v.).
                 males   males

EMILY: "It's about an antelope, you know, we call them bulls, *wandzi*. *Ndurua*, that means he's with his little ones, going down in the hot wave—so the dust—hot wave. They're going down, you know, in the plains you see them running. And *wandzi*, that's something like a bull. This Lander here [a nearby Wyoming town, off the reservation], that big hill on the other side, that's the name of that, *Wandzi Gariʔ*, [sits] where that bull sits and watches, *Wandzi Gariʔ*."

Naraya Song 71

Dorothy Tappay
Emily Hill

Wasüpi-t   n-dua-n-zi,
Game animals   young ones-(d.a.s.),

Wasüpi-t   n-dua-n-zi.
Game animals   young ones-(d.a.s.).

Dïna   huku   dïna   huku   yünzai   yo   wain   ena,
Down   dust   down   dust   ?   ?   ?down (e.v.),

Dïna   huku   dïna   huku   yünzai   yo   wain   ena.
Down   dust   down   dust   ?   ?   ?down (e.v.).

EMILY: "That's the game, mountain sheep and all them, *wasüpitïn.*
When they're going they're raising dust, raising dust when they're
going down."

Naraya Song 72

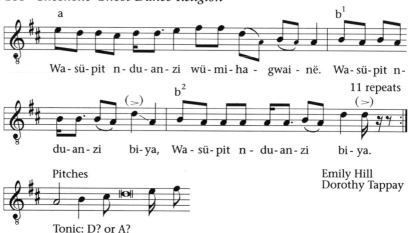

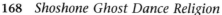

Pitches

Emily Hill
Dorothy Tappay

Tonic: D? or A?

Wasüpi-t   *n-dua-n-zi*   *wümihagwainë,*
Game animals   offspring-(d.a.s.)   keeps trying, but can't quite catch up,

Wasüpi-t   *n-dua-n-zi*   *wümihagwainë.*
Game animals   offspring-(d.a.s.)   keeps trying, but can't quite catch up.

Wasüpi-t   *n-dua-n-zi*   *?biya,*
Game animals   offspring-(d.a.s.)   ?mother/big,

Wasüpi-t   *n-dua-n-zi*   *?biya.*
Game animals   offspring-(d.a.s.)   ?mother/big.

EMILY: "That's the young ones, young different kind of game."

Emily believes this song to be from Nevada.

Naraya Song 73

♩. = ca. 66   (5th verse)

Doi-ya wa-sü-pen-ji   da-ve de-dok   wï-nï-ga-nò-

rë,   Doi-ya wa-sü-pen-ji   da-ve   de-dok

wï-nï-ga-nȯ - rë.   Doi-ya   wa-sü-pen-ji   wü-mi-ha-

b   7 repeats

nȯ - rë,   Doi-ya   wa-sü-pen-ji   wü-mi-ha nȯ - rë.

Pitches

Dorothy Tappay
Emily Hill

Doiya	*wasü-penji*	*dave*	*dedok wïnïganȯrë,*
Mountains	game animals-(v.s.)	sun/day	traveling,

Doiya	*wasü-penji*	*dave*	*dedok wïnïganȯrë.*
Mountains	game animals-(v.s.)	sun/day	traveling.

Doiya	*wasü-penji*	*wümihanȯrë,*
Mountains	game animals-(v.s.)	slowing down (barely catching up, GH),

Doiya	*wasü-penji*	*wümihanȯrë.*
Mountains	game animals-(v.s.)	slowing down (barely catching up, GH).

EMILY: "A lot of deer, elk, everything like that, going up towards the sun. *Winïgano* means they're tired of going up. They're spread out as they're going. A bunch of her, different kind, *wasüpi,* means different kind. *Dedok wanokin,* that's traveling, you know, climbing the mountains. Says, all day, all day, they're traveling. *Wümihanȯr* means slowing down. When the sun's going down those young ones, they're behind, way behind—way back. They're slowing down. Well, they're still going up, the sun's going down. They must be climbing big long mountains, high mountains."

Naraya Song 74

♩ = ca. 92   (6th verse)

Da -mën   do-sa   te   mo - zam-bi - an -zi   boi   wa

se-na na-roi-ya-bi-an-zi   yai - yo - wain-da,

a

Da - mën do-sa te mo-zam-bi-an-zi boi   wa   se -

b[1]

na na-roi-ya-bi-an-zi   yai - yo-wain-da.   Boi   ti wa-zum-

b[2]   6 repeats

bi-an-zi,   Boi   ti wa-zum - bi-an-zi yai-yo- wain-da.

Pitches

Dorothy Tappay
Emily Hill

Damën	*dosa*	*te*	*mozambia-n-zi*	*boi*	*wa*	*sena*	*naroiya-bianzi*
Our	white	?	ewe-(d.a.s.)	road	?	?aspens	going up (?s.)

yaiyowainda,
(e.v.),

Damën	*dosa*	*te*	*mozambia-n-zi*	*boi*	*wa*	*sena*	*naroiya-bianzi*
Our	white	?	ewe-(d.a.s.)	road	?	?aspens	going up (?s.)

yaiyowainda.
(e.v.).

Boi	*ti*	*wazumbi-an-zi*	*yaiyowainda,*
Road	?	game animals-(d.a.s.)	(e.v.),

Boi	*ti*	*wazumbi-an-zi*	*yaiyowainda.*
Road	?	game animals-(d.a.s.)	(e.v.).

EMILY: "Mountain sheep on the top of the ridge and the rocks. They stay up, way up in the high mountains. *Boi,* that's the road. On the back side there's a road where they go down, where they travel.

"They're the best-tasting meat, better than deer, antelope, elk, moose, cow—really taste good. No matter how much you eat, you still want more."

Naraya Song 75

Ho wia-ïna   *hombi*   *ena,*
?   ?mountain pass-(?v.s.)   ?wood (e.v.),

Ho wia-ïna   *hombi ena.*
?   ?mountain pass-(?v.s.)   ?wood (e.v.).

Damën dosa se mozambi-an-zi damë roni,
Our   white ?   ewe-(d.a.s.)   our   ?,

Damën dosa se mozambi-an-zi damë roni.
Our   white ?   ewe-(d.a.s.)   our   ?.

The Shoshone word for mountain sheep takes two forms, *duk* is "ram" and *mu´ʒambia* (*mozambia*) is "ewe" (Shimkin 1947b:277).[4] Songs 74 and 75, the only two songs that mention mountain sheep in Emily and Dorothy's repertoire, both take the female animal as their subject.

Naraya Song 76

♩.= ca. 72   (8th verse)

Yë- na dui yë- na yë- na dui yë- na.   Yë- na ba- zi- gi

yë- na ba- zi- gi- na,   Yë- na ba- zi- gi yë- na ba- zi- gi- na.   9 repeats

Pitches

Emily Hill
Dorothy Tappay

Yë-na   *dui yë-na*   *yë-na*   *dui yë-na.*
Woodchuck-(?v.s.) black woodchuck woodchuck black woodchuck.

Yë-na   *bazigi*   *yë-na*   *bazigi-na,*
Woodchuck-(?v.s.) shining/slick woodchuck shining/slick-(?v.s.),

Yë-na   *bazigi*   *yë-na*   *bazigi-na.*
Woodchuck-(?v.s.) shining/slick woodchuck shining/slick-(?v.s.).

EMILY: "That means woodchuck, black woodchuck, it's just fat.
Barazigwid, it's shining."

Gladys Hill compared the fat shiny woodchuck to the moose in summer, a time when it, too, is dark, fat, and sleek.

Naraya Song 77

♩ = ca. 72   (7th verse)

Ya- na he ya - na, Ya- na he ya - na. Ya- na he

ya - na, Ya- na he ya- na he yan.   Ya- na du - si-

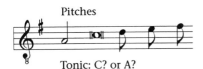

an,   Ya - na   du - si - an.   Ya - na   he

ya - na,   Ya - na   he   ya - na   he   yan.

Pitches

Dorothy Tappay
Emily Hill

Tonic: C? or A?

Ya-na	*he*	*ya-na,*		
Woodchuck-(?v.s.)	(?voc.)	woodchuck,		

Ya-na	*he*	*ya-na.*		
Woodchuck-(?v.s.)	(?voc.)	woodchuck.		

Ya-na	*he*	*ya-na,*		
Woodchuck-(?v.s.)	(?voc.)	woodchuck,		

Ya-na	*he*	*ya-na*	*he*	*yan.*
Woodchuck-?(v.s.)	(?voc)	woodchuck	(?voc.)	woodchuck.

Ya-na	*du-*	*sian,*		
Woodchuck-(?v.s.)	?black	?,		

Ya-na	*du-*	*sian.*		
Woodchuck-(?v.s.)	?black	?.		

Ya-na	*he*	*ya-na,*		
Woodchuck-(?v.s.)	(?voc.)	woodchuck,		

Ya-na	*he*	*ya-na*	*he*	*yan.*
Woodchuck-?(v.s.)	(?voc)	woodchuck	(?voc.)	woodchuck.

Emily thought that this song came from Idaho Shoshones.

Naraya Song 78

Dorothy Tappay
Emily Hill

Damën dave-dï sïneyugwid-ïd,
Our   sun   says,

Damën dave-dï sïneyugwid-ïd.
Our   sun   says.

Dewanga roiya   yamande dosa-ro   gëm-beya,
?   ?mountains ?   white[-tailed]-(?v.s.) jack rabbit,

Dewanga roiya   yamande dosa-ro   gëm-beya.
?   ?mountains ?   white[-tailed]-(?v.s.) jack rabbit.

EMILY: "That's our sun, seeing those jackrabbits running under it. You see those jackrabbits, when they're running you could see their white tails, you know. I don't know which that song belongs to, either Bannocks or Shoshones. I don't know whose song it is, 'cause it's a little different from the last part, it's a little different from ours."

Emily remained unsure whether this song originated in Idaho or Wyoming. As we will see in Naraya song 79, there are differences in the rabbit populations between Idaho and Wyoming. An overlap of rabbit terms used by Shoshone-Bannocks and Wind River Shoshones is a source of confusion.

Biya   dave[5]   waiyo   biya   dave   waiyo,
Big/mother sun/day ?down big/mother sun/day ?down,

Biya   dave   waiyo   biya   dave   waiyo.
Big/mother sun/day ?down big/mother sun/day ?down.

Du   gëm   um-biya du   gëm   um-biya ena,
Black   jack rabbit big   black   jack rabbit big   (e.v.),
(-tailed)   (-tailed)

Du   gëm   um-biya du   gëm   um-biya ena.
Black   jack rabbit big   black   jack rabbit big   (e.v.).
(-tailed)   (-tailed)

EMILY: "That's a song from Idaho. I know *gëmU*, black-tailed jack-rabbits. They're from Idaho. They're not from here."

Gladys Hill analyzed rabbit terms as follows. Wind River Shoshones use two terms: *dav* for rabbit,[6] and *dosa gëm* for white-tailed jackrabbit. Shoshone Bannocks from Idaho use the term *gëmU* for a rabbit, which, compared to a Wyoming rabbit, is bigger than a snowshoe hare, or cottontail, and smaller than the white-tailed jackrabbit. Naraya song 79 adds a further distinction, the animal's black tail. Wind River Shoshones refer to this type simply as an Idaho rabbit.

Naraya Song 80

Davege   warhigi,
Daytime   fox,[7]

Davege   warhigi.
Daytime   fox.

Dosa   mamaiyïgwidir warhigi,
White   spots   fox,

Dosa   mamaiyïgwidir warhigi.
White   spots   fox.

EMILY: "Do you ever see a fox? That's about that, *wã:hi*, a fox. In daytime you could see, [at a] distance, those white streaks out there. One time there was one up here, right straight across the river by that little pasture there, standing there when we was going down."

Naraya Song 81

Doi - ya- no war - hïn- ge,   Doi - ya- no war - hïn- ge.

Du- gum- ba- ga sai- ya- ga- nȯ- ra, Du- gum-ba- ga sai- ya- ga- no.

Dorothy Tappay
Emily Hill

Pitches

Doiya-no   *warhï-nge,*
Mountains-(?v.s.) fox-(?v.s.),

Doiya-no   *warhï-nge.*
Mountains-(?v.s.) fox-(?v.s.).

Dugumba *ga* *saiyaga-nóra,*
Sky   ?   Milky-Way-moving,

Dugumba *ga* *saiyaga-no.*
Sky   ?   Milky-Way-moving.

EMILY: "It's about the fox up in the mountains. I think it's when, kind of night's come. Looks like when it comes, the night, that those *saiyagan* comes, you know, those stars I talked to you about, [the Milky Way] when they're up there—the mountains—that's the thing that goes over them like that."

JUDY: "The fox is up in the mountains when the Milky Way is out?"

EMILY: "Hu huh, in the evening."

JUDY: "What's the word for Milky Way?"

EMILY: "*Wasaiyagano.*"[8]

Another explication of *dugumba-ga,* which begins the second line, might be that it is an elision of two words. It is possible that *dugumba?,* "sky," and *bagana,* one Naraya form of the word meaning "fog," create *dugum-baga,* "sky-fog," a poetic allusion to the Milky Way.

Naraya Song 82

Dorothy Tappay
Emily Hill

Damën de   gwitsu-no   sogop   mande sogop mande
Our   ?small buffalo-(?v.s.) earth/ground ?   earth ?
sogop   mande ena.
earth   ?   (e.v.).

Dono   ba-ru   sïgi   mande,
?Greasewood water-?black leaves   ?,

Dono   ba-ru   sïgi   mande ena yaiyowainda.
?Greasewood water-?black leaves   ?   (ending vocables).

EMILY: "White salty ground—those sticker plants that looks like . . . they're tall but they're different from sagebrush. That's what they eat, those buffaloes."

Gladys Hill adds that *dono* also could mean "alkali" and refer to white salt. *Dono-baru* may be the damp salty ground where the greasewood plant with its stickers, or thorns, grows.

Questions concerning the identification of the plant in this song will be explored fully in connection with songs 106 and 107. I believe that *dono* refers to greasewood; however, as the identification is not definitive, the question mark remains in its translation.

As noted in the introduction to this book, Naraya song 82 is the only Naraya song of Emily and Dorothy's repertoire that mentions buffalo.

Sky People

Song texts in which birds appear could logically be grouped and presented according to the species, for example, eagles or blackbirds. (A listing of the bird species that appear in Emily and Dorothy's Naraya repertoire is given later in this chapter.) However, I believe that the more compelling logic for this section derives from songs that mention birds and their relationship to various aspects of their habitats: birds and vegetation (Naraya songs 83–87), birds and water (Naraya songs 88–89), birds and mountains (Naraya song 90), birds and sun and stars (Naraya song 91–92), and a final, unique, category of one song, birds and the life cycle (Naraya song 93). Although, admittedly, the subcategories are mine, I have taken my cue from Shoshone and Great Basin taxonomy, with which these subcategories are congruent.

Naraya Song 83

♩ = ca. 92   (5th verse)

Ye- vai yï- zï- e-ï-në ye- vai yï-zï-ë-ï- në   e - na,

Ye- vai yï - zï - e-ï-në ye-vai yï- zï-e - ï- në   e - na.

b

Bu- hi s(h)o - go - vai - gi   bu - hi s(h)o - go - vai - gi   e - na,

b   7 repeats

Bu - hi s(h)o - go - vai - gi   bu - hi s(h)o - go - vai - gi   e - na.

Dorothy Tappay
Emily Hill

Pitches

Yevai   *yïzï(eï)në yevai yïzï-eï-në ena,*
Bird (unidentied) flying   bird   flying   (e.v.),

Yevai   *yïzï(eï)në yevai yïzï-eï-në ena.*
Bird (unidentied) flying   bird   flying   (e.v.).

Buhi   *s(?h)ogo-vaigi buhi   s(h)ogo-vaigi ena,*
Green/grass earth-above   green/grass earth-above (e.v.),

Buhi   *s(?h)ogo-vaigi buhi   s(h)ogo-vaigi ena.*
Green/grass earth-above   green/grass earth-above (e.v.).

This song was on one of the tapes that Emily had made years earlier of Dorothy and herself singing. There was static on it, which made it hard for Emily to hear.

EMILY: "It's something about a bird over our earth, earth that's got green grass. I don't know what kind of bird's flying over that green grass on the ground, earth. *Sogovaig* is earth, ground. Something about a bird flying. Can't catch it 'cause my ears won't work too good."

Naraya Song 84

♩. = ca. 84

a¹   a²   (2d verse)

Sï- nav gai- wai rü- vi   pü - gi,   Sï- nav gai- wai rü- vi

b¹

pü - gi.   Bu - hi wai bu - hi - wai rü - vi   pü - gi,

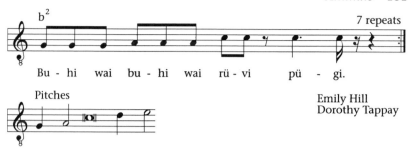

Sïnav   gaiwai   rüvi pügi,
Quaking-aspen   ?Brewer's blackbird[9] ?   ?,

Sïnav   gaiwai   rüvi pügi.
Quaking-aspen   ?Brewer's blackbird ?   ?.

Buhi   wai   buhi   wai   rüvi pügi,
Green/grass ?down   green/grass ?down   ?   ?,

Buhi   wai   buhi   wai   rüvi pügi.
Green/grass ?down   green/grass ?down   ?   ?.

EMILY: "Aspen trees, growing under it, green grass."

JUDY: "It's about *sïnavI*, aspen trees?"

EMILY: "Yeah. There's some things that oldtimers call—[which Emily couldn't recall] growing under it. A lot these—just like white people—hard jawbreaker words. Yeah, that's the kind they use sometimes. The oldtimers use that sometimes. Some people still don't understand it. *Dïvid*, but that's something that's growing on that thing there. Under that's the green grass."

JUDY: "Is that the *buhi, buhip*[h]?"

EMILY: "When that thing's green and the bottom of that thing is all green. Some things have hard words.

"There's birds on that [aspen trees]. *Gaiwah* means a bird, *gaiwah* [Brewer's blackbird; see note 9]. They go, they're around the foot of the mountains way up that way. And when they come down, when they're coming here, there's a lot of them. They just spread out here on trees, all over. It's a blackbird. I think it's a little bigger than them blackbirds, bigger."

JUDY: "Is it like a raven?"

EMILY: "Uh huh. In spring they were coming this way, going up where they stay, way up the foot of the mountains, down the mountains where they fly around the pine trees. They come back with spring. They come up this way. They go up, go around, and next day they go up, keep going, keep going. They eat those rosebud bushes, red ones. They were on those rosebud bushes when they were ripe all winter long. They were out picking all those out all over here. I mean those rosebud bushes' berries [?rosehips]."

JUDY: "Do they stay around all winter?"

EMILY: "No, they come from way down there someplace. I don't know where they are. Then pretty soon, along in—about this time, June, last part of June, July, those yellow birds. There were a lot of yellow birds here. They were flying around. Some are gray. The gray ones are the hens and them real yellow ones are the he-ones. They were all over here, all over the yard, all over—on trees. You could hear them noise, hear them down that river too, when I had good ears. You could hear them birds, like that song.

"One time, 1977—no, '76—there was real pretty birds. You know, those blue pretty birds. They got long tails like that. Bigger than the magpies and they got red up here, red up this way and gray and all over spots. Real pretty birds. Big! About that big. They were two of 'em. They were sitting in the back there. I seen them. I told Dorothy—she couldn't get up, she's in bed—'There's a real pretty bird.'

"You could see the robins all over here, too. Two people here visiting us, they said, 'Why your place here, you see all kinds of birds around here. Around our place it's nothing, just magpie and meadowlark.' Meadowlarks talks dirty. That Arapaho girl told me, 'That meadowlark sure has bad words. He talks dirty to you.' I said, 'Same with the Shoshones' language.'"

JUDY: "How is it that all the birds come by your place?"

EMILY: "Maybe they like it. They feel good here. All green."

(I sang the second line of Naraya song 84.)

JUDY: "What does *rüvi pügi* mean?"

EMILY: "I don't understand that. Green grass by these aspen trees."

Naraya Song 85

Gai-wai dï-va yo-ri-ke-na gai-wai dï-va yo-ri-ken,

Gai-wai dï-va yo-ri-ke-na gai-wai dï-va yo-ri-ken.

Emily Hill
Dorothy Tappay

Pitches

Dïva	*homando*	*dïva*	*homando*	*dïva*	*homando,*
Pine nut	?	pine nut	?	pine nut	?,
tree		tree		tree	

Dïva	*homando*	*dïva*	*homando*	*dïva*	*homando.*
Pine nut	?	pine nut	?	pine nut	?.
tree		tree		tree	

Gaiwai		*dïva*	*yorikena*	*gaiwai*	*dïva*	*yoriken,*
?Brewer's blackbirds		pine nut	fly	blackbirds	pine nut	fly,
		tree			tree	

Gaiwai		*dïva*	*yorikena*	*gaiwai*	*dïva*	*yoriken.*
?Brewer's blackbirds		pine nut	fly	blackbirds	pine nut	fly.
		tree			tree	

EMILY: "I can't think about these pine trees' different names. It's a pine tree, but there's different kinds. It's some kind of a white-man name. Good great big trees. *Dïva* means they get those for wood. They burn good. That *gaiwa^h*, that means birds, brown ones, pretty big sizes. There's a lot of them come through here. You could just see them all over. They're gathering up. They're going different ways, gathering up. There's a lot of *biya* [big] ones, you could just hear 'chu chu chu chui chui.' You could see them on the trees all over here. They look for rosebud berry bushes, them berries that's already ripe [?rosehips]. I seen them way up there at the foot of the mountains about this time [September]. They're looking for chokecherries too. Dark brown birds. *Gaiwa^h*, that's that bird. *Dïva homando*, that's those trees, they go on those trees for nights."

Naraya Song 86

♩ = ca. 88   (5th verse)

Hu -pin dan- zi - a   hu - pin dan- zi - a   ha - ve

e - na,   Hu -pin dan- zi - a   hu - pin dan- zi - a   ha - ve

e - na. Dï - vai yu-wï-nan- gwad   dï-vai yu-wï- nan-gwad   e - na,

6 repeats

Dï - vai yu-wï- nan -gwad   dï-vai yu - wï- nan- gwad   e - na.

Pitches

Emily Hill
Dorothy Tappay

Hupin	*danzia*		*hupin*	*danzia*		*have*	*ena,*
Wood	knocking together		wood	knocking together		lying	(e.v.),

Hupin	*danzia*		*hupin*	*danzia*		*have*	*ena.*
Wood	knocking together		wood	knocking together		lying	(e.v.).

Dïvai		*yuwïnangwad*[10]	*dïvai*	*yuwïnangwad*	*ena,*
Dïvwaiyòr birds	go down out of sight		D. birds	go down out of sight	(e.v.),

Dïvai		*yuwïnangwad*	*dïvai*	*yuwïnangwad*	*ena.*
Dïvwaiyòr birds	go down out of sight		D. birds	go down out of sight	(e.v.).

The use of *dïvai* in song 86 is not to be confused with *dïva,* which appeared in song 85 and means "pine nut." Emily explained that in this song *dïvai* refers to a certain type of bird for which she did not know the English translation.

EMILY: "It's about the wood, to the end of the wood; some birds, you know, on there."

JUDY: "On the wood [branches]?"

EMILY: "Uh huh. Those *dïvwaiyór* are them birds, what they call—. They especially get on them dry trees like that. They just bunch up at the ends."

Naraya Song 87

Dorothy Tappay
Emily Hill

Hupin	*danzia*	*hupin*	*danzia*	*ena,*
Wood	knocking together	wood	knocking together	(e.v.),

Hupin	*danzia*	*hupin*	*danzia*	*ena.*
Wood	knocking together	wood	knocking together	(e.v.).

Dïvavaiyo		*wane*	*dïvavaiyo*	*wane*	*ena,*
?*Dïvwaiyór* birds	?	?	D. birds	?	(e.v.),

Dïvavaiyo   wane   dïvavaiyo   wane   ena.
?*Dïvwaiyór* birds ?   ? *D.* birds ?   (e.v.).

Emily thought this song originated in Idaho or Nevada. It seems closely related in text and music to Naraya song 86.

Naraya Song 88

Pitches

Emily Hill
Dorothy Tappay

Bagan-bagan-nogan-zi   *ba*   *havi*   *wanoginóra,*
?Redwing blackbirds-(s.r.)-(v.s.)-(d.a.s.) water lie   standing-moving,
                                  [bathe]   [e.g., shaking]

Bagan-bagan-nogan-zi   *ba*   *havi*   *wanoginóra.*
?Redwing blackbirds-(s.r.)-(v.s.)-(d.a.s.) water lie   standing-moving.
                                  [bathe]   [e.g., shaking]

Bagan-bagan-nogan-zi   *ba*   *havi*   *wanoginóra,*
?Redwing blackbirds-(s.r.)-(v.s.)-(d.a.s.) water lie   standing-moving,
                                  [bathe]   [e.g., shaking]

Bagan-bagan-nogan-zi	ba	havi	wanogino.
?Redwing blackbirds-(s.r.)-(v.s.)-(d.a.s.)	water	lie	standing-moving.
	[bathe]		[e.g., shaking]

Emily commented that this song was from Idaho, and that the word for blackbirds, *bagantsuk^h*, was the same in Shoshone and Bannock. The final verb, *wanoginòra*, also appeared, in slightly variant form, in Naraya song 13. Emily explained its meaning there with an image. "It's standing, *wïnïgano*, you know, the trees, when the wind's blowing" (Vander 1986:43). Applying this image to the blackbirds in Naraya song 88, one sees the bird standing, dipping, and shaking water from wings and ruffled feathers.

Naraya Song 89

Sai ba-gan-tsu-kïn-tsi yï-zï nü-ïn-dï, Sai ba-gan-tsu-kïn-tsi yï-zï nü-ïn-dï. Du sai ba-ru ga-ni, Du sai ba-ru ga-ni.

Pitches

Emily Hill
Dorothy Tappay

Sai	bagantsukïn-tsi		yïzï	nüïndï,
?Cattails	?Redwing blackbirds-(d.a.s.)		flying	wind,

Sai	bagantsukïn-tsi		yïzï	nüïndï.
?Cattails	?Redwing blackbirds-(d.a.s.)		flying	wind.

Du	sai	baru[11]	gani,
Black	?cattails	damp	?home,

Du   sai   baru   gani.
Black ?cattails damp ?home.

EMILY: "Blackbirds, flying to wind. You know, something like the ground kind of damp, *barusaigïd*. That blackbird flying and going into the wind, going down into that kind of swampy place."

Naraya Song 90

Dorothy Tappay
Emily Hill

Saiwan   duduwa-tsi   ena,
?White-tailed ptarmigan many young ones-(d.a.s.) (e.v.),

Saiwan   duduwa   segïn.
?White-tailed ptarmigan many young ones ?chirping together (GH).

Sïhuwë   n-doiya   yiyigwint,
Bare, no vegetation mountains   all sitting,

Sïhuwë   n-doiya   yiyigwi-endë.
Bare, no vegetation mountains   all sitting-(v.s.).

EMILY: "It's some kind of bird, I think it's brown one. These birds are on top of the bare mountains, sitting on top of that bare mountains."

Naraya Song 91

♩ = ca. 88   (2d verse)

a

Dïm - pi sai-ya - ga- në dïm-pi sai-ya-ga-në e - na,

a

Dïm - pi sai-ya - ga - në dïm - pi sai-ya - ga-në e - na.

b ↓   ↓

Wai - ya - vo du - gu van - du sai - ya - ga - nan e - na,

b   3 repeats

Wai - ya- vo du - gu van - du sai-ya - ga - në e - na.

Pitches   Dorothy Tappay
Emily Hill

Dïmpi	*saiyaganë*		*dïmpi*	*saiyaganë*		*ena,*
Rocks	shiny, twinkling stars		rocks	shiny, twinkling stars		(e.v.),
	(Milky Way)			(Milky Way)		

Dïmpi	*saiyaganë*		*dïmpi*	*saiyaganë*		*ena.*
Rocks	shiny, twinkling stars		rocks	shiny, twinkling stars		(e.v.).
	(Milky Way)			(Milky Way)		

Waiyavo	*dugu*[12]	*vandu*	*saiyaganan*	*ena,*
Common night hawk	sky/night	above	shiny twinkling stars	(e.v.),
			(Milky Way)	

Waiyavo	*dugu*	*vandu*	*saiyaganan*	*ena.*
Common night hawk	sky/night	above	shiny twinkling stars	(e.v.).
			(Milky Way)	

Elsewhere, Emily explained *dïmpi saiyagan* as rocks in a row, one image for the Milky Way. To further explain *saiyagan,* Emily drew her fingers together over an imaginary ball and then opened her fingers as if letting it drop. Her fingers closed and opened many times, suggestive of a pulsing light, a twinkling star. In this song the nighthawk flies in the starry field of the Milky Way.

EMILY: "That's this [bird, the nighthawk]—what do you call it? It's like a big mouse, too; they lay their eggs in the rock. It's got spots all over it like rocks. If you see some kind of hawk, you see it laying over there, sitting on a rock, laying on a rock. You won't see it till it flies. It's a bird, it has a beak. About this time it's already flying in the evening. They get up and fly around. Kind of dark. [They're] some kind of nighthawks. They got a big mouth (?), too. It's got spots on it. They lay eggs in the rocks.

"They say old people tell stories a long time before, Indian stories, something like fairy stories. This eagle was chief of all the birds. He was telling them how to make nests for the eggs. And these two birds, that one, that *waiyavo* [nighthawk] and that little dove, these two—when everybody, these different kind of birds listened to the eagle telling them how to make, fix their nests—these two busy laughing, laughing. They didn't listen to him, what he was telling the different birds. These two didn't listen so they don't have [good] nests. That other bird [the dove], it just has two, three sticks on the branches, tree branch. Have their eggs like that. When the wind blows them, eggs fall out. That's why they—some people's like that, see. Some people when somebody's telling something—what's right and wrong—some people's busy laughing and talking about something else. That's what happened to those two birds. And now they don't know how to fix their nests. That's what the story is, oldtimer's story. That's why they can't make no nest. Them *waiyavos,* you see them along those fence and rock there. You could see some of them setting there. When you get close they could fly away. They lay eggs in the rocks, just because they didn't listen. Just the way people are, Indian and white. Or me or anybody. That's the way it is. They don't listen to what a person trying to tell you."

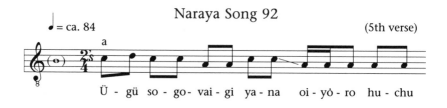

Naraya Song 92

♩ = ca. 84   (5th verse)

a

Ü - gü so - go- vai - gi ya - na   oi - yȯ - ro hu - chu

Pitches

Emily Hill
Dorothy Tappay

Ügü   sogo-vaigi yana[13]   *oiyóro huchu*[14] *naranga*[15] *semikai,*[16]
New   earth-on   every kind of   all   birds   sounding   all together
                                                                         at the same
[daybreak (GH)]   time,

Ügü   sogo-vaigi yana   *oiyóro huchu*   *naranga*   *semikai.*
New   earth-on   every kind of   all   birds   sounding   all together
                                                                         at the same
[daybreak (GH)]   time.

Ohan   gunwarua-kïn,
Yellow   edging, rim-?very small,

Ohan   gunwarua-kïn.
Yellow   edging, rim-?very small.

EMILY: "Next morning, *ügü sogo vai:chi,* daybreak, and all the different kind of birds singing. You know the light early in the morning, you see that light just coming up, that yellow along there. That's the time those birds all wake up and sing, different kind of birds. That's what it means."

Naraya Song 93

♩. = ca. 69   (5th verse)

Da bi-ya gwi-an - zi   yï - zï - nȯ - rë,   Da bi-ya gwi-an-

zi   yï - zï - nȯ - rë.   Bü - num dü - pïn du - i - wë-në

si - ya wën   si - ya wë - në,   Bü - num dü - pïn

du - i - wë - në   si - ya   wën   si - ya wën.

Pitches

Emily Hill
Dorothy Tappay

Da	*biya gwian-*	*zi*	*yïzïnȯrë,*			
Our	eagle-	(d.a.s.)	flying,			

Da	*biya gwian-*	*zi*	*yïzïnȯrë.*			
Our	eagle-	(d.a.s.)	flying.			

Bünüm	*düpïn*	*duiwënë*	*siya*	*wën*	*siya*	*wënë,*
?	?	?	feathers	? fall from	feathers	?fall from,

Bünüm	*düpïn*	*duiwënë*	*siya*	*wën*	*siya*	*wën.*
?	?	?	feathers	? fall from	feathers	?fall from.

EMILY: "It's about eagle, eagles flying. When they're growing them stumps, they lose some of their feathers. *Si: wënëds,* it's falling from them."

(Emily sings, "*Bünüm düpïn duiwën.*")

EMILY: "That means that they fly away together. They go slow and that's how those things come out, the feathers. I think about this time [September] they lose their feathers and have winter feathers grow.

"That eagle [feathers], that's the main one you use for praying and something like that."

Da   biya gwian-viva   bui   wai   dïvaro   yaiyowaindë,
Our   eagle-(?suff.)   looking   ?down   ?   (e.v.),

Da   biya gwian-viva   bui   wai   dïvaro   yaiyowaindë.
Our   eagle-(?suff.)   looking   ?down   ?   (e.v.).

Da   biya gwian-viva   yïzï   yïzïnörë,
Our   eagle-(?suff.)   fly   fly-moving,

Da   biya gwian-viva   yïzï   yïzïnörë.
Our   eagle-(?suff.)   fly   fly-moving.

Emily had no commentary on this song except to say that it came from Idaho.

Water People

Naraya song 95, the first song in this section, gave me entry into Shoshone animal taxonomy. In Emily's comment on the text, she clearly defined who the Water People are. Water, so important in a variety of contexts in Naraya songs, is here the domain for the wide range of animals who live and swim in it.

Naraya Song 95

♩. = ca. 72   (2d verse)

Ba nü - wï-tsi ba nü - wï- tsi ba nü- wën,   Ba nü - wï- tsi

ba nü - wï - tsi ba nü - wën.   Ba nü - wï - tsi

nü - wü wï - nen - ga doih yï - zi - gïn,   Ba nü -

wï - tsi nü - wü wï - nen - ga doih yï - zï - gïn.

Dorothy Tappay
Emily Hill

Pitches

Ba	nüwï-tsi	ba	nüwï-tsi	ba	nüwë-n,
Water	people-(d.a.s.)	water	people-(d.a.s.)	water	people,

Ba	nüwï-tsi	ba	nüwï-tsi	ba	nüwë-n.
Water	people-(d.a.s.)	water	people-(d.a.s.)	water	people.

Ba	nüwï-tsi	nüwü	wïnenga	doih	yïzïgïn,
Water	people-(d.a.s.)	people	stand in front of you	come up	about to rise or pop up,

Ba	nüwï-tsi	nüwü	wïnenga	doih	yïzïgïn.
Water	people-(d.a.s.)	people	stand in front of you	come up	about to rise or pop up.

EMILY: "*Ba: nüwïtsi* means beaver, muskrat, and fish, them ducks, weasel—all those Water People, and they come out, front of you."

Gladys Hill defined Water People as all things that go under water.

Notice that Emily places ducks with the Water People. It would seem that despite their ability to fly, ducks' association with water and their swimming behavior take precedence in the way they are viewed and categorized. Using this same rationale, I have placed geese in the water people section even though they, too, like ducks, can fly. Song 97, a text about goslings, reinforces this placement. It focuses on their watery nursery, the vegetation and wetlands surrounding Dinwoody and Bull Lakes.

Naraya Song 96

Emily Hill
Dorothy Tappay

Pengwi	*bai*	*anoga*	*pengwi*	*bai*	*anoga*	*pengwi*	*bai*	*anoga*	*enë,*
Fish	upon/ above	waves	fish	upon	waves	fish	upon	waves	(e.v.),

Pengwi	*bai*	*anoga*	*pengwi*	*bai*	*anoga*	*pengwi*	*bai*	*anoga*	*enë.*
Fish	upon/ above	waves	fish	upon	waves	fish	upon	waves	(e.v.).

Buhip	*bai*	*anoga*	*buhip*	*bai*	*anoga*	*buhip*	*bai*	*anoga*	*enë,*
Grass	upon/ above	waves	grass	upon	waves	grass	upon	waves	(e.v.),

Buhip	*bai*	*anoga*	*buhip*	*bai*	*anoga*	*buhip*	*bai*	*anoga*	*enë.*
Grass	upon/ above	waves	grass	upon	waves	grass	upon	waves	(e.v.).

EMILY: "Fish going like that [*Emily waves her hand sideways back and forth*], where those—you know, those kind of tall grass, like in the water. Them fishes go in there. You know how fish, when the fish in the water, that water kind of waves, like. *Buhip^h*, that's grass. That fish moving it like that."

Shoshone word order in this text differs from English. Paraphrased in English, the movement of fish causes waves in the water above them and above the grass through which they swim.

Naraya Song 97

Dorothy Tappay
Emily Hill

Buhi	nïgïnt	nana[17]		duan-zi,
Grass	wild geese	?all kinds, together		goslings-(d.a.s.),

Buhi	nïgïnt	nana		duan-zi.
Grass	wild geese	?all kinds, together		goslings-(d.a.s.).

Ba	sï	wia	sï	wia-ni,
Water	?willows	?drag	?willows	?drag-(v.s.),
	[?tall grass]		[?tall grass]	

Ba	sï	wia	sï	wia-ni.
Water	?willows	?drag	?willows	?drag-(v.s.).
	[?tall grass]		[?tall grass]	

As Emily's comments will show, *ba sïwia* could refer to small willows in water, high grass in water, or perhaps even a wet, sandy place. (*Ba:sïwamp*[h] is the word for sand.) Ambiguity of meaning remained unresolved after several conversations. In 1982 the following discussion took place:

EMILY: "*Nigïnd*, that's that large geese, wild geese. It's the song of the little ones. In those grasses (they grow in the water), them high ones—the little geese is in that high grass. I think that's where the little geese was born. Them wild geese, they don't have their little ones around here. They go down in Bull Lake and up there to Din-woody. They have them way back in the mountains where the lakes are. That's where they raise them, the little ones."

JUDY: "What does *ba sï-wia* mean?"

EMILY: "You know them little wild geese, they knock 'em down [the grass], dragging, you know. You know how tall those grasses in the water? That's where those little ones stay. *Sïwia sïwiani*, see, they're in the grass, tall grass. I don't know what they call them. It ain't like these big flat ones around here. It's kind of thin ones like that. Tall ones. I think that's where they hatch their eggs, them wild geese. Water springs, where the water springs. You know, marsh close to the lakes, so they can swim out to the lake. It's a kind of swampy place."

In our 1981 conversation, the following exchange took place:

EMILY: "It's the little trees, small trees where they got sand water under there and that wild geese, the little ones under there."

JUDY: "What does *ba sïwian* mean?"

EMILY: "That means under them trees, little trees. You know, when it's kind of a lot of trees is—[the geese] go under there, *wianikïn,* drag-ging, dragging trees.

"Wild geese, they fly over you and when they fly they say, 'huu huu.' About this time they'd be flying down that way. A little later, in fall, they make noise. They go up to the mountains to the lakes where they have their eggs. But later they'd be coming down, going way down below someplace—lakes down this-a-way.

"You know they really taste good, great big geese. They taste way better than turkey, chicken, and all those. Sage hens, they're way better than them. Same way with the mountain sheep. If you eat it, you want some more. Don't even fill you up. It's the same way that wild geese is."

Naraya Song 98

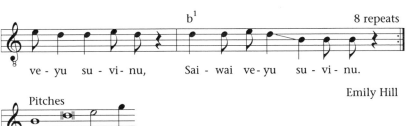

ve - yu su - vi - nu,   Sai - wai ve - yu su - vi - nu.

Emily Hill

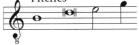

Ban	gara	noiya	havegïn,
Otter	?	mountains	lying,

Ban	gara	noiya	havegïn.
Otter	?	mountains	lying.

Saiwai		?veyu	suvinu,
?Melting snow	?		hissing sound,

Saiwai		?veyu	suvinu,
?Melting snow	?		hissing sound,

Saiwai		?veyu	suvinu.
?Melting snow	?		hissing sound.

EMILY: "Otter mountains, you hear that otter in the water. They got some kind of voice, 'sssssss' [a sibilant with a 'u' sound], when they see somebody. [The sound is] something like the rattlesnake, but louder. *Sikitʰ, sikitʰ*. There's otters by Bull Lake and Big Wind [River]."

This song and Naraya song 99, which follows, are companion songs in their subjects, use of onomatopoeia, mountain setting with melting snow, and problematic translations.

Naraya Song 99

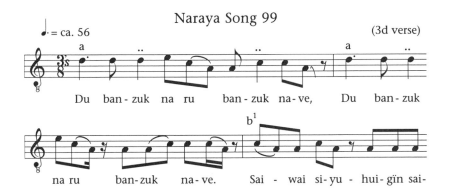

Du ban - zuk na ru   ban - zuk na - ve,   Du ban - zuk

na ru   ban - zuk   na - ve.   Sai - wai si - yu - hui - gïn sai-

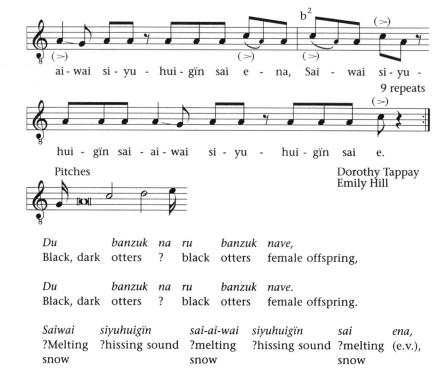

ai - wai si - yu - hui - gïn sai e - na, Sai - wai si - yu -

9 repeats

hui - gïn sai - ai - wai si - yu - hui - gïn sai e.

Pitches

Dorothy Tappay
Emily Hill

Du	banzuk	na	ru	banzuk	nave,
Black, dark	otters	?	black	otters	female offspring,

Du	banzuk	na	ru	banzuk	nave.
Black, dark	otters	?	black	otters	female offspring.

Saiwai	siyuhuigïn	sai-ai-wai	siyuhuigïn	sai	ena,
?Melting snow	?hissing sound	?melting snow	?hissing sound	?melting snow	(e.v.),

Saiwai	siyuhuigïn	sai-ai-wai	siyuhuigïn	sai	e.
?Melting snow	?hissing sound	?melting snow	?hissing sound	?melting snow	(e.v.).

EMILY: "It's the kind like the *banzuku.*"

JUDY: "The otter?"

EMILY: "Yes. The one that's with it, they makes noise. She ones, little ones, they got those *suyuhiugïtsi,* which makes those [noises]. They're in the water and they're looking at the noise."

Naraya Song 100

♪· = ca. 69   (6th verse)

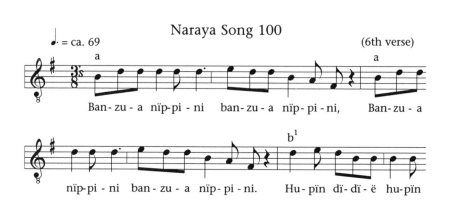

Ban - zu - a nïp - pi - ni ban - zu - a nïp - pi - ni, Ban - zu - a

nïp - pi - ni ban - zu - a nïp - pi - ni.   Hu - pïn dï - dï - ë hu - pïn

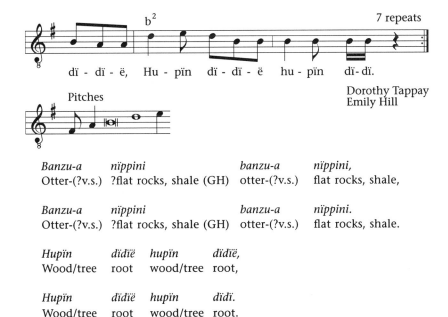

Dorothy Tappay
Emily Hill

Banzu-a	*nïppini*			*banzu-a*	*nïppini,*
Otter-(?v.s.)	?flat rocks, shale (GH)			otter-(?v.s.)	flat rocks, shale,

Banzu-a	*nïppini*			*banzu-a*	*nïppini.*
Otter-(?v.s.)	?flat rocks, shale (GH)			otter-(?v.s.)	flat rocks, shale.

Hupïn	*dïdïë*	*hupïn*	*dïdïë,*
Wood/tree	root	wood/tree	root,

Hupïn	*dïdïë*	*hupïn*	*dïdï.*
Wood/tree	root	wood/tree	root.

EMILY: "Otter in the water and that rock underneath the water. They're the rocks under the water, the ones that look like a sidewalk. That's that. And them trees, it's roots like that. That's where those things [otters] go under and go climbing on the trees; go outside. They're out of the water. They lay on the tree way up there. They see you, they're going to just jump for the water. They're going to dive. Now you can't see it. Well, from there it's going to stick its head out. They're hard to get. They say that's hard to get."[18]

Commentary

The animals found in Naraya songs, and the specific songs in which they appear, are listed in table 3.

Table 3. Animals in Naraya Songs

Ground people: edible   (25)
  13   *Wasüpi,* general term for game animals (elk, deer, antelope, etc.); songs 8, 48, 53, 64, 65, 66, 67, 71, 72, 73
   4   pronghorn antelope bulls, *Antilocapra americana;* songs 62, 63, 69, 70
   1   whitetail deer, *O. virginianis;* song 61

Table 3, continued

2　mountain sheep ewe, *Ovis canadensis;* songs 74, 75
1　buffalo cow, *Bison bison;* song 82
1　white-tailed jackrabbit, *Lepus townsendii companius;* song 78
1　black-tailed jackrabbit, *Lepus californicus;* song 79
2　woodchuck, *marmota flaviventris* (yellow-bellied marmot); songs 76, 77

Ground people: nonedible (3)
2　fox ?kit, *Vulpex velor,* or ?red mountain, *Vulpex macrouros;* songs 80, 81
1　mountain lion, *Felis hippolestes;* song 8

Animal young, principally game animals (10)
4　*wasüpi* (game animals); songs 8, 66, 71, 72
2　antelope; songs 69, 70
1　otter; song 99
1　ducklings; song 12
1　goslings; song 97
1　White-tailed ptarmigan; song 90

Sky people (16)[a]
4　eagles (bald), *Halaectus leucocephalos;* songs 6, 35, 93, 94
2　redwing blackbirds; songs 88, 89
2　Brewer's blackbird; songs 84, 85
2　*divaiyór* (?); songs 86, 87
1　*yevai* (?); song 83
1　white-tailed ptarmigan; song 90
1　common nighthawk; song 91
2　*huchu,* generic term for "bird"; songs 17, 92
1　butterfly (?); song 5

Water people: edible (4)
1　*ba nüwïtsi,* or *nüwë,* general term for water people; song 95
1　fish; song 96
1　goose, *Branta canadensis;* song 97
1　duck (?); song 12

Water people: nonedible (3)
3　otter, *Lutra canadenses canadenses;* songs 98, 99, 100

---

a. Eagles are definitely not eaten. I have no information on the other birds listed that leads me to believe that any were eaten.

Animal Taxonomy

"In the beginning there was nothing but water. . . . He [God] called out: 'Water-people, where are you?'" Beaver, Otter, and Muskrat responded to the call, in this creation story told by Shoshones in Idaho. Only Muskrat succeeded in his dive to the bottom, bringing up the mud from which God made the earth and everything on it (Liljeblad 1969:50). Emily's discussion of Naraya song 95 amplifies the Water People category. "*Ba nüwïtsi* means beaver, muskrat, and fish, them ducks, weasel—all those water people," she said.

We see the other two categories of animals in the Owens Valley Paiute telling of the race to Koso Springs. "There were many animals over by the ocean. The ground animals were to have a race with the sun, the stars, the birds, and the other people of the sky. Sun was leader of those in the air, and Fox was leader of the ground animals [Beetle and Frog]" (Steward 1936:436). Environmental habitat, not anatomical structure, is the criterion for animal classification, extending even to include celestial bodies of sun and stars.

Animal names reflect this taxonomy. Gladys Hill pointed out that the Wind River Shoshone name for animals that live in water all start with *ba,* or *pa.* Thus, we have seen *banzuk*[19] for otter in Naraya songs 98–100. Other Wind River Shoshone words in this same vein are *pa´sunuwiyo,* "water snake," and *pa: ´βiʒi,* "weasel" (Shimkin 1947b: 278). Vocabulary reported by Powell reveals the same pattern: otter is *pan-sūk´* in Ute (Powell 1971:172), *pats´ug* in Paviotso (Powell 1971:211); muskrat is *pa-mu´-si* in Paviotso, water snake is *pa-si´-gan* in Ute (Powell 1971:211, 173); trout is *pa´gu* and turtle, *to-pa´-gu,* in Southern Paiute Kaibab (Powell 1971:130).

Wind River Shoshone animal names include a variety of habitats: bat is *hɔ´nɔβic,* "gulch-being," snowshoe rabbit is *wɔŋguraβ* (Shimkin 1947b:276, 277). *Wongovĭ* is the word for pine tree, which, here, is a defining part of the snowshoe's habitat. Likewise the pine squirrel is called *wɔ´ŋgorac* (Shimkin 1947b:278). According to Gladys Hill, the word for mountain-sheep ewe, *mozambia,* or *mu´ʒambia* (Shimkin 1947b:277), derives from *muzare,* the rocky mountain cliffs where the sheep live. (See Naraya song 74.)

There is suggestive evidence that colors associated with environment are part of animal names as well. *Bu* can be "green" and/or "blue" in Wind River Shoshone.[20] It may be that *bu´ipeŋgwi,* "minnow," and *pu: ´yï,* "duck" (Shimkin 1947b:277, 276), begin with reference to the color of water.

Sarah Winnemucca's comment on Paiute training of the young—

"They are taught a great deal about nature; how to observe the habits of plants and animals" (Hopkins [1883] 1969:52)—leads us from habitat to habits of animals, their behavior. Powell reported further subdivisions of Northern Paiute animal taxonomy as follows:

tree climbers	wild cats, squirrels, bears, etc.
diggers (*tu´-hi-mit´*)	badgers, moles
divers (*kwu-mit´*)	beaver, muskrat, mink
wading birds (*kwa-nid*)	
diving and swimming birds (*pŭ-hŭ-kwŭ-min*)	wild geese, swan, ducks, brants
[larger birds] (*Kwit-na*)	eagles, buzzards, hawks, owls
little singing birds (*hu-zi-pa*)	

(Powell 1971:241)

This same orientation for taxonomy appears among the Klamath in Oregon. Spier observes that in shamanistic song texts, "The references to the [animal] spirits . . . are not random but center in some particular characteristic, habit, or association of the animal. Thus, the swimming of the mink, the underground habits of the weasel, woodchuck, and snake" (Spier 1930:133).

My discussion of animal names and their relationship to environment and behavior is an elaboration of what Shimkin has categorized as descriptive animal names. He proposes two other name types used by Wind River Shoshones. One is based on simple stems, usually Uto-Aztecan, and sometimes differentiated according to sex. *Wa:´nz*, "buck antelope," which appears in Naraya songs 62, 69, 70, and *kwa´hari*, "doe antelope," are examples of this type. A third type—*ka:k*, the modern word for crow—uses onomatopoeia (Shimkin 1947b:276).

Taxonomy based on anatomical structure, used in Western biology, is also a part of Great Basin classification. In Powell's list cited above, mammalian divers, such as beaver and muskrat, are in a separate category from nonmammalian swimming birds, such as geese and ducks. Big birds, such as eagles and hawks, are distinct from small birds.[21] Other categories based on the similarity of anatomical structure include cats, animals with horns, and animals with hooves (Catherine Fowler, 1992, personal communication). Mythic brothers, Wolf and Coyote, clearly reflect the biological resemblance between two members of the canine family.

There are also terms that reflect human relationship and perspective regarding animals.[22] Wind River Shoshones use the word *wasüpi* to refer to game animals—the elk, deer, antelope, moose, and mountain sheep—with whom they have a predator-prey relationship. Regarding the Shoshone term *wasüpi,* Fowler writes, "In nearly all the Numic languages, names for game animals appear to derive from what may be older respect names: . . . *wasippi* 'bighorn sheep' from *wasi* 'to kill (dl., pl. obj.)'" (Fowler 1986:96). Clearly, Wind River Shoshones, whose territory is rich in a variety of game, extended this term well beyond mountain sheep. (See Emily's comments for Naraya songs 60, 64, 65, 66, 71–73.) Mountain sheep remain one of many species included in the term.

Finally, Shoshones extend the Great Basin pattern for naming different human populations according to diet (for example, Pine Nut Eaters or Salmon Eaters), using that method also to name animal populations in relation to their diets. Wind River Shoshones call chicken hawks, *gu 'iarïka,* "chicken eater," and buzzards, *do 'gwarïka* "[? rattlesnake] eater" (Shimkin 1947b:276). The same naming principle applies equally to human and animals; there is no differentiation between the two. I suggest that it is another reflection of a close identity of people with animals.

Animals and Diet

The animals that inhabit Naraya songs were essential elements in Shoshone environment and diet. As Shimkin noted, "Ecology and economy in the broadest sense are synonymous. Both describe the total relation between culture and environment" (Shimkin 1947b:279). Shoshones and other Basin people subsisted on hunting and gathering. For all, the ratio of plant to animal food in the diet depended on local environments and historical factors, notably the impact of European immigration and migration on native people, environments, and the cultures they supported.

The diet of many Basin cultures was derived predominantly from plants. Fowler makes this point in her chapter on Great Basin subsistence (1986:91–93). Steward made the same point in his earlier study, noting that annual migrations for food were for plants, not animals (Steward 1938:33). At the same time, animals were an important dietary supplement and for some groups comprised a larger part of the diet than plant foods (Callaway, Janetski, and Stewart 1986:340, 341; Fowler 1986:91, 92; Murphy and Murphy 1986:293). Thus it was for Wind River Shoshones in the prereservation period. Their more easterly geographic territory provided a rich diversity of plant and animal life. Shimkin's study "Wind River Shoshone Ethnogeography" (Shimkin 1947b) focuses on this prereservation period. Figure 4 reproduces a chart in which Shimkin presented the Shoshones' yearly calendar of locality, social groupings, principal foods

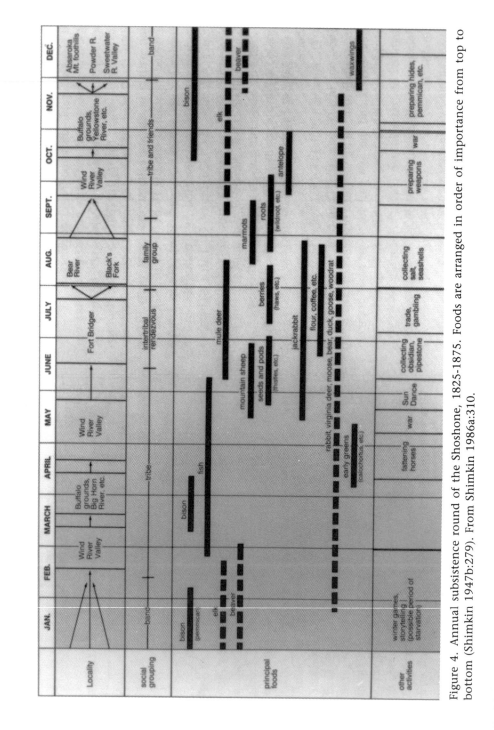

Figure 4. Annual subsistence round of the Shoshone, 1825-1875. Foods are arranged in order of importance from top to bottom (Shimkin 1947b:279). From Shimkin 1986a:310.

harvested, and cultural activities. In commentary about animals in Shoshone diet, Shimkin added explanatory material to supplement this chart. "Staples were the bison, fish (especially trout), elk, beaver, and mule deer. Major but occasional were the antelope, jackrabbit, mountain sheep, marmot, sage hen. Accessories were the Virginia deer, moose, bear, duck, goose, cottontail, badger, snowshoe rabbit, ground squirrel, and wood rat. The bobcat or lynx, mink, otter, and weasel had value as fur, but were not eaten" (Shimkin 1947b:265).[23]

Although the bison was the greatest resource, difficulties after 1840 interfered with hunting success. This was, in part, a consequence of competition and hostilities from other tribes. However, as Shimkin noted, "The primary limitation was the vulnerability of their horses. These, on one hand, quickly consumed available fodder in short-grass prairies; on the other, [the horses] could not be too widely dispersed for fear of theft. In consequence, the Shoshone could rarely gain as much as half their annual food supply from the buffalo" (Shimkin 1986a:317). Elsewhere, Shimkin wrote:

> Use of the antelope, jack rabbit, mountain sheep, marmots, sage hen, and waxwings was characterized by irregular peaks and long periods of nonoccurrence. All of these are gregarious and somewhat migratory; none are large enough or numerous enough to allow any considerable reserve to be built up from a mass slaughter. Thus the antelope could be caught effectively only in surrounds, as it was too fast even for horses. But a single killing would cut down the population for years. The jack rabbit waxed and waned in numbers, increasing a dozen-fold one year over the other. This undependability, plus the difficulty of preserving rabbit meat, made the animal only casually valuable. Mountain sheep necessitated arduous and dangerous climbs in summer; in winter, however, snowshoed hunters could trap them in the deep snow (this was the Sheep Eater specialty). Marmots were a prized tidbit in the summer and early fall. (Shimkin 1947b:268)[24]

Reservation life drastically altered Shoshone subsistence; the U.S. government worked at changing buffalo hunters into farmers and ranchers. Early successful crops in 1872 and cattle issued to the people had declined by 1886 for a variety of reasons. Simultaneously, the number of buffalo killed between 1882 and 1885 plummeted to 10 from 2,400. Reduction in government rations of beef and other staples as well as sickness added to the hardship of this same period in the late nineteenth century and on into the early twentieth century (Shimkin 1942:453–55).

My own intensive work with five Shoshone women, whose birth dates span the period from 1911 to 1959, reveals continuities of diet and hunting from prereservation life. Emily is a case in point. She hunted and ate woodchuck and prairie dog (*?Uinta,* "ground squirrel") as supplement to the cows, pigs, chickens, and turkeys that she raised. Angelina Wagon, born in 1921, recalled her grandfather's hunting deer, elk, mountain sheep, antelopes, pheasants, quails, rabbits, and jackrabbits. She and her grandfather also hunted small game on their land. "We had a lot of prairie dogs up there. He'll hold that shovel down and get all the water on this side and let it go. And then it'll go in there and flush 'em out. That's what the old man used to do, flush them prairie dogs out. People like those. They used to be really fat. It tastes good. I like prairie dog" (Vander 1988:53).[25] Despite this interest in prairie dogs, these animals do not appear in Emily and Dorothy's Naraya songs.

Hunting in the fall for game animals, *wasüpi,* is still common practice. Fresh and dried moose, elk, and antelope meat is served on many occasions. The hides from game animals are equally important, transformed through a labor-intensive process into soft, supple buckskin used for clothing and beadwork.

Food, place, time of year, and people are all embraced in Wind River Shoshone and Great Basin names for one another. Regarding animals, the hunter incorporated the name of the hunted as the distinguishing element. One can generalize Liljeblad's comments on Shoshones of Idaho beyond Idaho. "The Shoshone made it a point of geographic, or rather ethnographic, order to refer to the prevailing food habits within a sub-area when naming the indigenous population collectively. There is hardly a native term for any principal food throughout the common area which does not occur in these names" (Liljeblad 1957:54).

Some names that referred to animals were, *agáideka,* "salmon eaters"; *péngwideka,* "fish eaters"; *yáhandeka,* "ground-hog eaters"; *kámedeka,* "rabbit eaters"; and *túkudeka,* "sheep eaters" (Liljeblad 1957:54, 55, 113). Scholarly literature is rife with permutations of these as well as others. There are *Kuyuidökadö,* "black sucker eaters," and *Pakwidökadö,* "chub eaters" (Stewart 1939:138, 142); *kidü-dökadö,* "woodchuck eaters" (Stewart 1941:365); and *Duhu'teyatikad,* "deer-eaters" (Kelly 1932:72). Often scholars include information on the specific geographic area implied and understood by users of the designations. The *kámedeka* in Liljeblad's publication live in the area between the Snake River and Great Salt Lake, and the *péngwideka* are fish eaters of Bear River.

Comanches, Shoshones who lived on the Southern Plains from the early eighteenth century, maintained this same naming pattern. One of their divisions was *Ko´tso-tĕ´ka,* "Buffalo eaters," another, the *Kwa´hari* or *Kwa´hădi,*[26] "Antelopes." Mooney explains that the Antelopes received their name because they "frequented the prairie country and the staked plains" (Mooney [1896] 1991:1045). They shared antelope terrain, presumably hunted antelopes, and these associations became their identification.

The following comments by Liljeblad point to the fluid nature of names for people, a reflection of migratory patterns set in motion by seasonal appearance of plants and animals. "Nowhere among Northern Shoshoni did these or other names relating to special foods denote clearly defined local groups or individual bands. Rather, they referred to regional resources utilized by people who might travel widely. An individual, a family, or an entire band, could be named differently at different times according to temporary whereabouts or to the seasons and the corresponding foods" (Liljeblad 1957:56). Buffalo eaters, mounted migratory hunters of the Plains, became elk eaters when they resided in northwest Wyoming (Liljeblad 1957:55–56). These names took on nuances of status among groups. Liljeblad continues, "Indeed, as band organization and class distinction evolved, these terms sometimes came to indicate a person's social standing. As a mode of expression, 'buffalo eaters' became synonymous with 'well-to-do people'; a 'buffalo eater' would rank socially above a 'salmon eater,' as would a 'big-salmon eater'" (Liljeblad 1957:56). Horses were status markers. Buffalo eaters who possessed horses called people with few or no horses "mountain sheep eaters" (Liljeblad 1957:93).

At the same time, Liljeblad vehemently debunks literature on the *túkudeka,* Mountain Sheep Eaters, that portrays them as disorganized, impoverished, even renegades. "Quite to the contrary, the mountaineers were much better off than other Shoshoni, save the buffalo-hunters. The Fort Hall Bannock, who pitied the poor seed-gatherers in the western desert, respectfully referred to the mountain Shoshoni as 'hunters of big game'" (Liljeblad 1957:95).

Mountain Sheep

Mountain sheep is the subject of Naraya song 74, which prompted Emily's long discourse on the joys of eating mountain sheep. I turn now to connections that link Mountain Sheep Eaters, mountain sheep, and the Naraya.

Descendants of Wind River Shoshones today derive from a variety of groups or bands that coalesced around Chief Washakie in the nineteenth century. One such group was known as Sheep Eaters.[27] Polly

Shoyo, a Wind River Shoshone woman born around 1845, told Shimkin that the *Dukurka*[28] (Mountain Sheep Eaters) had two special dances. One was the Bear Dance. "The other special *dukurka* dance was the *Narayar*, or *Round Dance* [my emphasis of Round Dance]. It is now called the Ghost Dance" (Shimkin 1937). Mountain Sheep Eaters brought with them one particular tradition of the ancient Great Basin Round Dance.

During my fieldwork I received information about Togwotee, a well-known Sheep Eater who lived on the Wind River Reservation, that reinforces the Naraya–Mountain Sheep Eater connection. Richard Engavo was well into his eighties when he told an anecdote about Togwotee:

RICHARD: "Naraya songs was very different, you know. It's just like a dance, but the real old ones that used to dream that, they said they that for the people that's gone so they could come back. That was that dance. One ole man, he was going to make them believe that there is something to that. So I guess he—that was old Togwotee—he's the one. They said they was having a *Round Dances* [my emphasis] and he was kind of with them ones that's have that, in that belief. I guess one time he went and got old rotten wood. He took all that rotten stuff—the top was alright—rotten stuff out, that loose stuff, he push it out. He must of made it just part of it. And he made a hole and he cut eyes in it, where the nose is and the mouth. He must of made some kind of a thing in it so it would hold up that light, I guess, in there—candle. He put that in brush somewhere where he lived. I believe close where they have that Naraya—where they see it themselves. I guess there was a Naraya. And they saw that. Light down in the eyes, somebody down that. And then he told them, 'You people dance hard.' He said, 'The dead is coming back. That's the leader over there.'" [*Richard laughed.*]

JUDY: "He fooled them."

RICHARD: "Old Togwotee."

Richard, himself, did not believe in the Naraya because he noticed that it did not prevent illness. On the contrary, he felt that winter performance caused colds. Although the anecdote may be apocryphal and the product of humorous fantasy, nevertheless, it remains significant on two counts: first, the particular identification of Togwotee, a Sheep Eater, with the Naraya, and second, a previous focus of the religion on the resurrection of the dead—a vanished element in Emily's latter-day Naraya belief.

Hultkrantz interviewed some of the descendants of Mountain Sheep Eaters on the Wind River Reservation from 1948 to 1958. I quote from his characterization of who they were and their way of life:

By Sheepeaters we mean here the aboriginal pre-horse population of Shoshonean stock who occupied wide areas of the mountains and valleys of south-western Montana, eastern Idaho and north-western Wyoming. Their Shoshonean neighbors called them *tukudika,* "eaters of meat," that is, the meat of the wild mountain or bighorn sheep, *Ovis canadensis.* These sheep roamed the mountains and foothills. "Sheepeater" was not a name designating a particular tribe or self-governing group but a label to characterize all those Shoshoni who lived on mountain sheep and hunted sheep on foot. . . .

It is the Sheepeaters of Wyoming that will be dealt with here. . . .

Before they were placed on reservation in the 1870s Sheepeater Indians were found in the Yellowstone Park area, the Absaroka and Wind River ranges, the Owl Creek and—possibly—the Bighorn mountains. . . .

The Sheepeaters were gatherers, hunters and fishermen, but first of all hunters. They followed the mountain sheep on their seasonal migrations: in the summer, up to the highest mountain cliffs, and in the winter, down to the valleys and foothills. The hunters were equipped with bow and arrows and they loaded the packs on their dogs or on travois drawn by dogs. The dogs were also used in tracking down the game animals. (Hultkrantz 1981a:36–37)[29]

Hultkrantz noted that "although other animals were also hunted, such as bison, elk and deer, bighorn constituted mainly the staple game. It provided the Indians with food, materials for bows and possible snowshoes, and clothing" (Hultkrantz 1981a:37–38).

Duk, the linguistic root for the various forms of the term for Sheep Eater (for example, *Dukurka, Tukudeka*), literally means "meat" or "flesh." Because meat, for Sheep Eaters, meant the meat of their most important game—mountain sheep—one word became synonymous with the other. It reflected the importance of sheep to hunter and to those it fed (Liljeblad 1957:55).

Recent assessments of earlier patterns of subsistence in the Great Basin as a whole suggest bighorn sheep were "very important animals to native hunters and undoubtedly more common than formerly suspected" (Fowler 1986:79). Of course, this was true only in mountainous areas with habitat for the sheep.

Research by George Frison documents the early 1990s discovery of trapping complexes constructed by Sheep Eaters in Wyoming and elsewhere in the Central Rocky Mountains. Frison has analyzed the wooden remnants of these protohistoric traps in conjunction with the study of mountain sheep behavior in order to recreate the operation of the traps (Frison 1992).

Beyond the physical strategy for hunting mountain sheep are other cultural practices that accompany and abet the process. We see this among the Chemehuevi, for whom the Mountain Sheep Song belonged to a specific group, which passed it down through male inheritance from generation to generation. Ownership of the song brought with it territorial rights: song defined a man's kinship and his hunting preserve. Laird recorded other cultural characteristics of the song:

> Also the song described the hunter's equipment and the way in which these accoutrements moved in response to the swift and rhythmic movements of his body; and along with the character and "feel" of the land it conveyed a poignant sympathy for the animal hunted and a sense of the relationship between the hunter and hunted. From the songs and from the Chemehuevis' attitude toward them one learns that the connection between a man, his song, and his mountain (or his land, as the case might be) was sacred and unbreakable, and that the animal he pursued was included in this sacred unity. (Laird 1976:10)

In 1910 Sapir recorded and transcribed a fragment of a Mountain Sheep Hunting Song (no. 75), which Southern Paiutes sang the night before going hunting, along with other songs of the same genre. The text of the song and Sapir's commentary on its use seem suggestively similar to the power of antelope-charming songs and ritual.

> Keep standing up straight,
> White faced ones stand up in a row on the mountain divide,
> Stand up in a row.
> Keep standing up straight, keep standing up straight.
> (Sapir 1994:626–27)

Sapir commented in his notes on this song, "Makes mountain sheep come together to one place, so as to be easily rounded up" (Sapir 1994:627).

Mountain sheep motifs in rock art throughout the Great Basin area also bear testimony to the importance of the animal. However, interpretations of the meaning and function of these motifs differ markedly. Some scholars suggest that sheep moving into V-shaped elements represent hunting corrals described in the ethnographic literature. Other scenes with sheep and anthropomorphic figures might have been used in connection with rituals for hunting game (Schaafsma 1986:220–21, 226).

In contrast to these interpretations, Whitley argues that mountain sheep motifs in the Great Basin stem from the vision quest and, specifically, the acquisition of weather control (Whitley 1994:362–64). He explains that "not only did the weather-control shaman have the mountain sheep as his helper, much of his paraphernalia was derived from the sheep, too, further emphasizing the (supernatural) relationship between the two" (Whitley 1992:22). Whitley supports his thesis with data published by Kelly. She wrote that "a mountain sheep singer always dreamed of rain, a bull-roarer, and a quail tufted cap of mountain-sheep hide" (Kelly 1932:142). Kelly made the sheep-weather connection even more explicit, noting: "It is said that rain falls when a mountain sheep is killed. Because of this some mountain sheep dreamers thought they were rain doctors" (Kelly 1936:139).

Great Basin people not only sang about sheep and drew them on rocks; they read them into their stars of winter, the proper time for telling myths. Northern Paiutes recount how a mother, father, and child are transformed into mountain sheep, seen as three stars, probably a reference to Orion's belt. In another example, a group of women turn into sheep and appear in the sky as a cluster of stars in the east (Kelly 1932:154; Kelly 1938:429; Fowler 1990).

Rabbits

The proportion of plants, large game, and small game in the diet of various groups varied depending upon the environment. As is evident in the subsistence calendar chart for Wind River Shoshones prior to settlement on the reservation (see fig. 4), bison and other large game were major food sources. Rabbits and other small game (as well as a variety of plant foods) supplemented a diet already rich in protein. This was not the case for other Great Basin people, many of whom depended, in large part, on plant foods. Antelope were hunted "but such slaughter so reduced their number that years might be required to restore the herd" (Steward 1938:33). Thus the importance of rabbits and other small game, an important source of protein that could reproduce rapidly and replenish its population (Fowler 1986:82; Kelly and Fowler 1986:370; Steward 1938:33).

Two types of jackrabbit were the object of the hunt, and both make individual appearances in Naraya songs 78 and 79. In the Basin Plateau area, the gray blacktail jackrabbit, *Lepus californicus*,"was very important throughout its range, which included the entire area except parts of Idaho and northeastern Utah. The whitetail jackrabbit, *L. townsendii* Bachman, had a more restricted range within the area. The jackrabbit now occurs in enormous herds, having increased both in numbers and range in recent years. Natively, however, it seems to have been sufficiently numerous to have been of major importance" (Steward 1938:38).

As Steward described the rabbit hunt, a group of people would drive rabbits into a semicircular fence made of grass cord. Others within the enclosed area would kill the rabbits as they fled or were ensnared (Steward 1938:38–39). Drawing on this experience, Surprise Valley Paiutes interpreted the Big Dipper as constellation as follows: "Stars of the Big Dipper (*ta noa´di*) are Indians driving rabbits into a net; 'the two [rabbits] in front don't know where they are going'" (Kelly 1932:154).[30]

Rabbits "not only afforded considerable meat when taken in communal hunts, but provided skins which were utilized for the all-important Shoshonean garment, the rabbit-skin blanket or robe" (Steward 1938:38). In a later study of Shoshones in Idaho, Steward discussed the extension of blacktail jackrabbits into Idaho, which led to communal rabbit hunts there as well (Steward 1943a:267). Emily's comments on Naraya song 79 reveal that the range of the blacktail jackrabbits did not extend into Wyoming, which leads her to deduce the origin of the song. She said, "That's a song from Idaho. I know [*du*, 'black'] *gëm*, black-tailed jackrabbits. They're from Idaho. They're not from here."

In contrast, the whitetail jackrabbit in Naraya song 78 was hunted and eaten by Wind River Shoshones (Shimkin 1947b:277).[31] Emily's comments here indicate this to be true both in Wyoming and among the Shoshones and Bannocks in Idaho. Her difficulty in identifying the origin of this song stems not from the type of jackrabbit mentioned but from small differences in linguistics.

Cottontail rabbits were also hunted in the Basin and by Wind River Shoshones, although customarily by individuals rather than the community (Fowler 1986:82; Steward 1938:39).[32]

The communal hunt for rabbits in the fall was another special occasion in the Basin, often preceded by the pine nut harvest and the attendant Round Dance that both harvest and hunt made possible. Shoshones of Carson River Basin in Nevada continued to hold communal rabbit hunts until as recently as 1964 (Shimkin 1970:173). Shimkin tells us that "before setting out on the hunt, the people had a Rabbit dance (qamu no'qa') which was held all day" (Shimkin 1970:185). Further, we learn that Steve Dick, the "boss" of the occasion, called the people to dance for five days, the special number for many Basin people and the number of days for other Round Dance occasions, Wovoka's Ghost Dance, and the *Naraya*.[33] Even the duration of the rabbit drive, itself, was five days for eight of fourteen Northern Paiute groups (Stewart 1941:368).

Unlike the involvement of shamans and shamanistic ritual in antelope charming and that inferred from rock art regarding mountain sheep hunting, there is an absence of shamanistic activity associated with rabbit drives (Fowler 1986:268; Park 1938:139). Steward's description of the Rabbit Dance by Lemhi Shoshones suggests its playful nature:

> [Lemhi Shoshones] claimed not to have had it natively, saying that they learned it at Fort Hall when moving there in 1909. They thought Fort Hall had received it from the west. It was called *kahmu* (jackrabbit) *nukaiyu* (dance). Several men dressed in breechclouts, carrying mock bows and arrows, their faces and bodies painted with horizontal white stripes, and wearing false penises, large cloth rabbit ears, tails and other comic features. They performed individually, pretending to shoot spectators. They seized coins held by spectators in split sticks and placed their loot on a blanket in the center. They were called crazy rabbits and spectators pretended to strike them with sticks, whereupon they fell down. A "doctor" carrying a feather would then revive them. The singer stood in the center beside the "doctor." (Steward 1943a:289)

Shoshones and Bannocks of Fort Hall performed their variants of this dance, and both groups considered it to be an old dance. If there were shamanistic or religious aspects of this occasion, Steward's informants were silent about it.

More will be said of rabbits in the later section on animals, myth, and power.

Animal Young and Fertility

Fertility of animals, expressed in references to animal young, is an important Naraya topic. It appears in ten songs: numbers 8, 12, 66, 69, 70, 71, 72, 90, 97, and 99. Recall Emily's words, quoted earlier: "Everything: fish, anything. Sing for them. Let them, our elk and deer and all them. That's what it's for. It ain't any kind of song." The Naraya sings of animal young to promote animal young.

Shoshone and Paiute names for the months of the year reflect observation of animal behavior and, especially, the reproductive cycles. Northern Paiute nomenclature translated by Stewart (1941:445) includes:

Red-butte dwellers
    November, deer-breeding month
    December, buck-deer-stands-for-week-on-south-side-of canyon-
       month
    January, tracks-threw-out-on-one-side-month
Sagebrush-mountain dwellers
    November, deer-breeding-month
    January, jack-rabbit-urine-on-snow-month
    February, first-young-jack-rabbit-month

Western Shoshones from various locations in Nevada mark their calendar according to these events:

February, coyote young born
March, fence-antelope corral
April, mountain sheep lamb
May, antelope young born
June, fawn born
July, fat month (i.e., game)
October, deer breed
November, breeding.
　　　(Steward 1941:268–69)

The pattern continues with the Lemhi Shoshones of Idaho.

October, elk breeding moon or month
December, deer breeding moon, or month.
　　　(Steward 1943a:291)

Likewise, the Grouse Creek Shoshones of Utah:

April, coyote pups moon, or month
May, female mountain sheep moon, or month
June, antelope young moon, or month
August, fawn moon, or month.
　　　(Steward 1943a:291)

I have already given Lowie's account of Wind River Shoshone names for the seasons or months of the year and pointed out how these divisions were, in part, determined by the state of water in the environment. The presence of water in various forms was but one of many important events in the natural world. The time when animals bear young, the first appearance of vegetation, and the concordance of these events with the state of water were all closely observed and expressed. Thus, Lowie reports, there were the following two divisions of the year:

Wolves have young and ice gone from creeks
mountains sheep have their young and grass is beginning to come up.
　　　(Lowie 1924a:311)

I have cited native names for the months of the year in this chapter in order to suggest the importance of specific animals in Wind River Shoshone and Great Basin cultures. I will do likewise in the next chapter, suggesting there that for some groups, plants are even more important than animals, as indicated by the number of months whose names derive from plants. I have given all the published accounts for the Wind River Shoshones' calendar, both Lowie's listing of their own nomenclature and Shimkin's information concerning many facets of subsistence. Because I realize the inherent danger of distortion when one presents only selectively from data, I provide, in note 34, the complete native calendars for at least some of the other groups cited in both chapters.[34]

Animals, Myth, and Power

In Great Basin myth there were no dividing lines in nature. Animals, plants, and rocks were all "people." That is, all spoke one language.[35]

Language is at the center of two stories that account for the break with this mythic past. Lowie gives a Paviotso, or Northern Paiute, version in which "all the wild animals, rocks, greasewood, and so on, were like persons and spoke the Indian language. After the Indians had been made, then birds and beasts got wild, while the Indians used language and killed wild animals. They got their language from the animals. Rabbits, antelope, and other game of that sort belonged to men; ducks, swans, and geese belonged to the woman with vaginal teeth" (Lowie 1924b:228).[36]

Gladys Hill presented a Wind River Shoshone explanation for the end of a universal language and mythic times.

GLADYS: "See, that's what she's [Emily] talking about is water people. See, these [songs] are so old, she says, maybe two hundred [years], maybe more than that. At that time, you know, there was a story. You know, just like they do fairytales in school—that all the—everything talked, one language. Everything talked, like the birds. Oh, just everything—the coyotes. They say the coyote's the one that suggested somebody dying, you know. And he got it. His son was the first one to die. And then when he cried around, cried around, why he wanted to change it. But they told him, no, you know. And then that's how the birds get their colors too, you know.

"But what I was told [was] that they were trying to build a stairway to Heaven, you know. Everybody, they spoke the same language—trying to build a stairway up there. They were so far with that stairway that—there's one person or somebody, anyway, that talking dirty—using dirty language. And they said they went to bed and the next morning they couldn't understand one another. They say that's how it was. I always wonder how would it be if they finished that stairway? Maybe we wouldn't be here. Maybe it'd be altogether different."

JUDY: "But how does it have to do with these water people? They all talked, you mean?"

GLADYS: "Uh huh. Just like, long time ago, people related them. Like, maybe the otter'd be your uncle. Maybe weasel'd be your brother, Coyote be your uncle. And then he'd say, 'uncle,' to somebody else, you know. That's the way they were. They understood each other and could talk. Everybody understood one another. Well, too, you read in the Bible, too, like that, too, and I always think, 'Where did that come from?' And this is so old. It's got to be way before the Bible."[37]

In the first Northern Paiute account of the end of mythic times, given above, the power of speech passed from animals to humans and with it the dominance of one over the other. The story also describes an interesting subdivision of the hunt according to sex—"ground" people (rabbits and game animals) were the men's domain and "water" people (water fowl), the women's. In the Shoshone version, it is unclear whether humans were also present with other animals in mythic times. (Gladys Hill's comments suggests this to be the case.) Although Gladys was inspired to tell this myth in order to connect its antiquity with that of the Naraya, it also brings out two sharp differences between myth and the Naraya. First, animals do not speak in Naraya songs, although clearly the song texts themselves are felt to affect animals—indeed, every part of the natural world. Second, reference to "dirty" language with its bawdy suggestiveness and tinge of humor—commonplace elements in Shoshone myth—is totally absent in Emily's Naraya repertoire and her discussion of it.[38]

Despite the passing of this mythic past, a cultural remembrance of it continues to color emotional responses to the natural world. A subliminal sense of kinship—a feeling that the otter might have been your ancestor's uncle—remains.

Animals in some Naraya songs carry subtle allusions to the exploits of animal characters in myth. In Naraya song 71, the mention of dust raised by game animals coming down the mountains is reminiscent of the crucial scene in which Coyote liberated game animals for all time. In some earlier mythic time, Wolf secured all game animals in a cave, killing one as needed and always carefully shutting the cave after each kill. Coyote had no luck in hunting and asked Wolf how he was so successful. Wolf told Coyote where the animals were kept and cautioned him on the importance of shutting the cave before leaving. Coyote ignored this caution, and thus all the game animals were released. "Wolf looked out from his house and saw dust all over the mountains. All the game was gone. He knew that Coyote had let them escape" (Steward 1943b:298). As a consequence of Coyote's carelessness, people must spend much time and energy to hunt the game that has scattered far and wide over the earth.

The combination of sun and rabbits in Naraya songs 78 and 79 carries overtones of an important myth, in this case, about Cottontail/Jackrabbit and Sun. Jackrabbits and cottontails appear in myth as Kom, the Progenitor of the Large Rabbit nation (jackrabbits), or as *Tov-wots*, Progenitor of the Little Rabbit Nation (cottontails) (Powell 1971:89, 77). Of the two, it is usually *Tov-wots*, Cottontail, who is the important hero, even claimed, in one place, to be the father of the *Shin-au-av* brothers, Wolf and Coyote (Powell 1971:78). In one of Cottontail's most heroic exploits, he kills Sun and then creates a new Sun from the old Sun's gallbladder.[39] In the Northern Paiute version of the story, Cottontail's motive is to secure more daylight hours for hunting (Kelly 1938:424). In a Gosiute Shoshone version, the need was to set a new Sun higher in the sky so that it could no longer burn up vegetation and people (W. Miller 1972:46–51). Cottontail's speech to the new Sun exemplifies both the direct address between parts of the natural world and the potency of speech: "'You, Sun. You're not going to be like that anymore. You are going to be good. You are going to be good. You are going to give light all over the world. . . . You will be good, and under you people on this earth will gather all kinds of seeds and eat them. No more will they die from heat. Everything will be good,' he said" (W. Miller 1972:51). As a consequence of this exploit, Cottontail got burned, which accounted for his brown coat, his dark "stocking," and the color of the back of his neck (Kelly 1938:424; W. Miller 1972:51).

The rabbits in Naraya songs 78 and 79 are jackrabbits and not Cottontail of myth. However, Lowie reports a Northern Shoshone myth from Idaho in which Jackrabbit is, in fact, the hero who kills and re-creates Sun (Lowie 1909a:253). Emily believed that Naraya song 78 may have originated in Idaho, and she definitely identified Naraya song 79, with its black-tailed jackrabbit, as an Idaho song. Both texts evoke the mythic confrontation in their presentation of only two images: sun in the first line, jackrabbit in the second. Note, too, the personification of the sun in Naraya song 78, which bears another link to myth and the myth of Jackrabbit/Cottontail killing the Sun. The first line accords the power of speech to the Sun: "Our sun says." Emily added to this personification in her comment that the sun "sees" the jackrabbits running below on earth.

Animals in Great Basin myth are animals *qua* people. Notions about dance, song, speech or thought, dream, and power that appear in the exploits and experience of animals in myth counterpoint Great Basin people in their cultural perception of life and response to it. In myth, we see the Circle/Round Dance as a social occasion used to welcome a visitor, Fox (Steward 1936:434). Views of the Round Dance as a prehunting activity appear in Rat's invitation to Mountain Sheep to join him in a Round Dance. In this case the Round Dance itself and Rat's song are part of his deceitful ploy to attract and then kill Mountain Sheep (Lowie 1924b:194–95; Steward 1943a:284–85).[40] Coming closer to prehunt dances and songs, such as those performed as part of antelope charming, and prehunt songs, such as Buck Skin Joe's (see chapter 1), is the dance performed by Crow, Eagle, Wildcat, Yellow-hammer, and Big Rat. The words in the song that accompanied the dance state, "I am going to shoot mountain-sheep" (Lowie 1924a:214).

Like the weather shaman, animals in myth have power and use it through music and song text: "By means of his flute playing and his singing, Cottontail brought the wind down to the people in the valley" (Steward 1943b:285). In other examples Mallard and Goose sing to bring back light after Coyote destroyed Sun in fire; Owl and Duck sing to dispel stormy weather (Steward 1936:415, 417). Cottontail asks his Brush Rabbit uncles, "'How do you two eat?'" The Brush Rabbits reply, "'We ask it (to come to us) so we can eat.'" The storyteller says, "(I've forgotten the song for that. That has a song.)" (W. Miller 1972: 56).

Also like people, animals in myths have dreams, which are a source of information that dictates rules and behavior in waking life. In one myth all the animals held a council to determine what each should eat. *Ta-vu* (little rabbit) decided that all would go to sleep and let dream be the guide. Those who had good dreams would eat pine nuts; those who did not would have to search for something else to eat. Some who had bad dreams tried to disregard the ruling, but in the end all were forced to follow the predetermined consequence of their dream. Such was its power (Powell 1971:218).

Finally, there is a connection between one mythic explanation for the creation of the world and Naraya–Ghost Dance doctrine. Liljeblad recounts two creation myths of Idaho Shoshones. The so-called "Earth-diver myth," with its special involvement of Water People, has been mentioned earlier, in the section on animal taxonomy. In a second creation myth, Wolf creates the world in four layers, one on top of the other. Wolf and Coyote once lived on the top layer and dropped some earth down onto the water of the second layer. Wolf ordered Coyote to jump down onto the second layer and fashion a second earth. "'Now,' Coyote said, 'this will be enough earth for people to live on. It will last for two thousand years. Then it will be destroyed'" (Liljeblad 1969:51). Liljeblad comments, "In this worldview there is also embodied the idea that the world after a period of existence must be destroyed and recreated by the same high-god who created the former one, in this case by Wolf. Likewise, the world that existed before ours was also destroyed with all its inhabitants, whether by water or by fire is a matter of variation" (Liljeblad 1969:51). Ghost Dance and earlier Naraya belief in the destruction of this world and the promise of a new one dovetails with this mythic account of a series of worlds.

Even after a language barrier came to separate people and animals, an intimate relationship endured between them. Joe Green, Northern Paiute shaman, speaks of this special relationship in which people receive power from animals. Interestingly, he too alludes to the language barrier that divided people and animals, mythic and modern times. "Indians were put here on this earth with trees, plants, animals, and water, and the shaman gets his power from them. One shaman might get his power from the hawk that lives in the mountains. Another may get his power from the eagle, the otter, or the bear. A long time ago all the animals were Indians (they could talk). I think that is why the animals help people to be shamans" (Park 1938:16).

A Northern Paiute man described how the shaman receives power from animals. "Anyone can get to be a shaman by dreaming. In the dreams, spirits such as those from the eagle, bear, owl, snake, antelope, deer, mountain sheep, mole, or falling star appear. The spirit that comes in the dreams is the shaman's power. It helps him to doctor sick people (Harry Sampson)" (Park 1938:16). The animal seen in this dream-vision experience is often referred to as a guardian spirit.[41]

Animals and animal power help the shaman retrieve souls and bring them back to their body and life. The song text of a Northern Paiute shaman demonstrates this, saying that a "person's spirit emerges, white weasel carries it crosswise in its mouth, [through] sky hole at rolling descends" (Natches 1923:259).

Animals also have souls, which after death travel to the land of the dead. Shamans shunt human souls back from death to life. Conversely, in antelope charming (described in chapter 1) they capture antelope souls to bring them to their death; hunters merely finish the job. Steward reported various accounts of this process by Nevada Shoshones. The shaman "captured antelope souls (*suəp:*, breath) so that they were already 'dead' when they entered the corral and could not be frightened" (Steward 1941:220).

Song and song text lured the antelope souls. "The shaman rubbed a notched stick tied to the back of a tanned antelope hide . . . , which was stuffed with a grass (*watsip*) to resemble an antelope, and sang for about two hours. His song [text] was [referring to] a kind of brush (*sisovi*) that antelope eat and about young antelope and their food. People near the shaman also sang. Meanwhile, a line of boys, . . . danced in imitation of antelope. They finally pretended to be very tired, indicating that the shaman had captured the antelopes' souls" (Steward 1941:219).

Commentary by the Northern Paiute man who published the shaman's song quoted previously also implies potency of song and text. "Thus he [the shaman who sang the song about weasel's carrying the soul] shouted, so he sang, the person's soul brought back as he said, so sang" (Natches 1923:259). Some Nevada Shoshones explained the effect of the shaman's song on antelopes and other animals: "by singing, [they could] capture the souls of any animals, making them 'crazy' and easily killed" (Steward 1941:230).[42]

The transfer of power from animals to people takes place on a metaphysical level and is expressed in words and song. But it also takes a physical form, residing even in a part of the animal, and related to specific characteristics of the animal. Voget writes: "'Medicines' [power-endowed objects] varied in construction and in interpretation. Eagle feathers were basic to most medicines, along with weasel and otter hide, for they were 'tough little animals,' and like the eagle, were linked to the Sun Dance. . . . Weasel and otter provided prime war medicines in former times, and the purpose of the Crow Sun Dance was to mobilize medicine for revenge against the enemy" (Voget 1984:253, 253n.17).

These "power" associations with the otter are equally relevant to Wind River Shoshone culture and may explain, at least in part, why otters are the subject of three Naraya songs (numbers 88–90). Certainly dietary interest does not apply here; Shoshones do not eat otter.

Rattles, a standard item for shamans, were imbued with power from their animal parts. Rattles were sometimes made of deer ears filled with pebbles gathered at ant hills (Park 1938:33–34). Wind River Shoshones consider these pebbles as having power endowed with the strength of the ants beneath. Another type of shaman's rattle used deer hooves (Park 1938:33). In the following account of Wind River Shoshone antelope charming, a rattle made with antelope hooves helps the shaman lure antelopes to their deaths.[43]

Equipped with a gourd surrounded by lots of antelope-hooves the medicine-man went up to a pinnacle on the plain from which he could see, at a distance, the shy but curious antelopes. Standing on the hill he shook the gourd and sang antelope songs, ending each one of them with a sound imitating the antelope. As the antelopes in curiosity approached the singer, the members of the tribe, men, women, and children, surrounded them by horse and came closer and closer in circles. Finally, the swift animals could be caught by ropes or with the hand. This was the way the Plains Shoshone hunted antelopes along the Sweetwater. (Hultkrantz 1961:201)

Shamans were by no means the only ones to have visions of animals and to receive power from them. Hultkrantz learned some of the animals and the particular powers they conferred to Wind River Shoshones. Elk gave power (*wapiti-puha*) that protected one from wounds and injuries.[44] The antelope gave "running-medicine" and scouting ability. The jackrabbit gave the ability to run fast and to run on top of the snow. The beaver gave the ability to dam water (Hultkrantz 1956:198).

Buffalo

So far, significantly, the buffalo has been absent from my discussion of animals in relation to myth, language, shamanism, and power. The buffalo is rare in Emily and Dorothy's Naraya repertoire, appearing only in Naraya song 82. This seems an enigma since the buffalo was formerly a mainstay in prereservation days and continues to be respected as a source of power in the contemporary Sun Dance religion. I turn now to the buffalo and Wind River Shoshone culture, with relationship to the topics of my earlier discussion. The enigma will come into sharper focus, but will remain unresolved.

Mooney correctly appraised the importance of the buffalo in Plains life. "The buffalo was to the nomad hunters of the plains what corn was to the more sedentary tribes of the east and south—the living, visible symbol of their support and existence; the greatest gift of a higher being to his children" (Mooney [1896] 1991:980). Even in the mid-twentieth century, some Wind River Shoshones retained memories from nineteenth-century life. Hultkrantz writes, "Buffaloes were . . . until the 1870's richly represented on the Shoshoni hunting grounds. An old informant told me [in 1948] how in her youth the whole valley of the Wind River was filled up with buffaloes as far as the eyes could see" (Hultkrantz 1961:199).

In 1937 Polly Shoyo, a Wind River Shoshone woman born around 1845, described to Shimkin a type of shamanism used for buffalo. It reflects a fascinating blend of Plains and Great Basin traditions, using song, dance, and speech in ways reminiscent of antelope charming and other prehunting ceremonies already described. Shimkin wrote,

Another way to get game magically was this: when the people were starving, a medicine man (*pohogant,* i.e., holder of supernatural power, DBS) would be helped by four women and three men to bring game. The seven sat and sang; he danced all night long. They would smoke a pipe all around at first (it was not offered to the directions); then they sang four smoking songs, while the shaman danced. There were no rattles, no drum. He danced back and forth. Once in a while he would stop and say: 'Now, I want you to bring a lot of buffaloes.' Then they smoked, sang four songs, and smoked again. The next morning the shaman would tell the people that he had found the buffaloes. They were at a given place. The people went there, found them, killed them, and were saved. (Shimkin 1937)[45]

The importance of the buffalo in everyday life took on religious significance for Wind River Shoshones and other Plains tribes, with symbolic expression in the Sun Dance religion. The origin of the Wind River Shoshone Sun Dance religion itself involved the buffalo, who appeared in the vision of Yellow Hand. The buffalo was a messenger from Our Father, and in Yellow Hand's vision it imparted all information concerning the Sun Dance. "Our Father had sent it because the buffalo was foremost of all animals and superior to them all" (Hultkrantz 1987:68). Or, as an elderly Shoshone man expressed it to me, "He's the chief of everything on earth."

Hultkrantz, on at least two occasions, noted the importance of the buffalo, writing that "the Plains Sun Dance elevated two animals to a lofty supernatural level, the buffalo and the eagle" (Hultkrantz 1961:208) and that "the buffalo head and the eagle stand for two tiers of the universe, earth and sky" (Hultkrantz 1987:71).

Given all these associations, the buffalo is a source of power for Sun Dancers. Voget writes, "In the contemporary Sun Dance the buffalo radiates power and is renowned as a giver of good things" (Voget 1984:307).[46] Another anecdote about Yellow Hand brings out both points. Hultkrantz reports that Ben St. Clair said: "'Yellow Hand was gifted. He had a buffalo robe which he sometimes turned inside out. Then he covered his head and body with it and sat down for a while. When he raised himself there was a bunch of goose-eggs where he had been seated'" (Hultkrantz 1968:303).

In this story buffalo power addressed one primary Wind River Shoshone concern, abundance of food. Buffalo power could also address another, relief from illness: it could protect one from measles and smallpox (Hultkrantz 1956:199).

Sun Dancers see the buffalo in their vision. Tom Compton, a Wind River Shoshone Sun Dance chief in the late 1930s, described how a buffalo came to him and turned into a person, talking and giving instructions (Shimkin 1939:154–55). In 1978 I learned that Angelina Wagon's son "once danced in the Sun Dance, and he was getting a vision of a white buffalo running, and he could hear a song far away off—but the Sun Dance singers stopped singing so the vision slipped away, and she feels that because of it he never learned his vision song and wasn't 'blessed'" (Vander 1986:66).

Both visionary experiences add further examples of the transfer of power in words and song. Tom Compton's example turns back the clock to the time of myth when animals were people and could talk.

Yet, contrary to one's expectation, the buffalo barely appears in the myths of Shoshones, even those who subsisted, in large part, on it.[47] From this absence and from the presence of other myths (for example, The Origin of Death; see chapter 2), Lowie concluded that the myth of Idaho and Wyoming Shoshones bore a closer connection to that of the Great Basin and California than to the myth of the Plains (Lowie 1909a:236; Lowie 1923:155–56).

An old medicine man told Lowie that buffaloes do not appear in myth because "'the buffalo was never an Indian'" (Lowie 1909a:236). That is, the buffalo came after the time when animals spoke, too late to seep into myth.

Buffalo were, however, part of Wovoka's Ghost Dance prophecy. Delegates from different Plains tribes visited Wovoka and carried his message back to their people. Porcupine reported to the Northern Cheyenne "that the game and the buffalo would be brought back" (Grinnell 1891:65). Wovoka instructed a delegation of Sioux and Cheyennes that if they should kill a buffalo on their way home, "they must cut off its head and tail and feet and leave them on the ground and the buffalo would come to life again" (Mooney [1896] 1991:821). Members of the delegation testified that this did happen on their return trip. "The story of the revivified buffalo became so widely current as to form the subject of a Kiowa ghost song" (Mooney [1896] 1991: 822).

To return to the original issue: Why is the buffalo so minimally represented in Emily and Dorothy's Naraya repertoire? A likely explanation is that Naraya song texts sing of the natural environment and by the twentieth century, buffaloes were no longer part of it. In fact, this is true even if one moves back further in time to the late nineteenth century. The last major buffalo hunt by Wind River Shoshones took place in 1884 (Shimkin 1939:100).

Even though the buffalo is a rare subject in Naraya songs, note that its presentation in song 82 is congruent with all other Naraya song texts. People do not intrude. The buffalo is envisioned as one part of a healthy ecosystem.

The Sky and Sky People

The appearance of various Sky People (and other birds, like ducks, classified by Emily as Water People) in the Naraya reflects, to some extent, that some were a dietary source. Thus, Wind River Shoshones hunted ducks and geese; these fowl appear, respectively, in Naraya songs 12 (see appendix A) and 97. Bull Lake was identified by Emily and by Murphy (Murphy and Murphy 1960:308) as one place for hunting waterfowl. August and September were the proper time of year, as noted in Shimkin's 1825–75 subsistence calendar.[48]

However, of far greater importance for the Naraya is the power associated with the sky and its "People." The defining characteristics of Sky People come from two sources—their habitat, the sky; and their behavior, song and flight. These defining characteristics are power-laden, for both Great Basin and Plains cultures. Shamanism, health, and weather all take on particular form and meaning in their relationship to sky and its People. Although Emily placed ducks and geese with Water People, I include these Water-Bird People here in my discussion of Sky People. Like Sky People, Water-Bird People have wings, are equally at home in sky and water, and share the defining behavioral characteristics of Sky People—song (albeit "quack" and "honk") and flight.

I begin with the sky, a place of power and the environment of Sky People. The sky is associated with Our Father, *Tam Apo*. A Wind River Shoshone person explained this. "We think about him as the whole sky, he covers the whole world. He is a human being above the sky. His power extends over the whole earth" (Hultkrantz 1956:205). The sky is the realm of the highest power.

Goss (1972:128) has analyzed the relationships among animal, habitat, and associated color in a Ute ecological model, as shown in figure 5. The central triangle represents the sacred mountain in this hierarchy. The eagle sits at the zenith point of the sky. While I do not suggest that Shoshones share the same conceptual model in every regard, I do see Shoshone correspondence to this model in the hierarchical placements of mountain, sky, and eagle.

The sky is the realm of highest power and one that is pure. This latter point appears symbolically in the Wind River Shoshone Sun Dance as discussed in an article written by Lynn and Herman St. Clair for their own people. "Now each time the dancer blows his [eagle-

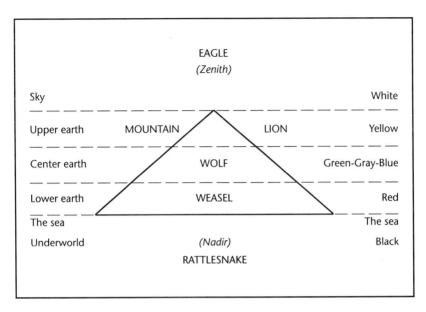

Figure 5. The Ute view of the world. From Goss 1972:128.

bone] whistle, he is praying for the earth to be clean and free from disease, like the air high, up where the eagle flies" (St. Clair and St. Clair 1977).

The sky is home to *Tam Apo,* pure air, eagle (which will be described in detail in the next section) and other birds, lightning, and thunder in a confusing array of power and interrelationships between those who possess the power. Two commonplace observations underlie the following discussion of weather and birds: The sky is the source or origin of weather—rain or sunshine—and birds are the only animals with power to fly up in the sky.

The Thunderbird is a single religious entity into which sky, weather, power, and bird are fused. Lowie notes that in North America there was widespread belief in the Thunderbird, a large bird who caused thunder. It was an important figure in Plains religion and appeared in the text of Plains Ghost Dance songs (Lowie 1924c:197, 268). Mooney provided details about the conception of the Thunderbird, writing that "among the Algonquian tribes of the east, the Sioux, Cheyenne, Arapaho, Kiowa, Comanche, and prairie tribes generally, as well as among those of the northwest coast and some parts of Mexico, thunder and lightning are produced by a great bird, whose shadow is the thunder cloud, whose flapping wings make the sound of thunder, and whose flashing eyes rapidly opening or closing send forth the lightning" (Mooney [1896] 1991:968). In another visualization the lightning comes from the flashing wings (Hultkrantz 1986: 632).

The Thunderbird that appears in petroglyphs near Dinwoody Lake on the Wind River Reservation attests to the longevity of belief by Wind River Shoshones, for whom it fits into a hierarchy of spirits that confers power. Writing of this hierarchy, Hultkrantz reports that "the most powerful is lightning whose force is the very essence of every vision. Next comes the thunderbird and then the eagle—the former is sometimes represented as an eagle, but most commonly as a humming-bird" (Hultkrantz 1956:200).

Thunderbird as eagle is a characteristic Plains transformation and this is true for Wind River Shoshones. However, these Shoshones, drawing on their Uto-Aztecan heritage, also manifest the thunderbird in other bird forms, as we have just seen. Small birds, rather than large, create cosmic forces. In one woman's account, thunder and lightning had independent bird origins; she spoke of "small brown birds that jump up and down close to the creeks—apparently blackbirds—control thunder" (Hultkrantz 1987:46). Emily identified the brown bird in Naraya songs 84 and 85 as a kind of blackbird. Of particular interest is another kind of blackbird, the subject of Naraya songs 88 and 89. This bird, *bagantsukʰ*, is described as bathing (song 88) and flying into the wind by a swampy place (song 89). I suggest that the first syllable of its name, *ba-*, is derived from the word for water, and, further, that this bird might be the one that jumps up and down close to creeks and controls thunder. Completing this woman's account was her saying that lightning was caused by the hummingbird.

Other Shoshones identified hummingbird with thunder: "the hummingbird collects the water in the clouds and makes them thunder" (Hultkrantz 1987:46).

Hultkrantz reports, "The idea that the thunder spirit looks like a hummingbird is apparently an old one among Indians of the Uto-Aztecan linguistic stock to whom the Shoshoni belong, for the ancient protective god of the Aztecs, Huitzilpochtli, was connected with hummingbirds. Actually, his name means 'hummingbird to the left'"[49] (Hultkrantz 1987:47).

Small birds play other important roles in Wind River Shoshone myth. In the creation story, Chickadee dives into the flood in order to bring up earth to Our Father (Lowie 1909a:273).[50]

Great Basin myth presents striking examples of Sky People, in some cases joined with Water-Bird people, who have enormous creative power as well as the power to influence weather through their song, and sometimes their dance. "Then the Whippoorwill who had a fine voice and was a wonderful enchanter sang one of his magical songs and danced one of his magical dances, whirling and eddying about the frog who stood in the center and who was slowly and wonderfully transformed into a moon" (Powell 1971:221).

In an Owens Valley Paiute myth, the world remained in darkness after Coyote killed the Sun. Coyote coaxed Mallard and Goose to help bring back daylight. As Steward recounts:

> Mallard and Goose began to sing. After they had sung a little while, they said, "Quack, quack, quack," and the third time they said it, a tiny light appeared in the east. Coyote said, "Ah, I knew my nephew was a great man and could do that. I am that great. I am greater. I will try." Coyote sang and said, "Wah, wah, wah," trying to make the light as bright as the full daylight. But when he did this, the little light disappeared. No one spoke. All were quiet. Then everyone scolded Coyote.
>
> He tried again and said, "A hi oi, a hi oi," but nothing happened. Coyote said, "I know I am not great. I thought I could make daylight come quicker. I didn't mean to discourage you. Everybody makes a mistake once in a while. It is a wonderful thing to make light. Not everybody can do that. I want Mallard to try again." . . . Mallard tried again. . . . He sang and then said, "Kwisah, kwish, kwish," and the third time he said it, daylight came. (Steward 1936:415)

In another story, Coyote wanted relief from stormy weather and asked Duck and Owl. "'Could you, nephews, do anything to stop this storm?' . . . They said, 'We will do what we can.' They started to sing. Owl sang, 'Mu, mu, mu,' in a deep low voice, and Duck sang, 'Kish, kish.' Every time they made these noises the weather cleared a little. . . . They sang louder and it became lighter all the time. Finally, Owl with his hoots and Duck with his quacks made the storm go away" (Steward 1936:417).

The special connection between Sky People and weather comes out in a Kaibab Southern Paiute tale of Wolf (*Shin-au-av*) and Snow bird (*Nu-wa-pa-kuts*). Wolf ignored Snow bird's warning of an impending snowstorm and did not stop his travel to wait it out. After Wolf barely recovered from his frozen condition, he told all the nations to heed Snow bird's words, "and since that day *Nu-wa-pa-kuts* has been revered for his great wisdom concerning the weather" (Power 1971:85). Among Wind River Shoshones, it is the chickadee, who is considered a "harbinger of severe snow storms" (Olden 1923:40).

Sky and Water-Bird People are associated with weather, and their song and feathers have power to influence it. Myth provides models for people in the everyday world. "By waving a feather or by singing, shamans may cause the clear sky to become cloudy, the wind to blow, or rain to fall. They can also stop wind and rain or banish the clouds that they have brought" (Park 1938:60). Shimkin reported the use of an eagle feather by a singer for the Sun Dance. A certain motion brought rain; a scattering motion made the clouds break up (Shimkin 1939:120).

Eagle

The eagle, which appears in Naraya songs 6, 35, 93, and 94, is extremely important in Great Basin culture. As noted earlier in the discussion of the buffalo, both the buffalo and the eagle have special religious roles in the Shoshone Sun Dance. Hultkrantz explains that the eagle was selected because "he is a manifestation of the sacred thunderbird . . . and obviously is a representative of the sky powers" (Hultkrantz 1961:208). Like the buffalo, the eagle played a special role in Sun Dance origins. The buffalo was messenger from Our Father in a first vision and "there was a second vision in which the eagle gave further instructions for the erection of the Dancing lodge" (Hultkrantz 1961:209). As Lynn St. Clair told Hultkrantz, the eagle was chosen because he was "the bird of birds" (Hultkrantz 1961:209). Hultkrantz concludes, "The eagle had been chosen as God's messenger because it is superior to all birds, soaring high above them in the sky, a symbol of purity" (Hultkrantz 1987:68).

As messengers, the eagle and other birds help shamans. Dick Mahwee, a Northern Paiute shaman, told Park, "The Indian doctor gets his power from the spirit of the night. . . . Eagle and owl do not give a shaman power. They are just messengers that bring instructions from the spirit of the night" (Park 1938:17). In line with this view is information that Hebard learned about the relationship between the thunderbird and Wind River Shoshones. She writes of Dinwoody petroglyphs, "The thunder-bird is present, which is the go-between for God and indian [*sic*]" (Hebard 1930:311). Voget discussed this point in reference to the Sun Dance: "Eagle is the primary servant of the Sun and in his spiritual manifestation takes the form of Thunderbird. Eagle is a bearer of messages from spirit to man, and from man to spirit" (Voget 1984:307).

Everything said thus far about Sky and Water-Bird People defines their roles as preservers of health and healers of sickness. The eagle draws together sky, power, flight, and song. Sky is the locus of Our

Father and the eagle, a place free of disease. Souls of the dead travel across the sky on the Milky Way road, which leads to the Land of the Dead. The shaman's soul must also rise into the sky to find and retrieve the patient's soul. Bird wings fly. Even detached feathers fly; seemingly weightless, they float in air and drift on wind currents. Eagle feather, plumes, and wings will be one topic in this section. Eagle "song"–human song will be a second: power in, as, and through song, song as a medium of exchange. Richard Engavo's comments to me about the eagle and the Shoshone Sun Dance flesh out some of these analytical abstractions and serve as bridge to data and further analysis that elaborate them.

RICHARD: "The [eagle-bone] whistle has the eagle's sound when he's flying around a ledge of a cliff. You hear them whistling. They got a whistle like that. That's the wind bone of eagle, the [Sun Dance] whistles. . . . When they're flying around, you hear them eagles. They make that noise and that's why they [the Sun Dancers] have those whistles."

JUDY: "Is it because the eagle is a sacred bird?"

RICHARD: "Yeah. And their feathers, too, the eagle plume. I see a lot of them old doctors used to have their whistle and if somebody wanted to get prayed for, then they walk out there.[51] Then they touch them and they blow their whistle. Maybe that represented the eagle. Probably the eagle's got that power, see, that good power. Just like somebody fanning you, [with eagle feathers] fan the sickness away."

John Truhujo, well known to Wind River Shoshones as a healer and Sun Dance leader, amplified these points after giving his eagle-bone whistle to the father of a soldier during World War II: "'Here's the whistle that I have used all through the [Sun] dance and several before. I suffered a lot with that whistle, and we used it a lot in doctoring in the Sun Dances. You take this and keep it for your boy.' Elmer Hill [the son, and no relation to Emily] returned safely from the war and recounted a war blessing at the Sun Dance of his father-in-law, John Cummins, in 1946 at Lodge Grass" (Voget 1984:193 n22).[52] Thus, the whistle served as curative and preventive medicine.

Park discussed the widespread use of eagle feathers in his study of shamanism:

> Feathers, usually the tail-feathers and down of eagles, form an extremely important part of the Paviotso shaman's paraphernalia, partly because of the common belief that they are symbolic of the shaman's power. These feathers, moreover, are used by all shamans in the curing performance, especially in connection with the stick which is planted near the patient's head during the rites.

The use of eagle-feathers in curing and other shamanistic performances is widespread. In fact it seems almost universal among the tribes
of western North America. . . . The scanty data on Great Basin usages
do not permit a definite statement for that region. Several scattered
instances of the use of feathers in curative rites suggest that the practice may be more general among these tribes. One shaman among the
Owens Valley Paiute is reported to have stuck long sticks bearing eagle-feathers into the ground around his patients, but this was not apparently done generally by shamans. Shamans among the White Knives
and Salmon Eater bands of Shoshoni commonly use eagle-feathers in
their curing ceremonies. Feathers are attached to a cane which is placed
in the ground by the patient's head. This practice is clearly similar in
details to the Paviotso custom. (Park 1938:134)

Eagle feathers cure by fanning away illness, or by touch (Stewart
1941:414) and stroking (Steward 1943a:345–46). They prevent illness
by keeping it at bay; Park learned the function of eagle feathers tied
to a stick outside the patient's home. "'It keeps the bad spirits away'"
(Park 1934:104).

Lowie noted similar use of feathers by Wind River Shoshones, who
generalized the power of feathers to many types of birds besides the
eagle. "The Wind River people seem to look upon many birds as
possessors and bestowers of *bu'ha* [power]. The tail-feathers of the
flicker, worn as headgear, ward off sickness and tend to restore health"
(Lowie 1909a:224).

As clearly demonstrated by Richard Engavo's and John Truhujo's
comments about the eagle, eagle-bone whistles, and eagle feathers in
the Shoshone Sun Dance, power from eagle is central to health and
healing. Steward reports that in the Fort Hall Shoshone Sun Dance,
"the doctor put an eagle feather in the dust, then on the invalid, then
blew the disease away" (Steward 1943a:289). Sun Dancers who, during the course of the ceremony, attained the power to heal used eagle feathers as part of their practice (Steward 1943a:283). Jorgensen
describes the use of eagle feathers by Sun Dancers throughout the
ceremony. On the second day and "the longer the dance progresses,
the more probable it is that renowned and powerful dancers will carry
special eagle feathers, or fans made of eagle wing or eagle tail. Ritual
objects which include eagle feathers are especially useful in controlling power and, in shamanistic practices, passing power on to other
dancers as well as to ill spectators" (Jorgensen 1972:187).

Eagle feathers were standard in shamanistic practice, whether or
not the shaman received power directly from the eagle in a dream
(Steward 1941:260).[53] Some shamans did, in fact, seek and receive

power from the eagles (Steward 1933:303, 308; Steward 1943:282). Eleven of twenty Paviotso shamans interviewed by Park received power from birds, principally the eagle. The shamans and their sources of power were:

Dick Mahwee	eagle, crow
Abraham Mahwee	large spotted bird which lives on the lake
Judy David	eagle
Johnny Calico	eagle and unidentified bird
Eugene Frazier	eagle and crow
Mary Garvey	crow and big mountain fly
Julia Robinson	eagle
Blind Bob	magpie
Paiute Harrison	eagle
Mary Harrison	eagle
Tom Mitchell	eagle, small unidentified bird living in the mountains.

(Park 1938:18)

Feathers are one talisman of eagle power. They could even be instrumental in acquiring power. Among Grouse Creek Shoshone of Utah, "The candidate tied eagle feathers to himself and the eagle came, giving him instructions and power for doctoring. He became a *puhagunt*" (Steward 1943a:282–83). In other accounts, the acquisition of song—a second talisman of power crucial for healing—combines with the use of eagle feathers. In one, a young man acquired eagle feathers by going to a location seen in a dream, and he later heard a voice say that he could cure his nephew. "He painted evi (white clay) on the boy's chest, arms and legs. Then a song came to him. He had never doctored before. People gathered to witness his performance. Five songs developed in his head and dances were revealed to him. He sang, danced, and smoked, while holding his eagle feathers" (Steward 1943a:283).[54]

Park tells us that the shaman "learns his songs when the spirit comes and sings to him" (Park 1934:99). The shaman learns additional songs and knowledge of curing from the spirit, who visits from time to time. For many, the eagle is the spirit and source of power. Kelly writes of eagles, shamans, and song:

A [Surprise Valley Paiute] shaman controls various kinds of animal spirits which come to him in dreams. The eagle is the most frequent one, consequently in treating, a doctor puts an eagle feather on the ailing part and "sings like an eagle. When he calls on the eagle it comes from the mountain and looks at the sick man, but no one is able to see it come." If a shaman dreams of a deer and hears a deer call, he imitates the cry when doctoring. I did not hear of any spirits other than animals. Sometimes the shaman has a feather or other token of his vision, but usually he has a song, in which event he does not carry the token. Every shaman dreams his own songs. (Kelly 1932:190)

Park wrote of Joe Green, a Northern Paiute shaman from Pyramid Lake Reservation, "He had eagle feathers that he put under his head when he slept. . . . He got his songs from the eagle feathers" (Park 1934:109).[55] The relationship of shamans to eagles, as regards song, varied: "Some claim that the songs come to them from their powers while they are doctoring and they cannot remember them afterwards. Dick Mahwee said that his songs came to him through the eagle-feather on the stick that is planted by the patient's head. [Recall that his power came from the eagle and crow.] Other shamans assert otherwise, testifying that their songs are derived directly from the powers and that the feather wand does not have any connection with the singing" (Park 1938:52).

In Kelly's account, given above, one use of song is as a call. The shaman "sings like an eagle" and the eagle comes. A variant on this may also occur with bone whistles made from the wing-bone of eagles and other large birds. Park states, "These instruments are used by some shamans at the beginning of the curing performance in order to call the powers. . . . It was reported that a shaman uses a whistle only if told to do so by his power" (Park 1938:36).

The transfer of power in a dream is not the only way to acquire shamanistic power. There is documentation for the transmission of John Truhujo's power to heal and his leadership role in the Sun Dance to Tom Yellowtail.[56] The account catches the essence of much of my discussion of the connection of power, health, and eagle, and eagle (and other Sky, Water-Bird People) flight and song. First, during the 1967 Sun Dance, John gave eagle feathers he had been using to Tom. Second, in 1969, John sang and recorded for Tom his three special songs. "The first or opening song was dedicated to the 'medicine fathers,' to the little people [perhaps a reference to *ninïmbi*, a Shoshone conception of an elflike people who possessed power], the elk, the otter, and the white goose. The second was connected with all the birds, since these were the ones who communicated with the dancers on the second day. The third song referred to the white goose from which power to cure was derived. This was the power that Tom should use at all times when doctoring" (Voget 1984:191).[57]

While eagles, power, and health are at the heart of shamanistic practice, they are by no means exclusive to that practice. Other areas of cultural life freely incorporate these same underlying notions. I believe this to be true for the Naraya as described by Emily with regard to the eagle, which is expressed in the text of Naraya song 35. I also believe this to be true for the Naraya's source, the Round Dance. Consider the Rabbit Dance of Idaho Shoshones described earlier (see Rabbit section, above), with its pantomime of striking down rabbits and then reviving them. In this enactment a "doctor" carrying a feather,[58] accompanied by a singer, effect the revival. Song, feather, and, by implication, power all come into play in a playful performance. The rabbit actors wear false penises and large ears (Steward 1943a:289). In a more serious vein, the prayer song sung four times at sunset prior to the evening's dance said, "'*Kwinaŋ* (eagle feather) *gwasi* (tail) *hupi* (stick) *nzia* (?),' which was addressed to nature or to the maker of green things. . . . These dances were usually held spring and fall and were to *promote health* [my emphasis] and make nature fertile. But a special dance might be held in time of *sickness* [my emphasis] or trouble" (Steward 1943a:287;). Once again, it is song, eagle feather, and their power that are invoked for health.

The eagle also had symbolic meaning for Wind River Shoshones as participants in Plains life and warfare. There are further manifestations of eagle power in this context. Some Shoshones wore eagle feathers in their hair to protect them from "missiles" (Lowie 1909a:224). Wind River Shoshones had medicine bundles especially for warlike purposes. Lowie reports, "These were composed of bear claws, otterskins, etc. Most of them contained eagle feathers as part of the sacred aggregate" (Lowie 1924a:296).[59]

Associations among the eagle, warfare, and warriors appear in the contemporary powwow. Eagle feathers adorn the dancers' outfits and sometimes they fall to the ground during the course of the dance. Lenore Shoyo, a Wind River Shoshone singer and dancer, described to me the correct way to pick up fallen feathers. In an account dependent upon a free flow of overlaying symbols, Lenore moved from honoring the American flag to the eagle, from the eagle to an implied identification with Our Father who watches over us, and back to honoring the eagle as well as the warrior-veteran: "Grand Entry song . . . you're bringing the dancers in behind the flag. . . . They're dancing behind the flag in respect. And the people are standing in respect of the flag. . . . It's just the same way as you would have respect for the eagle feather. Because the eagle flies above us and watches over us. That's why they have this Feather Dance when anyone drops any eagle plume. They usually have a veteran come on up and pray for the feather and owner. He also prays in all four directions and talks about his experience in war" (Vander 1988:223).

Just as war and peace go together as complementary opposites, so symbolic attachments to the eagle bear both connotations. Hultkrantz reports, "It remains that among the Wind River Shoshoni eagle feathers were held up as peace signs when other Indian groups were met" (Hultkrantz 1961:209). He suggests the associations behind this symbolic choice: "The eagle itself is respected by the Shoshoni as the bird of peace, connected with the sky and the Supreme Being" (Hultkrantz 1987:46). We have come full circle to birds, sky, power, and Our Father.

Three more Wind River Shoshone examples make these same points of connection. John Truhujo explained the meaning of the eagle-bone whistle and eagle plumes used in the Sun Dance to Voget, who wrote: "The whistle used by the dancers represented the birds, and was made from either the right or left humerus of the eagle. One prayed to the Creator through the whistle, regulated in sets of four. The long shrill blasts in combinations of four echoed the cry of the eagle when it swooped down to earth. The feather plumes worn by the dancer brought to mind the 'picture of Christ when he is standing on the clouds.' Christ said, 'You must wear the plumes to be a believer in my lodge'" (Voget 1984:77).[60]

Emily's comment about Naraya song 93 is pertinent here. "That eagle, that's the main one you use for praying and something like that." Naraya song 6 (see appendix A) is also germane. Emily paraphrased its Shoshone text, saying, "That eagle's flying, his wings way up there in the sky, looking down to the earth and seeing the water, shining. And the grass on the earth green" (Vander 1986:40). The extraordinary vision of the eagle is explicit in Emily's comments and is one physical demonstration of its power. I suggest that on a metaphysical plane, the human power to see in visionary experience is its spiritual counterpart. It, too, demonstrates power.

Emily described the eagle as "looking," which is different from Lenore's comment that the eagle "watches over us." However, in an alternate explication of Naraya song 6, Dorothy added meaning with Christian terminology that draws closer to the eagle–sky–Our Father configuration. She said, "'That's a song about angels flying up about Heaven, like that, flying'" (Vander 1986:40).[61]

In war and peace, in healing, and in the Sun Dance—even in myth as leader and teacher of nestmaking—the eagle assumes a variety of symbolic roles. One of the symbolic meanings for both buffalo and eagle in the Wind River Shoshone Sun Dance addressed concern for subsistence. The buffalo head hung on the center pole represented game furnished by God, and the eagle on the east-running "backbone" rafter stood for game birds (Shimkin 1939:107). The choice of the eagle in this role is interesting. In fact, neither Wind River Shoshones nor other Great Basin and Plains peoples hunted the eagle for food because it was held sacred.[62]

Sky People and the 1890 Ghost Dance

Mooney reported that "the crow . . . is the sacred bird of the Ghost dance, being revered as the messenger from the spirit world because its color is symbolic of death and the shadow land. . . . The eagle, the magpie, and the sage-hen are also sacred in the Ghost dance, the first being held in veneration by Indians, as well as by other peoples throughout the world, while the magpie and the sage-hen are revered for their connection with the country of the messiah and the mythology of his tribe" (Mooney [1896] 1991:982).[63]

Images of eagles, magpies, crows, and sage hens appeared on Ghost Dance clothing (Mooney [1896] 1991:823; Peterson 1976:39, 43, 56, 58). Interestingly, Emily's Naraya repertoire makes no mention of magpies or sage hens (it is not clear whether any unidentified birds are crows).

Because the magpie, like the eagle, was sacred to the Northern Paiute, Wovoka used both eagle and magpie feathers in the Ghost Dance. For many adherents these feathers became symbols of his power. Wovoka received their letters and requests for magpie and eagle feathers (Dangberg 1957:285; Dangberg 1986:43, 49).[64] Crow, eagle, or magpie feathers worn on the head in the dance were believed to enable people to fly to the new spirit world (Mooney [1896] 1991:970, 999). Colby learned from Sioux Ghost Dancers that eagle feathers were not only worn on the head, but the picture of the eagle was painted on the back of the shirts and dresses and eagle feathers were attached to the shoulders and sleeves as well. When the Ghost Dancers were in a trance, "the eagle comes to them, and carries them to where the Messiah is with his ghosts" (Colby 1895:139). When they returned to this world they brought back with them "water, fire, and wind with which to kill all the whites and the Indians who help the chief of the whites" (Colby 1895:139).[65]

Among the Southern Arapaho, Caddo, and Kiowa tribes on the Southern Plains, a special "giving the feather" ceremony developed. The person who first brought the Ghost Dance to the tribe gave a crow or eagle feather to seven or fourteen designated leaders. "After having thus received the feather the tribe began to make songs of its own, having previously used those taught them by the apostle from his own language" (Mooney [1896] 1991:919). Thus, the connection of birds, eagles, and song I discussed earlier had its own variant form in the Ghost Dance.

The use of eagle feather wands in Ghost Dance performance of the Kaibab also connects to previous discussion of eagles and Great Basin shamanism. "In this [Ghost Dance] performance a cedar pole about two feet high was planted in the center of the circle. Two feathers, one a tail-feather painted red, the other a soft white feather taken from under the tail of an eagle, were suspended by a string from the top of the pole" (Park 1938:135).

Wovoka's use of eagle and magpie feathers to control weather are another connection with Great Basin shamanism. A Paviotso (Northern Paiute) informant told Park, "Jack Wilson [Wovoka] could bring rain. At Sweetwater [Nevada], five Sioux came to see him. As soon as they arrived he took a magpie-tail feather from his hat. He waved it in front of his face. Right away the clouds came up in the sky. Rain started to fall. When Jack stopped waving the feather the clouds went away" (Park 1934:108).[66]

There is evidence that Wovoka used feathers in order to induce trance.

> After his great soul-shaking experience in catalepsy, Wovoka found the trance-state easier to produce, not only in himself, but in others. With the eagle feather, which became his badge of divinity, and the magpie tail-feathers he distributed to his neophytes as optical targets in his ceremonies, he found that he now had the tools which had built Smohalla, Squ-sacht-un, and a dozen other great Indian dreamers into fame and influence. In the trance-state, it was possible to will and suggest what the participant would see, and amazing indeed were the religious experiences his low, vibrant voice and his feathers were able to conjure into the consciousness of those who sought his council. (Bailey 1957:85)

Finally, Wovoka, himself, was envisioned as a bird:

> My children, my children,
> I am flying about the earth,
> I am flying about the earth.
> I am a bird, my children,
> I am a bird, my children,
> Says the father,
> Says the father.

In this song the messiah, addressing his children, is represented as a bird (crow?) flying about the whole earth, symbolic of his omniscience. (Mooney [1896] 1991:997)

The song text recorded by Mooney and his commentary on it bring us back to the associations among bird, sky, power, and Our Father. The messiah bird in this text, like the eagle, "watches over us," all-seeing, hence, all-knowing.

6 | *Plants*

Plants are at the heart of the Naraya, and Naraya performance promotes vegetation. Emily's comments bring this clearly into focus. Follow her thoughts as her mind seems to move on a cultural stream of consciousness and associations, channels that connect rain, water, sickness, health, plants, earth, song, and dance.

EMILY: "Them songs is for, it's for the grass to grow again and grow good and trees grow good, green. Flowers grow good and berries, our berries. Some people say when our trees and grass and no berries, old people says, 'Well, we'll dance. We'll make our earth come, grow up and make more water, more water.' *Datevuntëg* means wake 'em up, wake 'em up. That song is for that. Them Nevada Indians, Nevada Shoshones, Johnny Dick [a deceased Naraya leader] says, 'Well, let's have our berries, have berries on our earth. Let the water run, let the grass grow again. Let's dance and make our earth and everything, roots what we eat on our ground—let 'em come alive again.' That's what Johnny Dick said. That's what those Nevada Indians say. And they dance, he said.

"And I told her [Dorothy], I think it's the same thing like these [Wind River] Shoshones. When you don't feel good, too, you dance with them and you feel good."

JUDY: "Did you used to stamp the ground after you finished dancing?"

EMILY: "Yeah." [*Emily blew on her hand,* a motion to blow away sickness. This motion is also done in connection with the Sun Dance.]

JUDY: "Did they stamp their feet?"

EMILY: "Stomped the rain away, sick[ness]."

JUDY: "Did you wake up the roots in the ground, too?"

EMILY: "Yeah. That's how they dance. Nowadays these people don't believe in it, especially these young people. They don't know nothing about it. They think it's just a Ghost Dance."

Naraya Song 101

♩ = ca. 176

(1st verse)

Dorothy Tappay

Ba	*buhi*	*buhi-mande*	*ba*	*buhi*	*buhi-mande,*
Water	green	green-(?v.s.)	water	green	green-(?v.s.),

Ba	*buhi*	*buhi-mande*	*ba*	*buhi*	*buhi-mande.*
Water	green	green-(?v.s.)	water	green	green-(?v.s.).

Senav-av	*buhi*	*doiyav-ende*	*yaiyowainda,*
Aspens-(v.s.)	green	mountains-(?v.s.)	(e.v.),

Senav-av	*buhi*	*doiyav-ende*	*yaiyowainda,*
Aspens-(v.s.)	green	mountains-(?v.s.)	(e.v.),

Senav-av	*buhi*	*doiyav-ende*	*yaiyowainda.*
Aspens-(v.s.)	green	mountains-(?v.s.)	(e.v.).

Naraya Song 102

♩· = ca. 69   (6th verse)

Da - më   so - go - pë   na - za - më - rï - ki- no,   Da - më

so - go - pë   na - za - më - rï - ki- no.   Bu - hi

gwam - bai - yïn,   Bu - hi   gwam - bai - yïn.

Dorothy Tappay
Emily Hill

Pitches

Damë	*sogopë*	*nazamërïkino,*
Our	earth	it's turning,

Damë	*sogopë*	*nazamërïkino.*
Our	earth	it's turning.

Buhi	*gwambaiyïn,*
Grass	is waving,

Buhi	*gwambaiyïn.*
Grass	is waving.

EMILY: "Our earth is turning over and turning green. The grass is just—you know how grass is when it's tall—it goes like this when the wind blows. Yeah, that's the way it's doing it. When the grass is that tall like that, when it's got wind, looks like it's moving. Waves."

Naraya Song 103

♩ = ca. 100

(7th verse)

Dï- na we- gi- du bu- hip pa- ro wai- yo- wan

e- na, Du- ra we- gi- du bu- hip pa- ro wai- yo- wan

e- na. Buhi shï- na -ra na- wȯ- ra na - na- na

wa- süp- pen - ji na wa- süp- pen- ji, Buhi shï- na - ra na- wȯ-

9 repeats

ra na - na- na wa- süp- pen - ji na wa- süp- pen- ji.

Emily Hill
Dorothy Tappay

Pitches

Dïna	wegidu	buhip	pa-ro	waiyowan ena,
Down	on a slant, sideways	green/grass	water/damp (GH)	(e.v.),

Dura	*wegidu*	*buhip*	*pa-ro*	*waiyowan ena.*
Down	on a slant, sideways	green/grass	water/damp (GH)	(e.v.).

Buhi	*shïna-ra*	*nawòra*	*na-nana*	*wasüp-penji*
Green/grass	quaking aspen	?straight	?all kinds	game animals-(v.s.)[1]
na	*wasüp-penji,*			
?	game animals-(v.s.),			

Buhi	*shïna-ra*	*nawòra*	*na-nana*	*wasüp-penji*
Green/grass	quaking aspen	?straight	?all kinds	game animals-(v.s.)
na	*wasüp-penji.*			
?	game animals-(v.s.).			

EMILY: "Down, *dura* means down. Grass, there's grass, green, kind of damplike. *Dura wegidu,* that's the side of the hill or something like that. *Dura* means down that way, down. *Wegidu* means it's sideways like that. *Davor* means it's something like—you seen them tree up here, them straight ones?"

JUDY: "Aspens?"

EMILY: "Yes."

Gladys Hill suggested another word for the end of line one, *bazoind,* meaning "damp."

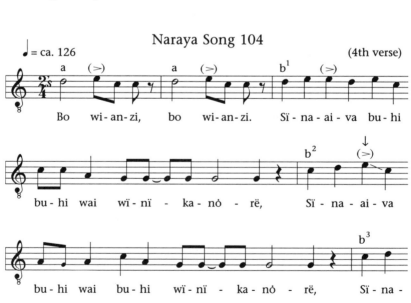

Naraya Song 104

♩ = ca. 126   (4th verse)

Bo wi-an-zi, bo wi-an-zi. Sï-na-ai-va bu-hi

bu-hi wai wï-nï-ka-nò-rë, Sï-na-ai-va

bu-hi wai bu-hi wï-nï-ka-nò-rë, Sï-na-

ai - va   bu - hi   wï - nï - ka - nȯ - rë.

Pitches

Dorothy Tappay
Emily Hill

Bo	*wia-n-zi,*
Sagebrush	gully, pass-(d.a.s.),

Bo	*wia-n-zi.*
Sagebrush	gully, pass-(d.a.s.).

Sïna-aiva	*buhi*	*buhi*	*wai*	*wïnïkanȯrë,*
Quaking aspen	green/grass	green/grass	?under	stand up moving, [blowing]

Sïna-aiva	*buhi*	*wai*	*buhi*	*wïnïkanȯrë,*
Quaking aspen	green/grass	?under	green/grass	stand up moving, [blowing]

Sïna-aiva	*buhi*	*wïnïkanȯrë.*
Quaking aspen	green/grass	stand up moving. [blowing]

EMILY: "You know that hill over there. It's steep like this. It's *wiaph* [a pass or low-sloping part of the hill] that's got sagebrush on it. See that sagebrush up there, that's like that. On top back there, these kind of trees [aspens] and green grass."

Naraya Song 105

Wë - nȯ - ro wë - nȯ - ro - bi   wë - nȯ - ro wë - nȯ - ro - bi,

Wë - nȯ - ro wë - nȯ - ro - bi   wë - nȯ - ro wë - nȯ - ro - bi.   Bu - i - wam

bu - i - wam - bi   bu - i - wam bu - i - wam - bi   e - na,

b   6 repeats

Bu - i - wam bu - i - wam - bi   bu - i - wam bu - i - wam - bi   e - na.

Pitches   Dorothy Tappay
                                           Emily Hill

Wënóro wënórobi wënóro wënórobi,
?   ?   ?   ?,

Wënóro wënórobi wënóro wënórobi.
?   ?   ?   ?.

Bui-wam   bui-wambi   bui-wam   bui-wambi ena,
Green-(?s.)   green-(?s.) green-(?s.) green-(?s.) (e.v.),

Bui-wam   bui-wambi   bui-wam   bui-wambi ena.
Green-(?s.)   green-(?s.) green-(?s.) green-(?s.) (e.v.).

EMILY: "I think that song's from Idaho."
JUDY: "Does it say *buhi*, 'green,' in the second line?"
EMILY: "Yes, green. Dorothy learned this song from her brother-in-law. I learned it from her.

"When you're singing you're supposed to kind of drag your song. Make that song pretty." *Emily sang the first line of the song very fast.*]
"That don't sound good. You gotta jazz like—kind of drag your voice. Make it pretty."

Naraya Song 106

♩ = ca. 76   (2d verse)

a¹   a¹

Do - no - va   do - no - va   yen - go - ni,   Do - no - va

Pitches

Emily Hill
Dorothy Tappay

Dono-va   *dono-va*   *yengoni,*[2]
?Greasewood-water (creek) ?greasewood-creek hanging down,

Dono-va   *dono-va*   *yengoni.*
?Greasewood-water (creek) ?greasewood-creek hanging down.

Waiyovi   *waiyovi*   *yengoni,*
(Vocable [GH]) (vocable) hanging down,

Waiyovi   *waiyovi*   *yengoni.*
(Vocable [GH]) (vocable) hanging down.

In this song, the identification of the bush, which first appeared in song 82 and will appear again in song 107, remains problematic. Gladys Hill and some other Shoshones thought it was greasewood. Steward lists *tonovi* for "greasewood" (*Sarcobatus vermiculatus*) in his Shoshone study (Steward 1938:309), and Sapir lists *tono-va-ts* as "greasewood spring" in his Southern Paiute dictionary (Sapir 1931:686). In his study of "Wind River Shoshone Ethnogeography," Shimkin lists *to:´napi* as "greasewood," with the same Latin identification as Steward's (Shimkin 1947b:275). Emily definitely denied the greasewood identification, although she could not remember the English name for the bush.

On one occasion Emily took me to see the bush and I broke off a branch from it. Years later I showed the branch to Professor Nelson, a botanist at the University of Wyoming. He thought that it was most likely greasewood. But, of course, by that time, positive identification of a dessicated, leafless stick was very difficult, if not impossible.

EMILY: "What do you call those brushes, they grow in the salt ground, tall ones. I forgot the name [in English]. Them things, they're like sagebrush but they're tall. It's got a lot of stickers on there. They grow in the salt ground. *Donova* means creek. . . . Them salted puffed grounds along, you know, the banks. They're kind of puffed like that."[3]

One year later Emily and I spoke again about the bush.

EMILY: "You know those kind of gray-looking—they grow in them salty ground. Next time I'll show you what it is."

JUDY: "Does it grow near your house?"

EMILY: "No, over on Sage Creek. They stick you when you walk by."

JUDY: "What does *yengoni* mean?"

EMILY: "When they got long—*yengo* means hanging down, *yenkʰ*."

JUDY: "What about *waiyovi?*"

EMILY: "I think that song belongs to either Idaho or Nevada. I can't understand some words. Those leaves are salty. Cows eat it. [Buffalo, too, in song 82.] There's Sage Creek on the other side of M's house. They call that *dono ogwe* ['river'], where the water, not very much water, just a very little stream."

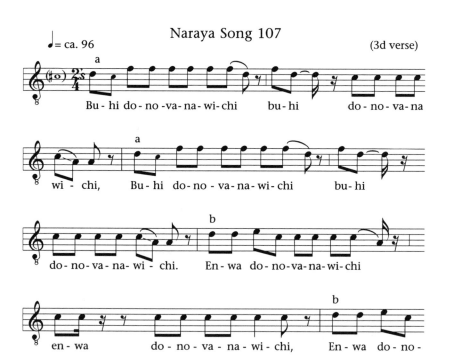

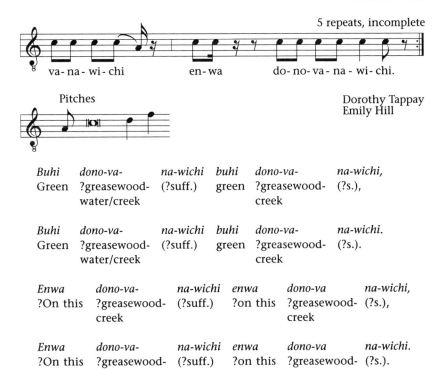

5 repeats, incomplete

va - na - wi - chi   en - wa   do - no - va - na - wi - chi.

Pitches

Dorothy Tappay
Emily Hill

Buhi   *dono-va-*   *na-wichi*   *buhi*   *dono-va-*   *na-wichi,*
Green   ?greasewood-   (?suff.)   green   ?greasewood-   (?s.),
             water/creek   creek

Buhi   *dono-va-*   *na-wichi*   *buhi*   *dono-va-*   *na-wichi.*
Green   ?greasewood-   (?suff.)   green   ?greasewood-   (?s.).
             water/creek   creek

Enwa   *dono-va-*   *na-wichi*   *enwa*   *dono-va*   *na-wichi,*
?On this   ?greasewood-   (?suff.)   ?on this   ?greasewood-   (?s.),
                  creek   creek

Enwa   *dono-va-*   *na-wichi*   *enwa*   *dono-va*   *na-wichi.*
?On this   ?greasewood-   (?suff.)   ?on this   ?greasewood-   (?s.).
                  creek   creek

EMILY: "It grows in the white ground, salty ground. Them things grow high like that. I forgot the [English] name of that. They're singing about that, that bushes—it's green, and the bottom, it's kind of drylike. Horses, cows eat it. It's sticky; it's got sticks, them things. I forgot the name for that."

JUDY: "How do you say it in Shoshone?"

EMILY: "*DonovI.*"

Naraya Song 108

♩ = ca. 96

(5th verse)

a

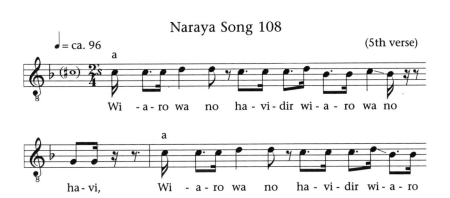

Wi - a - ro wa   no   ha - vi - dir wi - a - ro wa no

a

ha - vi,   Wi - a - ro wa   no   ha - vi - dir wi - a - ro

wa no ha- vi. Wi - a - ro ha - vi- dir wi- a - ro wa no

ha - vi, Wi - a - ro ha - vi- dir wi- a - ro wa no ha- vi.

Pitches

Emily Hill
Dorothy Tappay

Wia-ro   *wa*   *no*   *havi-dir wia-ro*   *wa*   *no*   *havi,*
Pass [in the hills]-(v.s.) cedar hill lie-(?s.) pass-(v.s.) cedar hill lie,

Wia-ro   *wa*   *no*   *havi-dir wia-ro*   *wa*   *no*   *havi.*
Pass [in the hills]-(v.s.) cedar hill lie-(?s.) pass-(v.s.) cedar hill lie.

Wia-ro   *havi-dir*   *wia-ro*   *wa*   *no*   *havi,*
Pass-(v.s.) lie-(?s.)   pass-(v.s.) cedar hill lie,

Wia-ro   *havi-dir*   *wia-ro*   *wa*   *no*   *havi.*
Pass-(v.s.) lie-(?s.)   pass-(v.s.) cedar hill lie.

EMILY: "*Wanovi* is 'hill,' cedar trees on there. They call it *wiav*,
'road'—hill on this side and hills on this side."
JUDY: "Is it a saddle or pass?"
EMILY: "Yes, and cedars all around."

Naraya Song 109

♩. = ca. 84   (4th verse)

Bi- ya won - go -no ha - vi   ye - na,   Bi- ya won - go-

no ha - vi ye - na.   Ba - ga don - zi - a

Emily Hill
Dorothy Tappay

Biya wongo-no havi yena,
Big pine tree-(v.s.) lie (e.v.),

Biya wongo-no havi yena.
Big pine tree-(v.s.) lie (e.v.).

Ba-ga donzia ba-ga donzia ena,
Water-(?v.s.) shiny water-(?v.s.) shiny (e.v.),

Ba-ga donzia ba-ga donzia ena.
Water-(?v.s.) shiny water-(?v.s.) shiny (e.v.).

EMILY: "It's about a pine tree, great big pine tree. *Ba wongovi,* it means real big trees, bigger than other timbers. Them big pine trees grow near water, a springlike, *ba wongovi,* it's about water. That's why it's up here by the river, way up there. You could see it from here, you could see it from Fort Washakie."

The image of needles floating in sun-shower pools, which appears in Naraya song 34, is another example of the coupling of water and pine trees.

Naraya Song 110

♩ = ca. 88   (4th verse)

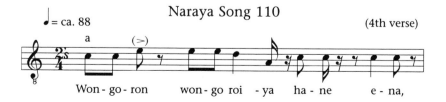

Pitches

Emily Hill
Dorothy Tappay

Wongo-ron   *wongo*   *roiya*   *hane ena,*
Pine tree-(?v.s.)   pine tree   mountain   ?   (e.v.),

Wongo-ron   *wongo*   *roiya*   *hane ena.*
Pine tree-(?v.s.)   pine tree   mountain   ?   (e.v.).

Rüvi pü   rüvi   pü   yë   hane   ena,
?   ?   ?   ?   ?   ?   (e.v.),

Rüvi pü   rüvi   pü   yë   hane   ena.
?   ?   ?   ?   ?   ?   (e.v.).

EMILY: "From Nevada or Idaho."
JUDY: "Does it say something about pine tree, pine mountains?"
EMILY: "I understood that part, too."

Naraya Song 111

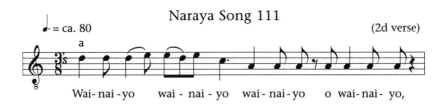

Wai - nai - yo wai - nai - yo wai - nai - yo o wai - nai - yo.

Da- më hu- pin doi- ïn- zi do- sa wü - wün - dü a wü - wün-

dü. Bu yu - wün - dü a yu - wün - dü.

9 repeats

Pitches

Emily Hill
Dorothy Tappay

Wain-aiyo   *wain-aiyo*   *wain-aiyo*   *o*
Coming down-(v.s.) coming down (v.s.) coming down-(v.s.) (v.)
    wain-aiyo,
    coming down (v.s.),

Wain-aiyo   *wain-aiyo*   *wain-aiyo*   *o*
Coming down-(v.s.) coming down (v.s.) coming down-(v.s.) (v.)
    wain-aiyo.
    coming down (v.s.).

Damë *hupin* *doiïn-zi*   *dosa*   *wüwündü*
Our   wood   ?come out (d.a.s.) white   many branches hanging over
    a   *wüwündü.*
    (v.) many branches hanging over.

Bu   *yuwündü*   *a*   *yuwündü.*
Green/grass   many branches hanging over   (v.) many branches hanging
                                                            over.

EMILY: "Getting down on something, pile of wood or something like
that. Where they're laying on the mountains. There's a lot of woods
and trees laying around. You could walk around. It means going down,
down that wood piled there. And when you get down there's a lot of
grass down there. . . . It's coming down a little hill there, there's a lot
of wood laying around, down there to the green grass."

One year later Emily remarked.

EMILY: "Coming down a hill where them wood are. You know how brown wood looks white? And there's grass around about, grass, *buhi yuwïd,* a lot of grass. Some of those trees have got green like that, just hang over like that. *Yu:wünde* means like that, hanging over like that, a lot of branches."

Naraya Song 112

Evïn   denüpi evïn   denüpi,
White clay man   white clay man,

Evïn   denüpi evïn   denüpë.
White clay man   white clay man.

Hupin   denüpi yórino,
Wood/stick man   keep flying on [together],

Hupin   denüpi yórino.
Wood/stick man   keep flying on [together].

EMILY: "That was a woman, she sang that song for them. That's Virginia [Grant] Bonatsie's song. She sang that when she was a young woman. She passed away a few years ago. [Virginia Bonatsie was born in 1890 and died in 1960.][4]

"She dreamt that song—just like Sun Dance or religious songs—she dreamt it. And she's got another one too, I think, her song. When they had a dance she sang that song for them. She got some of those old guys to sing it for it [the Naraya].

"*Evi* means that white chalk. It's under ground, you use it. It's mud, dough, they take it. They bring it out to dry. That's for dressing, putting on your buckskin. It's something like chalk. It's for the Sun Dance—white, smells good.[5] That man's made of that kind, and man made of wood. *Yòrino*—get up, up, flying on."

JUDY: "What does the song mean?"

EMILY: "It's something. We don't know what it is. She knows [Virginia Grant Bonatsie], but that's all I know."

This song is the most problematic and one of the most fascinating of the Naraya texts. Who are White-Clay Man and Wood Stick Man, and where are they flying to? Briefly, I believe that White-Clay Man personifies health and healing power, and that Wood Stick Man personifies plants and vegetative power. I will include each of these "men" and their symbolic meanings in the commentary on the song texts.

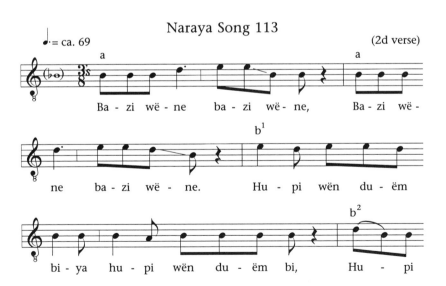

Naraya Song 113

Ba - zi wë - ne ba - zi wë - ne, Ba - zi wë -
ne ba - zi wë - ne. Hu - pi wën du - ëm
bi - ya hu - pi wën du - ëm bi, Hu - pi

3 repeats, incomplete

wën   du - ëm bi - ya   hu - pi   wën   du - ëm bi.

Pitches   Dorothy Tappay

Ba-zi   wëne   ba-zi   wëne,
Water ?   water   ?,

Ba-zi   wëne   ba-zi   wëne.
Water ?   water   ?.

Hupi   wën   duëm   biya   hupi   wën   duëm   bi,
Wood ?   ?   ?big/mother wood ?   ?   ?big/mother,

Hupi   wën   duëm   biya   hupi   wën   duëm   bi.
Wood ?   ?   ?big/mother wood ?   ?   ?big/mother.

I have no commentary from Emily for this text and it remains a fragment, with references to water and wood unexplained.

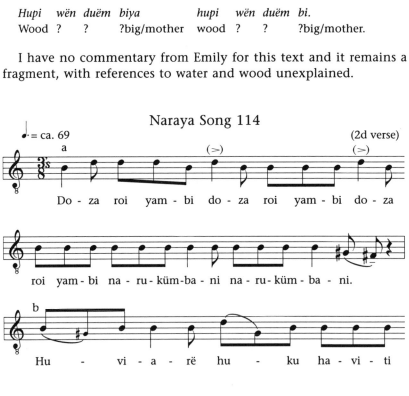

Naraya Song 114

♩. = ca. 69   (2d verse)

a   (>)   (>)

Do - za   roi   yam - bi   do - za   roi   yam - bi   do - za

roi   yam - bi   na - ru - küm - ba - ni   na - ru - küm - ba - ni.

b

Hu - vi - a - rë   hu - ku   ha - vi - ti

4 repeats, incomplete

na - ru - küm - ba - ni   na - ru - küm   ba - ni.

Pitches

Dorothy Tappay
Emily Hill

Doza   roi   yambi   doza   roi   yambi doza roi   yambi
White mountain root   white mountain root   white mountain root
narukümb-ani.   narukümb-ani.
has power to it [spirit] -(?v.s.)   has power to it [spirit] -(?v.s.).

Huviarë huku   haviti narukümb-ani   narukümb-ani.
Song   dust/ashes lying   has power to it   has power to it.
          [trail of dust]

EMILY: "I like that song. Idaho people knows it and people from here know it. Something white that grows up on the mountains. *Doza roi yamp*[h]."[6]

JUDY: "Some kind of root?"

EMILY: "Yeah. *Doza* means that Indian medicine. It ain't around here. It's put out up there to the mountains someplace, Bull Lake or Dinwoody someplace [sacred places for Shoshones, associated with power]. *Doza.* You have to pray for it before you dig the root out. It's for sores and everything."

The reference to "dust lying" in the second line is unclear. It might have associations with the whirlwind and the ghost of the dead—something dangerous and feared—and yet, at the same time, a potential source of power used for healing. Among the Wind River Shoshone and other Great Basin people, the trail of dust refers to the Milky Way, the path that leads to the Land of the Dead. This will be discussed further in chapter 7.

Naraya Song 115

♩ = ca. 88   (2d verse)

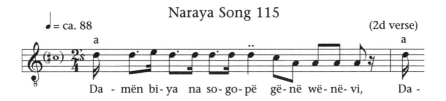

Da - mën bi- ya na so- go- pë gë- në wë- në- vi,   Da -

men bi-ya na so-go-pë gë-në wë-në-vi.   Da-men bi-ya na

so-go-pë   gu-si yëm-pë wë-në-vi,   Da-men bi-ya na

2 repeats, incomplete

so - go - pë   gu - si yëm - pë wë - në - vi.

Pitches

Dorothy Tappay
Emily Hill

Damën	*biya*	*na*	*sogopë*	*gënë*	*wënëvi,*
Our	mother	?	earth	bitterroot	(?voc.),

Damën	*biya*	*na*	*sogopë*	*gënë*	*wënëvi.*
Our	mother	?	earth	bitterroot	(?voc.).

Damën	*biya*	*na*	*sogopë*	*gusi*	*yëmpë*	*wënëvi,*
Our	mother	?	earth	gray, misty	?yampa	(?voc),
					[?wild root]	

Damën	*biya*	*na*	*sogopë*	*gusi*	*yëmpë*	*wënëvi.*
Our	mother	?	earth	gray, misty	?yampa	(?voc.).
					[?wild root]	

EMILY: "Mother earth, something about them roots. They're small but it looks like sunflowers. They're good to eat. It's like carrots. You get them up the mountains."

JUDY: "Is that *ohayamp?*"

EMILY: "[No,] *yamp*[h]. Carrots is *ohayamp*[h]. That one [in the song], that's *yamp*[h]. Same taste as that, [carrots], nice and sweet. You just cook it on the stove. Sometimes you boil them and then eat them. They taste good. They grow in the ground that's kind of moist."

Naraya Song 116

Dorothy Tappay
Emily Hill

Damë	*akën*[7]		*doiya*	*akën*		*doiyav-avin,*
Our	sunflower seeds		mountains	sunflower seeds		mountains-(ʔv.s.),

Damë	*akën*		*doiya*	*akën*		*doiyav-avin.*
Our	sunflower seeds		mountains	sunflower seeds		mountains-(ʔv.s.).

Du	*wai*	*du*	*wai*	*akën-*	*iküni,*
Black [seeds]	ʔto come down	black [seeds]	ʔto come down	sunflower seeds	(v.s.),

Du	*wai*	*du*	*wai*	*akën-*	*iküni.*
Black [seeds]	ʔto come down	black [seeds]	ʔto come down	sunflower seeds	(v.s.).

JUDY: "This is an Idaho song?"

EMILY: "Yes. *Ak* means some kind of seeds. They're little ones, little bits, black and white. They're something you cook, make gravy out of it. You sugar them, eat it. Really tastes good. I think they get them on the mountains. That's the song of that."

JUDY: "Do you get them here or do you have to go up Idaho way?"

EMILY: "No, they're around here, up in the mountains."

Na-na suyage hombi na-na suyage hom,
Looks good/pretty stick looks good/pretty stick,

Na-na suyage hombi na-na suyage hom.
Looks good/pretty stick looks good/pretty stick.

Sïnam[8]   *bogombi engana todowainda*   *sïnam*
?Wild rose hip berries   red   ripe and burst open ?wild rose hip
  bogombi engana todowainda,
  berries   red   ripe and burst open,

Sïnam   *bogombi engana todowainda*   *sïnam*
?Wild rose hip berries   red   ripe and burst open ?wild rose hip
  bogombi engana todowain.
  berries   red   ripe and burst open.

EMILY: "Sure looks pretty, it said. *Na: suyage hombi,* that means, good when you see it, *na: suyage hombi,* seeing that red one. *Todowainda,* that means something—red berries—they busted. They're still ripe."

Angelina Wagon sang the same song for me in 1981 and gave her translation for the text.

ANGELINA: "Something like those little red pine berries. Just like, you know, when you have holly—those same kind of berry. *Na:suyag* means it really looks good. You want it when you see it. *Engana* means something red, busting, bust, or whatever. Burst open, really ripe, and really nice" (Vander 1988:61).

Dick Washakie also sang this song in 1909. In 1988 I published a comparative score of all three performances for song 117, the dates for which span almost three-quarters of a century (Vander 1988:62).[9]

Naraya Song 118

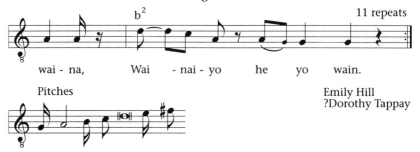

wai - na,   Wai - nai - yo   he   yo   wain.

Pitches

Emily Hill
?Dorothy Tappay

Engaparai   *yuwan*   *e-ï-na,*
Cinquefoil berries carrying something in pan, hand, etc. (e.v.),

Engaparai   *yuwan*   *e.*
Cinquefoil berries carrying something in pan, hand, etc. (abb.e.v.).

Wainaiyo[10]   *he yo*   *waina,*
?Going down (vocs.) ?going down,

Wainaiyo   *he yo*   *wain.*
?Going down (vocs.) ?going down.

JUDY: "Is that about a strawberry?"
EMILY: "Yes, got it in your hand, maybe pan or something."
JUDY: "What does *wai:no* mean?"
EMILY: "Going through where, you know, strawberries are down that way. In the hills, something like it—going down."

Information given by Shimkin indicates that the berry in song 118 is not actually the wild strawberry (*Fragaria*), *dɔ́săyahe:d*, but another similar berry of the cinquefoil (*Potentilla glandulosa*), *dɔyaɛ́ŋgaparaŋ* (Shimkin 1947b:273). The Shoshone word for the cinquefoil berry derives in abbreviated form from "mountain" (*doiyavi*), "red" (*engavitʰ*), and "water" (*ba:*). This word undergoes further abbreviation and alteration in song 118, appearing as *engaparai*.

Angelina Wagon, who sang this song for me in 1981, simply commented that the text mentions "something like a strawberry."

Naraya Song 119

♩ = ca. 100

(9th verse)

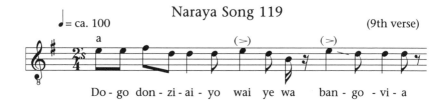

Do - go don - zi - ai - yo   wai   ye wa   ban - go - vi - a

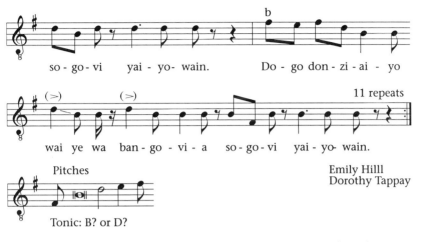

so - go - vi yai - yo- wain. Do - go don - zi - ai - yo

wai ye wa ban - go - vi - a so - go - vi yai - yo- wain.

11 repeats

Pitches

Emily Hilll
Dorothy Tappay

Tonic: B? or D?

Dogo	*donzi-aiyo*	*wai ye wa*	*ba-n-*	*go-via*	*sogo-vi*	*yaiyowain.*
White	flower	(?vocs.)	water	?earth-	earth-	(e.v.).
				?mother	?mother	

Dogo	*donzi-aiyo*	*wai ye wa*	*ba-n-*	*go-via*	*sogo-vi*	*yaiyowain.*
White	flower	(?vocs.)	water	?earth-	earth-	(e.v.).
				?mother	?mother	

EMILY: "*Dogo donzia* means those strawberries, on the ground, those flowers."

MILLIE GUINA: "Them white flowers. White flowers of strawberry plant."

Naraya Song 120

♩ = ca. 92

(4th verse)

Yï - vai doan - zi - a wü - wa doi e - na. Yï - vai doan - zi-

an wü - wa doi e - na. Yï- vai doan - zi - a wü - wa doi

d   7 repeats, incomplete

e- na.   De   doi- ya- vin- de   de   doi ya- vin- de   e- na.

Pitches

Dorothy Tappay
Emily Hill

Yïvai	*doanzia*	*?wüwa*[11]	*doi*	*ena.*
Fall	blossoms/blooms	?pine nut tree	mountains	(e.v.).

Yïvai	*doanzian*	*?wüwa*	*doi*	*ena.*
Fall	blossoms/blooms	?pine nut tree	mountains	(e.v.).

Yïvai	*doanzia*	*?wüwa*	*doi*	*ena.*
Fall	blossoms/blooms	?pine nut tree	mountains	(e.v.).

De	*doiyavi-nde*	*de*	*doiyavi-nde*	*ena.*
?Small	mountains	?small	mountains	(e.v.).

EMILY: "In the fall, you know, those flowers, something blooms in the fall. In the mountains where them, you know, those nut—pine nuts. That's pine nut tree, pine nut trees. You could find flowers blooming in the mountains. That's the kind of song it is. The fall flowers are blooming."

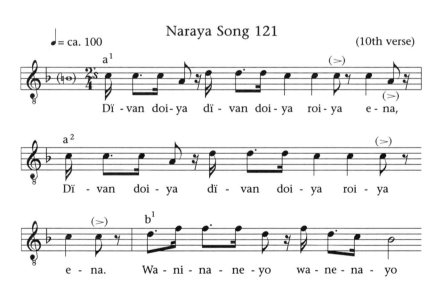

♩ = ca. 100   **Naraya Song 121**   (10th verse)

a¹   (>)

Dï - van doi- ya   dï - van doi- ya   roi- ya   e - na,

a²   (>)

Dï - van   doi - ya   dï - van   doi - ya   roi - ya

(>)   b¹

e - na.   Wa - ni - na - ne - yo   wa - ne - na - yo

Emily Hill
Dorothy Tappay

Dïva	*n-doiya*	*dïva*	*n-doiya*	*roiya*	*ena,*
Pine nut	mountains	pine nut	mountains	mountains	(e.v.),

Dïva	*n-doiya*	*dïva*	*n-doiya*	*roiya*	*ena.*
Pine nut	mountains	pine nut	mountains	mountains	(e.v.).

Waninaneyo	*wanenayo*	*ena,*
?Curving down	?curving down	(e.v.),

Waninaneyo	*wanenayo*	*ena.*
?Curving down	?curving down	(e.v.).

EMILY: "Those pine nut mountains, *dïvA,* pine nuts. I think that's from Nevada or someplace, that song. 'Cause they have pine nuts back there. They bring 'em out in the gunny sacks and they sell them here."

I suggest that Emily's comments about Naraya song 16 might have relevance for the second line of text in song 121. Emily paraphrased song 16.

EMILY: "That means mountains, going over the small mountains. . . . Just wander around in the mountains. *Waniya* is something like . . . down, like a curve . . . going down" (Vander 1986:51). *Waniya* also appeared in song 16 as *waneya. Wani-nane-yo* and *Wane-na-yo* may be two more elaborations, lengthening the word through vocable inserts.

Commentary

Plants as Calendar Markers

Plants are such important food sources that their sprouting and blossoming marked the yearly calendar for Great Basin people. Lowie learned that Wind River Shoshones reckoned *mo´dzaruə* as the time when mountain sheep have young and grass is beginning to come up (Lowie 1924a:311) (See chapters 3 and 5 for Lowie's complete listing of the months.) Shimkin's subsistence chart for Wind River Shoshones shows the place of plant food in their diet during the nineteenth century, prior to settlement on the reservation. Because of rich animal resources, the sprouting of early greens in April and May was not a matter of life and death to them as it was for others who lived in the Great Basin. Nevertheless, seeds and pods were important foods in May and June, as were berries in July and August and roots in August and September.

While pine nuts and sunflowers do appear in Naraya songs 62, 116, and 121, they are not calendar markers for the Wind River Shoshones. Northern Paiutes and Western Shoshones, on the other hand, depended heavily on plants for daily diet. Their names for the months of the year reflect a careful observation of what bloomed when. Pine nuts, sunflowers, rye grass, and a host of other plants, especially the life-saving early greens, were calendar markers for these people. I include a sampling of their names for the months of the year for comparison with the names used by the Wind River Shoshones. Such a comparison brings out both the differences between them—the greater Wind River focus on states of water and animals—and at the same time, the overlap—for example, the mention of new grass at lambing time. As my study assumes a deep historical frame, I believe that the Wind River Shoshone names for the months of the year and the names designated by other Great Basin groups, with their strong plant orientation, have relevance for Naraya song texts and concerns.

The following three calendar designations are from Northern Paiutes in Nevada (Stewart 1941:445). (See chapter 5, n. 34, for complete calendars of four groups, including example 1, below.)

1. sagebrush mountain-dwellers

March	everything-green-month (*puimöha*)
April	buckberry-leaves-out-month
May	flower-month
June	Indian-potato-month
August	rye-grass-month
September	piñon-nut-month

2. *wada*-seed eaters

[no month	first-green-shoots-through-snow-month
designation	(*poimaya müha*)
given]	grass-grows-high-month
	Indian-potato-month

3. red-butte dwellers

February	earliest-plants-push-aside-last-year's stalks-month
March	green-grass-growing-fast-month (*puiwaya möhü*)
August	rye-grass-ripe month
September	piñon-pine month (*tuva möhü*)

Kelly gives two Surprise Valley Paiute calendar markings (Kelly 1932:153). March was "plants germinating" (*Tokwü´tü-müha*) and April, "grass is sprouting" (*Puhi´-mayü-müha; puhi´,* "green"). Steward learned that Bannocks in Idaho called May "seeds sprouting [moon, i.e., month]" (*tokwö'nai muha*) and Shoshones of Grouse Creek in Utah called August "sunflower [month] (*kusiak müa*)" (Steward 1943a:291).

Shoshones from Death Valley called May "green brush" (*hu:pa-düa*) (Steward 1941:268). I believe that *hu:pa* is another version of *hupi*, which appears in songs 111–12. *Dua* means "son" or "child" in Shoshone and brings to mind vegetation in its early sprouting phase.

Shoshones of Egan Canyon, Nevada, called August "sunflower" [ripe] *akü-müa* [*müa* means "moon"], and six Western Shoshone groups from Nevada called September "pinenuts" [ripe] *tuba-müa* (Steward 1941:269).

Liljeblad writes of the Lemhi Shoshone of Idaho, "In the month they called *púhimeha,* the green month, when the grass was 'long as a finger,' the buffalo hunters left their valley. About midsummer they were on the hunting ground, where they remained until early fall" (Liljeblad 1957:106).[12] (This is one example of several to be described in which green stands for grass, and grass is food for the hunters' horses, not for the hunters.)

Plants as Names for Land and People

In the previous section I have suggested the importance of plants to Great Basin cultures, as reflected in their names for the months of the year. Another indication of the importance of plants is that, for many Great Basin people, land and people also bore names derived from various plants, including some of the edible roots and seeds that appear in Emily and Dorothy's Naraya repertoire. The yampa root mentioned in song 115 is one such example. Shoshones called Utes who lived near the White River *ya'mpadïkanï,* "Yamp-eating people" (Shimkin 1947b:251). Mooney rendered the Shoshone name for the Comanches as "*Yä´mpai-ni* or *Yä´mpai-Rï´ kani,*" explaining that it was a "Shoshoni name signifying 'yampa people,' or 'yampa eaters.' It is properly the name of only one division, but is used collectively for the whole tribe. The yampa plant is the *Carum gairdneri*" (Mooney [1896] 1991:1043).[13]

Sunflower seeds, which appear in song 116, gave their name to the Warraricas, Sunflower seed eaters in Oregon.[14] Another group of seed eaters from Utah and Idaho have personal ties to Emily and Dorothy. Steve Tappay, Emily's step-father and Dorothy's father, was a *Huku-dïka,* or Dirt Eater, as Emily translated it. Liljeblad shed light on this name and Steve Tappay's ancestry when he wrote that groups roaming between the Snake River and the Great Salt Lake—besides being referred to by a variety of other food names—were called *hékandeka* or *húkandeka*. The former term can best be translated with "seed eaters." In slightly varied form, the first part of the word in several Shoshoni dialects denotes one or the other of various grasses with edible seed (wheat grass, spear grass, wild rye, and probably others), all of which likewise occur under other names. *Huka*, on the other hand, means "dirt" or "dust." The term *húkandeka*, among contemporary reservation Indians, the commonly used appellation for the descendants of said groups, apparently originated as a pun; ingenuity in playing on words is much admired in Shoshoni lore. (Liljeblad 1957:55)[15]

Liljeblad says further that:

> To this day, descendants of *húkandeka* on the Fort Hall Reservation travel to the Goose Creek Mountains in early fall, when the pine nuts are ready for harvest. [See songs 62 and 121.] In prereservation times all the groups mentioned shared in the pine-nut harvest of this region. The local group, living as primitive food-gatherers in small and isolated villages along Grouse Creek, were called *tébadeka*, "pine-nut eaters," by the others. With this appellation, the Northern Shoshoni also referred to Shoshoni and Northern Paiute in Nevada—no discrepancy being involved, since in either case people with the same economy were alluded to. (Liljeblad 1957:113)

Plants, Women, and Equality

This section explores the results of the division of labor by men and women in the Great Basin and by Wind River Shoshones. My focus will be primarily on the role of women as gatherers of plant foods and the importance and impact of this role on female participation in shamanism, the Round Dance and Naraya, and other religious contexts.

Wind River Shoshones in the eighteenth and nineteenth centuries differed from most other Great Basin people because of their Plains-life reliance on hunting, especially buffalo hunting, for subsistence. As a consequence, the importance of the male hunter and warrior, who acquired horses and secured hunting grounds, made for a more strongly male-centered society. However, the division and complementary nature of labor remained. In 1879 Colonel Brackett reported that among the Wind River Shoshones, "The squaws collect roots, . . . They collect seeds and wood" (Brackett 1880:332). Later scholars amplified this. Lowie wrote in 1924, "The Wind River Shoshoni said that about August their women used to gather roots, storing them in bags for the winter" (Lowie 1924a:203). Shimkin added, "Women, especially in late summer and fall, picked currants, roseberries, hawthorns, and gooseberries" (Shimkin 1986a:317). Plant harvesting was the Wind River Shoshone woman's domain; hunting was the man's. Within their eighteenth- and nineteenth-century Plains world, plant foods supplemented meat and fish.

One finds a similar division of labor in the Great Basin,[16] but the dietary balance was often the reverse. Meat and fish supplemented plant foods. Such was the case for Southern Paiutes. "A great variety of plant foods was utilized. More important than game, they were largely the women's responsibility" (Kelly and Fowler 1986:370).

Interrelationships between the female-plant and male-animal dichotomy emerged in the restrictions and rules governing menstruation. For the Washoe, "Of particular significance was the consecration of the female role in the girls' puberty rites in which symbolic acts connected with gathering and domestic chores were given emphasis as well as taboos against eating meat and fish" (D'Azevedo 1986b:477). Lenore Shoyo, a Wind River Shoshone woman, explained the meat taboo to me. "We can't eat any kind of meat then [during menstruation]. Because if we do our brothers or whoever killed that meat won't be able to kill another one again. We wait like three days after it, before we touch meat" (Vander 1988:199). In a similar vein, Southern Paiute women observe the same taboo so that the animals will not take offense and allow themselves to be caught by the hunters (Franklin and Bunte 1992:2, 5).

Is there a special ritual for women in their roles as gatherers? D'Azevedo attempts to correct inaccurate assumptions regarding the lack of ritual within the Washoe woman's domain as plant gatherer:

> Downs suggests that gathering, a predominantly female activity, was less ritualized than hunting or other pursuits engaged in mainly by men. However, ethnographers have tended to overlook the religious and social aspect of women's subsistence activities. Prior to any gathering task, women (usually led by an elder member of the group) offered prayers to the plants and for the blessing of their utensils and other equipment. There were traditional restrictions on the amount that could be harvested from a given area, to insure future growth; and debris was removed out of "respect" for the local species. (D'Azevedo 1986b:477)

This implied equality of the sexes, here in regard to ritual and subsistence activities, is directly the point of Lowie's observation that "the frequent participation of both sexes in dancing may turn out to be a distinctive Shoshonean or Plateau or even Ultramontane feature" (Lowie 1924a:302). This included female participation as dancers in antelope charming rituals that preceded the hunt (Lowie 1924a:305).

Women participated as dancers in shamanistic curing rites of the White Knife and Salmon Eater Shoshones. Park writes, "As she [the dancer] follows the shaman in the ritual, the dancer carries a winnowing-tray containing seeds, a practice identical with the Paviotso [Northern Paiute] custom. This assistant among these Shoshoni is asked to serve only when the shaman is treating a female patient or in connection with a curing performance held to drive away an epidemic" (Park 1938:128). Here, the clear connection between women and plants, women as plant gatherers, is further linked to health, both curative and preventive.[17]

The possible equality between men and women, already suggested in subsistence ritual and in dance, extends to shamanism. Laird reports that in the past, there were as many women shamans as men among the Chemehuevi (Laird 1976:213). Park qualifies this point:

> The shaman's calling is open to both sexes among nearly all of the tribes west of the Rocky Mountains. As we have seen, the Paviotso have both men and women shamans, men, however, predominating in numbers. Although in theory female shamans can be as powerful and numerous as men, in practice the tendency is for a greater number of men to acquire shamanistic power and usually those possessing the greatest power are also of this sex.
>
> A very similar if not identical situation is found among most of the Great Basin and Plateau tribes. (Park 1938:88)

Other studies support these conclusions (Steward 1941:258; Stewart 1941:412). A Surprise Valley Paiute told Kelly of a female shaman who "cried like a stallion, took a firebrand of sagebrush, and pointed it toward the south, saying, 'Come on, rain; come on rain!' She did not dance. The wind blew, the rain came, and the snow began to melt" (Kelly 1932:201). A second informant testified to another female shaman's power of prophecy. "Doctors know when sickness is coming. Frank Naneo's mother is an old woman living near Paisley. She dreamed of a sickness and said, 'It's far in the east now, but it is coming here! It was influenza and it came here" (Kelly 1932:190).

Significantly, an equality of men and women in Great Basin culture also appears in religious ceremony. The Round Dance, itself, a circle of men and women, is a prime example. One sentence of the Round Dance prayer quoted by Harris brings us back to subsistence and the important contributions and roles of both sexes. "In the evening, between performances of the round dance, he [the leader and speaker] would admonish the people to be industrious, the men to provide abundant game and fish, the women to gather seeds and roots" (Harris 1940:53).

A comparison of Peyote religious practices on the Plains versus the Great Basin is revealing concerning the roles and status of men and women. La Barre discusses this issue for the Southern Plains.

> In the early days the Kiowa, Comanche, Tonkawa, Sauk, and Oto pro-hibited women from attending, and only old men used peyote, but forty or fifty years ago women started coming in to be doctored and gradu-ally came in for other reasons, though they could not use the ritual paraphernalia; under no circumstances may a menstruant woman en-ter. The restriction against women appears to apply only to groups who early had peyote, when it still had much of the flavor of a warrior's society about it; for example, the Arapaho, Cheyenne, Ponca, Kickapoo, Mescalero, Shawnee, Taos and Wichita apparently always allowed wom-en to attend. In the Iowa meeting the women formed the outer of two concentric circles, the men the inner, and the former were allowed only two buttons. Women never use eagle feather fans. (La Barre 1975:60)

Contrast this with Stewart's comments for Great Basin practice in Nevada: "The Peyote ritual changed very little in western Nevada. Perhaps the most unusual feature was the position accorded to wom-en: they led the singing while holding the staff and rattle, beat the drum, and sometimes acted as chief drummers. . . . A most surprising feature was dancing. At one meeting the members danced a few times around the Half Moon altar following the ritual and the morning recess" (Stewart 1987:279).

The roles and status of men and women in the Ghost Dance, like the musical style of its songs, bears the imprint of its Great Basin origins. This remained true even after the songs and religion took root in new cultural territory on the Plains. Mooney describes the ordi-nation of fourteen Southern Arapaho "priests," seven men and sev-en women, each given a sacred feather (either crow or eagle) and taught Ghost Dance songs and ritual. "Until the Ghost dance came to the prairie tribes their women had never before been raised to such dignity as to be allowed to wear feathers in their hair" (Mooney [1896] 1991:909). In his general discussion of the Plains Ghost Dance ceremony, Mooney adds that, in fact, nearly all the dancers, not just the chosen leader, wore feathers (Mooney [1896] 1991:919).

In addition to wearing feathers, female Ghost Dancers, like their male counterparts, had trance-visions and as a result of these expe-riences were the source of new Ghost Dance songs. For many tribes in the Plains, men were the ones who traditionally sought visionary experience from which they acquired special power, for such activi-ties as hunting or warfare. As in the Great Basin, power often came with or as song (Merriam 1967:3–9; Nettl 1989:96–99; Powers 1973: 16). That 20 of 161 Ghost Dance songs published by Mooney came from women who experienced visions is equally noteworthy (Mooney [1896] 1991:965, 1000, 1002, 1007, 1035, 1036, 1038, 1054, 1064, 1069, 1070, 1085, 1087, 1097–99). Naraya song 112, received by a woman (Virginia Grant Bonatsie), fits this pattern.

The importance of plants and, as a consequence, of women as plant gatherers in Great Basin society has been a given in this discussion. However, for balance, I would add that Great Basin scholars are not unanimous in their interpretations of the relative positions of power between the genders. Among the issues are not only different interpretations, but also both the complexity of the data from many different groups and the further difficulty of assessing historical factors, such as the changes within all these groups over time.[18]

Green/Grass

"Green" in Great Basin thought assumed a plethora of practical and symbolic meanings. The following observation by Steward brings out one series of associations, green-grass-spring-life. "In early spring, when stored foods were running low, people eagerly awaited the first growth of new plants to stave off starvation. The first edible plants were those whose stems or leaves were cooked or eaten raw as 'greens.' They occurred along streams, near lakes and in low hills, where snow had first disappeared and warmth had come earliest" (Steward 1938:19).

Green/grass is one of the most common Naraya images, appearing in songs 6, 10, 20, 35, 38, 39, 45, 47, 56, 66, 83, 84, 96, 97, 102, 103, and 104. The close association between green and grass appears in Shoshone language. For example, Crapo gives *pui"* (*-n*) for "green" or "blue" and *soni-ppyh* (*-a"*) for "grass," "hay." Green grass is *pui-soni-ppyh* (*-a"*), but it can also take a shortened form, *pui-ppyh* (*-a"*), one that emphasizes green by leaving that word intact (Crapo 1976:138–39). I have been given Wind River Shoshone words, *buhi* for "green" and *buhip^h* for "grass."[19] Tidzump gives Wind River Shoshone forms similar to Crapo's, but her translations suggest that different terms designate different types of grass. *Sonripe* means "hay," *puhui sonipe* means "alfalfa hay," and *puhipe* means "small grass" (Tidzump 1970:10SE, 12SE).

Olden suggests that the Shoshone name itself, used to describe Wind River people, derives from *Shont-Shonip*, "which means abundance of grass, because they always camped where the grass was plentiful. It was also the material with which they formerly constructed their wigwams" (Olden 1923:13).[20] (See plate 15 for Lowie's picture of a Shoshone grass lodge.) In this case, I believe the reference to camping near grass relates to Plains life and the need to secure food for horses, rather than Great Basin life and the harvesting of grass and its seeds for people (as I described in the section on plants and seeds).

Green/grass also vibrates with symbolic meanings and associations. For purposes of prognosis, grass signifies health. Dick Mahwee, a Northern Paiute shaman, told Park, "When [in a trance] I see a whirlwind I know that it caused the sickness. If I see the patient walking on grass and flowers it means that he will get well" (Park 1938:54).

Green also signifies longevity. Shoshones from Elko, Nevada, said that "people dream frequently, as omens; dreams of short life brought early death; dreams of green things indicated that one would live at least until the end of the year" (Steward 1941:264).

Green bespeaks resurrection, life. A Northern Paiute myth recounts how Coyote caused a wind, which blew to shore the bones of people who drowned in the water. "In a year or so green grass grew between those bones, and they became alive again" (Kelly 1938:414).[21]

Green corresponds to growth. Shoshones and some Northern Paiutes bury the "mild" or "baby" teeth lost in early childhood under grass or a green bush or tree (Steward 1941:410; Steward 1943a:342). Shoshones of Fort Hall chose rabbit brush or "any brush that grows fast so that the new teeth will grow fast" (Steward 1943a:387).

Green suggests spring and light. Various month names equate greenery with early spring. Myth adds the third element, light. In the race to Koso Springs, Coyote's team won and Coyote threw all the losers, including Sun, into the fire. Darkness covered the earth and all the creatures withdrew into a house. Darkness is an interesting parallel to the biblical flood. Coyote sends a lizard to find out what is happening outside, just as Noah sends out a dove to see if any land emerges from the water. The dove finally returns with an olive branch, vegetation and food source in the Middle East, and Lizard returns to Coyote and says, "There are plenty of berries already ripe on the hills and in the gulches" (Steward 1936:415). Then, at Coyote's urging, Mallard and Goose sing and bring back the light. "The world was bright now and everything outside was green as in the spring" (Steward 1936:415).

Finally, green is associated with water. I return here to the Northern Paiute myth for the origin of water, which links water with trees and grass. People searched for water but could not find any. "Then they went to a tree and opened it and out came the water. The father tells them that hereafter to look in the green spots on the ground and they will find water and to this day wherever there is a particularly green spot, there is always water to be found" (Powell 1971:219). The presence of greenery and water were prominent in my earlier discussion of Shoshone–Great Basin vision of the Land of the Dead. Both the 1870 and 1890 Ghost Dance movements carried this imagery over into the prophesied new world to come.

Wind River Shoshone examples of the associations of greenery with water, and by implication, power, appear commonly in religious visions already mentioned. Tom Compton's Sun Dance vision in, or near, the Land of the Dead placed him on a high mountain ridge, the lower half of which was "green with grass, sprinkled with flowers, and with a stream running" (Shimkin 1953:460). In the Sun Dance, Logan Brown saw "water and shiny green grass coming to his place in the lodge" (Vander 1988:64). Emily described the vision of a Shoshone man in which his soul temporarily departed in its moist foggy state and alighted onto a green grassy spot before ascending into the sky (Vander 1986:38). Toorey Roberts, a Naraya leader in the 1930s, had a vision of Jesus "and underneath him there was a pleasant spot with high green grass and green sagebrush" (Hultkrantz 1969:35). In this instance, water is unstated but implied by the presence of greenery. Richard Engavo's comments on the Sun Dance make explicit the link of greenery to water to power. "'The Shoshones used to have their Sun Dance in June, when the sweet sage leaves were damp and green. [Now it is generally held near the end of July.] Everything was green and everything was damp. But now, along in July, everything's burned up. Everything has no leaves on it; it's all dried up. Just has no power, nothing in it'" (Vander 1988:100–101).

Trees

The following trees are mentioned in Naraya songs

> "Wood," songs 86, 87, 100, 111, 112, 113
> Aspen (*Populus tremuloides*), songs 7, 20, 49, 84, 101, 103, 104
> Pine Nut (*?Pinus monophylla*), songs 62, 85, 110, 120, 121
> Pine (*?Pseudotsuga taxifolia*), songs 5, 34, 109, 110
> Cedar (*Juniperus*), song 108
> Cottonwood (*Populus augustafolia*) (see song text Sh-4, in chapter 10)
> Willow (*Salix*) (see song text Sh-4, in chapter 10)

Trees are obviously frequent images in Naraya songs and carry with them a wealth of associated properties: vegetation in general, strength, water, and long life. The all-important identification of trees qua vegetation began this chapter in the guise of Wood Man, the maker of green things. The symbolic association of trees with strength can be seen in the Wind River Shoshone practice of placing the sloughed umbilical cord of a baby close to or under the root of a tree in hopes that as the tree is strong, so shall the child be strong.[22] Surprise Valley Paiutes include the transfer of strength from tree to son as a secondary element in a ceremony performed after a boy's first kill. "My father came and asked me, 'what kind of tree would you like? Service?' I said, 'Yes, that is stout; maybe it will make me strong'" (Kelly 1932:80). As the son stepped back and forth over a ring of service branches entwined with slices of deer meat, the father named all the animals that the son would hunt in his lifetime. In this way the son was ensured good luck in hunting.

Trees also figure in myth. There was a time when trees, like rocks and animals, were people, and spoke (Powell 1971:241). Again, I remind the reader of the Northern Paiute myth for the origin of water—trees—and the association of trees and water with greenery (Powell 1971:219).

Finally, as we will see in the sections on specific trees, trees served as center poles in various contexts. The Round Dance, Naraya, Ghost Dance, Sun Dance, and Sun Dance lodge all use a circular form. A center pole defines the placement of the circle. Park reported, "People who were familiar with the old life insist that the [Round Dance center] pole had no other purpose than to provide a point of orientation for the circle of dancers" (Park 1941:184).

However, from other scholarly information, we learn, explicitly or implicitly, that the Round Dance center pole served more than just as a point in space. It also carried with it physical associations of its tree origins that related in a variety of ways to the metaphysical orientation and purpose of those who encircled it. In particular, as we will see in the sections on specific trees, many of the associations of grass and greenery carry over to trees that are used as center poles in various contexts. Wind River Shoshones sometimes attach flags to the top of the Sun Dance center pole. Edgar St. Clair, a well-known Shoshone Sun Dance chief, explained that if a green flag is flown, it stands for green grass. Even without a green flag, green branches and leaves that remain at the top of the Sun Dance center pole represent the "miracle of life" (Jorgensen 1972:211).

Cedar (Juniperus)   The cedar, which appears in song 108, is of particular interest with regard to the use of center poles in the Round Dance and Naraya. Dellenbaugh, an artist who accompanied Powell in 1872 during fieldwork among the Kaibab Southern Paiutes, described the Round Dance: "They had stripped a cedar tree of all branches but a small tuft at the top, and around this the whole band formed a large circle, dancing and singing" (Dellenbaugh 1908:178). Twenty years later, in 1892, Mooney visited the Wind River Reservation and subsequently wrote:

> Among the Shoshoni the dance [the Shoshone Ghost Dance, i.e., the Naraya] was performed around a small cedar tree, planted in the ground for that purpose. . . . the Shoshoni claim that the Ghost dance itself as performed by them was a revival of an old dance which they had fully fifty years before.
> The selection of the cedar in this connection is in agreement with the general Indian idea, which has always ascribed a mystic sacredness to that tree, from its never-dying green, which renders it so conspicuous a feature of the desert landscape; from the aromatic fragrance of its twigs, which are burned as incense in sacred ceremonies; from the durability and fine texture of its wood, which makes it peculiarly appropriate for tipi poles and lance shafts; and from the dark-red color of its heart, which seems as though dyed in blood. (Mooney [1896] 1991:809)

Like Mooney, Shimkin was informed on the use of a cedar tree in the Naraya. In 1937 he interviewed Toorey Roberts, a Naraya leader, and wrote, "The cedar (*wāpit*) in the center was used in the old days" (Shimkin 1937). The past tense of the verb and the reference to the "old days" suggest that this practice may have become obsolete by 1937. One can see a tree in the photograph of a Shoshone "Ghost Dance" (plate 10), originally published in 1895 with Colby's article. But a tree does not appear in the drawing made by Emily's sister, Millie Guina, and her family. Drawn in 1960, it portrays a 1924 Naraya (see plate 11). Emily and Dorothy did not mention the use of a cedar tree in their description to me of Naraya performance.

Park reports on the use of feather wands in healing,[23] an example of what seems to be a direct carryover of a shamanistic practice to the Ghost Dance: "The Ghost Dance of the Kaibab is reported to have involved the planting of a feather wand. In this performance, a cedar pole about two feet high was planted in the center of the circle. Two feathers, one a tail-feather painted red, the other a soft white feather taken from under the tail of an eagle, were suspended by a string from the top of the pole. Sometimes, instead of the pole, the prophet put up a stick of service-berry wood which had been nicely smoothed" (Park 1938:135).

Sarah Olden's 1923 publication documents the use of a cedar or hemlock tree in the Shoshone thanksgiving dance that she attended (Olden 1923:37). (See the Round Dance section in chapter 1 for Olden's complete description of the dance.) Hultkrantz connects Olden's information on the thanksgiving dance with Mooney's on the Shoshone Ghost Dance and writes, "The cedar tree of the Eastern Shoshone Round Dance was, like the dance itself, transmitted to the Ghost Dance" (Hultkrantz 1981b:264–81; Mooney [1896] 1991:809).[24]

Shimkin's information on the Wind River Father Dance (described in chapter 1) and the Naraya places emphasis on the shaman's role as leader and upon health as the primary purpose; it also highlights the relationship of shaman to center pole to dancers.[25] Shimkin writes that the dance "is initiated by a shaman who possesses mystical songs . . . which refer to his dream experience. A cedar is placed upright. . . . The shaman stands by the center pole, and the dancers form a circle [around the shaman and center pole]. . . . At the end of each dance, they shake their blankets to shake away illness" (Shimkin 1953:433n.41). Corroborating this shamanistic connection, Shimkin identifies the source of two Naraya texts he published as Frank Perry, "a powerful shaman" (Shimkin 1947c:350).[26]

Cedars have another important ritual function, called "cedaring." Thomas Johnson, an anthropologist who danced in the Wind River Sun Dance, described the process and its use by Sun Dancers. After the conclusion of a sunrise ceremony, "Sun Dancers . . . and others took turns 'cedaring' themselves. This consisted of bending over a pit which had been lined with cedar twigs and allowing the smoke of the ignited twigs to penetrate the body. 'Cedaring' is considered a source of strength, and indeed, as the smoke is inhaled the nostrils and throat feel refreshed" (Johnson 1968:34).

Edgar St. Clair commented to me that cedaring is not only beneficial for people, but also cleans the air. Cedaring is a widely used practice by individuals. While living in the home of a Shoshone family, I experienced an overwhelming feeling of suffocation one evening. I ran outside and breathed in deeply the cool night air. After returning to the house I learned that cedaring was taking place. Cedar had been placed in a pan on the stove. A family member had been having bad dreams; cedar fumes were the antidote to prevent their return.

Cedaring is one of several "therapeutic practices" that are part of almost all Peyote ceremonies (Stewart 1944:66). This is true of Wind River Shoshones and twenty-eight other groups studied by Stewart (1987:346–47). La Barre describes the incense-blessing ceremony in which the leader or his "cedar-man" sprinkles dried, rubbed cedar on the fire. "After cedar-incensing, the fireman makes a smoke, puffs four times and prays, thanking those responsible for the honor of being chosen fire-chief, and praying for the leader and his family, the sick and the absent" (La Barre 1975:48–51).

Pine Trees (?Pseudotsuga taxifolia) As suggested earlier, greenery is symbolically associated with longevity. Northern and Gosiute Shoshones associate the pine tree with longevity (Steward 1943a:283). Wind River Shoshones do likewise. The pine tree appears in Naraya songs 5, 34, 109, and 110. Herman and Lynn St. Clair published their explanation for the symbolic use of pine trees in the Wind River Shoshone Sun Dance. "The pine tree is very old among trees and promises the climb of man upwards" (St. Clair and St. Clair 1977:2:5, quoted in Vander 1988:296).

Second in importance only to the cottonwood center pole of the Sun Dance lodge is the east-running pine rafter. It is one of twelve rafters that radiate from the center pole as spokes of an open sky-roof. Ritual attends the cutting of this rafter, called the "backbone," or "chief" (Shimkin 1953:440). Excerpts of the following prayer used for the center pole were equally appropriate for the pine "backbone." Shimkin reports that T.W. said, "'The Creator has created this tree. . . . I ask you, Creator, to bless us so we may live until old age'" (Shimkin 1953:349).

Pine needles are also used as a medicine. They protect one from illness. Lowie reported, "A little girl came to Wawanabidi's lodge wearing, probably as a charm, a sausage-shaped buckskin necklace stuffed with pine-needles (*Wongo gwana*)" (Lowie 1924a:297).[27] The *wongo gwana* needles in the little girl's bag were combined with *doza* (*todza*), a medicinal plant and the subject of Naraya song 114, and used in the "smoking" procedure already described in connection with cedar.

The pine tree, like the cedar, was also used in Naraya performance. Coming almost twenty years after Mooney, Lowie learned from Wind River Shoshones that Naraya performance was sometimes so large that it was necessary to form a second concentric circle of dancers. "Within the (smaller) circle, though not in the center but rather near the circumference, there was a pine tree, this remained standing and was used for subsequent ceremonies" (Lowie 1915:817).

Willows (Salix) Willows do not appear in Emily and Dorothy's Naraya repertoire. However, I include a brief discussion of them since they do appear in the first line of a Shoshone Naraya song collected by Shimkin, which I quote in chapter 10. Willows grow near water and this is their prime association, notable within the Sun Dance. Water, in turn, is associated with power, thus, the sequence is willows-water-power.

Tom Compton, Sun Dance chief in 1938, explained the symbolism of willows placed in the crotch of the center pole. They are "Holy Water that Christ made in the mountains" (Shimkin 1939:107). In a more generalized Sun Dance study that included the Wind River Shoshones, Jorgensen writes, "The willow nests . . . represent a 'nest of water,' or 'JESUS' BODY,' or power" (Jorgensen 1972:182). The St. Clairs interpret the willows, sage, and mint as signs of abundance and luck (St. Clair and St. Clair 1977:2:5, quoted in Vander 1988:297).

Another use of willows in the Sun Dance brings us back to water and power. Women singers hold bunches of willows, which they wave back and forth as they sing. Alberta Roberts, an active Sun Dance singer, believes that the willows have power, and her Sun Dance singing companion adds that songs come to you while you are holding the willows. Ute women hold similar views. Jorgensen reports that "they use willows to attract power to themselves and to the dancers. Just as the willows in the crotch of the centerpole give water to the pole . . . so the women think that their willows will bring them power to sing well . . . and power for their own good health and happiness" (Jorgensen 1972:267).

Willows were also used in the Round Dance of at least one group of Nevada Shoshones. Harris writes of the White Knife Shoshones, "In the center of the circle, a green willow pole, which symbolized the verdure of the earth, was erected, and about this pole the dances were performed" (Harris 1940:53). The greenery-food connection is explicit in the leader's prayer, "that the earth bring forth berries, seeds, plants; that the hills be covered with green and growing things" (Harris 1940:53).

Aspens (Populus Tremuloides)   Aspens appear in six Naraya songs (7, 20, 49, 84, 101, 103, and 104) and are the most frequently identified tree in Emily and Dorothy's repertoire. Certainly they are an important feature in the Wind River Shoshone landscape, climbing the slopes of the Wind River Mountains that run through and border the reservation.

Aspens also appear in myth. For example, *To-go-av*, Rattlesnake, saved two fawns in a Southern Numic myth. "Then he led them . . . and showed them the rich grasses which they might eat, and took them to the clear spring where they might quench their thirst, and led them to the aspen groves where they might rest in the shade, and taught them a song" (Powell 1971:94).

Cottonwood (Populus augustafolia)   The cottonwood tree is not mentioned in Emily and Dorothy's Naraya repertoire, but it does appear in a Shoshone Naraya song collected by Shimkin, which I quote in chapter 10. The absence of the cottonwood in Emily and Dorothy's Naraya repertoire is very surprising given the prevalence of this tree on the reservation and its importance as the center pole of the Sun Dance lodge. I will nevertheless briefly summarize some of the meanings of the cottonwood center pole, as they exemplify many points made thus far: the tree's qualities of strength, longevity, and water, and the transfer of these qualities to people.

Quitan Quay, a Wind River Shoshone man, spoke thus to the cottonwood tree destined to be a Sun Dance center pole. "Now I am praying to you. I will cut you down. By means of you I am praying, praying well: You will bless youths. Make a sick person well through yourself!" (Shimkin 1953:439). Shoshones explain the metaphoric meaning of the cottonwood after it is cut down. "For the cottonwood lives after it is cut down and its new growth is a sign of one[']s life which goes on and on" (St. Clair and St. Clair 1977:2:5, quoted in Vander 1988:296).

Ceremony dictates the raising of the Sun Dance center pole in a certain manner, accompanied by prayers and songs. "The prayer songs that are sung when the center pole is lifted into place ask for help from the Spirit that the Dance might be successful, that the participants might have long lives—just as the center pole has had one" (Shimkin 1953:441).

Health and longevity are one set of meanings for the cottonwood center pole; water and power are another. "The center pole, which should always be a cottonwood, was chosen by the originators of the [Wind River Shoshone] dance because of its superiority over all other trees as a dry-land tree growing with little water. This tree represents God" (Hebard 1930:293). Jorgensen's Sun Dance study, which included the Wind River Shoshone Sun Dance, brings out the water-power connection implied in the above quote. "The center pole is the medium through which supernatural power is channeled. The center pole is also believed to have supernatural power of its own. . . . In all instances . . . power is equated with water" (Jorgensen 1972:182).

Thomas Johnson described the role of the Sun Dance chief and his assistant in the transfer of power from center pole to people: "Often they would scoop up dirt from the base of the center pole with the feathers or pat the center pole, presumably to convey the supernatural power contained in the pole and in the buffalo head hung on it to the recipients of the blessings. . . . Thus the center pole, as the major object of attention, symbolized this concentration of supernatural, emotive power; when the sponsor patted it with the eagle feathers he was merely acting as an intermediary for the conveying of supernatural power from the center pole to the people" (T. Johnson 1968:15).

Longevity, water, and power do not exhaust the wealth of interpretations that surround the cottonwood tree used as the Sun Dance center pole. I conclude with Jorgensen's admittedly incomplete listing: "the center pole represents life, the sacrifice of power so that others may live, a man's heart, Jesus Christ, Jesus' crucifix, God's brain, power itself, water, *sinawaf* [Wolf, Coyote's benevolent older brother], and probably several other things to which I am not privy" (Jorgensen 1972:210–11).

Edible Plants in Naraya Songs

Emily and Dorothy's Naraya repertoire includes seven edible plants:

bitterroot	*Lewisia rediviva*	Song 115
yampa	*Carum gairdineri B.*	Song 115
rose hip berry	*Rosa californica*	Song 117
wild strawberry	*Fragaria*	Song 119
cinquefoil berry	*Potentilla glandulosa*	Song 118
sunflower seeds	*Helianthus*	Song 116
pine nut seeds	*?Pinus monophylla*	Songs 62 and 121

The above list and the calendrical divisions discussed earlier, which marked the yearly cycle of greenery and plant food, testify to the importance of plants to subsistence. Fowler concluded, "On the whole a surprising proportion of the [Great Basin] diet was derived from plants and plant products" (Fowler 1986:93). Scholarly documentation of this is abundant. For example, "Plant procurement provided the economic mainstay for the Western Shoshone people" (Thomas et al. 1986:266) and "economy was grounded in a systematic and rather predictable seasonal round" (Thomas et al. 1986:268). Similarly, for the Northern Paiute, "Seed and other plant product collecting was very important everywhere in the region" (Fowler and Liljeblad 1986:441).

However, the dietary proportion of plant food to animal food varied from group to group, as did the relative proportions of seeds, berries, and roots. Liljeblad characterized a general pattern to these differences in his observation that "the metate of the seed-gathering peoples in the southern deserts was replaced in the north by the mortar, suitable for pounding roots and dried meat" (Liljeblad 1957:14).

This pattern aptly applies to Wind River Shoshones in the nineteenth century prior to settlement on the reservation. They subsisted primarily on buffalo and other animals and, as Shimkin points out, "these were supplemented by berries and roots, with seeds of minor importance" (Shimkin 1986a:316).

Shimkin's chart (see fig. 4) and commentaries provide a more detailed picture concerning the harvesting of plant foods. April and May are the time of early greens (*Calochorlius,* etc.), and Shimkin notes that "greens, in the forms of pistils and leaves, came as welcome changes from a monotonous winter diet" (Shimkin 1947b:269). Seeds and pods (thistles, for example) were associated with the period from mid-May to the end of June. "Thistles and some kinds of sunflower served as the only sources of seeds. Even they were gathered amateurishly. The gathering baskets of the Basin were unknown; ordinary sticks were inefficient beaters" (Shimkin 1947b:269). From mid-July through mid-August, berries (such as haws) were abundant. Shimkin reports that "women, especially in late summer and fall, picked currants, rose berries, hawthorns, and gooseberries. . . . Berries were eaten fresh, or in soups, or were pounded with buffalo or elk meat and fat to be preserved as pemmican" (Shimkin 1986a:317).[28] Finally, between mid-August and early October, roots (wildroots and others) were available. "Wild roots, camas, and wild onions, especially, were dug with digging sticks" (Shimkin 1947b:269), and "roots were commonly cooked in the earth oven" (Shimkin 1986a: 317). Lowie adds, "The Wind River Shoshoni said that about August their women used to gather roots, storing them in bags for the winter. Wild carrots were used all the time and are still gathered in the fall. They used a digging stick of greasewood" (Lowie 1924a:201).

What remains of these patterns in the twentieth century? Sustained research with five Shoshone women revealed some important points and trends (Vander 1988). The five women were born almost at ten-year intervals, from 1911 to 1959. Their music and life histories, which I gathered from 1977 to 1982, thus represent a large portion of the twentieth century. Emily, born in 1911, grew up eating plants mentioned in the songs: sunflower-seed soup, bitterroot soup, yampa (wild root), and some plants not specifically mentioned, such as wild carrots, buffalo berries, and chokecherries.[29]

Angelina Wagon, born in 1921, gives a vivid picture of the plants she and her family gathered and ate:

> A long time ago we used to get those wild onions, wild turnips, the wild potatoes, the wild carrots. And bitterroot and there's one other wild things—just about looks like a potato, too, but it tastes good. And the

wild rutabagas, it's got some sharp points on there, and it's got a purple flower. They skin them and eat that, but I don't know what it's called. They eat all kinds of wild food: chokecherries, bullberries, currants, elderberries, gooseberries, and there's another little red berry, and wild plums, wild raspberries. They used to grow along the river here, a lot of raspberries. Wild strawberries, I used to gather, too. There is really a lot of wild food around here. I don't think people ever know nothing about them things now. (Vander 1988:53–54)

Alberta Roberts, born 1929, remembers her mother and grandmother digging up bitterroot and how they prepared it in soup.[30] Alberta, herself, found bitterroot soup too bitter and never prepared it for her family. She described an average evening meal from when she was a young girl, which included "potatoes, dried meat that was boiled, bacon, and greasebread (or frybread). She comments: 'Of course they used to like to eat Indian way, you know. We're kind of modern-type now'" (Vander 1988:94). Berry picking remains popular, and Alberta, like other Shoshones, enjoys chokecherries, which she dries and pounds for future use.

Neither Helene Oldman, born in 1938, nor Lenore Shoyo, born in 1959, mention the wild roots that are memorable to Emily, Angelina, and Alberta. Chokecherries remain a traditional part of their diet, which is true for most Shoshones.

Roots Fowler writes: "Root harvesting took on more significance in the northern Great Basin than elsewhere in the region. This area, on the fringe of the root-abundant Columbia Plateau, was well supplied with various species of biscuit-roots (*Lomatium* spp.), yampa (*Perideridia* spp.), bitterroot (*Lewisia rediviva*), and camas. All were subject to intensive collecting activities in the spring of the year by the Northern Paiute, Bannock, and Northern Shoshone" (Fowler 1986:69).

Murphy extends this pattern to Wind River Shoshones and adds some details about the gathering process:

Roots, also, were a valuable adjunct to the diet. Yamp, the principal root, was found in the mountains. Bitterroot was dug on prairie hills, wild potatoes were found in the foothills, and the wild onion grew in the valley floors. Although special trips were not made to root grounds (in contrast to the congregations for camas in Idaho) the women dug them out with pointed sticks near favorable hunting camps. One informant spoke, for example, of the rich yamp grounds in the Big Horn Mountains. All the women of the camp group went out together to dig roots. This was for purposes of companionship: each woman dug and kept her own tubers. (Murphy and Murphy 1960:308–9)[31]

The importance of digging sticks and the roots they unearthed can be seen in the name "Diggers," which applied to portions of the Northern Shoshone (Lowie 1909a:187). Some authors have generalized the term "Diggers" loosely and broadly to mean Shoshones who lacked horses, that is, people in the Great Basin and Great Basin culture. This term distinguished and excluded Shoshones who had acquired horses and assumed Plains life, such as the Wind River Shoshones (Steward and Wheeler-Vogelin 1974:177; Trenholm 1972:4, 57).

Roots were cooked in two types of earth ovens: one, an underground pit into which roots and hot rocks were placed (Lowie 1909a:188) and, another, an underground pit into which roots, water, and hot rocks were placed, thus boiling or steaming the roots (Murphy and Murphy 1986:293). Fremont reported that Yampa was eaten green, dried, or simply pounded "to a mealy substance which thickened with boiling water" (quoted in Lowie 1909a:188).

Drying, mentioned in connection with yampa, was a common way to prepare and preserve other types of roots, such as bitterroot. Alberta Roberts, a Wind River Shoshone woman, described the process and the subsequent use of the dried bitterroot in soup, one of many wild foods eaten by both Alberta and Emily in their childhood. Alberta recalled, "My mother and grandmother used to dig those *gan?* [bitterroot] up with little iron pins. They grow way out on the deserts. They put it in water, and they peel the little pink toppings off. Then they'll dry it out in the sun. They have a little heart in there, little red ones, and they call that the heart. When my mother was living, she's the one that really picks them bitterroot. She used to cook it with soup, meat" (Vander 1988:94).

Some Shoshones continue to dig roots and dry them. Dried carrots, parsnip, and bitterroot were three of twenty-five possible entries for the 1980 Shoshone Tribal Fair.

Like people in everyday life, characters in myth dig and dry roots.[32] With much good humor, one Northern Shoshone myth describes Coyote's attempt to dig yampa with his tail:

> Coyote met Fox, who was eating yampas. 'Uncle, what are you doing?' asked Coyote. 'I am pulling up yampas with my tail. When I want to pull up a great many, I put my tail deep in the ground.' 'Well, I'll try this,' thought Coyote. He went to a place where the yampas were growing. He put his tail in, pulled out yampas and ate them. He went along. He wanted to eat yampas again and put in his tail very deep. This time he could not pull it out. 'Wai, wai, wai,' he shouted, 'Uncle!' Coyote went down until he was completely underground. The yampas pulled him in. [The yampas harvested Coyote!] (Lowie 1909a:272)

Plate 1. Emily Hill, 1981. Photograph taken outside Emily's house by the author (Vander 1986:4).

Plate 2. Emily and her sister Millie Guina, inside Millie's tipi encampment for the 1980 powwow at Fort Washakie, Wyoming. Photograph by the author (Vander 1988:Plate 2).

Plate 3. A photograph of Dorothy Tappay (center) taken in 1943, when she was twenty-three years old; she stands with some family members in front of the Crowheart store, Crowheart, Wyoming. Left to right: Millie Guina (Dorothy's half-sister) and her husband George Guina, Dorothy Tappay and her parents—Steve Tappay and Minnie Hill Tappay. Courtesy of the Shoshone Tribal Cultural Center.

Plate 4. Johnny Dick, 1904-71, was a Naraya leader in the 1930s. He was born in Nevada and eventually moved to the Wind River Reservation. This picture was taken sometime in the 1940s when he served in the armed forces. Courtesy of Margaret Dick.

Plate 5. Virginia Grant Bonatsie, who "dreamed" and received Naraya song 112. In 1910, when twenty years old, she posed as Sacajawea (Shoshone guide to the Lewis and Clark expedition) for this photograph taken by A. P. Porter. The star and crescent moon patterns in the blanket she wears were important motifs in Ghost Dance clothing and ritual objects (Petersen 1976:47–82). Courtesy of the Smithsonian Institution, National Anthropological Archives, no. 86-100.

Plate 6. J. K. Hillers's 1873 photograph of a Kaibab Paiute Round Dance: the *Ta-vo-ko-ki* Circle Dance, in summer costume. Hillers served as photographer for John Wesley Powell's anthropological expedition in the Great Basin. Courtesy of the Smithsonian Institution, National Anthropological Archives, no. 1622.

Plate 7. J. K. Hillers's 1873 photograph of a Kaibab Paiute Round Dance: *Ta-vo-ko-ki* Circle Dance, in winter costume. Courtesy of the Smithsonian Institution, National Anthropological Archives, no. 1623.

Plate 8. 1890 Ghost Dance at a Cheyenne-Arapaho camp near Fort Reno. C. C. Stotz's picture overviews the entire scene: tents, tipis, wagons, horses, and, at the center—just barely visible— the large circle of dancers. Courtesy of the Virginia Cole Trenholm Collection no. 32-97, American Heritage Center, University of Wyoming, Laramie, Wyoming, no. 25786.

Plate 9. Mooney's 1893 photograph of a Southern Plains Ghost Dance. Noteworthy features in this Ghost Dance picture include: dancers holding hands, dancers on the ground, unconscious, and feathers worn in the hair by men and women, a new tradition for Plains women. Courtesy of the Smithsonian Institution, National Anthropological Archives, no. 55,377.

Plate 10. An 1894 Ghost Dance photograph by Elwood Mead, showing "Shoshone and Arapahoe Indians at a ghost dance, summer of 1894, near Fort Washakie, Wyoming" (Colby 1895:246). Because Fort Washakie is a Shoshone location on the reservation, I believe this is a photograph of the Naraya. A cottonwood tree, which is important in the Shoshone Sun Dance, may be the deciduous tree that appears to be within the circle of dancers. (See plate 12.)

Plate 11. "Shoshone Ghost Dance—1924." In 1960, Emily's sister Millie, her son, husband, and husband's relatives made this drawing, recalling Naraya performance of the past. It points up humorous and social aspects of the dance—drawn hearts and amorous glances.

Plate 12. Shimkin took this photograph circa 1937 showing Wind River Shoshones raising the cottonwood center pole for the Sun Dance lodge. Courtesy of the Shimkin Collection 9942, American Heritage Center, University of
Wyoming, Laramie, Wyoming, no. 25794.

Plate 13. Wind River Shoshone Sun Dance circa 1937, photographed by Shimkin. Note the buffalo head on the center pole, believed to be an important source of sacred power, and the eagle paraphernalia (bone whistles and feathers on the hand), another source of sacred power, especially for healing. Courtesy of the Shimkin Collection 9942, American Heritage Center, University of Wyoming, Laramie, Wyoming, no. 25795.

Plate 14. Wind River Shoshones deem Dinwoody Canyon, with its petroglyphs depicting people, birds, mountain sheep, and other animals, a sacred place where one might go to seek sacred power. Shimkin took this photograph, showing a sample of the petroglyphic figures, circa 1937. Courtesy of the Shimkin Collection 9942, American Heritage Center, University of Wyoming, Laramie, Wyoming, no. 25796.

Plate 15. A "Model of a Wind River [Shoshone] Grass Lodge," photographed by Robert Lowie and published in 1924 (Lowie 1924:211). This older type of shelter brings to mind one derivation for the name "Shoshone," *Shont-Shonip*, meaning "an abundance of grass" (Olden 1923:13).

Plate 16. Shimkin took this photograph of a Wind River Shoshone woman (possibly Pandora Pogue) circa 1937. She is holding a digging stick and seems to be demonstrating how one uses it for harvesting edible plants. Courtesy of Shimkin Collection 9942, American Heritage Center, University of Wyoming, Laramie, Wyoming, no. 25785.

Plate 17. Roy Coleman has discovered mountain sheep traps, which Shoshones had built in Sunlight Basin, Wyoming. In 1971 George C. Frison, an anthropologist, photographed Coleman standing next to one such trap. Courtesy of George C. Frison.

In a Northern Paiute myth Coyote satisfies his yampa hunger more easily. Warned by Wolf not to go near the camp of some bad people, "Coyote thought they might have some *ya´pa´* roots. 'I'll go there anyway,' he said. . . . There was lots of *ya´pa´* drying outside. Coyote found a basket. He scooped up some *ya´pa´* and ran" (Kelly 1938:388).

The text of song 115, which mentions yampa and bitterroot, and Emily's quote of a Naraya leader, which opened this chapter, leave no doubt about the inclusion of roots within Naraya religious concern. She reported that Johnny Dick said, "'Let's dance and make our earth and everything, roots what we eat on our ground—let 'em come alive again.'" Liljeblad indicates other religious ceremony for roots: an annual first root-digging celebration with song, dance, and prayer (Liljeblad 1957:31).

Finally, roots also served a medicinal purpose, as shown by the following conversation I had with Lenore Shoyo, a Wind River Shoshone singer.

LENORE: "I usually use the bitterroot [mentioned in song 115] when I'm going to sing or if I get a sore throat, 'cause it numbs my throat up then. If somebody, in some cases, thinks bad about you, trying to hurt you."

JUDY: "That protects you from that, too?"

LENORE: "Uh huh. I chew on it. It's just like chewing gum" (Vander 1988:199).

Berries Berries, which are mentioned in songs 117, 118, and 119, were harvested throughout the Great Basin and assumed varying importance from group to group. For example, both the mention of buckberries in a Round Dance prayer (see chapter 1) and the development of a shaped basketry sieve for seeding and pulping them suggest the importance of this berry for certain Northern Paiute groups in Nevada (Fowler 1986:69). The Owens Valley Paiutes harvested six species of berries (Fowler and Liljeblad 1986a:416). Northern Paiutes had in their region many berry species, which people dried whole and added to soups or dried into cakes for trips (Fowler and Liljeblad 1986:443). People in Idaho ate chokecherries, service berries, and blackberries (Liljeblad 1957:29); Washoes ate chokecherries, elderberries, currants, and gooseberries—fresh, pounded and cooked in soup or baked into dry cakes (D'Azevedo 1986b:475).

Within the overall hierarchy of Wind River Shoshone subsistence patterns from the nineteenth century, berries, like roots, occupy the middle position: less important than bison and fish and more important then early greens and jackrabbits. (See fig. 4.) Currants, rose hip berries (mentioned in song 117), hawthorns, and gooseberries, chokecherries, and buffalo berries were eaten fresh, in soup, or dried and pounded with dried meat. To this list, Shimkin adds, "The sugary content of honey plants, gilia, cinquefoil [mentioned in song 118] and others was highly prized by children above all" (Shimkin 1947b:269). All these berries flourished in Shoshone territory of upland forests and high prairies, watered by rivers and streams.

In 1979 I spoke with Ethel Tillman, an elderly Wind River Shoshone, who reminisced about the succession of berries that she and the other women of her family used to pick:

ETHEL: "Well, when I was a little girl I remember we used to go berry picking. With my grandma and mother, we'd go berry picking, you know, early in the spring we used to go picking as soon as the fruits come out. We used to go picking gooseberries. That was the first part of the picking, the gooseberries. And they'd pick that and dry that. 'Cause they dried it, they didn't pound it. They just let it dry [whole]. That's the first part. Next was the sarisberry [service berry]. They got that. They dried that. Then that chokecherries comes the last. Chokecherries and buffalo berries. They dried that all the way through. They used to have dried fruit all winter long."

JUDY: "To dry it you would just lay it out in the sun?"

ETHEL: "Uh huh."

JUDY: "How did you eat that dried fruit? Just as is? Or did you soak it back up?"

ETHEL: "Yeah, you soak it back up and then when it's all ready, just like you cook [dried] beans, well, they come back up and then you cook them. Then you put your sugar and your flour and then that's it. Then you got *gotzap* [sauce, or gravy]."

Berries continue to be collected and dried. Dishes in the dried foods category of the 1980 Shoshone Fair included berry products such as whole chokecherry, chokecherry patties (pounded and mixed with dried pounded meat), whole buffalo berry, buffalo berry patties, currants, gooseberry, and service berry (Fair booklet 1980:24).

I picked buffalo berries (*enkoāmp^h*) with Millie Guina, Emily's sister, in back of Millie's house. Actually, we didn't pick the berries. We beat them from the branches with sticks, and they showered down onto a tablecloth that we had carefully laid around the base of the shrubby tree. Millie cautioned me not to hit the branches too hard, lest I break them. Her concern for diminishing next year's harvest seemed to be motivated by a desire to avoid not only any physical injury that I might cause but, in some sense and in equal measure, any nonphysical, metaphysical injury. Still, with plenty of daylight left in that early summer evening, we brought home our berries. Millie made buffalo berry jam.

The search for and enjoyment of berries sometimes moves beyond the reservation borders. People today travel in cars and pickup trucks in order to attend powwows and Sun Dances in Idaho, Montana, and Utah. This activity is at its height in the summer, a cultural harvest that coincides with the ripening of berries. "The location of berries . . . along roads frequently traveled to reservations in neighboring states is still part of the environmental knowledge which many Shoshones possess" (Vander 1986:65). Shoshones picking berries en route—traveling and gathering—is an ancient pattern that resonates softly in the twentieth century.

The origins of berries appear in Shoshone myth and in several instances these tales connect berries, eyes, and birds. According to one myth, the animals held a council in order to determine how to divide the year into seasons and what food they should eat. Kwitok-wits, a bird, pulled out his own eyes and threw them up among the trees, declaring, "'You shall be currants'" (Lowie 1924b:8). In other versions, the eye throwing is not meant to be permanent, but part of a game of eye juggling (Lowie 1924b:26). Coyote tried to do it, and others tricked him so that his eyes did not return and he was blinded. In the Paviotso (Northern Paiute) telling, Coyote then steals the eyes of a bird, saying, "'Get buffalo-berry seed and make eyes for yourself therefrom, I'll have your eyes'" (Lowie 1924b:222).[33]

We have seen that berries appear significantly in the race to Koso Springs. Lizard goes forth into the sunless world and reports back to Coyote that berries are ripe in a distant land. Light and spring are returning.

The rose hip berry mentioned in song 117 has interesting usage in Shoshone myth. Shimkin writes, "Other stereotyped actions [in myth] are reviving a comrade from death by rasping a wild rose branch vigorously in his mouth or anus. . . . [A footnote adds:] This plant was formerly placed on the chests of the deceased when they were interred" (Shimkin 1947c:343). It may be that there was a protective purpose to this custom in light of another use of wild rose by Harney Valley Paiutes. Their shamans, who cured patients suffering from "ghost sickness," kept the ghost from returning by placing bunches of wild rose by the door (Whiting 1950:41).

Berries appear in myth and in the idealized landscape of the dead. The soul of a female shaman traveled to that land in order to retrieve the soul of a boy. Her soul arrived at "a place where the land is green and fertile and berries and foods are always ripe" (Steward 1943a:283).

Berries even grow at the fork in the road that leads to the land of the dead, refreshing dead souls on their journey (Steward 1943a:287).

Another important berry is the chokecherry. Indeed, Ethel Tillman, who described the sequence of berrypicking earlier, called the chokecherry "our sacred food." I cannot explain the absence of the chokecherry in Emily and Dorothy's Naraya repertoire. The particular relationship of Wind River Shoshones to berries is expressed in the Chokecherry Dance, a ceremony in dance. The form of the ceremony for the chokecherry, the Plains style of its song and dance,[34] is very different from the Great Basin style of Naraya song and dance. But the intent, the religious contents of the two sit side-by-side, two seeds from the same pod. One Shoshone man described the Chokecherry Dance as a "dance of fertility, a dance of plenty, and a supplication for food. One remarkable man in his nineties [John Truhujo in the late 1970s] remembers that the ceremony was done in the spring *so that* the berries would ripen in the fall. . . . A long time ago the chokecherry sauce that was in the pot and used in the ceremony was thrown out with the belief that then there would be more berries" (Vander 1978:39).[35]

In his study "Indian Peoples in Idaho," Liljeblad also mentions "singing, dancing, and praying in connection with the first salmon catch, the first root-digging, or the first berry-picking of the year" (Liljeblad 1957:31).

As described in chapter 1, Lemhi Shoshones in Idaho had a special dance for berries called the *nū´akin* or *ta-nū´-in*. The purpose of the dance bears a striking resemblance to that of the chokecherry ceremony and the Naraya. "The *nū´akin* was celebrated for several days, either towards the end of winter or in the beginning of spring. Its object was to ensure plentiful supply of food, especially of salmon and berries" (Lowie 1909a:217). Lowie's description of the dance, even down to such fine details as women stepping back out of the circle at the end of the song and moving back in when the new song begins, precisely matches Emily's Naraya description. If not identical to Naraya, the *nū´akin* was a close variant in form as well as substance.

Seeds (Excluding Pine Nuts) "One fall we started out across the White mountains to gather a supply of wai for the winter." Thus speaks Jack Stewart in his Owens Valley Paiute autobiography. Steward, the scholar who conveyed this remark, added that "wai" was "*Oryzopsis huyenoides* or *O. miliacia,* a grass seed very important as food" (Steward 1934:425–26).

Seeds of all kinds were the mainstay for many Great Basin people, especially for those in the south. For example, Steward "lists some 40 food plants, mostly seed crops, harvested in Owens Valley" (Fowler and Liljeblad 1986a:416). Likewise, as Kelly and Fowler comment on Southern Paiute subsistence, "Seeds were basic" (Kelly and Fowler 1986:370).

This was not true for Wind River Shoshones, who hunted a rich diversity of animals. Roots and berries supplemented their diet, and seeds were of minor importance.[36]

Shimkin reports that "thistles and some kinds of sunflower seeds served as the only sources of seeds" (Shimkin 1986a:317). Collected from mid-May through the end of June, sunflower seeds "were gathered amateurishly. The gathering baskets of the Basin were unknown; ordinary sticks were inefficient beaters" (Shimkin 1947b:269).

Colonel Brackett wrote in his government report on the Wind River Shoshones, published in 1880, "Their bread was made of sunflower (*Helianthus annuus*) and lambs-quarter (*Chenopodium album*) seeds, mixed with service berries (*Amelanchier canadensis*)" (Brackett 1880:329). About seventy-five years earlier Lewis and Clark had seen Lemhi Shoshones also pound serviceberries and sunflower and Chenopodium seeds into a bread (Steward 1943a:271).

Sunflower seeds, their identification, harvest, and preparation, appear in more recent Great Basin literature. In his Basin-Plateau study, Steward writes, "*Helianthus,* sunflower. Seeds of several species, distinguished in native terminology but generically called *ak:,* were eaten." Steward continues with a detailed listing of many native terms for *Helianthus annuus* L. and *Helianthus aridus* Rydb. Sunflowers and their seeds, *ak,* are the subject of song 116.

Other scholars document the profusion of native terms that distinguish various types of sunflowers and the difficult task of matching them with scientific identification.[37] For Wind River Shoshones, Shimkin gives *dɔ́yaba:k* (literally, "mountain sunflower") for *Helianthus petiolaris* Nutt. In a category he calls "identification doubtful," he includes *ak'* and *kušiak* (the latter, literally, "gray sunflower"), which are identified as *Helianthus annuus.* Their seeds were used in soup; Emily describes this in her commentary on song 116. Shimkin gives *hi´ump* for *Helianthus peticolaris* and *pia´:ak'* (literally, "big sunflower") (Shimkin 1947b:273–74).

Some Wind River Shoshones still gather sunflower seeds and dry them. In the 1980 Shoshone Tribal Fair, a dried foods category included sunflower seeds and pine nuts.[38]

The origin and use of seeds, sunflowers included, find expression in myth. Northern Paiutes from Pyramid Lake recount "The Creation of the Indians." According to this tale, an ancestral first woman "made different kinds of seed into a soup for him [the ancestral first man]." Indians originated from this ancestral couple. "The old woman taught the Indians how to get seeds. They multiplied and had plenty of seeds but do not know them all" (Lowie 1924b:202).

Southern Paiutes tell how *Tov-wots* (Progenitor of the Little Rabbit Nation) and the *Shin-au-av* brothers (Progenitors of the Wolf Nation) played mythic roles in the planting of seeds after a flood had covered the earth and killed all plant life. *Tov-wots* led the *Shin-au-av* brothers into a hole, "and as he went, lo! a great way was opened before him and they all entered a vast chamber and found a great store of seeds. When they had eaten until they were full, they took of the seeds and scattered [them] over the earth, and the land was reclothed with vegetation" (Powell 1971:78).

Discovery and preparation of sunflower seeds appear in another Southern Paiute myth. "Cottontail turned a rock over and found something ground on it. [He asked his brothers,] 'What have you been grinding on that?' The boys said, 'That *aq* [sunflower] seed. It is close here and was stored up, then a big rock fell on it and we can only get out a little at a time by wetting a stick and pulling out some'" (Lowie 1924b:143).

The relationship of Round Dance performance and its associated prayers to vegetation and plant foods has already been cited in several places. It suffices here to reiterate this briefly and to present new evidence with specific reference to seeds. The following groups reported that the purpose of the Circle, or Round Dance, was to make seeds grow: Lemhi Shoshones, Northern Paiute Bannocks, Gosiutes of Skull Valley, and Gosiutes of Deep Creek (Steward 1943a:349); Shoshones of Snake River and Shoshones of Battle Mountain (Steward 1941:323); twelve of fourteen Northern Paiute groups (Stewart 1941:415).

Park singles out Round Dance prayers by White Knife and Salmon Shoshones for "abundance of wild seed" and adds that other Great Basin Shoshone groups held the "belief that the ceremony . . . assures a bountiful supply of seeds" (Park 1941:192). Shimkin supports this among the Shoshones of Carson River Basin. "They undertook . . . religious dances to promote game and seed harvests" (Shimkin 1970:177). Seven Northern Paiute groups made offerings of seeds at spring dances. (Full description of it is quoted in chapter 1.) Two groups gave offerings at meals when first seeds were gathered (Stewart 1941:415). Finally, a Northern Paiute group from upper Walker River, Nevada, made offerings to spirits "by sprinkling seeds during the spring dances and by sprinkling on grave [*sic*]" (Stewart 1941:444).

*Pine Nuts (?*Pinus monophylla*)* Pine nuts did not play a significant role in Wind River Shoshone diet. It may seem surprising, therefore, that pine nuts or pine nut trees appear in Naraya song texts (songs 62 and 121). I believe their source was the ongoing stream of Great Basin people and culture that continued to filter through Wind River Shoshone life—after they had adopted Plains life and even beyond, after they had settled on the reservation.

Beginning with an Owens Valley Paiute context, Fowler and Liljeblad expand their comments on pine nuts to include all of the Great Basin. They write, "Paramount among all the products that these mountain valleys afforded was the pine nut, the seed of *Pinus monophylla,* far and away the most important single food, which all Numic-speaking peoples called by cognates of the same word: Owens Valley Paiute *tiba,* Western Shoshone and Southern Paiute *tipa*" (Fowler and Liljeblad 1986a:416).[39] Wind River Shoshones call it *divA.*

Pine nuts assumed great importance for the Owens Valley Paiute and for other groups in the "central core of the Great Basin . . . especially in years of abundance (occurring in 3–7 year cycles, . . .)" (Fowler 1986:65). Steward estimated that, in an abundant year, a Western Shoshone family of four could gather 1,200 pounds of pine nuts during a few weeks of harvest in the fall (Steward 1938:27).

In late summer people used long hooked and straight poles to gather green pine cones. Lowie comments that Northern Paiute men and women picked pine nuts together; men climbed trees and threw pine nuts down to the women (Lowie 1924a:202). This is an exception to the general rule that women were the predominant gatherers. People could eat shelled seeds raw or parched, but most preferred to grind the seeds into a flour and mix it with water into a mush or gruel (D'Azevedo 1986b:474; Fowler 1986:65).[40]

The surplus of a bumper pine nut harvest in September and October was brought to winter residences and cached (D'Azevedo 1986b:474). Because the pine nut harvest was not annually predictable, its preservation was important through years of low yield. Seeds left unprocessed in the cones and stored in skin bags in pits could last as long as four or five years (Fowler 1986:65).[41]

Northern Shoshones and Bannocks from Idaho also harvested and cached pine nuts. Steward describes how they prepared and used them in conjunction with buffalo hunting. "The cones were always cooked at once on hot ashes, spread on a buckskin and broken and the nuts winnowed out and stored in buckskin bags. Procured on trips east for buffalo, these nuts could be stored in the mountains only when they were to be picked up on the trip home. Some were usually taken to buffalo country in buckskin bags" (Steward 1943a:362).

It remains unstated whether Shoshone Bannocks from Idaho exchanged or shared some of the buckskin bags of pine nuts with their Wind River Shoshone neighbors while traveling to the Plains in pursuit of buffalo. From Emily's comments in connection with song 121, it is clear that earlier in her life Western Shoshones from Nevada visited the Wind River Reservation and sold gunny sacks of pine nuts.

Important in everyday life, the pine nut also has a special place in Great Basin myth, which recounts its origins and favorite preparation as mush. In "The Theft of Pine Nuts," Wolf, Coyote, Crane, Crow, Hawk, Woodpecker, and Mouse are some of the characters who, like their Great Basin human counterparts, play the Handgame and perform the Round Dance together. Against this backdrop of social activities, those who do not have pine nuts deceive and steal from those who do. Despite unique details that mark each telling of the theft and planting of pine nuts, some general similarities draw them together.[42] The delicious aroma of cooked pine nuts draws Coyote's attention and arouses him to seek them out. Most frequently, the aroma comes from the north. Coyote and cohorts travel to this territory, where Crane is the leader of his people. Crane's people serve their guests pine nut mush, but so watered down that Coyote cannot steal pine nuts from it. As hosts and visitors play Handgame or Round Dance together,[43] Mouse secretly searches for the pine nuts. However, Crane's people have suspended them high off the ground for security. (Alternately, the pine nuts are concealed in a bow.) Either way, Woodpecker, alone or with compatriots, uses his beak to pierce and release the pine nuts. Coyote's people form a line and relay the pine nuts along it as Crane's people pursue and kill them. Crow or Hawk, who are the last in line, wish for and get one rotten leg into which they hide the pine nuts. The smell, this time the repugnant stench of the leg, causes Crane's people to discount it as a possible hiding cache for pine nuts. Sometimes the leg is knocked off and runs away on its own volition. Sometimes Crane's people also erect an ice block to prevent Coyote's people from escaping. Once again birds come to the rescue, heating stones and ramming them into the ice.

The escaped seed-bearing leg is responsible for the origin of pine nuts in a certain location and for a pine nut diet of the inhabitants of the place. Northern Shoshones say, "They [Crane's people] looked for the leg, but it was gone. It got to Coyote's Indians in the west, so all of them have pine-nuts now. The nuts used to grow here, but now they are among the *Dübadika* (Eaters of pine-nuts)" (Lowie 1909a: 247).[44]

Like Johnny Appleseed, Wolf and Coyote help disseminate the pine nut seed. Kelly tells us, "So these two brothers got some of the pine nuts. They chewed the nuts as they planted them. Wolf planted good ones, nice and big. Coyote chewed the nuts and swallowed most of them. He planted very little; he spat out only a little. The ones he planted were poor, and his planting came up as junipers" (Kelly 1938:398).

Another Northern Paiute version specifies the location of pine nut dissemination, in this case, by Wolf. "He sprinkled his pine nuts to the South and down there all pine nuts grow" (Kelly 1938:399). In Powell's earlier collection of a Northern Paiute version, it is *Itsa´* (Coyote) who says, "'I will chew the pine nuts and mix them with water in my mouth and spurt them out over the ground around the mountain and they shall grow'; and this pleased them all and it was done. And this is the origin of the pine nut trees about the *Tiv-A Kaiv,* pine nut mountain" (Powell 1971:248).

Myth explains the location of pine nuts and who shall eat them. As in everyday life, a dream was to be the source of knowledge, a validated and validating source. In one telling, it is Wolf who proclaims that all those who dream of pine nuts shall be pine nut eaters (Kelly 1938:398). In another, it is *Ta-vu,* little rabbit, who says, "I will tell you how we can find out what every one should eat; let us go to sleep and dream. All who have good dreams can eat pine nuts, and all who have not, must search for something else. So they fell into a deep sleep. . . . Those who had thus learned that they were to live on pine-nuts went away to the mountains where the pine-nuts grew" (Powell 1971:218).

Even the road that leads to the Land of the Dead has a connection with pine nuts. This road is often referred to as the Dust Road, as dust and whirlwinds are associated with ghosts and the dead. Recall that Wind River Shoshones believe the soul of the dead journeys upward inside the whirlwind. Bannocks and Gosiutes say the Dust road is "smoke from a fire made by two girls cooking pine nuts" (Steward 1943a:390).

Pine Nuts and Ceremony   As Kelly records, "They were going to have a dance after they had planted all the nuts" (Kelly 1938:398). This dance was to take place after Wolf had finished chewing and planting "nice and big" pine nut trees. The suggestive linkage between dance and nature in "The Theft of Pine Nuts" serves as my transition to Great Basin ceremonies that surround pine nut harvests and harvesting. Fowler says that "piñon harvesting is still associated with ceremony in the 1980s, and it remains as one of the key features of

Native identity" (Fowler 1986:65). Ceremonial acts take the form of song, dance, prayer, and offerings.

The connection between Round Dance performance and pine nut harvest is clear: As noted in chapter 1, Stewart reports that eight of fourteen Northern Paiute groups performed the Round Dance in order to make piñon nuts grow (Stewart 1941:416). Steward mentions two of nineteen Nevada Shoshone groups in this regard (Steward 1941:323).

Park describes Paviotso, or Northern Paiute, rituals from western Nevada. The chief of the dance "'wishes for pine nuts and other foods for the coming year. . . . As the head man walked around the dance circle he scattered seeds or pine nuts on the ground and over the dancers" (Park 1941:186). An informant explained, "'It is the big dance; it is to pray for good crops. . . . The dance is for a good time, for many seeds and pine nuts" (Park 1941:184–85). Park notes that for these people, "There seems to be no distinction made between rites and prayers in the spring and those of the dances held to celebrate the pine nut harvest" (Park 1941:186n.8).

Information about other Great Basin cultures reveals differing focuses of the Round Dance in relation to the time of year and the growing cycle of the pine nut and other plants. Western Shoshones of Battle Mountain held spring Round Dances to help seeds grow and summer dances to help seeds ripen. Snake River Shoshone at Owyhee, Nevada, Round Danced in early spring to dry up the snow, in May to make plants green, and later, when seeds and pine nuts were ripe, to produce a good harvest. One informant reported a dance at Belmont, "probably a circle dance, in which women jumped throwing grass seeds (*wai*), Mentzelia (*kuhwa*), and pine nuts, which they carried in baskets" (Steward 1941:265). Shoshones of Egan, Nevada, pulled up by the roots a young pine nut tree with green cones and used it as center pole for their summer Round Dance, with the belief that, "this helps insure good pine-nut harvest" (Steward 1941: 352).

Northern Paiutes performed special ceremonies in the early summer before harvest time in order to "set," or "fix" the crop. Water was a prime concern. Northern Paiutes called the ceremony *Kai Pasapanna*, "Do Not Dry Out," and it was part of a cycle of prayers and activities, including dances that used to be performed in order to insure the crop (Fowler 1986:65; Fowler 1992:n.p.).

The Washoe had similar observances, which they performed in the spring after pine cones had formed. "A branch with young cones was broken off and buried on the banks of a stream to insure against premature drying of the crop. Prayers were then offered for an abundant harvest and there was dancing for one or two nights" (D'Azevedo 1986b:492).

"Round dances were held at the time of harvesting and special prayers of thanksgiving were offered over the first seeds collected. The prayers ensured good harvests of other seeds and game for the remainder of the year" (Fowler 1986:65).

D'Azevedo describes in some detail Washoe thanksgiving observances of the past:

> Prior to harvesting there were four nights of dancing in which each person carried the gathering implements to be used such as hooked poles, burden baskets, manos and metates, stirring paddles, and thus these objects also received the blessings of the accompanying prayers and songs. During the day, rabbit drives were organized, and each family was allowed to pick some pine nuts for a feast on the last night of dancing. But this food was considered to be an offering: what was prepared by each family must not be eaten by them but distributed to others. The leader prayed over the food and exhorted the people to good behavior, warning that failure to follow prescribed procedures would affect the future productivity of the trees. (D'Azevedo 1986b:492)

The first pine nut mush of the year was given as an offering by various groups, including the Shoshones of Grouse Creek, Utah. Steward writes, "During the circle dance, however, the dance chief, who also directed the feast (kwini-gwani), put pine-nut mush made from the first nuts gathered on a stick and set it to one side for *Ap:* [Father]" (Steward 1943a:288).

Even after Plains traditions were part of Fort Hall Shoshone life, the Great Basin ritual of offering pine nut mush continued, albeit in a new context. According to Steward, Fort Hall Shoshones learned the War Dance from Wind River Shoshones around 1893. Descriptions of its performance suggest a fascinating blend of Plains elements—the warrior and ritual pointing to sky, earth, and the four cardinal directions—with Great Basin traditions centering on pine nut mush offerings by a "mush chief": "At the end of the dance, the *kwini* (mush) *dagwani* (chief), a warrior who directed the entire dance, danced with a bowl of mush, pointing a mush spoon first up (called *tugumbi*, sky; representing a soul going up during death), then down (*tsogopü*, earth; what we live on), the east ('the day,' that people may live peacefully throughout the day), then west ('sleep and rest'), then north (representing nothing), and finally south ('warm wind'). When pointing, he prayed for a good life and spoke of things associated with each direction" (Steward 1943a:290).

Offerings of pine nut mush mentioned thus far have been for people, Father, earth, sky, and the four directions. Offerings of pine nuts seeds were also sprinkled on the ground for the ghosts of the dead (Steward 1933:297). As Steward reports, for Shoshones of Hamilton, Nevada, "Pine nuts, like game, were offered to the 'country' to prevent sickness; offering called tuba (pine nut) *dü* (?)" (Steward 1941: 332).

The chain of cause and effect in this last example leads from people, through pine nuts, to the earth, and back to people. It connects food and human health. Human thought can enter the chain and influence pine nuts. Steward reports, "Good deeds or thoughts per se helped nature, e.g., brought rain and increased pinenuts" (Steward 1933:306). The Naraya is another example with the same underlying premise: that human thought and performance affected food, health, and weather in the natural world.

Doza and Sage

Fowler reports the medicinal use of more than three hundred plant species by Great Basin cultures and adds that "plants are also sources of 'spiritual well-being'" (Fowler 1986:96). Two of the most important that appear in the Naraya are *doza* (song 114) and sage (song 104).

Doza, an important medicinal plant, is the main topic of song 114. Like bitterroot, *doza* can help protect the singer's throat from soreness and hoarseness. Angelina Wagon described to me the special blessing that her father, Logan Brown, received, which accounted for his much-admired singing ability. "And this old man told him [Logan Brown] to use *doza* . . . when you sing. Each time your throat's not going to give away, you're going to sing really loud and good" (Vander 1988:58).

An elderly woman, a cousin to Emily, keeps a *doza* root taped to the wall of her house. She chews on a piece of *doza,* which is gummy inside, or boils it and drinks the juice to remedy a sore throat. Taped to the wall, *doza* has power to protect those in the household from harm of a bad spirit. For this reason some people crush it and put it in a necklace pouch.

There is etiquette for procuring *doza.* Those who gather the root should leave a gift, pray, and maybe sing a song. Another older woman told me that an appropriate gift might be beads, which are put into the ground where the root has been pulled out.[45] She, too, used *doza* for colds, chewing and swallowing this bitter-tasting medicine.

Gladys Hill, Emily's daughter-in-law, also commented on the requisite prayer and offering (she suggested a cloth offering) that one gives for any medicinal plant if it is harvested. She added another use of *doza:* it can be smudged on a person to protect against bad dreams.

A variety of scholarly articles documents the use of *doza,* alternately spelled as *toza* and *to´dza,* by many Great Basin groups.[46] Lowie wrote of the Wind River Shoshones:

> After discarding the rind of the root of a weed called *to´dza,* the natives boil the shavings of the root and drink this infusion as a remedy for smallpox, the measles, and eruptive affections [*sic*] generally. When a person is ailing, a little piece of the root is sometimes smoked and placed under the patient's face. This makes his nose run and cleanses it. . . . A very scarce medicine (*wo´ñgo-gwăna*) was obtained by boiling the needles of a small pine species growing on river banks. This was used a good deal for bad colds. The Shoshoni both drank the infusion and also smoked themselves with the needles. The latter method was used when this medicine was mixed with the *to´dza* mentioned above. (Lowie 1924a:310–11)[47]

Sagebrush (*Artemisia tridentata*), mentioned in song 104, and sweet sage (*Artemisia ludoviciana*) are also used by Wind River Shoshones as traditional means of curing and ensuring physical and spiritual well-being. Nick Wilson, a Euro-American boy who lived several years with the Wind River Shoshones, described how they would "heal a wound with poultice made of mashed weeds and bathing the wound with tea made of boiled sage leaves" (Wilson 1919:99–100).[48] Sagebrush infusions were also used to relieve fever (Shimkin 1947b:269).

People continue to use sage today. Lenore Shoyo talked to me about her use of the herb:

> Well, most of the time I'm traditional. I don't really care to take medicine from the clinic because it just seems to get worse. On the prescription, maybe I don't know how to take it. But usually I just take traditional, like boiled sage, and then we'd drink the juice. . . . When we come down with a cold or are on our period we usually chew on sage, too, if we want something like gum to chew on. That's one thing [of several dietary restrictions] we can't have either [during menstruation]. It's because of your teeth. We can't pick at our teeth 'cause your teeth is soft when you're having your period. (Vander 1988:199)

Alberta Roberts and others who sing each year for the Wind River Shoshone Sun Dance often chew sweet sage in order to prevent a sore throat. Sun Dancers also chew it to moisten their mouths. As one Sun Dance chief described it to me, "It makes juices run and moistens the alimentary canal" (personal conversation 1982). (Sun Dancers may only chew sage, as they are prohibited any food or drink throughout the ceremony.

Thomas Johnson, the non-Indian anthropologist who participated as a dancer in the Wind River Shoshone Sun Dance, adds this comment about the use of sage on the second day of the ceremony. "Wonderfully aromatic bunches of peppermint and sweet sage were provided, and when sniffed these herbs clear the throat" (Johnson 1968:13).

There are other meanings and uses of sage that go beyond its healing and refreshing qualities, in both the Sun Dance and everyday life. The center pole of the Sun Dance lodge is forked at its top and supports a circle of rafter poles that radiate out from it. The symbolism of sage and other plants that are placed in the center pole fork appears in a published article written by and for Wind River Shoshones. "A bundle of willows, sweet sage, wild mint are placed and tied in the large cottonwood fork as a sign of abundance or lots of luck, etc." (St. Clair and St. Clair 1977:5, quoted in Vander 1988:197).

Sage is also placed in the nostrils of a buffalo head that is attached to the center pole. Shimkin learned its meaning from Tom Compton in 1937: "the sagebrush is supposed to be a strong, healthy plant, and its purpose is to bring a long healthy life" (Shimkin 1953:440). Richard Engavo, an elderly Shoshone man, explained it to me this way: "They put the sweet sage on [and sticking out of] his nose. That's blowing his nose when he's on the fight, see. Phew!! Like that. They say he's got his head down. You just keep dancing around there, maybe he hook you and knock you down. That's when you're blessed" (Vander 1988:102). Here, sage is connected with the buffalo and its power, which is transferred to the Sun Dancer when he loses consciousness, is knocked down, and is blessed.

The Wind River Shoshone article quoted above also explains the presence of sage in the buffalo nostrils, noting that "its nose filled with sweetsage representing the foul air exhaled by the buffalo in the first vision by the medicine man" (St. Clair and St. Clair 1977:5, quoted in Vander 1988:297). Again, the reference is to power, specifically to knowledge of the Sun Dance religion and ceremony itself, received in dream. Buffalo head and sage represent the power source in the medicine man's vision.

Information on the transfer of the Wind River Shoshone Sun Dance religion to the Crow Indians by John Truhujo brings together health and power. Bird Horse "added silver sage to the sprig given him by Truhujo at the cutting of the [center pole] tree and placed this in the nostrils of the buffalo. . . . The sage was linked to medicine and protected the dancers and their medicine" (Voget 1984:225).

The very term "medicine" used in this context refers to the power to heal as well as to power in a more generalized sense. Physically and metaphysically, sage promotes health of the body. Its power can prevent theft of power by others and protect against the ill effects of other harmful power. Edgar St. Clair, the Shoshone Sun Dance chief, attached sweet sage over the doorway to his home to keep away evil and bad things—illness, arguments, harmful thoughts.

The physical and metaphysical power of sage to protect health was central to the Father Dance, which Shoshones performed in the late eighteenth and early nineteenth centuries (see chapter 1 for complete description). Recall that Shoshones performed the Father Dance in order to ward off smallpox and prevent illness among the children. Sage appeared in the performances in the following ways. The sponsor of the dance wore a crown of sage on his head and gave bundles of sage to the dancers, which they held in both hands throughout the dance. Ten prayers and prayer songs were addressed to various parts of the natural world, with "Sage" being one of the honored ten (Shimkin 1986a:326).

Sagebrush was equally important in the Great Basin, used for health and in ceremony. Harney Valley Paiutes conducted therapy for the ill inside specially constructed sagebrush enclosures (Whiting 1950:39). Eight of fourteen Northern Paiute groups used its leaves to make tea for colds (Stewart 1941:375, 428–29). Among Northern Shoshones, "A decoction of sage brush is prepared against colds and minor distempers" (Lowie 1909a:227). Western Shoshones used a different species of sage (*Artemesia gnaphalodes*) this way: "whole plant boiled for drink or for bath for small children with fever" (Steward 1938:310). Bannock and Gosiute shamans used sagebrush to sprinkle water on their patients (Steward 1943a:346, 389).

Sagebrush played important ceremonial roles at crucial points of the life cycle. "Its burning signifies purification of the living at the death of an individual or at times when ghosts may be present. It is often associated with girls' puberty ceremonies, being used as part of the costuming or as a wand with which girls are ceremonially sprinkled with water" (Fowler 1986:97).

In the Northern Paiute puberty ceremony the girl is bathed while she is seated on a pile of sagebrush. (Alternately, some groups have the girl jump over the pile of sagebrush or over a fire made from it.) In the boys' puberty ceremony the boy stood on a pile of sagebrush bark. His father chewed sagebrush along with the meat from the boy's first kill and "placed it on each of his joints to make him strong" (Fowler and Liljeblad 1986:450).

Sage has still other ceremonial forms and uses. Fowler writes, "Crushed sage can be a medium through which messages are taken to the spirits, for example, as an offering in the spring to ripen the pine nuts or as an offering for health after a specific illness" (Fowler 1986:97).

Finally, sagebrush plays important roles in the ceremony of the Native American Church or Peyote religion, in which many Wind River Shoshones participate. There it expresses a number of the same associations with health and protection that I have discussed so far. Not everything described as Wind River Shoshone, or more broadly as Great Basin, is restricted solely to these cultures and geographic areas. The Peyote religion and its use of sagebrush is a case in point. The religion originated in Mexico, moved north to the Apaches and then disseminated all over North America. La Barre summarized the many important uses of sage in the Peyote Ceremony:

> Sagebrush is used in several ways in peyote meetings: around the periphery of the tipi as a seat, in the cross or rosette under the father peyote on the altar, and in the perfuming ceremony before eating peyote, when it is rubbed between the palms, smelled and rubbed over the head and arms, body and legs. Sometimes a bunch of sage tied together is passed around with the singing-staff also. Dr. Parsons says that at Taos the perfuming is done to "keep the smell of it [on us] so we won't feel weak or dizzy," and as a similar protective function of sage is reported by Opler for the Lipan and the "Sun Dance weed" by Mrs. Cooke for the Ute, it is evidently wide-spread. (La Barre 1975:79)

The curative power of sage is clearly brought out in this statement. La Barre also noted, "The sage under the peyote may be passed to the patient, if there is one, or it may be requested for absent ailing relatives" (La Barre 1975:53n.117). Stewart's study of the Peyote religion verifies all these points for twenty-nine groups (Stewart 1987:346–49). He adds that sixteen of the twenty-nine, including the Wind River Shoshone, also chew sage during the ceremony (Stewart 1987:348–49). Stewart writes: "The purpose of the cult is to heal and to protect through the worship of God by means of peyote. . . . Eating peyote, praying, rubbing sage leaves on the body, fanning cedar smoke over the body, touching the ritual equipment to the body [including the sage on which father peyote sits], being sprinkled with 'holy' water, and smoking special cigarettes are therapeutic practices in nearly all peyote ceremonies" (Stewart 1944:64, 66).

There is an interesting footnote to this discussion of the Peyote religion in regard to the Naraya. Earlier in this century, these two religions were mutually exclusive. This is a unique relationship for the Shoshones who, in varying degrees, may adhere to multiple religious systems, for example, Sun Dance, Episcopalian, and Naraya. Emily, in part, blamed the loss of faith in the Naraya on the growing interest in the Peyote Religion. There was a direct correlation: the rise of one caused the demise of the other (Vander 1986:67–68).

Earth and Earth Mother

Earth as a female, Earth Mother, has widespread usage among many Native Americans, including the Wind River Shoshones. With specific reference to the Shoshones, Hultkrantz writes: "One of the most respected of all spirits is *tam sogobia*, 'Our Mother Earth.' The Supreme Being [*Damë Apë*, Our Father] and the powers associated with him, especially Mother Earth, completely dominate the Sun Dance. . . . Whenever there is a feast and the bowl is brought in, a little water is first poured on the ground for Mother Earth. She is identical with the earth itself and nourishes the plants and animals on which human beings live" (Hultkrantz 1987:47–48).

Earth appears in Naraya songs 19–23, 25–28, 52, 56, 82, 83, and 92, while the Earth Mother is found in songs 13 and 119.

Sam Gill challenges the notion that Mother Earth was an ancient religious belief in North America. He documents her to be a nineteenth-century response by Indian leaders (such as Tecumseh) and prophets (for example, Smohalla) to counter Euro-Americans and their seizure of land. Gill examines the adoption of Mother Earth as a quintessential Indian goddess by Euro-American scholars and, in a very different concept and context, by Indians themselves, as part of a pan-Indian movement in the twentieth century (Gill 1987). While debunking the notion of Mother Earth as a primeval goddess, Gill does recognize the importance of Mother Earth as a religious metaphor by Native Americans. A strong sense of kinship with all the elements of nature marks Wind River Shoshone and Great Basin religious thought, and Mother Earth, whether ancient or young, fits comfortably with these elements.

Certainly the role—even the existence—of Earth Mother in Wind River Shoshone religious thought of the distant past remains undocumented. But she is definitely present in this century in Naraya songs, the Sun Dance, and graveside funeral orations. Earth Mother receives prayers. Thomas Johnson writes that the prayer at the raising of the Sun Dance center pole "asked blessings from Mother Earth (*sogop bia*), from Our Father, (*dam 'apa*) also living water and our Elder Brother, Jesus (*bavi* Jesus) that they might bless this Sun Dance, so that it might cure people and bring peace" (Johnson 1968:6).

Reverence and respect carried over into everyday life. In 1980 I wrote in my fieldwork log, "Alberta says to drink water first thing in the morning—get a blessing. She might also drop some water on Mother Earth" (Vander 1988:100).

In myth Mother Earth is owner of water and fish (Clark 1966:175–77). A Gosiute Shoshone myth explains that "the Indians' father made this mother earth for Indians and scattered everything on it" (W. Miller 1972:144). In another account, a union occurs between a male heaven and female earth.

Earth, without any kin identification, is also the subject of prayer. Prayers and prayer songs in the Wind River Shoshone Father Dance addressed Sun, Moon, Trees, Queerly Shaped Rocks, Mountains, Berries, Sage, Sky, Waters, and Earth (Shimkin 1986a:326). Other Shoshone and Gosiute groups also offered prayers to earth (Steward 1943a:347).

Mooney also commented on the widespread Indian belief in earth as mother, and this included her destructive potential. "Earth quakes and underground noises are signs of her displeasure at the wrongdoing of her children" (Mooney [1896] 1991:721).

Earth, like a human mother, ages. Emily talks of this in connection with Naraya song 19.[49] She said, "Our old earth, just like when the trees, when they get old. . . . you see the trees, they get old, just like people." The same belief appears in a Shoshone speech to the dead. "You are going. A good land reach. . . . Don't return. This not good land (is), it is old. It is good for you to go" (Lowie 1909a:215).

The same image crops up in Wovoka's teachings. Porcupine, a Cheyenne convert to the Ghost Dance religion, reported, "My father [Wovoka] told me the earth was getting old and worn out and the people getting bad, and that I was to renew everything as it used to be and make it better" (Mooney [1896] 1991:785).

A Nespelim tale goes beyond the idea of an aging earth. "The Earth-Woman is now very old, and even her bones (the rocks) are crumbling away. Therefore the time cannot be far away when the earth will be transformed again, and when the spirits of the dead will come back" (Spier 1935:11). Spier felt that this and other beliefs from northwest tribes of the interior Plateau area both predated and influenced Ghost Dance doctrine.

The obverse of an old earth—a new or good earth—appears in songs 21, 22, 23. It is the ultimate destination of Wovoka's prophecy. "New earth" also appears in song 92, but Emily interpreted the phrase in this text as a poetic reference to dawn and without any reference to the new world of the Ghost Dance. It remains ambiguous whether it carried Ghost Dance meaning at some earlier time.

The dirt of Earth Mother has power and is a source of blessing. Dirt played a significant role in Angelina Wagon's story of how her father acquired power as an outstanding singer. "'A long time ago . . . when he was a young boy, he was blessed with singing songs—his throat. . . . Some old man blessed him—that dirt, and then up to him, and then the dirt up to the throat. An old man gave him all that. That's the way he was blessed, and that's the way he sings good'" (Vander 1988:58).

The restorative power of earth comes out clearly in many mythic accounts. Following a common pattern, Coyote resurrects his dead brother, Wolf, by burying him, or part of him, in damp earth (Kelly 1938:378; Smith 1939:167; Steward 1943b:298). In everyday life, damp earth is a remedy for bad dreams. One applies it to the body at sunrise, talks to the sun, and then brushes off the dirt toward the sun (Steward 1943a:389).

Wood Stick Man

"Vegetation" translates into Northern Paiute as *ho-pi*, a collective reference to all plants, trees, shrubs, weeds, and grass (Powell 1971:241). I believe this word bears relationship to *hupin* (from *hu:pi*) in Naraya song 112 and leads to a compelling connection between the Round Dance and the Naraya, in the following manner.

I return to a prayer song quoted previously, one that Lemhi Shoshones used in their "Circle dance": "'*Kwinaŋ* (eagle feather) *gwasi* (tail) *hupi* (stick) *nzia* (?),' which was addressed to nature or to the maker of green things." Steward underscored the meaning of this text within its context, writing, "These dances were usually held spring and fall and were to promote health and make nature fertile" (Steward 1943a:287). I suggest that Wood Stick Man in song 112 bears a close relationship, if not identity, with "nature" or the "maker of green things" addressed in the Lemhi prayer song.

Of course, only Virginia Grant Bonatsie, the woman who dreamed the song, could speak definitively on this matter. My fieldwork on the reservation, which began in 1977, precluded the opportunity to know and speak to Virginia, whose lifespan was 1890–1960. Emily was confident that the song had meanings and that Virginia knew them. But as is common in such cases of dreamed song with power, these meanings remained unspoken and unknown by others.

The personification of nature or the maker of green things is in keeping with Emily and Dorothy's explanation of the function of the religion—promoting grass, trees, greenery, and berries. On occasion they also personified nature. However, when they did so, nature was

Mother Nature, a female identification rather than male. As Emily said, "When you sing that song, when you dance, Mother Nature's going to give all the berries. They're going to grow good, and water [be plentiful] too."

Wood Stick Man, as the maker of green things, brings to mind the long list of cultural associations with greenery that I gave earlier in my commentary. Green = longevity, resurrection, life, growth, spring and light, and water. Let me conclude here by connecting these associations with the use of a scratching stick by Shoshones and other groups in the Great Basin (Stewart 1941:408, 410). A Shoshone woman is taught that, during menstruation and after childbirth, she must scratch her body and hair with a scratching stick rather than her own fingernails. Shoshones told me that the purpose of this observance was to prevent wrinkles and gray hair—signs of aging. Is it possible that the scratching stick shares with Wood Stick Man the associated power for greenness? Does it keep the body "green"—rejuvenated, ever-youthful?

White-Clay Paint, *Evi*, and White-Clay Man

Who is Wood Stick Man's flying partner, White-Clay Man?

Emily identified his mundane face, "That's for dressing, putting on your buckskin." The use of white paint by hunters suggests another, more than ordinary fact. The Northern Paiute hunter "painted himself with a white paint (*poeŋ osai ivi* [*evi*]) obtained near Dayton, Nevada, which made him invisible to deer" (Stewart 1941:422). Similarly, Surprise Valley Paiute hunted antelope in disguise, wearing an antelope head and hide and painting their bodies with white paint (Kelly 1932:82).

The specific use of paint made from earth is an essential part of the shaman's practice in the Great Basin and beyond. I believe it is shamanism that shapes the physical-metaphysical face of White-Clay Man.

In his study of shamanism, Park writes,

> The use of two native paints, red (*pi-jəp*) and white (*i-bi*), is very common in curing practices. Both of these paints are secured from natural deposits of earth. The uses to which the paints are put are manifold: the bodies and faces of both shamans and spectators are painted, the patient is sprinkled with the dry powder, and the feathers and the wand used in curing are painted. There are no fixed patterns that determine the way in which the paint is to be used, nor is one color preferred to the other. Either red or white paint, and often both, appears in every phase of the shaman's practice. The use of these paints, however, is by

no means confined to curing rites. In daily life these paints are employed for utilitarian as well as ritual purposes, and bodily decoration with these paints is also common on social occasions. Nevertheless, the paints are thought to be very potent in aiding the recovery of the sick. (Park 1938:56).

Park's statement mentions the use of both red and white paint by shamans. However, because my purpose here is to explicate the use of white paint in song 112 in order to understand its central image, White-Clay Man, my discussion will not include references and information on the use of red paint. The interested reader will find some of the parallel uses of red paint by both Shoshones and Wovoka in notes 50 and 53, respectively.

Twelve of fourteen Northern Paiute groups reported that the shaman received paint in a vision (Stewart 1941:413). Other shamans, such as Dick Mahwee, were instructed in a vision to "bathe in the water at the foot of the cliff and paint yourself with *i-bi* [white paint]" (Park 1938:28). Mahwee followed this and all other instructions and became a shaman.

In another example, Happy Jack made mistakes and was unsuccessful in his pursuit of shamanistic power. As an antidote, an owl "told" him that "he was to go down to the river and bathe and put *i-bi* [white paint] on the horse. This was to purify both the man and the horse [to prevent the sickness that would result from his improper conduct in relation with supernatural spirits]" (Park 1938:29).

White paint has many uses in the healing process. Paviotso (Northern Paiute) shamans took an eagle feather, smeared it with white or red paint, attached it to a willow stick, and planted it outside the patient's house. As one shaman explained, "'It keeps the bad spirits away'" (Park 1934:104).

Lowie reported this same procedure—an eagle feather attached to a stick planted by the patient's head—and learned the purpose for the use of white clay on the stick: "the idea of the clay was that it would cause moisture all over the patient's body" (Lowie 1924a:294). This statement is ambiguous: does the clay create wetness or draw it out of the patient? Let me anticipate here some information that I will cite on the use of white paint in the Sun Dance, as it is explicit and resolves this ambiguity. The clay is a drying agent. It draws the moisture—that is, the disease—out of the body. It dries it up. It cures.

Within the social context of the shaman's performance, even people in the audience might be asked to paint their faces with white paint (Park 1934:195). But it is the patient who is the central figure. As Park records, "Then the shaman tells the people to put white paint on the patient" (Park 1934:106). Direct application of white paint is key to many shamanistic performances. It is daubed around the area of the snake bite (Park 1934:106) or over the patient's heart (Steward 1943a:388). A sixteen-year-old shaman cured his cousin as follows: "He painted evi (white clay) on the boy's chest, arms and legs. . . . He sang, danced, and smoked while holding his eagle feathers" (Steward 1943a:283). There is one reference to eating white paint as a cure for diarrhea (Kelly 1932:197).

Even when the shaman's efforts failed, after death, there was a beneficial role for white-clay paint. "Purification after a burial or bad dreams was accomplished by taking a cold bath, painting, or in the north, applying white clay" (Steward 1941:263). This particular use of white clay also appeared in the Round Dance performance of Shoshones from Promontory Point, Utah. Their "circle dance was called *apənukəp* or *nazuŋgoyou* and was performed four nights and a half of the fifth day for relatives long since dead. It was concluded with a swim after which the people painted themselves" (Steward 1943a:288).

Dancers wore white and red paint in the Lemhi Shoshone *nū´'akin*.[50] As described in chapter 1, it is this form of the Round Dance that I believe comes closest to the Naraya. Dancing in late winter and early spring to ensure food, women wore red paint on their faces and men had white clay on their foreheads and hair. "An eagle, or at times a magpie feather, was inserted in the hair" (Lowie 1909a:217). The combination of white clay and eagle or magpie feathers draws on two of the shaman's potent sources for securing and protecting health.

Healing and the acquisition of healing power are at the center of the Wind River Shoshone Sun Dance today. White clay, *evi*, is essential to the achievement of these Sun Dance goals. As Shimkin learned from Tom Compton, "This white clay is the main paint of the Dance. It is so because it will dry the flesh quicker than any other. Any sickness will thus be dried out. Other paints won't do that" (Shimkin 1953:442).

I have suggested in chapter 3 that there is a dry-wet dichotomy in Great Basin conception. The positive connotations of wetness, fog, and the living soul, on the one hand, counterpoint negative connotations of dryness, dust-whirlwinds, and ghosts, on the other. However, the drying power of white clay and the goal of using white clay in shamanistic performance and in the Sun Dance turn this on its head. Dry = health = good; wet = disease = bad. The Sun Dance resolves the paradox of the two opposing conceptualizations by moving on to another plane. Jorgensen analyzes in great detail the dry-wet dichotomy in the Sun Dance (Jorgensen 1971:207).

Varying only in minor detail from his analysis,[51] I believe that the Sun Dancers endure abstinence from water in order to "dry out" and heal. Physically and spiritually, they cleanse and purify themselves. In that state, a special few may receive visions, which often includes visionary wetness and water—powerful and life-giving. In this way they acquire the power to heal.

Sun Dancers bathe and paint themselves with white clay as a preliminary step to entering the Sun Dance (Lowie 1919:392; Shimkin 1953:442, 475). The buffalo head attached to the center pole is also painted with white clay (Shimkin 1953:440, 475; Voget 1984:225).

Prior to 1912, white clay bracketed the Sun Dancer's experience. He painted his body before the beginning of the ceremony, and at its conclusion he drank water mixed with clay, which induced ritual vomiting. He was cleansed and purified, inside and out. Johnson wrote, "In former times the old men would recite their brave deeds after water mixed with clay had been drunk, ending the fast [required of all participants in the Sun Dance]. This would induce vomiting. . . . Now a large half-watermelon induces vomiting; the water that is distributed at the end of the ceremony is clear" (Johnson 1968:35). Shimkin dates the elimination of the older practice to at least 1912, as it was absent at that time when Lowie visited the reservation (Shimkin 1953:437).

Beyond purification there is an origin story of the Shoshone Sun Dance that links white clay with power. John McAdams, a Sun Dance chief of the 1930s, tells a story about his ancestor, Yellow Hand, whose Sun Dance vision was its source: "The main Sun Dance originated here, long ago. My great-grandfather [Yellow Hand] . . . said, 'I am going to look for *bɔx* [Power].' He had a buffalo robe, and he painted this grey with white clay. Then in the evening he went to a butte near Rawlins [Wyoming] and slept there overnight. . . . A man came from heaven and told him: 'You are looking for great power. I'll tell you what to do'" (Shimkin 1953:409).

Asleep and wrapped in his clay-painted robe, Yellow Hand learned all the details of the Sun Dance ceremony.[52] Steward forges another connection between white clay, power, and the Sun Dance. He notes that Fort Hall Shoshones who get the power to cure in the Sun Dance use white clay and eagle feathers in their curing practice (Steward 1943a:283).

White clay is an important part of Hittman's analysis of color symbolism in Northern Paiute shamanism, Wovoka's personal experience, and the 1890 Ghost Dance religion. I quote one set of symbolic sequences that seems directly relevant to all I have said about the uses and meaning of white clay. "Thus, the color white = *ebe* [white clay] = Thunder = rain = eagle feather = curing" (Hittman 1990:187). Although, as we have seen, white clay dries out disease, note that in the sequence here, it moves through water, and with it soul and life-giving associations, to curing and health.

White paint, like red paint, was important to Ghost Dance performance. For example, Wovoka's healing arts drew on this white-clay tradition. His son-in-law, "Andy Vidovich[,] . . . stated that Wovoka would 'chew it [white paint] up, but he didn't eat it. And while he was doctoring his patients he would use that for his purification. He'd blow it on his patients. . . . He'd put it over the sick over the part where the sickness was'" (Hittman 1990:186).

Even years after Ghost Dance performances were a thing of the past, Wovoka continued to receive requests by mail for red and white paint (Dangberg 1957:289; Dangberg 1968:42). Mooney writes that delegations of Indians who came to see Wovoka and learn the Ghost Dance religion during its heyday "must use the sacred red and white paint and the sacred grass (probably sagebrush) which he gave them" (Mooney [1896] 1991:821).[53]

Fieldwork by Wier repeats this even more forcefully: Ghost Dancers were "required to paint their faces red as well as white" (Wier, in Hittman 1990:185), and they did (Spier 1928, in Kelly 1932:116). Some, like Sun Dancers, also used it before the dance proper: "Hopi traders attended an 1891 Ghost Dance . . . . They were met by a Havasupai who informed them that his fellow tribesmen were all engaged in a very important ceremony. The traders were told that they must wash their bodies and paint them with white clay before they could go into the encampment, showing the diffusion to the eastern bands of the theme of ceremonial cleanliness" (Dobyns and Euler 1967:26).

The most poignant use of white paint in connection with Ghost Dance performance came as an aftermath to the tragic massacre of Lakota Ghost Dancers at Wounded Knee. "The survivors had fenced off the trench [a mass grave for the slaughtered] and smeared the posts with paint made from clay of Western Nevada given to Sioux delegates by Wovoka" (Moses 1984:63, in Hittman 1990:13). Nevada clay and its power held at bay the danger and contamination of death in a South Dakota field.

At last, we can answer our earlier question: Who is White-Clay Man? We see his symbolic visage in his power and work. He protects one from harm, he cures, he cleanses and purifies. He assists the seeker of vision. White-Clay Man is the protector of health. He *is* Health.

White-Clay Man and Wood Stick Man are flying off together in song 112, but what is their destination? I do not believe that Wood Stick Man, the maker of green things, and White-Clay Man, Health Man, are flying to the Spirit-land. This possibility makes no sense. I believe they are en route to the new world, just as Our Father, followed by our mother, flies to the new world in Naraya song 22. In song 112, there is a fascinating union that joins the Naraya to the Ghost Dance. The embodiments of vegetation and health, central concerns of this world, which Shoshones and other Great Basin peoples addressed in religious Naraya and Round Dance performance, fly to what will be the new locus of people and life—the new world prophesied by Wovoka. This alliance was not to last.

7 | Sun, Stars, and Night

The song texts in chapter 7 inhabit the sky. Sources of light—the sun and stars—and the absence of light—night—are their topics.

Naraya Song 122

♩ = ca. 100

(5th verse)

Da - më so - go - vai - gi da - ve ya - nu - gënt e - na,

Da - më so - go - vai - gi da - ve ya - nu - gënt e - na.

Ba - gu so - go - vai - gi ba - gu yï - më - gënt e - na,

6 repeats

Ba - gu so - go - vai - gi ba - gu yï - më - gënt e - na.

Pitches

Dorothy Tappay
Emily Hill

Damë	*sogo-vaigi*	*dave*	*yanugënt*	*ena,*
Our	earth-on/over	sun	waves	(e.v.),

Damë	*sogo-vaigi*	*dave*	*yanugënt*	*ena.*
Our	earth-on/over	sun	waves	(e.v.).

Bagu	*sogo-vaigi*	*bagu*	*yïmëgënt*	*ena,*
Clear	earth-on/over	clear	waves	(e.v.),

Bagu	*sogo-vaigi*	*bagu*	*yïmëgënt*	*ena.*
Clear	earth-on/over	clear	waves	(e.v.).

EMILY: "It's about the earth, *sogop^h*. Light, the sunlight. You know, when it's real hot, you see the waves over the earth when it's hot. You could see it. . . . It's clear when it's sort of like that. Waves. That's what it means. Clear waves."

I have no explanation for the variant form of "waves" in the second line of text. Gladys Hill derived *yanugënt* in line one from the spoken form, *yanugïnd^h*.

♩. = ca. 72

Naraya Song 123

(5th verse)

a

Nï- së su - a - ve- an- dë nï- së su - a - ve- an- dï- nȯ ge -

a

na, Nï- së su - a - ve- an- dë nï- së su - a - ve- an - dï- nȯ

b

ge - na. Da- mën na - ru- gum- ban- go da- ve- de doih- ïn - zi da- ve

b

da- ve doih ge - na, Da- mën na- ru- gum - ban- go da- ve- de

doih - ïn - zi   da - ve   da - ve   doih   ge - na.

Pitches

Dorothy Tappay
Emily Hill

Nïsë   suave-andë   nïsë   suave-andïnó   gena,
Myself thoughts-(?v.s.) myself thoughts-(? v.s.) (e.v.),

Nïsë   suave-andë   nïsë   suave-andïnó   gena.
Myself thoughts-(?v.s.) myself thoughts-(? v.s.) (e.v.).

Damën   narugumba-ngo   dave-de   doih-ïn-zi
Our   ?sky   sun[light]-(?v.s.) come out-(d.a.s.)
   dave   dave   doih   gena,
   sun[light]   sun[light] come out   (e.v.),

Damën   narugumba-ngo   dave-de   doih-ïn-zi
Our   ?sky   sun[light]-(?v.s.) come out-(d.a.s.)
   dave   dave   doih   gena.
   sun[light]   sun[light] come out   (e.v.).

EMILY: "That's my own thought, my own thought. Sun, you know, light—goes way up in the sky. Way up there the light, sunlight. His thoughts goes up that way. The person's thoughts [are] like that. Light goes like that. People don't know they're [i.e., human thoughts] like that."

At this point in our conversation, I misunderstood Emily's comment "That's my own thought," which led me to the false conclusion that song 123 was Emily's song. So I asked if she thought of this song while sleeping. Emily, in turn, did not fully understand my question or confusion. But her answer was revealing nonetheless.

EMILY: "I think that's what it means, dreams or something like that."

"Dreams" refer to visions in this context. Emily's comment and the song's imagery of rising thought underscore the mental nature of visionary experience on the one hand, and its physical likeness to light, on the other.[1]

This is a highly unusual Naraya text, being spoken in the first-person voice of the one who dreamed it. Introspective, it reflects on the visionary experience itself. I never did learn who dreamed this song.

Dorothy Tappay

Dave	dïn-dïn-dïn-dsi	roiya	dïn-dsi	roiyavi,
Sun	down/toward-(s.r.)-(d.a.s.)	mountains	down/toward-(d.a.s.)	mountains,

Dave	dïn-dïn-dïn-dsi	roiya	dïn-dsi	roiyavi.
Sun	down/toward-(s.r.)-(d.a.s.)	mountains	down/toward-(d.a.s.)	mountains.

Dave	doiyavi	dave	doiya	dïn-dsi	roiyavi,
Sun	mountains	sun	mountains	down/toward-(d.a.s.)	mountains,

Dave	doiyavi	dave	doiya	dïn-dsi	roiyavi.
Sun	mountains	sun	mountains	down/toward-(d.a.s.)	mountains.

EMILY: "It's about the sun in the mountains."

JUDY: "What does *dïndsi* mean?"

EMILY: "That's going towards the mountains. About this time it's going up."

JUDY: "Oh, late in the day."

EMILY: "Yes. See, like that—the pine tree things [pine needles are] like that, see—the light from the sun."

I believe Emily means that the sun rays streaming out from behind the mountain resemble the way pine needles spread out in lines from the point where they attach to the branch.

EMILY: "That's a song about the evenings when the sun's on the mountains."

Naraya Song 125

♩ = ca. 88   (3d verse)

Da - man da - ve yu -wï - nan- gwa yu - wï - ge - na,

Da - man da - ve yu -wï - nan - gwa yu - wï - ge - nòr.

Nu -wë nu - wë nu - wï - ge - nòr nu - wï ge - nòr,

7 repeats

Nu -wë nu - wë nu - wï - ge - nòr nu - wï - ge - na.

Pitches

Dorothy Tappay
Emily Hill

Daman   dave   yuwïnangwa   yuwï-gena,
Our   sun   sets in the west   sets-?moving,

Daman	*dave*	*yuwïnangwa*	*yuwï-genòr.*
Our	sun	sets in the west	sets-?moving.

Nuwë	*nuwë*	*nuwïgenòr*	*nuwïgenòr,*
Indian	Indian	taking one's time walking	taking one's time walking,
		(trudging)	(trudging)

Nuwë	*nuwë*	*nuwïgenòr*	*nuwïgena.*
Indian	Indian	taking one's time walking	taking one's time walking.
		(trudging)	(trudging)

EMILY: "Well, our sun's going down and when the sun goes down, there's an Indian walking around, over there where the sun went down. Indian walking around where the sun went down up by the shadows." Song 125 is one of the rare Naraya song texts that mentions people.

The sun is an important image in two Naraya song texts published previously (Vander 1986:48–50). Because I will discuss them in the commentary section of this chapter, I will quote here their literal translations and Emily's comments on them. I will then present song 126.

Song 4

> Our sun's face white set while moving,
> Our sun's face white set while moving.
> Our sun's going/moving sun set while moving,
> Our sun's going/moving sun set while moving.
> (Vander 1986:48)

EMILY: "It's a prayer song to sun. It's about the sun; the sun's face is white. You can't see it. . . . You can't look at the sun, it's too strong. . . . The sun's face is white, warming up the world. It's a-going—sundown. . . . When it's going down it cuts the light. Light shining like a can is shining" (Vander 1986:48).

Song 15

> Our morning star coming up,
> Our morning star coming up.
> Clear sun rays streaming out,
> Clear sun rays streaming out.
> Star sitting [lightly],
> Star sitting [lightly].
> (Vander 1986:49)

EMILY: "Morning Star, song about Morning Star. . . . Towards morning, when daylight's coming up—Morning Star coming up with that light. It's been sitting up there just before daybreak" (Vander 1986:49).

Song 15 fits equally well with the next two songs and their poetic description of the stars.

Naraya Song 126

♩. = ca. 76   (2d verse)

Pitches

Emily Hill
(Dorothy Tappay hums
or sings quietly)

Dïmpi	*wonge*	*dïmpi*	*wonge,*		
Rocks	?in a row	rocks	?in a row,		

Dïmpi	*wonge*	*dïmpi*	*wonge.*		
Rocks	?in a row	rocks	?in a row.		

Dïmpi	*wonge*	*dugu-n-dïvarë*	*vaigi*	*du-*	*parësai,*
Rocks	?in a row	sky-under [or lining]	above	dark/night [blue]	shining-twinkling,

Dugu-n-dïvarë   *vaigi*   *du-*   *parësai.*
Sky-under/lining   above   dark/night   shining-twinkling.
                   [blue]

EMILY: "That *dugu-n-dïvarë* is that blue sky, *dugu-n-dïva?* You see those *dïmpi won,* those . . ."

JUDY: "The Milky Way?"

EMILY: "Yes. *Dugu-parësed,* dark, you know, go like this in the dark." (Emily suggested the pulsing light of a star by rhythmically closing and opening all the fingers of one hand.)

JUDY: "Does *dïmpi* mean rock?"

EMILY: "Yes, rocks in a row. I think it says something like, it [the row of rocks] goes up there where those stars are. Indians call it backbone."

JUDY: "How do you say it in Shoshone?"

EMILY: "*Daziump* ['star'], *daziumbe gwahaiboromp* ['backbone'].[2] You see those stars that go straight across?"

JUDY: "The Milky Way?"

EMILY: "Yes. You see that blue sky up there? *Dugu-n-dïvarë* ['sky-lining'], you see that when there's no clouds, you see them *dugu-n-dïvarë.* They call it the Heaven way, you know. Something like that."

Years after Emily made these comments to me I finally understood them. "Backbone" of the sky is one Shoshone term for the Milky Way. *Dugu-n-dïvarë,* "sky-lining," the Heaven way, is another term and with a different context. It is literally the "way" or path that leads to Heaven—the land of the dead. In this song text the stars in the Milky Way path to Heaven are like rocks in a row.

EMILY: "You see that sky kind of blue, dark blue, *du-par, du-par*— that's kind of dark. You see them things [the stars] that go like this [*Emily's hand makes a pulsing motion*]?"

JUDY: "Twinkling? They're shining or twinkling?"

EMILY: "Yeah, yeah."

I believe that translated into everyday language the text says, "Rocks in a row of the sky lining—the Milky Way path that leads the dead to 'Heaven'—shine and twinkle above in the dark blue sky."

Naraya Song 127

Dugu   ba-gaganana   dugu   ba-gaganan,
Sky/up   water/fog   sky/up   water/fog,

Dugu   ba-gaganana   dugu   ba-gaganan.
Sky/up   water/fog   sky/up   water/fog.

Dugu   saiyog-anana   dugu   saiyog-anan   ena,
Sky/up   Milky Way-(v.s.)   sky/up   Milky Way-(v.s.)   (e.v.),

Dugu   saiyog-anana   dugu   saiyog-anan   ena.
Sky/up   Milky Way-(v.s.)   sky/up   Milky Way-(v.s.)   (e.v.).

EMILY: "That's about up there—water there, water. At night you could see those things, stars, *saiyaganoi(hiya)*."

JUDY: "The Milky Way?"

EMILY: "Yes. It's on the other side of the sky, way up there [the Milky Way or Heaven way mentioned earlier]. There's a little bit of water back there. A song about up there."

JUDY: "What is the Shoshone word for Milky Way?"
EMILY: "*Dugu saiyaganan, dugu saiyag.*"

Sai, which meant the shining and twinkling of the row of rocks in song 126, becomes *saiyag,* the central descriptive element in song 127, and another way to refer to the Milky Way. It may be that the derivation of *sai* and *saiyag* is to be found in Naraya song 11 (see appendix A). Its text begins with *Saiwai,* which Emily translated as melting snow, a wet shining surface (Vander 1986:41). Gosiute Shoshone has a similar word, "*saiG,* to melt (of snow only)" (W. Miller 1972: 132). Likewise, Natches gives *sa-'i´* for "melt" or "thaw" in Northern Paiute (Natches 1923:251). The derivation of *dugu,* which precedes *saiyag,* may have multiple roots: *dugumbaʔ,* "sky," *duganriph,* "night" or "black," and *dugup,* "up."

The first line of song 127 also contains other Shoshone words whose roots overlap. *Dugumbaʔ* is "sky"; *ba:* by itself means "water"; *vagïna* or *bagïna* means "fog." *Dugum-ba-gaganana* may compress all three words together.

The Milky Way along with the nighthawk also appear in song 82, which was presented in chapter 5. Its text—*dïmpi saiyagan*—"rocks that shine and twinkle"—combines the two Milky Way images in songs 126 and 127.

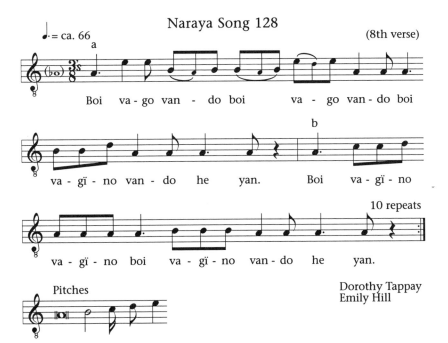

Naraya Song 128

Dorothy Tappay
Emily Hill

Boi   vag-o   vand-o   boi   vag-o   vand-o   boi   vagïn-o
Road   fog-(v.s.)   above-(v.s.)   road   fog-(v.s.)   above-(v.s.)   road   fog-(v.s.)
vand-o   he yan.
above-(v.s.)   (vocs).

Boi   vagïn-o   vagïn-o   boi   vagïn-o   vand-o   he yan.
Road   fog-(v.s.)   fog-(v.s.)   road   fog-(v.s.)   above-(v.s.)   (vocs.).

Emily thought this song to be from Idaho. Even without any commentary on it, its text is easy to hear and translate. Fog road, yet another image of and reference to the Milky Way, contrasts with the rocks in a row and the twinkling stars of the previous song texts.

Night, marked by the absence of the sun in the sky, is the time for stars, the implied setting for Naraya songs 91, 126, 127, and 128. Night, itself, is the main topic in Naraya songs 129 and 130.

Naraya Song 129

Dorothy Tappay
Emily Hill

Daman	duganangwa		ba	vesiyu-uvinu,
Our	towards or come night		water	?splashing-(?v.s.),

Daman	duganangwa		ba	vesiyu-uvinu.
Our	towards or come night		water	?splashing-(?v.s.).

Daman	duganangwa		neshiwai-uvinu,
Our	towards or come night		breeze-(?voc. suff.),

Daman	duganangwa		neshiwu-uvinu.
Our	towards or come night		breeze-(?voc. suff.).

EMILY: "In the night time when everything's quiet you could just hear very little water going, you could hear the water. Sounds like it's going through big rocks, splashing onto the rocks. Sounds like it's, 'shhhhh.' That's what it means. And at night there's a little breeze, a little wind."

The word *duganangwa*, "towards night," might also have folded into it *na´ŋga*, "to hear" (Shimkin 1949b:210). If true, the word would join the darkness of approaching night with what one hears at that time. In any case, this evening song is a counterpart to song 83, which pairs the special light of dawn with its chorus of bird sounds.

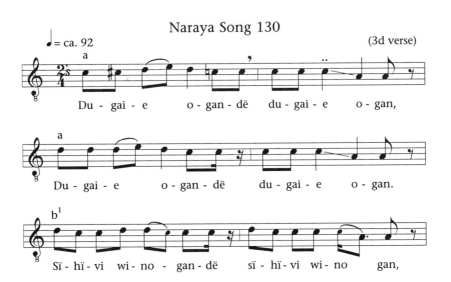

Naraya Song 130

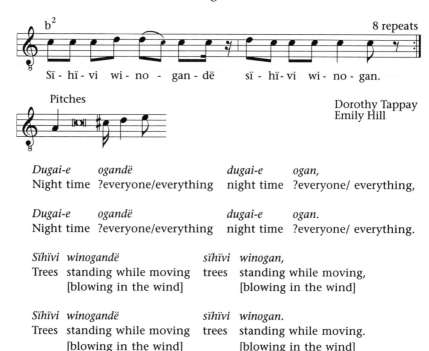

Sï - hï - vi wi - no - gan - dë   sï - hï - vi wi - no - gan.

Pitches

Dorothy Tappay
Emily Hill

Dugai-e	*ogandë*	*dugai-e*	*ogan,*
Night time	?everyone/everything	night time	?everyone/ everything,

Dugai-e	*ogandë*	*dugai-e*	*ogan.*
Night time	?everyone/everything	night time	?everyone/ everything.

Sïhïvi winogandë   *sïhïvi winogan,*
Trees standing while moving   trees standing while moving,
     [blowing in the wind]   [blowing in the wind]

Sïhïvi winogandë   *sïhïvi winogan.*
Trees standing while moving   trees standing while moving.
     [blowing in the wind]   [blowing in the wind]

EMILY: "That means when everybody's silent, you know, no noise. *Wi:nogantʰ*, you know, the trees, just the trees moving like that. Everything's silent. *Gai* time, it means night time."

The central verb in this text appeared in song 13 (see appendix A). For that song text, Emily explained, "standing, *wïnïganór*, you know, the trees, when the wind's blowing" (Vander 1986:43). Mooney renders what appears to be the equivalent Paiute verb as *wĭ'noghän*, which he translated as "shaken by the wind, waving in the wind" in his Paiute glossary (Mooney [1896] 1991:1057). In his poetic translation of the line that uses this verb, Mooney wrote, "The wind stirs the willows" (Mooney [1896] 1991:1054).

Nighttime in songs 129 and 130 is defined by its sounds—the movement of water over rocks and the wind in the trees.

Commentary

Sun

The sun occupies an important place in Great Basin and Wind River Shoshone religions—similar in many respects and significantly different in others. Sun appears in Naraya songs 4, 15, 34, 43, 78, 79, 92, and 122–25.

Sun and moon appear as one class of gods in Powell's discussion of Ute and Southern Paiute religion (Powell 1971:73). In her study of Great Basin mythology, Smith comments that in some Northern Paiute myths, the father, identified as the Creator, is associated with wolf and sun (Smith 1939:21). A Northern Paiute myth published by Kelly exemplifies this connection. The link was made as the earth began, when all was water with but one little island in its midst. "They had this Sun for a god. When the Sun came up, he told his people, 'Don't worry, come to me; I'll help you. Don't worry; be happy all your life. You will come to me'" (Kelly 1938:437). In 1990, Hittman discussed Northern Paiute cultural beliefs and symbols, suggesting a "formal if not functional correspondence between 'God' = Sun" (Hittman 1990:182).

Colonel Brackett's 1879 annual report on Wind River Shoshone religious belief would seem to testify to a similar belief by the Shoshones. "These Indians . . . believe in *Tamapah,* or Sun-Father, who is the Father of the Day and Father of us all, and lives in the sun" (Brackett 1880:330). However, as discussed in chapter 2, subsequent scholarship strongly denies the fusion of the two entities into one identity. The issue comes up in connection with the Sun Dance and its prayers. Bivo, a Wind River Shoshone, told Lowie that "the prayers were addressed to the Sun *and* [my emphasis] Apo (the Father), the latter being Coyote's elder brother [Wolf]" (Lowie 1919:399). Again I quote Tom Compton, a Shoshone Sun Dance Chief of the 1930s, who explained to Shimkin, "'In the Sun Dance there is no worship of the Sun. It is through the Sun'" (Shimkin 1953:463). In this view, Sun serves as an intermediary power, or an intermediary to power. Sun was not specifically addressed in the Wind River Shoshone prayer that Thomas Johnson reports was spoken in 1966 just prior to the ritual raising of the center pole for the Sun Dance lodge (T. Johnson 1968:6). (See chapter 6 for Johnson's quotation of the prayer.)

However, Wind River Shoshones did pray to the Sun, as well as to Moon, Trees, Queerly Shaped Rocks, Mountains, Berries, Sage, Sky, Waters, and Earth during the Father Dance, a religious dance performed in the late eighteenth and early nineteenth centuries (see chapter 1). Emily's comment on song 4, "It's a prayer song to sun," is in the same vein. I believe that all aspects of the natural world that are mentioned in Naraya songs are objects of Naraya prayer.

Although the conceptions of Sun as Father/God held by Wind River Shoshones and other Great Basin cultures may not be identical, all these peoples looked to the sun as a source of power. For Northern Paiutes, "Classes of spirits who might help shamans but who also were of more general reference in supernatural beliefs were Sun and Moon, Thunder, . . . Wind, Clouds, and Stars. Of all, Sun was the most powerful and most respected" (Fowler and Liljeblad 1986:452–53).[3]

Apart from shamans, ordinary people spoke to the sun directly in their prayers. For example, Fowler and Liljeblad write of the Northern Paiute, "Many people addressed morning prayers to the Sun, asking that it have a good journey through the sky, and that it take their troubles with it as it entered the 'big water' to the west" (Fowler and Liljeblad 1986:453). Both complementing and reinforcing this point, Hittman writes, "Numus [Northern Paiutes] also pray to *tamme pea*, or 'Our Mother,' but pointed out to me that their prayers more frequently were directed to the Sun" (Hittman 1990:194n.4). Ten Northern Paiute groups gave prayers and offerings to the sun (Stewart 1941: 414); six Northern and Gosiute Shoshone groups also gave prayers to the sun (Steward 1943a:347).[4]

Belief in Sun and praying to it are central in the Northern Paiute mythic origins of the sweat house. Eagle and other birds who entered the sweat house for the first time learned about its meaning and customs. "You talk to the sun while you're in the sweat house; that's your god" (Kelly 1938:376). In this way the birds acquired power for hunting. However, the sweat house, which replicates the heat of the sun, is also a place where one seeks relief from illness.

Sun as a source of health and healing takes many forms. After a bad dream, a Shoshone of Grouse Creek "talks to the sun against the dream" (Steward 1943a:389). Although the sun is not worshiped per se in the Wind River Shoshone Sun Dance, it is, nevertheless, crucial to the physical health and religious visionary experience of the Sun Dancer. Like the paint that the Sun Dancer smears on his body, the sun dries out the dancer and dries out illness (Shimkin 1953:442). By enduring the hardship of the sun's unremitting heat, and by abstaining from food and water, the Sun Dancer prepares himself. Hot and dry, he becomes eligible for visionary experience—often involving water, the talisman of power and his acquisition of it.[5] In this way, some Sun Dancers achieve power as healers.

Threading through the above discussion have been examples of direct address to Sun, in myth and in everyday life. I remind the reader of another myth, already cited earlier in connection with songs 78 and 79, in which Cottontail kills Sun, resurrects Sun, and then lectures Sun not to be too hot (Kelly 1938:424, 426; W. Miller 1972:51; Steward 1936:415). Finally, the sun is "greeted" after the all-night

Peyote Ceremony by several groups, including the Wind River Shoshones, Utes, and Gosiutes (Stewart 1987:352).

Wovoka drew on Great Basin beliefs and relationship to the sun in his own religious experience, and this had an impact on the course of the Ghost Dance. Wovoka's state of trance-unconsciousness on January 1, 1889, coincided with an eclipse of the sun. He told Mooney, "'When the sun died, I went up to heaven and saw God and all the people who had died a long time ago. . . . He gave me this dance to give to my people'" (Mooney [1896] 1991:764). If Wovoka believed that Sun was a god, then he believed in two gods—his visionary communication being with another, perhaps Christian, God. Wovoka roused to life and the sun came out from its eclipse; in tandem both moved from death to life. Edward C. Johnson, in a history of his own Walker River Paiute people, writes, "Numus [Northern Paiutes] living in the Walker River area interpreted the Prophet's spontaneous recovery on that date [January 1, 1889] as his having 'saved' the Sun, their principal deity; that is, Wovoka prevented the ending of this universe, an apocalyptic belief they held" (E. Johnson 1975:47). Northern Paiute understanding may have likened Wovoka to the shaman, who "dies" and retrieves the soul of the "dead" patient, in this case, Sun. Wovoka proved his power, and this served as strong validation for the Ghost Dance religion he preached. Hittman points out the Sun-God-Father associations with Wovoka by Northern Paiutes in the way they addressed him, using "their name for the Sun, Tamme Naa'a, or 'Our Father,' . . ." (Hittman 1990:184).[6]

We know from Mooney's publication ([1896] 1991:920) and later museum collections of Plains Ghost Dance clothing (see Peterson 1976) that the sun was a commonly used Ghost Dance design. However, there is no information that relates the sun design to either the eclipse of the sun in 1889 that coincided with Wovoka's trance or Northern Paiute belief in Sun. In connection with Lakota Ghost Dance shirts, Mooney suggests otherwise, that representations of sun, moon, and stars were "sacred things of their mythology, and the visions of the trance" (Mooney [1896] 1991:790). Thus their source was Lakota tribal lore and personal religious experience.

Stars and the Milky Way

Rich in metaphoric imagery, the Milky Way was important in Great Basin views of the cosmos. It was a road for the spirits of dead people to take to the land of the dead, the spirit world (Kelly 1932:154, 198; Mooney [1896] 1991:1053; Steward 1941:323; Steward 1943a: 348). Various Northern Paiute terms expressed this: *nümü po*, literally "Numus," "people"—specifically Northern Paiute—"trail" (Kelly 1938:372); *Nu-mü mo-go-a-po,* "Northern Paiute soul trail" (Powell 1971:242); and *muguabo,* "soul road" (Steward 1941:267). And, as Lowie suggested, shamans, too, used this road. "After death the souls go to the Milky Way, and that is probably where the shaman goes to bring back the patient's soul" (Lowie 1924a:295).[7]

The connection between the Milky Way and the soul has to do with the physical appearance of one and the conceptualization of the other. The Milky Way, a dense line of celestial bodies, gives the appearance of murkiness—as of a swathe of mist and fog dividing the night sky. Given Great Basin and Wind River Shoshone belief that the soul looks like fog when it leaves the body, the relationship between the two is self-evident. It is this image of the Milky Way that appears in song 128. Using English word order, the text says, "fog-road above."

Dust presents another physical likeness to the appearance of the Milky Way, and it, too, connects on a conceptual level. Dust is a different and feared embodiment of the dead. No longer retrievable to life by the shaman, whirlwind ghosts are powerful and dangerous. In his glossary of Northern Paiute terms, Mooney gives *Kosi´ba,* for "dust" and *Gosi´pa* for "Milky Way," the road of the dead (Mooney [1896] 1991:1056). Stewart's transcription is almost identical: *kusipo,* "dust road" (Stewart 1941:415). Northern Paiute Bannocks use the term *kösiwuyuwat,* "grayish line"; and Gosiute Shoshones of Deep Creek use an expression that translates as "Dust road" (Steward 1943a: 390). Similarly, Shoshones from Nevada use *kueci woyona,* "dust streak," and *tsoapobo,* "ghost road" (Steward 1941:267).[8]

Emily's commentary on the Milky Way, which appears in song 126, does not include any of the terms discussed thus far—soul road, dusty road, or ghost road. In place of these she referred to "Heaven way," a name that, at least on the surface, carries Christian overtones. Emily, like so many Wind River Shoshones, was baptized by Reverend John Roberts at the Episcopalian Mission on the reservation. However, I believe that her rare use of Christian terminology here and elsewhere was primarily directed at connecting with what she perceived as my Euro-American religious background. It was her way of also reminding me of the religious validity of her Naraya belief. In a similar vein, but without the Christian reference, there is a Southern Paiute name for the Milky Way, *tuwu´nawüv,* "sky path" (Steward 1941:267).

Wovoka, who was inculcated with Christian belief during the time he lived with David Wilson's family, moved easily between native Paiute and Christian religious terms and concepts. God, Jesus, and heaven were part of his Ghost Dance vocabulary. Like Emily, he combined the Milky Way with a heavenly destination. Stewart learned that "Jack Wilson [Wovoka's non-Indian name] got a song that said the Milky Way is a trail to heaven" (Stewart 1941:444). The first Paiute Ghost Dance song published by Mooney does, in fact, mention the Milky Way, and it was reported to be a favorite among the Northern Paiute (Mooney [1896] 1991:1052–53).

Given Ghost Dance prophecy for the resurrection of the dead and Wovoka's Great Basin heritage, it is not surprising that there is an anecdote that links him with the Milky Way. This connection is also consistent with Lowie's suggestion regarding the journey of the shaman on the Milky Way. Wovoka was said to be one "who could at will go to heaven by way of the Great Dipper and the Milky Way. ... This was one of Jack's claims to supernatural power, according to Robert Dyer" (Dangberg 1957:287, 287n.13).

Soul road, dust road, ghost road, sky road, and Heaven way are all roads for those who journey in the sky to a netherworld, be it the land of the dead or the new world of Ghost Dance prophecy. Emily also gave another term for the Milky Way, *daziumbe gwahaiboromp,* literally, "star backbone." This metaphor for the Milky Way draws on the structure of biological anatomy. It, too, had currency among other Great Basin people.[9]

The Milky Way and Milky Way–backbone imagery appear in the Wind River Shoshone Sun Dance. Clark brings this out, quoting material from a 1926 manuscript by Lynn St. Clair, a Wind River Shoshone tribal leader and well-known Sun Dance singer. Clark writes that the center pole of the Sun Dance lodge "symbolizes the Milky Way, 'a great path over which travel the people who have passed to the great beyond'" (Clark 1966:186).

Second in importance only to the center pole of the Sun Dance lodge is the east-west rafter, one of many poles that radiate out from the center pole to create a spoked covering. The Sun Dance Chief is always positioned under this rafter, which, like the Milky Way, is also called the "backbone" (Shimkin 1953:439–40, 443–44). It cuts across the top of the circular lodge just as the stars do across the night sky. Lowie's suggested connection between the shaman and the Milky Way seems relevant here. Healing is an important focus of the Sun Dance, and Sun Dance Chiefs are often noted for their power to heal. There is, therefore, conceptual logic to position the Chief directly under the Milky Way–backbone rafter.

The Milky Way as "rocks in a row" is, to my knowledge, an image unique to Naraya song 126. The shiny or shining quality of the rocks in song 126 and the focus on this attribute as the defining characteristic of the Milky Way in song 127 derive, I believe, from the root, *sai*, a reference to melting snow, its wetness and glistening appearance. In addition to this reference, song 127 specifically mentions water up in the sky. One can find other associations between water and stars in Great Basin thought. Surprise Valley Paiutes call the North Star *pa´düwüdüdü*, "'standing in the water,' because it does not move" (Steward 1933:288). However, the following Northern Paiute myth is more to the point regarding the shining image in songs 126 and 127: "The Sun and the Stars came with the Water. They had the Water for a home. The Indian doctor saw them coming. He let his people know that they were coming. There were many of them. The little streams of spring water are the places from which silver money comes. It comes from the Sun shining on the water" (Kelly 1938:437–38). Watery origins and the shining quality of water attach to sun and stars. There is a reciprocity of imagery: water gives a sheen to the sun and stars in the sky, and sun and stars shine on water and give shining silver—visually, physically—on earth.

The Milky Way as road and the travel of people on it after death was but one type of relationship between people and stars. Great Basin people also related directly to individual stars during their lifetime. Like the sun and clouds, stars are a source of power (Fowler and Liljeblad 1986:453; Park 1938:17). The Morning Star, in particular, enjoyed special prominence. In 1986 Liljeblad reported that "the Morning Star, always personified, was prayed to, and in rare cases still is" (Liljeblad 1986:642). One Owens Valley Paiute woman communicated with the Morning Star and received advice about gambling (Liljeblad 1986:642). In a dream, the Morning Star spoke to another Owens Valley Paiute person, who recalled: "Then I went home and lay down and while I was asleep the great morning star, which had just risen, said to me: 'What is the matter with you that you are sick? A little thing like that ought not to make you sick.' I went out the next day and was well. I had never dreamed of the morning star before" (Steward 1934:428).

The name "Morning Star" is a reminder that the star fades in the sky just as the sun rises. The ending of one coincides with the beginning of the other; two potent entities are in company. Naraya song 15 captures the special quality of the light from both sun and star at that moment of joint passage. In English, "Morning Star" notes this linkage of sun and star, and so do native terms. Owens Valley Paiutes call it *ta´viha'a*, "sun or dawn coming" (Steward 1933:288). Shoshones call it *ta·ttaci?umpi*, adding, I believe, an abbreviated form of sun, *ta*, from *tavai* (Tidzump 1970:1), before the word for star, *ttaciʔumpi* (Liljeblad 1986:642).[10]

Like the sun, the Morning Star serves as a time marker. This appears in the dreamed instruction of an Owens Valley Paiute man who was receiving a "call" to be a doctor. A certain mountain told him how he should cure people. "'I should sit by my patient all night, holding my hands on him and singing. When the morning star should rise, I should get up and dance a few rounds, and then hold out my hand, when something like snow would appear in my palm'" (Steward 1934:428).

The Morning Star also became a special time marker in the Ghost Dance. According to Mooney, Wovoka "gave instructions that the dance should be held only at intervals of six weeks, and should then continue four consecutive nights, lasting the first three nights until about midnight, but on the fourth night to continue all night until daylight of the next morning" (Mooney [1896] 1991:1011).

Mooney reported that the following song "to the morning star was sung just before daylight on the final morning of the dance" (Mooney [1896] 1991:1011):

> Father, the Morning Star!
> Father, the Morning Star!
> Look on us, we have danced until daylight,
> Look on us, we have danced until daylight.
> Take pity on us—*Hi'i'i!*
> Take pity on us—*Hi'i'i!*
> (Mooney [1896] 1991:1011)

The Morning Star was ritual timekeeper and became associated with Wovoka, himself. Arapahoes sang:

> My children, my children,
> It is I who wear the morning star on my head,
> It is I who wear the morning star on my head;
> I show it to my children,
> I show it to my children,
> Says the father,
> Says the father.
> (Mooney [1896] 1991:1007)

Naraya song 15 describes the waning light of the Morning Star as the sun's beams stream out. Did the Naraya, like the Ghost Dance, continue throughout the final night of its performance, ending as the Morning Star faded from sight? Emily remembered that Naraya performance took place on a series of four nights, like the Ghost Dance.

She further noted that the final performance took place in the day-time after the fourth night. However, she gave no indication that the fourth night was, in fact, an all-night performance. Naraya song 15 certainly raises the possibility that at some time in the past the final evening's dance continued until morning.

Sun, moon, stars (including the Morning Star), and birds—all in-habitants of the sky realm—were some of the most common designs painted by Ghost Dancers on their clothing and faces (Mooney [1896] 1991: 823, 916, 919). Virginia Grant Bonatsie, the woman who re-ceived Naraya song 112, posed for her photograph in 1910 wearing a shawl decorated with crescent moons and stars similar to those on Ghost Dance clothing (see plate 5). One wonders whether she wore this shawl for the Naraya.

Night

The time of day for performance was prescribed for certain Wind River Shoshone ceremonies.[11] This was true for the Naraya, which was per-formed on a series of nights and then concluded after a final session of daytime dancing. Great Basin notions about night and its primal origins may be relevant for this prescribed timing. They serve as back-ground for songs 129 and 130, whose subject is night and its poetic evocation.

Within the context of a study of Great Basin religion, Jay Miller brings out the importance of night and its power:

> According to Powell, the primal world consisted of the "original facts or primary concepts that there is a land and a sea, an abyss below, and a night above." Of these basic elements, night and water were among the most sacred.
>
> Night was the universal condition until the stars, moon, seasons, and sun were created. It was a night of both time and space, with "the face of the night meaning the sky or apparent firmament." Because it was of the very beginning, night remains the most appropriate time for curings, gatherings, and dances to capture power, especially around midnight and the blackness just before dawn. Northern Paiute person-ified night as the spirit who sent messengers and aid to the shamans. Olofson was told that the spirit of night "is everywhere and send ani-mal messengers to the doctor; it is for this reason that shamans prefer to work at midnight when their power is strongest." (J. Miller 1983:70)

Dick Mahwee, a Northern Paiute shaman, explained the special relationship between shaman and the night. He told Park, "The In-dian doctor gets his power from the spirit of the night. This spirit is everywhere. It has no name. There is no word for it. The Indians hold this spirit so sacred that they are afraid if they had a name for it the spirit would be angry. No one has ever dared give it a name.

"Eagle and owl do not give a shaman power. They are just messengers that bring instructions from the spirit of the night. . . . When shamans get power it always comes from the night. They are told to doctor only at night. This power has nothing to do with the moon or stars" (Park 1938:17).

Joe Green, another Northern Paiute shaman, elaborates: "There are two nights. The second one comes behind the night that everybody sees. This second night is under the darkness. It tells the shaman where the pain is and what caused the sickness. When the second night comes it makes the shaman feel that he is a doctor. The power is in him to doctor. Only shamans can see this second night. The people can only see the darkness. They cannot see the night under it" (Park 1938:17).

Even when night itself is not communicating with the shaman, it is the traditional time for vision and communication with other sources of power. This is equally true for those who are not shamans but who, nevertheless, may be recipients of vision and power. Lowie writes of the Northern Shoshone, "In the night, his medicine [source of power] speaks to him and counsels him" (Lowie 1909a:224).

Winter and night are the proper season and time of day for telling myths. Night itself plays a role in myth. In several Southern Paiute accounts Wolf has power over night and keeps it securely tied in a special bundle. After Wolf's death, Coyote opens this bundle and night rushes out over the world. Coyote then uses bird feathers also contained in the bundle, shooting them into the air, and in this way finally restoring the light (Franklin 1992:14; Laird 1976:200; Lowie 1924a:101, 163–64). Birds—inhabitants of the sky just as night is—are instrumental in bringing back the light. This was also the case in another myth previously cited (chapter 5) in which Coyote killed the Sun, calling on Goose and Mallard in this instance to sing back the daylight.

This concludes the presentation of Naraya texts and commentary on them. The next two chapters will examine the form of the songs, beginning with their texts.

8 | *Textual Analysis*

I would like to preface the detailed examination of verbal forms and patterns that follows with a few broader comments about the song texts in general. First, I reiterate a point concerning Great Basin and Wind River Shoshone notions about language, especially in religious contexts. The following remark by Witherspoon, cited in the introduction to this book, makes this point beautifully in reference to Navajo culture, but it is equally applicable to Great Basin culture and specifically the Naraya. "The language of Navajo ritual is performative, not descriptive. Ritual language does not describe how things are; it determines how they will be. Ritual language is not impotent; it is powerful. It commands, compels, organizes, transforms, and restores" (Witherspoon 1977:34).

This is the power of Naraya language, which leads to the next logical question: Who is the speaker? Except for speeches made by the Naraya leader, song texts are the main vehicle of verbal communication. From a physical standpoint, then, the "speaker" in the Naraya is the singer—the song leader and as many dancers who pick up the song and wish to join in the singing as they dance. It is communal communication.

Within the song texts themselves, who is the speaker? People are barely present.[1] Indeed, song 123 is the sole Naraya text with a human subject, sung from a first-person perspective. As I stated in the introduction to this book, nature is the subject of Naraya songs and with no reference to the "I" of the eye that beholds. Bahr comments similarly about Pima-Papago song poems in his article on Native American dream songs: "They tend to leave out the grammatical subjects of their sentences . . . thus, although these three songs are heavy with nouns, the nouns are not the subjects of the sentences or the doers of actions. Rather, the nouns name things or places that the actor, an 'I,' . . . comes upon. . . . [The result is] a subjective action oriented, pictorial and shamanic poetry" (Bahr 1994:82–83).

How do these observations on Pima-Papago songs relate to Naraya songs? According to Emily, all Naraya songs were received in dreams and, by implication, had power. To my knowledge, Virginia Grant Bonatsie, who dreamed song 112, was not a shaman. However, like the shaman, she, or any Shoshone, could dream and receive song with power. Naraya songs were "shamanic," with power to restore and revitalize nature. But there is this difference: Naraya songs were neither subjective nor action oriented from a human standpoint. Each song was the product of a personal dream experience, but once the song entered the Naraya circle the tie to its receiver was unimportant—in most instances, severed and forgotten.

There is, however, one important pronomial adjective in Naraya song texts and interestingly it, too, reinforces the communal rather than personal expression of the songs. Naraya songs sing of "our" mountains and "our" big river and "our" earth. Thirty-five songs contain *damë,* the inclusive form of "our," which in everyday discourse refers to the speaker and includes his or her listeners. In the Naraya, "our" means Wind River Shoshone. Naraya singers and the texts they sing are in unison. Physically and verbally the songs are Shoshone communal speech.

To whom do Naraya songs speak? Emily gives two answers. First, she said, "It's a religious song that you sing to God." Pandora Pogue, another Wind River Shoshone woman, made similar comments to Shimkin forty years earlier, in 1937. "Whenever they sing that [Naraya] song they pray first. They are God's songs" (Shimkin 1937). Our Father, *Damë Apë,* appears only in five Naraya songs (numbers 8, 9, 20, 22, 25). He is Our Father, the Creator, and as such, all are his— the animals (song 8) and the world he inhabits, be it this world, which is getting old (songs 19 and 25), or the new world of Ghost Dance doctrine (song 22), or an ambiguous land of the dead (song 9). (A reference to Christ, the unmentioned but understood subject of song 24, is unique.) Within this small number of texts, however, there are references to Our Father but never direct addresses to him.

Emily's second answer was her litany. Songs are addressed to the natural world that fills the song texts. For example, after singing about the sun in song 4, Emily said, "It's a prayer song to sun" (Vander 1986:48). Her comments quoted earlier imply this point over and over. "They say when you sing those songs it makes berries grow! And makes grass grow. Make water run. . . . Everything: fish, anything. Sing for them." Sing about them, to them, for them. Nature nouns are the major subjects of Naraya songs. They are both the subject of Naraya song texts and simultaneously the object of its performance.

The relationship is creative: sung green mountains help make real green mountains.

Repetition and "Dynamic Symmetry"

Repetition is a guiding principle in Naraya songs and texts. It was an overriding feature in Naraya performance. Recall that the circle of dancers sang for themselves as they performed at least one complete revolution before stopping. It would have required many repetitions of a song to accomplish this since most, if not all of the songs, take less than half a minute to sing. Many take a bare fifteen seconds.

Repetition creates and shapes the form of the verse, which is the basic unit of the song and its text. In its most common form, each verse contains two lines of two to six words and each line repeats, forming what Herzog termed a "paired pattern" or "paired progression" (Herzog 1935a:404). Herzog's study of Plains Ghost Dance songs characterized its formal symmetry and the simplicity of means to achieve it—repetition. The data and analysis in my 1986 monograph and the songs and texts presented in the present book amply support Herzog's basic analysis regarding repetition and symmetry. However, his statistical study of a relatively small number of selected parameters contains its own limitations. Because these songs are minute forms, only a detailed, microscopic study brings into focus their many facets. If one sees and synthesizes the unique, idiosyncratic features of individual songs, a very different characterization emerges. In equal measure, Naraya music and texts are rife with complexity and asymmetrical subtlety.

I came to this same conclusion in my earlier study of seventeen Naraya songs, and the greatly enlarged sample size in this book only serves to confirm it. "Dynamic symmetry," a term coined by Witherspoon in a discussion of Navajo art, seems equally apt for understanding the way in which Naraya songs and their texts integrate the asymmetrical with the symmetrical into a coherent, unified whole. Witherspoon defined his concept of dynamic symmetry: "Just as perfect symmetry in art is basically static, perfect equality and balance between two parts of a pair also produces a static result. . . . Dynamic symmetry is based on the ideas of similar and complementary but inexact, imperfect, and unequal pairing or balancing. . . . Dynamic symmetry is more characteristic of the dynamic flow and flux found in nature and in the proportions of the human body and in the growing plant" (Witherspoon 1977:197–200). This concept of dynamic symmetry informs my understanding and analysis of Naraya texts and music. The rest of this chapter and much of chapter 9 will explore the aesthetic nature of a poetic-musical form that is minute in size and, simultaneously, judged by its artistic achievement and religious intent, immense, beautiful, and powerful.

Form

In Emily and Dorothy's repertoire the form of almost all Naraya texts follows the general rule of the genre and is made of pairs of repeated lines, AA BB. Some exceptions to the rule include three repeated lines (song 53), a single line followed by a pair of repeated lines (song 24), and even a pair of repeated lines, which itself repeats (AA AA, song 88). In the latter case, the second repetition is set to a new line of music and in this altered state serves as the B part. In song 8 (see appendix A) a sequence of two different lines repeats, followed by a final repeated pair, AB AB CC.[2]

Song performance itself opens the possibility for formal instability. Emily and/or Dorothy would occasionally omit the repeat of a line in one or more repetitions of the song verse, a vagary that can happen more easily when there are one or two singers rather than a large group.

In addition to the paired lines, which make up the basic verse of each song, individual lines are themselves made up of smaller repeated units. This happens in a significant number of lines. Within 113 Naraya songs, 47 lines (my reference to lines of text always refers to individual lines and does not include their repetition) are made of two repeated units (for example, line one of song 18), and six lines consist of three repeated units (for example, line one of song 24). However, in these 53 cases, just 8 texts use the same subdivided form consistently in both of their lines (for example, song 65). In these 8 texts there is structural balance or symmetry between the lines, whereas in the majority of the 47 examples, a "mini"–two-part form occurs in only one of the two (or three) lines of a verse. Thus, the structural relationship between the lines of the verse is asymmetrical—an unequal pairing or balancing. Songs 49 and 69 present yet another interesting variant of unequal pairing in this regard. While both songs contain small repeated units in both lines of text, the number of repeated units is not the same. The first line of both songs contains three repeated units; the second line, two repeated units.

The length of the different lines of texts is another aspect of form that reveals unequal pairing or balancing. The numbers of words and their syllables that comprise each line are characteristically different.

Only 20 of 113 song texts have verses with lines of identical length (for example, song 47). Word accent and rhythm await further discussion in the next chapter, which examines these characteristics in relation to the musical settings of the texts.

A discussion of rhyme completes this overview of the basic form of the verse. The incidence of rhyme in 113 songs is as follows: 49 songs end both lines of text with the same word and not a true rhyme, 22 songs have true rhyme, 6 songs have assonance, and 36 songs have no ending rhyme. I will argue that Naraya poetic form centers at least as much, if not more, on the manipulation of word sounds within a line rather than between different lines and their word endings.

Incomplete, Inexact Repetition and Parallelisms

Repetition of the largest unit, the line, creates Naraya form and its vaunted symmetry. Within smaller units—parts of lines or individual words—incomplete or inexact repetition creates a "regular irregularity." I invite the reader to enter the forest of this realm, to begin to see it from inside out, from the perspective of its trees.

First, I consider incomplete repetition within individual lines the abbreviations that shorten the line. For example, this occurs in a line that appears in songs 62 and 121. Both songs omit "pine nut" at the end of the line: "Pine nut mountains, pine nut mountains, mountains *ena.*"

In the examples given thus far, whole words are missing in a repeated phrase. Another common type of abbreviation results from cutting off part of a repeated word. In song 52, the word "flat," *dïpëgaiyu,* is immediately repeated as *dïpëgai,* dropping the final syllable. In song 108, the verb "lie" (*havi-dir*) ends the first half of the first line. The second half repeats the first, but omits the verbal suffix, *-dir.* At this micro-level, the omission of a suffix in the two-part repeated form is significant. It foils what would have been a same-word "rhyme" within the line and it shortens the second half of the pair by one beat. In place of an AA form within the line, there is an A^1A^2 form.

This same process may also occur in the repetition of an entire line. For example, in song 28, the repeat of the second line of text omits the final suffix, *-ye.* As a consequence the form of line two and its repeat becomes B^1B^2. In this particular song there is a progression of abbreviated endings. Line A and its repeat end with a vocable suffix, *-yedu:* B^1 cuts it down to *-ye.* B^2 has no vocable suffix at all, marking the end of the B lines and the end of the entire verse as well. Abbreviation is one way of indicating the end of a line in Naraya texts. For example, *yorikena,* which ends the first half of the last pair of lines in song 85, is shortened to *yoriken* at the end of the line.

As suggested, repetition in Naraya texts may be a shortening process accomplished by omitting or abbreviating words. Repetition also makes possible the opposite process, a lengthening of texts through added words and word parts. For example, line two of song 52 says, "Rocks flat, rocks flat flat." The first line of song 123 is made of two repeated parts: "Myself thought, myself thought *gena.*" The Shoshone word for "thought" takes a suffix, *suave-andë,* which in repetition becomes *suave-andïnö.* The ending vocable, *gena,* is another added element that creates asymmetry in this and other lines made of two repeated phrases. In some songs, for example song 83, the ending vocable ends every line of text.

The second line of song 123, also a two-part form, shows the use of both omission and addition in its repetition, creating an interesting relationship between its parts. The line reads, "Our sky sun comes out, sun sun comes out *gena*"; omitting "our sky" in the second half, the text repeats "sun" at the beginning and adds *gena* at the end.

From a structural standpoint, one of the most complex examples of repetition—incomplete and inexact—occurs between the different lines of text. A bewildering array of parallelisms and borrowings creates a thicket of relationships that break the surface neatness and separation of its paired lines. This is true of both text and music and helps define Naraya stylistic essence and subtlety. There is a propensity for recycling patterns and pattern bits—larger branches, smaller branches, leaf structure, and individual leaves.

As preface to my discussion of parallelisms in Naraya song texts, I will briefly place the topic within the context of Wind River Shoshone linguistics and myth. I quote Shimkin, who has studied both subjects and has written: "Predication or apposition of nouns or verbs in parallel construction is a grammatical process of major importance in Shoshone" (Shimkin 1949a:177). "The ordinary *sequential devices* of Shoshone myths are four in number: parallel development to a climax, simple reiteration or repetition, sharp contrast, and parenthetical incorporation. As has been shown before, parallel development is the principal characteristic of plots" (Shimkin 1947c:339).

Naraya texts reveal a poetic realm that is rich in parallelisms. The most common type of parallel relationship between the different lines of text occurs at the beginning of the lines. In its simplest form, these beginning phrases are identical:

Our people . . .
Our people . . .
(song 18)

Our big mountains . . .
Our big mountains . . .
(song 43)

Mountains sit on . . .
Mountains sit on . . .
(song 44)

Water-black rock . . .
Water-black rock . . .
(song 55)

Game animals young . . .
Game animals young . . .
(song 72)

Mountains game animals
Mountains game animals
(songs 60, 73)

Water people . . .
Water people . . .
(song 95)

Our come night . . .
Our come night . . .
(song 129)

Another type of beginning parallelism substitutes one or two new words within what is otherwise the same grouping:

Our good earth . . .
Our new earth . . .
(songs 21, 23)

Our big river . . .
Our big hill . . .
(song 32)

Our big mountains . . .
Green water mountains . . .
(song 47)

Fish upon waves . . .
Grass upon waves . . .
(song 96)

A still smaller parallel adjective-noun unit begins several texts:

> Our Father . . .
> Our mother's . . .
> > (song 22)

> Side (of the) mountain . . .
> Quaking aspen mountain . . .
> > (song 49)

> Water mountains . . .
> Otter mountains . . .
> > (song 51)

> White-Clay Man . . .
> Wood Stick Man . . .
> > (song 112)

The smallest beginning parallelism uses the same first word:

Fog mountains under water *he*
Fog, fog, fog blown
> (song 36)

Rocks sitting, rocks peeling
Rocks, rocks
> (song 54)

Fall [i.e., autumn] antelope bulls, fall antelope bulls, fall antelope bulls
Fall hill above young, fall hill above young
> > (song 69)

Woodchuck black woodchuck, woodchuck black woodchuck
Woodchuck shining, woodchuck shining
> (song 76)

The parallel first word sometimes receives further emphasis through various types of repetition elsewhere in the line. In the above examples, "fog" takes over almost all of line two in song 36. Songs 54 and 69 repeat the parallel first word of both lines within each line due to their subdivided repeated form. The use of "woodchuck" in song 76 is noteworthy as there is parallelism not only between the beginning of the two lines but, within the first line, between the beginning and ending of the small repeated unit. Thus, the form of the two lines is ABA, ABA / AC, AC.

Another type of parallelism occurs between the endings of lines, often by the use of the same final word, for example, "flying" in song 35, and "shining lying-moving" in song 47. A rarer type of parallelism matches both beginnings and endings, bracketing the new word or words within identical boundaries:

> Game animals rocks *tiwaizi*, game animals rocks *tiwaizi*
> Game animals road *tiwaizi*, game animals road *tiwaizi*
>
> > (song 65)
>
> Our mother earth bitterroot *wënëvi*
> Our mother earth misty yampa *wënëvi*
>
> > (song 115)

Further permutations of parallelism relate parts of one line to parts of another:

> Sun showers mountains, sun showers mountains *ena*
> Pine needles pools low place, sun showers mountains *ena*
>
> > (song 34)
>
> Rocks in a row, rocks in a row
> Rocks in a row . . .
>
> > (song 126)
>
> *Wainaiyo wainaiyo*
>
> .   .   .
>
> *Wainaiyo*
>
> > (song 53)

All three examples use just half or one of the two repeated parts of a previous line. Song 34 adds a new first half before returning to the material from the previous line; song 126 adds a different conclusion to the second line. Song 53 forms line three simply by using half of line one. The repeat of line three also adds a concluding vocable, *wainda.*

Song 124, unique in its form, typifies the complex possibilities that even three words of text may achieve, straining at, perhaps bursting its parallel seams:

> Sun down mountains   down mountains
> Sun   mountains sun mountains down mountains.

The complexity of the parallelisms in this example is more striking in Shoshone, which presents three variants for "down" (*dïna?*) and "mountains" (*doiyavi*).

> Sun *dïn-dïn-dïndsi roiyabi*   *dïndsi   roiyavi*
> Sun   *doiyabi* sun *doiya dïn-dïndsi roiyavi.*

Song 108, like song 124, compresses the first part of line one in line two, and both lines share an identical second half:

Pass cedar hill lie, pass cedar hill lie
Pass　　　　　　lie, pass cedar hill lie.

The separation of lines begins to blur in much the same way that a tongue-twister of similar sounds can confound both tongue and mind. Other examples of parallelism, in which either the ending of one line becomes the identical beginning of the next, or a pattern begun late in one line carries over and into the next, forge links between the lines in ways that tend to smudge the boundary between them. For example, the first line of song 41 ends with *"van-vagïnan doi (seya),"* a phrase that then begins the next line. To take another example, in line one of song 56, the last two words are *pa-ro wai gondi,* "water under." This becomes the basis for all of line two:

　　. . . 　　　　　　　　　　　　*pa-ro wai-gondi,*
　　pa-ro-wai-gondi pa-ro wai-gondi pa-ro wai-gondi.

In line one of song 37, the last two words of the five-word line are "sky rocks." Line two substitutes "fog" for "sky," and the line becomes: "fog rocks, fog rocks." Similarly, the second line of song 52 derives from line one and in this example "rocks" substitutes for "earth." Also note in song 52 the differing degrees of repetition and parallelism within the second line and between the two different lines:

Our earth　　　　　　　　　　　　flat *(dïpëgaiyu)* flat *(dïpëgai),*
Rocks　　flat *(dïpëgaiyu)* [omits *dïpëgai*] rocks flat *(dïpëgaiyu)* flat *(dïpëgai).*

Song 45, like song 52, shows parallelism between the end of line one and the beginning of line two, as well as more examples of inexact repetitions and unequal balancing.

Our big mountains, big two mountains, big two mountains *yaiyowaindë*
　　Green two mountains, green two mountains *yaiyowanidë.*

Finally, in song 26 the last two of four words in line one, "earth shakes with rumbling sound," carry forward and develop further in line two, "earth crackling like thunder."

Sung versus Spoken Language

The title of this section focuses on one set of distinctions concerning the use and form of language in Naraya song texts. This set is actually one of three, and inseparable from the other two—poetry versus prose and sacred language versus everyday discourse. Naraya song texts are sacred sung poetry, which shapes their linguistic form.

Nouns

The language of Naraya song texts is strikingly different from that of everyday speech. If we look at the text of each complete musical line and its repeat, we find a predominance of nouns. In fact, roughly half of Naraya lines contains only nouns, sometimes with adjectives, and without verbs. Song 45 is a striking example of this. (*Yaiyowaindë* is a vocable pattern that often marks the end of a line, and I include it in this literal translation.)

> Our big mountains, big two mountains, big two mountains *yaiyowaindë*,
> Our big mountains, big two mountains, big two mountains *yaiyowaindë*.
> Green two mountains, green two mountains, *yaiyowaindë*,
> Green two mountains, green two mountains, *yaiyowaindë*.

Hinton reports similar findings in her linguistic study of Havasupai Circle Dance songs. Although the Havasupai are not a Great Basin culture, they live contiguous to the Basin in the Southwest. Their Circle Dance bears likeness to the Great Basin Round Dance in its form and function, and many of Hinton's analytical points regarding differences between sung and spoken Havasupai language are pertinent here. She, too, notes that "in the circle dance songs, . . . we find very few complete sentences by spoken-language standards. . . . The Havasupai clearly choose for nominal style in their sung language, especially in circle dance songs" (Hinton 1984:57–58). They "exhibit primarily concrete nouns in their texts; there are some words interpretable as verbs, except that they always lack the verbal suffixes, which makes them more noun-like" (Hinton 1984:59).

Whereas Naraya performance addressed nature, the Havasupai circle dance addressed group solidarity, an aspect of Great Basin Round Dance performance as well. With this shift of focus, Hinton adds, "Unlike the fully-worded songs . . . the circle dance songs do not approximate a spoken communication event. We have already seen . . . that no true sentences are present . . . and no separate entities of 'speaker,' 'addressee,' etc., exist. The message is from the group, to the group, by means of the group, and about the group" (Hinton 1984:106–7).

Bahr's analysis, cited earlier, regarding who is the speaker in Pima-Papago songs, suggests a similar prevalence of nouns in song texts.

Verbs

The absence of verbs in approximately half the lines of Naraya texts is both striking and at odds with normal patterns of Wind River Shoshone speech. Shimkin writes, "Shoshone sentences are of two types, the predicate sentence noted above [demonstrative verb + predicate, nominal subject + predicate], and the true verbal sentence. In the verbal sentence the basic word order is rigidly fixed: subject—object—verb" (Shimkin 1949a:177).

Verbs in Naraya texts appear at the ends of lines, consistent with the "true verbal sentence" structure as given above.[3] Approximately 95 of 238 lines in Naraya texts have verbs, and roughly 50 of these lines are in texts whose form is AABB. About half of these latter texts have verbs in both lines, and half have verbs only in the second line. Verb placement only in the second line of text is another powerful means of integrating and unifying the two different lines of text. The second line completes the first; both are dependent halves of the whole. Notice in the following examples the parallels or repeats between lines one and two, some of which have been cited above, and how this works together with the verb placement to make inseparable unions, each in its own way. (For clarity, in these examples my translations move beyond the literal to a slightly freer English version.)

The two lines of song 18 (omitting the repeat of each line) say, "Our people, our people / Our people, feeling good, are coming." (In this text "our people" refers to dead Shoshone relatives.) Paraphrased, the verse says, "Our people, our people / Our people are feeling good and coming [back to life and earth]." Whereas line one of song 18 introduces its characters, line one in song 36 sets the scene, mentioning fog, mountains (?under water)—static elements. Line two adds the action to the scene. The two lines say, "Fog on the mountains (?under water) / Fog, fog, fog, blown apart by the wind." Line one of song 81 introduces character and scene, "fox in the mountains"; line two enlarges the scene and adds movement to it: "Night sky above—Milky Way moving across." In line one of song 130, the natural world and night are both character and setting. Again, the second line provides the verb and action—"standing while moving"—which Emily explained by describing the silent motion of trees blowing in the wind. "Nighttime—everything, nighttime—everything / Trees stand silently moving in the wind, trees stand silently moving in the wind."

The solitary verbs at the end of songs 112 and 95 buttress the diverse cumulative effect of their subjects. Song 112 places two subjects, White-Clay Man and Wood Stick Man, in lines one and two, respectively. The verb in line two joins them in flight: "White-Clay Man, White-Clay Man / And Wood Stick Man keep flying on together." Line one of song 95 reiterates its one subject, water people, an insistence and intensification that build and move across the line through the beginning of line two. A string of three verbs follows, a flurry of actions in this uniquely verb-rich text that offsets the series of preceding repeats and balances its unequal parts. The effect is even more startling, with the usual repetitions of each of the two lines. I will give them for this text: "Water people, water people, water people, / Water people, water people, water people. / Water people, people— stand in front of you, come out, rise up, Water people, people—stand in front of you, come out, rise up."

Another type of relationship between two lines of text sets two subjects in apposition to one another, one in each line. The solitary final verb completes the presentation of the second subject and simultaneously clarifies its apposition and metaphoric relationship to the first. Song 123 says, "My own thoughts, my own thoughts *gena* / Up in our sky sunlight comes out, sunlight, sunlight comes out *gena*."

Finally, five songs (songs 1, 35, 47, 61, and 108) use the same verb to end their two lines of text, another way of integrating them. Song 35 is an interesting example, one that achieves integration by dividing two parts of a single sentence across the two lines of text. Line one gives the subject, "eagle," and verb, "flying." Line two says, "Grassy ponds flying." Clearly, the ponds are not flying; the eagle in line one, unstated but implied in line two, flies over the grassy ponds.

Examination of the repertoire of verbs in Emily and Dorothy's Naraya songs reveals an interesting prominence of a few verbs—"lying," "standing," and "flying." I begin with "lie" or "lie down," whose verbal stem is *havi*. Mountains lie (songs 13, 98); mountain passes lie (song 108); silver lies under the mountains (songs 50, 57); pine trees (song 109), green grass (songs 67), and dust lie (song 114). Blackbirds lie in water, that is, bathe (song 88).

Havi, like other verbs that I will mention momentarily, commonly takes a verbal suffix, -*nòr(ë)* (songs 1, 2, 6, 10, 32, 47). *Havi* and the suffix usually appear as *havenòrë* and mean "lying-moving" or "lying while moving."[4] Because this suffix is broad and general, it permits a wide range of interpretations, especially in the poetic context of Naraya songs. Consider song 47: "Our big mountains shiny lying while moving / Green water mountains shiny lying while moving." Green water in this context could mean "wet green grass" and/ or "small streams flowing down grassy slopes." *Havenòrë* suggests the stillness and activity of the scene and its parts. The mountains lie, grass and water lie on the mountains, water lies on the grass, and grass lies on or in the water. There is wetness, shine, shimmer, and movement of grass on water and water on grass. All lend their movement to the mountains whose rising contours contain their own interpretive suggestion for "lying-moving." Together and in different ways, all lie and move.

The verbal stem "(to) stand," *wën-* or *wënë-*,[5] is another common Naraya verb. It almost invariably takes the suffix *-nóre* and translates as "standing-moving." The combination of verb and suffix appears in many slightly different forms (for example, *wanëkinóra*, in song 40, and *wainanórë*, in song 22), and like *havenórë*, it translates in a variety of ways depending upon the poetic context. Gladys Hill explained verb and suffix with an example of someone's standing up in the back of a truck as it is moving. Song 22 follows this model; "standing-moving" in the third line refines the verb, "flying up," in line two. Paraphrased, it says, "Our Father *ena* / Our mother's footsteps behind Him, flying up / Standing while moving onto the top edge of our new world." This standing flight is not the result of using either arms or legs, but rather seems a passive response to some other power or source of movement.[6]

In other songs, Emily identified wind as the implied source of movement. With this understanding, Emily glossed "standing-moving" as "blown or blown apart by the wind" (songs 36, 40, 43, 104, 130). This, in turn, opened further translation possibilities of the subject-image, its state and appearance: blowing apart fog (songs 36, 40); creating the windblown or slanting angle of sunshowers on the mountains (song 43); blowing through aspen leaves, bending down the grasses that lie beneath them (song 104); and silently waving trees, branches, and all vegetation in the night (song 130).

In song 88, blackbirds are the source of their own movement as they "stand while moving" in water. Again, the nonspecific verb and suffix permit a variety of realizations of the bath. I have already given my own vision of this scene, "birds standing, dipping, and shaking water from wings and ruffled feathers."

Song 64 contains the word *wïnërë*, derived from "standing-moving," which Emily translated as "tracks."[7] I am uncertain whether this is a verb or verb-derived noun. In either case the word focuses on the result of animals' standing and moving about in the mountains, the tracks that their standing-motion creates. Song 64 takes place in early spring, where the game had recently been moving about. "Our mountains with game animals *yaiyai ena* / Snow-melt-water-black standing-moving tracks *yaiyai ena*."

The verbal stem *yïzï-* (and its plural form, *yori*) is another common verb in Naraya songs.[8] It has a pair of related meanings, "get up," that is, "rise" or "arise," and "fly." In his unpublished sketch of Wind River Shoshone grammatical forms, Shimkin added some further comments that bring out the different implications and nuances of meaning. *Yɔ´rik,* means "to arise," "awake," and *yɔ´ri,* "to awake," "to get up from bed." *Yï´zï,* means "to arise," "to fly up like a bird" (Shimkin n.d.:18, 1, 2). Although Shimkin noted whether these particular verb forms were singular or plural, I do not believe that any of these translations were exclusive to one form of the verb. Tidzump verifies this in her Shoshone Thesaurus: *yets,* "get up," *yeze,* "get up!," and *yeze-doiq,* "to fly" (future) (Tidzump 1970:18SE).

This is true for the Wind River Shoshones as well as for other Shoshone speakers. We see similar forms and meanings in Crapo's dictionary of Big Smokey Valley Shoshoni: *jycy˝,* "get up, arise," *tuku-jycy˝,* "airplane" (Crapo 1976:160). Wick Miller gives Gosiute Shoshone forms: *yetseG,* "to get up, to fly" (singular subject) and *yotiG,* for a plural subject (W. Miller 1972:151).

Birds fly in songs 83 (*yïzï-eï-në*), 85 (*yoriken*), and 89 (*yïzï*). Eagles fly in songs 35 (*yïzïnór*) and 93 (*yïzïnór*), and in these latter examples the suffix *-nórë* is once again added to the verb stem. How is the "flying" of birds in songs 83, 85, and 89 different from "flying while moving" in songs 35 and 93? I do not know.

This same form, *yïzïnór,* appears in song 22 and refers to our mother's footsteps flying up to the top of the new world. In this context the two different connotations of the verb—bird-flight and awakening-arising from bed—might come into play. Earlier, I discussed the close connection between death and sleep in Numic view, the awakening from death of its mythic characters, the perception of Wovoka's "death" (unconsciousness) and resurrection (awakening), indeed, the basic premises and procedure of the shaman's work. The arising and flying up of the mother may imply her awakening from death, her resurrection on the new world of Wovoka's prophecy.

Several other forms of "flying-arising" appear in song texts whose subjects, like the mother, may invoke more than one meaning of the verb. In song 3, the soul is flying up (*yïzïkanzi*); in song 10, whirlwinds that surround the soul on its journey are flying up (*yoriendë*). White-Clay Man and Wood Stick Man in song 112 are in flight to the implied new world. Might this suggest their death and destruction in the aging and eventually dead old world and their awakening, arising, flying onto the new? Surely they are a rejuvenated pair, if they are not resurrected.

Even water people, in song 95, may draw on the two meanings of *yïzïgïn,* but only in a physical way. They rise or pop up. Among their many members, only the ducks (and conceptually, geese) could rise up by flying up. The rest of their watery company, the beavers, muskrats, and weasels, would arise from the water on foot.

A final observation on the uses of *-nörë* in Naraya texts is that its placement at the end of verbs creates a same-suffix "rhyme" between the lines of text.

Another fairly common Naraya verb is *garï-* "to sit," and its plural form, *yïgwï-* (Shimkin 1949b:207), which appear in nine Naraya songs.[9] Game animals (songs 8, 61), birds (song 90), mountains (songs 20, 25, 44, 61), white rocks (song 59), and stars (song 15), all "sit."

Finally, a variety of Naraya verbs indicates motion and direction. For example, celestial bodies such as the sun (songs 2, 123) and Morning Star (song 15) come out, people come or come back (songs 2, 18, 19). Game animals come down (song 53), deer climb (song 61), mountain sheep go up (song 74), game animals travel (song 73), and an Indian walks (song 125).

Word Transformations

I move to the smallest level now: individual words, word parts, and their interrelationships within a line. I will try to point out what seem to me to be differences between Naraya song language and ordinary spoken language. To do this I will draw on the analytical framework and conclusions of linguists who have made similar sung-spoken comparisons. I will also respond to what I believe are aspects of rhyme and rhythm that have their own poetic logic. I alert the reader to the inherent risks of my approach as I am neither a Shoshone speaker nor able to provide a complete linguistic analysis of the texts. At some future time the forms that I ascribe to pure sound or aesthetic considerations may be shown to be morphemes and not phonetic play. At the same time, I am convinced that there will ever remain parts that cannot be analyzed, poetic and sacred parts that dictate form and push Naraya language to the edge and perhaps even beyond the boundary of linguistic communication.

Shimkin's comments on the Shoshone language, in his study "Wind River Shoshone Literary Forms," are basic to the Naraya texts and the changes one finds in them. He wrote: "The constant alternation of consonants and vowels, the phonemic differentiation of two vocalic lengths, and the regular patterning of three distinct degrees of stress infuse Shoshone with a distinct rhythmical swing. . . . Speakers of the language clearly appreciate its melody, for the rules of good elocution, in myth-telling and oratory alike, demand a smooth, continuous flow of words elided into one another" (Shimkin 1947b:338).

Abbreviation and elision occur in the songs, as, indeed, they do in everyday speech. "*Du,*" from *duhuvit*[h], meaning "black," which appears in song 99, is a common daily usage. A more extreme and beautiful example of Naraya elision and resultant shortening appears in song 69. The song mentions antelope young sitting on the hills above. This is literally expressed in three words: hill, above, offspring. The three Shoshone words, *no:vI, vand^h, dudua,* become *no-van-du.* The "v" is both ending and beginning of the first two words, respectively, and the "d" is both ending and beginning of the second two words, respectively. Liljeblad has analyzed a similar example of abbreviation and elision in a Northern Shoshone song, which by coincidence is song 117 in Emily and Dorothy's repertoire. He explicates the first words of line two, "wild rose hip berries": "The nominal phrase [*cinámboŋgóombi*] is apparently a contamination, typical of verse, of [*nanámboŋgó·mbi*] (found in a variant of this song; with *nana-* 'togetherness' or 'hanging together') and *ciampih* 'wild rose hip'; *pokompih,* elsewhere 'currant(s)', here means 'berry' or 'berries'" (Liljeblad 1986:648).

Another type of Naraya abbreviation, one that is not found in everyday speech, deletes "p" stops at the ends of words.[10] For example, "sage," *bohop^h,* becomes *bo* (song 104); "cedar," *wapI, wa* (song 108); "rain," *bauwap^h, bauwah* (song 34); "game animals," *wasüpi, wazaŋ* (song 48); "leaf/pine needle," *sügip^h, sügi* (song 34); and "foot of mountains," *nugap, nuga* (song 50). "Wild rose hip," *ciampih* (song 117), drops the final "p" and inserts an "n" between the "i" and "a," becoming *sïnam.* The dropped "p" as well as inserted nasal in the last example accords with the following analysis of Havasupai song texts and its song transformations.

Hinton notes this as one strategy within Havasupai song for the "maximization of resonance." She points to other changes that abet this aesthetic preference and relates them to Shoshone song as well: "one could hypothesize that the Havasupais are choosing for nasals and glides because they carry tone, whereas stops and fricatives, by definition, interrupt it. . . . Havasupais choose for consonants that either carry tone or produce the least noisy interruption of tone. . . . This is not a phenomenon that is limited to the Havasupais. Curtis Booth says that Shoshone accomplishes the increased use of nasal consonants in singing by turning all stops into prenasalized voiced stops" (Hinton 1984:38).

Liljeblad reiterates this same point. "The pronunciation of words in Numic songs differs from that in ordinary speech in certain systematic ways. . . . In Shoshone, the phonemic geminated consonants, *pp, tt, kk,* etc., are heard in verse sonorously prenasalized [mb, nd, ng], etc. exactly like the phonemic nasal-plus-stop sequences, *mp, nt, nk,* etc. This occurs in all Shoshone singing quite regularly" (Liljeblad

1986:647). Crum documents the change of "medial geminated consonants to their corresponding prenasalized form" in Western Shoshone poetry songs (Crum 1980:17). Her example is *huuppin,* which becomes *huumpin* in song. There are many examples of stops changed into prenasalized stops in Naraya songs, beginning with a variant of Crum's example, *hupI,* which becomes *hom* (song 117). Other examples are, *wasüpi* becoming *wasümbi* (song 68) and *wazumbianzi* (song 74); *wiap^h* becoming *wianzi* (song 104); and *garïd* becoming *garïmbi* (song 59). Note that in addition to the prenasalization of stops in these examples, vowels are also appended at the end of the word. In song 114, even a nasal suffix follows the spoken prenasalized stop: *narukümp^h* becomes *narukümbani. Gwamp^h,* in song 102, like *narukümp^h,* takes a suffix in song and, in this case, it ends with a nasal, *gwambaiyïn.* One of the most common insertion of nasals into Naraya texts occurs in the ending vocable, *ena.* It will be the central topic of a later discussion.

A few examples of spoken words ending with fricatives, which change to different consonant-vowel combinations in song, also suggest a selection determined by ease in singing and sustaining tone. Examples are *vaigi* (song 83) and *vaiyedu* (song 28), which replace spoken *vaix, baigi,* which replaces *baix* (song 35), and *gaz-ombi,* which suffixes *gaz* (song 43). All of these examples reveal some of the ways in which words are made longer and contrast with the shortening of words through abbreviation mentioned earlier in my discussion. The lengthening of words is a corollary process and, I believe, a more prevalent one.

Notice the particular substitution of "y" for "x" (*vaiẏedu* for *vaix*), just given, and *vai-ẏe* for *uvaix* (song 21), both of which exemplify the Naraya parallel to Havasupai selection for glides as well as nasals over stops and fricatives in their songs, a point quoted earlier from Hinton's study. Songs 90 and 129 include examples of text that insert "w," another glide, into the sung version of spoken words. *Dudu-wa* replaces *dudua* and *duganangwa* replaces *duganankW.* Aside from these occasional inserts or substitutions of "y" and "w" within words, the most striking use of these glides is in vocables (e.g., songs 50, 106, 119), especially the numerous and variant forms of the ending vocable, *yaiyowaindë* (song 82), and so on.

Hinton places Havasupai preference for nasals and glides within a broader framework of song aesthetics.

First, I have hypothesized that Havasupais have a model of the aesthetics of sound that can be expressed as a preference for the maximization of resonance. The preference for resonant segments is expressed as a choice of nasals and glides over stops and affricates, and as a choice of lower vowels over higher vowels. . . . Another hypothesis that is suggested by everything I have been talking about here is that some songs without words can be seen as embodying the aesthetic ideal for sound. Songs with real words have two constraints: the aesthetic constraint and the constraint of intelligibility. In genres such as sweathouse songs, the intelligibility constraint is essentially inoperative, and so the aesthetic factor is clearly observable. Real-word songs, trying to achieve both aesthetic quality and intelligibility, will be found to live somewhere between spoken language and unintelligible songs in their phonetic realization. (Hinton 1984:38, 39)

Song genres that Wind River Shoshones sing today—War Dance, Round Dance, Sun Dance, and Handgame—have no "real-word" texts, but rather nonlexical syllables, or vocables, as they are often called.[11] Applying Hinton's second hypothesis suggested above, I examine the vocable inventory in these genres to gain insight into the particular sounds and sound combinations favored by Shoshones in song. They provide the background for the subsequent discussion of Naraya word transformations. They also point to Shoshone concordance with Havasupai preference in song for maximizing resonance through nasals, glides, and lower rather than higher vowels.

Shoshone Vocables

Vocables in song texts are a series of single syllables, sometimes a vowel, but more commonly, a consonant-vowel unit that appears in a fixed order. Singers learn the particular vocable sequence of each song in conjunction with its melodic pitch and rhythm, and this sequence remains constant throughout a performance. Vocable texts are never meant to be separated from their musical settings. But if one does, in fact, view them separately, they are an abstract poetry, a play of phonetic sounds with no reference beyond themselves.[12] Vocable texts are analogous to abstract or nonobjective painting, wherein colors and shapes bear no reference or resemblance to real objects. Both are self-contained sensual patternings—one aural, the other visual.

The following vowels and consonants are the basis for the vocables that Shoshones sing:

a e ai i o
h
w
y

They create a vocable stock.[13]

a,	*e,*	*ai,*	*i,*	*o*
ha,	*he,*	*hai,*	*hi,*	*(ho)*
(wa)	*we,*	*(wai)*	*wi*	
ya,	*ye,*	*yai,*	*yi,*	*yo*

All of the above vocables are not used equally and there are conventions for their placement as well. The listing of the vowels and consonant-vowel combinations reflects my general impression of their frequency and moves from greater to lesser. *A* and *e,* equal mainstays, are principal foils for one another; *ai* is common, *i* is less frequent and often accompanies notes of shorter duration,[14] and *o* is usually reserved for phrase endings. The major placement of vowels that do not combine with consonants is in the opening phrase of the song, sung first by the lead singer and repeated by the rest of the singers around the drum.

Ho is almost nonexistent. It never appears in War Dance, Round Dance, or Sun Dance songs. I have recorded and transcribed what I view as its special and playful appearance in a few Handgame songs (Vander 1988:180–82). In these examples, *ho* is the first word of the song, notable both as a vocable rarity and for its upside-down placement of the *o* sound at the beginning rather than at the ending of the song.[15] I have never heard *wo* as a vocable, and for all intents and purposes, *we* and *wi* are the principal vocables beginning with *w*. *Yo,* like *o,* is a cadence marker, often occurring on the last note of the song, which fades as it trails down to an indeterminate lower pitch.

I believe this brief overview of Shoshone vocables relates positively to Hinton's first hypothesis. Two of the three consonants used to generate Shoshone vocables are glides (*w, y*) and the more frequent occurrence of vowels *a* and *e* in relation to *i* is consistent with Havasupai preference for nasals, glides, and lower vowels in song in order to maximize resonance. Although I do not have sufficient data for a separate analysis of vowel lowering in Naraya texts, I will, nevertheless, mention it in various places throughout the following analyses where it does occur. I find no examples to the contrary, that is, vowel raising.

Vocables in Naraya Texts   The most striking use of vocables in Naraya texts is as ending markers. They serve as poetic, phonetic punctuation. Because they are so formulaic, I prefer to write them as a unit, like a word, rather than as separate syllables. *Ena* is the most common ending and appears in thirty-two of the songs.

Because *ena* is an ending formula used exclusively in Naraya songs, it is, therefore, also a song genre marker. It contrasts sharply from War Dance song endings[16] and Sun Dance song endings.

Example A. War Dance song ending

Example B. Sun Dance song ending

It may be that the prevalence of *e* and *a* in the vocables used throughout War Dance and Sun Dance songs dictates the selection of a contrasting set of vowels, *e* and *o,* to mark their cadence. Following this same logic, there would be no problem of selecting *e* and *a* for the Naraya ending formula, *ena,* because in this case, the vocable unit itself stands out in relief from the rest of the lexical text.

The absence of *o* and the presence of nasal *n* distinguishes the vocable cadence of Naraya songs from those of other song genres Shoshones sing. It is interesting that Hinton also finds a similar presence of *m,* a nasal placed at the ends of lines and especially at the ends of verses in Havasupai songs with lexical texts. She points out their rarity in vocable songs (similar to the absence of *n,* in Shoshone vocable texts and song genres) and relates it to spoken language. She writes that,

> in speaking, /*m*/ carries the notion of "switch-reference" or "different-subject." In singing, the semantic field of /*m*/ is extended to something like "new topic"— . . . It seems that it can be extended to a purely syntactic function of signalling "new verse," . . . This is just one more of many cases where the meaning of a morpheme has been extended so much in singing as to make it almost semantically empty. Once again, /*m*/ as a nasal consonant, fits the aesthetic model for sound in song; we can see the aesthetic model as part of the motivating force for the semantic extension and increased usage of the /*m*/ morpheme. (Hinton 1984:65)

I do not know whether there is a similar semantic origin for the *n* in *ena*. However, the particular choice of a nasal accords with Hinton's aesthetic model mentioned in the passage quoted above, referring to the preference for nasals and glides in song.

Naraya songs differ from War Dance and Sun Dance songs not only in their conventional ending vocables but in the absence of the drum. The drum part plays an important role in defining the final cadence of War Dance and Wind River Shoshone Sun Dance songs. In War Dance songs, an accented drum beat occurs on the final vocable of the song. In Sun Dance songs, the male singers stop singing and drumming halfway through the second part of the final repetition of the song and allow the women singers to finish the song without drum accompaniment. The male singers then hit the drum with a flurry of one or two accented but nonsynchronous beats. The vocal part of War Dance and Sun Dance songs ends as singers land on a long penultimate note, then the much shorter last note, which almost immediately slides down in pitch and fades into silence. As we shall see momentarily, the release of the last note in Naraya songs is strikingly different.

Naraya songs have no drum accompaniment and therefore must rely on other strategies to signal the end. The selection and placement of *ena* is one. The musical setting and vocal performance of *ena*, which enhance the signal, is another. The first syllable, *e,* is held significantly longer than -*na,* which is both accented and clipped short. From musical and linguistic standpoints, the result is a staccato, glottal stop. The accented attack and especially the sharp break off of the last syllable and note are most pronounced in the final cadence of the song. (These same musical patterns carry over to the settings of other words and vocables that appear in ending position.) In a sense, the voice takes on the role of an accented drumbeat.

There is not one consistent pattern to the use and placement of *ena*. In 18 songs (e.g., song 62), *ena* marks the end of every line of text. In four songs (e.g., song 103), *ena* appears only at the end of the first line of text and its repeat. In six songs (e.g., song 71), *ena* appears only in the second line of text and its repeat, marking the second half of the text and end of the verse.

Because so many individual lines are themselves made up of two small repeated phrases, the line-ending tag of *ena* thwarts what would have been an identical repetition of parts. It is another example of inexact repetition discussed earlier in this chapter.

The form of *ena,* itself, is subject to variation. In song 109, it is both *yena* and *ena.* In songs 63 and 123, it is *gena.* Finally, *ena* sometimes combines with another ending vocable formula, widening the range of Naraya endings. In song 82, the repeat of the second line ends as *ena yaiyowainda.* Solitary, it signals the end of the entire verse. Elsewhere, the order of the combined formulas is in reverse, for example, *waiyowain ena* (song 103), which appears only at the end of line one and distinguishes the first half of the text from the second. Song 64 is another example; every line ends with *yaiyai ena.*

As one can see already, the form of the alternate line-ending vocable unit is not as stable as *ena.* It can be *wainda* (song 53), or *yaiyowainda* (song 74), or *yaiyowain* (song 119), and usually stands by itself. Although, like *ena,* nasal *n* is present, glides, *w* and *y,* predominate. Notice the inclusion of *yo* in a new environment although it is still used in connection with phrase endings. In place of the *e-a* vowel alternation in *ena,* there is a longer series, *ai-o-ai-a* (or *ai-o-ai*). *Ai* is a common diphthong in vocables of War Dance, Round Dance, and Sun Dance songs. The alternation of *ai-o* in *waiyowain* brings to mind the cadential *e-o* alternation in *he yo* of these other song genres.

Yaiyowain, or permutations of it, may come at the end of both lines of text (songs 45, 119) but more commonly comes only at the end of the second or final lines of text and their repeats (songs 8, 60, 74, 82). In song 53, *wainda* appears only at the end of the final line of text in the last repetition of the song and marks its completion.

The use of formulaic endings is by no means unique to Naraya songs. *Ena,* its most common ending, also appears in the second half of a Northern Shoshone Round Dance song.

> The large sunflower, the fully yellow flower spreading out
> The large sunflower, the fully yellow flower spreading out
> From the water-clear root
> From the water-clear root
> *Heena!*
> From the water-clear root
> *Heena!*
> From the water-clear root.
>
> (Liljeblad 1986:648)

Liljeblad analyzes *heena* in the above translation and suggests its wider use in the Great Basin. He defines it as "the expletive emphatic particle *hi-na* or *he-na,* which often occurs in both Numic and Washoe poetry" (Liljeblad 1986:648).

It is fascinating to see the extension of this convention in a scholarly paper written by Beverly Crum, a linguist and native Shoshone speaker from Nevada. After the last true sentence of her paper, *"Newe*

Hupia—Shoshoni Poetry Songs," she writes, "*Haina;* 'the end'" (Crum 1980:19). Crum's use of quotation marks around "the end" makes her meaning clear; *haina* is an ending convention and not the actual Shoshone word for "end."

Like songs, Shoshone stories have their own conventional ending marker. While recording Shoshone stories Wick Miller realized that storytellers were extending its use for his benefit, analogous to Crum's use of *haina* to signal the end of her scholarly paper. He recounts, "The ending of a Coyote Story is marked by the sentence kaan kwaisi kwaiyakkwa, The rat's tail fell off. Some of the storytellers have used this as a device for telling me that it is time to turn the tape recorder off. Thus it will be found at the end of other kinds of stories, where its use is normally not appropriate" (W. Miller 1972:26).

Wind River Shoshones have their own conventions for storytelling, including the ending. In place of "the rat's tail fell off," they say, "Coyote way out there is tracking through slush" (Shimkin 1947c: 335). Shimkin writes that the ending is "a statement obscurely hinting at melting snow, which results from properly told tales" (Shimkin 1947c:330). In this case, the sentence is an ending marker and although unrelated to the story it tells, it has not totally tossed aside its intrinsic meaning. It connects with a larger underlying purpose. Both in its imagery—melting snow—and in its power to influence weather, the act of storytelling and its conventional ending bear resemblances to Naraya imagery and function.

As an end to endings, I simply note that there is also an ending formula for Shoshone Sun Dance prayers: "*us* [That is] *su:Bega* [ended]" (Shimkin 1953:419). It means just what it says. But I wonder, might there be a relationship between -*Bega* and the vowel sequence in *ena?*

Word-Vocables   A long series of vocables such as one finds in War Dance or Sun Dance songs is rare in Emily and Dorothy's Naraya songs. One such series does occur, however, as the first line of song 50: *He yo na he yo he yo na he yo he yo na he yo.* If we use the *yo*'s as interior punctuation, the vocables coalesce into two units that repeat three times, *heyo naneyo* / *heyo naneyo* / *heyo naneyo.*[17]

Most vocables are used in conjunction with real words, being either infixes or suffixes whose form is strongly influenced by the host word and sometimes followed by more "classic" independent vocables.

Both Emily and Gladys Hill commented insightfully on the parts of the texts that they deemed untranslatable. In answer to my many queries about various problematic bits of text, Gladys would say,

"That's just a filler." The "filler" is in response to musical time. In unaccompanied vocal music, the duration and rhythms of melody need a text to carry it. Although it is possible to let one syllable carry across many notes and beats of the melody, which creates a melismatic setting of the text, Shoshones choose otherwise. Naraya songs, like most songs Shoshones sing, are primarily syllabic. A new syllable of text appears on every note of music. Vocable infixes and suffixes in Naraya songs serve as fillers that stretch real words of text to fit the melody.[18]

Emily brought out another consideration regarding the specific choice of fillers in Naraya texts. I had noticed that in song 64, the song word for game animals (*wasüp-penji*) differed from the spoken form (*wasüpi*) as I knew it.[19]

JUDY: "What about the '-*penji*' in the first line?"

EMILY: "Just to make it pretty. Just put 'pretty' on there."

Emily's eyes and voice were full of humor as she made the last pronouncement. But with her joke she hit the mark. In addition to musical time, fillers respond to aesthetic considerations—word sounds and rhymes that influence other aspects of their form.

The meshing of meaningful words with vocable forms is abundant in Naraya songs. Elaboration of word endings such as -*penji*, given above, is a common pattern for the placement and union of words and vocables. This particular example also demonstrates the difficulty of cleanly drawing the line between the two. Hinton observes the same problem in her analysis of Havasupai song texts and cautions that "no strict line can be drawn between vocables and meaningful elements" (Hinton 1984:56). *Wasüpi* means "game animals."[20] Wick Miller gives *waseppin* (-*a*) for this same word in Gosiute Shoshone (W. Miller 1972:147), which comes closer in form to the sung version, *wasüp-penji*. The vocable suffix substitutes lower vowel *e* for *i* after the *p*, includes the *n* given in Miller's version, and adds a *j* followed by the final *i* in the spoken version of the word. The addition of *j* in -*penji* is unique to *wasüp-penji* and was not included in the vocable stock given earlier. But the addition of *e* before *i* in the suffix and especially the musical setting, which places -*pen* on a longer note than -*ji*, fit the expected pattern of vocables in song. Certainly -*penji* demonstrates that vocables used in combination with word texts generate more and unexpected vocable possibilities. Powers makes the same point: "Songs containing vocables only are likely to contain fewer vocables than those containing a combination of vocables and meaningful texts" (Powers 1987:16).

Repetition, so central to many aspects of Naraya form, plays a role in the relationship between words and their vocable suffixes. In songs 53, 111, and 118, *waino* becomes *wain-aiyo*. Although vocables *ai* and *yo* appear in the vocable stock discussed earlier, I believe that *waino* plays a key role in determining its vocable suffix. *Ai-o* (in *waino*) becomes *ai-ai-yo* (in *wain-aiyo*). *O* at the end of *waino* changes to *yo*, a common vocable ending, and its ending function remains constant.

We see the same process in an analysis of Havasupai song texts. Hinton writes that whereas the consonantal environment determines the vowel in spoken language, song texts use a different criterion. "A much preferred process is that of assonance—i.e., the assimilation of one vowel to the feature of another vowel" (Hinton 1984:47). As one example, Hinton compares *'im yum* in spoken language to its sung form, *'imi̱ yumu̱*. The Shoshone example, *wain-aiyo,* follows the same process and in this case creates rhyme between *wai* and *nai*.

The repetition—exact and inexact—of *wainaiyo* becomes the entire basis for lines of text. In song 53, *wainaiyo* ("coming down") brackets the text. It repeats four times in an unrepeated first line and two times in an unrepeated third and final line. Between these unequal *wainaiyo* brackets are the subject and setting of the text. The following English translation can be only a crude representation of the Shoshone. Lacking a real tradition in English for vocable and word-vocable texts, I have repeated a diphthong and carried over untranslated the "-o" ending vowel from the original.

Song 53

> Coming dow-own-o, coming dow-own-o,
>   coming dow-own-o, coming dow-own-o.
> Game animals on mountain rock slides,
> Game animals on mountain rock slides.
> Coming dow-own-o, coming dow-own-o.

Song 111 has almost the identical first line to that of song 53 and does repeat, but its small difference makes all the difference. A single vocable "o" appears between the third and fourth repeat of *wainaiyo,* which interrupts the flow of the series by juxtaposing two "o" sounds. Musical punctuation underscores the text. A melodic rest after the third *wainaiyo,* a musical equivalent to a glottal stop, clearly marks and separates the ending of the third repeat from the "o" that announces the last repeat. This is an interesting and unusual role for "o," a poetic connector and separator with what has come before and what has yet to come. Very roughly, this line might read in English as follows: "Coming dow-own-o, coming dow-own-o, coming dow-own-o—o coming dow-own-o."

The second line of song 118 and its repeat also use *wainaiyo,* the vocable-enlarged form of *waino,* as well as an abbreviated form, *wain.* (Here, *wainaiyo* and *wain* translate as "going down" and refer to someone's carrying cinquefoil berries.) *He yo,* a common vocable ending, sits between the two forms of *waino.* In this song, and many others to come, the relationship of the interior sounds within the line is paramount. In song 118, *wain-* brackets its own line, between which lies *-ai-yo* (its vocable suffix) and *he yo* (free-standing vocables). I have already suggested the derivation of *-aiyo* from *waino.* I now suggest that *he yo* in song 118 is a vocable response to, or elaboration of, *-aiyo.* Both pairs share the same last syllable, *yo,* and contrast their preceding vowels, *ai* with *e.* From an internal perspective, the line reads:

> *Wain-*
> *ai yo*
> *he yo*
> *wain.*

Song 62 presents another example of a vocable suffix, which seems to arise from both the word it tags and the vocable pool. *Wadzi,* "male antelope," becomes *wadzi-wo.* *-Wo* repeats the *w* sound of the beginning of the word (also a prominent glide in the vocable pool) and ends with *o,* again consistent with the ending placement of *o* in other genres. (Although both *w* and *o* are part of the vocable pool, recall that their combination, *wo,* is not.) *Wadzi-wo* repeats and sets the alliterative pattern that continues throughout most of the line until its conclusion on *ena.* Derived from *wadzi* and following it, *wo* then seems to take on a life of its own in the line. An independent *wo* followed by *ya* pads the text until it reaches *wai* ("going down") and *ena* punctuation. Here, the choice of *wo ya* in line one may stem from its sound and placement, which are similar to that of *doiya* ("mountain") in line two:

> Wadzi-wo wadzi-wo   wo ya wai ena
> Dïva n-doiya dïva n-doiya n-doiya   ena

Song 119 follows this same pattern of word, vocable suffix, and "independent" vocables. *Donziap,* an everyday word for the white flower of the strawberry, becomes *donzi-aiyo* in song. *-Aiyo* replaces *-ia* (plus concluding *-p*) and sets up the pattern for a beginning "*-ai-y-*" sequence in the two other sets of vocables in the line that comes after *donzi-aiyo, wai ye wa* and cadential *yaiyowain.* The syncopated setting for *wai ye wa* is counterbalanced by the similar vocables and unsyncopated rhythmic setting for concluding *yai yo wain.*

Example C. Excerpt of Naraya song 119

wai   ye wa   yai - yo- wain.

Caught between these two vocables units are two sets of words or word-vocables that combine assonance with contrast and whose musical setting adds another level of correspondences. Again, the difficulty is to distinguish meaningful elements from vocables. *Ba-n-go* is either *ba:*, "water," nasal *-n* and suffix vocable *go*, which foreshadows *sogo-*, itself, an abbreviated form of *sogo* ^{h}, "earth." Or the *-go* is yet another and more radical abbreviation of *sogo* ^{h}. Both are followed by slightly variant forms of *via*, "mother." Other interlinear relationships exist between *dogo* and *sogo*, which rhyme, and their shared ending with *ba-n-go*. In sum, song 119 relates these sounds:

> *Dogo donzi-/aiyo/ /wai ye wa/ba-n-go-via sogo-vi/yaiyowain/*
> *Dogo donzi-aiyo wai ye wa /ba-n-go-via/ sogo-vi/ yaiyowain*
> *Dogo donzi-aiyo wai ye wa ba-n-go-via sogo-vi yaiyowain*

Song 116 presents the most extreme example of a vocable suffix that derives so closely from the word it follows that it is a vocable version of the entire word, its alter-ego. *Akën*,[21] "sunflower seed," becomes *akën-ïküni*. *K* and *n* alternate in both forms, a framework of consonants from which vowels hang, first those of the word, then a vocable play on them. With no vowel repeats, the *k* and *n* are flanked by vowels *a, ë, ï, ü,* and *i*.

In song 57, it is the vowels of the words that repeat in the suffix rather than the consonants. *Maruk* ^{h}, which locates silver as still under the mountains, becomes *maruk-andu,* reusing the *a-u* vowel sequence of the word. This repetition takes on added impact as *maruk-andu* follows the word *ruka,* in which the vowel sequence is just the reverse, *u-a*. The complete sequence is *u-a / a-u / a-u*.

The vocable suffix that appears in song 123 shares similarities with those just discussed, in song 57. Here, the word with its suffix is *suave-andë*. The suffix repeats one vowel (*a*) of the word it tags (*suave*), adds a prenasalized *d* and a concluding vowel. Notice the asymmetrical pairing of the vowel sounds between the word and suffix: *u-a-e / a-e*. This word appears in a line of text that is made of two repeated parts; the repeat of *suave-andë* in the second half of the line changes to *suave-andïnò,* lengthened further with the addition of cadential *yena*.

The differences between these two repeated parts exemplify dynamic symmetry: repetition that is inexact and pairing that is unequal. The choice of vowel sounds in the vocable suffix again suggests relationships within the line and to vocable placement: *Nïsë̱ suave-andë̈, nïsë̱ suave-andï̱nȯ yena.*

The end of the first word, *nïsë,* rhymes with the end of the suffix, *suave-andë,* which also concludes the first half of the line. The *i* sound in *nïsë* repeats as the second vowel in *-andïnȯ* and the final *"ȯ"* functions like vocable *"o."* It marks the end of the word and suffix as well as the entire line.

Songs 20 and 106 provide additional examples of vocable suffixes that lead to a variety of sound connections between lines and within lines. The final words of the four lines in song 20 are:

> *sogop-ade,*
> *yiyïgwidë,*
> *miëppüdo,*
> *yiyïgwidë.*

In song 106, *yeng-oni* ends both lines of text and, in the second line, creates assonance between the last two syllables of its two-word text, *wai-yovi* (which repeats) and *yeng-oni.*

A variety of transformations within words creates assonance or rhyme between word parts. *Gaiwah* (Brewer's blackbird) becomes *gaiwai* in song 84. The sung word for *wāhi* (fox) becomes *warhigi* in song 80. *Doiyavi* (mountains) becomes, *doiyavi-di* in song 66 and *doiyavavin* in song 116. *SïnavI* (quaking aspen) becomes *sïna-ai-va* in song 104.

This pattern carries across to different words within a line. In line one of song 69, *yeva,* (?autumn) and *wandzi-a,* (antelope bulls) are assonant with one another by the addition of suffix *a.* These two words repeat three times so that the entire line is assonant. Even *ena,* an ending vocable, abets the final *"a"* pattern for all the words in the line.

Sometimes, neighboring words influence transformations in one another and result in assonance. In song 59, *dïmpi,* "rock," and *garïd,* "sit," become *dïmpi garïm-bi.* In song 108, abbreviations of "cedar" and "hill," *wa no,* are preceded by *wiaph,* "pass," which becomes *wiaro.* "O" is consistent as an ending vowel and creates assonance between *wia-ro* and *wa no,* which follow. In song 74, word transformations create correspondences between two words that sit in the middle of lines one and two, respectively. *Mozambiats,* "mountain sheep," in line one, and *wasüpi,* "game animals," in line two, become *mozambianzi* and *wazumbianzi.*

The complexity of internal relationships within a line may also become intensified because of the prevalent pattern of subdividing lines. Both lines in song 34 are made of two parts: line one repeats its two parts and line two presents a new first part of the line and ends with one repeat or half of line one. In the first half of line one—*dave baüwah doiyave*—the final vowel of the last word differs from its spoken form, *doiyavi*, by lowering the "i" to "e." In so doing, *doiyave*, "mountains," rhymes with the first word, *dave*, "sun." The first half of line two begins with *wongo* and ends with *dogando*. The assonance between the beginning and ending of the first half of line two parallels the form of line one; as stated, the second half of line two is the same as that of line one. The rhyme scheme of song 34 holds these correspondences as well as *ena*, the ending vocable for both lines of text:[22]

> *dave* ... *doiyave*, *dave* ... *doiyave ena*,
> *wongo* ... *dogando*, *dave* ... *doiyave ena*.

The poetic relationship between words and vocable fillers is by no means unique to Naraya songs. Powers has commented on similar findings in Lakota song. "Infixes and suffixes have a strong tendency to rhyme with the preceding syllable, and the rules of influencing the ordering of phonemes in either language or vocables also hold when both words and vocables are combined" (Powers 1987:19). Similarly, Rothenberg observes that in Navajo song texts, "the vocables give a very clear sense of continuity from the verbal material; i.e., the vowels in particular show a rhyming or assonantal relationship between the 'meaningless' and meaningful segments" (Rothenberg 1969:299).

Hinton's analysis of Havasupai song texts suggests the larger principle at work in Naraya songs and the other Native American examples just given. Hinton writes, "Assonance (but not rhyme) may well be universal in poetic language. Different languages use different methods to attain assonance: for English, the major method of attaining assonance is through lexical choice; in Havasupai, as we see, it is the manipulation of the quality of variable vowels that is the most prominent strategy for attaining assonance" (Hinton 1984:48).

Stem Reduplications

The repeat of *na* in <u>*na-nana*</u> in song 103, brings us to another strategy for lengthening sung words in Naraya songs, one that has a grammatical base. It is possible that *nana* in this song is not meaningless repetition but an independent reduplicated form of *na-*, reflexive and correlative of a plural subject, and meaning "all kinds of," or "every kind of" (Shimkin 1949b:209–10). Liljeblad translates this word in song as "togetherness" (Liljeblad 1986:648), and this meaning would be appropriate in this text, bringing to mind a diverse group of animals.

Stem reduplication in connection with nouns and verbs either gives a distributive meaning to all members of a class or indicates a plural subject (Shimkin 1949a:177, 180). However, in practice, this principal applies to certain nouns (e.g., *cu´cug´e*, "old men" [Shimkin n.d.:14], *duduwa*, "sons" or "children" [song 90]) and verbs (*gi´giman*, "to come back," plural [Shimkin n.d.:7]), but not all. I believe that *van-vagïna*, "fog," in song 41 would not be used in everyday speech to indicate much fog; it is a new and poetic extension of stem reduplication. Similarly, in song 88, the stem reduplication of "blackbird," *bagan-bagan*, followed by a vocable insert and diminutive suffix, *-nogan-zï*, is only a song form. There is a certain energy generated by the vowel progression, the play of the *a-an-a-an-o-an-i* pattern. Rhythmic asymmetry enhances the impact of the vowel progression / *a-an-a-an* / *o-an-i* /, four beats plus three.

Stem reduplication may also be an "iterative intensive" (Shimkin n.d.:8) and its unique poetic usage in Naraya texts draws on this meaning as well as plurality. For example, in song 124, the text describes the sun going down over the mountains. *Dïna?*, "down," in everyday speech, actually repeats in the song three times, *dïn-dïn-dïn*, and adds *-dsi*, a diminutive suffix: "down, down, down, a little bit." The effect is verbal-visual—like three still photos of the setting sun, each one showing the sun slightly lower than in the previous one.

In song 127, reduplication of other word parts and the assimilation of vowels so that words and word parts rhyme may be the analytical keys for solving its poetic puzzle. *Dugumba?* means "sky": *ba:*, by itself, means "water": and *vagïna* or *bagïna* means "fog." The first line of text, divided into independent syllables, is: *du gu ba ga ga na na, du gu ba ga ga nan*. *Du gu ba* agree with spoken forms and can be "sky," elided with "water" as well as the first syllable of "fog." *Ga* could be the second syllable of "fog," which changes the vowel from *i* to *a* and rhymes with *ba*, or it might be a vocable that reuses the *g* from *-gu* in "sky" and adds the *a*, which rhymes with *ba*. *Ga* repeats or reduplicates. *Na na* is either the third syllable of the word for fog and repeats, or it is a vocable suffix made of repeated parts. The *a* sequence is: *ba ga ga na na*. It is longer and contrasts with the opening *u* sequence in *du gu*. *G* is the only consonant in *du gu* that carries over into the *a* sequence. Beyond sound and from a grammati-

cal standpoint, if *bagïna*, fog, is part of the line, might not the reduplication of some of its parts also allude to its pluralness—the dense
swathe of fog up in the sky, i.e., the Milky Way?

Independent syllables in line two of this same text are: *du gu sai
ya ga na na, du gu sai ya ga nan e na*. *Dugu* comes from *dugumbaʔ*,
meaning "sky," and/or *dugupʰ*, "up"; *saiyag* (or possibly *saiyaganan*),
refers to the Milky Way, and *ena* is the ending vocable. Like *ba ga ga
na na* in line one, *sai ya ga na na* in line two contrasts with *dugu*.
Between the two lines is a correspondent contrast of *u-a* sounds, use
of *g* and *n* consonants in reduplicative or vocable parts, and rhyming within as well as between the lines. *E-* (in *ena*) momentarily breaks
the *a* sequence in line two only to return to it with the final syllable, *-na*.

Notice that in line one the final syllable on *a* adds a nasal ending,
which differentiates the two repeated parts of the line and marks its
ending. This is also true in line two. *Ena* is an additional ending
marker for line two and also indicates that it is the final line of the
song. The two lines of syllables are:

> *Du gu ba ga ga na na, du gu ba ga ga nan*
> *Du gu sai ya ga na na, du gu sai ya ga nan e na.*

Bahr's comments on a particular comparison between song texts
and spoken language are germane here. "The latter will have more
words but paradoxically fewer syllables. This will be true if Yaqui 'song
language' is like Pima-Papago in reduplicating syllables 'for the music'" (Bahr 1993:13).

Word Endings and the Suffix -Tsi

In spoken language, Shoshone words end in a variety of ways. Some
words, like *waipëʔ*, end with a glottal stop. Others, like *yampʰ*, are
aspirated and still others, like *denüpI*, end with a voiceless vowel. In
Naraya songs, often the voiceless becomes voiced: *denüpI* becomes
denüpi (song 112), *nuHIyokïn* becomes *nuhiyogeno* (song 21). Concluding aspiration becomes a vowel, for example, *yampʰ* becomes *yambi*
(song 114); *bogompʰ* becomes *bogombi* (song 117); and *duganankW,
duganangwa* (song 129). The only place where something equivalent
to a glottal stop occurs in song is on the last syllable of the ending
vocable, *ena*, or the last syllable of the last word, which is most pronounced in the final repeat of the last line and verse.

I have already pointed out many suffixes that are unique to Naraya songs and that arise from word-vocable combinations. One of
these, *-Tsi* (and its variants *-zi* and *-dsi*), a grammatical suffix with

diminutive and/or affectionate connotations,[23] appears enough times in Naraya songs to warrant comment on it. As preface to this, I quote Beverly Crum, a native Shoshone speaker whose reflections on the use of this suffix in Western Shoshone poetry songs give insight into its use and meaning in Naraya songs.

> Grammatically, the *-ttsi* suffix is a diminutive noun suffix. However, Shoshoni speakers commonly use it for special emphasis denoting endearment, high esteem, reverence, as well as a poetic device. My opinion is based on the fact that Shoshoni people have a warm attachment to nature. For example, the Shoshoni word *Soko Pia* means "Earth Mother." Out of this warm attachment to nature comes a figurative way of communicating. Most Shoshoni poetry songs are about nature. They contain detailed descriptions of what the poet singers observed in nature, and they express the poet singer's warm feelings about it. The use of the suffix *-ttsi* is one way for the Shoshoni poet singers to express this warm attitude. However, it does not mean that the use of the suffix *-ttsi* makes the word *pentsi* translate to mean "dear little fur." The warm attitude is more general and directed toward nature at large. The poet singers are also expressing a shared attitude of the whole group. (Crum 1980:17)

I begin my discussion with songs that seem to draw more on the diminutive connotation of the suffix than the affectionate, although, of course, it is always possible for varying degrees of both to be at play. Song 64 describes the tracks of game animals in the mountains in late winter or early spring: literally, "snow-melt water-black-(diminutive)." Song 104 describes a pass in the hills or mountains that has sagebrush growing on it: "sagebrush pass-(diminutive)," that is, a small dip or saddle in the hill/mountain. Songs 123 and 124 describe the sunlight, coming out a little in 123 and going down little by little in 124.[24] The use of the suffix in connection with the sun may carry the connotations of reverence and high esteem mentioned in Crum's discussion. The Wind River Shoshone Sun Dance includes a Sunrise Ceremony that begins each day of the ceremony. All the dancers stand in rows facing the opening of the Sun Dance lodge to the east. They dance and lift their arms in front of them as the sun rises over the horizon. After the sun is up and the dance is finished, the dancers pat and brush their bodies with the fresh and newly sunlit air.

Given my commentary in chapter 5, there is no question that the suffix attached to *biya gwian-zi,* "eagle" (song 93), carries only meanings of reverence and high esteem appropriate for the sacred bird and is not a diminutive. Equally clear is the use of *-tsi* in song 18. *Damën* *nüwï-tsi,* "our people," refers to the dead relatives of the Wind River Shoshone people who are coming back to life. Here, *-tsi* has affectionate connotations, a sense of warmth and endearment for friends and kin.

People receive affectionate connotations with *-tsi* as do sheep, game animals (song 74), water people (song 95), and blackbirds (song 88). It becomes difficult to gauge when and to what degree the warmth combines with the diminutive—the little water people and little blackbirds.

Finally, and taking both senses, *-tsi* suffixes the word for son or child, *dua,* and its stem-reduplicated plural form, *dudua.* Notwithstanding Crum's caution given above, here I believe one possible translation is "dear little one," or as Gladys Hill expressed it, "really cute ones." This is the most common noun that combines with *-tsi* in Naraya songs and almost invariably applies to animal young: game animals (songs 8, 66, 71, 72), goslings (song 97), and a brood of white-tailed ptarmigan chicks (song 90). In song 16 (Vander 1986:51), *dua-n-zi,* "child," plus *-tsi* (here, *-zi*), is a metaphoric image applied to mountains. The first line reads, "Our mountains child(+zi) curving down." The first three words mean "our mountains' child+zi," that is, diminutive offspring (translated in the plural by Emily), the small mountains viewed with affection by the Shoshones. A nonliteral translation of this line could be, "Our mountains' children—the beloved small mountains—curving down." Momentarily I will return to the use of metaphor in Naraya song texts. It is not only an important poetic device but lies at the heart of Shoshone perception and relationship to the natural world and the Naraya itself.

Other Poetic Devices

Alliteration

Shimkin commented on the frequent alliteration in Shoshone myth-telling and its linguistic basis. "The small number of initial consonantal phonemes and the paucity of basic stems result in constant alliteration in Shoshone" (Shimkin 1949b:339). Alliteration is common in Naraya texts for two reasons. In the first place, there are few words in individual lines of text and sometimes one word repeats several times. For example, *vagïna,* in line two of song 36, repeats three times in a four-word line. Second, many lines of text are themselves made of two or three small repeated parts. Repetition of the one or two words in the basic unit occurs many times. Alliteration is especially prominent in several Naraya texts. Song 124 is almost completely made of words that begin with "d." The single exception to this is when *doiyavi*, "mountains," changes to *roiyavi*. Stem reduplication—actually triplication—of *dïna?*, "down," accentuates the alliterative effect. The two lines, unrepeated, are, *Dave dïn-dïn-dïndsi roiyavi dïndsi roiyavi / Dave doiyavi dave doiya dïndsi roiyavi*. Like song 124, song 52 is also almost completely made of words that begin with "d." Two words of the four-word text are *damë*, "our," and *dïmpi*, "rocks." *Sëpaiganu*, meaning "flat" in spoken language, becomes *dïpë-gaiyu / dïpëgai* in this song. (The vowel change of "ë" to "ï" in the sung form further enhances the beginning similarities between *dïmpi* and *dïpïgaiyu*.) *Sogopë*, "earth," is the only word that does not begin with "d" in both lines of song text: *damë sogopë dïpëgaiyu dïpëgai / Dïmpi dïpëgaiyu dïmpi dïpëgaiyu dïpëgai*.

Song 62 has contrasting alliteration in both lines of text. The first line repeats "w" through word selection, *wadzi*, "antelope bull," and *wai*, "climbing down"; vocable suffix, *-wo:* and "free-standing" vocables, *wo ya*. The line reads, *Wadzi-wo wadzi-wo wo ya wai ena*. The second line repeats "d" simply through word selection, "pine nut" and "mountain": *Dïva n-doiya dïva n-doiya doiya ena*. Song 121 is just the reverse of song 62. "D" alliteration occurs in line one, using essentially the same text as in song 62, *Dïva n-doiya dïva n-doiya roiya ena*. "W" alliteration in line two occurs by repeating two sung versions of *waniya*, "curving down." *Wani-na ne -yo wane- na -yo ena*. The two vocable infixes, *na ne* and *na*, which I believe spring from the "n" sound in the meaningful syllable it follows, *-ni-*, create alliteration at a lower level—within the word.

In some songs, just one line of text uses alliteration. In song 83, both words of line one begin with "y," *Yevai*, "bird" and *yïzï-eï-në*, "flying." In song 125, line two, all words begin with an "n": *nüwë*, "Indian," which repeats, and *nuwïgenòr*, "walking slowly." In this example there is beginning alliteration on "n" as well as the same vowel and subsequent consonant, "w," in both words.

The stem reduplication in song 88, *Bagan-bagan-nogan-zi*, blackbirds, results in alliteration of "b" and subsequent "g." The line and alliteration continue: *ba havi*, literally, "water lie," that is, "bathe." Beyond alliteration, there is also assonance between *ba havi* and *bagan-nogan-zi*.

Onomatopoeia

Shimkin writes, "The imitations of natural noises are an integral part of the [Wind River] Shoshone language, but to a small degree. Outside of interjections, onomatopoeia has originated only a few verbs, e.g. *wɔ́wɔ́*, to bark, and nouns, e.g., *su´akwakwa*, robin" (Shimkin 1947c:339).

Onomatopoeia in Emily and Dorothy's Naraya repertoire appears in three songs. It imitates the hissing sound of otters (songs 98, 99) and the sound of water splashing over rocks (song 129). These are sibilant sounds, and their phonetic representations seem interrelated. Explaining song 98, Emily imitated the sound of otters in the water when they see a person. "They got some kind of voice, 'sssssss' [a sibilant with a 'u' sound], when they see somebody." The word-sound in the song text, *suvinu*, with its "s," "v," and "u" sounds, seemed to match Emily's imitation. Gladys Hill gave me a Shoshone word in spoken language, *suhuikin*, which means a hissing sound, and this bore some likeness to the song word as well as Emily's imitation of the sound. In song 99, the noise, here identified with the young female otters, appears in song as *siyuhuigïn*, from spoken form, *siyu-huigïnt* (Gladys Hill). Emily commented, "They got those *suyuhiugi-tsi* which makes those [noise]." The alliteration on "s" in line two— *saiwai*, "melting snow," and *siyuhuigïn*, which repeats four times—is another poetic device that works with the onomatopoeia to simulate the hissing sound.

In song 129, *vesiyu* is the song word for splashing, which follows *ba*, "water." According to Gladys Hill, *bawasuw*, means "water splashing" in everyday language. If we extract the water syllable, *ba-*, from this word, *-wasuw* in spoken language becomes *vesiyu* in song. The "w" changes to a "v," glide to fricative, counter to the usual direction of change in song, but appropriate from an imitative standpoint. Following this is *uvinu*, repeating the "u" and "v" sounds and rhyming the final syllables, *-yu* with *-nu: vesiyu-uvinu*. On the one hand, *uvinu* might be a vocable suffix and spinoff from *vesiyu;* on the other, it seems very close in form to *suvinu*, the hissing-sound word in song 98.[25]

Finally, song 129 also mentions a breeze, *neshiwai*. Tidzump gives a spoken form for "breezy" as *neaysuwayfuinde* (Tidzump 1970:7SE). The song word adds the "sh" sound of a breeze where the stem of the spoken form, *neaysuway-*, has simply an "s."

Personification, Metaphor, and the Natural World

Naraya song language, with its personifications and metaphors, catches something of the special relationship between people and nature. Beverly Crum makes this point in her analysis of several Western Shoshone social-dance song texts. I repeat here some of her comments quoted earlier because they touch specifically on personification and metaphor. She remarks on the complexity and cultural importance of poetry songs sung for these occasions. She writes, "Poetry songs are composed in an elevated and figurative form of language . . . with several levels of meanings" (Crum 1980:5). Various poetic devices in these song texts relate to the "peoples' feelings about nature" (Crum 1980:11): "For example, the Shoshoni word Soka Pia means 'Earth Mother.' Out of this warm attachment to nature comes a figurative way of communicating. Most Shoshoni poetry songs are about nature. They contain detailed descriptions of what the poet singers observed in nature, and they express the poet singer's warm feelings about it. . . . The warm attitude is more general and directed toward nature at large. The poet singers are also expressing a shared attitude of the whole group" (Crum 1980:17).

Naraya personification of nature, be it male—White-Clay Man and Wood Stick Man (song 112)—or female—Earth Mother (songs 13, 115, 119)—links people to nature in a special relationship, something we have already noted in my commentary about animals, plants, and, even earlier, rocks. Recall Shoshone and Great Basin mythical time when birds and other animals, rocks, trees, and sagebrush were all people with language. Personification was part of the portrayal of its nonhuman characters and this pattern persisted in various forms even after myth time had come to an end. Liljeblad gives examples:

> Personification was the productive principle when appealing to nature for aid in everyday affairs. The mythological tales representing centuries of metaphoric fiction remained a never-failing repository of allegorical ideas. . . . Salt came to the Moapa Southern Paiutes in the shape of a man traveling through the country and putting his hand in the boiling food. . . . Typical also are the anecdotes about quarrels between different food plants and the prayers for success addressed to herbs with pharmaceutical properties. Viewing nature under the aspect of human conditions appears in a variety of comic sayings, as, for example, when the Northern Paiutes greet the chickadee with . . . ("how is your mother?"). (Liljeblad 1986:642)

Even more to the point, as regards Naraya song 112, Liljeblad continues, "Personification of natural phenomena was closely associated with individual access to supernatural aid and patronage, the principal doctrine in the religious system of the Great Basin Indians" (Liljeblad 1986:643). Chemehuevis (a Southern Paiute people), who gathered jimson weed for its dream-producing properties, "would approach the plant . . . , address it respectfully as 'old woman,' apologize for disturbing it, and explain fully just what revelation was desired" (Laird 1976:39). They also addressed prayers to Ocean Woman, who in their view, "is the prime creator of all things and the personification of the mysterious Ocean" (Laird 1976:46).

In addition to White-Clay Man, Wood Stick Man, and Earth Mother, Naraya songs personify the sun. It has a "face" in song 4 (Vander 1986:48; see appendix A) and the power of speech in songs 78, it "says." Liljeblad sees this as part of a broader pattern. "Cosmology in general but also various other inanimate phenomena and abstract ideas were subject to personification, creating an imaginary world of animate beings" (Liljeblad 1986:642). Goss provides an example from Ute cosmology, which illustrates their personification of the sun. "The sun was the moon's strong, energetic son in the prime of life" (Goss 1972:124).

In her explanation of the Naraya, Emily relied on metaphors, applying verbs appropriate for biological organisms, such as "growing up" and "awakening," in new ways. Emily: "Well, we'll dance. We'll make our earth come, grow up and make more water, more water. *Datevuntëg* means wake 'em up, wake 'em up. That song is for that. . . . Let's dance and make our earth and everything, roots what we eat on our ground—let 'em come alive again." Given Shoshone and Great Basin notions of death, discussed in chapter 1, it is not surprising that in the latter example the slenderest of lines divides sleep from death. Shoshone myth is rife with characters who "awaken" from death (Shimkin 1947c:342).

The relationship between people and the natural world is reciprocal. So far I have given examples of nature cast in human form or metaphoric images. The obverse is also possible. In Sarah Winnemucca Hopkins's description of the Northern Paiute Festival of Flowers, girls "became" the flower of their choice. "They all go marching along, each girl in turn singing of herself; but she is not a girl anymore,—she is a flower singing. . . . I, Sarah Winnemucca, am a shellflower, such as I wear on my dress. My name is Thocmetony" (Hopkins [1883] 1969:47). In Naraya song 123, human thought takes the form of sunlight that goes high up into the sky. More basic yet are the human transformations or incarnations into other forms of nature: the human soul as fog, the human ghost, a whirlwind.

Naraya songs also reveal metaphors that link different parts of the natural world, freely associating and likening one to the other. In chapter 4 I discussed similarity between fog and feathers perceived by Shoshone and Great Basin people and their cultural identification of both with the soul. Song 44, which talks of feathers on the mountains, may be a poetic reference to fog and a symbolic reference to the soul. In song 126 the stars of the Milky Way are rocks in a row. The more common term for the Milky Way, backbone of the sky, is yet another metaphor and, once again, drawn from biological organisms.

Emily explained some Naraya images by means of nature metaphors. In song 36, she likened the fog, blown apart by the wind, to petals or seeds of a flower scattered in the wind. In song 124 she compared the rays of the setting sun that radiate out behind the mountains to pine needles and the way they radiate out from the branch.

Liljeblad comments on the prevalence of figurative language in Great Basin culture and the translation difficulties it presents. "Figurative speech, common in the Numic languages, can seldom be interpreted by simply analyzing the literal meaning of a verbal sequence. The social context is decisive.... The use of metaphor is enhanced by the continued use of free composition, creating new, unexpected 'words' and ideas, producing compounds and phrases not otherwise found in the lexicon" (Liljeblad 1986:641).[26] There are two issues here. One is the context of figurative language, the other is the linguistic basis for its unique forms. In the case of Naraya texts, their figurative and sung-poetic language must be viewed within its sacred context and origin—something heard in vision.

Sacred Language: Intelligible, Unintelligible, Archaic, and Ambiguous

If one looks at all the descriptive texts of mountains, water, greenery, and animals in Emily and Dorothy's Naraya songs and listens to the women's explanations about the purpose of Naraya performance—the revitalization of nature—one can understand the relationship of texts to religious purpose. The dreamed origin of Naraya songs, a religious experience involving power that inheres in music and text, transforms Naraya words from the everyday to the sacred and powerful. Most, but not all Naraya texts are understandable. Some are problematic for a variety of reasons. For example, Emily easily gave a literal translation for every word of Naraya song 112, but she could give no explanation for what White-Clay Man and Wood Stick Man symbolized, nor their flight.

JUDY: "What does the song mean?"

EMILY: "It's something. We don't know what it is. She knows [Virginia Grant Bonatsie], but that's all I know."

In other words, only Virginia Grant Bonatsie, who dreamed the song, knows its full meaning. Shimkin received this same information during his fieldwork in the late 1930s. He subsequently wrote,

"The texts are cryptic descriptions of visions, fully understood only by their authors" (Shimkin 1947c:350).

Powers's study of Lakota sacred language sheds light on the translatable-incomprehensible enigma of Naraya song 112. Powers writes, "From the standpoint of verbal stylistics, however, most terms employed in sacred language are generated out of familiar words to which occult meanings have been assigned, as well as other kinds of verbal ornamentation. As one form of trope, metaphor plays an important part in the creation of sacred language" (Powers 1986:33).

Powers details other linguistic alterations that create sacred language. They are, in fact, some of the changes that I have already discussed in detail in my analysis of Naraya texts—such things as abbreviating words, attaching suffixes to them, and reduplicating words (Powers 1986:28–32). I have discussed these aspects as poetics, a reflection of my own personality and non-Shoshone upbringing. Obviously, from Emily's comment on the unusual suffix, -*penji*—"Just put pretty on there"—she, too, responded to Naraya texts aesthetically.

It is also true that for Gladys Hill, who helped me translate the songs, these changes in ordinary words often made them difficult for her to recognize. In many instances only Emily's comments on the songs made it possible for her to identify the underlying Shoshone words. Whether by design or serendipity, Naraya sacred language, sung and poetic, obscures everyday spoken language.[27]

Both Emily and Gladys mentioned the inclusion of archaic words in Naraya texts as another barrier for translation. Emily struggled to recall a particular plant mentioned in song 84, one that grows under aspen trees. She said, "There's somethings that oldtimers call—growing under it. A lot these—just like white people—hard jawbreaker words. Yeah, that's the kind they use sometimes. The oldtimers use that sometimes. Some people still don't understand it."

Emily's reference to "hard jawbreaker words" brings us back to Liljeblad's earlier observation on Shoshone creation of compound words by fusing two or more verbal stems. But her commentary that the hard words in question are words of the "oldtimers," words that some people don't understand, implies that they are obsolete, archaic, no longer current. Gladys Hill typified this state in her translation of song 54. She thought that *narueyagint* was the spoken form of the word mentioned in the text, but could not come up with its meaning. She thought that it was an old word.

This situation is by no means unique to Shoshone Naraya songs. McAllester writes of Navajo songs that "poetic texts are often in archaic or other unusual forms of language" (McAllester 1969:306).

Hinton states, "In [Havasupai] song, linguistic archaisms are often present" (Hinton 1984:4). Hinton quickly follows this statement with an important admonition. "However, caution must be used in the study of archaism in Havasupai songs (or any other tradition). Whenever one finds a difference between sung and spoken language, it can mean one of at least two things: either the sung form is archaic, or it is a poetic form, which may have nothing to do with archaism. Many constructions are studied here that must be defined as poetic, not archaic forms. That is, language in songs differs from spoken language because that is how one sings, not necessarily because that is how spoken language used to be" (Hinton 1984:4). I would add that the sacred dreamed origin of Naraya songs adds another dimension to the understanding of their linguistic form. I believe that archaic language, while included in Naraya songs, does not occupy a major place in its texts.

Finally, there is an ambiguous quality to Naraya texts and their sacred language. Some words keep their everyday meaning and, at the same time, the religious connotations that have been added to them may still sound for some listeners. Fog, in song 41, may be fog, nothing more nor less, and/or it might refer to the souls of the dead. The "new" earth, or world, mentioned in song 21 and other songs given in chapter 2, refers to the new world of Ghost Dance prophecy. But in her translation of song 92, Emily explained the "new" earth simply as a poetic reference to dawn, defined by its bird sounds and the rising sunlight. Did this adjective at some earlier time also carry connotations of the new world to come? Was *ügë* a pun, a new day on the new world—its bird songs and sunlight?

Repetition: Paired Phrases in Great Basin Culture

I began my analysis with paired phrases or progressions, the basic form of Naraya texts and music, and I return to them here. It is fascinating to see how many different contexts within Shoshone and Great Basin culture use this same form. I begin with Mooney's observation of Northern Paiute conversational style, which both impressed and annoyed him during his interview with Wovoka. Mooney wrote,

> Wovoka received us cordially and then inquired more particularly as to my purpose in seeking an interview. His uncle [and interpreter on this occasion] entered into a detailed explanation, which stretched out to a preposterous length, owing to a peculiar conversational method of the Paiute. Each statement by the older man was repeated at its close,

word for word and sentence by sentence, by the other, with the same monotonous inflection. This done, the first speaker signified by a grunt of approval that it had been correctly repeated, and then proceeded with the next statement, which was duly repeated in like manner. The first time I had heard two old men conversing together in this fashion on the reservation I had supposed they were reciting some sort of Indian litany, and it required several such experiences and some degree of patience to become used to it. (Mooney [1896] 1991:770–71)

This same pattern carried over to Northern Paiute communication that took place in more formal and public settings. Sarah Winnemucca Hopkins recounted, "At the council, one is always appointed to repeat at the time everything that is said on both sides, so that there may be no misunderstanding, and one person at least is present from every lodge, and after it is over, he gives and repeats what is decided upon at the door of the lodge, so all may be understood" (Hopkins [1883] 1969:54). Notice that, in this case, there is actually a designated "repeater."

We have encountered this before in connection with shamanistic performance. Recall that the shaman has a "talker" with him who repeats everything said by the shaman—even the song text of the shaman's song (Park 1938:50). In Northern Paiute, the repeater is called the *tuneggwukeadu,* the "designated shamanic repeater and interpreter" (Hittman 1990:69). Steward commented that among Northern and Gosiute Shoshones, "interpreting is unnecessary in most localities because the shaman can be understood. The assistant merely repeats the doctor's remarks about the sickness" (Steward 1943a:388).

Storytelling presents another example of paired phrases or progressions. Lowie reported, "In telling a story the [Northern Paiute] raconteur expects the listeners to repeat verbatim every paragraph" (Lowie 1924a:309). Liljeblad also described Northern Paiute storytelling practice. However, notice that in Liljeblad's account, first, it is the storyteller who does the repeating rather than the listener, and second, repetition of phrases could be either exact or *inexact:*

> After finishing a detail of the plot, the storyteller used to pause for response or questions, whereupon he repeated or rephrased his utterance. Thus, an episode or a single phrase would recur in the same or in a slightly different form, as the narrator continued his story step by step. Repetition also gave the narrator an opportunity to elaborate an incident with epic embellishment. The fact that storytelling used to occur within the frame of conversation between the narrator and his audience is obscured in published tale collections, owing either to incomplete recording or to omission of repetition. (Liljeblad 1986:650)

Wick Miller carefully makes this point in his publication of Gosiute stories. He informs the reader, "Repetitions, which is [*sic*] a typical feature of Mrs. Moon's oratorical style, were largely edited out in
the stories processed in 1971 with Mrs. Pete, sometimes resulting in
stories almost half as long as the original. . . . Repetitions were used
by Mrs. Moon in all her stories" (W. Miller 1972:25). A trace of this
remains in the story "Mourning Dove." Dove gathers seeds and says,
"'Those (seeds) are already ripe there. I will gather them, we will make
porridge, and then eat it. I will gather them, we will make porridge,
and then eat it,' she said" (W. Miller 1972:94).

Certainly, repeated phrases create the musical form of Round
Dance songs, and I shall discuss this more fully in the next chapter,
which is devoted to musical analysis. All evidence regarding Round
Dance song texts points in the same direction. Two of three Round
Dance song texts published by Liljeblad are made of repeated lines
(Liljeblad 1986:649). However, the sample size of published Round
Dance songs remains small and it is not clear whether some of these
were edited to remove repetition. For example, Liljeblad observes that
"an indefinite number of Powell's 'Songs and Chants' are to all appearance abridged Round Dance song texts with repetitive verse excluded" (Liljeblad 1986:649). I will explore this question further in a
final chapter devoted to a comparison of song texts.

9 | *Musical Analysis*

It is easy to see the poetic form of Naraya texts on the page. Each line is separate; repeated lines are printed one under the other. The eye follows the progression of paired phrases down the page. Musical transcriptions, on the other hand, obscure poetic form and the musical phrases that carry it. Convention and economy dictate that musical lines run across the entire page, indiscriminate of where the line ends in relation to musical-poetic phrases. Musical symbols, such as slurs, barlines, and rests, indicate phrase beginnings and endings.

I wish to preface this chapter on musical analysis with a visual representation of the musical-poetic form of Naraya songs. To do this, the musical transcriptions of songs 122 and 77 given below follow poetic conventions of presentation (ex. 1).[1] In this way, one can compare and see at a glance key points about Naraya musical style: the symmetry of its repeated phrases, the asymmetry of unequal phrase lengths, the inexactness of the repetition, and small variations—some

Example 1. Song 122

Example 1, continued. Song 77

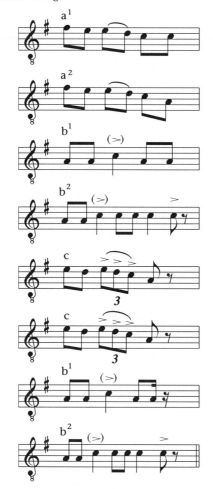

codified throughout every repeat of the verse (a^1a^2) and others unique to the verse. Finally, to repetition, symmetry, asymmetry, and variation I will add contrast as another important characteristic of Naraya musical style. All are basic to the songs and my discussion and analysis of their musical elements.

My transcriptions of Naraya songs are of one verse. Singing and recording for themselves, Emily and Dorothy repeated the verse from three to sixteen times, seven being the most common.[2] I have often chosen to transcribe a verse from the middle of their performance, as there seemed to be more tentativeness and "irregularities" in the beginning verses, which disappeared as the women selected and settled into a stable and more consistent version of the verse. The two women sang in unison and one of the two served as leader for the song. As I have noted elsewhere, "While listening to Naraya songs of herself and Dorothy singing together, Emily would sometimes state which of them was the 'leader.' The leader knows the song very well, starts it off, and makes the final performance decisions in a strong voice which the other singer or singers follow" (Vander 1986:21–22).[3]

Emily was explicit on the source of Naraya songs. "They dream it someplace way off, someplace in the mountains or hills someplace. Indians dream their songs. They dream it and they're going to sing it" (Vander 1988:13). In her comments on song 112, Emily described the transmission of a dreamed song during a Naraya performance. "That's Virginia [Grant] Bonatsie's song. She dreamt that song—just like Sun Dance or religious songs—she dreamt it. When they had a dance she sang that song for them when she was a young woman."

Another Wind River Shoshone woman, Angelina Wagon, provided further details about the origin and transmission of sacred dreamed song, in this case, a Sun Dance song.

> My mother, she found that song. When the sun was coming out and she came into our kitchen and then she heard that song. She was sleeping the first time she heard that song, so she start in singing that song. And when she sang that song, well, she thought that it was a prayer song. Something mentioned to her that it would be a prayer song. That's the way they do, too, for the Ghost Dance songs. It's got meanings to them or something like that, to somebody that found that song. So she got up and was singing that song, and she went in there to the room where my dad was sleeping, and she sang that song for him, and my dad just caught that song all at once [the sign of a true visionary song]. He just sang it once, and he knew that song and that's what they sing. And my dad sang that song 'cause it was my mother's song. The old man said, "Well, if it's given to you, maybe it's been a blessing for you. We should have it for a starting song, call it a Prayer Song, *Naishuntai Huvia*."(Vander 1988:66–67)

Congruent with these statements are those of Toorey Roberts, the Naraya leader in the 1930s who was interviewed by Shimkin in 1937. Excerpting from his own fieldnotes, Shimkin wrote to me: "Toorey's song come to his mind: an idea. . . . Sometimes, one dreams of a song at home. He himself made his up; didn't dream them [This is a conventional denial, DBS]" (Shimkin 1937). (See chapter 10 for three texts of Roberts's Naraya songs.)

In 1935 Herzog analyzed the musical style of Plains Ghost Dance songs available to him at that time, primarily the transcriptions of Mooney (1896), Densmore (1929), and Curtis (1923). He wrote:

> Practically all songs found associated with the Plains Ghost Dance are so closely related to each other that they must be conceived as representing a distinct type, forming an integrated "style" of their own. This style is foreign to the Plains; its patterns are different from those prevalent in Plains music. The style can be traced to the Great Basin: musical evidence reflects the diffusion of the Ghost Dance from that region to and through the Plains. In the Basin the style is not restricted to Ghost Dance songs; it is represented in other song categories so generously that its pattern may be regarded as the strongest and most characteristic element of some Great Basin musical styles. (Herzog 1935a:403)

Herzog ended his article with further conclusions about Plains Ghost Dance songs: "Ghost Dance songs form a style of their own, embedded within the various local styles of the Plains. That is, Plains music did not strongly affect the Paiute [Great Basin] musical patterns offered to it in the form of Ghost Dance songs. We have, to be sure, pointed to the occasional merging of Plains patterns with Ghost Dance patterns, . . . That this process did not progress further may be due in part to the exceedingly quick spread of the Ghost Dance movement and to its brief life in many places" (Herzog 1935a:415–16).

Naraya songs, performed with the dance until the late 1930s and still remembered and sung in the late 1970s, offer a latter-day opportunity to reexamine Herzog's questions regarding the durability of Ghost Dance musical style. First: Is Naraya song style congruent with that of Plains Ghost Dance songs studied by Herzog? And second: Does it show influence from Plains musical style, the War Dance, Round Dance, and Sun Dance songs, which comprise the bulk of the Wind River Shoshone song repertoire?

As the rest of this chapter will document, Naraya songs fit comfortably into Herzog's musical characterization, In his words, "The melodic range is usually narrow, essentially a fifth. As a rule there is no accompaniment. Many of the phrases end on the tonic. They fall into sections so symmetrical as to be startling in primitive material. This symmetry is achieved by the most essential feature of the style, a simple structural device: *every* phrase is rendered twice. The emphasis on 'every' is important . . . and is unique in Plains music" (Herzog 1935a:403–4). Table 4, which indicates melodic range, structure, and the frequency of melodic tones at the beginning and ending phrases in Naraya songs, uses Herzog's conventions for these same musical elements as its model and amply supports his data and conclusions (Herzog 1935a:406).

Table 4. Application of Herzog's Analytical Table of Plains Ghost Dance Songs to the Naraya.[a]

Melodic range				3	4	5	6	7	8	9
Total number of songs				6	14	50	43	8	7	2

Melodic tones	IV	V	VI	VII	1	2	3	4	5	6
Frequency as phrase finals	1	32	50	9	400	10	15	5	0	0
Frequency as phrase starters	0	10	26	9	123	87	98	120	42	6

Song structure
  64 songs have aabb
  44 songs have a¹a² and/or b¹b²
  22 songs have a variety of other structures

a. To facilitate comparison, I follow Herzog's conventions (Herzog 1935a:406): roman numerals stand for tones below the tonic, and arabic numerals for tones above it, starting with 1 on the tonic.

At the same time, I have already suggested in chapter 8 that there are limits to the scope of Herzog's study—its parameters and level of detail. Clearly, symmetry and simplicity are one side of the Naraya coin and they are easily seen. Asymmetry and complexity, the other side of this coin, are less obvious. Because Naraya songs are miniature forms, only very close attention to small details can bring individual irregularities into view. I believe that summed together, their diversity and multitude are equally impressive. If, at times, I labor long on this side of the coin, it is to bring it to light. A just characterization of Naraya music and poetry is incomplete and skewed without it.

Plains musical style has influenced Naraya songs in some ways, but the total impact has been relatively minor. With the exception of pulsation, which I integrate within my discussion of Naraya ending patterns, all other examples of Plains influence appear at the end of the chapter, after I have placed Naraya songs within the larger frame of Great Basin music.

Rhythm

Naraya songs use a variety of durations. Sixteenth notes, eighths, dotted eighths, quarters, dotted quarters, half and dotted half notes appear in combination with one another, commonly two to four in a song. One senses that the songs move in two's or three's (or multiples thereof), and that is how I write the time signature for these songs. I choose not to identify a particular meter or to use barlines that separate and subdivide the melody. Meter and barlines, notational conventions from Euro-American musical traditions, carry with them implied patterns of accents and a regularity that do not fit Naraya songs.

Of the songs presented in this book, 75 have duple rhythmic organization, 46 have triple, and 9 combine the two (see table 5).[4] Songs 51 and 67 (example 2) are examples that combine and contrast two rhythmic organizations, the even symmetrical movement in twos of the *a* sections with the asymmetrical and rolling movement in threes

Table 5. Rhythm and Tempo

	Duple	Triple	Combination
Total number of songs	75	46	9
Tempo range	♩ = 68–138	♩. = 56–88	

Example 2. Excerpts from songs 51 and 67

a. Song 51

b. Song 67

of the *b* sections. (Note the rhythmic subtlety in the six bracketed beats of song 67. Ties override the pattern of threes, suggesting groups of twos. At the completion of the repetition of *b,* their final placement in the section serves as a transition to the beginning of *a* and its return to duple rhythmic organization.)

In song 18, the combination of twos and threes does not break along sectional lines. Rather, the *a* section and first six beats of the *b* sections are in threes and the last fourteen beats of the *b* sections are in twos (ex. 3).

Example 3. Excerpts from song 18

The shifting between movement in twos and threes becomes even more entwined within sections in songs 75 and 140 (ex. 4).[5]

Example 4. Excerpts from songs 75 and 140

a. Song 75

b. Song 140

As a general rule, the length or number of beats in the two or three sections of Naraya songs is not the same. Only 27 of 130 songs are identical.[6] Irregular lengths, from the large and obvious down to the small and subtle, occur between sections of a song, repetitions of the same section, and smaller units within sections.

Another source of irregularity comes from the insertion of "extra" beats. For example, the repeat of the *a* section in song 20 (ex. 5) adds one beat to the first half of the section.

Example 5. Excerpts from song 20

Within an overall framework of movement in twos or threes, these so-called extra beats have an impact on rhythmic structure and flow. In song 25, an "extra" eighth-note duration creates a small bulge in the *a* section, which uses primarily quarter notes and pairs of eighth notes (ex. 6).

Example 6. Excerpt from song 25

In song 59, an extra pair of sixteenth notes occurs after the third beat in both the *a* and *b* sections (ex. 7). Although brief in duration, the extra pair takes on importance as it coincides with two other irregularities. Besides being an extra half-beat within a duple framework, it is the only pair of sixteenth notes in each section of the song, and the only place where one syllable of text carries through more than one note of the melody. These asymmetries play against the identical lengths of the two sections, 7½ beats, and the identical placement of the extra sixteenth notes in both sections of the song.

Example 7. Excerpts from song 59

Song 35 flows consistently in threes; however, an extra one-beat rest in the *b* section sets off its final six beats, which are identical to the ending of the *a* section (ex. 8). It opens a small gap in the rhythmic flow.

Example 8. Excerpts from song 35

In addition to extra beats, the steady underlying beat and move-ment in twos or threes is sometimes subject to syncopations—the unexpected placement of a longer note within a rhythmic setting. Used sparingly, this is one of several types of contrast in Naraya songs that contributes to its asymmetrical profile. One relatively common form of syncopation appears in song 55 (ex. 9).

Example 9. Excerpt from song 55

Notice that there are two settings for the word *doiyavi*, and just the first one (bracketed in the example) is syncopated. In song 65, every setting of *tiwaizi*, in both the *a* and *b* sections, is set to this same syncopated figure (ex. 10).

Example 10. Excerpts from song 65

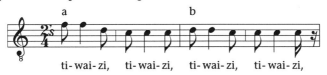

One of the most striking uses of this syncopation appears in song 119, two times in succession. Accented attacks on the long note in the pattern emphasize the syncopation (ex. 11).

Song 97 is another example of back-to-back syncopations (ex. 12). In this case, their placement at the beginning of the *b* section is an-other way to emphasize them.

In my earlier Ghost Dance publication, I reported the use of this particular form of syncopation (♪♩♪) in other musical genres from the

Example 11. Excerpt from song 119

Example 12. Excerpt from song 97

Great Basin: an Owens Valley Paiute Funeral Song, a song recitative from Kaibab Paiute myth, and a Paiute Hand Game Song (Vander 1986:25).[7]

Another type of syncopation occurs in songs whose underlying rhythmic organization moves in threes. Such rhythms as (♩., ♫, ♩♪) establish the sense of movement in threes and are the prevailing patterns. Within this rhythmic system, an eighth followed by a quarter note (♪♩)—a short-long pattern—creates an agogic accent on the second beat by virtue of its longer duration relative to the first beat. It plays against the standard three-beat patterns given above. This type of syncopation appears selectively in Naraya songs and as a consequence stands out in its rhythmic context. In songs 26 and 81 (ex. 13), it occurs just once at the beginning of the *b* sections (bracketed in the example).

In song 37, this type of syncopation appears two times at the beginning of the *a* section (ex. 14).

Example 13. Excerpts from songs 26 and 81

a. Song 26

b. Song 81

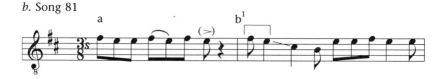

Example 14. Excerpt from song 37

In songs 40, 126, and 73 (ex. 15), the beginnings of sections and subsections, often with the same text, receive further parallel treatment with the same syncopated figure.

Example 15. Excerpts from songs 40, 126, and 73

a. Song 40

b. Song 126

c. Song 73

Again, in songs 47 and 28 (ex. 16), the same word of text in different sections receives this same syncopation. In these examples this occurs near the end of the section rather than at the beginning.

In songs 98 (ex. 17) and 102 (ex. 18), the syncopation appears once in the middle of both the *a* and *b* sections. But notice the balance of

Example 16. Excerpts from songs 47 and 28

a. Song 47

Example 17. Excerpts from song 98

Example 18. Excerpts from song 102

what is the same and what is different in both songs. In song 98, whose two sections are the same length (four groups of three beats), the placement of the syncopation in each section differs—falling on the third group in *a* and the second group in *b*.

In song 102, whose two sections are not the same length (five groups versus three), the placement of the syncopation is centered—falling on the third group of five and the second group of three.

Another type of syncopation occurs when the final beat of a one grouping ties over through the beginning of the next. In song 129, this type of syncopation is heightened further by the use of an accented attack (ex. 19).

Example 19. Excerpt from song 129

Song 74 uses two similar types of syncopation in a row (ex. 20); however, in this example they occur between two consecutive beats and are set off by rests that bracket them.

Example 20. Excerpt from song 74

In several examples this type of syncopation occurs at the beginning of a section and is one strategy for binding sections closely together (ex. 21). In song 138B, the anticipated third beat at the end of section a^2 becomes the first beat in section b^1, tied to beats one and two of the next group of three. Songs 64 and 118 are other examples of syncopations that straddle the boundary between the *a* and

Example 21. Excerpts from songs 138B, 64, 118, and 144

a. Song 138B

b. Song 64

Example 21, continued.

c. Song 118

d. Song 144

e - na,

b sections. In song 144, this syncopation occurs at the beginning of both *a* sections. In this case the boundary is between the first ending and beginning repetition of the same section.

In addition to syncopated rhythms, approximately one-fourth of the songs begin a new section on the last portion of the preceding section's final beat.

Rhythmic contrasts take many forms in Naraya songs. Some have already been suggested: duple or triple rhythmic organization and, in some instances cited earlier (songs 51, 67, and 18), the alternation of duple and triple rhythms in different sections of a song. Syncopations provide another source of contrast. Few in number and proportion, they stand in relief against an unsyncopated background.

Choices and combinations of durations provide another rich source of rhythmic interest and contrast. This may be on a large scale, for example, the contrast in song 48 (ex. 22) of section *a*'s (♩♩♩) with section *b*'s (♩♪ or ♪♩),

Example 22. Excerpts from song 48

or the contrast of the dotted rhythm in section *a* of song 83 (ex. 23) with the smooth string of eighth and quarter notes in section *b*, and vice-versa in song 66 (ex. 24).

The contrast may be on a small and subtle scale, as it is in song 74 (ex. 25), in which parallel, but not identical, musical settings match

Example 23. Excerpts from song 83

Example 24. Excerpts from song 66

Example 25. Excerpts from song 74

mo - zam - bi - an - zi, wa - zum - bi - an - zi

parallel, but not identical, words of text—*mozambianzi* (mountain sheep) in section *a* and *wazumbianzi* (game animals) in section *b*. Interesting, too, is the placement of the rhythmic contrast in the above example, which does not coincide with the contrasting parts of the text, but rather with the places where the two are identical.

By rights, the importance and use of rests in Naraya songs would logically be another topic within this analytical discussion of the various aspects of rhythm. However, because rests play such a key role in the articulation and demarcation of melody and song form, I will postpone my analysis of them until I focus discussion on melody and song form.

Tempo is my final subject regarding the rhythm of Naraya songs. Emily commented that the Naraya had fast and slow songs. A comparison of the tempos of the song performances presented in this book confirms this (table 5, above). Songs with duple rhythmic organization have metronome markings for a quarter note that range from 68 to 138. Songs with triple rhythmic organization have metronome markings for a dotted quarter note that range from 56 to 88.[8] However, in both cases, most of the songs actually fall within a considerably smaller range. Fifty-six of 77 songs with duple organization are marked in the 84–100 range and 35 of 48 songs with triple organization are in the 66–76 range. These choices of tempos are consistent with additional comments by Emily regarding tempo and her aesthetics of Naraya songs. The following remarks by Emily also include information from my fieldnotes, indicated by their dates of the entry.

Emily said: "'When you're singing [*Naraya* songs] you're supposed to kind of drag your song. Make that song pretty.' [August 18, 1977. 'Dorothy and Emily sang another Ghost Dance song. Also told me not to sing the Ghost Dance songs too fast. . . .'] Once, after listening to a *Naraya* song on her own tapes, Emily expressed particular pleasure in a song: 'I like that song—slow'" (Vander 1988:16).

In 1979, Emily and I listened to Edward Curtis's 1909 recording of Naraya songs, including song 117. The singer was Dick Washakie, son of Chief Washakie and a well-known Wind River Shoshone man of his time. Emily enjoyed the performance but did critique the tempo as being too fast. I have transcribed Washakie's performance of song 117 as well as Angelina Wagon's, which I recorded in 1981. Emily and Dorothy's performance was by far the slowest, ♩ = 84; Angelina Wagon's, considerably faster, ♩ = 104; and Dick Washakie's, the fastest, ♩ = 108 (Vander 1988:62).

Pitch Material, Intervals, Tonality, and Phrase Finals

Naraya melodies use relatively few pitches. Of the songs presented in this book, 47 have four pitches and 40 have five—accounting for more than half the songs. Less common are 23 songs with six pitches, 16 with three, and only 6 songs with seven pitches. As summarized in table 6, the number of melodic intervals from this pitch material is likewise modest in size. Major seconds (in 133 songs), minor thirds (119), perfect fourths (99), and major thirds (67) are the interval-backbone of the melodies. Perfect fifths (34) and minor seconds (32) are much less common; minor sixths (4) and octaves (1), rare.

In his study of Ghost Dance songs, Herzog tabulated phrase "finals," which he analyzed frequently as the tonic. A tabulation of

Table 6. Frequency of
Melodic Intervals

Interval	Frequency
m2	32
M2	133
m3	119
M3	67
P4	99
P5	34
m6	4
8	1

Naraya phrase finals (table 4) correlates positively with Herzog's data (Herzog 1935a:406–8). Four hundred of 522 sections of Naraya songs end on the tonic. Seventy-seven songs, more than half, end every section on the tonic.

But as is the case for all the musical elements in Naraya songs, closer scrutiny always brings out a host of contrasts and ambiguities that run counter to the prevailing characteristic. Phrase finals and tonality are no exceptions. I begin with song 66, a song in which three of four section finals are not on the tonic and a good example of my criteria for determining it (ex. 26). (Final notes of subsections are given in parentheses.)

Two factors establish the tonality in Naraya songs. First, the pitch of the final note of a section takes on importance by virtue of its position. Second, a pitch with longer total duration throughout a

Example 26. Song 66

song relative to other pitches reinforces its status as tonal center. In song 66, these two factors are at work and at play. Sections a^1, a^2, and b^1 end on VI, the second most common ending note (in fifty sections) after 1 (recall that I follow Herzog in using roman numerals for tones below the tonic and arabic numerals for tones above it, starting with 1 on the tonic). Notice that the first subsection of the *a* sections ends on 1—a secondary position of importance after the section final. The long reiteration of C prior to and on *ena,* in the last half of b^2, is a common ending pattern on the tonic. Section b^1 plays against this expectation and foils it, giving us once again a final on VI. In some songs there is a subtle hierarchy in the importance of section finals. The second final of a repeated section may be more important than the first, which is true for b^2 in song 66. The highest level in this subtle hierarchy is often the last final of the last section of a song. In song 66, the final 1 (C) in section b^2 is more important than the finals on VI (A) of b^1 and both *a* sections. Not only the final position of C is critical to its status as tonic, but also its total duration throughout the song relative to A: 17½ beats versus 3½. C is tonic.[9]

Section finals, which are important to song tonality, are equally important to melodic form. Consequently, I always distinguish repeated sections that are identical in all ways except for their final notes, as a^1, a^2, b^1, b^2, and so on.

The relationship between the different sections of a song takes many forms, one of which has an impact on phrase finals. Naraya songs repeat many times and, in this sense, are circular forms, like rounds. Except for the last repeat, the final note of the last section is followed immediately by the first note of the first section. It seems to me that in some songs the final note of the last section serves primarily to provide a smooth melodic transition between ending and beginning, rather than its usual function, to determine tonality as suggested above. In song 71 (ex. 27), and counter to my earlier comments on the primacy of the last section's final in regard to tonality, I hear the first three consecutive cadences on C as tonic finals, with the D final in b^2 leading to E in section *a*. My other test for tonali-

Example 27. Song 71

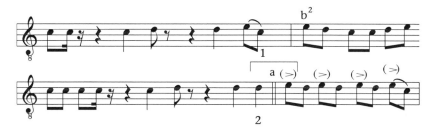

ty—total duration—is ambiguous here. Both C and D have identical total durations in the song.

Song 33 (ex. 28) is another example of what I hear as three cadences on the tonic C and a final cadence not on the tonic but on E, which makes a smooth transition to the next repeat of the song. This song is unusual in its use of major and minor thirds, C to E and E-flat, used separately in sections *a* and *b*¹ and side-by-side in *b*².

Example 28. Excerpts from song 33

Perception and musical background influence how one hears and analyzes what one hears. Song 30 (ex. 29) brings out some of the unanswered questions of my perception and analysis of Naraya songs.

Example 29. Song 30

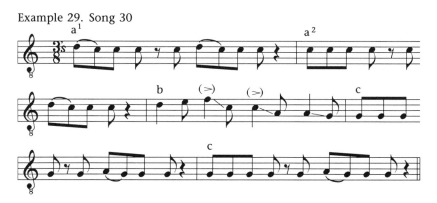

In this song both *a* sections clearly establish C as tonic, through total duration and phrase finals. Section *b*, unrepeated, is an interesting melodic bridge, which brings the melody down to, and cadences, on G. The melody of section *c*, which begins on G, is identical to section *a* except for being transposed down a fourth. If the *a* section clearly established C as the tonic, wouldn't—doesn't—the *c* section clearly establish G as a tonic? Does the fact that section *c* eventually ends the piece—will be the last word of the last repeat—bolster its bid for being the tonal center? However, it is hard for me not to hear this like a round that ends on V, the dominant. Beethoven has shaped my musical ear. Or are there two tonal centers in this song, C and G?

A total of nine Naraya songs have such ambiguity regarding their tonality, for example, songs 53 and 119. In each song transcription in chapters 2–7 I have indicated the tonal ambiguity with a question mark under the pitch material.[10] I end this discussion with two final examples, each unique in its sequence of phrase finals and tonal play.

Song 77 (ex. 30) plays with two tonal centers, C and A.

Example 30. Song 77

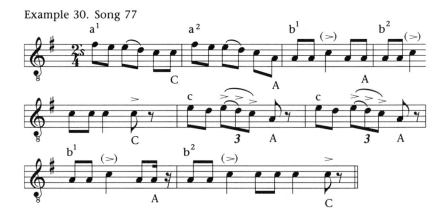

Before pointing out the pattern of phrase finals in this song, I call attention to its form, which is unusual. The song breaks into two parts and the last half of each part is identical to the other.

$$a^1, \ a^2, \ b^1, \ b^2$$
$$c, \ \ c, \ \ b^1, \ b^2$$

It might seem that A is the tonal center as five of eight cadences are on A. But it is not, for some of the same reasons given earlier in the tonal analysis of song 66. For one thing, the total durations, C for 11½ beats, A for 7½, suggest a C tonic. But more than durations, it is the importance of structural points, here noted in a variety of ways, that makes C the tonal center. The repeat of *b* (*b²*) takes on special importance in song 77 as it is not only the second presentation of the section but it also marks the end of the first half of the song and, with the return of the *b* sections after the *c'*s, marks the end of the entire song. The melody of *b²* distinguishes itself from all the other sections in three ways. It is two beats longer than sections *a*, *b¹*, and *c;* its five beats are little else than the reiteration of C for 3½ beats; the final beat, C, is accented.

The phrase final patterns in the two halves of the song—CAAC and AAAC—are slightly different, another example of unequal pairing or balancing. C finals bracket the sections of the song in an interesting way that is not the same for both halves of the song.

$$a^1 \quad a^2 \quad b^1 \quad b^2 \qquad c \quad c \quad b^1 \quad b^2$$
$$C \quad A \quad A \quad C \qquad A \quad A \quad A \quad C$$

C finals in sections *a¹* and *b²* bracket the first half of the song. C finals in sections *a¹* and the last *b²* bracket the entire song. I pointed out a melodic bridge in both song 71 and song 33 that smoothed the return to the beginning of the song for its next repeat. In song 77, the phrase final and tonal centering of the last *b²* section, which is identical to *a¹*, is another type of link that connects the end of the song to its next beginning.

Like song 77, song 53 also brackets the first and last sections with the same phrase final (ex. 31).

Example 31. Song 53

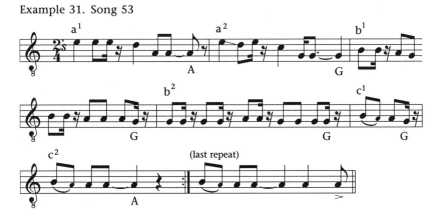

But in this song, the contest between tonal centers, A versus G, is more evenly balanced. The form and phrase finals are:

$$a^1 \quad a^2 \quad b^1 \quad b^2 \quad c^1 \quad c^2$$
$$A \quad G \quad G \quad G \quad G \quad A$$

Total durations of both pitches are almost identical throughout the song. However, in the final repeat of the song, c^2 expands with an extra 1½ beats of A at the end, making four beats of reiterated A. As further emphasis, the last beat of A is accented. The placement of the A finals and the longer cadence of the last repeat on A argue for A tonality. But G is a strong center within the A brackets and maintains a sense of tonal ambivalence in the song.

Songs with competing or ambiguous tonal centers are a minority. Most have a well-defined tonal center and a majority end every phrase with the tonic. However, in a small but significant group of songs, tonic (1) and nontonic (x) finals combine in interesting ways in relation to song form, suggesting at least five formulaic sequences:

song sections		a,a,b,b	
phrase finals	1)	x,x,x,1	(13 songs, e.g., songs 89, 72)
	2)	x,x,1,1	(7 songs, e.g., songs 26, 107)
	3)	1,x,x,1	(7 songs, e.g., songs 45, 31)
	4)	1,1,x,x	(4 songs, e.g., song 86)
	5)	x,x,x,x	(4 songs, e.g., songs 64, 25)

Melody

Four to five pitches within a narrow range are the bases of Naraya melodies. While the total melodic range of the songs is a third to a ninth, the norm is considerably smaller. Most of the songs encompass a fifth (49 songs) or a sixth (43 songs) and, more distantly, a fourth (14 songs). Songs with melodic ranges of a seventh (8), eighth (7), third (6), and ninth (2) are uncommon or rare. (See table 4.)

Drawing on these possibilities, the melodic contours of Naraya songs are characteristically undulating-descending. A numerical comparison of starting and final notes of phrases supports this, as summarized in table 4. Musical phrases frequently start on the tonic (123); however, the combined sum of phrases that begin on a fourth above (120), third above (98), second above (87 sections), and fifth above (42 sections) is almost three times that of the tonic. Phrase finals fall predominantly on the tonic (400), or below it on VI (53) and V (35). Herzog connected melodic range and contour in his discussion of Ghost Dance songs: "The gradually descending melodies do not have much freedom of movement when confined to a narrow space" (Herzog 1935b:409).

Song 40 (ex. 32) is typical of the narrow range and undulating-descending contour of many Naraya songs.

Example 32. Excerpts from song 40

Also notice in song 40 the slightly lower tessitura of the *b* section in comparison with the *a,* another common pattern of Naraya melodies. In this case, both the narrower range of the *b* section compared to the *a* (a third rather than a fifth) and its many reiterations of the tonic account for a lower tessitura.

Another practice accounts for a lower tessitura in *b* or subsequent sections: the reuse and transposition of a melody down on a lower level. In song 30 (ex. 33), the melody of section *c* is identical to *a,* except that it begins on a lower starting note a fourth below. The two melodic contours parallel one another.

Example 33. Excerpts from song 30

Small differences in the contour of the transposed melody may appear, due to the particular pitches that are available in the song. For example, in song 131 (ex. 34), all the intervals between the first four notes of section *a* are major seconds. The *b* section transposes these notes down one step, beginning on C. But because there is no B-flat in the song, the intervallic relationship between the last two notes is a minor third, as A rather than B-flat is the next available pitch below C.

Example 34. Excerpts from song 131

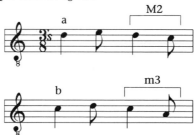

In other examples, including song 142 (ex. 35), the lower transposition of the *a* melody in the *b* section peters out as the melody returns to its original untransposed form.

Example 35. Excerpts from song 142

Many Naraya songs contrast two different types of melody between sections *a* and *b*, one that is active and uses the full range of notes, another that is more static and restricted in its range and movement. Songs 59 and 26 are good examples of this (ex. 36). Note that in both examples it is the *b* melodies that are static. With a few exceptions, for example, song 80, this is true when there is a contrast of these melody types, and it is another contributing factor to the lower tessitura of *b* sections relative to *a*. In these two examples, the *b* sections use scarcely more than one note.

Example 36. Excerpts from songs 59 and 26

a. Song 59

b. Song 26

In song 99 (ex. 37), the static *b* section oscillates between two notes, the tonic and a minor third above it, with only a brief touch on the note below the tonic as well.

Example 37. Excerpts from song 99

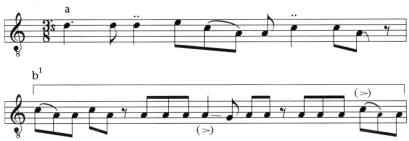

The static *b* section in song 51 (ex. 38) uses three notes—the tonic, circled by upper and lower neighboring tones.

Example 38. Excerpts from song 51

Finally, the oscillation in songs 105 and 128 begins on the tonic, alternates with other melody notes, strongly reiterates the tonic, and ends on the tonic (ex. 39). The tonic seems like a pedal tone, always reining the melody in and back to itself.

Example 39. Excerpts from songs 105 and 128

a. Song 105

Example 39. Song 105, continued.

b. Song 128

Rests and Melodic Form

The use of rests—measured silence—in Naraya songs is crucial to their form. Rests articulate and punctuate the melodic line. In song 19 (ex. 40), the melody of section *a* divides into three parts, each separated by rests.

Example 40. Excerpt from song 19

Our old earth ⁊ fading ⁊ fading ⁊

The longer rest comes at the end of the line and punctuates it. The shorter rests sculpt three smaller divisions of the music and text. Subsections 1 and 2 are the main part of the line, both musically and textually. Subsection 3 provides the cadence, a reiteration on the tonic and repetition of the verb "fading."

Rests create and reveal the molecular structure of the melody. They also break up the text in interesting and varied ways. Like the verbal command "stop," in a telegram, the rests in song 89 (ex. 41) govern the melodic and textual groupings of notes and words through pauses that separate them.

Example 41. Song 89

Using **stop** for rests, the poetic "telegram" reads:

> ?Cattails red-wing blackbird **stop** flying **stop** wind **stop**
> ?Cattails red-wing blackbird **stop** flying **stop** wind **stop**
> Dark ?cattails water-black **stop** ?home Dark ?cattails **stop**
> water-black **stop** ?home. **stop**

The lack of a rest between the two *b* sections, indicated here by the run-on sentence, is one of many ways to minimize or override the boundary between lines. This and many other relationships between sections will be examined separately in a later discussion.

Rests may emphasize one word of text by bracketing it. An example of this involves the word, "green," the first word of every section and subsection in song 39 (ex. 42).

Example 42. Excerpts from song 39

In song 107 (ex. 43), "green" is also the first word of both halves of section *a* text, but unlike song 39, this song's musical settings are not identical. The longer duration and concluding rest in the second presentation of "green" contrast with the first setting—shaping the second half of the melody and text in a slightly varied form.

Example 43. Excerpt from song 107

The poetic telegram for this line of text reads, "Green greasewood creek **stop** green **stop** greasewood creek."

In some Naraya songs, rests interrupt or intrude on the melody so frequently that they become an important musical element in and of themselves, rather than organizers and markers of musical phrases and sections (ex. 44).

Example 44. Song 53

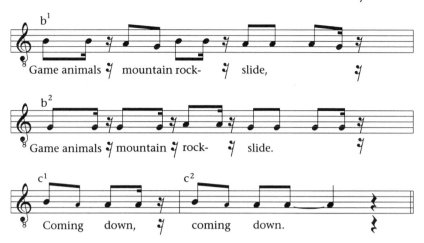

There is a halting, breathless quality to this song, especially in the *b* sections. Rests punctuate almost every word in section *b*[1], even breaking up "rockslide" into two parts. Section *b*[2] adds an additional rest after "mountain." The text as telegram reads:

> Coming down **stop** coming down **stop**
> Coming down **stop** coming down Game animals
>   **stop** mountain rock- **stop** slide **stop**
> Game animals **stop** mountain **stop** rock- **stop** slide **stop**
> Coming down **stop**
> Coming down **stop**

The "coming down" in this text refers to game animals. But in its poetic compression, "coming down" may also refer to the mountain rockslide itself. Is the disjunct movement, the many starts and stops, a musical response to these textual images? I do not know.

Elsewhere, the use of rests is a source of contrast. In song 139 (ex. 45), the extensive use of rests in the *b* section differs from the *a* section, which has no internal pauses. Every word in the *b* section takes a rest; even the final verb complex, "lying while moving," is split in two.

Example 45. Excerpts from song 139

Example 45, continued.

Other Naraya Ending Markers

Melodic form depends upon perceived beginnings and endings. Many Plains song genres clearly mark both beginnings and endings. The high solo call of the lead singer comes at the beginning of the song; the descending melodic contour encompasses a wide range, beginning high and moving progressively lower to a concluding reiteration of the tonic. Singers often use a distinctive vocal attack on the first note of a phrase (Vander 1988:42). The drum part, with its placement of accents, provides another set of cues indicating location within the melodic form (Vander 1988:252–53). Naraya songs, on the other hand, have no strong beginning markers. Although many songs do begin on a high note and end lower on the tonic, the contrast is minimal due to the narrow range of the melodies and their undulating contours. There is no equivalent lead singer part, no beginning vocal accents, no drum part. One perceives Naraya song form in two ways, from its well-marked endings and by recognizing repetition.

Rests, as described earlier, signal the ends of sections. Herzog commented on this in his study of Ghost Dance songs: "The rests between the phrases are more clear cut than in many Plains songs" (Herzog 1935b:25–26). Several other musical-textual conventions also work in conjunction with rests, as illustrated in an excerpt of Naraya song 109 (ex. 46).

Example 46. Excerpts from song 109

Ena (here, also *yena*) is the conventional ending vocable. Its musical setting is also conventional, a long note (often the longest duration used throughout the song) followed by a short note and rest. Sometimes a rest precedes as well as follows *ena*. In this example, the two notes on B that precede *ena* have the identical rhythmic pattern, a long note followed by a short note and rest. The double use of the ending rhythm reinforces it. Notice, too, that these four notes are all on the tonic. Reiteration of the tonic at the cadence is yet another melodic-cadential characteristic. (See the *b* section of song 79.)

Yaiyowainda, another ending vocable, uses nearly this same rhythmic pattern, the only difference being that it is twice as long (long-short-long-short-rest). In song 82 (ex. 47), one of the few songs that has both *ena* and *yaiyowainda* at the cadence, the extensive long-short-rest pattern on the tonic is as follows:

Example 47. Excerpt from song 82

e - na   yai - yo - wain - da

Other aspects of vocal performance coincide with one part of the rhythmic setting of *ena,* lending further emphasis to the constellation of ending cues. From a rhythmic standpoint, the long-short pattern on *ena* creates an agogic accent on the first syllable, *e-.* Counterbalancing this is an accented attack on *-na,* the short last note. The attack is strong, the decay, precipitous. However, this is not completely uniform, both in the degree of the accent and its placement. For example, in song 122, the final note is just slightly accented. Equally important, this occurs only at the end of the repeated *b* section and not in either of the repeated *a* sections or the first *b* section. The slightly accented ending is reserved for the end of the entire verse. In other songs, for example, song 109 in example 46, a strong final accent is reserved for the last note of the last repeated section of the last repeat of the verse. It marks the end of the entire song performance.

The long penultimate note on *e-* of *ena* may sometimes take two types of melodic ornamentation. Song 138B uses both of them (ex. 48).

Example 48. Excerpts from song 138B

Melisma—setting more than one melody note per syllable of text—is used sparingly in individual Naraya songs and is all the more noticeable as a consequence. The first setting of *ena* in song 138B replaces the expected three beats on C with melismatic elaboration of it: C; B, the lower neighbor, which is sung more softly; return to C and the original dynamic level. The second setting of *ena* has pulsation on the penultimate long G. Pulsation on long notes is an important characteristic of Plains singing style. Singers crescendo and decrescendo in uniform rhythmic surges, without ever breaking the tone. One could compare it to the trill, an ornament in Euro-American traditions of classical music. Whereas pulsation alternates different levels of amplitude, trills alternate different pitches. In both cases, the long note receives articulation.[11]

Although my discussion of musical ending patterns has so far been in connection with *ena*, the common ending vocable, the same points apply even when there is no ending vocable. In song 19 (ex. 49), both the *a* and *b* sections end with tonic reiteration and the rhythmic pattern of long-short-rest.

Example 49. Excerpts of cadences of song 19

Song 38 ends the *b* sections with tonic reiteration, long-short-rest, and pulsation on the penultimate long note (ex. 50).

Example 50. Excerpt from song 38

Interrelationships between Different Musical Sections: Borrowings, Boundary Points, and Parallelisms

Much of the musical analysis thus far has focused on various types of contrasts that separate different sections of Naraya songs: their differing lengths, rhythms and rhythmic organization, melody types, and tessitura. Beyond these characteristics is the bevy of structural ending markers discussed above that signal and separate. I turn now to aspects of Naraya song form that do just the reverse; they integrate through compositional interrelationships, cutting across different sectional divisions. This is analogous to the interlinear relationship in the texts examined in the preceding chapter.

Fragments of the melody and rhythm used in section *a* appear commonly in section *b*. These borrowings may be brief or they may develop and elaborate in various ways. In song 126 (ex. 51), the key melodic notes at the end of section *a* (F, C, A) form the middle part of section *b*; this is unusual only in the placement of the borrowing.

Example 51. Excerpts from song 126

Much more characteristically, melodic material from the end of section *a* appears at the beginning of section *b*, which is the case in song 147 (ex. 52).

Example 52. Excerpts from song 147

Notice the repetition of each of the two fragments—symmetrical pairing at the smallest level within section *b.*

This repetition of fragments also occurs in songs 62 and 49. In these examples (ex. 53), the borrowed repeated fragments are varied slightly from their original presentation in section *a.* The melismatic figure in section *b* of song 62 begins one step higher than in *a;* even eighth notes become a dotted-eighth and sixteenth note in song 49.

Example 53. Excerpts from songs 62 and 49

In song 92 (ex. 54), section *b* omits the beginning one-fifth of section *a* and reduces the remaining four-fifths down to its melodic essence—ACA—in four beats.

Example 54. Excerpts from song 92

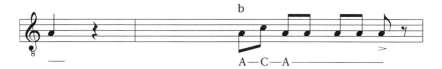

In other examples, such as song 125 (ex. 55), section *b* greatly expands its loan portion from section *a*.

Example 55. Excerpts from song 125

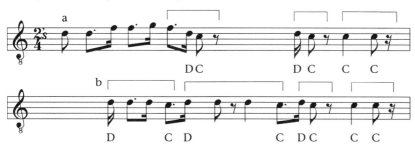

Song 111 is yet another example in which the melodic movement in the second half of section *a* (C to A), expands and becomes the melodic basis for all of section *b* (ex. 56). In addition, rhythmic patterns of section *b* are the same as those used in the first half of section *a*.

Example 56. Excerpts from song 111

In song 20 (ex. 57), sections *b*, *c*, and *d* derive from the melodic movement and dotted rhythms in the second part of section *a*. Set to new texts, they are expanded variants of the fragment.

Example 57. Excerpts from song 20

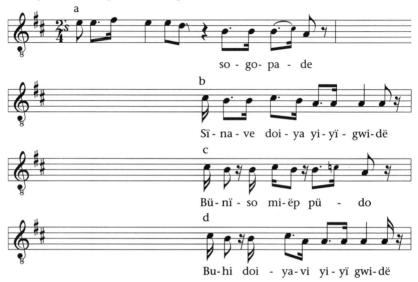

The prevalent pattern of borrowing melodic material from the end of the *a* section and reusing it in the *b* section has an impact on one's perception of Naraya form. It invites connecting the musical sections in a variety of ways that goes against the grain of its own clearly marked and separate sections. At issue is the question of musical boundaries, which I wish to consider at both the broader level and, subsequently, the narrower—the actual boundary point.

If one disregards the text in song 70 and looks at and listens to the music (ex. 58), the connection between the last half of section *a* and the beginning of section *b* is compelling. Instead of analyzing the form as *a, b¹, b²* (given above the staff in the example), one could argue another hypothesis: that its form is *a, b¹, b², b³* (given below the staff).

Example 58. Song 70, two analyses

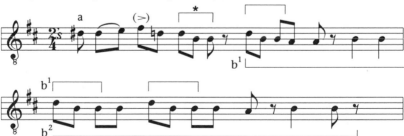

From this second vantage, one might further judge the connection between sections *b¹* and *b²* to be the closest on two counts. First, both begin with movement from D to B, rather than C-sharp to B as in *b³*, and second, there is no rest or break between them. This contrasts with the placement of rests at the end of *a, b²,* and *b³*.

There is one final point to be made regarding boundary points in the song. For this I return to the original and I believe correct analysis of the song, *a, b¹, b²,* which does take into account the text. Notice that notes D, B, B, which begin the second half of section *a* and the beginning and middle of *b¹* (bracketed in the example), first appear at the end of the first half of section *a* (marked with an asterisk in the example). There is a sense of development in the song, beginning with the germ idea at the cadence of the first half of section *a,* expanded in the second half, expanded further in section *b¹,* and varied in section *b²* by substituting C-sharp for D.

The practice of using the second half of section *a* as the first half of section *b* often has this result: the most similar, if not identical, portions of melody in the song sit side-by-side, although on opposite sides of the sectional fence. The second half of *b* may repeat the first half, but it often undergoes minor changes so that there is not the same correspondence between the two halves nor between the end and beginning of the two *b* sections. Given the pattern of repeated sections, the point of correspondence between the second *a* and the first *b* sections falls someplace near the middle of the song. Songs 87 and 93 exemplify these points (ex. 59).

Example 59. Songs 87 and 93

a. Song 87

e - na

Example 59. Song 87, continued.

b. Song 93

Text adds another element, which may combine with musical characteristics to obscure sectional boundaries. In song 144 (ex. 60), the first half of section *b* appropriates both melody and text from the second half of *a*.

Example 60. Excerpts from song 144

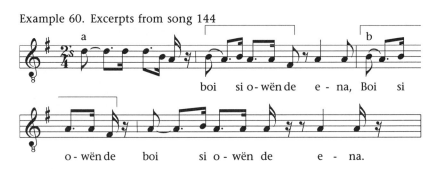

boi si o-wën de   e - na, Boi   si

o - wën de   boi   si o - wën de   e - na.

So far I have suggested the importance of borrowings and the special relationships between sections *a* and *b* in the interior of Naraya songs that influence one's perception of their form. I narrow my focus further to the boundary point, the one or two notes that appear on either side of the sectional divide. Here, too, at this minilevel, aspects of melody, rhythm, and tonality work in concert and influence the grouping of sections within a song. These are essential refinements if one is to move beyond the correct but oversimplistic representation of Naraya and Ghost Dance song form—*a,a,b,b*—which on the surface seems separate, equal, and neatly balanced, to the dynamics of these parts that lie beneath and shift the surface in uneven and irregular ways.

Endings become beginnings. The cadential notes for section *a* in songs 67, 108, and 81 (ex. 61) are the beginnings notes of section *b*.

Example 61. Excerpts from songs 67, 108, and 81

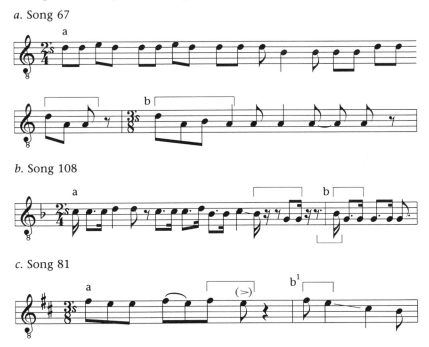

a. Song 67

b. Song 108

c. Song 81

In song 99 (ex. 62), the melodic beginnings and endings along with rhythmic and tonal factors make for a complex relationship between its four sections. The beginning of section *b*¹ adds an additional A to the final two notes of section *a*. These three notes (CAA) and their melismatic text-setting also serve as the ending of the section on the vocable, *ena*. Therefore, at the boundary between sections b^1 and b^2, the identical beginning and ending come back-to-back, and there is no rest between them. Sections b^1 and b^2 seem to meld into one large section of 42 beats. Notice the cadence of section b^2. It does not end with the CAA figure of b^1, nor even on tonic A. Abbreviated, it ends on C, setting it apart from section b^1 and both the *a* sections. The two-beat rest after the last note of b^2 clearly separates it from the beginning of section *a*. However, the choice of C as cadence note moves the melody higher (the single ascending cadence in the song) and facilitates a smooth transition to D, the opening note of section *a*.

Example 62. Song 99

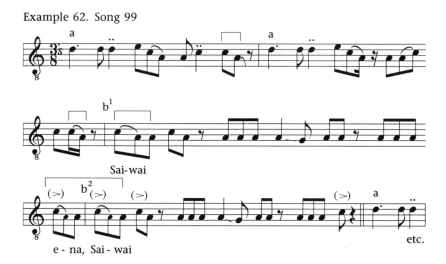

Earlier in this chapter I mentioned the common rhythmic practice of beginning a section on the last half of the beat from the previous section. This occurs in song 108, given above (ex. 61) (bracketed below the staff) and is particularly striking in song 64 (ex. 63), which starts on a syncopated and accented F. This makes for a tight connection between sections.

Example 63. Excerpts from song 64

The absence of rests, which one normally gets and comes to expect after the final note of a cadence, is another strategy that may confound perception of the boundary point. There is no silent space, no gap in sound. This may occur at cadences where the beat is not broken between sections, for example, in song 89 between b^1 and b^2 (ex. 64).

Example 64. Song 89

It may also occur in combination with a final beat that is divided over the boundary point. Melody streams through the boundary, making it less discernible. In song 34 (ex. 65), there are no rests between all of its sections and, with one exception, the final beat of one section concludes at the beginning of the next. Between the *a* and *b* sections, where there is no shared beat, a shared melody note abets the unbroken flow from *a* to *b*. E-flat, which ends section *a* on *ena*, continues across the boundary and begins the melody of section *b*.

Example 65. Song 34

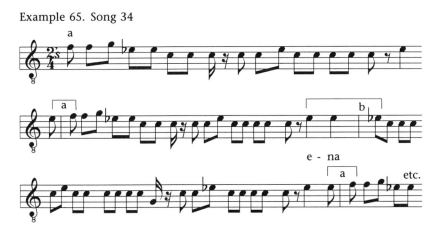

Like song 89, songs 36 (ex. 66) and 137 (ex. 67) combine melodic connectors at the boundary point with the absence of rests. Once again, their placement leads to a closer connection between the second *a* and first *b* sections. In song 36, the final A in section *a²* is the first note of *b¹*.

Example 66. Song 36

Song 137 is more complex. The melody notes of the second half of section *a²*, CEDC, are the basis for section *b* and repeat within it. From the standpoint of melody, the final C in *a²*, unbroken by a concluding rest, moves smoothly up to a D and the EDC pattern from section *a*. A rest separates the two repeated parts of section *b¹* and the boundary between *b¹* and *b²*.

Although there is no split of the final beat between a^2 and of b^1, there is a split in the larger rhythmic organization of the song. Song 137 moves in groups of three. The outer sections of the song—a^1 and b^2—complete this three-beat grouping at their cadence. The interior sections—a^2 and b^1—do not, which means that the first note of sections b^1 and b^2 begins on the third beat of the grouping.

Only the boundary point between a^2 and b^1 combines the lack of a cadential rest along with the melodic connector and over-boundary completion of the three-beat grouping.

Phrase finals and tonality present other opportunities for cross-sectional relationships. Earlier in the chapter, I have listed a variety of tonal patterns and their placement within Naraya song form, *a, a, b, b*. One of the patterns that cuts across sectional divisions is:

song form	a	a	b	b
finals	1	1	1	x.

This has already been discussed in examples 27 (song 71) and 28 (song 33). In these examples, the concluding nontonic final provides a smooth melodic transition back to the first note of the next song repetition.

A second pattern that cuts across sectional divisions adds yet another way in which interior sections *a* and *b* may enjoy a special relationship to one another. This is the case in song 90 (ex. 68).

a	a	b	b
1	VI	VI	1.

Example 68. Song 90

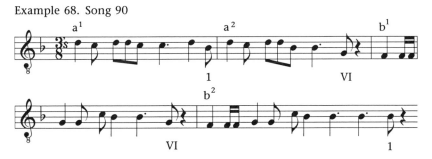

Song 18 uses a third pattern,

a	a	b	b
VI	VI	VI	1.

This is the opposite of that used in songs 71 and 33 yet similar in the smooth transition that links the last note (here, tonic C) of the final *b* section with the first note (D) of section *a*.

The reuse of the second half of section *a* as the first half of section *b* in song 18 is very striking (ex. 69). Texts are identical; with the exception of the lowered first two pitches, their melodies are the same. Cadence finals on VI are the same. The triple rhythmic organization is the same and contrasts sharply with the second half of section *b*, which is in duple rhythmic organization. The single place in the song where these two melodic subsections lie side-by-side is on either side of the division between the second *a* and first *b* sections.

Example 69. Song 18

Parallelism between the different sections of Naraya songs is another type of relationship that links them. I use this term in three senses, or orientations: horizontal comparison of melodic contour, vertical comparison of structural points (beginnings and endings), and comparison of the musical settings of identical texts. They may and do intersect.

I have already touched on horizontal parallelism in my earlier discussion of the use of melodic transpositions to lower levels. (See examples 33–35.) I now wish to elaborate this point, both musically and in combination with text. The use of parallel melodies for identical texts creates very close connections between sections. The melody of section *b* in song 119 (ex. 70) begins with a slight variant of the beginning of section *a* and then drops down to the next lower level. The lower transposition basically follows the same contour as in section *a*; however, as described earlier in example 34, constraints of available pitch material in the song result in some different intervals in the transposed version.

Example 70. Song 119

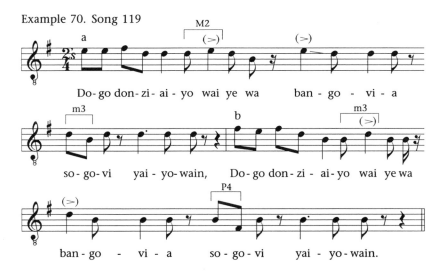

Sections *a, b,* and *c* of song 88 (ex. 71) share the same text. Their melodies form a staircase. Section *a* is the model for progressively lower transpositions in *b* and *c*.[12]

Example 71. Excerpts from song 88

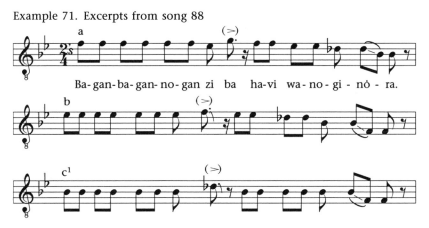

In every example given so far, the transposed melody is lower than the original one it parallels. This is the rule for which song 73 (ex. 72) is the exception.

Example 72. Excerpts from song 73

Example 72, continued

In song 38 (ex. 73), the basis for parallels between sections *a* and *b* is not melodic contour but text and rhythm, which are identical.

Example 73. Excerpts from song 38

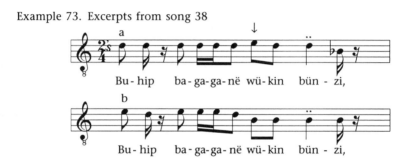

I move now from horizontal to vertical parallelism, specifically, parallel beginnings. The rhythm and melody of the first three notes in sections *a* and *b* of song 78 (ex. 74) are identical. Their texts, *Damën da-* and *Dewanga*, are interesting examples of assonance, pairing one word and a half (*da-*, from *dave*) with a second complete word.

Example 74. Excerpts from song 78

In song 28 (ex. 75), the first two words in sections *a* and *b* and their musical setting are identical.

Example 75. Excerpt from song 28

The parallel beginning of the same first two words in sections *a* and *b* of song 43 (ex. 76) is also parallel horizontally in its transposed musical setting.

Example 76. Excerpts from song 43

The vertical and horizontal parallels in song 94 (ex. 77) extend deeper into the first half of the *a* and *b* sections.

Example 77. Excerpt from song 94

Parallel endings of song sections should come as no surprise. I have already discussed the formulaic vocable ending, *ena*, and conventions for its musical setting. But parallel endings take many forms that go beyond *ena*. Even *ena* and its musical setting are not immune to variation and unexpected parallels. For example, the four endings in song 23 (ex. 78) present two different musical and textual forms of *ena* and two different phrase finals. The parallel endings fall between outer sections a^1 and b^2, which frame the paralleled inner endings of a^2 and b^1.

Example 78. Ending excerpts from song 23

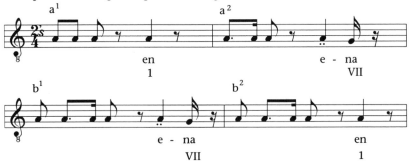

In song 128 (ex. 79), the transformation of *ena* to *he yan* at the cadence of section *a* is paralleled at the cadence of section *b*. Its musical setting is also identical, using the conventional ending for *ena*.

Example 79. Ending excerpt from song 128

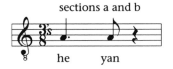

The vocable ending in song 29 (ex. 80), *madzo,* is unique to Emily and Dorothy's Naraya repertoire. According to Emily, it was idiosyncratic in the songs and singing of one old man. Like *ena*, it has its own musical setting, creating a parallel ending for sections *a* and *b*.

Example 80. Song 29

In place of vocable endings and their musical conventions, some songs (ex. 81) achieve parallel endings by using the same final word and musical setting of it in both sections.

Example 81. Excerpts from songs 35, 25, and 80

a. Song 35

b. Song 25

c. Song 80

In some examples, the correspondence of parallel ending text and music enlarges, moving back to the last two words of text (ex. 82).

Example 82. Excerpts from songs 57 and 47

a. Song 57

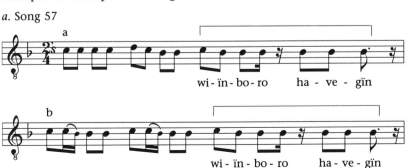

Example 82, continued. Excerpts from song 47

Finally, in song 34 (ex. 83), the entire second half of section *a* is also the second half of section *b*. Because section *b* does not repeat, the anticipated parallel symmetry of two sections with identical second halves is foiled. Instead of xy, xy, zy, zy, there is xy, xy, zy. ("X" represents the first half of section *a*, "z" the first half of section *b*, and "y" the second half of both *a* and *b*.)

Example 83. Song 34

Some Naraya songs parallel both beginnings and endings in their *a* and *b* sections. Textually, the beginning of section *a* in song 95 (ex. 84) is identical to that of section *b*, and its musical setting is similar. The musical cadence of both sections is almost identical; however, their texts differ.

Example 84. Excerpts from song 95

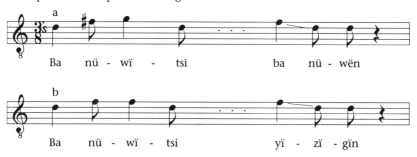

Song 65 (ex. 85) is rife with parallel beginnings and endings, as both sections are, in turn, made of repeated subsections. The beginning and ending of both sections parallel one another in several ways.

Example 85. Excerpts from song 65

The texts, *wazi . . . tiwaizi,* which, respectively, begin and end every section and subsection, are identical. Their rhythmic settings are identical. Musical parallelisms, while predominant, are not invariant. For example, while the musical settings for the beginning and ending of every section are identical, comparison of the interior cadence on *tiwaizi* and interior beginning on *wazi* (broken curved line in the example) reveals transposition in section *b* to a lower level.

Comparison of the two halves of section *a* reveals another relationship, one that reverses beginnings and endings and turns them upside down. The second subsection begins *wazi* by reusing the last two notes of the preceding cadence, FD. The final cadence of the entire section on repeated C hearkens back to DC, the opening notes of the section. In its melodic contour, the two halves of section *a* parallel one another, but in mirror image.

In songs 115 and 39 (ex. 86), parallel beginnings and endings expand to encompass most of the two sections. Vertical parallels, textual parallels, and horizontal parallels of melodic transposition (bracketed in the example) come together in different ways.

Example 86. Excerpts from songs 115 and 39

a. Song 115

b. Song 39

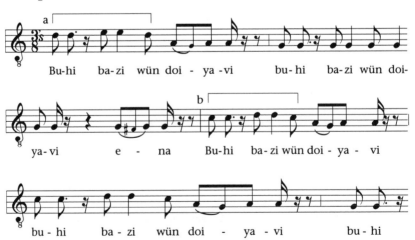

ba-zi wün doi - ya-vi   e - na

I end this discussion with an important textual parallel on the word for earth, *sogovi,* in song 26 (ex. 87). Old earth and new earth are contrasted in both lines of text and the placement of the word falls at neither the beginning nor the end of the lines. The identical musical setting for "earth," the sole parallel between the two sections, draws attention to this key textual image.

Example 87. Excerpts from song 26

so - go - vi

so - go - vi

Variation: Repetition in Performance

Repetition is an essential characteristic of Naraya song form, both within the basic verse and between different verses. In its performance, inexact, Naraya repetition embraces a range of many small substitutions of pitch and rhythm.[13] At one end of this spectrum are variations that come and go—acceptable play within narrow limits. At the other end are codified variations that are predictable and that return with every repetition.

I begin with an excerpt of song 122 (ex. 88), in which variation occurs within the verse itself. For example, in the repeat of section *a,* DC replaces CC. The substitution of a neighboring tone is perhaps the most common type of pitch variant in Naraya songs.

Example 88. Excerpts from song 122

Example 88, continued.

Variations between repetitions of the verse are of the same magnitude. The first part of song 84 (ex. 89) gives the opening two notes of section a^1, song 84, which are varied in a few of its verse repetitions. The most common form is EE, but occasionally it appears as DE, or even CE. The second part of example 89 gives two forms of the cadence for section a^2 from the same song. The first is the more common ending. The second leads smoothly into section b^1 by anticipating its first note, G.

Example 89. Excerpts from song 84

So far the comparisons have been between repetitions of the same performance. Not surprisingly, variation appears between different performances of the same song, for example, songs 138A and 138B (ex. 90).[14]

Example 90. Excerpts from songs 138A and 138B (in appendix B)

a. Song 138A

b. Song 138B

The significant difference in tempo between the two performances strongly affected my perception and transcription of their rhythmic organization. Notice the different melismatic ornamentation of *ena*. Consistent throughout their separate performances, they are variant forms of one another.

Codified variation, which appears in every repetition, may be within a section, for example, between repeated subsections in song 27 (ex. 91).

Example 91. Excerpts from song 27

Such variation commonly occurs in repeated sections of a verse. Song 104 (ex. 92) has three variant *b* sections.

Example 92. Excerpts from song 104

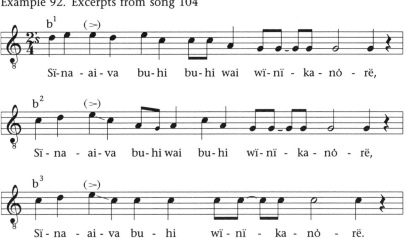

It is easy to understand how singers learn codified variations and can sing them in unison. But what of the sprinklings of spontaneous, uncodified variations during a performance? I remind the reader of Emily's comments given earlier, prompted by the two of us listening to recorded performances by her and Dorothy. She pointedly stated which of them served as song leader, the one who started the song off and in a strong voice shaped the performance. In the two different performances of song 138 given above (example 90), Dorothy was the leader of 138A and Emily of 138B. The different tempos and varied melismas on *ena* followed the preferences of each woman as song leader.[15]

Emily gave me clues as to how this worked in the past at actual communal performances of the Naraya. The Naraya sponsor was generally also a song leader. Others served as song leaders as well. But given the spatial dimension of the dance, with many dancers in a large circle singing the songs, it is hard to guess the dynamics of the performance. It is impossible to know to what degree the singing was in unison and to what degree song repetition contained irregular variation, such as I find in Emily and Dorothy's performances.[16]

There is one final point that needs to be made explicit regarding variation and song performance. Although I have chosen to transcribe just one verse of each song, this does not mean that it is the one and only true verse in the sense of its being a model against which all others are seen as variants. All the verses of a performance with all their slight variations are equally authentic. Were there world enough and time I would include complete transcriptions for all the repetitions in every song.[17]

Dynamics

Working hand in hand with variation are other aspects of performance that enliven it. Differing levels of sound that play a role in vocal attack and decay as well as pulsation are all important parts of Naraya performance.

Basic to these is the vocal quality of the singing style. As context for comparison, I quote Bruno Nettl's characterization of Great Basin–Ghost Dance singing style, which he contrasts with that of the Plains: "The vocal technique of the Paiute and Ghost Dance songs is generally free of pulsation and vocal tension and is roughly comparable to that used in most Western European folk music. This is true even in those Ghost Dance songs which are performed by tribes whose general style of singing contains pulsation and vocal tension, such as those of the Plains" (Nettl 1954:17).

Wind River Shoshones, with long residence on the Plains and full participation in Plains musical life, sing War Dance, Round Dance, and Sun Dance songs with vocal tension and prominent pulsation. Emily and Dorothy sing Naraya songs with some degree of vocal tension—certainly not as much as in their performance of Sun Dance songs, but neither in as relaxed a fashion as Nettl ascribes to Great Basin and Ghost Dance singing style. One can hear Emily and Dorothy's performance of four Naraya songs on the tape that accompanies these song transcriptions and translations in *Songprints* (Vander 1988). Hearing this tape it is possible to compare the vocal quality of the Naraya performances with that of War Dance song performances by Helene Oldman and Lenore Shoyo, which exemplify Plains singing style. One can also compare Emily's solo performances of Naraya song 5 with that of her performance of a Wolf Dance song and two Women's Dance songs, which are older versions of War Dance and Round Dance songs. Shimkin, who heard and recorded Naraya songs in 1937, described them as being "sung slowly in a high-pitched, and nasal voice" (Shimkin 1947c:350).[18]

Changes in dynamic levels must be understood against a general background of sound in Emily and Dorothy's Naraya performance. They sing these songs in a robust mezzoforte. In a few instances where song recall is a bit tentative during the first few verses, the dynamic level is commensurately softer. However, once the singers are secure and settled into the song, the dynamic level moves up to mezzoforte and remains there throughout the rest of the performance.

Accented vocal attacks and portamento stand out against this constant dynamic background, exemplified in song 122 (ex. 93).

Example 93. Excerpts from song 122

e - na

Accents in final position (the last syllable of *ena* in this example) are by far the most common and I have already discussed their function as ending markers. Beyond these, there are relatively few other types of accents in Emily and Dorothy's Naraya performances. Here and there one finds accents on high notes, such as occur on E and D in section *a* of song 122. This is also true in songs 32, 88, and 117.

Portamento release of notes is not unusual. It occurs between notes, the dynamic level lowering during the swift glide down from C to A shown in example 93. Notes with portamento release may also be followed by rests, for example, after C in the same example. In this case, the voice fades into silence while gliding down to an indeterminate lower pitch. This is the norm for the final notes that end large sections of such other song genres as War Dance and Sun Dance songs. Only a few rare Naraya sections use this conventional ending pattern, for instance, the final notes of section *a* in song 127 (ex. 94). Let me reiterate that the abrupt cut-off of the final note in Naraya songs is the norm and uniquely so within the Shoshone song repertoire.

Example 94. Excerpt from song 127

An opposite type of portamento, which moves into rather than out of a note, appears in song 135A. The first note of section *b* is approached from an indeterminate higher pitch and elevated dynamic level and then quickly fades as it glides down into the note. This type of attack indicates a phrase beginning in War Dance and Sun Dance songs (Vander 1988:42). Conspicuously absent in Naraya songs, it is interesting to see a rare carryover of this usage in an excerpt from song 135A (ex. 95).

Example 95. Excerpt from song 135A

Another rare form of portamento appears in songs 71 and 135B (ex. 96): the release of a note fades as it glides up to an indeterminate higher pitch.

Example 96. Excerpts from songs 71 and 135B

a. Song 71

b. Song 135B

Pulsation, the rhythmic alternation of crescendos and decrescendos on an unbroken tone, has been briefly mentioned as a cadential ornament. It requires time and falls on relatively long notes. One finds it in association with a variety of ending situations—section, subsection, word—and in varying degrees of consistency. Sections *a* and *b* of song 43 (ex. 97) contain classic examples of cadential pulsation, which reappear when the section repeats.

Example 97. Excerpts from song 43

ga - zom - bi   wï - nï - ga - nȯ - rë

In songs 78 and 87 (ex. 98), pulsation occurs only in the repeat of the two *a* and *b* sections, respectively. In these examples, pulsation marks the larger sectional division of the songs and is at the same time, a source of variation between the two *a* and *b* sections.

Example 98. Excerpts from songs 78 and 87

a. Song 78   *b.* Song 87

In some examples, final syllables of words receive pulsation. In songs 115 and 99 (ex. 99), these words are not at the end of their section. The pulsation treatment in song 115 is identical between the repetitions; in song 99, it is not.

Example 99. Excerpts from songs 115 and 99

a. Song 115   *b.* Song 99

Text Setting

Naraya songs are primarily syllabic. Each syllable of a word or vocable is set to one melody note and in this process the spoken language undergoes transformation. There are two sources of the transformation and they are inextricably bound to one another. Poetic changes in ordinary spoken words discussed in chapter 8 join with musical rhythms, dynamics, and melodic contour. Spoken language and sung poetic language run on two tracks, sometimes together or parallel, sometimes diverging or leading in opposite directions.

Shimkin characterized the rhythmic patterns of stress in spoken Shoshone: "In general, the initial vowel of each verbal stem in a word is stressed, with secondary stresses on succeeding odd vowels" (Shimkin 1947c:338). For example, the stress pattern for the four-syllable word *duduwatsi* would be: *dú-dŭ-wá-tsĭ*.

In speech, Shoshone syllables receive stress either by being slightly louder or longer. Song elaborates these two variables and adds a third, melodic pitch. All else being equal, higher notes are more prominent than lower notes.

I caution the reader that what follows is a smattering of interesting examples of song-play with words, places where song accent differs from its spoken equivalent. I have not done a systematic comparison and statistical analysis between the two. This notwithstanding, my overall impression is that the majority of sung texts are compatible with their spoken forms. At the same time, there are also many examples of common and important Naraya words, such as "Our Father," "sun," "mountains," "aspen trees," and "earth," that receive uniquely sung patterns of stress.

Consider the setting of *Damë Apë,* "Our Father," in song 20 (ex. 100).

Example 100. Excerpts from song 20

Da - më   A - pë   Sï - na - ve
Ow - er   Fa-ther

The duration of the second syllable in each word is more than twice
that of the first, reversing the stress of its spoken form. If we change
the English translation from "Our Father" to "Ow-er Fá-ther," the
rhymed two-syllable words with accent on the first would parallel the
Shoshone text, *Dá-më Á-pë*. The musical rhythm of the text changes
its stress pattern to *Da-më A-pë*, "Ow-ér Fa-thér."

The rhythmic setting of *sïnave* (aspen tree), in part *b*, is another
example in which the rhythmic durations—short-long-short—reverse
the spoken pattern of stress. In this example, the appearance of a
third syllable, *-ve*, further distinguishes the sung from spoken language. The final vowel sound in *sïnavI* is not only unstressed in
speech, it is whispered. There are just two spoken syllables. Musical
rhythm extends the length of the word to three syllables by sounding the whispered ending.[19]

Note, too, the lowering of the final vowel from "i" to "e," a point
that agrees with Hinton's observation of this practice in Havasupai
sung language.

In song 125 (ex. 101), the reversal of spoken accent by musical
duration encompasses most of the text of section *a* ("Our sun setting").
In four alternations of short and long notes, stressed spoken syllables
are consistently set on shorter notes and unstressed syllables on longer notes. It is as if the spoken text were turned inside-out.[20]

Example 101. Excerpt from song 125

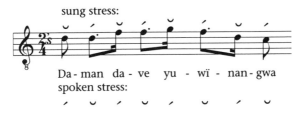

sung stress:

Da - man da - ve   yu - wï - nan - gwa
spoken stress:

In some songs—for example, song 19 (ex. 102)—one word (*damë*,
"our"), receives two different musical settings. In the first, the long-

short rhythm of the music coincides with the accents of the spoken form. In the second, the short-long rhythm does not.

Example 102. Excerpts from song 19

In song 73 (ex. 103), not only longer duration but movement to a higher pitch reinforces the musical importance of the second syllables in *doiya* (mountain) and *dave* (sun), which is at odds with the accent on the first syllables in their spoken form.[21]

Example 103. Excerpts from song 73

In another setting of *dave* (ex. 104), an accented attack on the second syllable coincides with the long of the short-long rhythm. Together they reinforce stress on the second syllable, which is at odds with the spoken form. In the *b* section of this same song, the accented, long, high note falls on the first syllable of *dosa*, "white." Here, musical and spoken stress converge. On the one hand are the similar musical settings of *dave* and *dosa* in different sections of the song, and on the other, their dissimilar relationship to spoken form. Counterparts or counterpoints, they define yet another kind of unequal balance in Naraya songs.

Example 104. Excerpts from song 78

In song 122 (ex. 105), the mix of accenting factors—high notes, longer notes, and accented notes—is not clearly apportioned to one note but divided between two. In such a mix, the factors tend to neutralize or cancel one another. In speech, the first syllables of *so-goph*, and *dave* receive the accent. In their musical settings, both move from a short to a long note, emphasizing the second syllable. At the same time, both begin the first syllable on a higher and accented note.

Example 105. Excerpts from song 122

Melisma is another way of altering spoken language. The importance of melismatic text-setting stems from its very selective usage in Naraya songs. It stands out from the syllabic context within any given song. Exceptional within a song, melisma is, at the same time, common in the repertoire. There are 83 songs with melisma. In a majority of these, melisma carries the syllable of text from one melody note to its lower neighbor (ex. 106).

Example 106. Excerpt from song 49

Often, the melody returns to the note from which the melisma began (ex. 107).

Example 107. Excerpt from song 48

Movement to upper neighbors in example 108 simply changes the direction of basically the same melismatic patterns.

Example 108. Excerpts from songs 54 and 124

a. Song 54   *b.* Song 124

ga - ra   roi - ya

The direction of the melisma may be a source of contrast within a song. In song 56 (ex. 109), the two melismas in section *a* contrast their direction and rhythmic placement, within the beat versus across the beat.

Example 109. Excerpt from song 56

si   bu- hi   pa- ro

In songs 111 and 103 (ex. 110), the contrast of melismatic directions is back-to-back.

Example 110. Excerpts from songs 111 and 103

a. Song 111   *b.* Song 103

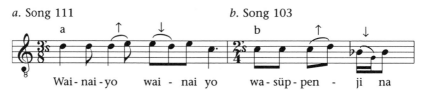

Wai - nai - yo   wai - nai yo   wa - süp - pen - ji na

Song 99 (ex. 111) uses contrasting melismatic directions several times in the repeat of section *a* and even continuing through the beginning of section *b*[1].

Example 111. Excerpts from song 99

na - ru   ban - zuk   na - ve   sai - wai

Naraya melisma takes two principal forms. First, it frequently anticipates the next melody note with new text (ex. 112).

Example 112. Excerpt from song 107

wi - chi

This sense of melodic anticipation is heightened when the "anticipating" melisma is sung considerably more softly than the "arrival" note, which frequently happens (ex. 113).

Example 113. Excerpts from songs 37, 57, and 109

a. Song 37   *b.* Song 57   *c.* Song 109

va - gï - na dïm - pi   Doi - ya   ru - ka   ha - vi   ye - na

In song 72 (ex. 114), there is even an extra and premature anticipation of the actual "anticipating" note and arrival note, on A.

Example 114. Excerpt from song 72

wü - mi - ha___ gwai - në

One of the most striking illustrations of soft, anticipating melisma appears twice in song 99 (ex. 115), back-to-back and across the sectional division. It was cited earlier for this reason.

Example 115. Excerpts from song 99

e - na   Sai - wai

A second type of melisma has already been introduced: one involving a lower neighbor tone, bracketed by its upper neighbor. In many songs, the melismatic lower neighbor is sung more softly than its syllabic upper neighbors. This change in dynamics draws attention to the melisma, to its decorative melodic function, and is an analog to the softer tone used in "anticipation" melisma, discussed above. Two examples of lower-neighbor melisma appear in songs 18 and 110 (ex. 116).

Example 116. Excerpts from songs 18 and 110

In song 114 (ex. 117), section *b* contains two examples of this type of melisma. They are settings for two different words, *hu-viara* and *hu-ku* that share the same first syllable, *hu-*. The melismatic settings, BG#B and DG#B, seem to parallel something of the similarity and dissimilarity of their texts.

Example 117. Excerpt from song 114

Song 128 (ex. 118) places three lower-neighbor melismas back-to back in section *a*, in contrast with section *b*, which has none.

Example 118. Excerpt from song 128

Also notice, in this same example, that the second melisma on *boi* is longer, as it extends throughout the three-beat grouping. Melismatic settings of *ena* in songs 22, 39, and 138B are further examples of melisma that lasts throughout a three-beat grouping.

In song 107 (ex. 119), the text in section *a* repeats two times. Each half ends with *wichi*. The melismatic setting of the same text is not the same, but rather contrasts where the melisma falls. This, in turn, creates a difference in where the word is accented.

Example 119. Excerpt from song 107

wi-chi   wi - chi

In the first setting, *-chi* takes the melisma and as a consequence is longer than *wi-*. This setting creates an agogic accent by virtue of the relatively longer duration on *-chi*. In the second setting, *wi-* takes the melisma and the agogic accent now falls on *wi-*.

Great Basin Musical Context

There were relatively few published transcriptions of Great Basin songs when Herzog wrote his 1935 study titled "Plains Ghost Dance and Great Basin Music." (He drew primarily on Densmore's Northern Ute study, Steward's transcriptions of a few Owens Valley Paiute songs, and Sapir's work with the Southern Paiute, both published and unpublished.) Vennum's 1986 transcriptions, which include one or two examples of different song genres from different parts of the Great Basin, are an important addition to the literature. The 1994 publication of 207 Southern Paiute songs that Edward Sapir recorded in 1910 adds a substantial new body of hitherto unpublished material. Sapir's father, Jacob Sapir, transcribed the music. He left behind no accompanying explanation about his transcription format nor any musical analysis of the songs. In the 1994 publication, Vennum has placed these transcriptions into the scholarly context of their time and brought out some of the technical problems concerning the recordings and the difficulties these posed for the transcriber (Sapir 1994:663–65). Other commentary by Franklin and Bunte in this same publication provides useful background information about the various song genres that are represented in this Southern Paiute repertoire. However, despite these significant gains, there still remains a paucity of in-depth studies and analyses of Great Basin music.[22]

Given this, Nettl's 1954 characterization of Great Basin musical style and Vennum's 1986 discussion of it do not differ significantly from Herzog's earlier observations. Vennum defined the style as including

> narrow melodic ranges, a relaxed vocal performance, undulating melodic contours with frequent returns to the tonic, a limited number of rhythmic values, and a tendency toward paired phrase structure. . . . Except for shamans' rattles and sticks beaten during hand games, musical instruments widely distributed elsewhere on the continent were either lacking in the Great Basin or comparatively late borrowings from adjacent peoples. . . . The old layer of Basin music is best represented by the Round Dance, the oldest and most widespread style in the Basin, known by many names, in which the performers' voices were the only regulators of dance steps. Songs for the Ghost Dance, the Uintah Ute Woman's Dance, the Washoe Girl's Puberty Dance, the Northern Paiute Hump Dance, and the Lemhi Northern Shoshone early spring *nuakkinna,* to name but a few, were all unaccompanied. (Vennum 1986: 682)

Vennum describes the musical characteristics of Handgame and Round Dance songs from the western Basin, all of which have correspondences in Naraya songs. For example, he mentions Handgame songs that use two or three phrases "that are related through repetitions of text and rhythmic motifs. But it is also common for half of each of two phrases to be identical, either in their beginnings or endings" (Vennum 1986:687). Analyzing specific examples of songs from the Washoe Girls Puberty Dance, Vennum notes their narrow range, brevity, many repetitions of the basic verse, undular motion, and syllabic text-setting. He adds: "Variety is achieved through several means: contraction . . , phrase B created from phrase A by omitting the second and third beats in its repetition; substitution of neighboring tone (or other pitches) at the end of a phrase . . . ; transposition . . . —phrase A repeated, is then essentially transposed to a lower level (phrase B) and repeated" (Vennum 1986:687–89).

Finally, Vennum cites Dellenbaugh's 1872 description of the Kaibab Southern Paiute Round Dance (quoted in chapter 1), which includes two Round Dance texts with paired phrases. He comments on the importance of this structure in the songs of the Ghost Dance, "the most famous of Basin Round Dances" (Vennum 1986:687).

I include below a small sampling of relevant Great Basin songs, for their comparative and contextual relationships to Naraya songs. My first examples are from Sapir's work. The following seven songs are all Southern Paiute with the exception of the first (ex. 120), which is identified as a Shoshone song (presumably, Western Shoshone). The singer was Tony Tillohash, a Kaibab Southern Paiute man.

Unfortunately, texts were not included with any of the musical transcriptions. The reader can find Edward Sapir's translations of the song texts in chapter 10, where they are compared with other Great Basin song texts. In order to facilitate locating these texts, I have assigned an identifying S-number to each, according to the order in which it appears in chapter 10. In the present chapter the S-number appears in parentheses after Sapir's original song number and title, for example, No. 200 Round Dance (S-4). I have added all the bracketed information on these transcriptions, for example, the formal analyses; this was not part of the original transcriptions.

Because it is my contention that the Northern Paiute Ghost Dance and the Naraya were rooted in Round Dance and shamanistic traditions, I begin with songs that were performed for these occasions. I then include two examples of what Sapir termed Southern Paiute Ghost Round Dance songs and two Ghost Dance songs.[23]

Example 120. No. 200 Round Dance Song (S-4)

Example 121. No. 76 Round Dance Song (S-3)

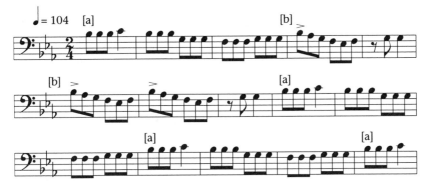

Example 122. No. 139 Medicine Song (S-34)

Example 123. No. 111 Ghost Round Dance Song (S-16)

Example 124. No. 110 Ghost Round Dance Song (S-14)

Example 125. No. 195 Ghost Dance Song (S-13)

Example 126. No. 192 Ghost Dance Song (S-20)

Certainly from a musical standpoint, the seven songs share a similar style and it would be difficult to distinguish among the genres based solely on the music. They are all made of pairings. In examples 122, 123, and 126, there are some differences between the two sections that comprise their repeated or paired progressions, but they are still relatively small and subtle and I therefore label them a^1 and a^2. Finally, in examples 120 and 121, there is greater contrast between the two repeated phrases and thus their labels, *a* and *b*.

Not only are the songs made of paired phrases or paired progressions; this propensity for pairing exists even within a section. It exists, for example, in the two halves within sections a^1 and a^2 of example 126, or in the two slightly unequal lengths but very similar halves of the *b* section in example 121 and the *a* section of example 125.

Small differences at the cadence point are similar to those described in Naraya songs. For example, the cadence of b^2 of example 120, unlike that of b^1, does not end on tonic C but rather on E, serving as a melodic connector to the next repetition of the song, which starts on G.

As in Naraya songs, rests clearly demarcate form: the *a* sections in example 125. The effect is striking in example 124, the rests cleanly and clearly separating each phrase. The final two notes and very short rest—(𝅘𝅥𝅮 𝄾)—abruptly break the flow of the melody and its repeated dotted rhythms.

The syncopated rhythm at the beginning of the Medicine Song, example 122 (𝅘𝅥𝅮𝅘𝅥𝅘𝅥𝅮), has been discussed earlier in connection with Naraya songs and other Great Basin examples. This rhythm is varied in a^2 where it becomes 𝅘𝅥𝅮𝅘𝅥𝅘𝅥𝅮.

Variation is everywhere apparent in these examples, and in varying degrees. This brings me back to my earlier comments on form and its frequent creation through small yet ordered and consistent variations.

Finally, one finds all the irregularities and asymmetries of Naraya songs in these examples. For instance, in example 121 the first *a* section in the song does not repeat as one would expect; and there is an "extra" fourth beat in the first measure of the repeat of section *a* in example 120.

Steward's 1933 study of the Owens Valley Paiute, a Northern Paiute group, includes several musical transcriptions.[24] Again I select those that seem most relevant for comparison with the Naraya, two songs concerned with health and two Circle Dance, or Round Dance, songs. Steward's original numbers for the songs appear in parentheses before each title.

Example 127. (1) Doctor's Song

"Recorded by E.L., who learned it from a Shoshoni doctor near Darwin (probably a Panamint) who cured his [E.L.'s] brother. This introductory part has no words [i.e., it is an all-vocable text]" (Steward 1933:278–79).

Example 128. (2) Bad Dream Song

Hi no i hi hi ya   ho yo   yu i na   ta yo ka tso tsi

Hi no i hi hi ya   ho yo   yu i na   ta yo ka tso tsi

"Recorded by B.M. Sung to remove the spell from persons who have dreamed 'evil'" (Steward 1933:279).

Example 129. (16) Circle Dance Song

ya di dô po ya na   ya di dô po ya na   ya di dô po ya na

ya da mi' i ya da   ya di dô po ya na   ya di dô po ya na

variant:

ya da mi'i ya da mi

"Recorded by H.T. and J. McB.... As recorded, [line] I was repeated 6 times, then [line] II 6 times, when the following variation [given in parenthesis in the example] was introduced in the second measure of [line] II. The words were translated: 'Our horse is dying'" (Steward 1933:283).

Example 130. (15) Circle Dance Song

"Recorded by T.S." (Steward 1933:283).

Every one of these four songs is made of repeated phrases, although not exactly so in every case. For example, the Doctor's Song has very similar repeated musical phrases, however, the vocable text for each line is different. In the Bad Dream Song, the repeat of the first phrase substitutes three upper-neighbor notes for those used in the first presentation—a small variation such as is so common in Naraya songs.

Even the obvious pairings in the first Circle Dance Song, example 129, have their slight and subtle variants. In the first line there is a difference between the form of the text and the music: the text repeats itself, the music is through-composed. The second line creates a longer line than the first by adding another pairing. The first half of line II repeats the music of the first line; however, the text for the second measure is new. The second half of line II repeats line I exactly. Steward tells us that for the final repeat of line II, the second measure was slightly varied once more, this time musically as well as textually.

The second Circle Dance Song, given in example 130, is much further along the variation continuum than the other examples. Still, I argue that once again the form is made of two repeated parts. After studying the text and the music, I believe that the original transcription given in example 130 obscures the form of the song.[25] I have, therefore, reformatted the transcription in example 131, changing no notes or rhythms but only the alignment of its sections on the page.

Example 131. Reformatted transcription of example 130

In this form, the musical pairings and variants in them, both important aspects of Great Basin musical style, can be seen. Textually and musically, the song has two paired sections. Although particular rhythms do vary in the repeat of both musical phrases, it is interesting to see that the number of beats allotted to each syllable of text remains constant. There is some melodic variation in the repeat of both phrases: the melody arrives sooner on tonic A, and reiterates it. This is more pronounced in section *b*², but not enough to override the perception of a pair of repeated phrases.

Example 132 is Vennum's transcription of a song performed by Dick Mahwee, which T. T. Waterman recorded in 1910 (Vennum 1986:704). As in so many Naraya songs, both sections *a* and *b* are subdivided into paired halves. Cadences on *hena* (and its abbreviated form, *he*) and its rhythmic setting—long-short-rest—are Northern Paiute equivalents to Naraya cadences on *ena*. I have bracketed them in the example.

Example 132. Northern Paiute Ghost Dance Song

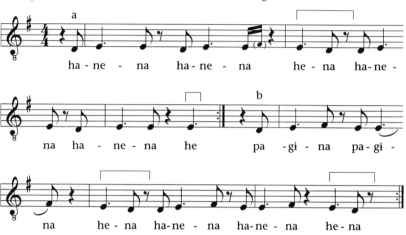

ha - ne - na   ha - ne - na   he - na   ha - ne -

na   ha - ne - na   he   pa - gɨ - na   pa - gɨ -

na   he - na   ha - ne - na   ha - ne - na   he - na

Like Naraya songs, this song has irregular features within a repetitive regular frame. Section *a* repeats, as one would expect; section *b* does not. Notice the text, too, regarding the boundary division between sections. The return to *a* from *b* is partially obscured by the foreshadowing of the *a* text, which appears with the music in the second half of *b*.

Rests in this song are an important element in the melody they punctuate. They have the same impact on the text analyzed earlier in regard to Naraya texts. Rests divide the text into its constituent parts. *Pagina*, "fog," is the Northern Paiute form of *vagina* in Shoshone. The text of section *b* reads, *pagina* (ɀ) *pagina* (ɀ) *hena* (ɀ). The rest of the text in section *b* and all of section *a* (all vocables?) is similarly broken into small bits. Mooney is perhaps referring to this quality, this frequent use of rests, when writing of his own aesthetic response to Great Basin versus Plains Ghost Dance songs. He commented, "The Paiute ghost songs have a monotonous halting movement that renders them displeasing to the ear of a white man, and are inferior in expression to those of the Arapaho and the Sioux" (Mooney [1896] 1991:1050).

Example 133 is Vennum's transcription of a recording of Zurick Buck made by Sven Liljeblad in 1943 (Vennum 1986:703–4). As a

Northern Shoshone song from Idaho, its origins are geographically closer to the Wind River Shoshone Reservation than the Northern Paiute song given in example 132 and its recording date places it closer in time to Emily and Dorothy's experience of the Naraya as young women.

Example 133. Northern Shoshone Ghost Dance Song

The song has two repeated sections, and section *b*, itself, contains two repeated sections. As is the case in most Naraya songs, sections *a* and *b* are of unequal lengths. The last three bracketed notes—DBA—at the cadence of the second *a* section, become the melodic basis for the two parts of the *b* section. Phrase finals for the two *a* and *b* sections, VI, V, V, 1, connect the interior *a* and *b* sections, which both cadence on V. These characteristics and relationships between parts should all be familiar echoes from earlier discussion of Naraya musical style.

Example 134 is my transcription of a recording made by Sven Liljeblad in 1949 of Archer Nappo, a Bannock singer.[26] Northern Shoshones and Bannocks have lived together in Idaho for centuries and with little distinction between their cultures other than linguistic: Bannocks are Northern Paiute speakers. The text of example 134 is, in fact, Shoshone.

Example 134. Northern Shoshone Ghost Dance Song

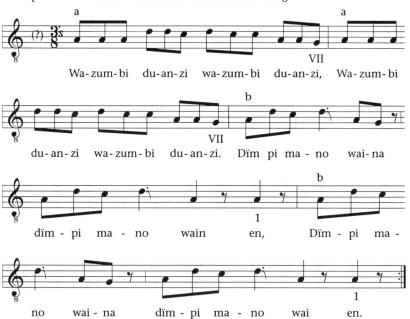

Musically and textually, this song is indistinguishable from the Naraya songs in Emily and Dorothy's repertoire. The fit is perfect. Its imagery—young game animals in a rocky mountain setting—are classic Naraya images. (See chapter 10 for the complete translation of this song.) The ending vocable *en*, a shortened form of *ena*, concludes both *b* sections. The song has two repeated sections, *aabb*; section *b* subdivides into two repeated parts. Sections *a* and *b* are of unequal lengths: twelve and twenty-one beats respectively. Section *a* cadences on VII, section *b* on 1.

Before leaving Great Basin music as context for the Naraya, I wish to spread my net most widely to include observations that Edward Sapir made on a very different genre, song recitatives in Southern Paiute mythology (Sapir 1910). Surprisingly—or not—there are correspondences between them and Naraya songs.

Edward Sapir was a meticulous transcriber and noted the minute variations that cropped up in the repetition of the song recitatives.[27] In some cases it was melodic, for example, EFG becoming EGG; in others, rhythmic, the insertion of a fourth beat where there had always been three (Sapir 1910:467). Sapir was also aware of the limits of using Western notation, the fractional division of time that did not always accurately represent the irregular rhythms he heard in the recitatives. He explained that "the eight pause of the last measure is accelerated, so that the measure does not receive the full value of four beats" and that "the pauses at the end of each section . . . are somewhat irregular in length. They are frequently a trifle too long to be metrically correct" (Sapir 1910:466, 460).

Other specific comments about a given recitative—for example, Badger-Chief's—also have relevance to Naraya songs. Sapir wrote, "Rhythmically it is characterized by the syncopation of the second beat and the decided staccato of the last note, to which corresponds the aspiration of the final vowel in the text" (Sapir 1910:461). Naraya songs use this same form of syncopation, excerpted in examples 12–14. Whether the staccato release at the end of *ena* is also rooted in language remains for me an intriguing unknown.

Finally, I quote from Sapir's musical summary of what he found in the song recitatives.

> From the musical point of view, perhaps the most remarkable fact to be noted in regard to these recitatives is the variety of rhythms employed. Out of only eleven examples obtained, no less that five meters can be illustrated—4/4 (Nos. 4, 6, 7, and 9), 2/4 (No. 11), 3/4 (No. 8), 5/4 (Nos. 2, 3, 5, and 10), and 11/4 (No. 1); the relative frequency of quintuple time, and the occurrence of an eleven-beat melodic unit, being particularly noteworthy. As regards musical form, the recitatives fall into two types—those whose period or largest melodic unit is not subdivided into sections (Nos. 2 and 3), and those whose period is built up of two balancing sections (Nos. 1, 4, 5, 6, 7, 8, 9, and 10). In every case but one (No. 6) these sections are of equal length, and in five cases (Nos. 1, 4, 5, 6, 7) the second section repeats material already made use of in the first. (Sapir 1910:470–71)

Plains Musical Style and Influence on Naraya Songs

Last and least, some Naraya songs do reveal the influence of Plains music on their musical style. In order to bring out these points, I briefly characterize Plains musical style, using the War Dance song as its prototype. Traditionally, male singers perform War Dance Songs around a large drum that lays flat on the ground, beating their own rhythmic accompaniment on it as they sing.[28] The vocal quality of War Dance songs is penetrating, tense, and nasal. Pulsation, the rhythmic surges of tone on long notes, is prominent. I have already discussed the influence of Plains vocal quality in connection with Emily and Dorothy's performance of Naraya songs, and the selective use of pulsation, principally at the cadence of Naraya songs.

Beyond these aspects of performance are properties of the song itself—range, contour, and form—which contrast sharply with Naraya and other Great Basin songs. War Dance songs encompass a large range, at least an octave and often more: for example, an eleventh in War Dance Song No. 10 and a twelfth in War Dance Song No. 18 (Vander 1988:227–28, 250–51). Songs begin high and end low. Nettl writes that "each phrase descends, and each begins somewhat lower than the previous one. Toward the end of a song the phrases do not usually descend as much as at the beginning, but they tend to flatten out, as it were, the last phrase lingering on the final lowest pitch for several notes. Frequently all of these descending phrases have the same, or similar, melodic contours, and may be simply transpositions of the initial phrase. This type of melodic movement as a whole is called the 'terrace-type' because of its visual resemblance to terraces in its graphic expression" (Nettl 1954:24–25). War Dance songs begin with a solo by the lead singer on the highest phrase of the song (*a*), which the rest of the singers immediately repeat (*a¹*). The song then continues its descent through subsequently lower and lower phrases, or "terraces," as described by Nettl. It is a two-part form, the second section being an incomplete repetition of the first, as it omits the open solo call and repeated response by the rest of the singers. In general, the War Dance song is also a larger or longer form than the typical Naraya song.

War Dance Song No. 18, given in example 135, is a typical War Dance song. One can hear it performed by the Big Mountain Singers (a Wind River Shoshone all-female drum group) on the tape that accompanies *Songprints: The Musical Experience of Five Shoshone Women* (Vander 1988).[29]

Example 135. War Dance Song No. 18

The melodic contour of several Naraya songs corresponds to that given in the above brief characterization and example of Plains War Dance songs. Song 98, still made of repeated sections, starts section *a* on the highest note in the song (ex. 136). The melody descends onto successively lower "terraces," from G to D in section *a* and from D to B in section *b*^{1}.

Example 136. Excerpts from song 98; the upper staff reduces the melody to its key melodic notes.

In songs 85 and 96, given in examples 137 and 138, respectively, the descending terraced contour occurs within section *a*. It ends with reiteration of the tonic, which corresponds to the "final flattening" Nettl mentioned in his description of Plains melodic contour. However, in all other regards, these two songs follow Naraya song style. Both sections *a* and *b* repeat; the melodic contour of the *b* sections undulates within a narrow range of a third.

Example 137. Song 85

Example 138. Song 96

Notice that in song 96 both sections *a* and *b* subdivide into three units, the final one being a reiteration of the tonic note.

Song 88 (ex. 139), moves further from the classic Naraya mold: sections *a* and *b* do not repeat, the two variant *c* sections do.[30] The melodic contours of sections *a* and *b* are descending terraces. Section c^1 continues the pattern set up in sections *a* and *b*; however, it does not move off the tonic except briefly at the cadence. Section c^2 two remains steadfastly on the tonic.

Example 139. Song 88

The melodic sweep of song 25 (ex. 140) is noteworthy within Emily and Dorothy's Naraya repertoire. The melodic range of section *a* encompasses a ninth. Beginning high, steadily descending, and ending low, the singer must leap up an octave to repeat this section, or to repeat the song after the completion of the repeated *b* section.

Example 140. Song 25

These examples of Naraya songs with Plains influence fit in with a few other rare examples in the literature. Colby's 1895 publication of Lakota Ghost Dance songs includes one musical transcription (Colby 1895:142), given in example 141.

Example 141. Lakota Ghost Dance Song

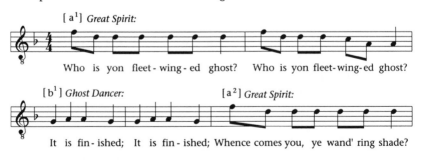

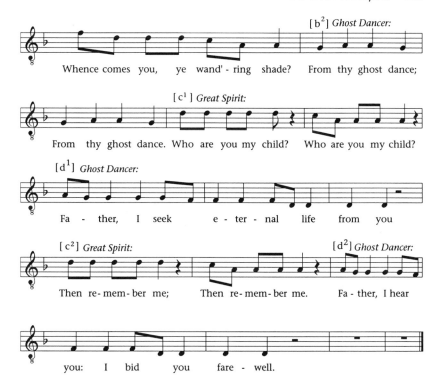

I have added structural labeling to the original transcription, which included none. I suggest that the song falls into halves, each made of paired progressions: *abab* and *cdcd,* respectively. In both cases, the repeat of the paired progressions sets different lines of text. Taking both text and music into consideration, the form of the song is $a^1b^1a^2b^2\ c^1d^1c^2d^2$.

Like Naraya song 25, the Lakota Ghost Dance song covers a wide melodic range, a tenth. Both of the *ab* and *cd* progressions start high and have a descending, terraced contour. However, the form of the song continues to adhere to the Ghost Dance model of paired phrases—here, paired progressions.

In 1941 Willard Rhodes traveled to Anadarko, Oklahoma, and recorded Kiowa songs, including two Ghost Dance songs. The Library of Congress made this material available to the public when it issued a recording of Kiowa songs (AAFS L35) in the early 1950s. In an accompanying booklet, Rhodes analyzed the impact of Plains style on the two Kiowa Ghost Dance songs and wrote:

The Opening and Closing songs of the Kiowa Ghost Dance present-ed here as sung by George Hunt are at variance with Herzog's conclu-sions. Both songs, extending through a range of a twelfth, are sung with accompaniment and though some phrases are literally repeated, the structure of terraced phrases and descending melodic movement sug-gest a strong influence of the prevailing Plains musical style. Most Ghost Dance songs are sung with words. Here the words are reserved for the concluding phrases of the songs, reminiscent of the Plains practice of singing a song through with meaningless syllables and introducing the words on the repetition of the song. (Rhodes n.d.:19)

Song Performance and Music Form

I conclude this chapter as I began it, returning to the paired phrases in Naraya songs. Here, I wish to connect this form with the perfor-mance practice of other song genres within the Great Basin and even other musical traditions outside the region.

Information on communal shamanistic practices and Round Dance performance suggests musical or, at least, textual antiphony—call and response between two entities. Park writes, "The interpreter [for the shaman] sitting at his left listens attentively and repeats the words clearly in order that the spectators may understand. He also follows the songs that the shaman sings, repeating the words loudly to en-able the spectators to follow them easily and join in the singing" (Park 1938:50). Similarly, Whiting describes how "a man, who is known as the repeater, leads the spectators in the singing and inter-prets the doctor's order concerning procedure" (Whiting 1950:40). From Kelly we learn that among Surprise Valley Paiutes, "the doctor chanted, and his son told in plain Paiute what he was saying. . . . The doctor started the singing, and his son led the people off" (Kelly 1932:193). Does this last description imply an alternation of the doctor, who sings a phrase, with the son and people, who repeat it as a response?

Or what can we infer from Dellenbaugh's description of a South-ern Paiute Round Dance? He writes, "In the centre stood a man, seem-ing to be the custodian of the songs and a poet himself. He would first recite the piece, and then all would sing it, circling round at the same time" (Dellenbaugh 1908:178). Did the custodian sing the en-tire verse? One line at a time? Commenting on the prevalence of paired phrases in the Ghost Dance texts published by Mooney, Ven-num suggests a connection with the earlier Round Dances in the Basin and Dellenbaugh's comments given above. "Dellenbaugh's description of a Kaibab Southern Paiute Round Dance in 1872 suggests that there may once have been some sort of antiphonal call and response pattern in performing its songs" (Vennum 1986:693). Evidence does not support more than this tentative suggestion.

Moving outside the Great Basin, yet staying within the large Uto-Aztecan language family to which the Shoshone belong, information on Aztec musical traditions is equally tantalizing in its suggestion of Aztec song performance and song form. Quetzlcoatl, the culture bringer, is the subject of a Nahuatl poetic text that dates from the mid-sixteenth century. One episode in this text describes a sorcerer who lures people through song and dance to their deaths. I draw the reader's attention to the implied call and response format in this poetic description of song performance.

> The sorcerer began to sing, to drum, to strike a beat for them upon his drum. At once there was dancing.
>
> And so they went leaping, hand in hand, turning back to back. Great was the rapture as everyone sang, as the song came surging and ebbing.
>
> And the song that he sang he invented right there. And as he sang out, they answered right then, taking the song from his lips.
>
> (Bierhorst 1974:50)

The sorcerer-composer sings out each line and the chorus of entranced people takes "the song from his lips," that is, repeats it: AA, BB, and so on.

In his translation of Aztec song texts that date from the late sixteenth century, Bierhorst discusses Aztec notions of song composition as a cooperative act between singer and otherworld source. "The singer 'begins' or 'strikes up,' the song, but the heavens must give the 'answer,' or the 'echo'" (Bierhorst 1985:21). That the answer is an "echo" strongly suggests that once again, the form builds through a sequence of paired phrases. Bierhorst reinforces this point by citing Aztec myth concerning the origin of music.

The notion of reciprocity, moreover, is not limited to ghost songs. The fact that it is described in the myth of the origin of song, as preserved in both Mendieta's *Historia* and the "Histoyre du Mechique," suggests that it was a general feature of Aztec music theory. According to the "Histoyre du Mechique," music was taken from the sun by Ehecatl, the god of wind: Seeing him approach, the sun said to his musicians, "No one must answer him, for whoever answers him must go with him."

These musicians were dressed in four colors: white, red, yellow, and green. And now, having arrived, the wind god called to them with a song [*les appela en chantant*], and one of them immediately answered it and went off with him, carrying the music that they perform to this day in their dances in honor of their gods. (Bierhorst 1985:21)

Antiphony is implied, but not necessarily a repeat of the call by the responder.

Motolinía, a priest, saw and described Aztec performance in his *Memoriales*. Using this source, Bierhorst writes, "As the drumming began and the dancers got into position, two 'choir directors' would lead off the singing. . . . Antiphonal singing could be inferred from Motolinía's description . . . . Antiphonal singing divided between two choirs is explicitly described by the Conquistador anónimo" (Bierhorst 1985:71, 532n.6). Bierhorst also quotes a Jesuit historian, Andrés Pérez de Ribas, who published in 1645 an eyewitness account of another Aztec ritual involving song and dance, the *tocontin*. "The vocal music, which does not stop, corresponds to that which is played on the teponaztli, with another choir that answers it and is hidden behind a curtain or blind, as though [the music] were of two choruses" (Andrés Pérez de Ribas, in Bierhorst 1985:89).[31] Again, one cannot know definitively from this description whether the second choir's answer repeats the first musical phrase or provides a new one.

There is a postscript to Naraya and Great Basin song performance, one that underscores the power and pleasure of group singing—already mentioned in connection with shamanistic, Round Dance, and Naraya performance. I conclude with a Chemehuevi myth in which Coyote and his allies prepare for war against Gila Monster.

> Sitting around the campfire on the night before battle, Coyote says, "Haik^{y}a, haik^{y}a, . . . it is customary-aik^{y}a, it is the proper thing-aik^{y}a, when people are going on the warpath-aik^{y}a, when they camp-aik^{y}a, for all of them to sing their war songs-aik^{y}a! You sing first, my Lizard-nephew-aik^{y}a!"
> Lizard sang:
> > From under coarse sand
> > (I) get up, get up
> > from under coarse sand
> > (I) get up, get up
> "Haik^{y}a, haik^{y}a," Coyote said, "It is not good aik^{y}a, it is not a war song-aik^{y}a, you are just singing about what you do-aik^{y}a!" He made fun of the song. "It is no good-aik^{y}a, it is no good-aik^{y}a!"
> "Very well, hand me down my moccasins," said Lizard, rising from his seat by the campfire, "I will return home."

"Haikʸa, haikʸa," Coyote protested, "you must stay with us-aikʸa, I was just fooling-aikʸa, your song will go nicely-aikʸa when we all sing it together-aikʸa!"

Lizard took his seat, and all the warriors sang his song. (Laird 1976:173)

The same scene happens over and over when the others take their turns to sing—Crow, Buzzard, Horsefly. Finally Coyote sings. Now all the creatures want to get even with him for his teasing rejection of their songs, so all shout out that his song is no good. He, too, is hurt and threatens to go home. "'No, no, Coyote,' all the people said, 'you must go with us, we need you! We were just fooling. Your song will go well when all of us sing it together.' The war party sang Coyote's song. Then they all went to bed" (Laird 1976:176). The story ends with success: Coyote's war party slays Gila Monster. Fighting together, singing together—all goes well . . . together.

10 | *Song Text Comparisons: Naraya with Great Basin Songs and Plains Ghost Dance*

The purpose of this chapter is comparative from two standpoints. I will first present selected Great Basin song texts—principally Round Dance and Ghost Dance—showing the resemblances between their imagery and form and those of Naraya song texts. The second comparison is one of contrast: I present a sampling of Plains Ghost Dance texts from the collections of Colby and Mooney.

As introduction to the many texts that follow as examples, I begin with three topic-imagery tables (tables 7–9), which summarize these points of similarity and contrast in a quantitative fashion. The first two tables summarize almost all Ghost Dance songs of which I am aware. As I emphasized in the introduction to this book, the frequency of the topics and images used in Mooney's texts carries the weight of my argument that Plains Ghost Dance texts do, indeed, differ qualitatively and quantitatively from those of the Great Basin. In the first topic-imagery table (table 7), therefore, I compare the rank ordering of these topic-images with those of the Naraya. I have separated out the statistics for the sole example of Great Basin texts in Mooney's publication—nine Northern Paiute songs—so that one can see the close correspondence between these texts and those of the Naraya on the one hand, and their contrast with those of the Plains, on the other. Note that the "father" who appears prominently in Plains Ghost Dance songs refers to Wovoka, the prophet of the Ghost Dance religion. "Our Father" in Naraya songs does not refer to Wovoka but rather to the Creator, God. The topic-images presented in other scholars' collections of Plains Ghost Dance texts (table 8) reveal a distribution of topics indistinguishable from that of Mooney, showing that Mooney's collection was not idiosyncratic.

Table 7. Topic Images in Mooney's Ghost Dance Songs and Naraya Songs

Plains[a] (152 songs)		Great Basin			
		Northern Paiute[a] (9 songs)		Shoshone Naraya (130 songs)	
people	134	water	3	water	52
father (Wovoka)	72	whirlwind	3	mountains	45
birds	35	greenery	2	animals	34
spirit world	21	trees	2	greenery	32
animals	13	mountains	2	trees	29
feathers	13	rocks	2	earth	17
dead relatives	13	earth	2	birds	17
gambling	12	animals	1	rocks	15
Ghost Dance	11	lightning	1	sun	14
resurrection	10	Milky Way	1	food plants	10
new world	9	new world	1	sky	7
food	8	wind	1	Milky Way	6
water	6	dust	1	people	6
paint	6			Our Father	5
buffalo meat	5			wind	5
pipe	4			new world	4
Whites	4			dead relatives	4
medicine	4			night	3
bow and arrows	4			medicine	3
earth	3			mountain spirit road	2
trees	3			soul	2
wind	3			spirit world	2
whirlwind	3			resurrection	2
plants	3			thunder	2
Ghost Dance clothing	3			silver	2
tipi	2			sacred power	2
ball	2			feather	2
Ghost Dance song	2			Morning Star	1
5 (number)	2			earthquake	1
Milky Way	2			whirlwind	1
sun or moon	2			sickness	1
rocks	1			song	1
thunder	1			Naraya performance	1
mountains	1				
bed	1				

a. Mooney [1896] 1991.

Table 8. Topic Images in Ghost Dance Songs Presented in Other Publications[a]

Plains		Great Basin	
Lakota (31 songs)		*Southern Paiute* (17 songs)	
people	20	water	4
father	13	mountains	4
resurrection	8	knoll, or hill	3
dead relatives	6	plants (includes berries)	2
food	3	birds	2
spirit world	2	sky	2
Ghost Dance	2	earthslide and quake	2
earth	2	sun	1
health-healing	2	rocks	1
buffalo	2	trees	1
bow and arrows	2	canyon	1
spirit ghost	1	land	1
spirit world	1	soul	1
Ghost Dance songs	1	?Milky Way	1
pipe	1	dead relatives	1
mocassins	1	Coyote (God)	1
tipi	1	people	1
birds	1		

Lakota, Pawnee, Southern Arapaho (8 songs)	
people	7
father	3
stars	3
Morning and Evening Star	2
Ghost Dance songs	1
dead relatives	1
resurrection	1
food	1
spirit world	1
bird	1
sun and moon	1
water	1

Pawnee
(4 songs)

people	4
father	1
birds	1
feather	1
animals	1
stick	1

a. Sources: For Lakota: Colby 1895; for Southern Paiute: Sapir 1994; for Lakota, Pawnee, and Southern Arapaho: Curtis [1907] 1968; for Pawnee: Densmore [1929] 1972.

In the third topic-imagery table (table 9), I present a sample of Great Basin Round Dance songs. Although the information comes from a relatively small sample size, I include it as I believe that the choice of textual images in these songs—drawn from the natural world—is significant. A few of the texts do not follow this pattern but focus instead on people. They are reminders that the Round Dance was a social occasion, a time for fun and playfulness, too. A complete picture of Round Dance song texts from the Great Basin still awaits an exhaustive study with much more data.

While the numbers on the topic-imagery tables are compelling, I want the differences between the two branches of the Ghost Dance to come alive poetically as well as statistically. It is for this reason that the remainder of this chapter will provide many examples.

Table 9. Images of Great Basin Round Dance Songs[a]

Southern Paiute					Northern Shoshone	
Powell, 1870s (3 songs)		Sapir, 1910 (9 songs)		Franklin-Bunte, 1988 (2 songs)	Liljeblad, 1940s (3 songs)	
people	3	water	7	water	2	plants	3
animals	1	trees	4	mountains	1	water	1
		mountains	3				
		plants	1				
		rocks	1				
		animals	1				
		people	1				

a. Dates given refer to years the songs were collected.

I believe that, taken together, all the parts and points of this chapter amply support the ideas presented in the introduction. First, Naraya song texts exemplify Great Basin song texts, in their form, in their selective imagery of the natural world, and, most important, in their relationship to that world. Second, Great Basin Ghost Dance song texts bear important similarities to Round Dance texts. Third, the Plains Ghost Dance assumed a distinctly different focus and emphasis. People are the subjects of its song texts: either in the land of the dead, coming back to life, or as participants in Plains culture—setting up tipis, riding horses, and hunting buffaloes—a way of life that by the late nineteenth century was as irrevocable as the dead.

Great Basin Song Texts
Powell, 1870s

I begin with Kaibab Southern Paiute song texts collected by Powell in southern Utah in the 1870s. With few exceptions, there is no precise identification of the song texts. Liljeblad writes, "Most songs in Powell's classic collection prove to be 'song recitatives,' that is, songs with mythological association detached from the tale types to which they originally belonged. Nevertheless, an indefinite number of Powell's 'Songs and Chants' are to all appearance abridged Round Dance song texts with repetitive verse excluded" (Liljeblad 1986:649).[1]

Of the seventy-two song texts in Powell's collection, I quote three texts for which there is information to indicate that they were, in fact, performed at a Round Dance. I include thirty-eight additional texts, some of which may have been Round Dance songs, and others that were extracted from mythological renderings. I do so because the poetic images in all these song texts—drawn from nature, brief and yet deftly suggestive of a complete ecological scene—seem similar to those in Naraya song texts.

I have selected and grouped the songs according to their topic-images. I begin with seven texts that refer to people, song, and dance. In order to facilitate locating and discussing these texts, I have given them an identifying P(owell)-number label. In the original manuscripts, some texts had titles, many were untitled. I will present the songs first, followed by comments on them.

P-1 (Our Song)

Our song will enter	U-wot´ sin tu-wīp´ pu-a´
That distant land	U-wi´a wu-ni-ga´-va
That gleaming land	A-vwīm´ pai-ar ru-wīp-a

That gleaming land   A-vwīm´ pai-ar ru-wīp-a
And roll the lake in waves U-wa´ pa mon-ti-ri´ va
                            (Powell 1971:124)

P-2 (Music)

Over the land at night   Tu-wīp u-wan´ tuk
Slowly the music floats   Ya´gām´ im-pa
                            To-gwau-o-gúmp
                            (Powell 1971:125)

P-3 (The Spirit)

The spirit   Mo-go´av
Is swaying and singing   Yan-tu´-na-gi-kai
                            (Powell 1971:125)

Song, itself, is at the center of these first three song texts. In text
P-1, song has the power to travel from this world to "that distant
land," which Hill interprets as the Spirit Land, or Land of the Dead
(J. Hill 1992:120, 128). Song has the power not only to travel from
this world to another; it can create waves in the lake of that "distant
land." Song, with its power, affects water, another power, or source
of power. Text P-2 connects song with the land of this world. The
impact of the one on the other is not stated. In my reading, it seems
intimated, floating over the text like music over the land. In text P-
3, we see the spirit—the essence of life and medium of power—manifested in song and movement.

P-4 (The First Song of the Dance)[2]

Friends let the play commence   Ki´-ap-pa tu´-gu-vwav
All sing in unison   Pi´-vi-an-a Kai´-va
                               (Powell 1971:126)

P-5 (Patience)

Let a man talk   Um-pa´-ga´-va
A very long time   Sho-ra´-ga-va
A hole he will bore   Uon-ti´-ri-gai
Into a cliff   Uu-kwa´-ni-kai
                       (Powell 1971:127)

Dellenbaugh, who traveled with Powell, also learned this last song
and wrote down his own, different, transcription of it:

Montee-ree-ai-ma, mo-quontee-kai-ma
Umpa-shu-shu-shu-ra-ga-va
Umpa-shu-shu-shu-ra-ga-va

Umpa-shu-shu-shu-ra-ga-va
Montee-ree-ai-ma
(Dellenbaugh 1908:178)

Dellenbaugh noted, "This . . . signifies that a long talk is enough to bore a hole in a cliff" (Dellenbaugh 1908:179).

P-6 (Untitled)

If you don't kill a rabbit	Ka-shak´-um pu-Kai´-vwan
You don't eat a rabbit	Ka´-shak-um ti-kai´-vwan
	(Powell 1971:127)

Dellenbaugh also wrote this song down in his book, which included repetition of both lines. He wrote:

Another popular one was:

Ca, shakum, poo kai
Ca, shakum, poo kai
Ca, shakum tee kai
Ca, shakum tee kai,

these lines being repeated like the others over and over and over again. They were highly philosophical, for they explain that you must kill your rabbit (shakum) before you eat him. I do not remember that they sang these particular songs on that occasion, but they will serve as examples. (Dellenbaugh 1908:179)

One can identify songs P-4 through P-6 as Round Dance songs. Song P-4 opened the evening, inviting all to dance and sing.

Dellenbaugh, who participated in a Southern Paiute Round Dance, learned and published P-5 and P-6 as examples of their Round Dance songs. Round Dance humor is very much in evidence in these two song texts, especially P-5. Powell gives us the word-for-word translation in two lines, "Let a man talk" (*Um-pa´-ga´-va*) / "A very long time" (*Sho-ra´-ga-va*). Dellenbaugh gives us the form, in which the two lines combine, shortening here and lengthening there, with humorous result. *Umpa-* (shortened version of *Um-pa´-ga-va*) shu-shu-shu- (stem reduplication of "A very long time", the vowel here given as "u" making the whole line alternate "u" and "a") *ra-ga-va*. This line repeats three times. Word play imitates word meaning. I do not know the exact meaning of the words, but the spirit of the translation should be something like: "Long talk-talk-talking / Long talk-talk-talking / Long talk-talk-talking."

Despite Dellenbaugh's comment about the "highly philosophical" nature of text P-6—perhaps made with tongue in cheek—I think it is humorous. Again, I turn to Dellenbaugh's version, as I guess that its repeated text is closer to the sung form than Powell's translation of the words. Literally, the text says:

> Not, rabbit, you kill
> Not, rabbit, you kill
> Not, rabbit, you eat
> Not, rabbit, you eat.[3]

A modern, rough equivalent might be:

> No ticket you have,
> No ticket you have.
> No shirt you get,
> No shirt you get.

P-7 (Untitled)

It is smokey on the cliffs	Ta-shi´-gai-ra´ toung ping´-wants
We dance in the smoke	Ta-shi´-yan-tok´-i-na-vich
	(Powell 1971:127)

The image of smoke, which appears in both lines of P-7, could refer either to dust or to clouds. The text to P-29 given below may assist us here, as its third line says, "And the Smokey clouds drift away." The smoke on the cliffs in P-7 might also refer to clouds. If so, it brings to mind Naraya images of fog on the mountains and all the associations that go with water—power and vegetation—and specifically for clouds or fog—the soul.

This song may have been performed at a Round Dance. The text suggests that the "we" who dance are also the singers, the customary practice at Round Dances.

The grouping and order of the remaining thirty-four song texts parallel, in abridged form, that used for Naraya songs. Water is as ubiquitous in these Southern Paiute song texts as it is in the Naraya. I begin with P-8 and P-9, a brief water sampler that points to the sky as the source of rivers and mud-red eddies.

P-8 (The Home of the River)

The edge of the sky	To-gūm´-pai kung-wa´ra
Is the home of the river	Nu-kwin´-kai ka-ni´-gu
	(Powell 1971:122)

P-9 (The Storm)

The sky is falling	To-gum´-pai-av
The red water eddies	Ats-ai´-kai-i-va
	Kūnt ai´-kai-i-va
	(Powell 1971:126)

Texts P-10 through P-33 use images of fog, mountains, and rocks.

P-10 (Untitled)

The blue water rolls on the Mountains	Shak-war´ pa-nouk´-i-kai´-vwa
(meaning the clouds are rolling on	(Powell 1971:128)
the Mountain)	

P-11 (The Storm Crown)

It rains on the mountains	War´-ru-um kai´-va
It rains on the mountains	War´-ru-um kai-va
A white crown encircles the mountain	Wi-gīv a vwīm kwi-nu-ai kai-va
	(Powell 1971:125)

Clouds on the mountains in these texts suggest two very different images and metaphoric references: waves in the sea in P-10 and a crown encircling the top of the mountain, its head, in P-11. I remind the reader that four texts collected by Powell and quoted earlier in chapter 4 (P-12 through P-15), liken fog, clouds, and foam or spray from a river, to feathers. The white crown in P-11 is reminiscent of the red-cloud feathers on the mountains in P-14 and the rain or snow feathers on the head of the mountain in P-15.

Shoshones conceptualize the soul either as fog or feathers. I do not know if these images in Powell's Southern Paiute texts had a double reference. However, like Naraya texts, those texts respond to the resemblance between feather and fog as visual images and have selected this form of water as their subject.

P-16 (The Lost Feather)

My feather was lost	Wu-shi´-av pu-ro-kwa-gi-kai-va
At dusk on the hills	Shu-an´-tu u-no-whu-kai-i-nok
	(Powell 1971:127)

Again, one wonders whether the feather in text P-16 refers to the soul of a person.

P-17 (A Paradox)

The crest of the mountain	Wi-gīv´ a ka-ri´-ri
Forever remains	Yu-gu´ kai mai u-uk
Forever remains	Yu-gu´ kai mai u-uk
Though rocks continually fall	Ma-mūm´-pa-ri tum-pa
	(Powell 1971:123)[4]

Another text—seemingly a variant of the above—is:

A feather on the
Hill will remain continuously

> But the rocks slide down
> (Powell 1971:123)

Is the feather in this text another poetic metaphor for fog or clouds?

P-18 (The Earthquake)

In the land, in the land	Tu-wīp´ pu-a-tu-wip pu-a
In that glittering land	A-vwīm-pai ar-ru-wip pu-a
Far away, far away	Tu-ra´-gu-ok tu-ra´-gu-ok
The mountain was shaken with pain	Kai´vwa mu-tu´-rai-ka-nok
	(Powell 1971:126)

Powell's alternate English version is:

> In the land
> The land which is white
> Across the country
> The mountains tremble

Notice the mountain-water images in texts P-19 through P-23.

P-19 (The Kai-nu-shuk)

Through the cleft of the rocks	Tum-pi´-pa-go´-a
In the land far away	U-wot´-sin tu-wēp-u-ni
The water was dashed from the mountain	Pong-wu´-mum tish-i-kai-vwa
	(Powell 1971:125)

P-20 (Untitled)

The red water of the Mountain Stream	Un-kar´-pa nu-kwint´-in-kaivw
In the summer time	Ta-ma´-ru-int
The rills are singing	Nu-kwi´-kai-ing´-u-ni
	(Powell 1971:128)

P-21 (Untitled)

Rainwater at the foot of mountain	Wa-pa´-ka-ni´-gav
Rainwater singing (making a noise)	Wa-pa´ toung wa´-vok
	(Powell 1971:128)

Where there are mountains there are valleys:

P-22 (The Beautiful Valley)

The Paranagut Valley	Pa-ran´-i-gi yu-av´-i
The Valley	Yu-av´-in-ni
The Paranagut Valley	Pa-ran´-i-gi yu-av´-i
The Valley	Yu-av´-in-ni
Is a beautiful valley	U-ai´-in-ni yu-av´-i
The Valley	Yu-av´-in-ni
	(Powell 1971:125)

Text P-23 adds plant life, the cane that grows by the stream that runs down the mountain.

P-23 (Untitled)

By the cane on the mountain	Pa-gu´-tan-ga Kaivw-va
The Muddy water	Tu-weap-pu-a´
Rolls down continuously	Whu-Tu´-nu-nunk´ Kwi-ni´-va
	(Powell 1971:128)

Texts P-24 through P-34 sing of animals. Their order and taxonomy, ground, sky, and water people, accord with those used in chapter 5.

P-24 (Song of the Mountain Sheep)

My curved horns	Ap-a´ gu-nuv´
Like a necklace stand	Wu-wu´ Ka-gi´ a Kai´-ing
	(Powell 1971:123)

P-25 (Song of the Deer)

The reeds grow in the Mountain glades	Pa-gum pai-av to-i ni-va
The reeds grow in the Mountain glades	Pa-gum pai-av to-i ni-va
The reeds grow in the Mountain glades	Pa-gum pai-av to-i ni-va
The reeds grow in the Mountain glades	Pa-gum pai-av to-i ni-va
And the poplars stand on the borders	Shi-av pai-av i-ni
And the poplars stand on the borders	Shi-av pai-av i-n
And the poplars stand on the borders	Shi-av pai-av i-n
They eat the reeds and get shade in the aspens	(Powell 1971:123)

In the Song of the Deer, Powell does indicate the number of repetitions for the first two different lines of text. Because the third line ("They eat . . .") has no corresponding line of Southern Paiute text, I suspect that it is information that Powell learned about the song rather than an unrepeated third line of its text.

P-26 (Untitled)

The blue water in	Sha´-kwar war´-pu
The Mountain cañon	Shi-Kats´-i Kai-vwa
The grizzly bear on the mountain	Kwi-at-si Kai-vwa
Is digging	Ou-rout´-sen
	(Powell 1971:128)

Texts P-24, P-25, and P-26 are strikingly different. P-24 has a single and arresting simile for the curved horns of a mountain sheep. They are likened to a necklace, human adornment that sits around the neck, horizontal to the ground. In P-24, the horn necklace stands, perpendicular to the ground. The sheep is the speaker in the text, using the first-person pronoun, "*My* curved horns." This strongly suggests that the text was from a myth and the time when the animals were people and could speak.

If, as I believe, P-25 does not include in its text the final unrepeated line of commentary, then is this text the song of the deer—the deer's thoughts on food and habitat? Does it, like P-24, come from myth when animals spoke? Or is this a song sung by humans about the food and habitat of the deer? Is the intent to attract the animal? If so, this would be similar to the shaman's song used for antelope charming quoted in chapter 1. "His song was of a kind of brush (si-sovi) that antelope eat and about young antelope and their food" (Steward 1941:219). In any case, P-25 visualizes a particular scene of vegetation, an ideal habitat for deer.

P-26 brings together neighboring habitats and animal behavior. Below, a river runs through a mountain canyon; above, on the mountainside, a grizzly bear grubs for food.

Sky people are the subjects of texts P-27 through P-31.

P-27 (Eagle's Tears)

At the morn the eagle will cry	Ta-vi´-kwai-nant´-si ya´-ga-wats
On the farther shore of the sea	Si-chōm´-pa kung war´-ru
And the rainbow will be in the sky	Tu´-yung-wi-ra´-vats
	(Powell 1971:122)

P-28 (The Mountain Peak)

On the peak of the mountain	Kaivw-ok´ kwai-nants´ we-pa´-gi-ni-va´
The eagle is dancing	War´-ru shong-ai´-mi-ni-va´
The tempest is roaring	
	(Powell 1971:125)

Commentary on the relationship of the eagle to power and weather, especially lightning and storms, given in chapter 5, is germane to texts P-27 and P-28. The power of song and dance discussed in chapter 1 is likewise germane. According to my interpretation, both texts associate the eagle with sky and weather and, by implication, with power. The eagles are located at places of power—by the sea and on the mountain peak. We see their power manifested in a cry, or song, and dance. One brings rain, prisms for coloring the morning sunlight, and the other, a tempest. Even if the relationship is not directly causal, there is, at the very least, close association between the two.

Birds and their song are at the center of texts P-29 and P-30. Notice the mountain and cliff settings in the texts and the inclusion of clouds in text P-30.

P-29 (The Blue Bird)

At the foot of the cliff	Tūm-pwi´ to-nai´-ga
On the face of the cliff	Tūm-pwi´-wa-ro´-kwa
The blue bird sings	Shok´-wai-ants´ u-yo´-kwi
	(Powell 1971:125)

P-30 (Untitled)

When the Americans dwell in the mountains	Mer-rung-Kats Kaivw-ai-yu-gi-Kane
The flickers sing	Um-kar-kivo-nau-ants Ya-Kik-Kwo-ni
And the Smokey clouds drift away	Kwi-pog-yu-nav As-Kane
	(Powell 1971:128)

Winter Song seems an appropriate title for P-31. "Feathers" on the ground, which here refer to the dead tops of the reeds, help establish the season. Quails in the pines complete this scene of the natural world.

P-31 (Winter Song)

The feathers of the reed	Pa-gump´ pi-av´
Are lying on the ground	A-vwi´ mi-ni´
And the quails are perched on the pines	Yu-im´ ka' ka´ rum-pu-i-gunt
	(Powell 1971:124)

Geese and their song, the subject of P-32, share characteristics of both the sky and water people. Their placement here serves as a bridge between the two.

P-32 (The Song of the Wild Geese)

We go to the south land	Houm-wi´ Kwa-ni´ tan-tun´ tu-weap´
To eat Kwai-mu-rant	Kwai-mu´ rant tu-kum´ i-a-gai´
	(Powell 1971:124)

Like people, the geese migrate in the winter in order to harvest another food source. The first-person pronoun "we," in the first line, indicates that this song is from the mythic time when animals spoke.[5]

P-33 (The Trout)

In the blue water	Shag-wa pa-wu´yu-unt
The trout wags its tail	Pa-gu´ kwa-sing´ Chu-nu´-wu-gi
	(Powell 1971:125)[6]

P-34 (Cave Lake Song)

The twilight has a home	Shant´-an Ka-ni´-wa
And the black fish has a home	To-pa´-gu Ka-ni´-wa
	(Powell 1971:126)[7]

Fish, their movement and specific habitat, are the subjects of P-33 and P-34. P-33 is quite similar to Naraya song 96 and Emily's descriptive commentary on the song text.

Plants are my final grouping of Powell's Southern Paiute texts.

P-35 (The Tobacco Plant)

The tobacco plant is standing	Ku-au´ a-gun-tūr
Where the babbling water runs	Nu-ni´ ga-kai-na
On the side of the mountain	Pa-ku´ wi-ing-kai-va
	(Powell 1971:124)

The combined images of plant, running water, and mountain location in this text are indistinguishable from other Naraya combinations drawn from nature.

P-36 (The Pines)

The lofty pines	Pan-tin´-ni-yu-imp´
The tops of the lofty pines	Wi-ga´-gun tu-mai-u-ni
The lofty pines	Pan-tin´-ni yu-imp
Are swaying with the winds	Yan-tai´-ku-ni-va
	(Powell 1971:125)

P-37 (Untitled)

In the pines on the sides	Ya ing kaivw ping wa-uk
Of the Mountains	Sha kwar ni-ur
The Blue wind sighs	Ting wa va ka ni va
	(Powell 1971:128)

P-38 (Untitled)

In the land of the Spaniards	Hu´-kwats tu´-weap pu-a
The young pines	Shu-ai´ yu-wimp´
Stand around on the mountains	Uw´-wind-ni´-ga Kai-va
	(Powell 1971:128)

P-39 (Untitled)

The grass, on the Mountain	U-gwiv Kaivw i-va
Moves in the Mountain Breeze	Wu wun na rin i Kaivw-i-va
	(Powell 1971:128)

The image of pines in the mountains, standing, swaying in the wind,

soughing in the wind, which appears in P-36 through P-38, has counterparts in Naraya song texts.[8] Aspens and other trees stand and move
with the wind in Naraya songs 104 and 130. Windblown grass, the subject of P-39, is also to be found in Naraya songs 102 and 130.

P-40 (Untitled)

On the bushes	Ma-sing´ ´mai
The Blossoms are hanging	Yu-wai´-Ka-va
	(Powell 1971:128)

In Emily and Dorothy's Naraya repertoire, only greasewood branches, grown long in Naraya song 106, hang down. The sole mention
of blossoms or flowers in Naraya songs is the white strawberry blossom in song 119.

P-41 (Untitled)

The dove seeds	Yu-vi´ pu-i´
Are falling down	Shong-its´-i-ka´-ni
	(Powell 1971:127)

The text of Naraya song 116 is the analogue for P-41. In it, sunflower seeds, rather than dove seeds, are coming down.

It is not my purpose and certainly beyond my ability to provide a
detailed analysis of the Powell texts presented in this chapter. Also,
the texts, as we have them, limit aspects of analysis. They are not
always complete in that they omit the repetition of lines in the text.
What follows are some brief observations about the Southern Paiute
texts that seem relevant to Naraya texts.

Given the uncertainty regarding the completeness of Powell's texts,
it is difficult to comment with assurance on the presence or absence
of paired phrases in them. Paired phrases are infrequent in the sampling of Powell's texts that I present. However, note that in Dellenbaugh's transcriptions of the same two Round Dance texts given by
Powell, repeated phrases do appear, classically so in P-6—AABB. In
Dellenbaugh's rendering of P-5, the second line repeats three times
and the final line is a shortened version of the first. At least in the
repetition of the basic verse, the last and first lines would come con-
secutively—shortened A followed by complete A. The only other song
in my sampling that includes information for the repetition of individual lines is P-25, Song of the Deer. If I am correct and the last line
of English text is Powell's commentary and not part of the song proper, then the text has two lines. The first repeats four times and the

second, three times, creating the asymmetrical form, AAAABBB. Finally, there are a few texts where one line repeats, for example, the first line of P-11 and the third line of P-1.

Parallelisms, an important structural devise in Naraya texts, appear in some of the Southern Paiute texts. There are parallel beginnings, for example, *wa-pa´*, "rainwater," in P-21; *tum-pwi´*,[9] "the cliff," in P-29; and *ta-shi´*, smoke, in P-7. In P-36, the parallelism occurs between the first line in a pair of progressions. The first line in each progression begins identically, "The lofty pines," making the form of the entire text AB-AC.

In other examples, parallelism occurs at the end of the line. *Kai-va*, "mountain," in P-11, ends both line one (which repeats) and line two. Similarly, *Ka-ni´-wa*, "has a home," ends both lines of text in P-34. P-22, like P-36, is made of a paired progression, line *a*, *Pa-ran´-i-gi yu-av´-i*, "The Paranagut Valley," and line *b*, *Yu-av´-in-ni*, "The Valley." This progression repeats. The last progression changes only the first part of the *a* line, which becomes, "Is a beautiful valley," and then ends with line *b*. The form is AB-AB-CB.

The most striking use of parallelism appears in P-6. The beginnings and endings of its two lines of text are the same, with only the root of the two verbs, *pu-kai´* (*poo kai*), "kill," versus *ti-kai´* (*tee kai*), "eat," differing.

Finally, notice the poetic sensitivity to the sound of water mentioned in two of the texts. A mountain stream (P-20) and rainwater at the foot of a mountain (P-21) "sing" in Powell's personified translation. Recall that the sound of water figured prominently in the first line of Naraya song 129, one of the rare examples of onomatopoeia in Naraya songs. I repeat Emily's comments about it: "In the night time when everything's quiet you could just hear very little water going, you could hear the water. Sounds like it's going through big rocks, splashing onto the rocks. Sounds like its, 'shhhhh.'"

Mooney, 1896

Mooney's Ghost Dance book, published approximately twenty years after Powell's fieldwork, included texts for nine Ghost Dance songs of the Northern Paiute. They are the oldest and only examples of their kind (with one exception, in Vennum 1986:704), gathered from Wovoka's home territory. The genesis for my book came from a recognition of the striking resemblance between the imagery and form of Northern Paiute and Naraya texts (see topic-imagery chart, table 7). I quote all of them here so that the reader will feel, as I did, a strong sense of *déjà vu*.

Mooney numbered these texts and used each text's first line, or part of it, for the song's title. I have reordered the texts and grouped them according to their topic-imagery, which parallels the order and grouping of Naraya texts. Therefore, I have added my own M(ooney)-number and put the original number and title in parenthesis. I have included Mooney's comments for each text. I intersperse my comments between the different groupings of texts.

M-1 (5. Pägü´nävä´)

Fog! Fog!	Pägü´nävä´! Pägü´nävä´!
Lightning! Lightning!	Tûngwu´kwiji´! Tûngwü´kwiji´!
Whirlwind! Whirlwind!	Wûmbe´doma´! Wûmbe´doma´!

Mooney commented, "This song is an invocation of the elemental forces. It was composed by an old woman, who left the circle of dancers and stood in the center of the ring while singing it" (Mooney [1896] 1991:1054).

M-2 (7. Kosi´ wûmbi´ndomä´)

There is dust from the whirlwind,	Kosi´ wûmbi´ndomä´,
There is dust from the whirlwind,	Kosi´ wûmbi´ndomä´,
There is dust from the whirlwind.	Kosi´ wûmbi´ndomä´.
The whirlwind on the mountain,	Kai´-va wûmbi´ndomä´,
The whirlwind on the mountain,	Kai´-va wûmbi´ndomä´,
The whirlwind on the mountain.	Kai´-va wûmbi´ndomä´.
	(Mooney [1896] 1991:1054–55)

M-3 (6. Wûmbĭ´ndomä´n)

The whirlwind! The whirlwind!	Wûmbĭ´ndomä´n, Wûmbĭ´ndomä´n,
The whirlwind! The whirlwind!	Wûmbĭ´ndomä´n, Wûmbĭ´ndomä´n.
The snowy earth comes gliding,	Nuvä´rĭ´p noyo´wană´, Nuvä´rĭ´p
the snowy earth comes gliding;	noyo´wană´,
The snowy earth comes gliding,	Nuvä´rĭ´p noyo´wană´, Nuvä´rĭ´p
the snowy earth comes gliding.	noyo´wană´.

Mooney believed that "this song may possibly refer to the doctrine of the new earth, here represented as white with snow, advancing swiftly, driven by a whirlwind. Such an idea occurs several times in the Arapaho songs" (Mooney [1896] 1991:1054).

M-4 (1. Nüvä´ ka ro´răni´)

The snow lies there—ro´răni´!	Nüvä´ ka ro´răni´!
The snow lies there—ro´răni´!	Nüvä´ ka ro´răni´!
The snow lies there—ro´răni´!	Nüvä´ ka ro´răni´!

The Milky Way lies there,	Gosi´pa´ hävi´gĭnû´,
The Milky Way lies there.	Gosi´pa´ hävi´gĭnû´.

(Mooney [1896] 1991:1052)

I quote Mooney's lengthier commentary on this text:

> This is one of the favorite songs of the Paiute Ghost dance. The tune has a plaintive but rather pleasing effect, although inferior to the tunes of most of the ghost songs of the prairie tribes. The words as they stand are very simple, but convey a good deal of meaning to the Indian. It must be remembered that the dance is held in the open air at night, with the stars shining down on the wide-extending plain walled in by the giant sierras, fringed at the base with dark pines and with their peaks white with eternal snows. Under such circumstances this song of the snow lying white upon the mountains, and the Milky Way stretching across the clear sky, brings up to the Paiute the same patriotic home love that comes from lyrics of singing birds and leafy trees and still waters to the people of more favored regions. In the mythology of the Paiute, as of many other tribes, the Milky Way is the road of the dead to the spirit world. *Ro´răn´i´* serves merely to fill in the meter. (Mooney 1965:290)

Great Basin topic-imagery and symbolic associations are the foundation of these texts. Wovoka's conceptualization of the Ghost Dance built another layer of symbolic elaboration on top of it. The images in these texts are code words for a host of interpretive meanings. For example, take the imagery of M-1: fog, lightning, and whirlwind, elements that I discussed in some detail in chapters 1 and 2. Fog is the embodiment of the soul, still moist and potentially retrievable by the shaman. Lightning, which comes with thunder and rainstorms, is power, a source of power, either for good or ill. Whirlwind is a ghost, dry, something to be feared, a dangerous source of power. According to Ghost Dance prophecy, lightning storms and earthquakes are part of the destruction of the old world. The return of the dead, the whirlwind—dry and hitherto irretrievable from death—coincides with the death of earth as we know it and the appearance of the new world. The whirlwind will become at that time a retrievable soul, like its former foggy self. These are some of the Great Basin–Ghost Dance meanings and associations for the code words. However, the precise meaning of the text, the precise nuance of each word and its order, remain forever in code, known only by the old woman who received and sang the song.

Whirlwinds also appear in M-2. They are on the mountain. Emily's explanation of Naraya song 10, which also describes a whirlwind in the mountain, may have relevance to the imagery used in M-2. She said: "When a person dies they [the soul] go in a dust whirlwind. They go up in the mountains. There's a road for that, there's a green pass through there, where they go" (Vander 1986:53).

In Naraya song 10, the soul in the whirlwind is leaving this world. In M-2, there is no way to know whether the dusty whirlwind over the mountain is leaving or coming back to earth.

The text of M-3 brings together the whirlwind (dry, dead ghost) with the snowy earth. Mooney suggests that "snowy earth" refers to the new earth to come. Does the text suggest Ghost Dance prophecy through a symbolic contrast of its images: whirlwind dust with snowy-watered earth, dry with wet, death with resurrection?

M-4 also combines snow images with a reference to the dead—the Milky Way path that leads to the Land of the Dead. As part of my earlier discussion of the Milky Way, I noted closeness, if not identity, between Mooney's transcription of Northern Paiute words, *Gosi´pa* for "Milky Way" and *Kosi´ba* for "dust" (Mooney [1896] 1991:1056). Stewart's transcription and translation of *kusipo* for "dust road," given in his Northern Paiute publication (Stewart 1941:415), lends support to this connection. Stewart also reported, "Jack Wilson [Wovoka] got a song that said the Milky Way is a trail to heaven" (Stewart 1941:444). I suggest that M-4 may be the text to that song. Translated literally, it is an allusive road map. The first line, "The snow lies there . . . ," is spoken as though someone were pointing the general direction to the snowy new earth or "heaven." The second line, "The dust road (the Milky Way) lies there," provides the specific route. Does the traveler from this earth traverse the dust road of the Milky Way through the land of the dead and on to the new earth?

M-5 (8. Dombi´na so´wina´)

The rocks are ringing,	Dombi´na so´wina´,
The rocks are ringing,	Dombi´na so´wina´,
The rocks are ringing.	Dombi´na so´wina´.
They are ringing in the mountains,	Kai´va so´wina´,
They are ringing in the mountains,	Kai´va so´wina´,
They are ringing in the mountains.	Kai´va so´wina´.

Mooney wrote, "This song was explained to refer to the roaring of a storm among the rocks in the mountains" (Mooney [1896] 1991:1055).

M-6 (3. Do´ tĭ´mbi)

The black rock, the black rock,	Do´ tĭ´mbi, Do´ tĭ´mbi-nä´n,
The black rock, the black rock,	Do´ tĭ´mbi, Do´ tĭ´mbi-nä´n,

The rock is broken, the rock is broken,	Tĭ′mbi bai′-yo, Tĭ′mbi ba′i-yo-ä′n,
The rock is broken, the rock is broken,	Tĭ′mbi bai′-yo, Tĭ′mbi ba′i-yo-ä′n.

Mooney tells us that "this song may refer to something in Paiute mythology. *Nä′n* and *ä′n* are unmeaning syllables added to fill out the measure" (Mooney [1896] 1991:1053).

Rocks and mountains, which are important natural features in Naraya songs, are the central images in M-5 and M-6. Mooney added that there is water implied in M-5—a mountain rainstorm that accounted for the "ringing" of the rocks. Such a violent rainstorm may possibly refer to Ghost Dance doctrine, the cataclysmic events predicted to occur as the new world slides over and replaces the old one. We see this cataclysmic scene in the rumbling and crackling storm described in Naraya song 26.

M-7 (2. Dĕna′ gayo′n)

A slender antelope, a slender antelope,	Dĕna′ gayo′n, Dĕ′na ga′yoni′,
A slender antelope, a slender antelope,	Dĕna′ gayo′n, Dĕ′na ga′yoni′,
He is wallowing upon the ground, He is wallowing upon the ground,	Bawă′ doro′n, Ba′wă do′roni′,
He is wallowing upon the ground, He is wallowing upon the ground.	Bawă′ doro′n, Ba′wă do′roni′.

In his comment, Mooney reports, "This song evidently refers to a trance vision in which the sleeper saw an antelope rolling in the dust, after the manner of horses, buffalo, and other animals" (Mooney [1896] 1991:1053).

The antelope in M-7 is the sole animal in these Northern Paiute texts. Its importance to Great Basin cultures has already been discussed in chapter 1, in connection with shamanistic antelope charming.

M-8 (9. Sû′ng-a ro′yonji′)

The cottonwoods are growing tall,	Sû′ng-ä ro′yonji′, Sû′ng-a ro′yon,
The cottonwoods are growing tall,	Sû′ng-ä ro′yonji′, Sû′ng-a ro′yon,
The cottonwoods are growing tall.	Sû′ng-ä ro′yonji′, Sû′ng-a ro′yon.
They are growing tall and verdant,	Pu′i do′yonji′, Pu′i do′yon,
They are growing tall and verdant,	Pu′i do′yonji′, Pu′i do′yon,
They are growing tall and verdant.	Pu′i do′yonji′, Pu′i do′yon.

Mooney writes, "This song seems to refer to the return to spring. Throughout the arid region of the west the cottonwood skirting the borders of the streams is one of the most conspicuous features of the landscape" (Mooney [1896] 1991:1055).

M-9 (4. Päsü´ wĭ´noghän)

The wind stirs the willows,	Päsü´ wĭ´noghän,
The wind stirs the willows,	Päsü´ wĭ´noghän,
The wind stirs the willows,	Päsü´ wĭ´noghän,
The wind stirs the grasses,	Wai´-va wĭ´noghän,
The wind stirs the grasses,	Wai´-va wĭ´noghän,
The wind stirs the grasses.	Wai´-va wĭ´noghän.

Mooney makes these identifications: "*Wai´-va* (or *wai* in composition) is the sand grass or wild millet of Nevada (*Oryzopsis membranacea*), the seeds of which are ground by the Paiute and boiled into mush for food" (Mooney [1896] 1991:1053–54).

Trees and greenery, two major topics and images in Naraya songs, appear prominently in M-8 and M-9. Their associations with water and other qualities have been discussed in chapter 6.

Mooney's observation that cottonwoods are conspicuous features of the Great Basin landscape has linguistic ramifications. Trager notes that for many Native American cultures in the southwest, the word for cottonwood is also the generic word for "tree" (Trager 1964:467). Both Wick Miller and Richley Crapo document this for the Gosiute and Smokey Valley Shoshones,[10] *soho-pin,* carrying the double reference (W. Miller 1972:134, 171; Crapo 1976:188).

Mooney identifies the particular grass mentioned in M-9 and comments that its seed was part of the Northern Paiutes diet. This song and Mooney's comments bring to mind Naraya song 116, which also mentions an edible seed (sunflower) that Shoshones prepared in soup.

From a formal standpoint, there are many correspondences between the texts of the nine Northern Paiute songs and Naraya songs. Eight out of the nine are based on two different lines of text that repeat. In four and one-half songs (M-2, M-5, M-8, M-9, the first line of M-4) both lines repeat three times[11] and in three and one-half songs (M-3, M-6, M-7, the last line of M-4) they repeat two times. Like Naraya songs, many individual lines, themselves, subdivide into two repeated parts. Examination of the Paiute rather than English texts reveals that the repetition of parts may be exact (M-1 and M-3) or inexact (M-6, M-7, M-8). Again, like many Naraya songs, the point of the inexact repetition takes place at the ending, which is either slightly lengthened or shortened. For example, compare the mid and final endings of both lines of M-6, *tĭ´mbi* versus *tĭ´mbi-nä´n* and *bai´-yo* versus *ba´i-yo-ä´n,* and M-8, *ro´yonji´* versus *ro´yon* and *do´yonji´* versus *do´yon.*

The lengthening or shortening of words is not restricted to ending words. We learn from Mooney's glossary of Paiute words that *päsü´*, the first word of M-9, is a shortened form of *päsü´bi*, meaning "willow." Similarly, *pu´i* in M-8 is a shortened form of *pu´igai´-yu*, "green."

Mooney comments on the use of vocables in connection with M-4 and M-6. In his glossary of Northern Paiute words, in which the sung form of a word is given and then its spoken form, we can discover more examples of vocables and even a vowel change in the following: "*Dombi´na*—for *Tĭ´mbi* [M-5] . . . *Noyo´wana*—for *Noyo´ä* [M-3]" (Mooney [1896] 1991:1056). In the last example, the added parts include glide, "w," and nasal "n," linguistic elements that are important in Naraya sung forms discussed earlier in chapter 8. Two further examples of nasalization and vowel changes in the Paiute song texts are *tûngwü´kwiji,* which is the sung nasalized form of spoken *tăkwû´kwij* (M-1) and *wûmbe´doma, wûmbi´ndoma´,* and *wûmbi´n-doma´n,* three sung nasalized forms of *wûbi´doma,* whirlwind (M-1, M-2, and M-3) (Mooney [1896] 1991:1056–57).

In the original Paiute texts, four of the nine have parallel endings between their two different lines of text:

M-2, dust (*kosi´*) whirlwind (*wûmbi´ndomä´*)
mountain (*kai´-va*) whirlwind (*wûmbi´ndomä´*)
M-5, rocks (*dombi´na*) ringing (*so´wina´*)
mountains (*kai´va*) ringing (*so´wina´*)
M-8, cottonwoods (*sû´ng-a*) are growing tall (*ro´yon*)
green (*pu´i*) are growing tall (*do´yon*)
M-9, willows (*päsü´*) wind stirs (*wĭ´noghan*)
grasses (*wai´-va*) wind stirs (*wĭ´noghan*)

The use of rhyme in Paiute Ghost Dance texts frequently results from the parallel same-word endings such as those given above. There is true end rhyme in M-7, *ga´yoni´* and *do´roni´,* and assonance between the vocable endings of M-6, *-nä´n* and *-ä´n.*

As in Naraya texts, neither people nor the activities of people appear in these Northern Paiute texts. Their images come from the natural world—fog, snow, rocks, mountains, whirlwinds, the Milky Way, antelopes, trees, grasses, and greenness.

Notice the verb used in M-9, *wĭ´noghän,* which Mooney defines in his Paiute glossary as "shaken by the wind, waving in the wind" (Mooney [1896] 1991:1057). I believe this is the same verb that takes many different forms in Naraya texts (for example, songs 13, 40, 43, and 130) and is rich with interpretive meanings. (See chapter 8.) In Shoshone, the image is of standing-moving, which in many contexts implies the wind as the source of movement for a standing object, such as the willows and grasses in M-9.

Finally, I conclude with Mooney's only two comments about the source of these Paiute songs and their texts. He reports that M-7 came in a trance vision and M-1 was composed by a woman. Regarding the last point, I remind the reader of Naraya song 112, which also originated from a woman, and discussion in chapter 6 about the role and status of women in the Great Basin and their influence on the Ghost Dance movement.

Lowie, 1909

From his work with the Northern Shoshone, Lowie published one song text (L-1) of the *nu´akin,* a type of Round Dance. I have already quoted in detail Lowie's description of this dance in chapter 1. I repeat here Lowie's commentary on the text, which followed his transcription and translation of it.

> The following very imperfectly translated nu´akin song was secured:
>
> Ma´zambi a   un-du´a, wa´sipi   un-du´a-tsi,
> Mountain-sheep her son, mountain-sheep's son,
>   du´mbi   ma-to´owEn.
>   on the rock goes out.
> E´nga-m-bo pa go´nait wu´kum-bai yo´ina, pado´nobina.
> A red ball cloud   wind has   (?)   go outside.
>
> (At this point of the song several of the singers knelt down on the ground.)
>
> Bi´a-gwina umbi´oi   un-du´atsi pa´wucorotogin.
> Eagle   white (?) her son   (?)
>
> Ta´ham bi´agwina   bi´oi du´atsi.
> Our   white-   eagle's son.

A very vague, general resemblance might be noticed between the style of this song and that of some recorded ghost-dance songs. Together with the informant's statement that some Shoshone called the nu´akin dzo´a-nogakin, ghost-dance, the slow movement, the characteristic position of the women, and the clasping of hands, it might be taken as evidence of a recent development of the dance. But Mooney's statement, that the Shoshone ghost-dance was merely a revival of an older dance practised fifty years ago, is supported by the testimony of Lemhi informants, re-enforced both by the mention of the nu´akin in mythology and the explanation of its object. There can thus be little doubt as to its antiquity. (Lowie 1909a:218)

Even though there are some holes and problematic spots in the translation of this *nu´akin* text, it is still possible to see a relationship between it and eleven Naraya texts, which also center on animal offspring.[12] In chapter 5 I wrote, "The Naraya sings of animal young to promote animal young." I suggest that this *nu´akin* text is similar to Naraya texts not only in its subject matter but, in some similar sense, in its intent. The following comment by Lowie and his use of the verb "insure" seem to support this interpretation: "the *nu´akin* was celebrated to insure the coming of the fish" (Lowie 1909a:218).

With few changes, I wish to redo the English translation in order to bring out what I think are some of the nuances of the text and to make its form more visible. Let me explain the rationale for the changes I have made. First, notice that in line one, Lowie translates both *ma´zambia* and *wa´sipi* as "mountain sheep." I believe that *ma´zambia* is almost identical to *mozambia* in Naraya song 74, and from this I conclude that the reference is to a ewe. Lowie's use of the pronoun, "her," confirms this. The second term, *wa´sipi*, may also be correctly translated as "mountain sheep," but it can also mean "game animal,"[13] which broadens the reference, implying or alluding to the other members of the same category—the deer, the elk, the moose, and antelope. In any case, that mountain sheep should be synonymous with game animal indicates its importance for some Shoshone groups.

I believe that the last line has mistakenly reversed the translation of *bi´agwina* as "white" and *bi´oi* as "eagle's." It should be the same as in the preceding line, *bi´a-gwina*, "eagle," and *umbi´oi*, "white (?)." Lowie was unsure of his translation of *umbi´oi*, and added a question mark in parenthesis after the translated word. The word for "white" in Shoshone is *dosavit*[h]. Perhaps *umbi´oi* refers to the white tail feathers of the eagle, those used by shamans in healing. A Wind River Shoshone woman suggested that *bi´oi* might derive from *biya*, which means "mother." Again, Lowie's use of the possessive pronoun, "her son," is consistent with this suggestion. Unlike the Shoshone word for "mountain sheep," which indicates sex, "eagle" has no separate male-female forms. There are general terms for male and female animals, however, and *ombiafe*, the female form (Tidzump 1970:8), does bear some resemblance to *umbi´oi* in the text.

Lowie's translation of *un-du´a*, or *un-du´a-tsi* (with a diminutive, affectionate suffix), as "son" is correct. But the word can also include broader meanings of "child" or "offspring." Keep this in mind when reading the following presentation of the text, which incorporates some translation changes and leaves in untranslated form those words that are questionable or lacking translation.

> Mountain-sheep her son, game-mountain-sheep's son, on the rock
> goes out.
> A red ball cloud wind has *yo′ina,* go outside.
> *(kneeling)* Eagle *umbi′oi* her son *pa′wucorotogin.*
> Our eagle's *bi′oi* son.

Animal young are the main topics of the text—mountain-sheep–game animal and eagle. The text progresses from earth to sky and embraces the features and creatures of its shifting environment. The first three lines are earthbound: sheep–game animal young on the rocks, i.e., climbing on the rocks in the mountains. The next three lines move above the mountain rocks up to the sky. "A red ball cloud" is, I believe, a poetically compressed reference to the red sun and sunset clouds over the mountain. Note the similarity between this line and the first line of P-15, the key Shoshone roots being *enga-,* "red," and *pa:,* the water element in "cloud."

> P-15 Un-ka′   pa-ris,   The red sunset clouds
> L-1   E′nga-m-bo pa go′nait, A red ball cloud

Wind, another element that moves over earth, comes out with the red clouds of the setting sun.

The kneeling down of the singers before they sing the last two lines of text is perhaps a sign of their reverence to the sacred eagle mentioned in these lines. The text has moved on to the highest level, the powerful realm of the eagle. Recall Goss's hierarchy for the Ute ecological model, with the eagle sitting at the zenith point in the sky.

Parallel beginnings and endings frame the text. It begins with a line the two parts of which are slight variants of one another (mountain sheep her son) and ends with a parallel pair of variants (eagle her son). The two verbs in the text, "goes out" and "go outside," are also parallel. The first refers to mountain sheep on the rocks and the second to the cloud and wind on the mountain.

Waterman, 1910

Waterman recorded the following song in 1910, but it was not until Vennum transcribed it that it was finally published in 1986. Besides Mooney's publication, this is the only other Northern Paiute Ghost Dance text in the literature. The singer was Dick Mahwee, who lived on the Pyramid Lake Reservation in Nevada and was one of twenty shamans interviewed by Park in his study of Northern Paiute shamanism.

In Vennum's presentation the text appears under the music and not separately as I present it here. Music and text have already been given in example 133 in chapter 9.

W-1   ha-ne-na ha-ne-na he-na
      ha-ne-na ha-ne-na he
      pag*i*na pag*i*na he-na
      ha-ne-na ha-ne-na he-na

Regarding its translation, Vennum writes, "TEXT: vocables plus *pakɨnna* 'fog, cloud on the ground'" (Vennum 1986:704). Fog, *pagina*, is almost identical to my various transcriptions of it in Naraya songs 36–42. I have discussed it abundantly throughout this book because it is such an important image in Naraya songs. Let me recall its many associations and meanings in a stream of consciousness.

Fog and mountains:
   Fog as form of water:
      water and power
      water and plants
      fog-watery soul:
         retrieval by shaman
         resurrection in the Ghost Dance.

The form of the text is AABA; however, the form of its musical setting is *aabb*, classic paired phrases. The use of the A text on the second *b* musical phrase textually anticipates the return of the A section when the song repeats. It is yet another way of obscuring sectional divisions and foiling expectations.

Like Naraya songs, each section ends with *hena*, a variant form of *ena*. In the repeat of line A, *hena* is shortened to *he*. Finally, notice the cluster of three vocables and how it relates to the three syllables of *pagɨna*.

line A   ha-ne-na   ha-ne-na   he-na
line B   pa-gɨ-na   pa-gɨ-na   he-na

Ha- and *pa-* rhyme; *ne-* and *gɨ-* are both consonant-vowel formations but do not rhyme; *-na* and *-na* are identical endings.

Sapir, 1910

The following texts are but a small fraction of the 207 songs that Sapir recorded in 1910. The singer was Tony Tillohash, a Kaibab Southern Paiute, who at that time was a student at Carlisle Indian School in Pennsylvania. These texts remained unpublished until 1994, when Franklin and Bunte carefully prepared them for publication, and I quote from their edition of the texts. I have included the original Southern Paiute text only when there was no English translation for it. Otherwise, I quote the complete translation for the texts, including all vocables that were part of the original line. Those parts of the text that appear in quotation marks are from Sapir's original manuscript; those parts without quotation marks are Franklin and Bunte's close rendering of Sapir's transcription and translation analysis of the text. Finally, I have noted as "annotations" (the term used by Franklin and Bunte) comments made by Sapir about the song, which I cite whenever relevant to my discussion.

I present ten Round Dance texts first and then twenty-two Ghost Dance texts.[14] Within this division I have again grouped the texts by their topics and imagery, which accords with my presentation of Naraya texts. My own commentary intersperses the various groupings.

The S-number represents the order of Sapir's Southern Paiute texts as they appear in this chapter. Following it in parentheses is the original number used by Sapir and his titling of the text according to song genre. As musical transcriptions for S-3, S-4, S-13, S-14, S-16, S-20, and S-34 appear in chapter 9, I thought it helpful to include the musical-example numbers used there, along with the other parenthetical information.

S-1 (No. 116 Round Dance)

Willow[-bordered] stream, á: há   [-hɛ́] o: há [-hɛ́] e: ho: [ho:]
                           (vocables)
Willow[-bordered] stream, á: . . .
                           (vocable)

Annotation: "Not Ghost [Dance]" (Sapir 1994:633–34).

S-2 (No. 185 Round Dance Song)

Strangers' water-mountain, strangers' water-mountain,
The (melting) snow-rivulets will flow down, the snow-rivulets
will flow down.
(Sapir 1994:653)

Texts S-1 and S-2 are water texts—flowing by willows, snow-melted and flowing down.

S-3 (No. 76 Round Dance Song, Example 121)

"Mountains whose flanks are black with clouds"
"Mountain without trees, when mt. has been deprived of trees."

Annotation: "Not Ghost Dance" (Sapir 1994:627).

S-4 (No. 200 Round Dance [Shoshone], Example 120)

From off of little pinyon mountain, little mountain,
From off of little pinyon mountain, little mountain,

Cloud mountain ǰi:i:
Cloud mountain ǰi:i:

Annotation: "Shoshone; no Ghost Dance" (Sapir 1994:657).

Sapir did not give the repeats for both lines of this text, but as it was audible on the recording, Franklin and Bunte have added it (Sapir 1994:662n.31).

S-5 (No. 119 Round Dance)

"When does a cloud stand up and walk on the edge of a fir tree?"

Annotation: "Not Ghost [Dance]" (Sapir 1994:635).

S-6 (No. 115 Round Dance)

"[It is] a white peaked person."
e: yahe: ʔyahe: h[h][ʔ]e:ʔe: ya . . .
(vocables)

Annotation: "Not Ghost [Dance]" (Sapir 1994:633).

Clouds are the central image in S-3 through S-5, combining with mountains and lack of trees in S-3, mountains and pinyon pines in S-4, and fir trees in S-5.

Notice that Sapir identifies S-4 as a Shoshone song, which includes the Shoshone words for mountain and pine nut. The first Southern Paiute word of the second line, *æmpágɪna*, equates with various forms of *bagïna* or *vagïna*, translated as "fog" in Naraya songs. In its language, form, and imagery this text is indistinguishable from Naraya texts in Emily and Dorothy's repertoire. Sapir must have recognized the great similarity between Round Dance and Ghost Dance texts, so much so that he frequently felt impelled to write, "not Ghost Dance," on eight of the ten Round Dance texts to make sure that there could be no mistaking their correct genre identification.[15] S-4 is one of the eight that contains such a note.

I suggest that the central image in S-6, a white-sitting person, a white-peaked person, is a poetic reference to clouds. I have deduced this after studying two Ghost Dance texts, S-16 and S-17, one of which contains wording almost identical to that used in S-6. Further discussion of this interpretation follows these Ghost Dance texts. For now, let me simply comment that just as clouds stand up and walk on the edge of fir trees, so they may also sit and peak.

S-7 (No. 118 Round Dance)

Like small gravel, "dust in the air."

Annotation: "Not Ghost [Dance]" (Sapir 1994:634).

S-8 (No. 205 Round Dance)

The pumpkin which I struck repeatedly.
(Sapir 1994:659)

S-9 (No. 117 Round Dance)

a:,   Blue mare   a: + o: . . .
(vocable)   (vocables)

Annotation: "Not Ghost [Dance]" (Sapir 1994:634).

S-10 (No. 114 Round (Squaw) Dance)

yi:ʔɩ [-ye:ʔɩ] yá:ʔa yé:ʔe: ya:ʔa yé:ʔɩ ya:ʔa ye:e:, . . .
(vocables)
ɾa: o: . . .
(vocables)

Annotation: "Not Ghost Dance" (Sapir 1994:633).

There is no coherent pattern for the last four Round Dance texts (S-7 through S-10) and their images. Sapir notes that S-7 is not a Ghost Dance text, and from this I conclude that there is no reason to believe that "dust in the air" refers to a ghost or the dead. The text likens two similar natural phenomena, small gravel and dust. I have no clue for understanding the repeatedly struck pumpkin in S-8 and the single meaningful word, "mare," in S-9. S-10 is an all-vocable text and I will examine the choice and placement of its vocables in a later discussion.

S-11 (No. 113 Ghost Round Dance)

"In the middle of the land,"
"[About to] touch around from place to place."
(Sapir 1994:633)

S-12 (No. 154 Ghost Dance Song)

The mountain person will lie down,
? is revolving, revolving continually.

Linguistic Notes: "tɔyá´yɩ̥ = mt. (used only in songs)" (Sapir 1994:642).

S-13 (No. 195 Ghost Dance, Example 125)

Coming sliding, coming sliding.

Linguistic notes: "coming sliding (glass, stones, snow, ice)" (Sapir 1994:656).

Land and mountains are the subjects of texts S-11 through S-13. In S-12 and S-13, the scenes suggest dynamic, cataclysmic events. The personified mountain in S-12 continually turns or revolves—that is, its rocks fall, or it undergoes upheaval from earthquake. This image fits the Ghost Dance prophecy for the end of the world and brings to mind the old earth in Naraya song 25, which is wavy and swirling. The sliding in S-13, be it of glass or stones, snow or ice, also carries apocalyptic notions, and connects with Naraya song 27 and its vision of ground slides in the mountains during violent storms.

S-14 (No. 110 Ghost Round Dance, Example 124)

"Coy., God's (old) track" [is] wont to be cloud-spotted.
(Sapir 1994:632)

Text S-14 is rich with meanings and contexts. First, notice that Sapir equates coyote, literal translation of the Southern Paiute word, with mythic Coyote and God. Naraya songs never refer to Coyote as God, but rather, Our Father. However, recall that in other contexts, Wind River Shoshones interchange a variety of terms, including Our Father and Creator for Wolf and/or Coyote. (See chapter 2.)

"God's track" in S-14 is very close to Our Father's footprints or tracks mentioned in the first line of Naraya song 9 and a similar reference to Our Father, Our mother's footprints, in song 22. In both Naraya songs, the mother follows Our Father on a path up in the sky, either to the Land of the Dead (song 9) or the new world of Ghost Dance prophecy (song 22). I suggest that the cloud-spotted track in S-14 refers to the Milky Way in two possible senses. It may refer to the road itself; if so, note that it is moist and replaces another common Basin term for the Milky Way, the dry dust road. It also may refer to the foggy souls of those who travel the road—their souls in retrievable form—perhaps on the way to resurrection in the snowy new world.

The text of S-14 also brings to mind the final statement in Wind River Shoshone myth. "The ending of all mythological tales is a prescribed magical formula, . . . 'Coyote way out there is tracking through slush.' . . . a statement obscurely hinting at melting snow, which results from properly told tales" (Shimkin 1947c:335, 330). Although situated at opposite ends of time—past and future—a parallel exists between myth and Ghost Dance prophecy in its textual sequence of Coyote-God, his tracks, and a form of water.

S-15 (No. 112 Ghost Round Dance)

[A] soul is walking along, walking along, "our relation is coming back."
(Sapir 1994:632)

S-15 is the only text that specifically mentions the return of the dead soul, a return to life. Songs 18 and 2 are the rare Naraya examples that are equally explicit on this point.

S-16 (No. 111 Ghost Round Dance, Example 123)

The clear water makes a sound like pierced paper.
Cloud, cloud.

Linguistic Notes: "it makes sound of paper when something is thrust through it" (Sapir 1994:632).

S-17 (No. 194 Ghost Dance [Shoshone])

?"little spring"
"White—he is coming to sit down," white.

Annotation: "Shoshone" (Sapir 1994:655).

S-18 (No. 193 Ghost Dance)

Moving through the mountain plateau, moving through the
    mountain plateau,
"[The] crowned one, he peeps out now and then as he goes."
(Sapir 1994:655)

The images in S-16 through S-18 come from different forms of water. S-16 provides the key to the group, juxtaposing clear spring water on the ground with clouds, airborne water in the sky.

I suggest that S-17 is a similar juxtaposition. However, in place of the word for "cloud," the second line presents a poetic personification of cloud, white-he is coming to sit down. The first two words of the second line are virtually identical to the first two words of S-6, "white-sit." Sapir translated that line as, "[It is] a white peaked person," an apt image for clouds.

Moving even further out onto a limb, I suggest that S-18 may also have clouds as its implied subject. Recall text P-11 from Powell's collection of Southern Paiute texts, "It rains on the mountains, / A white crown encircles the mountains." I propose that clouds move through the mountain plateau in S-18. The "crowned one" is the mountain peak, which one glimpses now and then as the clouds move along.

S-19 (No. 109 Ghost Round Dance)

Edge of the mountain(s).
(Sapir 1994:632)

S-20 (No. 192 Ghost Dance, Example 126)

"From on the eagle mountain,"
"From on the eagle mountain."
(Sapir 1994:655)

Mountains, a sacred place for visions, are one of the most important images and settings in Naraya texts. (See topic-imagery chart (table 1) in the introduction.) Eagles, a traditional source and symbol of power, are the topic of S-20. Eagles appear in Naraya songs 6, 35, 93, and 94. See chapter 5 for a detailed discussion of the importance of the eagle in Ghost Dance belief.

S-21 (No. 144 Ghost Round Dance)

"[The] brownish knoll keeps coming together in two chunks."
(Sapir 1994:639)

S-22 (No. 145 Ghost Round Dance)

Through the drowsy canyon, at the canyon, through the canyon.
(Sapir 1994:639)

S-23 (No. 183 Ghost Dance)

"From squaw-bush spring rock"
Appeared scattered spots of sunlight.
(Sapir 1994:652)

S-24 (No. 188 Ghost Dance)

"On to that,"
"On to that,"
"red-berry (sp.?) knoll"
"red-berry knoll."
(Sapir 1994:653–54)

I have no commentary for the brownish knoll in S-21 or the drowsy canyon in S-22.

The images and complete scene presented in S-23 epitomize what one so often gets in Naraya texts: particular vegetation (here, squaw bush), water (spring), rock, and sky-weather conditions (fog, or dappled sunlight, in this text). Song 34 is a Naraya counterpart to S-23, afternoon sunshowers on the mountain, pine needles floating in pools on the mountainside.

S-24, which refers to a particular place where a particular berry is plentiful, also reminds one of Naraya songs, in this case, the berry texts of songs 117, 118, and 119.

S-25 (No. 156 Ghost Dance Song)

The sky [it is] that is sitting, the sky [it is] that is sitting,
The sky [it is] that is sitting, the sky [it is] that is sitting,
What silently struts like a pigeon? what silently struts like a pigeon?
What silently struts like a pigeon? what silently struts like a pigeon?
(Sapir 1994:643)

S-26 (No. 157 Ghost Dance Songs)

Pine covered knoll in the sky,
Pine covered knoll in the sky,
The sky that is flat and white, the sky that is silent and flat
The sky that is flat and white, the sky that is silent and flat.

(Sapir 1994:643)

In an editorial note, Franklin and Bunte suggest that the last repeated lines of the text "can be reanalyzed as: the sky [it is] that is silently sitting, the sky [it is] that is silently sitting" (Sapir 1994:661n.14).

The sky, itself, is the subject of S-25 and has no Naraya equivalent. However, its silence does bear resemblance to that of nighttime described in song 130, when trees and vegetation stand-moving in the wind without sound.

The text of S-26 envisions vegetation in the flat, white world of the sky. The central image is the pine tree, symbol of longevity, which Great Basin people used in connection with health. Pines also appear in Naraya songs 5, 34, and 109.

S-27 (No. 196 Ghost Dance [Shoshone])

GáŋaŋGaŋaŋGaŋaŋGáŋaŋ to:ro:andᶻi: tivʷaaɩvazo:annaʰ
[~ . . . vaso: . . .] á:yo:aɩnna

Annotation: "(text not glossed by Sapir; appears to be comprised of vocables or possibly Shoshone)" (Sapir 1994:656).

S-28 (No. 186 Ghost Dance)

ó:wɩnɩ ó:wɩnnɩ. . . . o:wɩnnó:
(vocables)

(Sapir 1994:653)

S-29 (No. 187 Ghost Dance)

ó:wɩyahaɩnɩ? ó:wɩya hó:wɩyahaɩnɩ?. . . .
(vocables)

(Sapir 1994:653)

S-30 (No. 197 Walapai Round Dance [Ghost Dance]), untranslated

siyo:ná:vɩ amattaʰ ||
siyo:ná:vɩ aɩyo:we:waʰ ||. . . .

(Sapir 1994:656)

S-31 (No. 198 Walapai Round Ghost Dance), untranslated

í:nnaɩndo:a sɩgígɩn?na:
í:nnaɩndo:a sɩgígɩn?na:

mia vɔ́a sɪsáɪnna[:]aa
mia vɔ́a sɪsáɪnna[:]aa
(Sapir 1994:656)

Note: "This strophic pattern (AABB) follows the cylinder recording. Sapir wrote each verse only once" (Sapir 1994:662n.29).

S-32 (No. 199 Walapai Round Ghost Dance), untranslated

í:nnaɪdo:a sɪʔέ:
í:nnaɪdo:a sɪʔέ:
yá:nʔnaɪndo:ŋ [~ . . . dɷ:ŋ] qáram?ᴵᵛᴵ̦ɪné:
yá:nʔnaɪndo:ŋ [~ . . . dɷ:ŋ] qáram?ᴵᵛᴵ̦ɪné:
(Sapir 1994:657)

Annotation: "This strophic pattern (AABB) follows the cylinder recording. Sapir wrote each verse only once" (Sapir 1994:662n.30).

I have included S-27 through S-32 even though they are untranslated texts and vocable texts. If nothing else, one can at least see their form. Regarding the untranslated Walapai songs, Sapir's annotation for S-30 is also relevant for S-32 and S-33: "Walapai round-dance song sung by Walapais in 1892 who came to Cedar City for last great ghost dance" (Sapir 1994:662n.28).

Franklin and Bunte comment on the form of the Round Dance and Ghost Dance songs after analyzing Sapir's transcriptions and comparing them, whenever possible, to the recordings. With the aid of the recordings they could verify that the texts of S-2, S-4, S-25, S-26, S-31, and S-32 are made of two paired phrases, AABB (Sapir 1994: 661nn.13, 14, 662nn.29, 30). Sapir's textual transcriptions for these texts indicated the complete repeated form only for S-2. In their presentation of these texts Franklin and Bunte have added line repetitions whenever the recordings warrant it. However, because the recordings for many of the songs are either lost or inaudible and Sapir's transcriptions do not necessarily include repetitions, the exact form of many of these song texts remains unknown.

Pairing, or repetition of lines, is not restricted to songs with two lines of text. The form of the basic stanza or verse of a song may simply be one line and its repetition, AA, for example, S-1 and S-20. Jacob Sapir's musical transcriptions suggest this is true in other songs as well. In several examples, Sapir writes a double bar after giving a repeated phrase, and then indicates the number of times that the *aa* musical unit repeats. In other words, the basic song is a single line of music and text, which repeats. This is true of examples 124, 125, and 126, the music for S-14, S-13, and S-20. It is also true for musical transcriptions numbers 144 and 145 (Sapir 1994:698; not included in the musical examples given in chapter 9), which are the musical transcriptions for texts S-21 and S-22.

Notice that in S-13 (example 125), the single line of text divides into two repeated subsections. The musical setting of the two-part text also repeats, but not exactly. This resembles Naraya form both in the paired subdivision of a section and in the slight differences in repeated parts—here, the music. S-25 and the second line of S-26 are further examples where lines of text subdivide into two repeated parts.

The use of vocables in these texts covers the gamut, from all-vocable texts to various combinations of vocables with lexical texts. S-10 is at the all-vocable end of the spectrum. *Y*, a glide that is common in Shoshone vocables, is used repeatedly in this text. The *r*, used just once in S-10, is uncommon in Shoshone vocables.[16] The vowels are *i* and *ι*, *a*, *e*, and *o*. The single and final *o* sound would seem to fit Shoshone use and placement of this vocable vowel; however, the dots after it suggest that the vocable line continues and it is therefore impossible to comment on this point. S-28 begins with *o*, and uses only one other vowel, *ι* which combines with *n* and another glide, *w*. S-29 adds to this inventory *h*, *y* (another glide), and *a*, all common elements in Shoshone vocables.

S-9 frames its meaningful text with vocable *a* at the beginning and *a* and *o* at the end. Again, a series of dots after the *o* suggests that the vocables continue, but the transcription does not. In S-6, the first line is lexical, the second line is vocable. The vocable stock is small and predictable: *y* and *h* combine with *a* and *e*. Vocables appear sparingly in S-4, used only at the end of the second pair of repeated lines. The combination of *j* and *i* as a vocable is unique within Sapir's texts and it is interesting to note that this Round Dance song is not, in fact, Southern Paiute, but Shoshone. An equally striking use of this unusual vocable combination appears in Naraya songs 60 and 64. In both cases *-ji* suffixes the word for game animals: *wasüpi* becomes *wasüp-pen-ji.*

Sapir also noted that S-27 is a Shoshone song and considered the first long pattern, *GáŋaŋGaŋaŋGaŋaŋGáŋaŋ*, to be vocables. I believe that this text combines meaningful Shoshone words with vocables, but that over time and shifting from Shoshone to Southern Paiute singers, changes in it blurred distinctions between its use of lexical and nonlexical portions.

It clearly ends with one of the formulaic vocable ending patterns, a variant form of *yaiyowaindë,* such as one finds in Naraya songs 45,

60, 74, and 82.[17] Even its musical setting is identical to that used in Naraya songs, for example, song 45.

Excerpts from S-27 (No. 196 Ghost Dance) and Naraya song 45

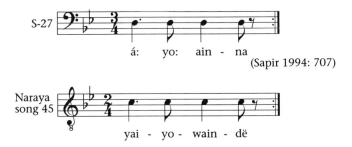

S-27

á: yo: ain - na

(Sapir 1994: 707)

Naraya song 45

yai - yo - wain - dë

I suggest that the first long *Gaŋaŋ-* pattern is a repeated portion of a word, "fog" being a likely candidate. In Naraya songs, "fog" appears in variant forms, such as *vagïna* (song 36) or *bagana* (song 40). ("Fog" also appears in the Shoshone Round Dance text in Sapir's collection, S-4, which he transcribed as *æmpágïna*.) "Fog" is stretched out in Naraya songs in a number of ways: by repeating the word—*vagïna vagïna vagïna* (Naraya song 36), by repeating the first syllable—*va-n-vagïna* (Naraya song 41), and by repeating the second syllable—*baga-ga-në* (Naraya song 38). Or, coming closer to the pattern of S-27, the second and third syllables both repeat in Naraya song 127: *baga-ga-na-na*. In this same text, the word for Milky Way is also lengthened, becoming *saiyaga-na-na*.[18] The reiteration of *Gaŋaŋ-* in S-27 may simply have been a manipulated word fragment cut loose from its lexical anchor.

I also suggest that the beginning of the last "word" of this text might be "pine nut." Sapir's transcription for it appears in almost identical form in Naraya songs 62 and 121 (*dïva*).

Sapir's rendering of the Southern Paiute song texts shows the many small variations that I have noted as an important feature in Naraya songs. Franklin and Bunte remark that he included "slight variations in repeated verses within single song performances" (Sapir 1994:593). We see this even at the level of repetition within a line. For example, "Cloud, cloud" in S-16 is, *pa:ɣïnavɪ paɣïnav*. The omission of the final *ɪ* in the repeated word is similar to the abbreviation of *hombi* to *hom* in the first line of Naraya song 117.

Also in S-16, Sapir gives the variant forms of a word, distinguishing them by their poetic or nonpoetic use: "*pa:vúmpass* = clear water (in poetry)"; "*pa:vúmpaʰ* = clear water." The additional sibilant *s* sound seems particularly appropriate in this text, as the line refers to the sound of the clear spring water. It is onomatopoeic and brings to mind the use of *s* and *v* for water sounds in Naraya song 129. (See chapter 8.)

Personification, such as one finds in Naraya songs, appears in the Southern Paiute songs. Clouds walk, stand (S-5), and sit (S-6, 17); a mountain person turns around (S-12). Like Wood Stick Man of Naraya song 112, there is also a personified tree, a pine, who appears in the following Bird Song.

S-33 (No. 63 Bird Song "with Rattle")

On the other side of an old ponderosa stump (is one that is standing, Tears will start falling.

(Sapir 1991:623–24)

Bird songs are one of four genres performed in the Southern Paiute Cry ceremony. "The essential elements of the ceremony are the singing of numerous mourning songs and the offering of valuables . . . in memory of the dead" (Sapir 1994:595). Sapir's annotation for the meaning of S-33 suggests how the pine person shames the human mourners by behaving more appropriately, given an analogous situation. "On the other side of an old pine-tree stump (away from people) stands another tree with tears rolling down (i.e., dirty red pitch exuding). I.e.: You people have come to have a good time, but the relation (2nd tree) of the dead man (stump) stands mourning" (Sapir 1994:624).

The reciprocity between all parts of the natural world appears in the Southern Paiute songs. Personification is just one form of it. In S-25 the sky struts silently like a pigeon. Sapir's annotations for two other Bird Songs reveal how singers imitate different aspects of bird behavior for each song. The Rooster Song (No. 42) "is sung only in morning to correspond to a rooster's crowing" (Sapir 1994:620). In performing the Quail Song (No. 43), "Singers strut back and forth like quails, holding their hands clenched to bodies below breasts" (Sapir 1994:620).

I would like to conclude with one Southern Paiute Medicine song in Sapir's collection, because I believe that like the Round Dance, shamanistic performance and songs are part of the essential grounding for the Ghost Dance and Naraya

S-34 (No. 139 Medicine Song, Example 122)

On elk mountain, on elk mountain,
Moving through the red pines,

The wind passes quickly, the wind passes quickly,
"Carrying snow on its head," "carrying snow on its head."
(Sapir 1994:638)

The combined imagery of this text bears a strong resemblance to that in Naraya songs. It touches all the natural bases—mountains, animals, trees, wind, and snowy water. It evokes a healthy scene from nature. Sapir tells us that this song was actually used to cure Tony Tillohash, "Sung by a medicine-man alone, mostly while sitting, sometimes dancing" (Sapir 1994:638). Song, dance, and this particular text—all the elements of Naraya performance with its song, dance, and similarly imaged texts—were to restore Tony's health. Even the name of the medicine man, *maáššax^warih* = "[plant-] green," seems significant. Recall the associations with greenery and the comment by one medicine man that if he sees greenery in connection with a patient, the prognosis for recovery is good.

This text is reminiscent of Naraya texts in its imagery and personification of nature as well as in its blend of small asymmetries within a symmetrical frame. Three of the four lines of text have two repeated parts. These four lines of text are set to two repeated musical lines. Each line subdivides in two, the second part repeating the first exactly except for one and one-half beats before the cadence.

Shimkin, 1937

Shimkin did his Shoshone fieldwork on the Wind River reservation in 1937, recording several Naraya songs. English translations for four of the texts and a Shoshone transcription for one were published in 1947. In 1977 Shimkin sent me all the information on these texts that he had written down in his fieldnotes, including their Shoshone transcriptions. The version I give here includes this additional material.

Two of the songs (Sh-1 and Sh-3) were recorded from Toorey Roberts, born in 1881 and a Naraya leader from 1932 until 1937, when Shimkin interviewed him. They were his songs, songs that "came to his mind: an idea." Shimkin recorded the other two songs (Sh-2 and Sh-4) from Pandora Pogue, born in 1863. She told him that the songs were from Frank Perry, "a powerful shaman" who dreamed them.

Sh-1 Naraya Song Text

White-rock rivers	dosa tïmbi ógwet
All kinds of rivers	na´na ógwet
Warm rivers (Repeat whole verse)	yuwaixent ógwet
(Shimkin 1947c:350)	(Shimkin 1937)

Sh-2 Naraya Song Text

Water-black rock,	pa:ˊrutïˊmbi
Water-black shining;	pa:ˊruʒïga:ˊʹyu
Two water-grass fishes	pa:ˊšoni peˊŋgwinux
On the water's edge.	pa:ˊŋgë maβiˊ
(Shimkin 1947c:350)	(Shimkin 1947c:350)

Sh-3 Naraya Song Text

Green goose's son	puˊhiwa nïgïnt nduˊa
Green goose's son	puˊhiwa nïgïnt nduˊa
(Shimkin 1937)	(Shimkin 1937)

Sage-brush goose's son
Sage-brush goose's son, etc.
(Shimkin 1947c:350)

Sh-4 Naraya Song Text

Yellow willow waving	oha šïhiβi gwambikiŋ
Rye grass, giant rye grass waving	šonip, pia šonip gwambikiŋ
Alder waving	hugwiʒap gambikiŋ
Cottonwood waving	šohop gwambikiŋ
Spruce, big spruce waving	woŋap, pia woŋap gwambikiŋ
Quaking aspen waving	šïnap gwambikiŋ
Spruce waving	woŋogwana gwambikiŋ . . .
(Shimkin 1937)	(Shimkin 1937)

Yellow willow is waving
Yellow willow is waving
Grass, big grass is waving
Grass, big grass is waving
Alder is waving
Alder is waving, etc.
(Shimkin 1947c:350)

Cottonwood is waving
Cottonwood is waving
Spruce, big spruce is waving
Spruce, big spruce is waving
Quaking aspen is waving
Quaking aspen is waving
Spruce is waving
Spruce is waving
(extrapolated from Shimkin's 1937 fieldnote version)

The imagery in these four texts fits perfectly with that in Emily and Dorothy's Naraya repertoire. Sh-1, a water text, focuses on rivers. Sh-2 is a common Naraya scene: water, rocks, animals (fish), and vegetation (grass). (See, for example, song 96.) Sh-3 combines vegetation and animals, specifically animal offspring, an important subdivision in Naraya songs (songs 66, 69–72) and also central to the *Nuʹakin* text, L-1. Goose's son or offspring is the subject of Naraya song 97, and like Sh-3, the text includes the associated environment—green vegetation at the water's edge.[19] Sh-4 focuses exclusively on vegetation, primarily trees. The image of trees and grass waving in the wind is very similar to the image of grass waving in Naraya 102 (both texts using the same verb) and other texts with windblown vegetation, such as in songs 104 and 130. These bring to mind the scene of windblown willows and grass in the Northern Paiute text, M-9, and the grass blowing in a mountain breeze in Powell's Southern Paiute text, P-39.

Before giving the text of Sh-4, Shimkin wrote in his fieldnotes, "it was to all the trees" and then after the text, "And so on for all the trees. Whenever they sing that song they pray first. They are God's songs. Every song is supposed to kill disease and help bring the dead back" (Shimkin 1937). The juxtaposition of these statements with this song text suggests many meanings. First, there is the power of song and thought-prayer; then, the power of trees and the interrelatedness of all things—abundance and health of trees with health of people, even resurrection of people.

Shimkin discussed the form of these texts and other matters pertaining to them in the 1947 publication in which they appeared, and I quote from it.

> The singers are shamans who dream or compose their songs. The music is a mere alternation of two themes of simple structure and narrow tonal range sung slowly in a high-pitched nasal voice. The texts are cryptic descriptions of visions, fully understood only by their authors. These texts are built up of units of single lines which rhyme through simple, final repetition, through alliteration or assonance, or through true rhyme. Two varieties of Ghost Dance texts exist, one, which simply repeats each line and another more complicated in structure, which repeats each verse. (Shimkin 1947c:350)

Shimkin cited Sh-3 and Sh-4 as examples of texts made of repeated lines and Sh-1 as a three-line verse that repeats. He then analyzed Sh-2 as follows: "In this instance meter and stress are well balanced. The lines are of five, seven, seven, and five morae, respectively. The stresses are on the second and fourth, second and sixth, second and fifth, and second and fifth morae. But such balance is accomplished only through poetic license. In normal Shoshone the adjective precedes the modified noun; the suffix *a´yu* is short and unaccented; intervocalic *m* becomes a nasalized *w;* and so on" (Shimkin 1947c:350–351).

I would add that there is striking use of parallelisms in these texts. In Sh-2, it is at the beginning of the text; every line starts with *pa:*, "water." Literally,

> water-black rock,
> water-black shining;
> water-grass two fishes
> water on the edge of.

In Sh-1, Sh-3, and Sh-4 the parallelism appears at the end of each line, repeating the same last word or words: "rivers" in Sh-1, "son" in Sh-3,[20] and "is waving" in Sh-4.

Liljeblad, 1940s

Liljeblad recorded Northern Shoshone songs in the 1940s. In 1986 he published transcriptions and translations for four of them, three Round Dance texts and one Ghost Dance text. I have listened to one of his tapes and transcribed the music and text for an additional Ghost Dance song. (See example 134 in chapter 9 for its musical transcription.)

I include Liljeblad's introductory remarks to his presentation of the three Round Dance texts and his analytical comments that followed each text.

> The following three examples of Round Dance song texts in Northern Shoshone have been chosen for illustration because they are representative in style and are matched by variants on the same themes elsewhere. In these songs the entire poem consists of only one stanza, which for the sake of parallel construction has four, six, or eight verses or lines. The fully developed stanza in this conservative song style usually begins with two cola [plural of colon, which refers to the unit of verses and its form] held together in one musical phrase ending on the tonic and repeated at least once, often three times with the additional vocable fillers in the context. The final syllable of the last verse of the strophe is abbreviated by apocopation [through omission of the last sound or syllable of a word]. Alternatively, one or two syllables may be added to the last verse in order to denote the end of the stanza. Any reiteration of the stanza is separated from what precedes by a caesura representing one dance step. The texts are in phonetic transcription to illustrate the phonetic modifications of verse, which would not be apparent in a phonemic transcription. (Liljeblad 1986:648)[21]

Li-1 (I.)

pí·aʔáŋginándɨ óhandóŋgimbínȝi
pí·aʔáŋginándɨ óhandóŋgimbínȝi

pábu·ndí·diná·nʒi
pábu·ndí·diná·nʒi
hí:na
pábu·ndí·diná·nʒi
hí:na
pábu·ndí·diná·nd

The large sunflower, the fully yellow flower spreading out
The large sunflower, the fully yellow flower spreading out
From the water-clear root
From the water-clear root
Heena!
From the water-clear root
Heena!
From the water-clear root.

(Liljeblad 1986:648)

This song begins with two hexasyllabic phrase cola, each one under one principal stress on the first syllable, forming one syntactic nominal sentence repeated once and followed by three identical hexasyllabic verses, a final abbreviated pentasyllabic line, and the expletive emphatic particle *hi·na* or *he·na,* which often occurs in both Numic and Washoe poetry. (Liljeblad 1986:648)

Li-2 (II.)

nanás·u·yáɣɨ húumbi, nanás·u·yaɣɨ húumbi
nanás·u·yáɣɨ húumbi, nanás·u·yaɣɨ húumbi
cinámboŋgóombi éŋgandɨ túduwán·ɨ
cinámboŋgóombi éŋgandɨ túduwán·

Pretty one, the bush; pretty one, the bush
Pretty one, the bush; pretty one, the bush
Root above the ground and rose hips
In string of red
Root above the ground and rose hips
In string of red.

(Liljeblad 1986:648)

Li-3 (III.)

tɨ·sidó·yací·ya· tó·yanɨ·ga·rúŋga
tɨ·sidó·yací·ya· tó·yanɨ·ga·rúŋga
tɨ·sidɨkwá·ruŋgíu
tɨ·sidɨkwá·ruŋgíugin·a

(Liljeblad 1986:648)

Freely translated: "Bluegrass hill, under the side of the hill, the bluegrass waves [in the wind]." The *-kinna [gin·a]* added to the last line indicates "motion toward the speaker." The song was recorded also in an eight-line stanza by the same singer.

The structure in "paired progression" of the examples given above (x representing the metric filling particle) are:
(1) aabbxbxb
(2) aabcbc'
(3) aabb'
Naturally, this does not exhaust the occurrences of paired patterns in Shoshonean poetry, metrical configurations that are well nigh uncountable. Variants with the same motifs as the second and third song texts were widely known and remained popular into modern times. (Liljeblad 1986:648)

The reader can compare Liljeblad's Round Dance texts with references he mentions, Mooney (M-1 through M-9) and Shimkin (Sh-1 through Sh-4), given above.

Plant images in the three Round Dance song texts are completely congruent with those in Naraya songs. The sunflower plant is the subject of both Li-1 and Naraya song 116. However, their images center on different stages of the life cycle, the blossom in Li-1 and the seeds after blossoming in Naraya song 116.

Li-2 presents the fruited stage of the wild rose. I believe that this song and Naraya song 117 are, in fact, variants of the same song. I listened to Li-2 on Liljeblad's tape and noted with interest that on the accompanying sheet with documentation, Liljeblad labeled it a Ghost Dance song. However, its publication as a Round Dance song is, nonetheless, completely consistent with information that Liljeblad received regarding the interchangeable use of terms by Northern Shoshones, specifically, Round Dance (Spring Dance and Grass Dance) and Ghost Dance (Liljeblad 1969:54). Earlier in this century Wind River Shoshones also used one term, Naraya—the shuffling step and common element between the Round Dance and Naraya—for both dances. However, and at the same time, they knew the differences between the two and clearly distinguished them. Song repertoire was one crucial separator.

I have transcribed two other Wind River Shoshone performances of this song, one by Angelina Wagon in 1981 (Vander 1988:61) and one by Dick Washakie, Chief Washakie's son, whom Edward Curtis recorded 1909. A comparative score of the three transcriptions is a lesson in constancy (Vander 1988:62). Music and text in Emily and Dorothy's performance vary in only the smallest details from Washakie's, despite the more than sixty years that separate them. This likeness remains consistent between Northern and Wind River Shoshone performances as well.

L-3 concludes the Round Dance set. Like Naraya song 102, Sh-4, M-9, and P-39, its central image is grass waving in the wind.

The following Northern Shoshone Ghost Dance text appeared only in conjunction with Vennum's musical transcription of the song. (See example 133 in chapter 9.) I present it here as a separate text. The sung text deviates strikingly from the spoken form of it, which Liljeblad provided along with its translation.

Li-4   Ghost Dance Song

> ho rem·anayaha giβan·aya:re
> ho rem·anayaha giβan·aya:re
> horemβanuŋgan·a horemβanuŋgan·a hoβæ·na
> horemβanuŋgan·a horemβanuŋgan·a hoβæ·na
> (Liljeblad, in Vennum 1986:703–4)

The spoken form of this text and its translation without repeats are:

> *kusippancaya?a kipantaya·ti/*   *kusippɨnnunkanna/*
> "Grayhawk is turning on stiff wings—gray one, his whirling—
>   *hupianna*
>   as the song goes."
> (Liljeblad, in Vennum 1986:703–4)

Li-5 Ghost Dance, Vander's Transcription and Translation

Wazümbi	*dua-n-zi*	*wazümbi*	*dua-n-zi,*	
Game animals	offspring- (d.a.s.)	game animals	offspring-, (d.a.s.)	
Wazümbi	*dua-n-zi*	*wazümbi*	*dua-n-zi.*	
Game animals	offspring- (d.a.s.)	game animals	offspring-. (d.a.s.)	
Dïmpï	*mano*	*waina*	*dïmpï*	*mano*	*wain*	*en,*
Rocks	?	going down	rocks	?	going down	(e.v.),
Dïmpï	*mano*	*waina*	*dïmpï*	*mano*	*wain*	*en.*
Rocks	?	going down	rocks	?	going down	(e.v.).

Animals are the topics in both Ghost Dance texts. The text of Li-4 seems to bear out points made in chapter 5 regarding the importance of two key qualities of birds—flight and song—in a variety of contexts, including the Ghost Dance. In Li-4, these images link poetically. "Grayhawk is turning on stiff wings—gray one, his whirling—as the song goes" (Vennum 1986:704). Like the flight of the bird, the song is whirling around and around, repeat after repeat.

Animal offspring, the subject of Li-5, are important in the Naraya song texts that both Shimkin and I have published (Sh-3 and Naraya songs 8, 66, 69–72). They are also the central image in L-1, another

Northern Shoshone song, and identified specifically with the *Nu´akin* Dance. In Li-5, young game animals are going down over rocks. In addition—or perhaps as an alternative reading—might the text suggest that rocks are coming down? The singer or the person who received the song would be able to clarify such textual ambiguities.

Both Ghost Dance texts are made of two repeated lines, AABB. Li-5, like many Naraya songs, subdivides each line into two repeated parts. In the first line, the repeated parts are identical; in the second line, there is a slight difference between the two. The first half of the line ends with *waina;* the second half shortens it to *wain* and adds *en,* an abbreviated form of the ending vocable, *ena.*

Steward, 1943

Steward included a Round Dance song text in his publication of Western Shoshone myths. Rat invites the Mountain Sheep to "join his circle dance and have a big feast. . . . When they arrived, Rat began to sing his circle dance song in a monotone." As Steward presents Rat's song (Steward 1943b:284):

Ka-wá ad-a tsu-na (I am rat),   ka-wá ad-a tsu-ná,

hú wí' wi - a,   hú wí' wi - a.

Not surprisingly, the form of Rat's Round Dance text is AABB.

Franklin and Bunte, 1988

In 1988 Franklin and Bunte recorded the following two Round Dance songs from Anna Whiskers, a Southern Paiute singer.

FB-1 (1.)

Pásitúi-yu	Pásitúi-yu
Foggy-when	Foggy-when
Pásitúi-yu	Pásitúi-yu
Foggy-when	Foggy-when
Nïvwá-raví	Nïvwá-raví
Snow-strike	Snow-strike [make footprints in unbroken snow]
Nïvwá-raví	Nïvwá-raví
Snow-strike	Snow-strike
	(Franklin and Bunte 1988:1)[22]

FB-2 (2.)

(ya) hái yáheyá yáheyáheyá   *pátsi*   *nónokwí'ni-kó-vachɨ*
    [vocables]   stream   run-inceptive-might/should

pátsi   *nónokwí'ni-kó-vani*
stream   run-inceptive-will

káivya-mánapaŋwi   *pátsi*   *nónokwí'ni-kó-vani*
mountain-down through from   stream   run-inceptive-will

pátsi   *nónokwí'ni-kó-vani*
stream   run-inceptive-will
(Franklin and Bunte 1988:2)

A free translation of this song is given by Jane Hill (J. Hill 1992:120–21):[23]

> Ya hai yaheya yaheyaheya streams should begin running
> Streams will begin running
> Down through the mountains streams will begin running
> Streams will begin running

Forms of water—fog, snow, and streams—are quintessential Naraya images. They are the spare and striking images in the texts of FB-1 and FB-2.

In these two texts one also sees all the formal elements so typical of Naraya texts. From a base of repetition arises symmetry, the two repeated lines of FB-1, AABB each line, in turn, made from two repeated parts. From a base of incomplete, inexact repetition arises the subtly complex asymmetry of FB-2. Lines two and four are the same. These two B lines parallel one another and divide the text into two paired progressions, ABCB.

Interrelationships among the four lines add another level of connection and development. The endings of all four lines are parallel in that they all share the words "streams . . . begin running." But notice the difference in the verb tense, which moves from "should begin running" in line one to a more compelling form, "will begin running," in lines two, three, and four. The power of words, observed by Witherspoon and quoted earlier—"Ritual language does not describe how things are; it determines how they will be" (Witherspoon 1977:34)—seems relevant to this text. It is the same power that appears in Numic myth when Cottontail says to the Sun, "You, Sun. You're not going to be like that anymore [too hot]. You are going to be good" (W. Miller 1972:51). With that critical change of verb tense, the second half of line one becomes independent line B. The third line matches the first in its general length, adding a new beginning and taking the revised form of the ending, "streams will begin running." The repeat of line B completes the second progression and the text.

Plains Ghost Dance Song Texts

Important collections of Great Basin song texts remained unpublished until relatively recent times, but major collections of Plains Ghost Dance texts had already been published by the late nineteenth century. Mooney's publication of 161 Ghost Dance texts (14 with musical transcriptions) appeared in 1896, one year after Colby's publication of 31 texts. I provide the reader here with a limited selection of 16 Plains texts. I choose 8 songs from the Southern Arapaho and 8 from the Lakota, as songs from these groups comprise the majority of songs in the two collections.[24]

I will not comment on the textual form of Plains Ghost Dance texts because the topic requires its own separate and detailed examination. Therefore, I give only the translations of the texts and do not include their original language transcriptions.

It will be obvious to the reader, even in the small sampling of Plains texts reprinted here, that the prevalence of paired phrases, so important in Herzog's characterization of the musical style of Plains Ghost Dance songs, is equally significant in their texts. One can also see, here and there, examples of small differences in the repetitions of lines and other exceptions to the basic pattern. However, I leave all of these matters to others, who will have time and space for their study and presentation.

Mooney, 1896

M-1 (12. Ha´ yana´ -usi´ ya´)

How bright is the moonlight!
How bright is the moonlight!
Tonight as I ride with my load of buffalo beef,
Tonight as I ride with my load of buffalo beef.
(Mooney [1896] 1991:966–67)

Annotation: "The author of this song, on meeting his friends in the spirit world, found them preparing to go on a great buffalo hunt, the prairies of the new earth being covered with the countless thousands of buffalo that have been swept from the plains since the advent of the white man. They returned to camp at night, under the full moonlight, with their ponies loaded down with fresh beef" (Mooney [1896] 1991:967).

M-2 (13. Ha´ti ni´bät—E´he´eye´)

The cottonwood song—*E´he´eye!*
The cottonwood song—*E´he´eye!*
I am singing it,
I am singing it,
He´yaya´ahe´ye!
He´yaya´ahe´ye!
(Mooney [1896] 1991:967)

Mooney's lengthier annotation says:

> The cottonwood *(Populus monilifera)* is the most characteristic tree of the plains and of the arid region between the Rockies and the Sierras. It is a species of poplar and takes its name from the white downy blossom fronds, resembling cotton, which come out upon it in the spring. The cottonwood and a species of stunted oak, with the mesquite in the south, are almost the only trees to be found upon the great plains extending from the Saskatchewan southward into Texas. As it never grows out upon the open, but always close along the borders of the few streams, it is an unfailing indication of water either on or near the surface, in a region well-nigh waterless. . . . In winter the camps of the prairie tribes are removed from the open prairie to the shelter of the cottonwood timber along the streams. The tree is held almost sacred, and the sun-dance lodge is usually or always constructed of cottonwood saplings. (Mooney [1896] 1991:967–68)

M-3 (51. Ni´chi´a i´theti´hi)

(There) is a good river,
(There) is a good river,
Where there is no timber—
Where there is no timber—
But thunder-berries are there,
But thunder-berries are there.
(Mooney [1896] 1991:995–96)

Annotation: "This song refers to a trance vision in which the dreamer found his people camped by a good, i.e., perennial, river, fringed with abundant bushes or small trees of the *baa-ni´bin* or 'thunder-berry,' which appears to be the black haw, being described as a sort of wild cherry in size between the chokecherry and the wild plum. It was eaten raw, or dried and boiled, the seeds having first been taken out. It is very scarce, if found at all, in the southern plains" (Mooney [1896] 1991:996).

M-4 (67. Ni´nä´nina´ti´naku´ni´na na´ga´qu)

My children, my children,
It is I who wear the morning star on my head,
It is I who wear the morning star on my head;
I show it to my children,
I show it to my children,
Says the father,
Says the father.

(Mooney [1896] 1991:1006–7)

Annotation: "This beautiful song originated among the northern Arapaho, and is a favorite north and south. In it the messiah [Wovoka] is supposed to be addressing his children" (Mooney [1896] 1991:1007).

M-5 (1. Opening Song—Eyeye´! nä´nisa´na)

O, my children! O, my children!
Here is another of your pipes—*He´eye´!*
Here is another of your pipes—*He´eye´!*
Look! thus I shouted—*He´eye´!*
Look! thus I shouted—*He´eye´!*
When I moved the earth—*He´eye´!*
When I moved the earth—*He´eye´!*

(Mooney [1896] 1991:958)

Mooney's annotation says:

This opening song of the Arapaho Ghost dance originated among the northern Arapaho in Wyoming and was brought down to the southern branch of the tribe by the first apostles of the new religion. By "another pipe" is probably meant the newer revelation of the messiah, the pipe being an important feature of all sacred ceremonies, and all their previous religious tradition having centered about the seicha or flat pipe, to be described hereafter. The pipe, however, was not commonly carried in the dance, as was the case among the Sioux. In this song, as in many others of the Ghost dance, the father or messiah, *Hesûna´nin,* is supposed to be addressing "my children," *nänisa´na.* . . . The second reference is to the new earth which is supposed to be already moving rapidly forward to slide over and take the place of this old and worn-out creation. (Mooney [1896] 1991:958–59)

M-6 (49. A-bä´qati´ hä´nichä´bi hinä´na)

With the bä´qati wheel I am gambling,
With the bä´qati wheel I am gambling.
With the black mark I win the game,
With the black mark I win the game.

(Mooney [1896] 1991:994)

Annotation: "This song is from the northern Arapaho. The author of it, in his visit to the spirit world, found his former friends playing the old game of the *bä´qati* wheel, which was practically obsolete among the prairie tribes, but which is being revived since the advent of the Ghost dance. As it was a favorite game with the men in the olden times, a great many of the songs founded on these trance visions refer to it, and the wheel and sticks are made by the dreamers and carried in the dance as they sing" (Mooney [1896] 1991:994).[25]

M-7 (3. Ate´bĕ tiăwu nănu´)

My children, when at first I liked the whites,
My children, when at first I liked the whites,
I gave them fruits,
I gave them fruits.
(Mooney [1896] 1991:961)

In his annotation, Mooney records that "this song referring to the whites was composed by Nawat or Left Hand, chief of the southern Arapaho, and can hardly be considered dangerous or treasonable in character. According to his statement, in his trance vision of the other world the father showed him extensive orchards, telling him that in the beginning all these things had been given to the whites, but that hereafter they would be given to his children, the Indians. *Nia´tha,* plural *Nia´thuă,* the Arapaho name for the whites, signifies literally, expert, skillful, or wise" (Mooney [1896] 1991:961–62).

M-8 (30. Nihi´nata´yeche´ti)

He´yoho´ho´! He´yoho´ho´!
The yellow-hide, the white-skin (man).
I have now put him aside—
I have now put him aside—
I have no more sympathy with him,
I have no more sympathy with him.
He´yoho´ho´! He´yoho´ho´!
(Mooney [1896] 1991:978)

Annotation: "This is another song about the whites, who are spoken of as 'yellow hides' or 'white skins.' The proper Arapaho name for a white man is *Nia´tha,* 'skillful'" (Mooney [1896] 1991:978).

In my choice of texts I have tried to select those that use some of the same topics that are central in Naraya texts. But in every case, the relationships are so different that there is actually little correspondence. For example, M-1 presents a nighttime scene with the buffalo. But it is not the buffalo in its environment with the plant life that supports it, as it is in Naraya song 82. The place in M-1 is not the real world, but the spirit world. The buffalo is off the hoof, meat, which the successful horseback hunter carries back home. The cottonwood in M-2 is not visualized waving in the wind, as it is in Shimkin's Naraya text, Sh-4. It is removed from nature. The text of M-2 sings about singing and the cottonwood has become cottonwood lyrics, song words. Even M-3, which combines river and berries, water and plant, seems similar to Naraya texts. However, Mooney tells us that the scene takes place in the spirit world and it is the camping spot for the people. Humans and Plains life, sometimes unstated, are ever-present at the center.

M-4 through M-6 are more directly about the Ghost Dance religion. I have already given M-4 in chapter 7 and commented on the Morning Star as ritual timekeeper for the ending of Ghost Dance performance. I repeated the text earlier in this chapter so that one can compare it to Naraya song 15.

Naraya Song 15

> Our Morning Star coming up,
> Our Morning Star coming up.
> Clear sun rays streaming out,
> Clear sun rays streaming out.
> Star sitting lightly,
> Star sitting lightly.
> (Vander 1988:24)

In M-4, the Morning Star is human adornment. Wovoka, the father, wears it on his head and appropriately so, as it was he who set the schedule for Ghost Dance performance: that the final dance should continue throughout the night until dawn (Mooney [1896] 1991:781). In Naraya song 15, the Morning Star sits in its sky environment with the sun. The text relates the two, the waning light of one with the waxing brilliance of the other.

So different in their poetic contexts for the Morning Star, the two songs both originated on the Wind River Reservation in Wyoming. They are a testament to the integrity of their cultural rather than geographical origins. Northern Arapahoes, traditional enemies of the Shoshone, were placed on the reservation by the government in 1878. The two tribes chose to live apart in separate areas of the reservation and their Ghost Dance and Naraya performances remained separate events; thus, the cleavage in their song texts.

M-5 is another Northern Arapaho song, which establishes the direct religious lineage of their Ghost Dance from Wovoka, something that Emily stoutly denied in regard to the Naraya. The text is filled with people and cultural allusions. There are the Arapaho believers (children), Wovoka, the pipe—an object rich with Arapaho religious traditions and associations—and a reference to the predicted earthquake that precedes the coming new world.

Mooney tells us that M-6 (also a Northern Arapaho text) takes place in the spirit world. It, too, is filled with Arapaho people and culture, deceased friends playing an old gambling game.

I suggest that Arapaho and other Plains Ghost Dance texts focus on people and all the important elements of cultural and daily life, especially from the past. The spirit world is, therefore, a congruent backdrop for these texts and additionally connects with Ghost Dance prophecy for the future resurrection of its inhabitants.

People in Plains Ghost Dance texts are invariably fellow tribal people—such as the Arapaho, Cheyenne, and Kiowa. (Wovoka is an exception to this, crossing tribal boundaries and appearing as the father in many different Ghost Dance texts and languages.) The inclusion of Euro-Americans in M-7 and M-8 is both rare and revealing. Like M-6, M-7 takes place in the spirit world and continues to focus on the past. It records a former time of amity and generosity toward Euro-Americans and a subsequent change of heart. Mooney quickly tries to assuage his Euro-American readers, assuring them that the text need not arouse fear. He points out that the term used for "Euro-American" in the text literally means "expert, skillful, or wise" in Arapaho. However, no trace of amity remains for the Euro-American in M-8. One can conclude that the substitution of "yellow-hide" and "white-skin" for the proper and complimentary term used in M-7 carries a pejorative connotation. The text is explicitly antiwhite, saying, "I have no more sympathy with him."

Powers, 1990 (Colby, 1895)

In 1990, Powers published his retranslations of Lakota Ghost Dance texts, primarily those published by Mooney and Colby in the mid-1890s. I will quote several of Colby's (1895) texts as well as those from two other sources used by Powers, Frederick Weygold's 1909 collection of Ghost Dance songs and the group gathered by Eugene Buechel, S.J., published posthumously in 1978.[26]

In his introduction, Powers discussed how the song texts and Ghost Dance religion underwent a "Lakotification" process.

> It was after these [Ghost] dance sets, that some fell into trances and believed that they died (just as Wovoka had done in the beginning), and traveled to *Wanagi Oti* "Spirit Camp" across the *Wanagi Canku* "Spir-

it Trail" (the Milky Way) where they met and communed with their deceased relatives. When the dancers awoke, they described some of their visionary experiences through the medium of song. Songs therefore contain almost exclusively the underlying significance of the Ghost dance from the Lakota point of view. In particular, references to the old way of life, which in the doctrine of the Ghost dance was believed to be returning after white people were exterminated during a cataclysmic event, are symbolic of an earlier time period which is irrefutably Lakota, and underscore the fact that although the Ghost dance is frequently referred to as a movement, there was very little connection between the Ghost dance of the Lakota and that of other tribes. In fact, little remained of Wovoka's teachings once the dance arrived in Lakota country, although leaders such as Sitting Bull, Big Foot, Short Bull, and Kicking Bear were all familiar with the original teachings. Although the peculiar belief that the Ghost dance shirts and dresses were bullet proof has led some authors to consider the Lakota version hostile, in fact all the designs on the attire represent protective animals, birds, and other species. The designs were decidedly defensive, not offensive. While there are references to kinship, games, religion, and hunting, there are none to warfare. (Powers 1990:11–12)

Powers divides his fifty-five song texts into four groups, based on their Ghost Dance themes. As he describes the groups, which he calls "parts":

Part I, "I Give You My Way," is composed of songs that make reference to the more general features of the Ghost dance given to Lakota disciples by Wovoka. . . . Part II, "You Will See Your Relatives," contains songs which describe meetings with deceased relatives during the trance. . . . Part III, "The People are Coming Back Home," focuses on the belief that deceased humans and animals will return to the world of the living after the white man has disappeared. . . . Part IV, "Now You Will Flourish," describes what the dreamers perceived life will be like after the world is restored. Of particular interest is the sharp focus on themes related to the old ways of life—hunting, camp life, games, and foods. (Powers 1990:14)

In the following translations, vocables from the original text that appeared in boldface are rendered in italic. My labels for these texts, PC, PW, and PB, combine Powers's initial followed by that of the original author, principally Colby, but in a few instances, Weygold or Beuchel.[27] The "endnotes" quote information given in the notes at the end of Powers's publication.

Part I, "I Give You My Way"

PW-1 (1. Miyoĥ'an cic'u we)

"I give you my Way,

I give you my Way."
Father said it so,
Father said it so.
(Powers 1990:20)

In an endnote for this text, Powers explains,

Way is capitalized because it signifies a prescribed manner of belief. . . . Furthermore, in Lakota the phrase *Lakol wicoȟ'an,* heard frequently in prayers, speeches, and songs, is normally translated "The Indian Way."
  The final paired phrase *Ate heye lo* [Father said it so] is one of the major diagnostic features of Ghost dance songs. . . . The texts in the songs are essentially quotes attributed to "The father" (or in some cases, a relative of the dreamer). "Father" also refers to the Christian concept of God the Father originally preached by Wovoka. My own feeling is that the phrase as it is used among the Lakota is more of a cadential formula, separating major themes in the songs, or simply ending them. There is simply no empirical evidence that in 1889–90 most Lakotas participating in the Ghost dance were Christianized (Powers 1990:61n.1).

PC-2 (7. Ateyapi kin maka owancaya lowanniśipe lo)

Our Father commands you to sing throughout the universe
All of you say it!
All of you say it!
All of you talk about him! *he*
All of you talk about him! *he*
(Powers 1990:23)[28]

Endnote: "The connotation of the texts here is that of 'spreading the word' (i.e. a gospel, or preachings of Wovoka)" (Powers 1990:62n.7).

Part II, "You Will See Your Relatives"

PB-3 (12. Nitakuye wanyeglakin kte lo)

"You will see your relatives,"
Father said it so *e ya yo e ya yo*
Father said it so *e ya yo yo*
(Powers 1990:27)

Endnote: "The 'relatives' referred to here are of course the deceased who are to return after the white man has disappeared" (Powers 1990:63n.12).

PC-4 (19. Howo micinkši)

All right, my son
All right, my son

> Now that I've called you, you've come
> You've come
> Take this earth
> Take this earth
> Upon it you shall flourish
> Upon it you shall flourish
> *Ha ye e ya yo*
> *Ha ye e ya yo*
>
> (Powers 1990:32)[29]

Endnote: "The Father is addressing the dancer telling him to take (back) his (rightful) land from the whites" (Powers 1990:64n.19).

Part III, "The People Are Coming Back Home"

PC-5 (33. Micinkši tahena kupi ye)

> "My sons, come back home to this side,
> My sons, come back home to this side,
> You will walk on good land,
> You will walk on good land,"
> Father said it so,
> Father said it so.
>
> (Powers 1990:42)

Endnote: "Again the reference to the 'good land' i.e., land to be occupied exclusively by Lakota. To this side refers to the world of the living" (Powers 1990:67n.33).

PC-6 (43. Ka koyan wiceška ali na)

> "Quickly, climb up the tipi!
> Quickly, climb up the tipi!
> Meanwhile, I shall cook the food,
> Meanwhile, I shall cook the food,
> All around the bottom,
> All around the bottom,
> Drive in the pegs!
> Drive in the pegs!"
> Your mother said it so,
> Your mother said it so.
>
> (Powers 1990:48)

Endnote [Powers writes that his note for a previous text applies equally to this text]: "In this song, the dreamer sees the deceased reenacting vignettes from old times. The texts are clearly the words of a woman who is telling her family to raise the tipi and stake it down while she cooks the evening meal" (Powers 1990:68n.42). "A young boy usually climbed up to [an] erected tipi in order to place the tipi pins in place to secure the front flap" (Powers 1990:68n.43).

> PC-7 (40. Iglaka au we)
>
> "They are moving camp,
> They are moving camp,
> To this side,
> To this side,"
> Father said it so,
> Father said it so.
> (Powers 1990:45)

Endnote: "The first two lines conjure up the great movement of people, horses, dogs, and all their belongings from one camping place to another. Moving camp was a time of great excitement and is a perfect metaphor for the return of the deceased as if they were all collectively pulling up stakes and heading for the world of the living" (Powers 1990:67n.40).

> Part IV, "Now You Will Flourish"
>
> PC-8 (53. Wakanyan inyankin kte)
>
> "It will roll sacredly,
> It will roll sacredly,
> The hoop will roll quickly,
> The hoop will roll quickly,
> All come see it!
> All come see it!"
> Father said it so,
> Father said it so.
> (Powers 1990:56n.53)

Endnote: "Many of the references to old time traditions revolve around games that the dreamers played when they were children. The hoop and javelin game was one such favorite. The hoop also has a number of sacred connotations, in particular, the unity of the tribe and totality of the universe" (Powers 1990:69n.53).

Although Powers does not mention the possibility that the Father in PW-1 refers to Wovoka, he does make this point in regard to PC-2. Mooney makes this specific point regarding several Sioux—i.e., Lakota—Ghost Dance texts. For example, in his commentary after the first song of the collection, he writes, "'Grandfather,' as well as 'father,' is a reverential term applied to the messiah" (Mooney [1896] 1991: 1061). This also appears in comments for songs 12 and 22 (Mooney [1896] 1991:1069, 1073).

It is interesting to see what the Father, Wovoka, commanded of his children in PC-2, that they "sing throughout the universe." The implied cosmic power of song in this text seems fitting to notions of power and song in Wovoka's cultural universe of the Great Basin.

Powers's commentary for PB-3, PC-4, and PC-5 brings to light Lakota implications for these three seemingly different texts. The texts revolve around Lakota relationship to Euro-Americans and Lakota interpretation of Ghost Dance prophecy. Powers explains that the relationship in PB-3 is a direct correlation: the resurrection of dead Lakota relatives coincides with the "disappearance," i.e., demise of Euro-Americans. One comes, the other goes. In PC-4, Lakotas are told to take this earth; the subtext adds: from the Euro-Americans who have usurped it. In PC-5, Powers defines the "good land" of its text as land occupied exclusively by Lakota.

Ghost Dance prophecy in Naraya texts promises a good and new earth (songs 21–23, 26). But unlike in the Lakota texts, the focus here is on earth itself, its state, its newness—healthy and pristine. As Emily said of song 23, "That means our Heaven." It was an idealized version or vision of this world, which contrasted with its unidealized decline in songs 19 and 20. The earth in these songs has grown old, just as trees and people grow old. Even Our Father eventually abandons it in song 20 and flies up to the new earth in song 22. Starting afresh on a new world, such matters as prior ownership or use are irrelevant. Whether it was an all-Shoshone or all-Indian new world, I cannot say. Emily and Dorothy's presentation of the Naraya religion had everything to do with the relationship of Shoshones to the natural world and virtually nothing to do with the relationship between people, be it Shoshone, Indian, or Euro-American. Naraya texts bear this out.[30]

PC-6 and PC-7 focus on nineteenth-century Lakotas' lives as nomadic hunters on the Plains. Wind River Shoshone were also nomadic hunters on the Plains at that time; nevertheless, there are no Naraya equivalents to these songs in Emily and Dorothy's song repertoire.

PC-6 presents some of the details of a family setting up camp in the spirit world. In PC-7, the scene is shifting from the spirit world to this world. Tribal members, no longer in the individual family unit but part of the larger encampment, are about to move back to their living bodies and continue their way of life in this world. PC-8 maintains the Lakota focus, the hoop game, which carries symbolic identification for the entire tribe, even encompassing the universe.

Plains Ghost Dance songs focus on people and their nineteenth-century Plains life. Naraya songs focus on the natural world. In the texts and intent of these songs, the Wind River Shoshone looked beyond their life on the Plains and continued modes of thought and behavior from their more distant origins in the Great Basin. These modes of thought and behavior are of the same stuff as Wovoka's own Ghost Dance vision, which also took shape and meaning within the cognitive world of the Great Basin. In Naraya songs, the place is the natural world, the time, the present, which looks to the near future: tomorrow's berries. Naraya and Plains Ghost Dance song texts, and the religions they embody, stand in sharp relief to one another—worlds apart, or more accurately, worldviews apart.

Epilogue

Some of the most important earlier writings on Great Basin culture dismissed the presence of religious ceremony and artistic expression. Focusing on land, food, and a simple way of life, the authors of these writings seemed to deny a full range of cultural possibilities among Great Basin peoples. Steward characterized Shoshone culture by saying, "So far as its basic orientation is definable it was gastric" (Steward 1938:46). Drawing on her own Western Shoshone upbringing for reference, Beverly Crum replied to this: "By leaving out any mention of the importance of round dances which integrates music, poetry, and dance into a unified whole, Steward left his non-Shoshoni reader with little alternative but to accept his statement that Shoshoni culture was indeed gastric and not much more. This is not so. Poetry songs are still a vital part of Shoshoni life" (Crum 1980:19).

Like Crum, I believe that the Naraya songs add weight to a different viewpoint regarding Great Basin culture. The Naraya songs presented in this book reveal artistic achievement of the highest order in the service of profound religious conviction. They document the richness, complexity, subtlety, and fullness of culture. To quote Crum again:

> These songs were handed down as heirlooms, while very few material objects were. There were a number of reasons for this, the most important being their life style. Much of the land on which the pre-White Shoshoni people lived was desert. The people had to continuously travel a wide area in their quest for food. . . . Thus the people had to travel lightly. Only the things they considered essential were moved along with them. Hence, poetry songs became very important because they required only "mental storage." This is why so much care was taken with the poetic expression in Shoshoni poetry songs. (Crum 1980:19)

While it is true that the Naraya are the particular expression of the Wind River Shoshone, it is also true that nothing springs from nothing. Great Basin traditions and ways of viewing the world provided the heritage, the cultural soil, from which the Naraya sprang. The Naraya was one of its extraordinary blooms.

I wish to end this book where I started, visiting with Emily and Dorothy in their bedroom and hearing Naraya songs for the first time. My fieldnote log entries for that day and the next, when the depth of my emotional response spilled over into a poem, marked the beginning of my journey, although I did not know it at the time. It is a sweet remembrance and seems a fitting ending here and now.

July 20, 1977

Went to see Emily—gave her the stew which she really liked. I sang the Giveaway Song and she had me go into the bedroom to sing to Dorothy. They liked it and then Dorothy had her play a tape of themselves which they had made 3 Easters ago. Old songs which they say no one knows—Sun Dance and a lot of Ghost Dance music. They sometimes play it before they go to bed. Dorothy was all gnarled and scratched herself with a stick. The smile on Dorothy's face as she sang along with the tape. Emily's look of concern as she looked at Dorothy. Beautiful. Their laughter when they heard a mistake on the tape.

July 21, 1977

Shoshone Sisters

Plaid kerchief on her head
The scratching stick used to
ease her troubled brow
evoked an earlier time

Was she avoiding the wrinkles of
old age
Or was it to replace the fingers
which were now curled in
arabesques of
pain

The sisters rested on their twin beds
listening to their breath of
Easters past
Caught on tape
the songs they learned from the
old ones

Drifting into sleep perhaps
to see the green mountains

green grass
ripe berries
Damë Apë, Himself
welcoming
Dorothy and Emily
into their Naraya song

Judith Vander

ena

Appendix A
Literal English Translations of Naraya Songs 1–17

Song 1

Our mountains above fog lying while moving,
Our mountains above fog lying while moving.
Fog fog fog lying while moving,
Fog fog fog lying while moving.
(Vander 1986:38)

Song 1 was also published as Naraya song 2 in my 1988 study (Vander 1988:17-18). The recorded performance of this song is on the cassette tape that accompanies that book. I have also recorded two other Shoshone performances of this identical song: VN in 1977 and Angelina Wagon in 1981. In 1981 I recorded Helene Furlong singing what seems to be a variant of this song (Vander 1988:133–34).

Song 2

Our mothers day/sun coming out lying while moving,
Our mothers day/sun coming out lying while moving.
Looking around, down for us [from] above, coming coming,
Looking around, down for us [from] above, coming coming.
(Vander 1986:54–55)

In 1988 I also published song 2 as Naraya song 11 (Vander 1988:26–27). The recorded performance of this song is on the cassette tape that accompanies the book.

Song 3

Soul fog soul fog,
Soul fog soul fog.
Soul floating, flying up, soul floating, flying up,
Soul floating, flying up, soul floating, flying up.
(Vander 1986:52)

Song 3 was also published as Naraya Song 10 in my earlier book (Vander 1988:25-26). The recorded performance of this song is on the cassette tape that accompanies the book.

Song 4

Our sun's face white set while moving,
Our sun's face white set while moving.
Our sun's going sun sets while moving,
Our sun's going sun sets while moving.
(Vander 1986:46)

Song 5

Pine tree butterfly pine tree butterfly,
Pine tree butterfly pine tree butterfly.
Dark pine tree holes underneath dark flickering/fluttering,
Dark pine tree holes underneath dark flickering/fluttering.
(Vander 1986:45)

Song 6

Eagle's wing is skying,
Eagle's wing is skying.
Green water shiny under lying-moving,
Green water shiny under lying-moving.
(Vander 1986:39–40)

Elsewhere I have published song 6 as Naraya song 4 (Vander 1988:19).

Song 7

Quaking aspen tree mountain quaking aspen mountain,
Quaking aspen tree mountain quaking aspen mountain.
Through water dragging across through water dragging across *he*,
Through water dragging across through water dragging across *he*.
(Vander 1986:40)

Song 8

Our Father's mountain lion,
Mountain side below walking down yowling *waindë*.
Our Father's mountain lion,
Mountain side below walking down yowling *waindë*.
Our Father's game animals child sitting *wainda*,
Our Father's game animals child sitting *wainda*.
(Vander 1986:45–46)

Song 9

Our Father's footprints/tracks,
Our mother's footprints/tracks making herself rise/fly up
My mother making herself rise/fly up,
My mother making herself rise/fly up.

(Vander 1986:56)

Song 10

Small dust [= whirlwind] whirlwind flying up,
Small dust [= whirlwind] whirlwind flying up.
Road mountain's green lying while moving,
Road mountain's green lying while moving.

(Vander 1986:53)

Song 11A

Snow melting mountain snow melting mountain,
Snow melting mountain snow melting mountain.
Mountain rock rock slide rock slide *enë,*
Mountain rock rock slide rock slide *enë.*

Song 11B

Snow melting mountain snow melting mountain,
Snow melting mountain snow melting mountain.
Mountain rock rock cliff point water zigzagging down *enë,*
Mountain rock rock cliff point water zigzagging down *enë.*

(Vander 1986:41)

Song 12

Duck's ducklings duck's ducklings,
Duck's ducklings duck's ducklings.
Good water swimming,
Good water swimming.

(Vander 1986:42)

Song 12 was also published as Naraya song 5 (Vander 1988:19-20). The recorded performance of this song is on the cassette tape that accompanies the book.

Song 13

White mountain lying,
White mountain lying.

Mother earth standing while shaking,
Mother earth standing while shaking.
(Vander 1986:43)

Song 14

Snow mountain melting,
Snow mountain melt-
-*No waro* saddle of mountain water melting saddle *e-*
-*No waro* saddle of mountain water melting saddle *ena.*
(Vander 1986:43–44)

Song 15

Our morning star coming up,
Our morning star coming up.
Clear sun rays streaming out,
Clear sun rays streaming out.
Star sitting,
Star sitting.
(Vander 1986:49)

Song 16 was also published as Naraya song 9 (Vander 1988:24).

Song 16

Our mountain child curving down,
Our mountain child curving down.
Curving down curving down curving down,
Curving down curving down curving down.
(Vander 1986:51)

Song 17

Huchi nüwiran dean nare toda dewan e-
-*Na wirapeya nangan e-*
-*Na nare toda dewan ena.*
(no translation)
(Vander 1986:51)

Appendix B
Seventeen Naraya Songs without English Translations

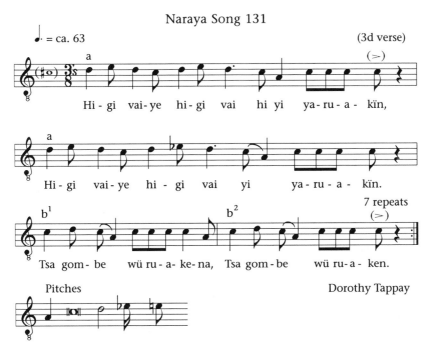

Naraya Song 131

Hi - gi vai-ye hi-gi vai hi yi ya-ru-a- kïn,

Hi - gi vai-ye hi - gi vai yi ya-ru-a- kïn.

Tsa gom-be wü ru-a-ke-na, Tsa gom-be wü ru-a- ken.

Pitches

Dorothy Tappay

Translation comments: *tsa*, "good"; *gombe*, possibly from *sogopʰ*, meaning "earth."

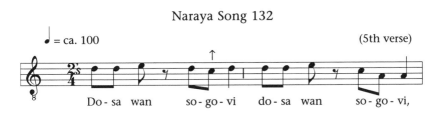

Naraya Song 132

Do - sa wan so - go - vi do - sa wan so - go - vi,

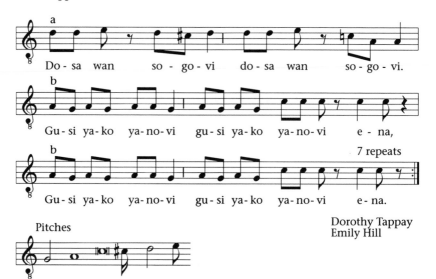

Do - sa wan   so - go - vi   do - sa wan   so - go - vi.

Gu - si ya- ko   ya- no- vi   gu - si ya- ko   ya- no- vi   e - na,

Gu - si ya- ko   ya- no- vi   gu - si ya- ko   ya- no- vi   e - na.

7 repeats

Pitches

Dorothy Tappay
Emily Hill

Translation comments: *dosa,* "white," i.e., "snowy"; *sogovi,* "earth"; *gusi,*
"?gray."

Naraya Song 133

♩ = ca. 92   (5th verse)

Da - man do - ga   nan - gwa ma   go - ve ve - ta

wa rü   man - do   e - na,   Da - man do - ga   nan - gwa ma

go- ve ve- ta   wa rü   man - do   e - na.   We- gi man - do

we   yan   we- gi man- do we   yan,   We- gi man - do

we   yan   we - gi man - do   we   yan.

Emily Hill
Dorothy Tappay

Pitches

Translation comments: *daman,* "our"; *gove,* "?face"; *wegi,* "sideways."

Naraya Song 134

$\bullet$ = ca. 138   (4th verse)

Gu - si doan - zi du - a man - ïl - ka - no,

Gu - si doan - zi du - a man - ïl - ka - no.

7 repeats, incomplete

Doi- ya ma - nïl- ka - nȯ - rë,   Doi- ya ma - nïl- ka - nȯ - rë.

Dorothy Tappay

Pitches

Translation comments: *doiya,* "mountain."

Naraya Song 135A

$\bullet$ = ca.100   (4th verse)

Wa - sü - pit - ïn ba - dïl - wi en - ga ba - dïl - wi en - zai   ge -

na,   Wa - sü - pit - ïn ba - dïl - wi   en - ga ba - dïl -

wi en - zai   ge - na.   Yo wa - rï - na ma   na gwar ïn - dë

en - zai   vi yï - gwe   ge - na,   Yo wa - rï - na ma

                                                        5 repeats

na gwar ïn - dë en - zi   vi   yï - gwe   ge - na.

Pitches   Dorothy Tappay
                                           Emily Hill

Translation comments: *wasüpitïn*, "?game animals."

Naraya Song 135B

♩ = ca. 96   (2d verse)

En - ga - pit - ïn ba - dïl - wi   en - ga ba - dïl - wi en - zai   ge -

na,   En - ga - pit - ïn ba - dïl - wi   en - ga - ba - dïl - wi en - zai   ge -

na.   Yo wa ni   ai   e   vi ai yai   yai   ge -

na, Yo wa ni ai e vi ai yai yai ge - na.

I recorded this same song from Angelina Wagon in 1981. She did not know what the text meant but did translate the first word of the song with this comment, *"Engapit*h, I think it's kind of a red paint or something."*

Naraya Song 136

Ye va va hom - bi ye va va hom,

Ye va va hom - bi ye va va hom - bi.

Ye va güt sï ni në, Ye va güt sï ne.

Translation comments: *hombi*, ?from *hu:pi*, "?wood."

Naraya Song 137

Won - go - vi ya na a rë mën e - na, Won - go-

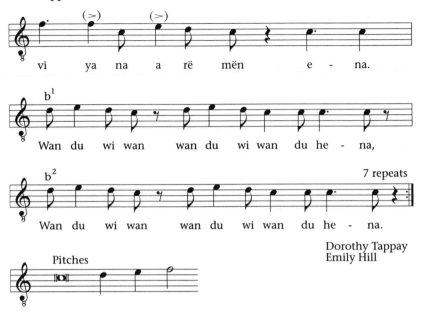

Dorothy Tappay
Emily Hill

Translation comments: Emily did not believe this text mentions pine tree, my guess for the first word of the song *(wongovi).*

Naraya Song 138A

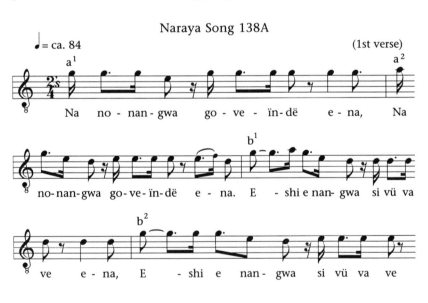

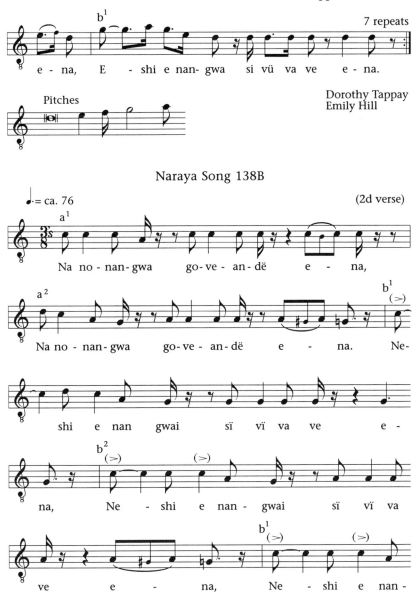

7 repeats

e - na,   E - shi e nan- gwa   si vü va ve   e - na.

Pitches

Dorothy Tappay
Emily Hill

Naraya Song 138B

♩. = ca. 76

(2d verse)

Na no - nan- gwa   go- ve - an- dë   e - na,

Na no - nan- gwa   go- ve - an- dë   e - na.   Ne-

shi   e   nan   gwai   sï   vï   va   ve   e -

na,   Ne - shi   e   nan - gwai   sï   vï   va

ve   e - na,   Ne - shi   e   nan -

gwai   sï   vï   va   ve   e - na.

Pitches

Emily Hill
Dorothy Tappay

Naraya Song 139

♩ = ca. 69   (4th verse)

Ye to do vi   ye   to do vi,   Ye to do

♩. = ca. 72

vi   ye   to do vi.   Bu - hi - wai   bu - hi - wai

ha - ve - nó - rë,   Bu - hi - wai

7 repeats

bu - hi - wai   ha - ve - nó - rë.

Dorothy Tappay
Emily Hill

Pitches

Translation comments: *buhi*, "?green"; or possibly *bui*, "?looking"; *wai*, "?down"; *havenórë*, "lying-moving."

Naraya Song 140

♪ = ca. 176   (7th verse)

Ge wai wai hoin   yoin   zi - a   ge   wai wai ron,

Ge   wai   wai hoin   yoin   zi - a   ge wai wai ron - zi.

Ge   wai   wai ron - zi   ge   wai   wai ron - zi,

8 repeats

Ge   wai   wai ron - zi   ge   wai   wai ron - zi.

Pitches   Dorothy Tappay
                                             Emily Hill

Naraya Song 141

♪ = ca. 192   (3d verse)

Wi   am   ba - dïl   wi   am   ba - dïl   wïn,

Wi   am   ba - dïl   wi   am   ba - dïl   wïn.

Wïn ba - dïl wi - no   wïn ba - dïl wi - no - a - gïn,

6 repeats, incomplete

Wïn ba - dïl wi - no   wïn ba - dïl wi - no - a - gïn.

Pitches

Dorothy Tappay
Emily Hill

Naraya Song 142

♩ = ca. 92

(3d verse)

Yo wai ï mai yo   wa do - san do - ve - do.

Yo wai ï mai yo   wa do - san do - ve - do,

6 repeats

Yo wai ï mai yo   wa do - san do - ve - do.

Pitches

Dorothy Tappay
Emily Hill

Translation comments: *dosan,* "?white."

Naraya Song 143

♩ = ca. 100 (7th verse)

O - wën du - ri - a wï - nȯ - ro vai - yo,

O - wën du - ri - a wï - nȯ - ro vai - yo.

O - wën du - ri - a o - wën du - ri - a wï - nȯ - ro vai - yo,

8 repeats

O - wën du - ri - a o - wën du - ri - a wï - nȯ - ro vai - yo.

Pitches

Emily Hill
Dorothy Tappay

Naraya Song 144

♩ = ca. 92 (8th verse)

Boi si o - wën de boi si o - wën de e - na,

Boi si o - wën de boi si o - wën de e - na.

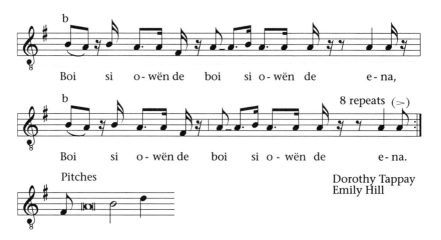

Boi si o-wën de boi si o-wën de   e-na,

Boi si o-wën de boi si o-wën de   e-na.

8 repeats (>)

Pitches

Dorothy Tappay
Emily Hill

Translation comments: *boi,* "?road."

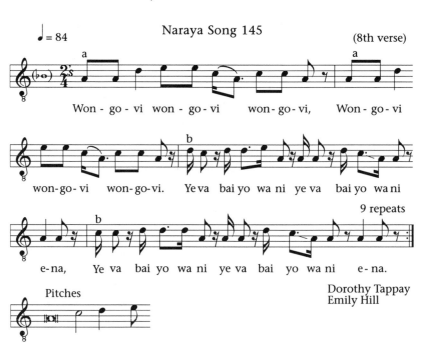

♩ = 84

Naraya Song 145

(8th verse)

Won - go - vi won - go - vi   won - go - vi,   Won - go - vi

won - go - vi won - go - vi.   Ye va bai yo wa ni ye va   bai yo wa ni

9 repeats

e - na,   Ye va   bai yo wa ni ye va bai yo wa ni   e - na.

Pitches

Dorothy Tappay
Emily Hill

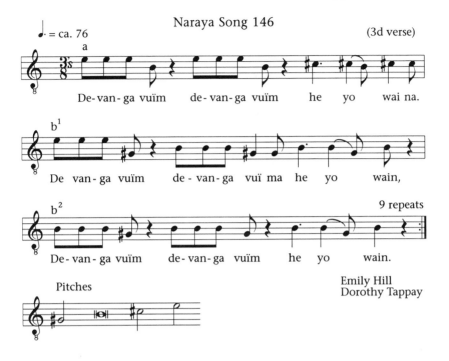

Naraya Song 146

Emily Hill
Dorothy Tappay

EMILY: *"Devanga bui*—about seeing something."

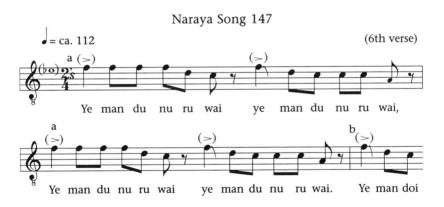

Naraya Song 147

EMILY: *"Bi yanogant*—something like a wave."

Appendix C
Shoshone-English and English-Shoshone Glossary

Part 1: Shoshone-English

All these words come from the texts of Naraya songs. Words on the same line include the various forms that appear in the same song. Words in brackets are other forms that appear in spoken language. Several different Shoshone words have the same English translation. One can see all the Shoshone words with the same meaning by looking up the English word in the English-Shoshone glossary; the various words are gathered in each appropriate single entry.

akën, akën-ïküni [aka, akamp^h]. sunflower seeds
anoga. waves
Apë. Father, Father's

babai-eya [babaiyu, babaiyigwip]. pools
bagadïdë. small lake, pond
bagaganana, bagaganan [bagïnaip^h]. fog
bagaganë [bagïnaip^h]. fog
bagana-via, bagana-vi [bagïnaip^h]. fog
bagan-bagan-nogan-zi [bagantsuk^h]. ?redwing blackbirds
bagosi. rain
bagu [bavunged]. clear
bai [bedïmp^h]. old
bai [vaix]. upon/above
baigi [baix]. high
baiwë [ba:ënwap^h]. rain
ban [banzuk]. otter
banzu-a [banzuk]. otter
banzuk. otter
baru. damp
ba-ru [ba:-duhuvit^h]. water-black
barukande [?baruk^h (GH)]. ?under water
basiwambitta [ba:siwamp^h]. sand
bauwah [bauwap^h]. rain

bazi [bagïnaipʰ]. fog
bazigi [barazigwid]. shining, slick
be-. [ʔbedïmpʰ]. ʔold
biya. big; mother, mother's
biya gwian-viva, biya gwian-zi [biya gwian]. eagle
bo [bohopʰ]. sagebrush
bogombi [bogompʰ]. berries
boha. sacred power
boi [boiʔ]. road
boihoigeno [boihoikïn]. running slowly
bu [buhi/buhipʰ]. green/grass
buhi [buhigïnt, buhipʰ]. green/grass
buhi [buhipʰ]. grass
buhi [buhuvitʰ]. green
buhi-mande. green
buhip [buhipʰ]. grass
bui. looking
bui-wambi [buhi, buhuvitʰ]. green
bünïs-o. he himself
bünzi. ʔeagle-down feathers (RW)

da. our
daman. our
damë, damën. our/we/us
danzia [danzigan]. knocking together
danzian. crackling (like thunder)
dave. sun/day
dave-dï [dave]. sun
davege. daytime
de [ʔdedïtsi (GH)]. ʔsmall
de [ʔneïdʰ]. wind
dedok wïnïganòrë [dedok wanokin]. traveling
denüpi [denüpë]. man
dï-. ʔold
dïdïë [dïdïnE]. root
dïmbe [bedïmpʰ]. old
dïmpi. rocks
dïmpi-do [dïmpi]. rocks
dïmpimëndoi-ya [dïmpimëndoihgiʔ]. rocks climbing
dïmp-vanzingo. rock slide
dïna. down
dïn-dïn-dïn-dsi, dïn-dsi [dïnaʔ]. down/toward
dïpëgaiyu, dïpegai [sëpaiganu (ʔsïpegandʰ)]. flat
dïva [dïvA]. pine nut, pine nut tree
dïvai [dïvwaiyòr]. unidentified bird
dïvarë [dïvarëruk or dïvana]. under or lining

dïvaroi [gewa:rin (Emily), günwa (GH); see chapter 2, note 13]. edge barely
    showing
doanzia [doanziyang]. blossoms/blooms
dogando [?dugand]. ?low place (deep)
dogo [dosavitʰ]. white
doi. mountain(s)
doih [doihgïn]. come up
doiya. mountain(s)
doiya-penji [doiya]. mountain(s)
doiyaro [doiyavi]. mountain(s)
doiyav-avin [doiyavi]. mountain(s)
doiyave [doiyavi]. mountain(s)
doiyave-dë [doiyavi]. mountain(s)
doiyavi. mountain(s)
doiyavi-di [doiyavi]. mountain(s)
dono [dōnovī]. greasewood
dono-va [dōnop ba:]. ?greasewood (GH) water (creek)
dónzi [doanzi]. shining, blooming
dónzia [doanzi]. shiny
donzi-aiyo [donziap]. flower
dosa [dosavitʰ]. white
dowano [dowïrhiya?]. washing down (?washes, pours down, GH)
doza [dosavitʰ]. white
du [duhuvitʰ]. black
du, n-dua-n-zi [dua]. child
duduwa-tsi [dudua]. many young ones
dugai-e [duga?i]. nighttime
duganangwa [duganankʰ]. toward or come night
duganripʰ. night
dugu, dugum [dugumba?/dugumbānr]. sky
dugumba-ga [dugumba?/dugumbānr]. sky
dugu-n [dugupʰ]. up, above
du-i [duhuvitʰ]. black
düna-na. downhill
duru, durua. young males

engana [engavitʰ]. red
engaparai [engapadankʰ]. ciquefoil berries
enwad. rain
evïn [evi]. white clay

gaiwai [gaiwah]. ?Brewer's blackbird
gani [ganī]. ?home
gara [garïd]. sitting
garïdë, garïd, n-garïd. sit
garïdëmënt, garïdë. sitting there

garïmbi [garïd]. sit
gaz-ombi [gaz]. end of group of mountains (GH)
gemano. coming
gëmbeya, gëm [gëmU]. jackrabbit
gënë [gën?]. bitter root
gewainörë [ge:wano]. getting old (fading away)
go-via [?sogop^h ?biya]. ?earth ?mother
gunwar. (on the) edging/rim
gusi. gray, misty
gwambaiyïn [gwamp^h]. is waving
gweshi. tail
gwian-zi [biya gwian]. eagle
gwitsu-no. buffalo

have [havi]. lying
havegïn. lying
have-nörë. lying while moving
havi-dir [havi]. lie
havi-endë [havi]. lying or showing
havi-gï-nörë. lying-moving
haviti [havi]. lying
hinën. ?what
hombi, hom [hu:pi]. wood, stick
huchu. birds
huku [hukümp^h]. dust/ashes
hupin [hu:pi]. wood/tree
huviarë [huvia (singular), huvianï (plural)]. song

mamaiyïgwidir. spots
maruk-andu. still under it
miëp. went
mozambia-n-zi [mozambiats]. female mountain sheep (ewe)
mugua. spirit/soul

naishünde [naishünte]. prayer
nambe. ?foot(steps)
nambürü [nanambuip^h]. footprints, tracks
nana. all kinds, together
na-na-suyage. looks good/pretty
narai-yïzïnörë [narai-yïzïno?]. rising, flying up
naranga [nananga]. sounding
nare-nagüx [nai:nagük (Emily), nagüx (GH)]. showing up
naroiya-bianzi [naroihïnt]. going up
narugumba-ngo [?dugumba?/dugumbãnr]. ?sky, or [?dugup] ?going up
narukümb-ani [narukümp^h]. has power to it/spirit
nave [naivi]. female offspring

nazamërïkino. it's turning
n-doi, n-doiya [doiya]. mountain(s)
n-doiyavi [doiyavi]. mountain(s)
neshiwu [neaysuwayfuinde (Tidzump 1970:1)]. breeze
nïgïnt. wild geese
nïkkë [nïkëpʰ]. dance
nïppini [?sïpegand]. ?flat rocks, shale (GH)
nïsë [nïsës]. myself
no [no:vi]. hill
noiy [doiya]. mountain(s)
nórë. moving
novi [no:vi]. hill
nuga [nugap]. foot of mountains
nuhiyogenë, nuhiyogeno [nuHIyokïn]. coming or moving in
nüïndi [neïdʰ (GH)]. wind
nuki. ?running
nüwë. Indian
nuwïgenór, nuwïgena [nuwikin]. taking one's time walking
nüwï-tsi, nüwü [nüwë]. people
nuyihïgïn. rumbling-shaking (after thunder)
nüyïhïgïndë. shakes with rumbling sound

ogandë, ogan [oiyëndë]. ?everyone/everything
ogwe. river
oha-n [ohapitʰ]. yellow
oi [oiyïdïs]. all (over)
oiyóro. all

pa [ba:] water
parësai. shining/twinkling
pa-ro. damp
pa-ro [ba:-dukand]. water-deep
paroagen [paroage (GH)]. rain shower
pengwi. fish

roi [doi]. mountain(s)
roiya [?doiyavi]. ?mountain(s)
roiyab-en, roiya [doiyavi]. mountain(s)
roiyavi [doiyavi]. mountain(s)
ru [duhuvitʰ]. black
ruka [dugantʰ]. under (?deep)

sai [?saipʰ]. ?cattails
sai [saigënt]. melting
saiwai. snow melting, wet
saiwai-wai [saiwai]. melting snow

saiwan. ?white-tailed ptarmigan
saiyag-anana, saiyag-anan. Milky Way
saiyaganë, saiyaganan. shiny, twinkling stars (Milky Way)
saiyaga-nòra [wasayagano]. Milky Way-moving
saiyawan [?saiyagant (GH)]. ?mesh/sieve, or [?sai]. ?wet, or
    [?saiyaganan]. ?Milky Way
sam-baro-mbi [ba:]. water
semikai. all together at the same time
sena [sïnavI]. quaking aspens
senav-av [sïnavI]. quaking aspens
shïna-ra [sïnavI]. quaking aspen
si [?sigip (GH)]. ?leaf
sï [?sëhëvI]. ?willows
sïgi. leaves
sïhïvi [sëhëvI]. trees
sïhüwe [sihuwët]. bare, no vegetation
sïna-aiva [sïnavI]. quaking aspen
sïnam [?ʒi´-amp (Shimkin 1947b:274)]. ?wild rose hip
sïnav [sïnavI]. quaking aspen
sïnave [sïnavI]. quaking aspens
sïneyugwid-ïd [simehugwid]. says
siya. feathers
siyuhuigïn [siyuhuigint]. ?hissing sound
sogo-bende [sogopʰ]. earth (ground)
sogop-ade [sogopʰ]. earth/world
sogopë [sogopʰ]. earth/ground
sogopi [sogopʰ]. earth
sogo-vai, sogo-vai-ye, sogo-vai-yedu, so-vai-yedu [sogopʰ vaix, uvaix]. earth-on
sogo-vaigi [sogopʰ vaix, uvaix]. earth-on, over
sogove, sogovi-në [sogopʰ]. earth/land
sogo-vendë [sogopʰ ?bai]. earth-?next to it (GH)
sogovi [sogopʰ]. earth
sogo-vi [sogopʰ-?biya]. earth-?mother
suave-andë, suave-andïnò [suavegind, suapʰ]. thoughts
sügi [sugipʰ]. needles
suvinu [suhiukun (GH)]. hissing sound

todowainda. ripe and burst open
tsa [tsant]. good
tsiyuwano. peeling, slicing

ügë. new
ügü [ügë]. new

va. water
vag-o, vagïn-o [vagïna]. fog

vagïna [bagïnaip^h]. fog
vagïna, van-vagïnan, vagïnë. fog
vaigi [vaix, uvaix]. above, on
vai-yo [vaix, uvaix]. on
vand-o [uvand^h, vand^h]. above
vandu [uvand^h, vand^h]. above
varu-kë, varukë-penji. ?water rising
vesiyu. ?splashing
viya [biya]. big

wa [wahadu]. two
wa [wap^h]. cedar
wadzi-wo [wandzi]. antelope bull
wai-gondi [wai:no]. down
wainaiyo [wai:no]. coming down
wainanòrë, wainano [wïnïno]. standing-moving
waiyavo. common nighthawk
waiyo, wai [wai:no]. coming down
waiyo, wain [wai:no]. going or climbing down
wandzia [wandzi]. antelope bulls
wanëkinòra [wïnïganòr]. blown by the wind
wani-goïnòrë [?goino]. ?stand–?coming back
waninaneyo [?waniya]. ?curving down
wanoginòra [wïnïno-nòra]. standing-moving
warhigi, warhï-nge [wãhi]. fox
wasümbita, wasümbi [wasüpi]. game animals
wasüp-enji, wasüp-penji [wasüpi]. game animals
wazan [?wasüpi]. ?game animals, or [?wandzi] ?antelope
wazi [?wasüpi]. ?game animals, or [wandzi] antelope
wazi [wasüpi or ?wazigad]. game animals or hiding
wazümbi-an-zi [wasüpi]. game animals
wegïd [wegip^h]. sideways/slanting
wegidu [wegip^h, wegipunt]. on a slant, sideways
wegidukano [wegidukand^h]. sideways
wegïn [?wegi]. ?side
wën, wënë [?wened]. ?fall from
wi [wih]. silver
wia-ïna [?wiap^h], ?mountain pass
wia-n-zi [wiap^h]. gully, pass
wia-ro [wiap^h]. pass
wïnenga [wïnankW]. stand in front of you
wïnëre [wïnërek from wïnïno]. standing-moving (with reference to animal
    tracks)
wïnïganòrë [wïnïganòr]. blown by the wind, or [wïnïnor (GH)] coming over
wïnïkanòrë. stand-moving
wïno [wenre (Tidzump 1970:18)]. stand

winogaiye [wïnïganòr]. blown (apart) by the wind

winogandë, winogan [wïnïganòr]. standing while moving (blowing in the wind)

wïto [?wïtüroi (GH)]. ?shelter, sheltered

won-ge. ?in a row

wongo-no, wongo-ron [wongovI]. pine tree

wongo [wongovI]. pine

wümihagwainë. keeps trying but can't quite catch up

wümihanòrë. slowing down (barely catching up, GH)

wüwa [?dïvA (GH)]. ?pine nut tree

wüwü. small amount

wüwündü [yuwündu]. many branches hanging over

yambi [yamp^h]. root

yana [nana]. every kind

yanome [yano:mi]. wavy

yanugënt [yanugïnd^h]. waves

yëmpë [?yëmp^h]. ?camas or wild root

yë-na, ya-na [yëh]. woodchuck

yengoni [yenk^h]. hanging down

yevai. unidentified bird

yïmëgënt [?yanugïnd^h]. waves

yiyïgwidë [yiyïgwid]. many sitting (together)

yiyïgwïnd [yiyïgwid]. many sitting together

yiyigwint. all sitting

yïva [yïva?]. fall, autumn

yïvai [yïva?]. fall, autumn

yïvam [yïva?]. autumn

yïzï. fly

yïzï-eï-në [yïzïne]. flying

yïzïgïh. rising

yïzïgïn [yïzïkïnïz/yïzïgïnt]. about to rise or pop up

yïzïnòrë. flying

yogai, yogavi, yogavit-a [yogavit^h/?yogëp^h]. "gooey stuff," i.e., mucus

yorikena, yoriken. fly

yòrino. keep on flying

yuwan [yunano]. carrying something in pan, hand, etc.

yuwïnangwa, yuwï. sets in the west

yuwïnangwad. go down out of sight

zani-suano-ve [tsant suano]. good feeling

Part 2: English-Shoshone Glossary

Shoshone words in brackets indicate spoken forms that do not appear in the song texts.

above. vand-o, vandu [uvand[h], vand[h]],
above/on. vaigi [vaix].
all. oiyóro
all (over). oi [oiyïdïs]
all kinds, together. nana
all sitting. yiyigwint
all together at the same time. semikai
antelope (?). wazan wazi [wandzi]
antelope bull. wadzi-wo [wandzi], wandzia

bare, no vegetation. sïhüwe [sihuwët]
berries. bogombi [bogomp[h]]
big. biya, viya [biya]
bird (unidentified). dïvai [dïvwaiyór]
bird (unidentified). yevai
birds. huchu
bitter root. gënë [gën?]
black. du, du-i, ru [duhuvit[h]]
blossoms/blooms. doanzia [doanziyang]
blown (apart) by the wind. winogaiye [wïnïganór]
blown by the wind. wanëkinóra [wïnïganór]
breeze. neshiwu [neaysuwayfuinde (Tidzump 1970:1)]
Brewer's blackbird (?). gaiwai [gaiwah]
buffalo. gwitsu-no

camas or wild root (?). yëmpë [?yëmp[h]]
carrying something in pan, hand, etc. yuwan [yunano]
cattails (?). sai [?saip[h]]
cedar. wa [wap[h]]
child. du, n-dua-n-zi [dua]
cinquefoil berries. engaparai [engapadank[h]]
clear. bagu [bavunged]
come up. doih [doihgïn]
coming. gemano
coming down. wai, wai-gondi [wai:no], wainaiyo, waiyo,
coming or moving in. nuhiyogenë, nuhiyogeno [nuHIyokïn]
coming over. wïnïganórë [wïnïganór]. blown by the wind, or [wïnïnór (GH)]
common nighthawk. waiyavo
crackling (like thunder). danzian
curving down (?). waninaneyo [?waniya]

damp. baru, pa-ro
dance. nïkkë [nïkëp[h]]
day/sun. dave
daytime. davege
down. dïna

down/toward. dïn-dïn-dïn-dsi, dïn-dsi [dïna?]
downhill. düna-na
dust/ashes. huku [hukümpʰ]

eagle. biya gwian-viva, biya gwian-zi [biya gwian]
eagle-down feathers (?) (RW). bünzi
earth. sogopi, sogovi [sogopʰ]
earth/ground. sogopë, sogo-bende [sogopʰ]
earth/land. sogove, sogovi-në [sogopʰ]
earth-?mother. ?go-?via, sogo-vi [sogopʰ-?biya]
earth-?next to it (GH). sogo-vendë [sogopʰ ?bai]
earth-on. sogo-vai, sogo-vai-ye, sogo-vai-yedu, so-vai-yedu [sogopʰ vaix, uvaix]
earth on/over. sogo-vaigi, sogo-vai-ye [sogopʰ vaix, uvaix]
earth-rock. sogo-rïmbïmpi [sogopʰ-dïmpi]
earth/world. sogop-ade [sogopʰ]
edge barely showing. dïvaroi [gewa:rin (Emily), günwa (GH); see chapter 2, note 13.]
edging/rim. gunwar
end of group of mountains (GH). gaz-ombi [gaz]
every kind. yana [nana]
everyone/everything (?). ogandë, ogan [oiyëndë]

fall, autumn. yïva, yïvai, yïvam [yïva?]
fall from (?). wën, wënë [wened]
Father, Father's. Apë
feathers. siya
female mountain sheep (ewe). mozambia-n-zi [mozambiats]
female offspring. nave [naivi]
fish. pengwi
flat. dïpëgaiyu, dïpegai [sëpaiganu (?sïpegandʰ)]
flat rocks, shale (?) (GH). nïppini [sïpegand]
flower. donzi-aiyo [donziap]
fly (*see also* rising). yïzï, yoriken, yorikena
flying. yïzï-eï-në [yïzïne], yïzïnòrë
flying (keep on). yòrino
fog. bagaganana, bagaganan, bagaganë, bagana-vi, bagana-via, bazi [bagïnaipʰ]; vagïna, vagïnë, vagïn-o, vag-o, van-vagïnan, [vagïna]
foot of mountains. nuga [nugap]
footprints, tracks. nambürü [nanambuipʰ]
foot(steps) (?). nambe
fox. warhigi, warhï-nge [wãhi]

game animals. wasümbi, wasümbita, wazümbi-an-zi, wasüp-enji, wasüp-penji [wasüpi]
game animals (?). wazan, wazi [wasüpi]
getting old (fading away). gewainòrë [ge:wano]

go down out of sight (*see also* sets in the west). yuwïnangwad
going or climbing down. wain [wai:no], waiyo
going up. naroiya-bianzi [naroihïnt]
good. tsa [tsant]
good feeling. zani-suano-ve [tsant suano]
grass. buhi, buhip [buhip^h]
gray, misty. gusi
greasewood. dono [dõonovĪ]
greasewood (?) (GH) water (creek). dono-va [dõnop ba:]
green. buhi, buhi-mande, bui-wambi [buhuvit^h]
green/grass. bu [buhi/buhip^h]
green/grass. buhi [buhigïnt, buhip^h]
gully, pass. wia-n-zi [wiap^h]

hanging down. yengoni [yenk]
has power to it/spirit. narukümb-ani [narukümp^h]
he himself. bünïs-o
hiding (?). wazi [wazigad]
high. baigi [baix]
hill. no, novi [no:vi]
hissing sound. suvinu [suhiukun (GH)]
hissing sound (?). siyuhuigïn [siyuhuigint]
home (?). gani [ganĪ]

in a row (?). won-ge
Indian. nüwë
is waving. gwambaiyïn [gwamp^h]
it's turning. nazamërïkino

jackrabbit. gëmbeya, gëm [gëmU]

keeps trying but can't quite catch up. wümihagwainë
knocking together. danzia [danzigan]

leaf. ?si [?sigip (GH)]
leaves. sïgi [sigip]
lie. havi-dir [havi]
looking. bui
looks good/pretty. na-na-suyage
low place (?) (deep). dogando [dugand]
lying. have, havegïn, haviti [havi]
lying-moving. havi-gï-nȯrë
lying or showing. havi-endë [havi]
lying while moving. have-nȯrë

man. denüpi [denüpë]

many branches hanging over. wüwündü [yuwündu]
many sitting (together). yiyïgwidë [yiyïgwid], yiyïgwïnd
many young ones. duduwa-tsi [dudua]
melting. sai [saigënt]
melting snow. sai-wai-wai [saiwai]
?mesh/sieve. saiyawan [?saiyagant (GH)].
Milky Way. saiyaganan, saiyagan-an, saiyagan-ana, saiyaganë, ?saiyawan
Milky Way–moving. saiyaga-nòra [wasayagano]
mother, mother's. biya
mountain(s). doi, doiya, doiya-penji, doiyaro, doiyav-avin, doiyave, doiyave-
    dë, doiyavi, doiyavi-di, n-doi, n-doiya, n-doiyavi, noiy, roi, roiya, roiyab-
    en, roiyavi [doi, doiya, doiyavi]
mountain pass (?). wia-ïna [wiap^h]
moving. nòrë
mucus or "gooey stuff" (GH). yogai, yogavi, yogavit-a [yogavit^h/?yogëp^h]
myself. nïsë [nïsës]

needles. sügi [sugip^h]
new. ügë, ügü
night. duganrip^h
nighttime. dugai-e [duga?i]

old. bai, dimbe [bedïmp^h]
old (?). be- [bedïmp^h]
old (?). dï-
on. vai-yo [vaix, uvaix]
on a slant, sideways. wegidu [wegip^h, wegipunt]
otter. ban, banzu-a, banzuk
our. da, daman
our/we/us. damë, damën

pass (mountain). wia-ro [wiap^h]
peeling, slicing. tsiyuwano
people. nüwï-tsi, nüwü [nüwë]
pine nut, pine nut tree. dïva [dïvA]
pine nut tree (?). wüwa [dïvA (GH)]
pine tree. wongo, wongo-no, wongo-ron [wongovI]
pools. babai-eya [babaiyu, babaiyigwip]
prayer. naishünde [naishünte]

quaking aspen(s). sena, senav-av, shïna-ra, sïna-aiva, sïnav, sïnave [sïnavI]

rain. bagosi, baiwë, bauwah [ba:ënwap^h, bauwap^h]; enwad
rain shower. paroagen [paroage (GH)]
red. engana [engavit^h]
redwing blackbirds. ?bagan-bagan-nogan-zi [bagantsuk^h]

ripe and burst open. todowainda
rise (about to), or pop up. yïzïgïn [yïzïkïnïz/yïzïgïnt]
rising (*see also* fly). yïzïgïh
rising, flying up. narai-yïzïnòrë [narai-yïzïno?]
river. ogwe
road. boi [boi?]
rocks. dïmpi, dïmpi-do
rocks climbing. dïmpimëndoi-ya [dïmpimëndoihgi?]
rock slide. dïmp-vanzingo
root. dïdïë [dïdïnE];
root. yambi [yampʰ]
rumbling-shaking (after thunder). nuyihïgïn
running (?). nuki
running slowly. boihoigeno [boihoikïn]

sacred power. boha
sagebrush. bo [bohopʰ]
sand. basiwambitta [ba:siwampʰ]
says. sïneyugwid-ïd [simehugwid]
sets in the west (*see also* go down out of sight). yuwïnangwa, yuwï
shakes with rumbling sound. nüyïhïgïndë
shelter, sheltered (?). wïto [wïtüroi (GH)]
shining, blooming. dònzi [doanzi]
shining, slick. bazigi [barazigwid]
shining/twinkling. parësai
shiny, twinkling stars (Milky Way). saiyaganë, saiyaganan
shiny. dònzia [doanzi]
showing up. nare-nagüx [nai:nagük (Emily), nagüx (GH)]
side (?). wegïn. ?wegi
sideways. wegidukano [wegidukandʰ]
sideways/slanting. wegïd [wegipʰ]
silver. wi [wih]
sit. garïdë, garïd, n-garïd, garïmbi [garïd]
sitting. gara [garïd]
sitting there. garïdëmënt, garïdë
sky. dugu, dugum, dugumba-ga [dugumba?/dugumbãnr]
sky (?). narugumba-ngo [?dʉgumba]
slowing down (barely catching up, GH). wümihanòrë
small (?). de [dedïtsi (GH)]
small amount. wüwü
small lake, pond. bagadïdë
snow melting, wet. saiwai
song. huviarë [huvia (singular), huvianï (plural)]
sounding. naranga [nananga]
spirit/soul. mugua
splashing (?). vesiyu

spots. mamaiyïgwidir
stand. wïno [wenᵲe (Tidzump 1970:18)]
stand (?)–coming back (?). wani-goïnòrë [goino]
stand–moving. wïnïkanòrë
stand in front of you. wïnenga [wïnankW]
standing-moving. wainanòrë, wainano [wïnïno]; wanoginòra [wïnïno-nòra]
standing-moving (with reference to animal tracks). wïnëre [wïnërek from
   wïnïno]
standing while moving (blowing in the wind). winogandë, winogan [wïnï-
   ganòr]
still under it. maruk-andu
sun. dave-dï [dave]
sun/day. dave
sunflower seeds. akën, akën-ïküni [aka, akampʰ]

tail. gweshi
taking one's time walking. nuwïgenòr, nuwïgena [nuwikin]
thoughts. suave-andë, suave-andïnò [suavegind, suapʰ]
toward or come night. duganangwa [duganankW]
traveling. dedok wïnïganòrë [dedok wanokin]
trees. sïhïvi [sëhëvI]
two. wa [wahadu]

under (?deep). ruka [duganᵗʰ]
under or lining. dïvarë [dïvarëruk or dïvana]
under water (?). barukande [barukʰ (GH)]
up, above. dugu-n [dugupʰ]
upon/above. bai [vaix]

washing down (?washes, pours down,GH). dowano [dowïrhiyaʔ]
water. pa, sam-baro-mbi, va [ba:]
water-black. ba-ru [ba:-duhuvitʰ]
water-deep. pa-ro [ba:-dukand]
water rising (?). varu-kë, varukë-penji
waves. anoga; yanugënt [yanugïndʰ]
wavy. yanome [yano:mi]
went. mïëp
what (?). hinën
white. dogo, dosa, doza [dosavitʰ]
white clay. evïn [evi]
white-tailed ptarmigan (?). saiwan
wild geese. nïgïnt
wild rose hip (?). sïnam [?ʒi´-amp (Shimkin 1947b:274)]
willows. ?sï, sïhïvi [sëhëvI]
wind. de [?neïdʰ]; nüïndi [neïdʰ (GH]
wood, stick. hom, hombi [hu:pi]

woodchuck. ya-na, yë-na [yëh]
wood/tree. hupin [huːpi]

yellow. oha-n [ohapitʰ]
young males. duru, durua

Notes

Introduction

1. See Shimkin (1986b:308–35) for a scholarly overview of Wind River Shoshone history and culture, and the bibliography of Shimkin's publications covering many important specific aspects of Wind River Shoshone culture (p. 806). See Trenholm and Carley (1972) for a documented but more general overview of Wind River Shoshone history and culture.

2. *Numu-tibo'o* appears as *Tävivo* in Mooney's account and is incorrectly identified as the prophet for the 1870 Ghost Dance (Mooney [1896] 1991: 764). See Du Bois 1939:3–4 for the correct identification of the prophet of the 1870 Ghost Dance (Wodziwob) and her understanding of the relationship of Wovoka's father (called *Numataivo* or *Tavivo* in her publication) to the religion as believer and assistant.

3. Mooney believed that Wovoka's trance-vision coincided with a total or partial eclipse of the sun that occurred on January 1, 1889 (Mooney [1896] 1991:16). Hittman suggests that Wovoka's vision was probably a trifle earlier, in late December 1888 (Hittman 1990:102).

4. Another Plains account that also contradicts any anti-white interpretation of the Ghost Dance religion comes from Porcupine, a Cheyenne man who visited Wovoka in 1889. A military officer interviewed Porcupine several months after this visit and quoted him as saying, "He [Wovoka] told us not to quarrel or fight or strike each other, or shoot one another; that the whites and Indians were to be all one people" (Mooney [1896] 1991:785).

5. "Sioux" was an older name used by Euro-Americans, which referred to any one, or all, of three groups: the Lakota, or western division; the Dakota, or eastern division; and the Nakota, or middle divison. It is a derogatory term, and contemporary members of the groups prefer the use of their specific native names as given here (Powers, personal communication, 1995). Regarding the Ghost Dance, it was the Lakota who were massacred at Wounded Knee, and it was the Lakota songs that Mooney, Colby, and Curtis published. For these reasons I use the name "Lakota" rather than "Sioux" throughout this book, except when directly quoting other authors and their use of "Sioux."

6. Wovoka's daughter and son-in-law did eventually become Mormons, but

this was late in their lives and well after the Ghost Dance movement in Nevada had ceased to exist (Hittman 1990:84).

7. See Vander 1986:12–14 for connections between this Prophet Dance complex and the Naraya.

8. Indeed they even changed its name. Lakota and other Plains tribes called the religion the Ghost Dance (Mooney [1896] 1991:791), and ironically, that is how it became known in English translation. The Paiute name for the religion was simply *Nänigükwa*, "dance in a circle," perhaps a reference to the Great Basin Round Dance tradition.

9. For a detailed account of the life history, songs, and musical experience of Emily Hill, see Vander 1988. Also included in that book is information regarding the recording and working relationships of the author with Emily and Dorothy (Vander 1988:xiv, xv, xviii, xxi, 10).

10. Bannocks, who speak a dialect of Northern Paiute, have lived in long association with Northern Shoshones in Idaho.

11. *Nanrisundaih*, "pray," in Tidzump 1970:41.

12. See Vander 1986:7–14 for additional information on Naraya performance and history.

13. Tassitsie, unlike Emily and other Wind River Shoshone cited by Shimkin and Lowie, also stated that the Naraya originated with Wovoka.

14. This counterclockwise motion may relate to a shamanistic practice discussed in chapter 2 in connection with sickness from ghosts/whirlwinds. Michael Hittman suggests that Turner's concept of liminality, which includes the use of countercultural patterns in religious ritual contexts, might be another explanation for the selection of counterclockwise motion as a closing pattern in Naraya ritual (personal communication, 1993).

15. For an example of a nonreligious Naraya song text that I recorded from Angelina Wagon in 1981, see Vander 1988:65.

16. The mutually exclusive relationship between the Naraya and Peyote religions among Wind River Shoshone people was exceptional to the ease with which Shoshones incorporated and participated in a variety of religious traditions. Shimkin has documented this mutually exclusive relationship in his Sun Dance publication (Shimkin 1953:467). That William Washington, a former Naraya leader, quit the Naraya altogether after he took up the Peyote religion is another specific example of this point. Information on the views of Quanah Parker, a Peyote leader among the Comanche, and Wovoka suggests that both leaders subscribed to this mutual antipathy. Mooney reported that Quanah Parker opposed the Ghost Dance and prevented its spread among the Comanches (Mooney [1896] 1991:902). Andy Vidovich, Wovoka's son-in-law, reported Wovoka's antipathy toward the use of peyote and quoted Wovoka as saying, "If you keep on using it you will walk on your hands and feet like a dog. Don't use it [peyote]. I don't like that" (Hittman 1990: 165). However, Hittman expressed his doubts to me regarding the quote by Vidovich. He thought that it was probably an anachronism (personal communication 1993). (For further discussion of Naraya decline, see Vander 1986:65–69 and Vander 1988:27.)

Chapter 1: Great Basin Context

1. Other spellings and scholarly references for this term are: *nümü* (Fowler and Fowler 1971:96), *nimi* (Murphy 1986 Handbook:305), *neme* (Liljeblad 1957:23), and *Nümä* (Mooney [1896] 1991:1056).

2. Although scholars of Great Basin culture use the terms "Round Dance" and "Circle Dance" interchangeably, Round Dance is the more frequent choice. For this reason I shall follow suit. However, the reader should be aware that "Round Dance" is also the name for a social dance of the contemporary powwow, which has its own distinctive Plains music, history, and use (Lowie 1915:821, 822; Powers 1961:97–104; Vander 1988:36–38; Wissler 1913:455). In this book, all reference to Round Dance assumes a Great Basin context.

3. For Wind River Shoshones, Dinwoody Canyon, with its lake and rocks bearing ancient petroglyphs, is a place associated with power (Lowie 1924a: 296; Shimkin 1986a:325).

4. For more examples and detailed elaboration of this analysis, see Vander 1995:179–83.

5. Among Harney Valley Paiutes, the shaman who specializes in breath-catching first "dances until his breath begins to leave him, then he either falls or lies down besides the patient" (Whiting 1950:41). Park tells us that only the best and strongest Northern Paiute doctors have the power to go into a trance (Park 1934:104).

6. In her study of Basin mythology, Smith comments on the common occurrence of death and resurrection by individual characters in myth (Smith 1939:167). This literature also reveals some examples of large-scale resurrection as well (Lowie 1924b:229–31; Powell 1971:91, 92; Steward 1936:420, 421; Steward 1943b:282, 283, and 287–90). Although few in number, they are, nevertheless, interesting mythic analogues to Paiute Ghost Dance prophecies.

7. The power of prophecy practiced by Wodziwob and Wovoka was not a new element in Paiute culture.

8. There are always skeptics. This myth actually parodies the use of dance to drive off illness. Coyote tricks the dancers into dancing with their eyes closed and kills some for his own consumption.

9. Shoshones were not the only Plains tribe to practice game charming. Park comments that it is a link that connects "Paviotso-Shoshoni with the western Plains" (Park 1938:152).

10. Not all shamans had power to influence weather. For some, it was a separate and solitary power (Steward 1943a:285). I discuss it here because Wovoka claimed power to both predict and cause weather. It has relevance to the 1890 Ghost Dance and the Naraya.

11. Edward A. Dyer Sr., a non-Indian storekeeper in Yerington, Nevada, who served as Wovoka's secretary in his correspondence to far-flung Ghost Dance believers, wrote down his own eye-witness account of this event and the trickery employed. In the heat of July, Wovoka had concealed a block of ice high up in a cottonwood tree. Eventually the melting block slipped down

from the tree to the amazement of those who were gathered underneath the tree. It seemed to be a miraculous event and proof of Wovoka's power (Hittman 1990:213–14).

12. Wovoka's predictions also included seismic events, for example, the earthquake that was to take place after he died and went to heaven. A severe earthquake did, in fact, occur in Mason Valley exactly three months after his death, and Yerington Paiutes attributed the quake to Wovoka and his power (Hittman 1990:172–73).

13. Even ordinary people who are not shamans may help control the weather. Millie Guina and Angelina Wagon, Shoshone women that I have lived with, spoke on different occasions to clouds, asking them to move off. The clouds heeded their requests.

14. A possible translation of *Badsai* may be *Ba:*, "water," plus *sai*, "melting." Naraya song 3 begins *Saiwai*, which means "snow melting" (Vander 1988:18).

15. Mooney suggested that bulletproof Ghost Dance shirts may have been influenced by Mormon practice regarding an "endowment robe," an undergarment that Mormon initiates wear (Mooney [1896] 1991:790). According to an 1890 Mormon source quoted by Barney, "This garment protects from disease, and even death, for the bullets of an enemy will not penetrate it" (Barney 1986:214). Bailey suggested that Wovoka learned of the Mormon undergarment from Northern Paiute converts (Bailey 1957:122–23). Mooney suggested Wind River Shoshone converts to Mormonism as an alternate line of influence leading, ultimately, to the Lakota Ghost Dance shirt. This route bypassed Wovoka altogether (Mooney [1896] 1991:790–91). Mooney reported that "whites and Indians alike agreed that it formed no part of the dance costume in Mason valley [Nevada]" (Mooney [1896] 1991:791). In the most recent examination of the relationship between the Mormon and Ghost Dance religions, Barney cautions that there is still no conclusive proof that Mormon influence was the source of Wovoka's claim to invulnerability or of Lakota Ghost Dance shirts (Barney 1986:155).

16. Smaller details of specific dances—such as women stepping back a step or two after a song finished, then moving back up into the circle for the next song—connect the Round (Grass) Dance (Steward 1943a:287; see also Steward 1941:353) with the Naraya (Vander 1988:13). Two references to counterclockwise movement of the dance are: Lowie 1909a:219, and Crum 1980:15.

17. In myth, Rat's Circle [Round] Dance song follows this Basin song form (Steward 1943b:284). This is also true in Naraya songs, in Paiute Ghost Dance songs, and even in the Ghost Dance songs of Plains tribes whose musical style for all other song genres differed significantly from those of the Basin.

18. Powell (1971:121–28) did not indicate the use of most of the Southern Paiute song texts that he gathered. Two texts are titled "Dance Songs"; we know that at least two other songs were also used at the Round Dance, for they appear in Dellenbaugh's Round Dance account. Although Powell's

sample probably includes many songs for occasions other than the Round Dance, they provide further evidence for the careful observation of the natural world and a variety of responses to it.

19. The term literally derives from the word for talk. *TaikwaG*, "talk," becomes *taikwahni*, "chief" (Miller 1972:170, 157).

20. Mooney gives the meaning of "*Nümi´naă´*—'our father'; the mythic ancestor of the Paiute" (Mooney [1896] 1991:1056).

21. For further Round Dance information, see E. Johnson 1975:9, 10; Kelly 1932:178; Murphy and Murphy 1960:319; Murphy and Murphy 1986:296; Shimkin 1970:177; Steward 1938:107, 139, 193, 237; Steward 1939:265.

22. Wovoka carried this five-day tradition over into Ghost Dance doctrine regarding performance of the religion (Mooney [1896] 1991:772, 802).

23. Recall that Comanches are Wind River Shoshone people who separated from their Wyoming relatives in the early eighteenth century and moved down to the Southern Plains.

24. Other references that mention concern for rain in Round Dance performance are Hittman 1973:260; E. Johnson 1975:10; Lowie 1915:817; Powell 1971:87, 270; Steward 1938:107; and Steward 1941:262, 265.

25. Harris notes the decline of religious and fertility rites in the White Knife Shoshone *Gwini* ceremonies by the time it became known as the fandango (Harris 1940:84). Hinton's discussion of the Havasupai version of the Round Dance, which they perform at their Peach Festival, is another example, and one that enfolds the Ghost Dance within its complex history. Havasupais learned the Ghost Dance from the Southern Paiutes. Although the notion of the return of the dead was foreign and rejected, other aspects of the dance transmitted from the Southern Paiute took root. They are another piece of evidence that supports the religious purpose of the Round Dance and its close connection to the Great Basin version of the Ghost Dance. Hinton writes in 1984, "The dance was said in Spier's time [the late 1920s] to ensure prosperity and good crops and rain; it was also, as it still is, simply a time when the community gathers for entertainment and fellowship" (Hinton 1984:18). In its final days, the Naraya also lost religious significance (Vander 1986:65–69; Vander 1988:63, 64). Eventually it ceased altogether, as other Plains dances supplanted it and even its social functions.

26. Steward gives further information on various forms of the Father Dance in this same publication (1943a:287–88) and in an earlier publication (Steward 1941:265–67).

27. In a 1909 publication, Lowie compared the Lemhi Shoshone *Nū´akin* and Father Dances and specifically contrasted their songs. "The *ā´pö-nö´kakin* (Father's dance) was danced like the *nū´akin*, but with different songs, which were usually without words, [inferring an exclusive use of vocables] but partly in the nature of a prayer" (Lowie 1909a:219).

28. See a discussion of the dance step of both the Father Dance and Naraya in relation to Spier's analysis of dance style in the Prophet Dance complex of the Northwest (Vander 1986:14).

Chapter 2: Naraya Songs Related to the 1890 Ghost Dance Movement

1. Although ghosts could cause illness and even death, they were also a potential source of power used for curing ghost-induced illness (Park 1938:79, 97).

2. There are also some exceptional examples of large-scale resurrection in Great Basin myth. See Lowie 1924:229–31; Powell 1971:91–92; Steward 1936: 420–21, 431; Steward 1943b: 282–83, 287–90.

3. Bailey makes clear in a previous paragraph that "my father" refers to *Numi'na,* the Paiute mythic father. See Bailey 1957:113, for a variant presentation of the same scene and speech given here.

4. I heard this verb complex as *wanï-ganörë,* similar to other versions of this in Naraya songs and which translates as standing-moving. If this were correct, the second line could translate as "Our, above, our, above, sun—standing-moving."

5. See Hultkrantz 1987:42–46 for elaboration on the complexity of these religious configurations among the Wind River Shoshone.

6. See Hultkrantz 1954:134; Hultkrantz 1956:209–12; Hultkrantz 1961:42; Hultkrantz 1981:560, 561, 568, 569; Hultkrantz 1986:632; Lowie 1909a:233, 235–37, 265, 272, 273; Shimkin 1947c:331.

7. See chapter 1 for an examination of the confusion surrounding the various uses and meanings of the Father Dance as performed by different groups.

8. Bailey's source of information was Wovoka's secretary, Edward A. Dyer Sr. Dyer gives the Paiute name for Wovoka, Numa-naha, which clearly documents the mythic reference for the English translation given in Bailey (Hittman 1990:215).

9. See topic-imagery chart for Mooney's publication (table 7), chapter 10.

10. It is possible that the final syllable, *-no,* in *boihoigeno* is a suffix of continuous action. If so, its translation would be, "keeps running slowly." This may also be true for the last syllable of *nuhiyogeno* in the second line of text and it would translate as "keeps coming or moving in." The repetition of the second line changes the final syllable of the word to *nuhiyogenë,* replacing the suffix of continuous motion with a form that makes the last two syllables of the word almost identical to *ena,* a common ending vocable.

11. Hultkrantz reports Northern Shoshone and Ute belief that Wolf escorts the dead to the other world (Hultkrantz 1986:637).

12. Shimkin comments, "Unfortunately, the same informant told that Wolf, after reviving from death, departed, telling Coyote, 'When people die, they're going to me.' Is Wolf 'Our Father' then? Most persons deny such a theory vehemently. But reconciliation of these fundamental conflicts is beyond their interests or abilities" (Shimkin 1947c:331).

13. There is a wide discrepancy between what I hear as the sung version of this word and the way that Emily says it in her talk about the song. Gladys Hill also hears it in the song the way Emily talks about it. I give both spoken versions: Emily's conversational rendering as well as Gladys's.

14. Emily tells a story of the journey in reverse. A man's soul left his body and rose high in the sky. Eventually angel wings carried the soul back down to earth, body, and life. See Vander 1986:38, 39.

15. For an interesting discussion of Christian reinterpretation of the Wind River Shoshone Sun Dance, see Hultkrantz 1969:38; Shimkin 1953:435–36.

16. Shoshone response to Christian proselytizing, indeed to Euro-American culture in general, is ambiguous. Hultkrantz reports a perceived hostility by some Shoshones between Christianity (and modern technology) and native Shoshone religion. "According to the Shoshoni the spirits of Nature have thus fled from both electricity and the Christian Gospel; an Indian told me how the powers had moved far up to the mountains in fear of the Christian Cross" (Hultkrantz 1969:30). In the late 1980s the location of the Shoshone Sun Dance was moved from its traditional field near Fort Washakie up to Winkelman's Dome, a remote place with no electricity or proximity to water. I was told that the old field had become too close to the encroaching development of houses and lights. It was no longer a place for spiritual power.

17. This first Ghost Dance experience "immunized" California tribes to its later and more famous successor (Kroeber 1925:869).

18. Interestingly, *prevention* of earthquakes was, in fact, the centerpiece of several principal dance ceremonies among the Yurok, Hupa, and Karok in northern California. In native terms, these ceremonies were "firm the earth," or "refixing of the world" (Kroeber and Gifford 1949:1, 6). Kroeber analyzed their three underlying goals: sufficient food, good health, and freedom from such natural disasters as earthquakes (Kroeber and Gifford 1949:105). One is immediately struck by the similar intent between these ceremonies and the Naraya as described by Emily Hill—although their outward forms were very different.

19. See Olden 1923:64 for a variant statement of this same point.

Chapter 3: Water

1. Songs 6–14, which appear on this list, were among the seventeen Naraya songs I published in 1986. The English translations for these texts are given in appendix A of this book.

2. Throughout this calendar, the term for moon is *Möə*. Steward adds that *pôsitc* means "soft snow" and corresponds to the month of March (Steward 1943a:291).

3. For example, Hinton commented that the Havasupai "have the notion that springs and rivers have *sumáaga* [having power, knowledge, or spirit]" (Hinton 1984:12).

4. This relationship is not restricted to males or shamans. Millie Guina and Angelina Wagon, Shoshone women with whom I have lived, talked to the wind and clouds, telling them to move off. (See also Buck Skin Joe's address to the wind in chapter 1.) Nor is this relationship unique to the Shoshone and Great Basin people. Hinton writes that "Havasupais converse with the powerful forces of nature much as they would with human beings" (Hinton 1984:9).

5. Many other Native American cultures share these beliefs in one form or another. For example, Coast Salish people, such as the Nooksack, bathed before seeking a vision. The bath is for health and helps one endure hardship (Amoss 1978:13). Gayton comments on the daily bath of the foothill people in south-central California. "It had a salutary effect, especially in the acquisition of supernatural power by both shamans and laymen. A boy or girl approaching puberty was roused from sleep and made to swim three times during the night for six days, usually in the coldest months. This was supposed to give them a long life as well as harden their characters. Water was venerated and regarded as immortal" (Gayton 1930:76).

6. Although health and general well-being are the principal goals of the Peyote Ceremony, it is interesting that some Washo and Northern Paiute people also believed that peyote had power to bring rain—ever a concern in the Basin (Stewart 1944:81).

7. According to Hultkrantz, water offerings by Wind River Shoshones to Mother Earth, *tam sogobia,* occurred at other larger gatherings, such as feasts (Hultkrantz 1987:47).

8. More details of this myth and additional scholarly references appear in the introduction and in chapter 2.

9. With humor, Wind River Shoshone myth suggests a different stimulus for resurrection: rubbing a wild rose branch vigorously in the mouth or anus (Shimkin 1947c:343).

Chapter 4: Fog, Mountains, and Rocks

1. A variant of this word appears in the text of Naraya song 13. Emily glossed the derivation of that word, "It's standing, *wïnïganór,* you know, the trees, when the wind's blowing" (Vander 1986:43). A seemingly related word appeared in the text of Paiute Ghost Dance Song No. 4 (Mooney [1896] 1991:1053–54). Mooney glossed *wï'noghän* as "shaken by the wind, waving in the wind" (Mooney [1896] 1991:1057). Gladys Hill did not recognize *wïnïganór* and suggested *wïnuagïn,* "moving along," as the spoken derivation for the song word.

2. This word comes from the spoken word *wïnïganór.* Another derivation may be from *wïnïnór,* which, in turn, comes from *wenre,* "standing," plus *-nór,* "while moving." *Wïnïganórë* also appears in song 40 in connection with rain that is blown by the wind—standing while moving.

3. I believe that "va" with an added nasal insert, "van," derives from the first syllable of *vagïna.* Stem reduplication is used in Shoshone to denote plurals. I believe that the usage here is a poetic one.

4. Although Emily identifies this as an Idaho song and mentions the "different words" that one may find in these songs, I see no evidence for this in song 45. Her comment may simply refer to the slight dialectical differences that sometimes distinguish these texts, but with no implication that they appear in this particular song.

5. *Wi* is from the spoken word *Wih,* which means "knife" and can refer more broadly to silver or any kind of metal. See Tidzump 1970:31.

6. Emily is referring to long braids of otter fur that girls and women attach as extensions to their own hair or braids. This is part of the female's dancing outfit and commonly worn for powwow performance.

7. This word appears in Naraya song 11A and Emily commented in connection with its use there that "those rocks that slide . . . cliff-like, they're underground" (Vander 1986:41).

8. Powell renders *ci-a-tub* as "slab rock" in his list of Northern Paiute vocabulary (Powell 1971:249). Kelly renders *topi´* or *tüpi´* as "stone" for the Surprise Valley Paiutes (Kelly 1932:202). (*Dïmpi* is the Wind River Shoshone word for rock.) The Paiute word for slab rock can be broken down: *ci-a*, "slab," and *tub*, "rock." *Ci-a* would seem to relate to *tsiyu* of *tsiyuwano*, which Emily translates as "peeling" or "slicing," in Naraya song 54.

9. Reviewing the transcription of this conversation at a later time, Gladys Hill understood Emily's comments as meaning the rocks at the bottom of the water had some soil and grass growing on top of them.

10. This could mean "a knife," or any kind of metal, such as steel or iron.

11. *Buih* means "eye" and "seeing" (Tidzump 1970:10SE). *Ohapuwiw* means "gold" (Tidzump 1970:8SE), which combines an abbreviation of *ohapite*, "yellow," *buih*, "looking," or "to the eye," and *wih*, "metal." *Buiwih*, the word Emily uses, omits the specific reference to the yellow color of gold and describes a metallic appearance applicable to either silver or gold.

12. The color white in Naraya songs is usually used to describe mountains and refers to snow. As Emily makes no mention of snow in her comments, it may be that in this instance the rock itself is white rather than snow-covered.

13. However, there are differences of belief as to whether each person has one or two souls, as well as about the placement of the soul(s) in the body. Powell writes that Northern Paiutes believe in two souls: *Mu-go-a*, Spirit of the heart, who is a man, and *Cu-na-min*, the Spirit of the head, who is a woman. Both souls exit through the nose at death (Powell 1971:242). Elsewhere in the same publication, Powell translates *Mo-go-a* as "Spirit of the liver" (Powell 1971:270). I wonder whether this has nothing to do with the anatomical organ but rather refers to the spirit of the live person in a general sense, i.e., to the body. If this is the case, then perhaps the distinction is between body (*Mo-go-a*, "seated in the heart") and mind (*Cu-na-min*, "seated in the head").

14. Millie Guina, Emily's sister, gives *navujieip* as *navushiep*.

15. I have given a "P" number to each of the forty-one song texts that I quote from Powell's published manuscripts (1971). The number refers to the placement of the text in my chapter 10, where there is a large section devoted to Powell's collection. His original titles for the texts, or an "untitled" heading for those lacking titles, appear in parentheses after the "P" number.

16. Note that the word for "soul" in this text is *mo-go´-av*, rather than *navujieip*. The latter term, to the best of my knowledge, is unique to the Wind River Shoshone.

17. In her Wind River "Shoshone Thesaurus," Tidzump gives *suape* for "breath" (Tidzump 1970:12).

18. Kelly and Park also received a pair of words for "soul." Kelly transcribes Surprise Valley Paiute terms for it as *sonupᵘ*, "breath," and *mugwa*, "the soul" (Kelly 1932:198). The following remark by Kelly leaves unresolved the issue of one versus two souls. "When a man dies his mu′gwa leaves and never returns. His soñüpᵘ breaks up and goes when he dies. If a man is half dead his sonu′p is still there; his mu′gwa is half gone. The doctor tries to put it back. When the mu′gwa leaves it hovers around" (Kelly 1932:198). Park reports a similar pair of words for the soul, either *sɔyəp* or *numəmuguʹᵃ*. Information on two possible placements of the soul in the body, head and chest, brings us back to Powell's information (heart and head) and the issue of one versus two souls. Park says nothing explicit about this; his presentation suggests differing forms of belief in one soul (Park 1938:39).

19. Smoke, another airy substance whose appearance and motion closely resemble fog and clouds, is another image of the soul. Father DeSmet observed a Ute cremation in 1843 and wrote, "The moment that the smoke rises in thick clouds, they think that the soul of the savage is flying towards the regions of spirits" (quoted in Steward 1943a:281). Mooney recounts that in 1890 dense smoke from forest fires in the mountains drifted down over the Wind River reservation. "This was regarded by the Indians as an indication of the approach of the great change, and the dance was continued with increased fervor" (Mooney [1896] 1991:808). Kroeber places this meaning of smoke within an even broader context of Native American mythology. "Rising smoke is a sign of the creation or momentous event" (Kroeber 1908:224).

20. The Aztec comrades mentioned above were warriors. Wind River Shoshone experience also included warfare as an important element in life on the Plains. Therefore, I suggest that beyond the Great Basin notion of fog as soul, the overlay of Plains culture on Wind River Shoshone culture added another and different context for the meaning and association of fog with feather. Voget reports, "In the traditional context of war, downy plumes evoked the idea of a fog that hid warriors from pursuers or otherwise made them invisible. The lightness of eagle feathers and plumes also suggested a weightlessness that carried horses swiftly over the ground" (Voget 1984:308).

21. Much to my surprise, I discovered the identical series of associations between breath, mist, and feathers in the epic poetry of Derek Walcott. The fit is perfect with Wind River Great Basin poetic perception. He writes, "So, first jam in our jacket, cause the heights was cold and our breath making feathers like the mist, we pass the rum" (Walcott 1990:3).

22. Powell translates "foam" from the first word of line two, *Pa-gaʹi-ani*. It closely resembles the Shoshone Naraya word for fog, *bagana* or *vagïna*. The root of the Shoshone word, and perhaps the Southern Paiute word as well, is *ba*, meaning "water."

23. The frequency of mountains in Naraya song texts is, in fact, second only to water. (See topic-imagery chart, table 1)

24. The absence of fasting, self-torture, and other practices differentiates Great Basin from Plains experience (for example, that of the Lakota) in the pursuit of power.

25. Amoss writes that among the Nooksack, a Coast Salish people, songs received by the shaman were associated with ritual objects, rocks being one such example (Amoss 1978:67). I add this as a reminder that many aspects of shamanistic belief discussed in relation to the Great Basin are by no means exclusive to that area, from both geographic and cultural standpoints.

26. Helene distinguished *bazidïmpi* from *wazidïmpi*. Both are round stones, but *bazidïmpi* are found in water while *wazidïmpi* are found on the ground.

27. Liljeblad includes this unusual category of rocks in his interesting distinction between the sources of shamanistic power. "In California, west of the Sierra Nevada sources of spirit power for treating sickness mostly were from animals, whereas east of the Sierra they were often inanimate objects and phenomena: mountains, trees, and peculiarly shaped rocks as well as meteorological forces and mythical beings, living in nature" (Liljeblad 1986:644).

Chapter 5: Animals

1. This refers to their tracks, from where they were standing and moving about. This word is abbreviated in its final appearance in the repeat of the second line.

2. This word comes from the spoken *no:vi*. Tidzump transcribes it as *noofi* (Tidzump 1970:2).

3. This word comes from the spoken *vand^h*. Tidzump transcribes this word as *uvande* (Tidzump 1970:47).

4. See discussion of the derivation of the female form in chapter 10). The Northern Paiute word for mountain sheep, *koipa*, is unlike *duk;* however, there may be a female form similar to the Shoshone. Kelly writes, "A band of stars in the east is called *müza´ᵃ* and is a band of mountain sheep who were once Paiute women" (Kelly 1932:154). Also, the word for mountain sheep, *koipa*, is yet another example in which its root, *koi*, like *wasi*, means "to kill" (Fowler 1986:95).

5. The correct translation choice for *dave*, "sun" or "day," remains unresolved. Gladys Hill notes that a literal translation of *biya dave* is "big day," the modern term for Sunday. She does not think that "sun" is the correct translation choice in this instance. However, Emily's comments about Naraya song 2 (Vander 1986:54–56) have relevance for the translation of Naraya song 79 and suggest otherwise. Emily gave two translations for "*Damën biyani . . . dave-de*, Our mothers day/sun" in Naraya song 2. The first is, "our mothers on Judgment Day," and/or, as Emily described it, "'When the sun comes up Mother Nature, our Mother comes looking'" (Vander 1986:55). In the second interpretation, the sun is identified with, or as, Mother Nature.

6. The word for cottontail has been transcribed respectively as *dabü̈ᵘ* and *tavü̈´tsi* in collections of Northern and Owens Valley Paiute myth (Kelly 1938:422; Steward 1936:371).

7. Of all the ground animals that appear in Naraya songs, the fox was one of two animals not eaten by Wind River Shoshones (Shimkin 1947b:276–77).

Indeed, many Great Basin people did not eat wolf, coyote, or fox (Fowler 1986:93). Sheep Eaters in Idaho, who ate coyote meat, are an exception to this general rule (Liljeblad 1957:97).

8. Elsewhere, Emily gave *daziumbe gwahaiboromp*, "star backbone," as the Shoshone word for the Milky Way. Other Great Basin tribes also used this same expression. I investigate this topic further in connection with Naraya song 126 in chapter 7.

9. I thank Professor James Lovvorn of the University of Wyoming, who brought his knowledge of Wyoming birds and their habitats to bear on the information given in Naraya texts. From them he has made educated guesses for identifying the birds in songs 84, 85, 88, 89, 90, and 91.

10. Gladys Hill added a range of meanings for this word: the sun goes down, sinking, going down, the side that anything's going down, that's where the sun goes down—the west. Tidzump gives the word for sunset as *tavaiyuuwixu* (Tidzump 1970:3). In this compound word *tavai* is the word for sun. Crapo gives *tapai jya-nankwa"* for west (Crapo 1976:81) and *nankwa"* for in the direction of, toward (Crapo 1976:57).

11. Another literal translation of *ba-ru* is "water black," from *ba:,* "water," and *ru,* abbreviated form of *duhuvitʰ,* "black."

12. This comes from the spoken word *dugumba*. I have also been told that *dugumbānr* is the word for sky. Tidzump transcribes it as *tegumbanrqa* (Tidzump 1970:1). Another possible derivation for *dugum-vandu* in the text is *duganripʰ,* "black," "night," plus *vandʰ* (*uvande* in Tidzump 1970:47), "above, up there."

13. This comes from the spoken word *nana*. In Shimkin's publication "Wind River Shoshone Literary Forms" he translates *nana* as "all kinds" (Shimkin 1947c:350). Elsewhere he analyzes it as a "reduplicated form of na-, reflexive and correlative of a plural subject" (Shimkin 1949b:209. *Nana* also appears in a song text published by Liljeblad, which in that context he translates as "'togetherness' or 'hanging together'" (Liljeblad 1986:648).

14. Hage and Miller suggest Shoshone bird nomenclature based on size: *kwinaa* is "eagle" and/or "large bird," and *huittsuu* is "small bird." *Kwinaa* also serves as the generic word for bird (Hage and Miller 1976:481, 483). Wind River Shoshones differ from this somewhat. An elderly Shoshone man explained to me that *gwina* was formerly the word for eagle, but in more recent times it means chicken. As a consequence, *biya* (big) *gwina* became "eagle." The generic word for bird is *huchu* and, to my knowledge, has no implication of smallness. The term for "little bird," *huchuchi,* adds a diminutive suffix to *huchu*. Malinda Tidzump, a Wind River Shoshone speaker and linguist, corroborates these points, although she varies somewhat from the author in orthography: *huuchuuh,* "bird"; *huuchuuchiih,* "little bird"; *kwinyah,* "chicken"; and *piagwinyaq,* "eagle" (Tidzump 1970:8).

15. Gladys Hill translated *naranga* as "sounding or hear 'em, you could hear 'em." Shimkin gives *naʹŋga-,* as a verbal stem, which he translates "(to) hear" (Shimkin 1949c:210); Tidzump gives *nangayku* for "hear" (Tidzump 1970:19).

16. I suggest that *semikai* may derive, at least in part, from *semeq,* Tidzump's rendering of the word for "one" (Tidzump 1970:45).

17. See note 13 for discussion of this word.

18. See Naraya song 56, in which the type of rock Emily likens to a sidewalk is the subject of the song. The rock may be limestone.

19. Shimkin translated *pa:´nʒux* as "mink"; however, he added a question mark to indicate his uncertainty regarding this translation. He rendered "otter" from *du´pasaiwï* (Shimkin 1947b:277). In this instance, *pa*, "water," is the second syllable. The first syllable, *du-*, is a common abbreviation for the word "black," or "dark."

20. Likewise, Big Smokey Valley Shoshones of Nevada use *pui"* (Crapo 1976:139) and Gosiute Shoshones of Utah, *pui* (Miller 1972:161).

21. See discussion on this point regarding Naraya song 92.

22. In this realm Northern Paiutes classify animals as edible, *ka-hu-a-wai-it* (birds, fish, insects, jumpers, etc.) and nonedible, *kai-na-wha-wait* (skunks, gophers, lizards, frogs, horned toads, worms, butterflies, mosquitoes, etc.) (Powell 1971:241).

23. Shoshones tell a myth for the origins of trout, which Shimkin terms a staple. Coyote, impatient to see all his Indian children, violated a warning and opened the water jug where they were kept. Most of them ran away. Coyote's wife searched for these lost children and found that some, like the Wind River Shoshones, lived where there were buffaloes to hunt. However, still concerned for their welfare, she told them, "There is a high mountain. I'll go up and cause water to be on the top with trout in it for you to live on" (Lowie 1924b:211).

24. In the summer of 1982 I was served marmot, or rock chuck, as Shoshones referred to it, at the breakfast concluding an all-night meeting of the Native American Church.

25. People enjoy prairie dog today. One summer evening while attending a powwow I bought a prairie dog—roasted and wrapped in newspaper—at a refreshment stand. It is, indeed, tasty. Western Shoshones also hunted ground squirrels, flooding being one of three techniques used to capture the animals. "Burrowing rodents such as pocket gophers and ground squirrels were dug out with rodent skewers, or flooded and smoked out" (Thomas et al. 1986: 268).

26. This is the female linguistic form of "antelope." In Naraya songs I have recorded, only song variants of the male form, *wandzi,* appears.

27. Emily Hill has told me her own lineage. Her father, Edrian Hill, was a *Hukudïka,* "Dirt Eater." Her mother, Barbara Minnie Neff, was from the *Doiyai,* "Mountain People." I believe the latter term, in fact, to be another name for Sheep Eater. Habitat, rather than the animal, is the name-giving distinction.

28. The term *Dukurka* is Shimkin's transcription of "Mountain Sheep Eaters" from Wind River Shoshone sources, with reference to their locations in the Wind River Rockies and Yellowstone (Shimkin 1937). The linguistic derivation for the various transcriptions of native terms for Mountain Sheep Eater will be given below.

29. Millie Guina, Emily's sister, told me that dogs were trained to bark or not to bark depending upon the large or small size of the animal spotted.

30. Similarly, Northern Paiute of Fish Springs and Fish Lake Valley called the Big Dipper, *yahidu,* meaning "is driving rabbits" (Steward 1941:267).

31. Shimkin transcribes the Shoshone name for the rabbit as *dɔ´sakam* and identifies it as *Lepus townsendii campanius.*

32. Liljeblad noted the aesthetic preference of Northern Shoshones for the zigzag pattern of white tails in blankets made from cottontail fur (Liljeblad 1957:37).

33. The number five also applied to Wovoka's Ghost Dance vision in which he received five songs to bring five different types of weather.

34. The following calendar names are from one Northern Paiute group from Nevada (Sagebrush mountain dwellers), two Shoshone groups from Nevada (Beatty and Egan Canyon), and one Shoshone group from Utah (Grouse Creek). These names appear in abbreviated form as Sa, S-Bty, S-Egan, and S-GrsCr. I provide only each author's English translation for the names except when there is none.

	Sa	S-Bty	S-Egan	S-GrsCr
Jan.	jack-rabbit-urine on-snow mo.	big mo.	big mo.	cold mo.
Feb.	1st-young-jack-rabbit-mo.	growth begins mo.	big snow-fall mo.	frozen mo.
Mar.	everything-green-mo.	spring mo.	coyote [young born]	soft snow mo.
Apr.	buckberry-leaves-out-mo.	mt. sheep lamb mo.	mt. sheep lamb mo.	coyote, i.e., pups mo.
May	flower-mo.	*tukap:* (ripe) mo.	antelope young [born] mo.	male mt. sheep mo.
June	Indian-potato-mo.	green brush mo.	fawn [born] mo.	antelope young mo.
July	summer mo.	dried mo.	fat (i.e., game) mo.	fawn mo.
Aug.	rye-grass-mo.	very hot mo.	sunflower [ripe] mo.	sunflower mo. *(kusiak)*
Sept.	piñon-nut-mo.	ripe pine nuts	pine nuts [ripe] mo.	sunflower mo. *(biak:)*
Oct.	autumn-mo.	crack (pine nuts)	hole mo. [i.e., rodents dig in]	*nagadazo* (?)
Nov.	deer-breeding mo.	*paʰumpi* seeds ripe mo.	small mo.	little mo.
Dec.	winter mo.	winter mo.	big mo.	big mo.
	(Stewart 1941:445)	(Steward 1941:268–69)	(Steward 1943a:291)	

35. For further information see Sapir 1910:457; Shimkin 1947c:329; Smith 1939:119; Steward 1943b:257.

36. Lowie has published Shoshone myths that recount the creation of the Shoshone people from the union of Coyote with two women, a mother and daughter, who both had vaginal teeth (Lowie 1909a:236–39).

37. Gladys's reference to animals in myth and kinship relationships seems related to Southern Ute taxonomy as analyzed by Goss. Goss presents a "Table of Semantic Fields of Kinship, Mythology, and Nature," areas that relate to one another through one shared root. For example, from the basic root form *kwana-*, comes *kwana-ni*, "my father-in-law"; *kwana-pi-ci*, "Myth Eagle"; and *kwana-ci*, "Eagle" (*Aquila chrysaetos*) (Goss 1990:15).

38. For discussion of the appearance of humor and sexual allusion in the waning days of Naraya performance and songs, see Vander 1988:27, 63–64.

39. Steward suggests a relationship between Cottontail's re-creation of Sun and the offering of gall by Nevada Shoshones after the hunt. "The offering often seemed somewhat to placate evil forces or to insure future hunting and gathering success. There may be a connection between the offering of gall in several localities and the common Shoshonean folk tale in which the sun, after having been killed by Cottontail, was created anew from the gall of the old sun; and also that gall had no use and would generally have been discarded in any event" (Steward 1941:230).

40. In "The Hoodwinked Dancers," already cited (chapter 1), Coyote fools a village of prairie dogs with the same ploy. Coyote calls for the dance ostensibly to prevent illness. Shimkin believes that the dance in this myth refers to the Naraya, which he translates as "the Shuffling Dance" (Shimkin 1986a:326–27).

41. Park documented the source of power for many Paiute shamans, for example, the otter for Joe Green, the antelope and eagle for Paiute Harrison, the rattlesnake for Rosie Plummer, the eagle and weasel for Tom Mitchell, and the eagle and crow for Dick Mahwee (Park 1938:18). John Truhujo, a Wind River Shoshone shaman and Sun Dance leader, received his power from the elk (Hultkrantz 1961:202).

42. Elsewhere Steward notes that the singing and shamanizing made the antelope "docile and stupid" (Steward 1938:34).

43. See Hultkrantz 1961:201–5 for discussion of the conflicting views regarding a taboo against killing any member of the species of one's guardian spirit.

44. Chief Washakie possessed this power (Hultkrantz 1956:198).

45. Whereas five is the special number in Paiute culture, as evidenced in the five weather songs that Wovoka received and the five-day duration for Round Dance and Ghost Dance performance, four is the sacred number on the Plains. In the above example, the singers perform sets of four songs after smoking. Smoking a pipe and offering it to the four directions is a common ritual on the Plains; Shimkin notes the omission of the presentation in this particular instance.

46. This quote from Voget's book on the Shoshoni-Crow Sun Dance is equally relevant to the Wind River Shoshone and the Crow Sun Dance. The Crow, who had lost their own earlier tradition for the religion, learned the Sun Dance anew from the Wind River Shoshones in 1941.

47. See Lowie 1909a:267–68, 276–77, 293.

48. Western Shoshones hunted doves, mockingbirds, sage hens, and quail.

Waterfowl were targeted in communal hunts (Thomas et al. 1986:268). Fowler discussed the hunting of land birds and waterfowl who inhabited the significant wetland areas in eastern and western Great Basin, or who migrated across on major north-south flyways (Fowler 1986:82). Northern Paiutes hunted sage and blue grouse, ducks, geese, and American coots (called mudhens) (Fowler and Liljeblad 1986:441; Stewart 1941:369).

49. It is interesting that Utes, who had their own particular Great Basin-Plains history, associate both the eagle and the hummingbird with the sky level of the cosmos (Goss 1990:13).

50. The Widjege, a species of titmouse, discovers the world. Lowie reports, "It is considered 'bad medicine' to kill this bird" (Lowie 1909a:235).

51. During the Wind River Shoshone Sun Dance, people from the community may enter the Sun Dance lodge at certain appropriate times in order to be "blessed" by the Sun Dance Chief.

52. John Truhujo's name also appears in scholarly literature spelled Trehero or Treheo.

53. The dream experience of the shaman determined the objects used in healing and so these objects varied from person to person. Park lists typical objects used by shamans: "a rattle (wisábaya), the tail feathers of eagle or magpie, or some other bird, down from the same bird, stone, shell, or bone beads, a tubular pipe, wild tobacco, often a peculiarly-shaped stone, and the large hollow wing- or leg-bone of the duck or pelican. . . . Some parts of the paraphernalia, however, are standard equipment and are to be found in the possession of all shamans. These include the pipe, tobacco, rattle, beads, feathers and down" (Park 1938:33).

As was always the case, the acquisition of power and objects used in connection with it carried potential danger for its recipient. "The loss of the eagle-feathers or other parts of the paraphernalia will result in the unfortunate shaman's sickness and loss of power" (Park 1938:131). "If a man disobeyed the orders of his *bu´ha*, it would leave him forever" (Lowie 1909a:224). Wind River Shoshones explained to Lowie the decline of the shaman's power in the twentieth century because of improper behavior toward the sage-hen. Lowie reports that "a certain male of a species of sage-hen is explicitly stated to impart the gifts of a healer, seer, and exorcist. This bird was offended some time ago because a Shoshone shot at it; hence the relative weakness of the *bu´ha* of modern, as compared with ancient, medicine men" (Lowie 1909a:224).

54. The five songs that developed are another example of the primacy of the number five in Great Basin cultures.

55. It is interesting to note the association of the eagle with song beyond the Great Basin in California. Maricopa people believe in discrete power from particular spirits. Coyote and Buzzard have the power to cure, Mocking Bird the power to orate, and Eagle the power to sing (Park 1938:101).

56. This is in reference to the Crow Sun Dance, reintroduced to the Crow by Truhujo.

57. *Ninïmbi* were, on the one hand, feared, and on the other, a potential source of power for beneficial purposes.

58. Whether it was actually an eagle feather or not was immaterial; the reference would have been clear to the amused audience.

59. Voget suggests another war association for eagle plumes. "In the traditional context of war, downy plumes evoked the idea of fog that hid warriors from pursuers or otherwise made them invisible. The lightness of eagle feathers and plumes also suggested a weightlessness that carried horses swiftly over the ground" (Voget 1984:308). Voget's comments are not about the Shoshone but the Crow, who did not originate in the Great Basin. This would seem to suggest a wider distribution for the fog-feather transformational image, which I discussed in chapter 3 in relation to Great Basin and Mezoamerican culture. However, around 1858, Wind River Shoshones defeated the Crow in the battle of Crowheart Butte and subsequently established a close and friendly relationship with them. Therefore, the Crow connection between fog and feathers may, alternatively, stem from Shoshone influence.

60. This is yet another example of the coupling of plumes with clouds.

61. I have noted elsewhere, "The two different verbal translations [by Emily and Dorothy] present a fascinating instance of symbolic translation between Shoshone and Christian religious thought" (Vander 1986:40).

62. Eagles were captured temporarily or killed for their feathers (Lowie 1924a:199; Steward 1941:224; Stewart 1941:370).

63. See E. Johnson 1975:15 for a Walker River Paiute version of the creation story in which sage hen saved fire for the people. (This is also in Kelly 1938:265.) See Steward for a Northern Paiute myth in which Magpie decrees henceforth the life patterns for coyotes, mud-hens, doves, and magpies (Steward 1936:382–83).

64. One such correspondent added a postscript, "P.S. I would like to find out if you have any kind of rules for your medicins [*sic*] that you send me if so let me know too . . . the feathers let me know please" (Dangberg 1968:49).

65. This open hostility to whites, and a general war-orientation shared by many Plains tribes, influenced Lakota interpretation of the clothing just described. Eagle pictures and eagle feathers engaged protective power. "They said that the bullets would not go through these shirts and dresses, so they all have them for war" (Colby 1895:139). The notions of protective garments appears in earlier discussion of shamanism (chapter 1) and in more recent mention of the protective power of eagle feathers, for example, against "missiles" (Lowie 1909a:224). Ghost Dance doctrine toward whites took a variety of forms on a wide spectrum. Clearly, for the Lakota, whites were the enemy and this was incorporated in their Ghost Dance belief. In contrast, Wovoka's speech to visiting Indian delegations, quoted by Mooney, argued for peace and nonviolence: "You must not hurt anybody or do harm to anyone. You must not fight. Do right always. It will give you satisfaction in life" (Mooney [1896] 1991:781). Wovoka cautioned his followers not to tell white people of his prophecy, coupling it with advice for the proper relationship to whites: "Do not refuse to work for the whites and do not make any trouble with them until you leave them" (Mooney 19656:23). With specific reference to bullet-proof Ghost Dance clothing and to whites, Wovoka "disclaimed all respon-

sibility for the ghost shirt which formed so important a part of the dance costume among the Sioux" (Mooney [1896] 1991:772).

66. Another example of Wovoka's power to control weather appears in a tribal history book written by and for Walker River Paiutes. Quoting Wuzzie George's 1974 taped interview, Edward C. Johnson states, "The People on the reservation lost some respect for the prophet when he was unable to prevent his infant son's death after a wagon accident between Mason Valley and Schurz. . . . It is said though that Wovoka became very angry and caused a wind storm to come up. The People's tents and summer shades were blown away while the prophet's brush shade barely moved in the wind because he had placed an eagle feather at each corner" (E. Johnson 1975:54).

Chapter 6: Plants

1. See song 64 for Emily's comment about this suffix, "just put pretty on there."

2. Gladys Hill commented that the older spoken word from which this is derived is *yenk* but that the modern word that has replaced *yenk* is *wehük*.

3. The identification of the bush in songs 106 and 107 remains problematic because Emily maintained that it was not greasewood. However, all other Shoshones consulted on this word agreed that it was greasewood. Scholarly literature reinforces this identification and fits with Emily's description of where it grows. Compare Emily's description with Steward's description of Northern Paiute territory, "characterized by small streams which flow into landlocked, brackish, or salt lakes. . . . On the floor of the basin, shadscale, sagebrush, salt grass, and greasewood dominate the flora" (Steward 1939:127). In a study of the Owens Valley Paiute, Steward writes, "Salt, Öŋä'vi, was scraped up with the hand from certain alkali flats (e.g., the south side of Big Pine lake), where a characteristic species of brush, to'navi, grew" (Steward 1933:250). Published transcription of native terms for greasewood are numerous: *tonobi* (Park 1989:157) and *to'-nuv* (Powell 1971:267), *tonovi* (Steward 1938:79, 309).

4. This song and essentially the same commentary that follows appear as song 1 in Vander 1988:14–15.

5. The use of *evi*, "white clay," for religious, health, and hunting purposes will be examined at the end of this chapter.

6. Song 114 appears as Naraya song 8 in Vander 1988:22–23.

7. Gladys Hill gave *akampʰ* for "sunflower seeds." Miller gives *akken*, which he identifies as *Helianthus* (Miller 1972:170).

8. From Liljeblad's transcription and translation of what seems to be the same song text (1986:648), the word is *ciampih*. (See the entire text, Li-2, which appears in chapter 10.) Shimkin gives *ʒi'amp* as the Wind River Shoshone word for rose *(Rosa californica)* and its Shoshone use, "Berries, religion, etc." (Shimkin 1947b:274).

9. Song 117 appears in Vander 1988:62–63 as song 12. Three musical transcriptions of this same song compare performances by Emily and Dorothy

with that of Angelina Wagon in 1981 and Dick Washakie in 1909. See Lilje-blad 1986:648, for transcription and translation of a Northern Shoshone ver-sion of the same song text.

10. Two words that seem to relate to *wainaiyo* are *waiG*, Gosiute Shoshone word meaning to come down, climb down (W. Miller 1972:146) and *waini"*, Big Smokey Valley Shoshone word meaning to take something down (Crapo 1976:97).

11. Gladys Hill suggested that what I heard as *wüwa* was *dïvA*, or derived from it. This would agree with Emily's mention of the pine nut tree in her comments on the song. However, it is sometimes difficult to separate sur-rounding information that Emily provides about a text from words that are actually in the text.

12. *Pùhimeha* is almost identical to *puimōha*, which is the word for the month of March among the Northern Paiute.

13. This plant is in the parsley family and sometimes is referred to as false caraway or squawroot. As described in a wildflower guidebook, "Yampa, one of the finest wild plant foods of the Rocky Mt. region, has a parsnip flavor, raw; cooked it is sweet and mealy. Though this plant was known by differ-ent names among the various Indian tribes, all collected the fleshy roots for food and trade. Lewis and Clark used it, as did the explorers and mountain men who followed them" (Craighead, Craighead, and Davis 1963:130–31).

14. The Warraricas are mentioned in Lander's 1860 report to the Commis-sioner of Indian Affairs and cited in Steward and Wheeler-Voegelin 1974:188.

15. Rupert Weeks, Wind River Shoshone author of Shoshone tales, tran-scribes the name *hùkandeka* as Hoo Coo Dic Kaw and translates it as "Dirt Eaters, name of one of the bands" (Weeks 1981:102).

16. Numerous citations specifically indicate that women were plant har-vesters in the Great Basin: For the Indians of Idaho, "Gathering and prepa-ration of vegetable foods were limited to what each woman was capable of producing for her own family" (Liljeblad 1957:38). Among the Surprise Val-ley Northern Paiute "Women went each day to dig . . . roots" (Kelly 1932:99). For the Ute, "Gathering was done by women although men might help in the gathering of piñon nuts" (Callaway, Janetski, and Stewart 1986:343). Owens Valley Paiute women "working in groups, gathered seeds by beating them from plants with seed beaters" (Steward 1933:239). Among the Washoe, "The digging stick was the universal implement for procuring roots; this task was entirely undertaken by women. A great variety of seeds and nuts were gathered and processed, mainly by women" (D'Azevedo 1986:477).

17. The identification of plants with women in everyday life and shaman-ism also occurs in myth. For example, Northern Paiutes trace the mythic origin of the Indian tribes from a man who hunted deer and a woman who made seed soup. By the time their children were grown and had to separate due to unending quarrels, the progeny had received the knowledge they needed to survive. "The old woman taught the Indians how to get seeds. They multiplied and had plenty of seeds but do not know them all" (Lowie 1924b:201–2). To take another example, Tuhuki'ni, hero of an Owens Valley

Paiute myth, journeys out to challenge and kill an infamous gambler-killer. The first day Tuhuki'ni (Black Hawk-Man) and his wife "traveled to where Gophers lived. Gophers were Tuhuki´ni'ˁⁱ's aunts, sisters of his father. [A footnote adds,] Gophers were women because they gathered seeds such as *tüpüsiˁⁱ*, grass nuts" (Steward 1936:389). A third myth takes place at the moment when the mythic characters are permanently transformed from animal-people into animals without the power to speak. Roadrunner, who in this myth is Wolf's brother, says to his wife, "'Wife, you be *tüara* [a small grass used for food]. You will be eaten.' His wife said, 'You be roadrunner. You will run along the foothills, crying.' Roadrunner said, 'I'd rather be that, a sort of person, than be grass like you.' His wife became grass and he went to the foothills" (Steward 1936:424). The progression in the three myths is from woman as source of plant knowledge to woman as gatherer of plants to woman as plants.

18. To exemplify this point I will cite three opinions, one concerning a specific Great Basin group, and two on the Great Basin as a whole. Laird writes of the Chemehuevis, "In the primal tetrad of Ocean Woman, Mountain Lion, Wolf, and Coyote, Ocean Woman definitely outranks her companions. She creates, while the others (in the stories recorded here, only Wolf and Coyote) play their parts in setting the earth in order, establishing its times and seasons, and determining a way of life for the people who were to come. Even in the time of the hunters women were (as to a great extent they still are) the prime movers in Chemehuevi society. In very primitive times, in the time of the gatherers, they were possibly dominant. Later, every woman needed a man to hunt big game for her; but conversely, every man needed a woman to gather and to grind for him. So while it came about that women yielded their husbands proper respect and (when convenient) obedience, they never occupied a position of inferiority. Women's voices were heard in the Gatherings, and fierce and implacable women incited their men to take the warpath. The Chief, so it is said, was always a man. But in the older, darker, and more awesome world of the shamans there were at least as many women as men" (Laird 1976:213). In 1976 Knack also commented on the continuing importance of Great Basin women in contemporary life and stated that they are still "mainstays and the buffers against economic and psychological uncertainty" (Knack 1976, in J. Miller 1983:82). Whitley, on the other hand, suggests a very different outcome from women's key role as plant-gatherers. Economically, women were independent, but marriage "tied them to a relatively strict plant gathering regimen, as well as burdened them with primary responsibilities for child care, and the hauling of water and firewood. . . . Although women were not necessarily considered inferior to men, the prescribed Numic means for acquiring and maintaining respect, prestige and ultimately authority essentially excluded them from it. Prestige, for example, was measured by the number of wives a person (of course, meaning 'male') could obtain and hold, . . . It is apparent that women were the objects of prestige, not the subjects of it" (Whitley 1994:9–11).

19. Likewise, Miller gives *pui* for "blue," "green," and *pui", pui-ppeh (-a)* for "grass" (Miller 1972:131–32).

20. A 1983 workbook written by Shoshones for students who attend the high school on the reservation (Wyoming Indian High School) elaborates on this. "The name 'Shoshone' probably comes from the Cheyenne Indians, who called the tribe 'Sus-son-i,' meaning 'grass lodge people.' The Shoshone often lived in grass, sage, or willow lodges, and were called 'grass lodgers' by many of their neighbors. The Eastern Shoshone also call themselves 'So-so-nee,' from the words 'sown-du' (lots, plenty of) and 'sow-neep'" (grass, hay) (Kruse 1983:8). Tidzump gives *soonde* for "much," "many," and *sonripe* for "hay" (Tidzump 1970:12SE).

21. Bierhorst's translations of Aztec song texts from the late sixteenth century reveal interesting parallels to Great Basin cultures in their use and connotations for greenery. Like the 1870 and 1890 Ghost Dance movements, the Aztec "ghost songs" attempted to resurrect the dead. However, unlike the Ghost Dance, the desire to resurrect the dead focused on male warriors who would then join the living as comrades in arms. A war of survival in this world was the object, not the achieving of peace and bounty in an idealized new world to come. These differences aside, Bierhorst writes, "The word *xopan*, literally 'green location,' denotes the growing season and is usually translated 'spring' or 'summer.' In ghost songs it refers to the greening [i.e., the resurrection] of spirits newly arrived from paradise—or it may refer to paradise itself or to *huehuetitlan*" (Bierhorst 1985:24).

22. An alternate location is on an anthill, recognizing and seeking the industry and strength of its ant inhabitants.

23. For example, the Northern Paiute shaman "directs the preparation of the stick . . . which is to be placed upright by the patient's head. The relative who summons the shaman cuts and prepares this stick, which is of willow and is three or four feet long. The shaman takes a feather from his kit (usually the tail-feather of the eagle) which, together with a bone or shell bead and down from the breast of the eagle, is attached by a buckskin thong to the blunt end of the stick. Red and white bands may also be painted on the wand. The precise way in which it is prepared and decorated depends upon the instructions received by the shaman in his dreams. The relative now returns home, and the wand that he has prepared under the direction of the shaman is stuck in the ground beside the patient's head with the feathers and the bead hanging by several inches of string from the top of stick. During the day the wand may be kept outside the house, but it is taken in and placed by the patient before the doctoring begins" (Park 1938:49). White Knife and Salmon Eater Shoshones had similar practices to those just quoted (Park 1938:134).

24. Regarding the Paiute practice of the Ghost Dance, Hittman writes that "no evidence exists that cedar *(waape)* poles were employed in Wovoka's ceremonies in Nevada. Nor, in fact, does cedar appear to be sacred in Numu cosmology" (Hittman 1990:49).

25. Shimkin views both dances as basically the same ceremony. See chapter 1 for discussion of this question.

26. See the Naraya texts Sh-2 and Sh-4 in chapter 10.

27. Shimkin identifies *woŋgogwa´na* as "Douglas spruce," *Pseudosuga mucronata* (Shimkin 1947b:275). Elsewhere Lowie explicitly describes a bag of spruce needles hung around a baby's neck used as a "safeguard against illness" (Lowie 1909a:229).

28. Lowie learned otherwise. "Chokecherries and sarvisberries were pounded up and dried, and gooseberries were dried, but neither cherries nor berries were mixed with meat" (Lowie 1924a:201).

29. Vegetable gardens were an important supplemental source of plant food, especially earlier in this century. All five women had gardens at various times, but by the time I met them, only Emily consistently put one in every year. For the other four women, summer travel to powwows or Sun Dance performances in neighboring states interfered with gardening efforts. At a certain point gardening and traveling become mutually exclusive. Of course, the amount of summer travel varies from family to family. Some of those who stay home and garden enter their products in the Shoshone Tribal Fair, held each year in late August.

30. See Vander 1988:94, for description.

31. From bits of scattered information one learns details about the various types of digging sticks used by different groups. It could be made of hardwood (Fowler 1986:69), sharpened and fire-hardened (Murphy 1986:293), curved (Liljeblad 1957:27), formerly sharpened mountain mahogany and now iron (Kelly 1932:101). Wind River Shoshones made their digging sticks from greasewood (Lowie 1924a:203). In his Northern Shoshone publication, Lowie also cites earlier information on the digging stick published by Wyeth in 1851. "In gathering roots, the women observed by Wyeth employed crooked sticks with curved ends sharpened by firing and rubbing against a rough stone. Sometimes the implement consisted of an elk or deer horn attached to a stick. I saw three digging-sticks, varying from two to three feet in length. All were of iron and pointed at the bottom. Two had an iron knob at the top; the third was provided with a horizontal piece of wood for a handle, which was clasped with the left hand palm-up, and in reverse fashion by the right" (Lowie 1909a:188).

32. A Southern Ute myth gives humorous expression to the wondrous power of the digging stick itself. Wild Goose asks for his wife's digging stick, strikes his own knee while saying "turnips, turnips," and lo and behold, wild turnips fall into the basket (Lowie 1924c:21).

33. A Wind River Shoshone version of the juggling myth varies in several important ways from the preceding examples. Coyote chances upon two girls who each toss one eye up and say magic words. Camas flowers sprout where the eyes land; the girls pick the blossoms and then retrieve their eyes. Coyote tosses his eyes up, but they get stuck in the willows because he had not learned the magic words. Coyote finally recovers eyesight by taking the eyes of a dead buffalo calf, rather than the eyes of a bird, as in the Paviotso myth (Spoonhunter 1980:n.p.). It is interesting to see that the Wind River Shoshone transformation of the myth draws on their Plains experience as buffalo hunters.

34. A complete description of this ceremony and the dance, and a musical transcription of the Chokecherry Song, are in Vander 1978:39–42, 122.

35. This sacrifice of the pot of sauce is similar to a custom of the Northern Paiutes reported by Powell. "The first fruits of the forest, the meadows, the chase, etc. are sacrificed, thanking the *Na-tu´-ni-tu-a-vi*" (Powell 1971:246). However, the editors of Powell's publication from which this is quoted qualify Powell's statement: "Later ethnographies indicate that such practices were not formalized to the degree implied here" (Powell 1971:287n.122).

36. Seeds are mentioned in Lander's 1860 government report on the "Eastern Snakes" (Wind River Shoshones). "Their principal subsistence is the roots and seeds of the wild vegetables of the region they inhabit, the mountain trout, with which all the streams of the country are abundantly supplied, and wild game" (cited in Murphy and Murphy 1960:305). However, Lander does not weight the relative importance of these foods to Shoshone diet as Shimkin does in his study.

37. For example, see Park 1989:47; Stewart 1944:375.

38. Various scholarly publications include information on the harvesting and preparation of sunflower seeds. "Sunflowers are rolled between the hands to break them and any other seeds that you want to grind up fast. Roast them before you grind the seeds. Sometimes it is mixed with other seeds" (Park 1989:47). Or, "Large seeds, such as sunflowers, had their seed coats cracked on the metate with an elongated mono *(tusun·u)* and then were winnowed and ground into flour" (Fowler and Liljeblad 1986:441). Steward writes of native peoples in Idaho that "people got different kinds of sunflowers, which were gathered with a seed beater, the flowers perhaps being rubbed on a metate to remove the seeds. These seeds were parched before storing to prevent their sprouting if the ground became damp" (Steward 1938:168). (See also Lowie 1909a:187–88.) In addition to serving as ingredients in soup, baked cakes, and bread, sunflower seeds were also eaten raw (Liljeblad 1957:28).

39. Besides gathering this single-needled piñon, the *pinus monophylla,* Great Basin people also harvested *Pinus edulis,* and less frequently, limber, sugar, and ponderosa pine, *P. flexilis, P. lambertiania,* and *P. ponderosa* (Fowler 1986:65).

40. The processing of pine nuts required several steps: 1. pit roasting if the cones were green, to open the bracts for seed release; 2. beating the cones to release all the seeds; 3. parching to make the seed coats brittle; 4. winnowings to separate the seeds from debris and nonedible parts (D'Azevedo 1986a:474; Fowler 1986:65).

41. Nowhere was the incompatible and tragic relationship between Great Basin Indian and Euro-American cultures more telling than in the 1860s and 1870s, and this in regard to food. Settlers used wild seeds for their cattle and cut pine nut trees for fuel. As Wick R. Miller points out, only grasshoppers remained as an undisturbed source of native food (W. Miller 1970:26).

42. See Kelly 1938:395–403; Lowie 1909a:244–47; Powell 1971:247–48; Steward 1943b:256–61.

43. The Western Shoshone version mentions such detail as the five-night

duration of the Round Dance in the myth (Steward 1943b:259), the same duration as the Round Dance in everyday life, Ghost Dance performance, and the Naraya. In the Northern Shoshone myth "Theft of Fire," which includes the theft of pine nuts, the Round Dance is identified as the *nu´akin* dance (Lowie 1909a:244). This form of the Round Dance is discussed in chapter 1. The Naraya is strikingly similar to it in form and substance.

44. Northern Paiutes from Winnemucca also note the north-south movement of Pine nuts. "The pine nuts [which had been scattered when the leg was thrown] grew fast. There used to be pine nuts in the north, but now they are all gone. They ground around Winnemucca now" (Steward 1943b:260).

45. Liljeblad's description of "prayers for success addressed to herbs with pharmaceutical properties" and the proper way to gather medicinal plants by Great Basin people is consistent with all the above comments and differs only in detail. Prior to gathering the specimen, "The supplicant went out at sunrise, sat facing east on the shady side of the plant, telling about his need and asking for cure and protection" (Liljeblad 1986:643).

46. Stewart describes the use of *toza*, or Indian balsam, by fourteen Northern Paiute groups. He gives the scientific identification as *Leptotaenia multifida* Nutt. and describes its use as "fish poison; smoked and chewed by Indians to cure a cold" (Stewart (1941:429). D'Azevedo reports Washoe use of the roots of Indian balsam as a medicine, "which older Washoe people still search for in the spring as a highly regarded remedy for colds and body aches" (D'Azevedo 1986a:474). He identifies it as *Leptotaenia dissecta*. Kelly writes of Surprise Valley Paiute use of *do´´saᵃᵇü*, Leptotaenia multifida Nutt. The root was crushed and used on sores and swellings (Kelly 1932:196). Keith Dueholm, a botanist, has informed me that *doza*, referred to with a variety of names in the scholarly literature, may very well be *Lomatium dissectum var. multifidum*, which he has collected in Wyoming (personal communication 1993).

47. Lowie provides more information on other Wind River Shoshone medicines in this same reference. He gives Shoshone terminology but no scientific identification.

48. See also Lowie 1924a:311.

49. See also Naraya songs 18, 20, 25, and 28 for additional expressions of an old earth.

50. Wind River Shoshones use red paint for health and protection in dances and in other contexts. In the Father Dance, which sought to ward off smallpox, the sponsor of the dance wore red paint (Shimkin 1986a:326). In the Naraya, which sought protection from a variety of diseases and natural disasters, women painted the part in their hair red (Vander 1986:8). Even as recently as 1981, red paint was one of the presents given to a young Shoshone woman as part of her special name-giving ceremony. The paint was to help protect her (Vander 1988:224).

The son of Tinzant Coando, deceased Naraya leader, mentioned to me the use of red paint by Shoshones who are going to be blessed, for example, for war or health. He gave another example: if you pray once a day in the morning, red paint is used in conjunction with your prayer. The comments of one elderly Shoshone man—Richard Engavo—sum up a generalized response to the use of red paint: "If you paint yourself red—you know this Indian paint it comes from the earth—it's good."

51. Jorgensen sees a "synthesis" of the dry-wet dichotomy. I see a linear progression, from one physical state of dryness and suffering in order to reach another spiritual state of wetness and blessing. Perhaps this is only a difference of semantics.

52. The use of white paint in this story is similar to the use of red paint in the Ghost Dance, which was "to assist the mental vision in trance" (Mooney [1896] 1991:779).

53. We learn about Wovoka's use of red paint, both in healing and in the Ghost Dance, from the following accounts. Andy Vidovich described how Wovoka used red paint in order to prevent swelling from a gunshot wound (Hittman 1990:185). Mooney mentioned the use of red paint in the Ghost Dance in connection with the presents that Wovoka had given to him: "the rabbit-skin robes, the piñon nuts, the gaming sticks, the sacred magpie feathers, and above all, the sacred red paint . . . which the Paiute procure from the neighborhood of their sacred eminence, Mount Grant. . . . It is the principal paint used by the Paiute in the Ghost Dance, and small portions of it are given by the messiah to all the delegates and are carried back by them to their respective tribes, . . . and used in decorating the faces of the participants in the dance, the painting being solemnly performed for each dancer by the medicine-man himself. It is believed to ward off sickness, to contribute to long life, and to assist the mental vision in trance" (Mooney [1896] 1991:778–79).

Chapter 7: Sun, Stars, and Night

1. Discussing the texts in shamans' songs, Bahr writes, "The songs used by Pima-Papago shamans for divination and curing generally feature first person journeys, and the journeys commonly involve light" (Bahr 1994:83). Whether this observation is germane to song 123 remains tantalizing but unknowable.

2. "Backbone," used in everyday language, is rendered as *kwahinzuhipe* by Tidzump (1970:1ES). Gladys Hill rendered it as *gwahaimp*h. Miller gives *kwaihaim-peh* as the Gosiute word for "back" (Miller 1972:156), and Crapo supplies *kwa'in-cuhni-ppyh(-a")* for "backbone" as spoken by Big Smokey Valley Shoshones (Crapo 1976:108).

3. Dick Mahwee, himself a Northern Paiute shaman, described the celestial sources of power used by another shaman. "'I knew one woman who used the sun, moon, and stars for her power. I saw her fill her pipe and just as the sun came up she puffed and started to smoke. I saw her do this several times. I watched her closely but she did not use matches. Her power lighted her pipe'" (Park 1938:17).

4. Direct address to various parts of the natural world is by no means unique to Great Basin cultures. Hinton writes, "In prayer, Havasupais direct-

ly address the sources from which power comes—the sun, a spring, the wind—and tell that source precisely what they want. There are still quite a few Havasupai that still pray to the sun or moon" (Hinton 1984:186n.6).

5. See Jorgensen 1972:206–16 for an excellent and slightly different interpretation of Sun Dance ideology and religious experience.

6. Wovoka also became "Father" to his Plains converts, who invoked his name in a majority of their songs.

7. Dick Jonas and Dr. Howard, two Harney Valley Paiutes, document this trip by both patient and shaman. Dick "was bucked off a wild horse which fell on top of him. Dr. Howard was summoned to restore him to consciousness. According to Dick's dim recollections, Dr. Howard said that his breath had left his body and gone up the Milky Way. He chased the breath and restored it to Dick's body" (Whiting 1950:46).

8. The belief that the Milky Way was the road of spirits was also held by many other cultures outside the Great Basin, for example, in California (Kroeber 1925:440). Beyond death, associations or explanations for the dust on the dusty road differed according to the cultural contexts from which they arose. For Gosiute Shoshones, the dust comes from smoke of a fire cooking pine nuts (Steward 1943a:390); for Pawnees, "it is the dust of the buffalo, in apparent reference to the cloud of dust that the buffalo kick up in running across the prairie" (Williamson 1984:233).

9. Some called it *tugumbit* (sky) *ta* (the) *ŋgwaihim* (backbone), *tugumbana* (sky) *wá'àada* (vertebrae) (Steward 1943a:390) and *waoda* (backbone?) (Steward 1941:267).

10. Malinda Tidzump, a linguist and native Wind River Shoshone speaker, gives *taziumbi* for "star" (Tidzump 1970:1). In an earlier publication I quoted Emily's term for Morning Star in reference to Naraya song 15. "*Navoi dazüümb* means towards morning, when daylight's coming up—Morning Star coming up with that light" (Vander 1986:49). I have no further explication of *navoi*.

11. Daytime performance is prescribed for the War Bonnet Dance and was for the Pointing Dance, the latter no longer being performed (Vander 1978: 45).

Chapter 8: Textual Analysis

1. Three songs mention dead mothers (songs 2, 9, and 22), three songs mention a person walking or running (21, 67, and 125), song 19 likens the aging of earth to people, and song 29 refers to dancing sideways, a reference to the Naraya itself. Song 123 is the solitary Naraya song cast from a first-person perspective—my thoughts rise up like sunlight.

2. The form of Naraya songs collected by Shimkin follow the same patterns with some interesting differences. Frank Perry's first song about trees (chapter 10) contains seven repeated lines, AA, BB, CC, DD, EE, FF, GG. Toorey Roberts's song is a sequence of three different lines that repeats, ABC. (See chapter 10 for these song texts.)

3. Bahr notes the similar final position of the verb in Pima-Papago songs, stating that it is a "general principle of the people's songs" (Bahr 1994:82).

4. *Nörë* appears in Crapo's study of Big Smokey Valley Shoshone as *-noh*, one of several directional adverbs. Crapo writes, "Directional adverbs qualify a verb in terms of the direction in which the actor is moving when the act is performed. Directional adverbs may be suffixed to verbs which do not themselves indicate any geographical motion." Crapo glosses *-noh*: "while moving or being moved (e.g. in a vehicle)" (Crapo 1976:8).

5. Shimkin gives both *wën-* and *wënë-* as the verbal stem for "to stand" in his unpublished and undated manuscript, "Wind River Shoshone Grammatical Forms (A Rough Sketch)." Tidzump (1970:18) gives *wenre* for "stand" and *weniku* for "stand up."

6. Interestingly, reference to the sunset in song 4 (Vander 1986:48) follows this same pattern, adding other associated characteristics to the verb complex. *Yuwenöre* breaks down into *yu-*, "warm" (or quiet), and *-wenörë*, "standing-moving."

7. *Nambürü*, which appears in song 22, is a similar word but is used in reference to humans. It means "footprints" or "tracks" and is a song form of *nanambuipʰ*, a word that derives from *nambe*, meaning "foot."

8. Shimkin gives *yïʹzï*, singular verbal stem "(to) fly," "rise," and *yuri-* for a dual or plural subject (Shimkin 1949c:212).

9. Tidzump gives *kade*, for "sit," "reside," in her [Wind River] *Shoshone Thesaurus* (1970:17). Miller gives *kateG*, "to sit," for singular subjects, and *yekwiG* for dual and plural subjects in his dictionary of Gosiute Shoshone words (1972:112). Crapo transcribes Big Smokey Valley Shoshone versions as *katyʺ* and *jykkwittih* (1976:41).

10. Similarly, the sung version of *banzuk*, "otter" (song 100) drops the final "k" stop. However, in this example there is no abbreviation, as an "a" substitutes for the deleted "k," *bunzu-a*.

11. Even Peyote songs, that may include some Shoshone or other Native American words, are also primarily vocables.

12. See Vander 1978:17 for a transcription and discussion of the vocable text of the Shoshone Giveaway Song.

13. These vocables are by no means exclusive to the Wind River Shoshones. They are part of a shared musical and vocable tradition on the Plains. Powers gives what he calls the prototype for Plains vocables: *a, e, i, o* (with and without glottal stops), either alone or combined with h, w, and y (Powers 1987:13). He also points out the relationship of the vocable to native languages, which is a source of variation from the prototype. "The distinctive features of the vocable are homologous to the distinctive features of the singers' language. Therefore, phonological rules governing one govern the other" (Powers 1987:16). For example, Lakota vocables include the consonant "l," making possible *la, le, li,* and *lo* (Powers 1987:14). Shoshones, who lack the "l" sound in their language, have no vocables beginning with "l."

14. Similarly, Hinton writes about the musical setting of "i" in Havasupai song, "The vowel is [i] most often in the short off-beat syllables, and [e] in long or on-beat syllables" (Hinton 1984:47).

15. My comments here remain anecdotal as they lack the context of an exhaustive study of Handgame song texts for a point of reference.

16. Powers gives *we yo he ye he ye yo* as the prototypical cadence for Plains War Dance songs (Powers 1987:13). Merriam (1967:315) gives a common cadential pattern in Flathead songs as follows:

He yo   He yo   He yo

17. The use of "n" in a vocable is not part of the Shoshone vocable stock outlined earlier. One does find it characteristically in Peyote songs that Shoshones sing, and this religion and the songs that are part of its ritual were imported and loaned. Wind River Shoshone people learned Peyote songs from intermediate sources, the Northern Arapaho and the Comanche, their southern kin (Stenberg 1946:146). In his study of Peyote music, McAllester gives Comanche examples for the vocable beginning of songs, *he ne ne na, he ne ne,* and concluding formula, *he ne neyowa* (McAllester 1949:67). Although all this may seem to suggest an influence of Peyote song texts on Naraya songs, everything else that I know regarding the relationship of these two religions argues against it. There was, in fact, strong antipathy between Shoshone adherents of these two religions. Emily, in part, blamed the Peyote religion for the demise of the Naraya. See Vander 1986:67–68 for further discussion of these points. As already discussed, the most important use of "n" in vocables in Naraya songs is in ending patterns, for example, *ena* and *waiyowain,* and is part of the broader musical aesthetic already described by Hinton.

18. Charlotte Frisbie reports comments by a well-known Navajo singer that imply this same strategy in Navajo music. "Frank Mitchell recognized that some syllables in the songs are meaningless, to be sure. These he calls 'tones' or 'links,' for 'they get you to the next word.' At times he also called them 'stretchers': 'These stretch out the words and make them last longer'" (Frisbie 1980:370–71). According to Hinton, this is also true in Havasupai song. "There are usually two or three words in a song, accompanied by extra, nonlinguistic syllables that fill out the melody" (Hinton 1984:18).

19. *Wasüp-penji* also appears in songs 60 and 103.

20. Tidzump gives *waaseepi* for this word in her Wind River Shoshone dictionary (Tidzump 1970:8).

21. In spoken language, "sunflower seeds in the mountains" would be said, *ak? ndoiya.* In the song text this becomes *akën doiya.* My analysis is of the sung form, *akën,* already one step removed from the spoken form.

22. Another subtlety in the second line of this text is the assonance between neighboring words, *babai-eya wegïn,* achieved by changing the spoken form, *babaiyu,* to *babai-eya.* "E" is inserted before the "y" and "u" is lowered to "a."

23. Shimkin gives *-ci* as "diminutive suffix, little, dear" (Shimkin 1949c: 211).

24. The use of *-tsi* in songs 123 and 124 is unusual in that *-tsi* does not suffix nouns but a verb (song 123) and an adverb (song 124). Naraya song 2

is identical to song 123 in the use of the suffix attached to the same verb and taking the same form, *doih-n-zi* (Vander 1986:54). This use of *-tsi,* which departs from its customary attachment to nouns, is, I believe, another example of poetic license.

25. It is interesting to compare the onomatopoeia for splashing water in Naraya songs with its representation in myth. In a Gosiute Shoshone version of "Sun and Cottontail," Cottontail awakens close to a stream. "The water made a lot of noise. 'Swhshsh,' said the water" (Miller 1972:50).

26. Shimkin documents this in his analysis of Wind River Shoshone language. "Stem-composition is extensively used and greatly developed. . . . Multiple composition is a noteworthy phenomenon; in these cases, two or more stems are prefixed to the basic morpheme" (Shimkin 1949a:176).

27. In her study of Navajo religion, Gladys Reichard learned from one informant that "disguising" vocables in songs sometimes replaced meaningful words (Reichard 1963:282, in Frisbie 1980:352).

Chapter 9: Musical Analysis

1. Natalie Curtis used this format for her transcriptions in *The Indians' Book,* first published in 1907. Curtis wrote, "This system makes the form of the songs to flash before the eye like the form of a stanza in poetry. For this idea, the recorder is indebted to Mr. Kurt Schindler" (Curtis [1907] 1968:n.p.). I, in turn, am indebted to both Kurt Schindler and Natalie Curtis.

2. I indicate with every transcription which verse I have transcribed and the total number of repeats in the performance. On a few occasions during fieldwork I did not have sufficient tapes on hand and made the unfortunate decision to collect more songs by copying only a few verses, or repetitions, of a song. My copy of these performances was incomplete. I have indicated this in my transcriptions and given the number of repeats that I did record.

3. The song leader's name is always the first one given in my transcriptions. In song 24 I have noted a rare example of divergence from unison singing. It occurred at the cadence where a final word or syllable is sometimes omitted. One of the women followed this practice, the other did not.

4. Of the 17 Naraya songs presented in my monograph (Vander 1986), 9 were triple, 6 were duple, and 2 a combination of both. The complete tally for 147 songs is: 81 duple, 55 triple, and 11 combinations.

5. The rhythmic organization of song 75 is particularly difficult to analyze with certainty.

6. Similarly, only two of seventeen songs published in my monograph had sections of the same length (Vander 1986:23).

7. Also see Naraya songs 58 and 120 for further examples with this type of syncopation.

8. There are five songs (songs 18, 75, 94, 140, 141,) that combine duple and triple organization in a complex way, and for this reason I have used the eighth note as the basic beat throughout these transcriptions. The metronome marking for these songs is for the eighth note and would need to be divided

by two in the duple parts and three in the triple to make it accord with the tempos given in the rest of the songs. Because of the complex mixing of duple and triple movement in these songs, I do not include them in my Naraya tempo tallies.

9. See songs 18 and 127, further examples that are almost identical to song 66 in their pattern of finals and tonal center.

10. See also Naraya songs 10, 13, and 14 in Vander 1986:28.

11. One can hear pulsation in War Dance Songs Nos. 8 and 12, which are on the accompanying tape for *Songprints: The Musical Experience of Five Shoshone Women* (Vander 1988). It is particularly prominent on the vocable, *he,* at the top of p. 159 and, for the third repeat of War Dance Song No. 12, at the end of the first line, p. 236, in that study. (See comments on the relationship between vocal pulsation and the drumbeat in footnote 15, p. 166.)

12. The cadences of sections *b* and *c* are identical because the transposition in section *c* ends at that point. This accords with comments made earlier in regards to song 142 in example 35.

13. See Vander 1986:17–22 for further examples and analysis of variation in Naraya songs.

14. Also see Naraya songs 6, 11, and 14 in Vander 1986 for transcriptions of two different performances of each of them. Page 19 of the same publication has a comparative score for excerpts of Naraya song 6.

15. See Vander 1988:62 for a comparative score of three different performances of song 117 by different singers. (Song numbers in the 1988 publication differ from this publication. In the former, song 117 is number 12.)

16. Close ensemble singing is a strong tradition among the Shoshone. Drum groups who sing for the powwow and Sun Dance have a lead singer who starts off the song. My transcriptions of these performances also reveal small variations that crop up in the many repetitions of a song. (For example, compare the text and melodic rhythm of verses one and two of War Dance Song no. 8, which appear on the bottom staves respectively of pages 158 and 159, Vander 1988.) Supporting singers are expected to follow and match the leader in all ways—melody, vocal quality, and drum accompaniment.

17. My transcriptions of seventeen Naraya songs in *Ghost Dance Songs and Religion of a Wind River Shoshone Woman* (Vander 1986) do include variations of the different repetitions of the verse. Four of these songs appear in *Songprints: The Musical Experience of Five Shoshone Women* (Vander 1988) and on an accompanying cassette tape. The numbering between the two publications is not identical. Songs 1, 12, 3, and 2 in the Ghost Dance monograph appear as songs 2, 5, 10, and 11, respectively, on the tape and in *Songprints*.

18. Unfortunately Shimkin's recordings are no longer audible due to their deterioration.

19. See songs 49 and 84 for further similar examples of the musical setting of *sïnavI*.

20. Liljeblad has also noted this point in his discussion of word-setting in Numic songs. "Another poetic license is the prosodic lengthening of short vowels and the breaking of long ones, if the melody so demands. As a con-

sequence, in verse the stress may shift freely from one syllable to another" (Liljeblad 1986:647–48).

21. See songs 41, 43, 48, and 121 for further similar settings of *doiya*.

22. Pietroforte's book, *Song of the Yokuts and Paiutes*, published in 1965, is one such exception.

23. Edward Sapir included the genre identification for all of the songs along with the textual transcription and translation of them. It is not clear what distinction he made between a Ghost Round Dance song versus a Ghost Dance or Round Dance song. Adding to this confusion, he also labeled two Walapai songs (nos. 198 and 199) as Round Ghost Dance songs. For a third Walapai song (no. 197) he wrote, "Round Dance (Ghost Dance)," adding that the Walapais had attended a particular Ghost Dance performance in 1892 (Sapir 1991:656). I infer from this that the Walapai Round Dance song was sung at a Ghost Dance performance. Examples 120–26 appear in Sapir 1994 as follows: examples 120 and 125–26 on page 707, example 121 on page 683, example 122 on page 697, and examples 123–24 on page 691.

24. Steward writes, "The following songs were recorded in the field and later transcribed in the laboratory" (Steward 1933a:278). As no one else receives credit for them, I presume that Steward did the musical transcriptions; however I have no further verification for this.

25. In my view, the original transcription distorts this form by putting the first part of a^1 as the conclusion of the song. If, in fact, the final repetition of the final verse really ends this way, then perhaps I have put the song into a Procrustean bed of my own liking. But I suspect that the original transcription comes from the first or some verse other than the final one. At some point, Steward decided that the first part of a^1 was the ending of the song, and therefore made its first appearance at the very beginning as a one-time-only introduction. I begin my reformatted transcription with the ending of the original transcription. Because it is included within the repeats for the entire song, I surmise that it must be the more common form for the first half of a^1 used throughout the performance. I believe that the beginning of the original transcription, which is not included within the repeat sign for the song, is simply a variant for the first half of a^1 that appeared only in the first verse of the performance. For this reason I place it below the transcription.

26. Because I made this transcription away from home and without the aid of a tuning fork, I had to approximate the starting pitch. There was no later opportunity to verify it, so it remains just an approximation. Likewise, I was without a metronome and am, therefore, unable to indicate the tempo of the song.

27. Unlike the large corpus of songs quoted earlier, the transcriptions in this publication were made by Edward Sapir and not his father.

28. In the past, only male Shoshones performed as both singers and drummers around the drum. Women could and sometimes did sing in back of the drum, but never actually sat with the men and beat the drum. Women have their own singing role when accompanying male singers. Since the 1970s, this

has changed. Some Wind River Shoshone women have moved into male roles at the drum—both as singers and drummers. (See chapters on Helene Furlong [now Oldman] and Lenore Shoyo in Vander 1988 and the book's accompanying tape for examples of War Dance song performance.)

29. The book and tape also contain several other examples of War Dance songs.

30. See the analysis of song 9 (Vander 1986:34–36). Like song 88, it is another Naraya example that combines Plains and Great Basin musical forms.

31. Bierhorst refers to the teponaztli as a log drum. According to ethnomusicological terminology, it is an idiophone, often referred to as a slit-gong. Bierhorst provides more detailed information about the instrument and the way it is played. "Beaten with rubber-tipped mallets on the tongues of an H-shaped slit, the teponaztli also produced two tones, yielding a fifth, a fourth, or some smaller interval, according to the individual instrument" (Bierhorst 1985:72).

Chapter 10: Song Text Comparisons

1. Whereas I use the term "verse" to refer to the complete text of a song, the term can also mean a single line of a poem—a single line of verse. I believe that Liljeblad uses the term in this sense, that is, Powell omits the repetition of individual lines within the text and not in the sense that he omits repetition of the entire text.

2. In different manuscripts, Powell wrote variant forms for the title of this song and its transcription and translation. Another title was "The First Song on the Night of the Dance." With reference to the first line, *Ki´ai* can mean "to play, sometimes to dance." An alternate translation of the second line is, "All sing together." In another rendering, Powell wrote, "They dance, / All together" (Powell 1971:127).

3. Sapir gives *qa* for "not" (Sapir 1930:625), which I think is his spelling and equivalent for *ka* and *ca*, given by Powell and Dellenbaugh, respectively.

4. The editors, Catherine and Donald Fowler, write the translation "Forever remains, forever remains" as one line with a comma in the middle. However, the Southern Paiute text appears in two lines. Following the form of the Paiute text, I have also written the English translation in two lines.

5. Fowler and Fowler suggest the coyote myths from which this song text might derive (Powell 1971:124).

6. Powell adds that when the expression "to wag (*chu-nu-wu-gi*) its tail (*kwa-sing*)," applies to a fish (*Pa-gu*), it means, "to swim."

7. Catherine and Donald Fowler report that Cave Lake "probably refers to a small body of water by that name found in upper Kanab Canyon. . . . The pool lies partly in an overhanging alcove in the sandstone wall of the cliff" (Powell 1971:126).

8. Although not necessarily described in connection with the wind, Naraya texts that do mention pine trees include songs 5 (Vander 1986:45), 34, 109, and 110.

9. Powell puts the English translation of this word at the end of the line, but in the Southern Paiute text, it is the first word. Sapir transcribes what appears to be the same or similar word as *tümpʷí-p·aia-i´ura´*, and defines it, "cliff-side (obj.) toward, towards the side of the cliff" (Sapir 1930:674).

10. Crapo gives a second generic term for tree used in the Cherry Creek dialect of Smokey Valley Shoshones. *Syhy-pin-tta"*, "willow tree," another tree associated with water, can also mean "tree." Tidzump documents similar usage by Wind River Shoshone speakers. *Sehevi* is her transcription for both willow tree and trees (Tidzump 1970:5).

11. The use of three rather than two repeated lines is striking and unlike Naraya songs. Hittman's comment on Wovoka's use of the number three in another context may have relevance to the use of three repetitions in the song texts. In 1889 Wovoka responded to a petition to relieve the drought-stricken Walker River Reservation. Drawing on his weather power, he predicted rain in three days, which came to pass. Hittman pointedly notes here that three is "the Christian integer, not the Northern Paiute sacred numbers of four and five" (Hittman 1990:9). Hittman also mentions the use of the number three in connection with Methodist-Episcopal baptismal practices in Smith and Mason Valleys. He reports that "Methodists favored sprinkling three drops (or 'three waves') of holy water" (Hittman 1990:59). One wonders whether Wovoka saw this practice, and if so, might it have been another reinforcing influence for his symbolic use of the number three. Obviously, the relationship of Christian symbolism to the use of three repeated lines in Northern Paiute Ghost Dance songs is conjectural.

12. See songs 8, 12, 66, 69–72, 90, 97, 99, and discussion of the importance of animal young in Naraya texts discussed in chapter 5.

13. To my knowledge, Wind River Shoshones use *wasüpi* to mean "game animals" and do not use it for "mountain sheep." Tidzump gives *waaseepi* for "animals" and *wasepi* for "game" (Tidzump 1970:16SE, 17SE). Shimkin gives *duk* for "ram" and *mu´ʒambia* for "ewe" (Shimkin 1947b:277). However, Miller and Crapo document that for other Shoshone dialects the same, or almost the same, word means both "mountain sheep" and "game," similar to the usage in the Lemhi text and Lowie's translation of it. Gosiute Shoshones use *waseppeh* for "mountain sheep" and *waseppin*, a closely related form, for "game" (Miller 1972:147). Big Smokey Valley Shoshones use *wasy" -pin(-tta")*, for both "mountain sheep" and "game" (Crapo 1976:97). (See chapter 5 for Fowler's derivation of this word in Numic languages.)

14. As mentioned in note 23 for chapter 9, there remain unanswered questions regarding Sapir's names for some of his different genre categories. The 22 Ghost Dance texts given in this chapter place Sapir's original titles in parentheses, which includes 12 Ghost Dance songs, 7 Ghost Round Dance songs, and 3 Round Ghost Dance songs.

15. Texts S-1, 3, 4, 5, 6, 7, 9, and 10 are annotated with "Not," or "no Ghost Dance."

16. One hears it occasionally in Shoshone Sun Dance songs, the flapped *r* sounding like *d* in the vocable sequence, *ha da*.

17. *Ena,* the most common vocable ending in Naraya songs does not appear in these Southern Paiute songs. It is interesting to see Sapir's annotation for S-25, which describes two strategies used to indicate its ending: "At end: *-raraina^h* with decided rise in pitch on last syllable, followed by word: *wĭnĭyĭnɩ* = I stop, lit. I stand" (Sapir 1994:643). Roan, or Salt Songs, which are part of the Cry ceremony, seem to have their own equally distinctive vocable ending. Sapir annotated many Roan Songs, for example No. 10, with the comment, "Last word *yau^h.*" He was more explicit in his annotation for No. 30 Roan Song, writing, "End: *yau^h*" (Sapir 1994:613, 617).

18. A similar effect also occurs in song 88, with reiteration of part of the word for blackbird plus a suffix: *bagan- bagan-noganzi.*

19. In his fieldnotes for Sh-3, Shimkin transcribed the first word of the text as *pu'hiwa,* which he translated as "green." In publication he changed the translation to "sage-brush." To my knowledge, *bohop^h* is the Shoshone word for sagebrush. The greenery mentioned in Naraya song 97—*buhi,* "grass and willows at the water's edge"—seems a more likely association for the goose's son, the gosling, than sagebrush, which flourishes in dry areas. The Shoshone word in both texts is almost identical. However, it is always possible that Shimkin received further information that the greenery in Sh-3 referred specifically to sagebrush. In any case, visionary juxtapositions have their own internal logic and need not conform to expectations from the natural world.

20. Notice the "etc." that Shimkin adds at the end of the published English translation of Sh-3. He also did this at the end of the published translation of Sh-4, and in this case his fieldnotes provide the other examples, which were left out in the published form. The "etc." in Sh-3 hints that there may be more lines of text for this song with other examples of animal offspring. The fieldnotes, however, give no additional information.

21. As defined by *The American Heritage Dictionary,* a colon is "a section of a rhythmical period in Greek and Latin verse, consisting of two to six feet and having one principal accent" (1973).

22. Franklin informs me that this song was originally a Havasupai song. However, he adds that it has been "renalayzed as Paiute" in Anna Whiskers's rendering of it (Franklin, personal communication, 1995).

23. I have used Jane Hill's English translation for "streams should begin running" and "streams will begin running" (Hill 1992:120–21). However, in all other ways I strictly follow the form and layout of the text as indicated in the original by Franklin and Bunte, which differs slightly in Hill's presentation of it.

24. All 31 song texts of Colby's collection are Lakota. Mooney's collection includes 73 Arapaho song texts, 26 Lakota, 19 Cheyenne, 15 Kiowa, 15 Caddo, 9 Paiute, and 4 Comanche. See appendix of "Ghost Dance Recordings and Published Musical Transcriptions" in Vander 1986 (pages 71–72) for information on additional publications that include song texts, e.g., Densmore's *Pawnee Music* ([1929] 1972) and Curtis's *The Indians' Book* ([1907] 1968).

25. The rest of this annotation goes on to describe the game in great detail.

26. See Powers 1990:71n.1, 72n.9, for complete information on these two sources.

27. The concordance of PC texts with their numbers as they appear in Colby's 1895 publication is as follows: PC-2 = No. 4, p. 145, and No. 6, 148; PC-4 = No. 5, p. 145; PC-5 = No. 4, p. 148; PC-6 = No. 13, p. 146, and No. 5, p. 148; PC-7 = No. 14, p. 147; PC-8 = No. 19, p. 147.

28. Powers notes that this text appears two times in Colby 1895: (I), No. 4, p. 145; (II), No. 6, p. 148, as well as in Curtis [1907] 1968, p. 47. Curtis also gives the musical transcription for it on pp. 63–65. In this transcription, the song is sung two times, the first time to an all-vocable text, the second time to the lexical text given in PC-2.

29. The use of vocables in PC-2, PC-4, and PB-3 is consistent with my discussion in chapter 8 of the form and placement of vocables in Shoshone song genres that have all-vocable texts. In the three Lakota texts, *h* and *y* combine with *e, a,* and *o*. In PC-4, the *o* sound in *yo* cadences the vocable line. It is tempting to interpret the use of *yo* in PB-3 as a hierarchy of ending markers. In this hypothesis, a single *yo* corresponds roughly to a comma and repeated *yo*'s correspond to a period. If this hypothesis were correct, the last two lines would be: "Father said it so *e ya yo, e ya yo,* / Father said it so *e ya yo yo.*" The musical setting of these lines would provide key evidence, either validating or invalidating this hypothesis. Unfortunately, it is not given. For detailed analyses and discussion of the use of vocables in Lakota songs by a specialist in Lakota language and culture, see Powers 1987:7–36; Powers 1992:293–310.

30. Naraya song 2 (Vander 1986:34–35) is the only exceptional text, which mentions a relationship between people. In it, dead Shoshone mothers who are about to come back to life look around from above for their children below. In the few other texts that mention people, they are returning to life or flying on to the new world to come and not relating to one another.

References

Aberle, David F. 1959. "The Prophet Dance and Reactions to White Contact." *Southwestern Journal of Anthropology* 15, no. 1: 74–83.

Amoss, Pamela. 1978. *Coast Salish Spirit Dancing: The Survival of an Ancestral Religion.* Seattle: University of Washington Press.

Bahr, Donald. 1993. "Musical Poems in America." Photocopy from the author.

———. 1994. "Native American Dream Songs, Myth, Memory, and Improvisation." *Journal de la Société des Americanistes* 80:73–93.

Bahr, Donald, Juan Smith, William Smith Allison, and Julian Hayden. 1994. *The Short Swift Time of Gods on Earth: The Hohokam Chronicles.* Berkeley: University of California Press.

Bailey, Paul. 1957. *Wovoka, the Indian Messiah.* Los Angeles: Westernlore Press.

———. 1970. *Ghost Dance Messiah.* Los Angeles: Westernlore Press.

Barney, Garold D. 1986. *Mormons, Indians and the Ghost Dance Religion of 1890.* Lanham, Md.: University Press of America.

Bierhorst, John, ed. 1974. *Four Masterworks of American Indian Literature.* New York: Farrar, Straus, and Giroux.

———. 1985. *Cantares Mexicanos: Songs of the Aztecs.* Stanford, Calif.: Stanford University Press.

Brackett, Colonel Albert G. 1880. "The Shoshonis, or Snake Indians, Their Religion, Superstitions, and Manners." In *Annual Report of the Smithsonian Institution for 1879,* 328–33. Washington, D.C.: Smithsonian Institution.

Callaway, Donald G., Joel C. Janetski, and Omer C. Stewart. 1986. "Ute." In *Handbook of North American Indians,* edited by William C. Sturtevant. Vol. 11, *Great Basin,* edited by Warren L. D'Azevedo, 336–67. Washington, D.C.: Smithsonian Institution.

Canonge, Elliott. 1958. *Comanche Texts.* Norman: University of Oklahoma Press.

Clark, Ella E. 1966. *Indian Legends from the Northern Rockies.* Norman: University of Oklahoma Press.

Colby, General L. W. 1895. "Wanagi Olowan Kin: The Ghost Songs of the Dakotas." *Proceedings and Collections of the Nebraska State Historical Society* 1:131–50.

Craighead, John J., Frank C. Craighead Jr., and Ray J. Davis. 1963. *A Field Guide to Rocky Mountain Wildflowers.* Boston: Houghton Mifflin.

Crapo, Richley H. 1976. "Big Smokey Valley Shoshoni." *Desert Research Institute Publications in the Social Sciences* 10.

Crum, Beverly. 1980. "Newe Hupia, Shoshoni Poetry Songs." *Journal of California and Great Basin Anthropology Papers in Linguistics* 2:3–23.

Curtis, Natalie. [1907] 1968. *The Indians' Book*. Reprint. New York: Dover.

Dangberg, Grace M. 1957. "Letters to Jack Wilson, the Paiute Prophet, Written between 1908 and 1911." *Anthropological Papers* 55, *Bureau of American Ethnology Bulletin* 164:283–96.

———. 1968. "Wovoka." *Nevada Historical Society Quarterly* 2:1–53.

D'Azevedo, Warren L. 1986a. "Introduction." In *Handbook of North American Indians,* edited by William C. Sturtevant. Vol. 11, *Great Basin,* edited by Warren L. D'Azevedo, 1–14. Washington, D.C.: Smithsonian Institution.

———. 1986b "Washoe." In *Handbook of North American Indians,* edited by William C. Sturtevant. Vol. 11, *Great Basin,* edited by Warren L. D'Azevedo, 466–98. Washington, D.C.: Smithsonian Institution.

Dellenbaugh, Frederick S. 1908. *A Canyon Voyage*. New York: G. P. Putnam's Sons.

Densmore, Frances. [1922] 1972. *Northern Ute Music*. Reprint. New York: Da Capo.

———. [1929] 1972. *Pawnee Music*. Reprint. New York: Da Capo.

Dobyns, Henry F., and Robert C. Euler. 1967. *The Ghost Dance of 1889 Among the Pai Indians of Northwestern Arizona*. Prescott, Ariz.: Prescott College Press.

Du Bois, Cora A. 1939. "The 1870 Ghost Dance." *University of California Anthropological Records* 3:1–151.

Fabre, Henri J. 1991. *The Insect World of J. Henri Fabre*. Translated by Alexander Teixeira de Mattos. Boston: Beacon.

Fowler, Catherine S. 1986. "Subsistence." In *Handbook of North American Indians,* edited by William C. Sturtevant. Vol. 11, *Great Basin,* edited by Warren L. D'Azevedo, 64–97. Washington, D.C.: Smithsonian Institution.

———. 1990. "Mountain Sheep in the Sky: Orion's Belt in Great Basin Mythology." Paper read at Great Basin Anthropological Conference at the University of Nevada, Reno.

———. 1992. "Kai Pasapanna ('Do Not Dry Out'): Pine Nut Ceremonies among the Northern Paiute." Paper presented at the Great Basin Anthropological Conference, Boise, Idaho.

Fowler, Catherine S., and Don D. Fowler. 1971. "Notes on the History of the Southern Paiutes and Western Shoshonis." *Utah Historical Quarterly* 39:95–113.

Fowler, Catherine S., and Sven Liljeblad. 1986. "Northern Paiute." In *Handbook of North American Indians,* edited by William C. Sturtevant. Vol. 11, *Great Basin,* edited by Warren L. D'Azevedo, 435–98. Washington, D.C.: Smithsonian Institution.

Franklin, Robert J., and Pamela A. Bunte. 1988. "Southern Paiute Round Dance Songs." Paper read at American Anthropological Association Conference, Chicago, Illinois.

———. 1992. "Animals and Humans, Sex and Death: Toward a Symbolic

Analysis of Four Southern Numic Rituals." Paper read at Great Basin Anthropological Conference, Boise, Idaho.

Frisbie, Charlotte F. 1980. "Vocables in Navajo Ceremonial Music." *Journal of the Society for Ethnomusicology* 24:347–92.

Frison, George. 1992. "Communal Mountain Sheep Procurement in the Central Rocky Mountains." Paper read at Great Basin Anthropological Conference, Boise, Idaho.

Gayton, A. H. 1930. "The Ghost Dance of 1870 in South-Central California." *University of California Publications in American Archaeology and Ethnology* 28:57–82.

Gelo, Daniel J. 1990. "Topographic References in Comanche Narrative." Paper read at Great Basin Anthropological Conference, University of Nevada, Reno.

Gill, Sam D. 1987. *Mother Earth.* Chicago: University of Chicago Press.

Goss, James A. 1972. "A Basin-Plateau Shoshonean Ecological Model." *Desert Research Institute Publications in the Social Sciences* 8:123–28.

———. 1990. "Ute Myth as Cultural Charter." Paper read at Great Basin Anthropological Conference, University of Nevada, Reno.

Grinnell, George Bird. 1891. "Account of the Northern Cheyennes Concerning the Messiah Superstition." *Journal of American Folk-Lore* 4:61–69.

Hage, Per, and Wick Miller. 1976. "'Eagle' = 'Bird': A Note on the Structure and Evolution of Shoshoni Ethnoornithological Nomenclature." *American Ethnologist* 3:481–88.

Harris, Jack. 1940. "The White Knife Shoshoni of Nevada." In *Acculturation in Seven American Indian Tribes,* edited by Ralph Linton, 39–118. Gloucester, Mass.: Peter Smith.

Hebard, Grace Raymond. 1930. *Washaki: An Account of Indian Resistance of the Covered Wagon and Union Pacific Railroad Invasions of their Territory.* Cleveland: Arthur H. Clark.

Heizer, Robert F. 1970. "Ethnographic Notes on the Northern Paiute of Humboldt Sink, West Central Nevada." In *Languages and Cultures of Western North American: Essays in Honor of Sven S. Liljeblad,* edited by Earl H. Swanson, 323–48. Pocatello: Idaho State University Press.

Herzog, George. 1935a. "Plains Ghost Dance and Great Basin Music." *American Anthropologist* 37:403–19.

———. 1935b. "Special Song Types in North American Indian Music." *Zeitschrift für vergleichende Musikwissenschaft* 3:23–33.

Hill, Jane H. 1992. "The Flower World of Old Uto-Aztecan." *Journal of Anthropological Research* 48:117–44.

Hinton, Leanne. 1984. *Havasupai Songs: A Linguistic Perspective.* Tübingen: Gunter Narr.

Hittman, Michael. 1973. "The 1870 Ghost Dance at the Walker River Reservation: A Reconstruction." *Ethnohistory* 20:247–78.

———. 1990. *Wovoka and the Ghost Dance.* Carson City, Nev.: Grace Dangberg Foundation.

———. 1992. "The 1890 Ghost Dance in Nevada." *American Indian Culture and Research Journal* 16:123–66.

Hoebel, E. Adamson. 1938. "Bands and Distributions of the Eastern Shoshone." *American Anthropologist* n.s. 40, no. 3: 385–415.

Hopkins, Sarah Winnemucca. [1883] 1969. *Life among the Paiutes: Their Wrongs and Claims,* edited by Mrs. Horace Mann. Reprint. Bishop, Calif.: Sierra Media.

Hulse, F. S. 1935. "Bishop Paiute Notebooks," notebooks 153, 154.2–5. Bancroft Library, University of California, Berkeley.

Hultkrantz, Ake. 1951. "The Concept of the Soul Held by the Wind River Shoshone." *Ethnos* 16:18–44.

———. 1954a. "The Indians and the Wonders of Yellowstone: A Study of the Interrelations of Religion, Nature and Culture." *Ethnos* 19, no. 1–4:34–68.

———. 1954b. "The Origin of Death Myth as Found among the Wind River Shoshoni Indians." *Ethnos* 19:127–36.

———. 1956. "Configurations of Religious Belief among the Wind River Shoshoni." *Ethnos* 21:194–215.

———. 1961. "The Masters of the Animals among the Wind River Shoshoni." *Ethnos* 26:198–218.

———. 1968. "Yellow Hand, Chief and Medicine-man among the Eastern Shoshoni." *Verhandlungen des 33 Internationalen Amerikanistenkongresses,* 293–304.

———. 1969. "Pagan and Christian Elements in the Religious Syncretism among the Shoshoni Indians of Wyoming." In *Syncretism,* edited by Sven S. Hartman. *Scripta Instituti Donneriani Aboensis* 3:15–40.

———. 1976. "Religion and Ecology among the Great Basin Indians." In *The Realm of the Extra-Human: Ideas and Actions,* edited by A. Bharati, 137–50. The Hague: Mouton.

———. 1981a. "Accommodation and Persistence: Ecological Analysis of the Religion of the Sheepeater Indians in Wyoming, U.S.A." *Temenos: Studies in Comparative Religion* 17:35–44.

———. 1981b. "Religious Aspects of the Wind River Shoshoni Folk Literature." In *Culture in History: Essays in Honor of Paul Radin,* edited by Stanley Diamond, 552–69. New York: Octagon Books.

———. 1986. "Mythology and Religious Concepts." In *Handbook of North American Indians,* edited by William C. Sturtevant. Vol. 11, *Great Basin,* edited by Warren L. D'Azevedo, 630–40. Washington, D.C.: Smithsonian Institution.

———. 1987. *Native Religions of North America.* San Francisco: Harper and Row.

Hymes, Dell. 1965. "Some North Pacific Coast Poems: a Problem in Anthropological Philology." *American Anthropologist* 67:316–41.

Johnson, Edward C., ed. 1975. *Walker River Paiutes: A Tribal History.* Salt Lake City: University of Utah Printing Service.

Johnson, Thomas H. 1968. "The Wind River Shoshone Sun Dance, 1966 and 1967." Master's thesis, Department of Anthropology, University of Illinois.

Jorgensen, Joseph G. 1972. *The Sun Dance Religion.* Chicago: University of Chicago Press.

———. 1986. "Ghost Dance, Bear Dance, and Sun Dance." In *Handbook of*

North American Indians, edited by William C. Sturtevant. Vol. 11, *Great Basin,* edited by Warren L. D'Azevedo, 660–72. Washington, D.C.: Smithsonian Institution.

Kehoe, Alice B. 1968. "The Ghost Dance Religion in Saskatchewan, Canada." *Plains Anthropologist* 1:13–42.

Kelly, Isabel T. 1932. "Ethnography of the Surprise Valley Paiute." *University of California Publications in American Archaeology and Ethnology* 31:67–210.

———. 1936. "Chemehuevi Shamanism." In *Essays in Anthropology Presented to A. L. Kroeber in Celebration of His Sixtieth Birthday,* edited by Robert Lowie, 129–42. Berkeley: University of California Press.

———. 1938. "Northern Paiute Tales." *Journal of American Folk-Lore* 51:364–438.

———. 1939. "Southern Paiute Shamanism." *University of California Anthropological Records* 2:151–67.

———. 1964. "Southern Paiute Ethnography." *University of Utah Anthropological Papers 69, Glen Canyon Series 21.* Salt Lake City.

Kelly, Isabel T., and Catherine S. Fowler. 1986. "Southern Paiute." In *Handbook of North American Indians,* edited by William C. Sturtevant. Vol. 11, *Great Basin,* edited by Warren D'Azevedo, 368–97. Washington, D.C.: Smithsonian Institution.

Kroeber, A. L. "A Ghost-Dance in California." 1904. *Journal of American Folk-Lore* 17:32–35.

———. 1908. "Catch-Words in American Mythology." *Journal of American Folk-Lore* 21:222–27.

———. 1925. "Handbook of the Indians of California." *Bureau of American Ethnology Bulletin 78.* Washington, D.C.

Kroeber, A. L., and E. W. Gifford. 1949. "World Renewal: A Cult System of Native Northwest California." *University of California Anthropological Records* 13, no. 1: 1–156.

Kruse, Babs. 1983. "Shoshones in the Wind River Area: Student Workbook." Wyoming Indian High School Title IV-A Curriculum Development Project. Photocopy. Ethete, Wyoming.

La Barre, Weston. 1975. *The Peyote Cult.* 4th ed. New York: Schocken Books.

Laird, Carobeth. 1976. *The Chemehuevis.* Banning, Calif.: Malki Museum Press.

Lesser, Alexander. [1933] 1978. *The Pawnee Ghost Dance Hand Game.* Reprint. Madison: University of Wisconsin Press.

Liljeblad, Sven. 1943. Tapes of Northern Shoshone and Bannock singers, Getchell Special Collections, Library, University of Nevada, Reno.

———. 1957. "Indian Peoples in Idaho." Photocopy. Pocatello: Idaho State College.

———. 1969. "The Religious Attitude of the Shoshonean Indians." *Rendezvous: Idaho State University Journal of Arts and Letters* 4:47–58.

———. 1986. "Oral Tradition: Content and Style of Verbal Arts." In *Handbook of North American Indians,* edited by William C. Sturtevant. Vol. 11, *Great Basin,* edited by Warren L. D'Azevedo, 641–59. Washington, D.C.: Smithsonian Institution.

Liljeblad, Sven, and Catherine S. Fowler. 1986. "Owens Valley Paiute." In

Handbook of North American Indians, edited by William C. Sturtevant. Vol. 11, *Great Basin,* edited by Warren D'Azevedo, 412–34. Washington, D.C.: Smithsonian Institution.

Lowie, Robert H. 1909a. "The Northern Shoshone." *Anthropological Papers of the American Museum of Natural History* 2:165–306.

———. 1909b. "Notes and Queries." *Journal of American Folk-lore* 22:332–33.

———. 1909c. "Shoshone and Comanche Tales." *Journal of American Folk-Lore* 22:265–82.

———. 1915. "Dances and Societies of the Plains Shoshone." *Anthropological Papers of the American Museum of Natural History* 11:803–35.

———. 1919. "Sun Dance of the Shoshoni, Ute, and Hidatsa." *Anthropological Papers of the American Museum of Natural History* 16:387–431.

———. 1923. "The Cultural Connection of California and Plateau Shoshonean Tribes." *University of California Publications in American Archaeology and Ethnology* 20:145–56.

———. 1924a. "Notes on Shoshonean Ethnography." *Anthropological Papers of the American Museum of Natural History* 20:185–314.

———. 1924b. *Primitive Religion.* New York: Boni and Liveright.

———. 1924c. "Shoshonean Tales." *Journal of American Folk-Lore* 37:1–242.

———. [1954] 1963. *Indians of the Plains.* Reprint. Garden City, N.Y.: Natural History Press.

Malouf, Carling I., and John Findlay. 1986. "Euro-American Impact Before 1870." In *Handbook of North American Indians,* edited by William C. Sturtevant. Vol. 11, *Great Basin,* edited by Warren L. D'Azevedo, 499–516. Washington, D.C.: Smithsonian Institution.

McAllester, David P. 1949. *Peyote Music.* Viking Fund Publications in Anthropology 13. New York: Viking Fund.

———. 1969. "The Tenth Horse Song." *Stony Brook* 3, no. 4: 306–15.

Merriam, Alan P. 1967. *Ethnomusicology of the Flathead Indians.* Viking Fund Publications in Anthropology 44. New York: Wenner-Gren Foundation for Anthropological Research.

Miller, Jay. 1983. "Basin Religion and Theology: A Comparative Study of Power (*Puha*)." *Journal of California and Great Basin Anthropology* 5:66–86.

Miller, Wick R. 1970. "Western Shoshoni Dialects." In *Languages and Cultures of Western North America: Essays in Honor of Sven S. Liljeblad,* edited by Earl H. Swanson Jr., 17–36. Pocatello: Idaho State University Press.

———. 1972. "Newe Natekwinappeh: Shoshoni Stories and Dictionary." *University of Utah Anthropological Papers* 94. Salt Lake City.

———. 1983. "Uto-Aztecan Languages." In *Handbook of North American Indians,* edited by William C. Sturtevant. Vol. 10, *Southwest,* edited by Alfonso Ortiz, 113–24. Washington, D.C.: Smithsonian Institution.

———. 1986. "Numic Languages." In *Handbook of North American Indians,* edited by William C. Sturtevant. Vol. 11, *Great Basin,* edited by Warren L. D'Azevedo, 98–106. Washington, D.C.: Smithsonian Institution.

Mooney, James. [1896] 1991. *The Ghost-Dance Religion and the Sioux Outbreak of 1890.* Reprint. Lincoln: University of Nebraska Press.

Murphy, Robert F., and Yolanda Murphy. 1960. "Shoshone-Bannock Subsistence and Society." *University of California Anthropological Records* 16:293–338.

———. 1986. "Northern Shoshone and Bannock." In *Handbook of North American Indians*, edited by William C. Sturtevant. Vol. 11, *Great Basin*, edited by Warren L. D'Azevedo, 284–307. Washington, D.C.: Smithsonian Institution.

Nash, Philleo. 1955. "The Place of Religious Revivalism in the Formation of the Intercultural Community on Klamath Reservation." In *Social Anthropology of North American Tribes*, edited by Fred Eggan, 377–442. Chicago: University of Chicago Press.

Natches, Gilbert. 1923. "Northern Paiute Verbs." *University of California Publication in American Archaeology and Ethnology* 20:243–59.

Nettl, Bruno. 1954. *North American Indian Musical Styles*. Memoirs of the American Folklore Society 45. Philadelphia: American Folklore Society.

———. 1989. *Blackfoot Musical Thought*. Kent, Ohio: Kent State University Press.

Olden, Sarah Emilia. 1923. *Shoshone Folk Lore*. Milwaukee, Wis.: Morehouse Publishing.

Park, Willard Z. 1934. "Paviotso Shamanism." *American Anthropologist* 36:98–113.

———. 1938. *Shamanism in Western North America*. Evanston, Ill.: Northwestern University.

———. 1941. "Cultural Succession in the Great Basin." In *Language, Culture and Personality: Essays in Memory of Edward Sapir*, edited by Leslie Spier, A. I. Hallowell, and Stanley S. Newman, 180–203. Menasha, Wis.: Sapir Memorial Publication Fund.

———. 1989. "Willard Z. Park's Ethnographic Notes on the Northern Paiute of Western Nevada, 1933–1944," edited by Catherine S. Fowler. *University of Utah Anthropological Papers* 114.

Park, Willard Z., et al. 1938. "Tribal Distribution in the Great Basin." *American Anthropologist* 40:622–38.

Peterson, Harold, ed. 1976. *I Wear the Morning Star: An Exhibition of American Indian Ghost Dance Objects*. Minneapolis: Minneapolis Institute of Arts.

Pietroforte, Alfred. 1965. *Songs of the Yokuts and Paiutes*, edited by Vinson Brown. Healdsburg, Calif.: Naturegraph Publishers.

Powell, John Wesley. 1971. *Anthropology of the Numa: John Wesley Powell's Manuscripts on the Numic Peoples of Western North America, 1868–1880*, edited by Don D. Fowler and Catherine S. Fowler. Smithsonian Contributions to Anthropology 14. Washington, D.C.: Smithsonian Institution.

Powers, William K. 1961. "The Social Dances." *American Indian Tradition* 7:97–104.

———. 1973. *Indians of the Northern Plains*. New York: Putnam.

———. 1977. *Oglala Religion*. Lincoln: University of Nebraska Press.

———. 1986. *Sacred Language*. Norman: University of Oklahoma Press.

———. 1987. *Beyond the Vision: Essays on American Indian Culture*. Norman: University of Oklahoma Press.

———. 1990. *Voices from the Spirit World: Lakota Ghost Dance Songs.* Kendall Park, N.J.: Lakota Books.

———. 1992. "Translating the Untranslatable: The Place of the Vocable in Lakota Song." In *On the Translation of Native American Literatures,* edited by Brian Swann, 293–310. Washington, D.C.: Smithsonian Institution.

Rhodes, Willard. N.d. Notes on Library of Congress Recording: Kiowa AAFS L35.

Roberts, Reverend John. 1900. "Questions and Answers in Shoshone," translated by Enga-Barrie and Reverend John Roberts. Wind River Reservation, Wyo.: Episcopal Mission.

Rothenberg, Jerome. 1969. "Total Translation, An Experiment in the Presentation of American Indian Poetry." *Stony Brook* 3, no. 4: 292–301.

Sapir, Edward. 1910. "Song Recitative in Paiute Mythology." *Journal of American Folk-lore* 23:455–72.

———. 1931. "Southern Paiute Dictionary." In *Proceedings of the American Academy of Arts and Sciences* 65:539–730.

———. 1994. *The Collected Works of Edward Sapir.* Vol. 4, edited by Regna Darnell and Judith Irvine. Berlin: Mouton de Gruyter.

Schaafsma, Polly. 1986. "Rock Art. In *Handbook of North American Indians,* edited by William C. Sturtevant. Vol. 11, *Great Basin,* edited by Warren L. D'Azevedo, 215–26. Washington, D.C.: Smithsonian Institution.

Shimkin, Demitri B. N.d. "Wind River Shoshone Grammatical Forms (A Rough Sketch)." Photocopy.

———. 1937. "Wind River Shoshone Fieldnotes."

———. 1939. "Some Interactions of Culture, Needs, and Personalities Among the Wind River Shoshone." Ph.D. diss. in Anthropology, University of California, Los Angeles.

———. 1940. "Shoshone-Comanche Origins and Migrations." In *Proceedings of the Sixth Pacific Science Congress of the Pacific Association of the University of California, Berkeley, Stanford University, and San Francisco, July 24–August 12, 1939,* 4:17–25. Berkeley: University of California Press.

———. 1942. "Dynamics of Recent Wind River Shoshone History." *American Anthropologist* 44:451–62.

———. 1947a. "Childhood and Development among the Wind River Shoshone." *University of California Anthropological Records* 5:289–325.

———. 1947b. "Wind River Shoshone Ethnogeography." *University of California Anthropological Records* 5:245–88.

———. 1947c. "Wind River Shoshone Literary Forms: An Introduction." *Journal of the Washington Academy of Sciences* 37:320–52.

———. 1949a. "Shoshone, I, Linguistic Sketch and Text." *International Journal of American Linguistics* 15, no. 3: 175–88.

———. 1949b. "Shoshone, II, Morpheme List." *International Journal of American Linguistics* 15, no. 4: 203–12.

———. 1953. "The Wind River Shoshone Sun Dance." *Anthropological Papers* 41:397–491. Bureau of American Ethnology Bulletin 151. Washington, D.C.: Smithsonian Institution.

———. 1970. "Socio-cultural Persistence among Shoshoneans of the Carson River Basin (Nevada)." In *Languages and Cultures of Western North America: Essays in Honor of Sven S. Liljeblad,* edited by Earl H. Swanson Jr., 172–99. Pocatello: Idaho State University Press.

———. 1986a. "Eastern Shoshone." In *Handbook of North American Indians,* edited by William C. Sturtevant. Vol. 11, *Great Basin,* edited by Warren L. D'Azevedo, 308–53. Washington, D.C.: Smithsonian Institution.

———. 1986b. "Introduction of the Horse." In *Handbook of North American Indians,* edited by William C. Sturtevant. Vol. 11, *Great Basin,* edited by Warren L. D'Azevedo, 517–24. Washington, D.C.: Smithsonian Institution.

Smith, Anne M. Cooke. 1939. "An Analysis of Basin Mythology." Ph.D. diss. in Anthropology, Yale University.

Spier, Leslie. 1930. "Klamath Ethnography." *University of California Publications in American Archaeology and Ethnology,* vol. 30. Berkeley: University of California.

———. 1935. "The Prophet Dance of the Northwest and Its Derivatives: The Source of the Ghost Dance." *American Anthropological Association General Series in Anthropology* 1. Menasha, Wis.

Spoonhunter, Bob, ed. 1980. "Shoshone Legends." Title IV-A Curriculum Development Project. Ethete, Wyo.: Wyoming Indian High School.

St. Clair, Lynn, and Herman St. Clair. 1977. "Shoshone Indian Religion: Sun Dance Da-goo-win-net." In *Songprints: The Musical Experience of Five Shoshone Women,* by Judith Vander, 295–99. Urbana: University of Illinois Press, 1988.

Steward, Julian. 1933. "Ethnography of the Owens Valley Paiute." *University of California Publications in American Archaeology and Ethnology* 33, no. 3: 233–350.

———. 1934. "Two Paiute Autobiographies." *University of California Publications in American Archaeology and Ethnology* 33, no. 5: 423–38.

———. 1936. "Myths of Owens Valley Paiute." *University of California Publications in American Archaeology and Ethnology* 34, no. 3: 355–440.

———. 1938. "Basin-Plateau Aboriginal Sociopolitical Groups." *Bureau of American Ethnology Bulletin* 120. Washington, D.C.: Government Printing Office.

———. 1939. "Some Observations on Shoshonean Distributions." *American Anthropologist* 41, no. 2: 261–65.

———. 1940. "Native Cultures of the Intermontaine (Great Basin) Area." In *Essays in Historical Anthropology of North America, Published in Honor of John R. Swanton, Smithsonian Miscellaneous Collections* 100:445–502. Washington, D.C.: Smithsonian Institution

———. 1941. "Culture Element Distributions 13: Nevada Shoshoni." *University of California Anthropological Records* 4:209–360.

———. 1943a. "Culture Element Distributions 23: Northern and Gosiute Shoshoni." *University of California Anthropological Records* 8, no. 3: 263–392.

———. 1943b. "Some Western Shoshone Myths." *Anthropological Papers* 31, *Bureau of American Ethnology Bulletin* 136:249–99.

———. 1970. "The Foundations of Basin-Plateau Shoshonean Society." In *Languages and Cultures of Western North America: Essays in Honor of Sven S. Liljeblad,* edited by Earl H. Swanson Jr., 113–51. Pocatello: Idaho State University Press.

Steward, Julian, and Ermine Wheeler-Voegelin. 1974. "The Northern Paiute Indians." In *Paiute Indians* 3:9–328. American Indian Ethnohistory: California and Basin-Plateau Indians. New York: Garland.

Stewart, Omer C. 1939. "The Northern Paiute Bands." *University of California Anthropological Records* 2:127–49.

———. 1941. "Culture Element Distributions 14: Northern Paiute." *University of California Anthropological Records* 4:361–446.

———. 1944. "Washo-Northern Paiute Peyotism: A Study in Acculturation." *University of California Publications in American Archaeology and Ethnology* 40:63–142.

———. 1970. "The Question of Bannock Territory." In *Languages and Cultures of Western North America: Essays in Honor of Sven S. Liljeblad,* edited by Earl H. Swanson Jr., 201–31. Pocatello: Idaho State University Press.

———. 1987. *Peyote Religion: A History.* Norman: University of Oklahoma Press.

Thomas, David H., Lorann S. A. Pendleton, and Stephen C. Cappanari. 1986. "Western Shoshone." In *Handbook of North American Indians,* edited by William C. Sturtevant. Vol. 11, *Great Basin,* edited by Warren L. D'Azevedo, 262–83. Washington, D.C.: Smithsonian Institution.

Thornton, Russell. 1986. *We Shall Live Again: The 1870 and 1890 Ghost Dance Movements as Demographic Revitalization.* Cambridge: Cambridge University Press.

Tidzump, Malinda. 1970. *Shoshone Thesaurus.* Grand Forks: Summer Institute of Linguistics, University of North Dakota.

Trager, George L. 1964. "'Cottonwood' = 'Tree': A Southwestern Linguistic Trait." In *Language in Culture and Society: A Reader in Linguistics and Anthropology,* edited by Dell Hymes, 467–68. New York: Harper and Row.

Trenholm, Virginia Cole, and Maurine Carley. 1972. *The Shoshonis: Sentinels of the Rockies.* Norman: University of Oklahoma Press.

Underhill, Ruth. 1941. "The Northern Paiute Indians of California and Nevada." *Indian Life and Customs.* Washington, D.C.: Branch of Education of the Bureau of Indian Affairs.

Vander, Judith. 1978. "A View of Wind River Shoshone Music through Four Ceremonies." Master's thesis, Department of Musicology-Ethnomusicology, University of Michigan.

———. 1986. *Ghost Dance Songs and Religion of a Wind River Shoshone Woman.* Monograph Series in Ethnomusicology, no. 4. Los Angeles: University of California.

———. 1988. *Songprints: The Musical Experience of Five Shoshone Women.* Urbana: University of Illinois Press.

———. 1995. "The Shoshone Ghost Dance and Numic Myth: Common Heritage, Common Themes." *Journal of California and Great Basin Anthropology* 17, no. 2: 174–90.

Vennum, Jr., Thomas. 1986. "Music." In *Handbook of North American Indians,* edited by William C. Sturtevant. Vol. 11, *Great Basin,* edited by Warren L. D'Azevedo, 682–704. Washington, D.C.: Smithsonian Institution.

Voget, Fred W. 1984. *The Shoshoni-Crow Sun Dance.* Norman: University of Oklahoma Press.

Walcott, Derek. 1990. *Omeros.* New York: Farrar, Straus and Giroux.

Wallace, Ernest, and E. Adamson Hoebel. [1952] 1986. *The Comanches: Lords of the South Plains.* Reprint. Norman: University of Oklahoma Press.

Warren, Claude N., and Robert H. Crabtree. "Prehistory of the Southwestern Area." In *Handbook of North American Indians,* edited by William C. Sturtevant. Vol. 11, *Great Basin,* edited by Warren D'Azevedo, 183–93. Washington, D.C.: Smithsonian Institution.

Weeks, Rupert. [1961] 1981. *Pachee Goyo: History and Legends from the Shoshone.* Reprint. Laramie, Wyo.: Jelm Mountain Press.

Wheat, Margaret M. 1968. "Pinenut Prayer." Margaret Wheat Collection, Getchell Special Collections, Library, University of Nevada, Reno.

Whiting, Beatrice Blyth. 1950. *Paiute Sorcery.* Viking Fund Publications in Anthropology 15. New York: Viking Fund.

Whitley, David S. 1992. "The Vision Quest in the Great Basin." Paper read at Great Basin Anthropological Conference, Boise, Idaho. Photocopy.

———. 1994. "By the Hunter, for the Gatherer: Art, Social Relations and Subsistence Change in the Prehistoric Great Basin." In *World Archaeology* 25, no. 3: 356–73.

Williamson, Ray A. 1984. *Living the Sky: The Cosmos of the American Indian.* Norman: University of Oklahoma Press.

Wilson, E. N. 1919. *The White Indian Boy: The Story of Uncle Nick among the Shoshones,* in collaboration with Horward R. Driggs. New York: World Book Company.

Wissler, Clark. 1913. "Societies and Dance Associations of the Blackfoot Indians." *Anthropological Papers of the American Museum of Natural History* 11, pt. 4: 361–474.

Witherspoon, Gary. 1977. *Language and Art in the Navajo Universe.* Ann Arbor: University of Michigan Press.

Index

JUDITH VANDER is an ethnomusicologist based in Ann Arbor. She is the author of *Ghost Dance Songs and Religion of a Wind River Shoshone Woman* and *Songprints: The Musical Experience of Five Shoshone Women.* She has written about Shoshone music for the *New Grove Dictionary of American Music* and has published several articles and essays.

Books in the Series Music in American Life

Mormonism and Music: A History   *Michael Hicks*

Voices of the Jazz Age: Profiles of Eight Vintage Jazzmen   *Chip Deffaa*

Pickin' on Peachtree: A History of Country Music in Atlanta, Georgia
Wayne W. Daniel

Bitter Music: Collected Journals, Essays, Introductions, and Librettos
Harry Partch; edited by Thomas McGeary

Ethnic Music on Records: A Discography of Ethnic Recordings Produced in
the United States, 1893 to 1942   *Richard K. Spottswood*

Downhome Blues Lyrics: An Anthology from the Post–World War II Era
Jeff Todd Titon

Ellington: The Early Years   *Mark Tucker*

Chicago Soul   *Robert Pruter*

That Half-Barbaric Twang: The Banjo in American Popular Culture
Karen Linn

Hot Man: The Life of Art Hodes   *Art Hodes and Chadwick Hansen*

The Erotic Muse: American Bawdy Songs (Second Edition)   *Ed Cray*

Barrio Rhythm: Mexican American Music in Los Angeles   *Steven Loza*

The Creation of Jazz: Music, Race, and Culture in Urban America
Burton W. Peretti

Charles Martin Loeffler: A Life Apart in Music   *Ellen Knight*

Club Date Musicians: Playing the New York Party Circuit
Bruce A. MacLeod

Opera on the Road: Traveling Opera Troupes in the United States, 1825–60
Katherine K. Preston

The Stonemans: An Appalachian Family and the Music That Shaped Their
Lives   *Ivan M. Tribe*

Transforming Tradition: Folk Music Revivals Examined
Edited by Neil V. Rosenberg

The Crooked Stovepipe: Athapaskan Fiddle Music and Square Dancing in
Northeast Alaska and Northwest Canada   *Craig Mishler*

Traveling the High Way Home: Ralph Stanley and the World of Traditional
Bluegrass Music   *John Wright*

Carl Ruggles: Composer, Painter, and Storyteller   *Marilyn Ziffrin*

Never without a Song: The Years and Songs of Jennie Devlin, 1865–1952
Katharine D. Newman

The Hank Snow Story *Hank Snow, with Jack Ownbey and Bob Burris*

Milton Brown and the Founding of Western Swing
Cary Ginell, with special assistance from Roy Lee Brown

Santiago de Murcia's "Códice Saldívar No. 4": A Treasury of Secular Guitar
Music from Baroque Mexico *Craig H. Russell*

The Sound of the Dove: Singing in Appalachian Primitive Baptist Churches
Beverly Bush Patterson

Heartland Excursions: Ethnomusicological Reflections on Schools of Music
Bruno Nettl

Doowop: The Chicago Scene *Robert Pruter*

Blue Rhythms: Six Lives in Rhythm and Blues *Chip Deffaa*

Shoshone Ghost Dance Religion: Poetry Songs and Great Basin Context
Judith Vander